ADOLESCENT DEVELOPMENT
Early Through Late Adolescence

ADOLESCENT DEVELOPMENT
Early Through Late Adolescence

David E. Balk
KANSAS STATE UNIVERSITY

Brooks/Cole Publishing Company
I(T)P™ An International Thomson Publishing Company

Pacific Grove • Albany • Bonn • Boston • Cincinnati • Detroit • London • Madrid • Melbourne
Mexico City • New York • Paris • San Francisco • Singapore • Tokyo • Toronto • Washington

Sponsoring Editor: *Vicki Knight*
Project Development Editor: *Eileen Murphy*
Marketing Representative: *Mark Edwards*
Marketing Team: *Margaret Parks, Frank Barnett*
Editorial Associate: *Lauri Banks Ataide*
Production Team: *Joan Marsh, Kathi Townes, Stephanie Kuhns*
Manuscript Editor: *Michele Betsill*
Permissions Editor: *Elaine Jones*

Interior Design: *Brian Betsill*
Cover Design: *Vernon T. Boes*
Cover Photo: *Thomas Heinser*
Art Coordinator: *Brian Betsill*
Photo Researcher: *Michele Betsill*
Typesetting: *Stephanie Kuhns*, TECH*arts*
Cover Printing: *Color Dot Graphics*
Printing and Binding: *Arcata Graphics/Hawkins*

For more information, contact:

BROOKS/COLE PUBLISHING COMPANY
511 Forest Lodge Road
Pacific Grove, CA 93950
USA

International Thomson Publishing Europe
Berkshire House 168–173
High Holborn
London WC1V7AA
England

Thomas Nelson Australia
102 Dodds Street
South Melbourne, 3205
Victoria, Australia

Nelson Canada
1120 Birchmount Road
Searborough, Ontario
Canada M1K5G4

International Thomson Editores
Campos Eliseos 385, Piso 7
Col. Polanco
11560 México D.F. México

International Thomson Publishing GmbH
Königswinterer Strasse 418
53227 Bonn
Germany

International Thomson Publishing Asia
221 Henderson Road
#05–10 Henderson Building
Singapore 0315

International Thomson Publishing Japan
Hirakawacho Kyowa Building, 3F
2-2-1 Hirakawacho
Chiyoda-ku, Tokyo 102
Japan

Printed in the United States of America.

10 9 8 7 6 5 4 3 2 1

Library of Congress Cataloging-in-Publication Data

Balk, David E., [Date]
   Adolescent development: early through late adolescence/David E. Balk.
          p. cm.
   Includes bibliographical references and indexes.
   ISBN 0-534-20040-0
   1. Adolescent psychology.   I. Title.
BF724.B25   1994   94-25195
155.5—dc20   CIP

To Mary Ann Balk, for her support and love and encouragement.

To Janet Renee Balk, for her faith and love and interest.

To Garth J Blackham, for his influence and friendship and teaching.

PREFACE

My rationale for writing this book is the need to view adolescence as a normal part of the human life span, connected to both middle childhood and young adulthood. The conceptual orientation emphasizes developmental transitions. These transitions during adolescence make this period of life both qualitatively distinct from other periods and significantly connected to continuous change in an individual's life.

In the United States, adolescence is viewed as a normal developmental sequence, clearly tied to expectations and resources of an industrialized society. This period consists of three separate phases: early, middle, and late adolescence. The demands of each phase are incorporated in and discussed throughout the text. Thus an organizing principle in this text synthesizes information about early, middle, and late adolescence consistently in each chapter.

Changes that characterize adolescent development are covered extensively in separate chapters: physical, cognitive, self-concept, and social/moral reasoning changes. Adolescent development occurs within specific ecological milieus, and a tacit issue throughout adolescence is establishing one's niche within the ecological milieus presented by society—family, school, peers, work and, increasingly, the media.

Although this developmental period of life needn't be an uncommonly stressful time, adolescents do encounter stressors. These stressors are clearly described in the comments of many parents that their adolescent children have become "difficult strangers." Based upon compelling research, however, I contend that the great majority of youth do not turn into "psychological werewolves" when they reach adolescence. Most adolescents are well-adjusted rather than depressed, possessing rather than lacking self-confidence, and maintaining rather than losing self-control. At the same time, I recognize that refusal to see that some adolescents exhibit signs of severe disturbance is injurious to them and their families.

I contend that sex biases place many adolescent females at disadvantage in terms of both achievement and establishing a valued societal niche. This book contains extended discussion about the impact of gender intensification in our society. I have also looked at some of the negative implications for males as well as some of the counterintuitive results of socialization based on gender roles and expectations.

Outstanding Features of the Text

The following topics are integral to a contemporary discussion of adolescent development and are given special consideration throughout the text.

■ **Cultural diversity.** A mandate for college texts on human development is to look carefully at issues of cultural diversity. The text incorporates extended references to cross-cultural research data, both in the main text and in topic boxes.

■ **Links between childhood, adolescence, and adulthood.** Too often discussions of specific phases in human development—especially adolescence—ignore what development has preceded and what will follow. Unfortunately, such discussions leave the impression that the aspects of adolescent development are divorced from the human life span. Links to childhood and adulthood are discussed in the main text and in some topic boxes.

■ **Development of moral reasoning.** For some time there has been an ongoing debate about whether the prevailing system to study the development of moral reasoning, as developed by Lawrence Kohlberg, discriminates against females, as has been suggested by Carol Gilligan. It is time for a lengthy review of the Kohlberg-Gilligan debate on moral reasoning. I have placed the issues in terms of an overlooked implication of Gilligan's criticism; upon careful scrutiny her position provides unexpected and (I imagine) unintended support for the argument that females are not suited for scientific and mathematical pursuits. The evidence indicates that Kohlberg's revised manual and scoring method do not place females at a lower stage of moral development than males. My analysis of Gilligan's perspective offers a critical orientation favoring rather than opposing gender equity.

■ **Adolescent self-concept development** is a major theme in the mainstream of research on adolescence, and a significant figure in this research is Daniel Offer. Although no text has previously provided an extended review of Offer's longitudinal and cross-cultural studies, this book discusses his position extensively.

■ **Television** has considerable influence in contemporary society, and so the text includes an extended treatment of the influence of television on adolescents.

■ **Life crises.** It is not uncommon for adolescents to have to deal with life crises, such as parental divorce and the death of a family member or friend. Chapter 11 presents a comprehensive model for understanding how adolescents cope with life crises, using bereavement as the prototypical crisis. Also reviewed are several types of crisis situations that often tax adolescent coping mechanisms and promote growth and development.

■ **Evaluations of schooling and adolescents.** The text looks carefully at the issues surrounding middle schools, the transition from elementary schools, and the transition to high school. The effects of college on late adolescent students is also reviewed.

■ **Work.** A forgotten portion of late adolescent youth are individuals who join the work force rather than enter college. This textbook considers these forgotten youths, as well as those late adolescents who enlist in the Armed Forces.

■ **Violence** has attracted national concern, and I devote Chapter 13 to the role of violence in adolescent development. Some adolescents are violent predators, and many adolescents are victims of violence.

- **Human sexuality** is a significant dynamic during adolescence, and the text presents various elements comprising the current phenomena of adolescence and sexuality—the incidence and prevalence of sexual activity, sexually transmitted diseases, adolescent pregnancy, and sex education.

The following features are included in each chapter:

- Current sources are used as a basis for much of this textbook, but I have also referred to older pieces, because they were groundbreaking at publication, set the stage for current thinking in an area, or deserve to be read again for the clarity they bring to an issue. A contribution should not be ignored simply because it is "dated." Since it is imperative for a textbook to be current, the balance of the research leans clearly toward current work.

- At the beginning of each chapter a case study is used to synthesize the issues and information addressed within the chapter. Each of these case studies provides information given by individuals who spoke to me in confidence.

- The chapters contain topic boxes. Some boxes deal with cross-cultural information, some present connections between adolescents and other points in the life span, and others provide knowledge about specific subjects. Separate logos designate cross-cultural, life span continuity, and knowledge topic boxes.

- Key terms are highlighted throughout the text.

- Each chapter closes with a summary, which is written to provide a reliable review of the chapter content. It is not, however, written as a substitution for reading the chapter.

Acknowledgments

Identifying and thanking the persons who made this project possible is very enjoyable. Many persons have read portions of the manuscript in various draft versions. I thank Elaine Daugherty, Laurie Harrington, Rick Miller, Ann Murray, John Murray, Candyce Russell, Brenda Thomas (now Brenda Sharpe), and David Wright for their insight, suggestions and encouragement. If I remember protocol correctly, here is where I say any mistakes in the book are my own and not theirs.

Each of the 15 case studies in the book involves personal information. These cases were taken from individuals whom I may not name but to whom I am grateful for their interest in this book and their trust in me.

Several faculty at colleges and universities around the United States have read the manuscript and offered extensive critical comments. Most often their ideas have spurred me to rethink sections of the manuscript. I appreciate the encouragement expressed in their comments, and I thank them for their help in finishing this effort.

My wife, Mary Ann Balk, has been of immeasurable help, not only encouraging me to continue writing but also listening to my ideas. She pitched in at the end of the final manuscript revisions, entering many changes into the computer files. We made the deadline because we worked together on this project. Mary Ann also knows a lot about adolescents, and I have always found her ideas to be insightful. I am getting suspicious that she is smarter than I am. Don't tell anyone.

My 16-year-old daughter, Janet Renee Balk, let me bounce ideas off her. She became a sounding board for me regarding adolescents. She would speak with pride —always wonderful for a dad to hear—when she mentioned this book to others. Although she wanted me to write this book, she has let me know she did not appreciate the amount of time my writing this book took away from being with my family, which is a lovely compliment to me. She wanted me to write the book, but she also wanted me to be around her. Well, not always.

Looking around my house and my office, I am reminded that books make up a great part of my life. It is amazing to have used books this long and yet have had so little appreciation of what it takes to put together a book. Now I understand the immense role my editor, Vicki Knight, has played in producing this book. She has been forever supportive and enlightening. Perhaps only a textbook author can appreciate how important that support and enlightenment are in the midst of an unfinished manuscript. Vicki has also been clear in what she needed from me. She has been fun to work with, and she is a true professional in her profession. When I informed someone from another publisher that Vicki Knight was my editor, she said, "Oh, you're very lucky. Vicki's one of the best in our business."

Vicki Knight also introduced me to Eileen Murphy, Developmental Editor at Brooks/Cole. Boy, does Eileen know how to improve unclear prose and how to organize more clearly the whole contents of a chapter. I ask myself, "How did she get so good at writing?" Eileen has poured herself into this project, giving me ideas and advice, and she has taught me her method for reworking text. Like Vicki, Eileen has been consistent in her praise and support. I feel fortunate that she gave my project her careful reading and want to let people know I appreciate how very well she performs her job.

Joan Marsh, production editor at Brooks/Cole, I have met only via the phone and the U.S. mail near the end of this project. She has offered her warmth, encouragement, humor, and considerable organizing skills in getting this project done.

Vernon Boes, art director at Brooks/Cole, picked a remarkable cover for the book. Elaine Jones helped with the thankless task of getting permissions. Faith Stoddard helped me understand the expectations Brooks/Cole had regarding an instructor's manual.

Now, finally my praise and admiration for the people at TECH*arts*, a firm in Boulder, Colorado, that worked with me and Joan Marsh to get my manuscript into published form. I want to single out Michele Betsill for her copy editing, Stephanie Kuhns for her production coordination and typesetting, and Kathi Townes, the TECH*arts* leader. We faced and met a deadline together. Hooray for all of us!

DAVID E. BALK

Contents

CHAPTER 6

THE DRAMA PLAYED OUT ON THE FAMILY STAGE 230

CHAPTER 7

PEERS, FRIENDS, AND ONGOING INTERPERSONAL SOCIALIZATION 274

ADOLESCENT DEVELOPMENT
Early Through Late Adolescence

AN OVERVIEW OF ADOLESCENCE

Case Study

The Story of Richard: Recovery in Adulthood from A Stormy Adolescence

Richard, a 43-year-old high school English teacher, remembers his adolescence with mixed feelings, mostly with regret. Although talented academically and athletically, Richard was self-conscious and felt uneasy around his peers, particularly around girls. He wanted his peers to like him, to be part of the leading crowd in his high school, but he was never accepted by those students. He felt as if he lived on the fringe of experience and now says he truly did.

Richard was raised in a devout Christian family and attended church schools until high school. He remembers his grade school years fondly; it was only in high school that he began to have serious self-doubts. He liked his sisters but felt distant from his parents—a homemaker and an attorney. Like his father, Richard kept his feelings to himself. He remembers feeling utterly astounded one day when his mother told him that his father loved him.

Richard entered puberty at age 11, earlier than many of his peers. He became increasingly interested in sex and enjoyed looking at "dirty pictures." One day, his Sunday-school teacher warned that people would go to hell for looking at such pictures. This news filled Richard with dread, and he became convinced that he was sinful and in danger of going to hell. He began to fear all sexual thoughts and feelings and became alienated from his own body and from his manifest physical development.

Richard's movement through adolescence provides a good example of what some researchers call the *storm and stress* years of development. He was moody and would swing suddenly from feeling light and at ease to feeling morose. He would lash out at his mother, say dreadful things, and then feel embarrassed.

Richard tried to keep his feelings to himself, voluntarily disclosing very little about himself to anyone. Later, some acquaintances told him that during high school they hadn't any idea what his feelings were because his appearance always seemed the same.

Like many other boys, Richard spent a lot of time playing sports. He was a better athlete than most, and many believed he was good enough for the varsity basketball team. In eleventh grade, he was cut from the squad on the last day of tryouts. Richard was extremely disappointed. Other boys told him it was unfair, but that did little to ease his pain. Richard buried his disappointment deep within.

3

He turned to academics with a vengeance and began moving up in his class standings. By the end of his senior year, his ranking had improved from 78th to 13th in a class of 129. Students began asking him for assistance in preparing for exams, and he enjoyed giving them help.

Toward the beginning of his senior year, Richard realized that he hadn't a clue what he wanted to do after high school. He'd thought about being a doctor, but had taken very little science and math. He decided to enter college and study liberal arts with an emphasis on English and philosophy.

College helped Richard turn around. He had two English teachers who he particularly admired. He began spending time chatting with them in their offices and eventually decided to become a high school English teacher.

Richard credits his real growing up to his wife, Martha, whom he met while in college and who has helped him overcome his fear of friendship and intimacy. Richard and Martha married shortly after they graduated and found teaching jobs in the same school district. They recently celebrated their 21st wedding anniversary.

Richard and Martha have three children, all boys. Joe is 13, Greg is 16, and John is 19. Because Richard recalls his own adolescence as a time of pain and remembers how much he would have liked to be close to his father, he has worked to maintain communication with his sons. He would do anything to prevent them from enduring the troubles he experienced, which he now feels were self-imposed, and he takes great pride in the joy for life each boy expresses.

One thing Richard won't do is infect his sons with guilt about sin and sex; however, he does worry about the way adolescents play with sex and the dangers to which they expose themselves. He wondered out loud to me if all those messages about sex from his church (which he no longer attends) were not a bit helpful. But then he shook his head and said, "No, they were really harmful."

Richard's story is not the story of all adolescents, but it does highlight some topics that interest adolescence researchers: responses to puberty, self-concept development, relations with peers, intimacy, and separation from parents. Richard would concur that his adolescent years were a time of turmoil, but he now sees that many adolescents develop in relative stability and calm.

ABOUT THIS BOOK

This book is about a period of life called adolescence. Most readers of this book will be in the last stages of adolescent development (18 to 22 years old) and may find it odd to read about issues that only recently formed part of their lives—issues such as the onset of puberty or coping with middle school, for instance. Some topics, such as separating from parents, recovering from rape, or dealing with an eating disorder, will reflect real-life, current issues in some readers' lives. What seems singularly true is that every college student has had experiences that provide a frame of reference from which to judge this book.

I have based this book on research. Considerable research is being conducted on adolescence these days, and I believe statements made in textbooks on adolescent development must be backed by evidence. While reading this book, I expect you to be asking whether I have provided credible evidence to support my assertions.

This book contains numerous case studies and portraits of adolescents. These stories are intended to provide a memorable framework and to highlight issues important in adolescent development. As in all case studies, the importance of these issues for an outsider to the story lies in how applicable and credible the story is to the reader's understanding of adolescence. Each chapter begins with a case study, and each case study is a true story told to me in confidence. No single story encompasses every issue important to adolescence, but each story does capture at least one issue that will be discussed at length in the ensuing chapter. All but the first story were told to me by adolescents.

The first story was told by an adult who remembers his adolescent years as a time of emotional turmoil. For many of the leading thinkers who have written about these years, the clear mark of adolescence is turmoil. However, as we shall discover in this book, there is growing debate about whether the adolescent years are a time of turmoil for most individuals.

We begin by looking at the span of years that encompass adolescence. These years are divided into three age periods: early, middle, and late adolescence.

THREE PERIODS OF ADOLESCENCE: EARLY, MIDDLE, AND LATE

The adolescent years extend roughly from age 10 to age 22. Although it is convenient to mark the beginning of the teenage years as the entrance to adolescence, most people consider that the onset of puberty, or the beginning of sexual maturity, heralds an individual's passage from middle childhood to adolescence.

The average age for the onset of puberty has declined steadily over the past century. As a consequence, any sixth grade classroom in the United States surely includes girls who have started to menstruate and others who have not; some sixth grade boys have had nocturnal emissions and others have not. Recall your own sixth grade experience. You may remember some girls and boys who physically were no longer children, although they had not yet finished growing and thus were not yet physically mature. While the physical changes of puberty are a critical marker signaling adolescent development, many other kinds of changes also occur during the adolescent years—changes in thinking about one's self, in understanding the ideas of other people, and in ability to think abstractly.

The initial period of change that marks the adolescent years is called **early adolescence**, which extends roughly from age 10 to age 14. During these years, the individual is expected to make certain transitions. In the United States, for instance, an early adolescent is expected to move from the security of an enclosed, elementary school classroom to the bustle and variety of either a middle school or a junior high school. However, in preindustrial societies, where the notion of teachers and schools differs from that in industrial societies, education occurs by working closely with skilled adults, often as an apprentice. Formal education may be available but limited to a small portion of male youths (as among the Iranian Kurds) or to a few hours weekly at the village mosque (as provided for male youth in rural communities in Turkey). Unlike American youths, who spend a great portion of their time with peers, adolescents in preindustrial societies spend more time in the company of same-sex adults (Schlegel & Barry, 1991).

Adolescence is comprised of three age periods: early, middle, and late adolescence

Middle adolescence coincides with the majority of time spent in high school—namely, ages 15 through 17. These years are marked by increased independence in decision making and increased time away from home and with peers. By the middle adolescent years, individuals whose puberty has been delayed will "finally" begin to mature physically. This delay can cause psychological trauma for some individuals, as we shall see in Chapter 2.

Late adolescence comprises the final years of the adolescent period—ages 18 to 22. Separating from one's parents and gaining independence are tasks that mark the lives of many young people during their late adolescent years. However, because many individuals enter college and remain dependent on parental support, their separation and independence from parents and family may be delayed. Of course, some adults, even in their 30s and 40s, seem never to have entered adulthood and have remained adolescents in terms of their ambivalence toward responsibility, identity, and interpersonal maturity. Perhaps you know one or two adults who strike you as having never grown up. You may also know some adolescents who are in danger of never growing up unless something critical happens to initiate the process. It is obvious that physical maturity alone has *not* made these individuals promising candidates for adulthood. These exceptions to fulfilled adolescent development accent the links between adolescence and young adulthood.

The end of adolescence is less easily identified than its beginning, although separation from home and financial independence are the markers that typically herald an individual's passage from late adolescence to young adulthood. For a large proportion of late adolescents, college provides a moratorium from entering young adulthood. Meanwhile, millions of other adolescents do not go to college, but enter the work force or the armed forces once their high school years have ended.

Throughout this book, I have used research that permits comparison of the responses of early, middle, and late adolescents to the many markers of the adolescent years. Many differences, subtle and obvious, distinguish an early, middle, and late adolescent. The research reported in this book illustrates these contrasts and clarifies the distinctions between the early, middle, and late adolescent years.

THE VIEWPOINT PRESENTED IN THIS BOOK

Links of Adolescence to Middle Childhood and Young Adulthood

Adolescence is bounded by middle childhood at one end and young adulthood at the other. Developments during middle childhood—socialization, changes in reasoning skills, and development of coping skills in response to stress—prepare individuals for the changes that occur during adolescence. While adolescence is a separate, indeed unique, period of change in a person's life, the changes of adolescence point not only back to middle childhood but also ahead to the greater maturity expected of a young adult.

Disregarding the links of adolescence to its immediate past and future may present the conceptual danger of ignoring the importance of adolescent development in the human life span—as though these years occur in a vacuum, with no developmental history, no link to other human experiences, and thus, providing no pattern for understanding the development of the human being. While linked to its past and future, adolescence involves developments that (*a*) differ qualitatively from the behaviors and capabilities that children exhibit and (*b*) prepare individuals for the tasks that young adults are expected to perform.

Over emphasizing the adolescent links to middle childhood and young adulthood may also be dangerous, inadvertently implying that adolescence is but a time of transition, with no uniqueness or integrity of its own. In a bleak interpretation, it is as though adolescence is a period one must endure to get from childhood to adulthood. Similarly, the adolescent years may be viewed as a way station in which to loiter until adulthood arrives. Societal rules lead some adolescents to think adults have contrived barriers to keep them from fully enjoying the rights and privileges of society. We will look at this view of adolescence in greater detail when discussing whether adolescence is a cultural artifact or a genuine period of human development.

A Contemporary Surge of Interest in Adolescence

Researchers have shown growing interest in adolescents and adolescent development. This can be seen in the formation of professional organizations, such as the Biennial Conference on Adolescent Research, which has met five times since 1982, and the Society for Research on Adolescence, which has attracted a multidisciplinary membership. Numerous research journals devoted to adolescence have emerged since the late 1970s. These include the *Journal of Adolescence, Journal of Adolescent Research, Journal of Early Adolescence*, and *Journal of Research on Adolescence*. In addition, several recent books have focused on specific adolescent concerns, such as adolescent suicide (Curran, 1987), drug use (Johnston, O'Malley, & Bachman, 1988), sex and pregnancy (Byrne & Fisher, 1983; Coles & Stokes, 1985), runaways (Lefkowitz, 1987), and work (Greenberger & Steinberg, 1986).

Student interest in adolescence has also surged—between January 1985 and June 1991, 569 doctoral students in education and psychology wrote dissertations that focused on adolescence. In part, this interest is a result of the growing number of careers available to individuals who specialize in adolescent development, such as counselors, social workers, juvenile probation officers, psychologists, marriage and family therapists, recreation specialists, and guidance workers. One young woman I know works in the school district of a rural county and develops programs for youth considered to be "at risk." (**Youths at risk** come from homes that involve alcohol or substance abuse, domestic violence, sexual abuse, and/or an impoverished single parent).

TWENTIETH CENTURY DIVERGENT VIEWS ON ADOLESCENCE

Strikingly divergent views about adolescence have emerged in the 20th century. Some scholars consider adolescence to be a time of exceptional conflict and difficulty (Barker, 1976; Blos, 1976/1979j; A. Freud, 1958/1969; S. Freud, 1935/1960; Gallagher & Harris, 1958; Haim, 1974; Hall, 1904; Hurlock, 1955; Kiell, 1964; Mohr & Despres, 1958; Parsons, 1959; Pearson, 1958; Stone & Church, 1973). James Coleman (1961), for instance, influenced several researchers to consider adolescents as members of a subculture at odds with adults and to view peer influence as negating, if not simply diminishing, the influence of parents on their adolescent children. However, a growing body of research has challenged the notion that adolescence is typically a time of turmoil and strain, asserting instead that the adolescent years are marked by relative calm and stability for most individuals (Bandura, 1964/1980; Connell, Stroobant, Sinclair, & Rogers, 1975; Offer, 1969, 1984; Offer, Ostrov, Howard, & Atkinson, 1988).

Most books about adolescents written for the general public characterize adolescence as a time of conflict, a time of **storm and stress** (that is, a time filled with turmoil). These books cover such topics as growing up (Atanasoff, 1989; Gordon, 1981), self-esteem (Ockerman, 1979; Schave & Schave, 1989), parental relations with teenagers (Bell & Wildflower, 1983; Brusko, 1987), sexuality and pregnancy (Wolf, 1988), drug use (Andre, 1987; Baker, 1982), runaways (Ritter, 1988), eating disorders (Macht, 1990), and suicide (Crook, 1988; Gordon, 1985). Many current religiously oriented books and video programs focus on adults' concerns about teenagers. A major figure in this market is James Dobson (1984, 1986, 1988, 1990).

Many parents seem to have accepted the storm and stress view of adolescence. Not uncommonly, parents express dread that their son or daughter will soon enter adolescence. These parents seem to think the adolescent years are filled with tension and conflict, children are transformed into some sort of monsters, and family life will be particularly stressful once their child enters into this "werewolf" stage of development. When informed that some researchers consider the adolescent years to be relatively free of turmoil and stress, parents look upon such claims as fairy tales they wish they could believe. A powerful assumption guides many individuals' expectations about adolescence. To paraphrase Anna Freud (1958/1969), the one thing we expect to be normal about adolescents is that they will be abnormal. Some conclude that there is something peculiar about an adolescent whose life is not filled with turmoil and stress.

The storm and stress model of adolescent development was originally presented by American psychologist G. Stanley Hall. We turn to his views.

The Pioneering Views of G. Stanley Hall

G. Stanley Hall (1844–1924) was one of the most influential psychologists of his time. Along with his contemporary, William James, Hall was, in the mind of the American public, the model of a psychologist. He was instrumental in bringing Sigmund Freud and Carl Jung to the United States to lecture on psychoanalysis. He was one of the founders of the American Psychological Association and is acknowledged for giving credibility to the critical study of adolescence. His writings had enormous public and professional influence. In particular, Hall's idea that adolescence is a time of unusual turmoil and conflict—storm and stress—captured the imagination of the public and provided a framework within which scholars could explain adolescent changes.

Hall was an ingenious, well-educated, and articulate product of Victorian times. He spent time studying in Germany and developed a noticeable appreciation for German culture. He was influenced by Darwin's powerful writings on evolution and by the poet Goethe's romantic themes concerning human existence. He incorporated ideas of these scientific and literary giants into his notions of adolescence.

Adolescence as the Recapitulation of Human Evolution

Hall makes explicit the influence Darwin's ideas had upon him. In fact, he became an apologist for Darwin, arguing that Darwin's contributions to psychology deserved more recognition (Hall, 1909). In the first chapter of his two-volume work, *Adolescence*, Hall began his discussion by saying that "individual growth recapitulates the history of the race" (1904, p. 1). Throughout his writings, he developed this assertion as a fundamental explanatory principle to account for every individual's growth and development. Hall claimed that the emergence of the human race can be explained through evolution, and further asserted, much more radically, that every individual repeats evolutionary stages that formed the human species in the ancient past. According to Hall (1909), a key function of civilized adults is to eliminate bestial, hereditary traits from children. Such traits, if left unchecked, produce social problems such as juvenile crime.

According to Hall, infancy recapitulates the animal version of the human race's existence. Childhood recapitulates the hunting and fishing epoch, and preadoles-

Hall said adolescent development at the turn of the century was endangered.

cence recapitulates "humdrum savagery." Adolescence recapitulates the introduction of civilization, with all its attempts to overcome chaos.

Hall believed adolescents are more responsive than any other age-group to positive growth and adult direction, and his optimism about the power of education to influence adolescents permeates his writings (Hall, 1904, 1909, 1920). However, he cautioned readers that contemporary adolescents live in times that endanger development in unprecedented ways. Referring to his recapitulation theory, he argued that adults could enable adolescents to overcome the savagery and the "insidious dangers" of their evolutionary heritage primarily by altering education to fit the contemporary needs of adolescents (Hall, 1904, p. xix).

Hall (1904) tended to use Christian terms and images in his discussion of adolescence. He referred to these years as "a new birth" and devoted several pages in *Adolescence* to the topics of sin, conversion, and religious confirmation.

In reading this account of Hall's recapitulation ideas, you may have thought that he used a colorful metaphor to describe human development, but that he could not possibly have believed his recapitulation view was literally true. The fact is, however, that Hall extended his knowledge of Darwinian evolutionary theory far beyond what any empirical evidence could support in order to explain the growth and development of human beings.

One irony in this matter is that Hall praised Darwin because "Darwin's method is always and everywhere objective and observational, never subjective or introspective" (1909, p. 252). Unlike Darwin's evolutionary ideas, Hall's recapitulation theory is more the result of speculation than of creative imagination applied to empirically tested data.

Adolescence as a Time of Storm and Stress

The German poet Goethe developed a compelling portrait of emotionally tortured, troubled, and sensitive youth. The protagonist of Goethe's work *The Sorrows of Young Werther* was beset by a life of storm and stress (in Goethe's words, *sturm und drang*). Overcome by the troubles portrayed throughout Goethe's literary master-piece, Werther commits suicide. This fictional portrait had a powerful influence on the imagination of educated individuals, and its influence can be seen in Hall's ideas about adolescence.

Hall viewed adolescence as a time of hope and optimism. However, despite his optimistic overview of the adolescent years, he depicted adolescence as a time of storm and stress. In *Adolescence*, he provided several biographical and autobiographical sketches to illustrate that storm and stress was a pattern during the adolescence of several famous authors.

The storm and stress theme has been one of Hall's enduring contributions to people's ideas about adolescence. As we shall see, it is a theme that has been criticized by some psychologists, anthropologists, and other social science researchers. At the same time, this theme has strong staying power. To use the evolutionary perspective that was so dear to Hall, storm and stress is an idea that has gained a firm foothold in the intellectual ecology. One school of thought in this intellectual ecology that has had a strong influence on keeping the storm and stress theme alive has been psychoanalysis.

Some Psychoanalytic Views: Sigmund Freud, Anna Freud, Peter Blos, and Erik Erikson

Sigmund Freud's (1856–1939) influence on contemporary Western culture has been profound. Perhaps one sign of this influence is the widely divergent reaction to the man and his ideas. He has been dismissed for being a male chauvinist, an ethnocentric, and a class-bound, Viennese intellectual (Lerman, 1986; Volosinov, 1976), lionized as a figure of uncompromising intellectual and moral courage (Jones, 1953, 1955, 1957; Kaufmann, 1980), and attacked for failure of personal courage and for intellectual dishonesty (Masson, 1984).

Whatever evaluation of Freud you consider appropriate, there can be no doubt that he has had a monumental influence on the images that shape modern thought. Ideas that originated with him include *defense mechanisms*, the *id*, the *ego*, and the *superego*. While he did not originate the notion of the human unconscious, he did make the influence of the human unconscious an ongoing assumption in modern thought. He persuaded several generations that dreams are communications from the unconscious. Further, the role of sexuality in personality formation and human motivation took a fundamentally new turn in Freud's powerful conceptual analyses of human behavior. Withstanding much opposition and even prejudice, Freud lived to see his theory about human behavior and personality become a dominant force in the thinking and practice of psychiatrists, psychologists, nurses, and social workers.

Sigmund Freud's Views on the Human Psyche

We will look at three concepts Freud developed about the human psyche: the unconscious, defense mechanisms, and stages of psychosexual development.

The unconscious. Freud maintained that existence in society impels each human being to engage in a relentless conflict between fulfilling unconscious, instinctual needs for pleasure and meeting acceptable standards of behavior. He postulated that initially, a human infant is motivated solely to have its needs met, with no ability to assess consequences or to delay gratification. This motivation emerges from unconscious mental processes that Freud called the **id** (S. Freud, 1920/1966, 1933/1964). The basic drive of the id is to achieve pleasure. Energy for the id comes from what Freud called the **libido**—namely, the basic energy of life. Keeping the id under control becomes a primary occupation of the individual.

As environmental realities (primarily the responses of parents) impinge on an infant's ability to achieve pleasure, some management of demands of the id becomes necessary. Through experience having demands met, an infant also learns that it is possible to actively manipulate the objects (both people and things) that gratify its needs. These lessons culminate early in the rudimentary and, thereafter, quickly developing mental processes that enable an individual to meet simultaneously the demands of the id and the expectations of the external world. Freud called these mental processes the **ego** (S. Freud, 1920/1966, 1933/1964). As a simple analogy, we may think of the id as a powerful racehorse and the ego as the jockey.

A third mental process is slower to develop but emerges fairly clearly by the age of 5 or 6 as young individuals begin to internalize the expectations of those who care for them. In short, an individual begins to develop a conscience. This mental process Freud called the **superego** (S. Freud, 1920/1966, 1933/1964). Freud considered the superego to be the young individual's accommodation to the demands of parental authority—that is, the internalization of the demands of external authority figures. Freud noted that the superego more readily and "paradoxically" internalizes "parents' strictness and severity, their prohibiting and punitive functions, whereas their loving care seems not to have been taken over and maintained" (S. Freud, 1933/1964, p. 62).

A common mistake is to assume that these three mental processes—id, ego, and superego—are separate persons or have an existence independent of the individual's mind. Freud considered the id, ego, and superego to be the fundamental processes whereby a person develops and interacts with self, others, and the world. Another analogy to explain these processes, one not available to Freud but, I believe, one he would have accepted readily, comes from the world of computer programming: the id, ego, and superego are akin to three very intricate software programs whereby the human personality acts. Since most of the commands that make up a computer software program are never displayed to an individual using the software, this analogy to Freud's three mental processes is apt. According to Freud, most of our mental processes remain below the level of awareness.

Defense mechanisms. Freud maintained that much of our existence is determined by unconscious interactions between the id, ego, and superego. For instance, all desires to fulfill needs—which are primarily sexual in nature—are called the **pleasure principle** and emerge from the completely unconscious mental processes of the id. Whereas the infant begins as completely id and has no qualm or concern that some desires might be punished if acted upon, by early childhood the individual finds him- or herself in a continual effort to keep "unacceptable" desires from being acted upon and, in some cases, from even becoming known to the individual.

How does the individual "recognize" on the unconscious level that a desire is unacceptable? The superego acts as a moral judge regarding the demands of the id. How do unacceptable desires remain out of consciousness? The ego develops what Freud called **defense mechanisms** (S. Freud, 1920/1966), or operations of the ego "to prevent an inroad of the id" (A. Freud, 1946, p. 32).

Freud's daughter Anna Freud, who became an internationally noted child psychoanalyst, provided an extended and influential exposition of the defense mechanisms used by the ego to protect against the anxiety of desires that run counter to parental approval. She traced the term *defense* to her father's early efforts to explain the development of **neuroses,** that is, emotional disturbances characterized by extreme efforts to avoid anxiety. According to A. Freud, her father later qualified his ideas to specify neuroses as unconscious efforts to prevent unacceptable desires and intolerable memories from becoming conscious (A. Freud, 1946).

But the question remains: Why would the ego develop defense mechanisms? The reason Freud provided is "to help the ego cope with anxiety, frustration, and unacceptable impulses and help relieve tension and inner conflicts" (Muuss, 1988, p. 41). The defense mechanisms are considered to be only temporarily successful in warding off unconscious threats, and some can even prove detrimental to long-term development (Blackham, 1967).

Psychoanalysts identify ten types of defense mechanisms (A. Freud, 1946). Rather than discussing them all here, I summarize three in order to emphasize the central importance of defense mechanisms in psychoanalytic theory. Two authors who lucidly and concisely review defense mechanisms are Garth J. Blackham (1967) and Rolf Muuss (1988).

One type of defense mechanism is **repression**—the exiling to unconsciousness of emotions or thoughts that create anxiety for the ego. An example of repression is illustrated by the case of an adolescent whose strong, unconscious desire for sexual relations with a neighbor is so anxiety-provoking that the adolescent's ego ensures that the desire never becomes known, to either the adolescent or anyone else.

Another type of defense mechanism is **intellectualization**, sometimes called *isolation of affect*. This mechanism involves thinking about threatening impulses, but in a way that represses feelings. Individuals remain unaware that their thoughts are not matched by their feelings on the subject. Intellectualization is illustrated by an anorexic adolescent who analyzes her eating disorder symptoms with a school counselor while having no real emotional investment in the discussion.

A third type of defense mechanism is **asceticism**, the denial of physical needs and engagement in practices that punish one's body. An example of asceticism is an adolescent who considers his physical impulses to be evil and who "disciplines" his body by fasting, losing sleep, and beating himself with a whip.

Freud noted that we become continually aware of our unconscious desires through various forms of behavior that reveal, in disguised form, what our id wants. He called these behaviors the **psychopathology of everyday life** (S. Freud, 1938b). The term *psychopathology* means mental disorders. Some examples of everyday psychopathology are forgetting someone's name, forgetting a promise, and making a slip of the tongue. The term *Freudian slip* has become part of ordinary vocabulary and refers to mistakes made while speaking or writing that Freud would suggest reveal unconscious thoughts and feelings. For instance, a young woman means to write "my boy friend," but instead writes "my boy fiend."

Freud also devoted considerable effort to exploring the world of dreams, which he saw as the major means whereby the individual's unconscious life emerges into consciousness (S. Freud, 1938a).

Stages of psychosexual development.   Instinctual drives take different courses as a child grows physically and psychologically. Psychoanalysts call these different courses **stages of psychosexual development.** Freud postulated five such stages: oral, anal, phallic, latency, and genital.

Freud said that infants focus first on **oral** means of getting pleasure (for instance, sucking a nipple) and later, on **anal** means (for instance, eliminating waste) (S. Freud, 1932/1964, 1938c). Around the age of 3, children become dominated by interest in their genitals, a stage Freud referred to as the **phallic** phase of psycho-sexual development (A. Freud, 1946; S. Freud, 1938c). By the start of middle child-hood, Freud said children go into a **latency** period that lasts until the onset of puberty. During this period, sexual interests and drives are supposedly directed into out-lets such as intellectual pursuits, and the superego gains greater control over the instinctual desires of the id (A. Freud, 1946; S. Freud, 1933/1964). With the onset of puberty, an individual's sexual drives and interests reawaken. Freud called this final stage of human psychosexual development the **genital** stage.

The fundamental conflict that determines future development occurs in early childhood. Freud says young children's love for their parent of the opposite sex cre-ates a libidinal desire to do away with their same-sex parent in order to have sole possession of "the parental love object." Freud termed this psychological develop-ment in boys the **Oedipus complex**, a reference to the figure from Greek tragedy who unwittingly killed his father and married his mother. He identified a comple-mentary development in girls, which he called the **Electra complex,** a reference to the figure from Greek tragedy who conspired to murder her mother. (For simplicity, the term *Oedipus complex* is often used for both boys' and girls' attractions to their opposite-sex parents.) The ego understands that such love for the parent of the oppo-site sex is prohibited and dangerous if acted upon. In the psychoanalytic view, the Oedipus complex is the fundamental crisis of psychosexual development, and if unresolved, can lead to neuroses.

Freud argued that the child's ego copes with his or her Oedipus complex by react-ing energetically on an unconscious level in an effort to repress the oedipal desires. The superego is formed as a result of this coping activity. In short, the origin of the superego is the need to do away with the unconscious desires represented by the Oedipus complex (S. Freud, 1923/1961). The superego is usually very successful in repressing oedipal desires until puberty. Psychoanalysts argue that the reappearance of the Oedipus complex in the adolescent years is the major reason for the turmoil of adolescence.

The preceding overview of Freudian thought prepares us to discuss Freud's views on adolescence. A danger inherent in such a cursory explanation is to delude uncritical readers into thinking that they are now masters at understanding Freud's complex, intricate theory on human personality. However, one of the beauties of Freud's theory is that it possesses remarkable coherency. Thus, from this overview about Freud, we have several basic concepts from which to examine his ideas about adolescent development.

Sigmund Freud's Views on Adolescence

Freud argued that psychosexual development proceeds through four stages—oral, anal, phallic, and latency—and culminates in the genital stage. This final stage of development has both physical and psychological manifestations. The stage begins with puberty, marks the start of adolescence, and "assigns very different functions to the two sexes" (S. Freud, 1938c, p. 604). During puberty, males become interested in sexual intercourse and seminal discharge, whereas females experience a strengthening of sexual inhibitions.

For Freud the obvious growth of the genitals is the most characteristic and striking process of puberty. These physical changes lead to an increase in physical tension, particularly in the male adolescent. This increase is accompanied by aroused interest in releasing this tension through sexual activity. However, unconscious drives also produce a new tension in the adolescent's life. The superego forbids acting on the instinctual demands to achieve sexual release. Thus, in Freud's view, turmoil and turbulence mark adolescence because unconscious prohibitions are raised against releasing tensions brought about by puberty.

Freud spent considerable effort discussing the **narcissism** of adolescence and the renewal of the Oedipus complex during the adolescent years. *Narcissism* literally means infatuation with oneself—the term is a reference to Narcissus, a figure from Greek mythology who fell in love with his reflection in a pool of water. Narcissism in adolescence serves to strengthen the ego's **attachment to ideals**; that is, to go beyond one's selfish interests in immediate gratification and to form *ego ideals* which include social institutions such as family and country (S. Freud, 1914/1957; see also Blos, 1974/1979c).

Successful resolution of the Oedipus complex enables an adolescent to develop a mature ego, to stabilize defenses, and to let go of infantile attachments to parents. A reorientation from parents to peers is an outgrowth of renewed oedipal conflicts and the arrival of sexual maturity. Furthermore, successful resolution of the Oedipus complex produces greater ego control over the superego. According to Freud, none of these accomplishments can occur without what many have called the *adolescent rebellion* (S. Freud, 1938c). Anna Freud more fully developed this idea of adolescent rebellion.

Anna Freud's Views on Adolescence

Anna Freud (1895–1982) spent her adult life in England as a psychoanalyst working with children. She and her father had come to England from their native Vienna in the late 1930s to escape Nazi persecution. Her theoretical work stemmed from clinical observations. She adhered to orthodox psychoanalytic ideas, wrote extensively on the psychoanalysis of children, provided an extended discussion of defense mechanisms, and wrote several papers on adolescence. The following discussion focuses on her ideas on adolescence.

Anna Freud described adolescence as a developmental disturbance and (as mentioned earlier) a period of turmoil. She cast suspicion on adolescents who did not manifest signs of upheaval in their lives (A. Freud, 1946, 1958/1969).

Anna Freud addressed three questions about adolescent upheaval and turmoil: (*a*) whether such upheaval is inevitable or avoidable; (*b*) whether the form adolescent upheaval will take can be predicted from a person's behavior as an infant and child; and (*c*) whether it is possible to distinguish disturbed adolescents from normal adolescents.

Is adolescent upheaval inevitable?   Anna Freud was certain that increased sexual drive and efforts to release the libidinal energy which accompanies puberty create anxiety for an adolescent's ego and produce inevitable and obvious upheaval in that person's life. Although an individual has achieved a balance between the id, ego, and superego during latency, the pressures of puberty require the individual to discard that balance and achieve new internal adjustments. Adolescent upheaval is necessary in order for the individual to incorporate a mature sexual identity into his or her personality. In Anna Frued's view, an adolescent who displays no signs of upheaval may not be making the necessary internal adjustments (A. Freud, 1958/ 1969).

During latency, some children adjust by adopting the mask of "good children." These children's excessive defenses against impulses of the id cripple their development by obstructing the "normal processes," the upheaval, of adolescence. Freud said "good children" need therapy more than any other adolescents because their defenses against the pressures of puberty pose a serious "delay to normal development" (A. Freud, 1958/1969, p. 150). The duty of the psychoanalyst is to remove the child's resistances, introduce him or her to how upsetting adolescence is, and provide assistance in appropriately modifying the child's defenses (A. Freud, 1958/ 1969).

Is adolescent upheaval predictable?   According to Anna Freud, knowing a person's infantile, early childhood, and latency period behavior does not ensure accurate predictions can be made about the form his or her adolescent upheaval will take (A. Freud, 1958/1969). She likened any form of upheaval to an illness and said that adolescent development "occasionally brings about something in the nature of a spontaneous cure" (A. Freud, 1958/1969, p. 151). Given her use of the illness metaphor, it is logical to question whether Freud made any distinction between psychologically disturbed adolescents and normal adolescents.

Can pathology be distinguished from normality during adolescence?   Freud considered this third question to be much more important than the first two. This evaluation reflects her clinical interests. She acknowledged difficulty in demarcating normality from pathology in adolescents (A. Freud, 1969/1971).

Anna Freud tempered her answer to this third question by saying that with skill and sensitivity a psychoanalyst could determine if an adolescent's defenses would promote or inhibit growth. One concludes from her discussion that adolescent pathology is not the same as adolescent normality, but she insisted that an adolescent who steadily manifests harmony and balance would, in reality, be manifesting abnormality (A. Freud, 1958/1969).

Is abnormality different from pathology? If all "normal" adolescents are "abnormal," making distinctions between pathology and abnormality is grasping at straws or employing what logicians call *a distinction without a difference*. You can imagine what Freud's reaction would be to researchers who conclude that most adolescents neither experience turmoil nor describe their lives as filled with turmoil and upheaval.

Anna Freud remained faithful to her father's theory that conflict is at the core of human personality. While some psychoanalysts also accept the Freudian emphasis on conflict, others who have specialized in adolescence do not consider these years to be marked by pathology or abnormality. In the next sections, we examine the views of such specialists, including Peter Blos and Erik Erikson.

Peter Blos's Views on Adolescence

As a practicing psychoanalyst, Peter Blos (b. 1904) saw adolescents in a private clinical setting. Formerly, he worked for Anna Freud in a school she had established for children of patients being seen by her and her father. Like Sigmund Freud and Anna Freud, Blos developed theoretical views based on clinical observations.

Blos used the concepts fundamental to orthodox psychoanalysis—id, ego, superego, oedipal complex, defense mechanisms, and stages of psychosexual development—as reference points and building blocks for his neo-Freudian views. He acknowledged the significant intellectual legacy provided by Sigmund Freud and then set out to modify and extend that legacy to explain development during adolescence.

The acceptance of conflict is an important theme in the thinking of Blos (1971/1979d). When speaking about the psychological development of individuals, Blos said "only through conflict can maturity be attained" (1971/1979b, p. 14). A constant, therefore, for Blos (and for the psychoanalytic movement as a whole) is the central role of conflict in development, whether of individuals, interpersonal relations, or the history of ideas. Like his psychoanalytic colleagues, Blos considered adolescence to be a period of time necessarily defined by turmoil and stress. However, unlike Anna Freud, he did not depict adolescent development as a type of illness.

The following discussion of Blos's views focuses on his ideas about the phases of adolescent development. Two essential elements of this discussion are what he has identified as the second individuation process and character formation in adolescence.

Phases of adolescent development.   Blos (1979g) identified five phases of development unique to adolescence: preadolescence, early adolescence, adolescence proper, late adolescence, and postadolescence. Muuss (1988) points out that a systematic presentation of these phases is missing from Blos's writings.

Preadolescence.   Blos uses the term **preadolescence** to describe the developmental phase following the latency period and preceding the onset of puberty. During preadolescence, an individual experiences psychic imbalance because instinctual demands are revived and are met with disapproval from the ego and superego. What most characterizes preadolescence is the renewed struggle to resist instinctual desires and the crisis of having to develop means of coping that extend beyond the defense mechanisms developed during early childhood and the latency period.

The initial reactions of preadolescent boys and girls to revived instinctual demands are to *regress* (to move backward or to revert) to earlier forms of defenses. I will discuss Blos's concept of regression more fully when reviewing his ideas about early adolescence and adolescence proper. To whet your curiosity, however, consider what Blos could mean by the assertion that adolescents mature because they revert to using defenses from their childhood (Blos, 1979f).

According to an early discussion of these matters, Blos (1941) described preadolescents as restless, moody, and aggressive. However, he later noted gender differences in how preadolescence manifests itself. He pointed out that preadolescent boys resist heterosexual attractions "with an uninhibited, public display or often elaborate recapitulation of pregenital drive modalities, apparent in such traits as smuttiness, neglect of body care, gluttony, and motor excitability" (Blos, 1957/1979h, p. 228). He saw female preadolescents approach heterosexuality more quickly and directly than their male counterparts, although preadolescent girls are more likely to keep their changing feelings private.

In summary, Blos emphasized that preadolescence is critical for the whole adolescent process and deserves to be considered as an exclusive developmental phase. During preadolescence, the individual sets the stage for resolving the developmental challenges that emerge later in adolescence, particularly the return of the oedipal complex.

Early Adolescence.   If you have observed students at a middle school, you have seen the signs of **early adolescence**: lessened identification with parents, increased identification with peers, intense (although often transitory) involvement in causes, infatuation with hero figures, and investment in a relationship with an opposite-sex peer. These early adolescent phenomena herald the efforts to form new ego ideals, separate from dependency on parents, gain more focused heterosexual relations, and develop a mature identity (Blos, 1965/1979e).

Blos used the concept of early adolescence to comprehend more fully the differences between individuals who develop normally and those whose development goes awry. He traced developmental failures in early adolescence to failure to surmount obstacles that emerge during this phase of life. Failure to overcome these obstacles constitutes a permanent barrier to maturity.

Blos drew attention not only to the challenges and dangers during adolescence, but also to the prospect of actual change and growth. For someone who successfully traverses the early adolescent course, the tasks and challenges of adolescence proper beckon, while someone who stumbles on the early adolescent course will be plagued by poorly resolved tasks and challenges.

In the psychoanalytic view, all of human development is beset with challenge and crisis. Thus, at any stage of development an individual may resolve a conflict favorably or unfavorably and carry the legacy of that resolution into the future. This sense of normal development versus developmental failure is not the sole property of early adolescence.

Adolescence Proper.   **Adolescence proper** is the period of time usually referred to as *middle adolescence*. Blos considered disengagement from parents and development of a distinctive, mature identity to be the fundamental obstacles to be surmounted during adolescence proper (Blos, 1974/1979c). In psychoanalytic terms, the task is to resolve definitively the Oedipus complex, which traumatized the individual in the early years of life.

Resolving the Oedipus complex produces what Blos has termed **the second individuation process,**which involves considerable reorganization of the superego (Blos, 1967/1979i). To posit that the superego alters considerably during adolescence is a major break from orthodox psychoanalytic writers, who insist that the superego is immutable to change after the latency period.

The changes that produce the second individuation process occur only because the individual experiences turmoil and stress. Blos described adolescence as a time of vulnerability, ambivalence, and, above all else, conflict. Without this conflict, a mature individual would not be impelled to develop. The vicissitudes of adolescence, according to Blos, enable maturity to emerge. This maturity is marked by greater resourcefulness in handling inner conflict.

As a result of the second individuation process, the adolescent acquires an ego more resourceful than the ego developed during middle childhood. The challenges of the preadolescent and early adolescent phases provide the impetus for acquiring a more resourceful ego. Having weathered and coped with these previous challenges, an adolescent experiences the oedipal conflict in a way qualitatively different than in early stages of development. The new resourcefulness of the ego enables the adolescent to rectify earlier, immature resolutions to psychosexual conflict; Blos therefore referred to adolescence as a "second chance" (Blos, 1979f, p. 475).

Unlike his predecessors, Blos did not describe adolescent development as merely the stage for reliving earlier conflicts, enduring upheaval, and looking pathological. He was optimistic about the developmental possibilities of adolescence.

We now return to Blos's assertion that adolescents mature because they regress. Blos emphasized that adolescents inevitably revert to earlier forms of coping, but rather than evaluating such regression negatively, Blos contends that it is normative and necessary. Adolescent regression provides the opportunity to address more adequately unresolved issues from childhood with a more fully developed ego. Thus, not only does regression inevitably occur during adolescence, but it is the catalyst for developmental progress.

Late Adolescence.   During the developmental phase of **late adolescence**, individuals accept that striving toward their ego ideal is really a journey without end (Blos, 1979f). Ambiguity and approximation become acceptable and, more importantly, are understood as a realistic assessment of human existence.

A stable **character formation** emerges as the end product of this final phase of adolescent development (Blos, 1968/1979a). Character formation is achieved by meeting four distinct developmental challenges. The first of these challenges is the second individuation process.

The second developmental challenge is the **response to traumatic experiences**, which some have called *unanticipated and undesirable life events.* (Danish & D'Augelli, 1980; Moos, 1986; Silver & Wortman, 1980) These events are commonly called *traumatic experiences.* Coping with traumatic experiences provides the means to achieve increased personal strength.

The third developmental challenge is to establish that the ego possesses **historical continuity.** In Blos's thinking, individuals must accept their past in order to possess a future (Blos, 1968/1979a). Difficulties in maturing occur when defense mechanisms prohibit individuals from resolving episodes in their childhood and, they thus do not come to terms with their past.

The fourth developmental challenge necessary for the formation of character in late adolescence is the emergence of a **sexual identity.** Blos differentiated sexual identity from gender identity. He said gender identity develops at an early age due to cultural messages about how males and females are supposed to behave, while sexual identity becomes possible only with the appearance of physical maturity, the loss of ambiguity regarding the object of sexual drives, and the ability to acquire heterosexual partners (Blos, 1968/1979a). You may have noted that Blos gives no mention to the prospect that sexual identity could be homosexual.

According to Blos, the formation of character, that is, a **stable psychic structure,** denotes the end of adolescence. He asserted that this closure is the natural outcome of development. However, he also implied that the individual will continue to develop during adulthood because new challenges will present themselves and earlier challenges not met successfully will be carried forward, "keeping alive an on-going effort of the ego at the harmonization of sensitivities, vulnerabilities, and idealizations that make up the essence of each individual self" (Blos, 1968/1979a, p. 497).

In summary, Blos accepted that adolescents experience conflict and develop by meeting challenges that produce turmoil. Unlike Anna Freud's view that adolescence is an abnormal time of life, Blos's model of adolescence focuses on ever-increasing maturity, individuality, and independence. We now turn to the ideas of Erik Erikson, a friend and colleague of Blos, who produced the most influential views on adolescence to emerge from the psychoanalytic tradition.

Erik Erikson's Views on Adolescence

Erik Erikson (1902–1994) grew up in Germany, the son of a Danish mother and father. His father abandoned his mother while Erikson was still in the womb, and for most of his childhood, he did not know that his mother's second husband, a German pediatrician, was not his natural father (Erikson, 1975).

As a young man, Erikson worked at Anna Freud's school in Vienna and became friends with Blos. Erikson credited Blos with rescuing him in his late twenties from a life without industry or direction (Erikson, 1975). Blos introduced Erikson to Anna Freud, and she guided him through psychoanalysis. In the early 1930s, Erikson graduated from the Vienna Psychoanalytic Institute, despite never having earned a bachelor's or advanced graduate degree.

Erikson emigrated to the United States in the mid-1930s and accepted a position as a clinical researcher at Harvard University. Throughout the rest of his adult life, Erikson held academic positions at several of the most prestigious private and public universities in North America.

Erikson wrote extensively on life-span human development from the vantage point of what he termed a **psychosocial model.** By psychosocial model, Erikson meant that psychological development occurs because the individual must adapt to the demands and expectations of society. He used his psychosocial concepts to produce studies of Martin Luther (Erikson, 1958) and Mahatma Gandhi (Erikson, 1969). He investigated childhood (Erikson, 1963), adolescence (Erikson, 1968), and old age (Erikson, Erikson, & Kivnick, 1986). While not contributing any specific work to middle adulthood, his writings clearly inspired major efforts by Daniel Levinson and his associates (1978), George Vaillant (1977), and Roger Gould (1978).

Erikson's psychosocial model.   The psychosocial model of development maintains that psychological growth occurs because of conflicts that are specific to the human species. Humans experience these conflicts throughout their lives. The source of the conflicts is biological, but they take shape because of societal demands that require psychological adjustment. Thus, the model posits psychosocial conflict as the impetus for fundamental human development.

Erikson maintained that a **genetic ground plan** directs the human search for psychological identity. He proposed the genetic ground plan as a means to bridge Sigmund Freud's theory of psychosexual conflict with his own knowledge of the physical and social growth of children (Erikson, 1968). This genetic ground plan manifests itself in eight crises fundamental to human development. Living in society impels each human being to master these **eight developmental crises**. These crises which he also called the **eight ages** of man, form the core of Erikson's view of psychosocial development.

The eight ages are presented in Table 1-1. The irreversible and invariant sequence proposed for these eight ages enables us to call Erikson's view *a stage theory of*

TABLE 1-1   Erikson's Eight Ages of Man

STAGE OF DEVELOPMENT	CRISIS	RESOLUTION
OLD AGE	Integrity *vs.* Despair	Wisdom or Disdain
ADULTHOOD	Generativity *vs.* Self-absorption	Care or Rejectivity
YOUNG ADULTHOOD	Intimacy *vs.* Isolation	Love or Exclusivity
ADOLESCENCE	Identity *vs.* Confusion	Fidelity or Repudiation
SCHOOL AGE	Industry *vs.* Inferiority	Competence or Inertia
PLAY AGE	Initiative *vs.* Guilt	Purpose or Inhibition
EARLY CHILDHOOD	Autonomy *vs.* Shame and Doubt	Will or Compulsion
INFANCY	Basic Trust *vs.* Mistrust	Hope or Withdrawal

SOURCE: Adapted from *Childhood and Society* by E. H. Erikson, 1963, p. 273 and *Vital Involvement in Old Age*: *The Experience of Old Age in Our Time* by E. H. Erikson, J. M. Erikson, and H. Q. Kivnick, 1986, p. 45.

development. The table names each stage, the crisis accompanying each stage, and the psychosocial strength or malignant tendency resulting from how the crisis is resolved. Capable resolution of a crisis produces competencies, which enable the person to take advantage of new opportunities, whereas poor resolution of a crisis restricts the individual in future interactions (Erikson, 1963, 1968, 1982; Erikson et al., 1986).

In Erikson's view, **crisis** refers to a critical point in development, an opportunity for growth or a refusal to grow. Thus, each crisis is a *turning point in development*. Each developmental crisis presents dichotomous possibilities, and there is no guarantee that an individual will resolve any crisis well. Capable resolution results in a specifically new psychosocial strength (Erikson, 1963). As an example, let's look at Erikson's analysis of the psychosocial crisis faced during the latency period.

In middle childhood, individuals enter school and face the crisis of applying themselves to learning and using skills to produce things. "School" may differ from culture to culture; that is, it may not be the organized classroom known in American society. In advanced, complicated societies, children learn to adapt to the unique culture of the school itself.

At this stage, the developmental crisis is between industry and inferiority. If the child resolves the crisis capably, the new psychosocial strength of competence emerges, whereas inertia grips the child who resolves the crisis poorly (Erikson, 1982). If children resolve the crisis poorly, they may become so constrained that as parents they frustrate the growth of their own children.

Whereas Erikson identified adolescence as the time for dealing with the crisis of **forming an identity,** in reality, Erikson presented identity as the fundamental stake in each stage of development. The infant's decision to trust or distrust the external world is a fundamental choice in forming an identity, as is the elderly person's decision to view his or her life with integrity or despair. Each age of man is a successive step in a hierarchical progression, and each age carries with it the potential for identity development or stagnation (Erikson, 1968).

Depending on how an individual resolves a crisis, the emergent favorable or unfavorable capacities "become full-grown components of the ever-new configuration that is the growing personality" (Erikson, 1968, p. 96). By the end of life, a person who has capably resolved all the developmental crises will possess eight significant **psychosocial strengths**: hope, will, purpose, competence, fidelity, love, care, and wisdom. How these strengths affect a person's life will depend on how the individual makes use of opportunities that emerge for him or her. Individuals who capably resolve all the developmental crises will use their psychosocial strengths in unique ways.

The crisis of adolescence presents the **bi-polar danger** of rushing into a premature commitment or indefinitely prolonging decision making (Erikson, 1961). The challenge in the person's life is to achieve **fidelity** in one's commitments while retaining **diversity** in one's approach. Unless diversity and fidelity are balanced, the person becomes the victim of narrow constraints (no diversity) or of "an empty relativism" (no fidelity) (Erikson, 1961, p. 11).

Erikson's linking of the term *crisis* to adolescent development caught the eye of a receptive public and fit in well with the storm and stress version of adolescence

School is not always in an organized classroom.

offered by Freud and the neo-Freudians. Erikson (1963) clearly accepted that the Oedipus complex, which reemerges during adolescence, presents conflicts in need of resolution.

Rapid physical development leads adolescents to be concerned primarily with their appearance in the eyes of others rather than their self-evaluation (Erikson, 1963). A second issue of concern is applying roles and skills learned in school to available occupational choices.

Erikson's argument for the emergence of a new ego identity in adolescence bears a striking resemblance to Blos's views regarding the second individuation process (Blos, 1967/1979i). Whereas Blos argued that the adolescent's ego is more resourceful than the child's ego, Erikson argued that the "integration now taking place in the form of ego identity (is) more than the sum of the childhood identifications. It is the accrued experience of the ego's ability to integrate all identifications with the vicissitudes of the libido, with the aptitudes developed out of endowment, and with the opportunities offered in social roles" (Erikson, 1963, p. 261).

There are also similarities between Erikson's ego identity formation and Blos's sense of historical continuity (Blos, 1968/1979a). Blos called the development of a sense of historical continuity a necessary condition for the formation of character in adolescence. Erikson said ego identity in adolescence comes from "the accrued confidence that the inner sameness and continuity prepared in the past are matched by the sameness and continuity of one's meaning for others, as evidenced in the tangible promise of a 'career'" (Erikson, 1963, pp. 261–262).

The adolescent looks for imaginative guidance, trusting in both peers and adults to provide focus, on some goal to hope and work for. The other side of this desire for imaginative guidance is resistance to narrow and impractical ideas (Erikson, 1968).

The greatest threat to any individual's resolution of the developmental crisis of adolescence is the inability to settle on an occupation. Choosing an occupation becomes much more important than simply making money or achieving social status. Adolescents who do not select occupations that capture their imaginations become victims of **role confusion** (Erikson, 1963, 1968).

Adolescents in a society awash with new technologies and ideas live in the best of times for capably resolving the **identity formation versus identity confusion crisis**. Not only do such times present vital, dynamic opportunities, but also increase prospects of adolescents being technologically literate and able to take advantage of these opportunities (Erikson, 1968).

In addition to the concept of an adolescent identity crisis, Erikson made popular another way of portraying adolescence. He talked of the adolescent years as being essentially a delay, or moratorium, between childhood and adulthood. During this moratorium, the individual becomes attracted to ideas, interested in peer approval, and eager to belong to a moral order identifying what is good and what is evil. During adolescence, the individual tries on new guises, new commitments, and new relationships, all in an effort to develop a unique identity (Erikson, 1963).

In summary, Erikson saw adolescence as a natural part of human development. Demands emerge for adolescents as part of interaction with society. Adolescents face choices which can produce strengths of individuality or leave the person impaired and immature. Issues from childhood, particularly the oedipal complex, reemerge in adolescence, but are dealt with more effectively using the greater resourcefulness of the ego. Like Blos, Erikson saw a strengthened sense of purpose and interest in life as the natural outcome of adolescence, whereas, for Sigmund Freud and Anna Freud, adolescence was a time of turmoil and surgent psychopathology.

We turn next to a school of psychology utterly at odds with psychoanalysis. These thinkers prefer to attend to observable behavior rather than to speculate about unconscious motivations. I am speaking about the behaviorists.

The Main Behaviorist Explanations

The three main behaviorist explanations for the acquisition of behavior are social learning, classical conditioning, and operant conditioning. The classical and operant conditioning models do not allow human cognition any place in human learning. In fact, the most famous of all behaviorists, B. F. Skinner, condemned psychologists' appeals to cognition as matters of superstition that retard the growth of psychology as a science (Skinner, 1990). However, the social learning theory of behavior accepts that cognitive processes are substantially involved in human performance.

Classical Conditioning

Classical conditioning, employed by Ivan Pavlov in his well-known experiments with dogs, explains behavior as the response of an organism to previously neutral stimuli that have become associated with some stimuli that naturally and automatically elicit this response. For instance, Pavlov noted that dogs begin to salivate when they are shown food; when a bell was rung directly before the dogs were given the food, the dogs soon salivated at the sound of the bell itself. Television advertising often employs classical conditioning principles by pairing the product being sold with sexual stimuli.

Blackham (1977) gave a clear example of classical conditioning in the life of a child whose father swatted him with a fly swatter when the boy misbehaved. The paddling itself hurt and frightened the child; however, the child began to associate other neutral stimuli with his punishment: his bedroom where the punishment always occurred, his father, and the fly swatter. "Previously neutral stimuli . . . developed the capacity to produce fear themselves" (Blackham, 1977, pp. 112–113).

You may know of the experiments conducted by John Watson, the behaviorist from the 1920s, who conditioned a young boy (called "Little Albert" in the study) to fear rabbits by making a loud sound whenever the boy spotted a rabbit. Within short order, not only did the boy fear rabbits but also other objects (such as dolls and stuffed animals) that resembled rabbits. Watson's treatment of Little Albert would today be considered a serious violation of the rights of human persons in psychological experiments, even a matter of child abuse.

Operant Conditioning

Operant conditioning, for which Skinner became internationally famous, explains that behavior is the *result of consequences.* In other words, what follows the performance of behavior increases the likelihood that the individual will repeat that behavior if the consequence is rewarding. Whereas classical conditioning indicates that behavior occurs because of stimuli that precede it, operant conditioning indicates that behavior occurs because of consequences that follow. For instance, Skinner noted that pigeons can be taught to peck a lever in a cage when they learn that pecking releases food pellets. The food is a reinforcer that strengthens the likelihood that the pecking behavior will occur. Skinner studied the many forms behavior takes as a consequence of reinforcement and insisted throughout his professional career that psychology as a science should concentrate on studying only **schedules of reinforcement** (Skinner, 1990).

A common example of operant conditioning in human beings is illustrated by an interaction between a mother and her daughter. The mother informs the girl that she can watch her favorite TV program only if she first washes the dishes. If enforced consistently, the parent's rule will teach the child that what she desires (watching her TV program) is contingent upon a specific behavior (washing the dishes). In short, operant conditioning is the theory that behavior is controlled by consequences.

Social Learning Theory and the Views of Albert Bandura

Social learning theory maintains that much—probably most—human learning occurs without any immediate reinforcers but rather through *observation* of people engaging in behaviors that produce consequences desirable to the observer. In effect, behavior is in the eye of the beholder.

Albert Bandura (b. 1925), a professor of psychology at Stanford University, is best known for his writings on the principles of behavior modification (1969) and, particularly, for his developments in social learning theory (1977, 1986). Bandura was president of the American Psychological Association in 1974.

Early in his career, Bandura did considerable research on adolescent aggression (Bandura & Walters, 1959). This work was followed by research on the effects on children of observing aggressive behavior in others (Bandura, 1965). Bandura later authored a book in which he analyzed human aggression from the social learning point of view (Bandura, 1973).

Bandura opposes behaviorist positions that rule out human cognition and contends that his is a social learning rather than a neo-behaviorist position. Bandura emphasizes that **vicarious reinforcement** (observing someone else obtaining consequences one would like to obtain) plays a very substantial role in learning, a role far surpassing extrinsic rewards or conditioned responses (Bandura, 1969, 1977). Social learning theory highlights (*a*) the ability of humans to use symbols and to analyze their own behavior, (*b*) the influence of various cognitive operations, such as self-regulatory processes, in psychological functioning, and (*c*) the self-initiated actions of humans to act on their environments, rather than remain passive responders to their environment (Bandura, 1977). The emphasis on cognitive processes and the active role of humans in influencing their lives and selecting their own behavior makes social learning theory differ radically from classical and operant conditioning.

Blackham provided an example of social learning in his daughter's life. One day when he took his daughter to get mail from a post office box, she asked if she could open the combination lock. Much to his surprise, his daughter opened the post office box, although she had never tried to open it before. Her explanation of how she had learned to unlock the box fits well into a social learning model; weeks before, she had observed her father opening the box, remembered the combination, and retrieved it from memory when the situation presented itself (Blackham & Silberman, 1975).

Bandura on adolescence.   Unlike the theorists who maintain that adolescence is a time of exceptional chaos, stress, and difficulty, Bandura argues that continuity and stability, rather than discontinuity and turmoil, normally mark adolescence (Bandura, 1964/1980). Bandura does not suggest that "adolescence is a stress- or problem-free period of development. No age group is free from stress or adjustment problems" (1964/1980, p. 31).

Adolescent behaviors emerge from childhood behaviors. Bandura extends this conclusion by asserting that adult behaviors are consistent with adolescent behaviors. He firmly believes that longitudinal research data and behavioral theory confirm that adolescents in turmoil were preadolescents in turmoil and likely will be adults in turmoil (Bandura, 1964/1980).

Bandura's views on adolescence emerge from his theory that developments in behavior are related to a history of reinforcement, observing other people's behavior, imitating what other people do, and remembering salient features about performance. Rather than displaying signs of turmoil that have no link to the laws of behavior, an adolescent in trouble possesses a history of reinforcement, behavioral models, mental representations, and imitative performances that account for what other persons mistakenly allege to be the sudden appearance of turmoil in the adolescent's life.

Bandura's ideas can be illustrated by his research on aggressive adolescents (Bandura & Walters, 1959). This research spanned more than a decade and culminated in a social learning analysis of aggression in humans of all ages, not only in adolescents (Bandura, 1973). Bandura noted two fundamentally consistent things about aggressive adolescents: (*a*) substantial evidence had demonstrated that modeling is the critical principle at work for adolescents in learning antisocial, aggressive behavior and (*b*) as a corollary of this first observation, watching others act aggressively proves sufficient to learn new ways of being aggressive (Bandura, 1969).

Bandura found that aggressive adolescents had been taught by their parents since early childhood that physical and verbal aggression are the preferred means to enforce compliance with one's wishes (Bandura, 1973; Bandura & Walters, 1959). Typically, the parents of aggressive adolescents provided graphic examples of assaultive behavior. In some cases, the parents verbally condemned aggression, while in other ways (for instance, by their rejection of their children and use of physical punishment as discipline), they encouraged their children to be aggressive (Bandura, 1973; Bandura & Walters, 1959).

Not all adolescents become aggressive, hostile, and antisocial. Some adolescents become very withdrawn. Bandura considers these withdrawn adolescents to be very unlike the majority of adolescents. Bandura found that withdrawn adolescents had been exposed since childhood to "pervasive inhibitory training in relation to aggression, dependency, and sex behavior" (Bandura, 1973, p. 96). Their parents kept careful control of emotions and discouraged any display of feelings.

Bandura argues that the majority of adolescents, however, do not become antisocially aggressive, withdrawn, or enmeshed in chaos and turmoil. They come from families in which discipline is fairly consistent and punishment rarely physical. Parents show their emotions and family members share feelings with one another. Consistency and stability mark the preadolescent years of these youth, and their adolescent years continue primarily in the same vein.

Why do so many people remain convinced that the adolescent years are a cauldron of trouble? Bandura (1964/1980) maintains that it is the few adolescents who are antisocial who grab the attention of adults, leading them to make invalid generalizations that all adolescents cause problems and create turmoil. In essence, Bandura expresses confidence that most parents influence the development of stable children who became stable adolescents. In contrast to the psychoanalytic expectation of adolescent disturbance and the popular belief in the horrors of adolescent life, Bandura asserts that adolescents in turmoil were preadolescents in turmoil. Surely you can remember one or more students in your elementary school whose behavior was so disruptive that their tumultuous adolescent years did not surprise you. On the other hand, did most of your elementary school peers experience a tumultuous adolescence or was it a continuation of stable growth? Consider the example best known to you; on the whole, was your own adolescence marked by storm and stress or by stability and continuity?

The Cultural Anthropological Views of Margaret Mead

In the 1920s, behaviorism began a relentless attack on the psychoanalytic supposition that biology determines behavior. A repudiation of the storm and stress interpretation of adolescence was implicit in this attack.

Another challenge to biological determinism also appeared in the 1920s. This challenge came from cultural anthropologists, who argued that societal practices, rather than heredity, explain human behavior. The cultural anthropologists particularly argued against the psychoanalytic supposition that all individuals experience difficulties in adjusting during their adolescent years (Boas, 1928/1950). The test case for cultural anthropology became the study of adolescents in a primitive society, drawing comparative generalizations regarding the influence of modern society. Such a study made Margaret Mead world famous.

Mead (1901–1978) was a graduate student of Franz Boas, one of the world's leading cultural anthropologists. In her early twenties, Mead went to the islands of Samoa to examine Boas's thesis that culture, rather than biology, determines behavior. The book that resulted from her stay in Samoa, *Coming of Age in Samoa*, came to be seen as a significant contribution to cultural anthropology and has been read by several generations of students. With the acclaim for her study, Mead's career was set. She held numerous prestigious appointments and for the rest of her adult life retained recognition as one of the foremost cultural anthropologists of this century.

Mead (1928/1950) noted in the first pages of *Coming of Age in Samoa* that she intended to test the idea that adolescence is a period of inevitable conflict and turmoil. Because controlled experiments in laboratories could not be applied to test whether adolescents experience inevitable distress regardless of their society, Mead asserted that such questions could be addressed only by the anthropologist. By studying human beings in other cultures, the anthropologist could begin to test whether conflict and turmoil were the result of a specific society or were an inevitable part of adolescent development.

Mead decided to study female adolescent development in Samoa by spending time with Samoan adolescent girls, observing the households in which the girls lived, and gaining material that would justify generalizations to all Samoan adolescents. She spent nine months in Samoa, with one predominant question guiding her work: "Are the disturbances which vex our adolescents due to the nature of adolescence itself or to the civilization?" (Mead, 1928/1950, p. 11). Note Mead's acceptance that adolescents in modern European and American societies were in turmoil. She did not question whether modern adolescents were in turmoil, only the causes of that turmoil.

Mead said Samoan society presented adolescent girls with coherent values and standards and did not hurry them into making important life decisions (Mead, 1928/1950, 1930/1952). Menstruation was not considered a matter to be hidden and, from their early childhood years, adolescent girls had understood about human reproduction (Mead, 1930/1952). Mead claimed that female adolescent turmoil was the exception, rather than the rule, in Samoa because Samoans encourage patience. Samoan adolescence was "perhaps the pleasantest time the Samoan girl will ever know" (Mead, 1930/1952, p. 533).

Mead did note that some adolescent Samoan girls were in conflict. She said that their deviancy occurred because of exceptional emotional needs and unresponsive home conditions (Mead, 1928/1950). Using her principle that culture determines behavior, Mead speculated that these delinquent girls would not have been in conflict in more favorable milieus.

Mead's ideas have not gone unchallenged. In fact, during the early 1980s, the cultural anthropologist Derek Freeman, who had spent several years in Samoa, published a book attacking Mead for sloppy methodology, naivete, and failure to learn the intricacies of Samoan culture (Freeman, 1983). Freeman concluded that Mead's analysis of Samoan society was in error and that her picture of an untroubled Samoan adolescence was therefore incorrect.

Freeman indicated that educated Samoans consider the storm and stress view to be an apt description of adolescence in the Samoan islands. He said interviews with Samoan adolescent boys and girls confirmed that their lives were filled with turmoil, resentment of adults, and intense emotional distress. He challenged Mead's assertion that suicide was rare among Samoan adolescents. Based on research gathered among adolescents in Australia, New Zealand, and Samoa, Freeman concluded that the incidence of adolescent suicide in Samoa was relatively high.

Referring to Mead's study and Mead herself as myths, Freeman asserted that she had produced a seriously flawed portrait of Samoan adolescent development. Freeman dismissed all of her conclusions, contending that she had based them on inaccurate portraits of Samoan life. Rather than having provided a challenge to biological determinism, Freeman believed that Mead had produced a false portrait of adolescent behavior (Freeman, 1983).

Mead asserted that the culture of modern societies profoundly affects adolescents for the worse. So many aspects of modern life are in flux, from changing standards and mores to economic fluctuation to the very heterogeneity of American society itself. To address such problems, she called for rituals whereby adolescents can move into adulthood (Mead, 1930/1952).

Mead contended that the vexations of adolescence are enhanced by modern society. Mead seemed to be reaching the same pessimistic conclusions as Freud about civilization's effects on individuals and nations (S. Freud, 1929/1946). Rather than seeing the prospect of a successful resolution of conflict in adolescence, Mead said modern society prevented the acceptance of responsible adulthood because rites of transformation did not exist. While individuals would become adults as far as chronology is concerned, "many of our most potentially gifted individuals will die adolescent, unplaced, and without realizing any of the promise of their genius" (Mead, 1930/1952, p. 539).

PARADIGMS AND THE STUDY OF ADOLESCENCE

We turn now to the historian of science, Thomas Kuhn, whose thoughts on how natural science develops were once considered revolutionary in the history and the philosophy of science. In themselves, Kuhn's ideas are not directly associated with the study of adolescent development. However, as a reflection on how scientists think about their endeavors, Kuhn's ideas illuminate how scholarship on adolescence has developed over the years.

The Model of Thomas Kuhn

Kuhn (b. 1922), a professor of the history of science at Princeton University, revolutionized contemporary thinking about change and progress in the natural sciences. In *The Structure of Scientific Revolutions*, he describes what influences chemists, physicists, and astronomers to change their minds about plausible scientific explanations of reality (Kuhn, 1962, 1970). According to Kuhn, fundamental change in scientific thinking occurs due to the triumph of a new model of reality rather than as the result of a rational, logical process of discourse about evidence.

Kuhn used the term **paradigm** to identify all those assumptions and beliefs about reality that capture the imaginations of scientists. A paradigm provides the keys to decode puzzles, and once a paradigm captures scientists' imaginations, work within that paradigm becomes a matter of puzzle solving. Kuhn called this form of scientific work "normal science." Scientists with a paradigm possess confidence that their model of reality holds the keys to unlocking whatever puzzles arise in their field.

It is only when (*a*) a scientific puzzle continually baffles scientists and (*b*) the inability to solve the puzzle challenges the fundamental plausibility of the paradigm that scientists begin looking for a new explanation—that is, a new paradigm. A *paradigm shift* is set into motion. The outcome of a paradigm shift is that a radically different theory of reality wins the imaginations of scientists and propels normal science in a new direction. In the 20th century, Einstein's theory of relativity and the theory of quantum mechanics are commonly acknowledged as exemplars of a paradigm shift in physics. The Copernican model of the solar system is the primary example of the triumph of a new paradigm in astronomy, and Darwin's model of evolution caused a paradigm shift in biology.

Two notions of Kuhn's thinking seem pertinent to the field of adolescent development. First, Kuhn's writings have persuaded me that assumptions about reality govern and influence how scholars explain adolescent development. This notion is manifest in the current scholarly arguments over the proper way to conduct scientific inquiries into human matters—the quantitative versus qualitative approach—and can be read clearly in the arguments for a feminist understanding of science and cross-cultural studies of human development, and even in the debate on whether adolescence is a stage of human development or a cultural artifact. Second, one way to judge that a paradigm has triumphed is to see whether textbooks in the discipline are organized according to that paradigm. In the remainder of this chapter, we will discuss these two paradigmatic issues.

Research and the Study of Adolescent Development

Quantitative and Qualitative Approaches

There is much debate about the appropriate way to study human beings. The tradition that has dominated scholarly work for most of the 20th century is the **quantitative tradition** in which scientists use rigorous experimental designs that employ statistics to determine whether research findings differ significantly from chance occurrences.

But what *is* a **statistically significant difference**? Commonly, researchers report that results are significant when the findings could have occurred due to chance less than 5 times in 100 tries (written $p < .05$); that is, the likelihood that the results should be trusted is at least 95%. Some researchers restrict themselves to reporting only results that could have occurred by chance less than 1 time in 100 tries ($p < .01$). If you knew your chances of winning the lottery were greater than 99%, might that information influence you to make a significant purchase of a lottery ticket?

Quantitative researchers design studies with the intent of statistically testing whether findings may be inferred beyond the sample of individuals studied. For instance, when political polls are taken, the intent is to apply the results to more people than those who were polled. The sample's responses should be representative of a much larger group of people who did not participate in the study. In other words, researchers want to go beyond the data and make broader conclusions about individuals considered similar to those in the study. Such conclusions are called **statistical inferences.**

Statistical inferences are vulnerable to error, and findings produced due to error lead to unsound conclusions. Some conditions that lead to errors of inference are sampling bias, wishful thinking, and confusing statistical significance with social significance. We will take up each of these conditions in turn.

The first condition is **sampling bias**. The sample chosen to be studied must represent the population about which statistical inferences will be made. A study can be so poorly designed that, even though results indicate statistically significant findings, the results are spurious. How the sample was chosen may have been so biased that the results are not representative of a larger group.

Imagine conducting a political poll on a college campus to investigate whether a course unpopular among some students should be abolished. If the students asked to participate in the poll were only those opposed to the course, the result could not be inferred to represent the total student body, even if the findings are said to be significant at the .01 level. The researchers polled only persons who already agreed with one point of view. In doing so, they eliminated the prospect of inferring that the results apply to the entire college student body.

An example from the field of human development is research conducted to look at parent-child interactions. Significant findings from studies that looked only at mother-child interactions could be inferred only to maternal interactions with children, not to all parental interactions. A similar issue emerges when research participants come from only one racial or ethnic group, but the results are inferred to apply to members of other racial or ethnic groups.

A second condition that may lead to errors of inference is **wishful thinking**. Some published reports suggest (or even boldly assert) that the findings indicate important differences, despite a lack of statistical significance. Read those types of claims with skepticism. A common ploy in these cases is for the researcher to say that the findings are "tending toward significance" or are indicative of a "trend." Researchers who claim that statistically nonsignificant findings indicate or suggest significant results are simply not playing by the rules.

A third condition that affects inference errors is **confusing statistical significance with social significance**. This type of inference error can occur because the sample is so large that a very slight variation in responses leads to statistically significant differences. The prospect for such findings are quite good in large surveys.

Imagine that a nationwide survey of 10,000 high school students was conducted in two consecutive years and that one question asked about knowledge of illegal drugs. If in the second year, a 1% increase occurred regarding knowledge of illegal drugs, such a change would be statistically significant given the size of the sample, but would this statistically significant finding have any social significance? Perhaps, but the meaning is not immediately apparent. A researcher might use this finding to claim that more money was needed for drug prevention programs, but what would be the foundation for such an assertion? Certainly not the statistically significant change found in the survey. The mere fact of statistical significance, in other words, does not explain what the findings mean nor even whether they have practical import.

Another tradition for studying human beings has been present, but less dominant, and its adherents maintain that researchers can understand human beings only within the natural contexts in which humans live; only by investigating the hopes, intentionality, and ideas human beings possess; and only by acknowledging that the multiple variables that influence human behavior always resist laboratory control. This approach emulates the success of historians and is seen primarily in the work of anthropologists. This approach is the **qualitative tradition** whereby researchers present information in the form of narratives. After conducting extensive interviews, observing naturally occurring behaviors, and writing voluminous field notes, the researchers construct vignettes and scenarios to facilitate the reader's comprehension of findings.

Quantitative adherents emphasize the *objectivity and precision* of their results and caution against the *subjectivity and imprecision* they see in qualitative studies. Qualitative adherents underscore that human actions are *ultimately subjective*. They question the prospect of attaining objectivity in any human endeavor, and they note that numbers have the allure of appearing true whether they provide insight or not.

The way I have cast this section on quantitative and qualitative approaches has struck some readers as dichotomous. Experience with researchers has persuaded me that many scholars do not appreciate the value of both the quantitative and qualitative traditions. Within the past several years, some scholars have urged their colleagues to use both quantitative and qualitative procedures in the same study, but mechanisms that encourage qualitative studies of adolescence have emerged only recently.

Most of the research published about human development comes from the quantitative tradition, and many of the research studies I consulted to write this textbook are citizens of the quantitative nation. However, I have also included qualitative studies. The triumph of the quantitative tradition within the human sciences can be seen as indicative of a paradigm. Given the dominance of the quantitative tradition in human development research, what strikes me as remarkable is the utter influence of Freud, Erikson, Piaget, and Darwin on our models of human development; the work of each of these thinkers is mostly, if not completely, qualitative. We now turn to some of the specific research approaches stemming from the quantitative and qualitative traditions.

The quantitative tradition provides three basic approaches for investigating human development: cross-sectional, longitudinal, and sequential.

Cross-sectional approach.   The **cross-sectional approach** involves gathering data from several people of different ages at one point in time and then making statistical analyses to see if answers differ according to age. For instance, a researcher might investigate whether answers to an intelligence test differ according to the ages of the subjects. If the answers did differ significantly, the researcher would report that age differences had been found. The results, for instance, might indicate that intelligence test scores of 20- to 29-year-olds differed from the scores of 60- to 69-year-olds. While age differences could be determined, these differences would provide no justification to conclude that the intelligence test scores of the 20- to 29-year-olds will become like those of the 60- to 69-year-olds (or to conclude that the scores of the 60- to 69-year-olds used to be like those of the 20- to 29-year-olds).

A cross-sectional study does not enable the researcher to determine whether differences in people's scores indicate change over time, that is, whether development has occurred. While cross-sectional studies allow a researcher to collect data efficiently and to make judgments about age differences, this approach does not enable a researcher to make any valid conclusions about development within an age group or between different age groups. Data must be gathered more than once from the same individuals in order to talk with validity about changes over time.

Longitudinal approach.   **Longitudinal studies** provide the most common approach to studying people over time. A longitudinal investigation involves gathering data at least twice from each study subject and comparing responses to see if changes have occurred. For instance, a researcher might investigate whether the intelligence of some children changes between the ages of 10 and 16. Data could be gathered on each child every year and then analyzed to see if later responses differ from earlier responses. Differences in scores would allow the researcher to conclude that change had occurred over time. The researcher could not conclude from these data, however, how people from another generation would respond at any age.

Longitudinal studies are more difficult to conduct than crosssectional studies. Having to gather data more than once leads to greater expense, more time, and greater risk to the integrity of the study. The primary risk in longitudinal research is that participants will not complete the study. Another risk is that memory of earlier responses will influence later responses, thus creating differences that are literally the effect of the study. In research jargon, such results are *test reactive*.

Sequential approach.   Investigators have developed a third approach that combines the cross-sectional with the longitudinal. The **sequential approach** involves gathering data more than once from several individuals grouped according to age. For instance, a researcher might study whether the intelligence test scores of children aged 10, 12, and 14 changed over a two-year period. Results could be analyzed for differences over time within a specific age- group and for differences between age-groups. Members of a specific age-group are called **cohorts**.

The sequential approach allows for the testing of *age differences* and for *changes over time*. The former is the province of the cross-sectional approach and the latter, the longitudinal. While cohort influences cannot be ruled out by the sequential approach, they can be identified by showing the extent of changes over time within a cohort and between cohorts. For instance, a younger cohort that was given more effective instruction in mathematics than an older cohort would thereby have an advantage over an older group in tests of mathematical comprehension; as the cohorts take more tests regarding mathematics, differences over time would become more pronounced and would eventually favor the younger group.

Triangulation.   Growing attention has been given to using multiple sources of data when conducting research. This idea is sometimes referred to as **triangulation**, the method whereby sailors use three separate points to obtain a true fix on the position of a ship at sea.

Qualitative and quantitative researchers endorse the use of triangulation. Sociologists, educators, and program evaluators who use qualitative methods insist that a reliable portrait can be obtained only by rigorous efforts to allow a variety of sources to confirm or disconfirm conclusions about what is being studied (Glaser & Strauss, 1967; Guba & Lincoln, 1989; Hendricks, 1982; Marshall & Rossman, 1989; Stake, 1967, 1978, 1986; Strauss & Corbin, 1990). Quantitative methodologists in these fields also insist that only through triangulation can a reliable fix be obtained in the complex reality of human individuals, groups, and institutions (Cook, 1985; Glass, McGraw, & Smith, 1981; Rossi, 1989; Rossi & Freeman, 1989).

Case studies.   Qualitative researchers have made use of a specific type of method, the **case study**. Robert Stake (1978) of the University of Illinois has argued that, frequently, case studies are preferred because they are "in harmony with the reader's experience" and thereby provide a natural basis for making conclusions (Stake & Trumbull, 1982). Stake (1987; Stake & Trumbull, 1982) has maintained, in fact, that the most common form of learning occurs in what he calls **naturalistic generalizations**. A naturalistic generalization occurs when a person makes conclusions by comparing one's own experience to what one understands about the experience of someone else. Case studies are singularly adapted to provide a basis for naturalistic generalizations.

A case may be a single person, a group of people, an organization, or anything whose boundaries can be deciphered. Some examples of cases are a youth gang, a family, a high school, a course on self-defense tactics, a fraternity, and a university program to prevent sexual harassment. It is crucial to define the boundaries of the case and to distinguish what is and is not the case. Several case studies will be presented in this book, both as the opening pieces for each chapter and as important pieces within specific chapters.

The emphasis of case study research is uncovering **issues**—matters of importance about which people disagree. For instance, an issue in many communities is whether birth control information should be provided in high schools. A case study of a community's response to proposed sexual education in the public schools would be expected to inquire about attitudes toward birth control information.

Some issues emerge only within the context of a particular case. These emergent issues are sometimes called **emic issues** (Stake, 1978). Researchers can learn about emic issues only by immersing themselves in the natural setting of the case. Such immersion is possible only by understanding the boundaries of the case. An example of an emic issue is the way students at a particular high school use styles of clothing as a means to determine social groupings.

Case studies come alive for readers as the writers use ordinary, nontechnical language. Case study research uses descriptions, portrayals, and metaphors. The focus of case study research is to enlighten readers about the case and thereby to increase understanding.

Vignettes and **scenarios** are the frequently used tools of case study researchers. A vignette is the retelling of an actual event as it happened. A scenario is a fictionalized account of an event, perhaps the accumulation of several observations. A scenario is true to the spirit of the case, while a vignette provides a literal rendition of a specific episode.

Potential uses of case studies.   Case study research can make strong contributions to social science by enlightening readers about exceptional cases. Three prominent uses of case study research are *Sybil* (Schreiber, 1973), the study of a woman with multiple personality disorder, *The Varieties of Religious Experience* (James, 1901/1985), in which William James presented in-depth studies of the experiences of a few extraordinary individuals, and "Personality under Social Catastrophe" (Allport, Bruner, & Jandorf, 1941), an analysis of the lives of 90 refugees.

Case study research is also used to preserve the uniqueness of the individual. Exceptional biographies and histories accomplish this purpose. An example is *The Last Full Measure* (Moe, 1993), a study of a regiment of Minnesota volunteers in combat during the Civil War.

A vivid use of personal documents to understand human psychology is found in two works of the Harvard psychologist Gordon Allport. In *Letters from Jenny*, Allport (1965) presented letters from an older woman to a younger married couple over a 12-year period. He called the letters "the most effective case material I have ever encountered for provoking fruitful class discussion of theories of personality" (Allport, 1965, p. vi). In the other work, "The use of personal documents in psychological science," Allport (1951) provided a lengthy argument favoring the use of personal documents in the study of psychology and discussed the limits and strengths of the case study method.

A third use of the case study approach is to generate theory, and one finds such applications common in the work of anthropologists and psychoanalysts (S. Freud, 1925; Mead, 1928/1950). A strong case for using case studies to generate theory can be found in a short article by Barry MacDonald and Rob Walker (1975) and, of course, in the works of Allport (1951, 1965) mentioned previously.

Potential abuses of case studies.   The potential gains offered by case study research do not eliminate potential abuses. One potential abuse is to make **false causal inferences**—that is, to apply the findings incorrectly to other cases. For instance, it would not be valid to conclude that more religious instruction with youth gangs is needed after learning that a religious conversion turned one gang member from a life of crime to a life of self-sacrifice.

Another potential abuse is to have one's **biases affect how one interprets findings**. Consider, as an example, the issue dividing researchers about adolescence as a time of turmoil versus adolescence as a time of relative calm and stability. A researcher with a bias toward either side of the issue may simply "reinterpret" case observations that challenge his or her biases.

A third potential abuse is to be **biased in the very collection of data**, to look only for observations that confirm what one wants to discover. A researcher intent on proving males are not capable of sensitivity to the feelings of others may look only for situations in which males act selfishly and insensitively.

In summary, two distinct research traditions have emerged in the social sciences. One tradition emulates the success of the natural sciences in representing reality through numbers. The other emphasizes the inherently subjective nature of human beings and attempts to capture the meaning of human activity in words.

Basic and Applied Research

Another distinction differentiates basic and applied research. **Basic research** is considered the realm of the *knowledge generator*, who is interested in producing theoretical explanations. Two examples are the works of Charles Darwin, who developed the theory of evolution, and Martin Seligman, who developed the theory of learned helplessness (Seligman, 1975). **Applied research** is considered the realm of the *knowledge user*, who is interested in making practical use of theoretical knowledge. An example is the work of Carol Dweck (1975, 1986) to help school-age children who give up when they encounter difficulties even though they have the ability to complete their assignments. **Applied professionals**, such as counselors and psychotherapists, are clear examples of knowledge users who translate theory into practical use. One example of a person whose basic research has stimulated considerable applied research with adolescents is Lawrence Kohlberg (1969) who developed a theory of moral reasoning (see Chapter 5).

Critical analysis of traditional scientific procedures has emerged in recent years. This development allies readily with the criticisms raised against the quantitative approach. We now examine this development, focussing on feminist interpretations of science.

Feminist Interpretations of Science

When Allen Bergin and Hans Strupp (1972) investigated the prospects of conducting multisite research on psychotherapy, one of the persons they interviewed was Marvin A. Smith, a biochemist at Brigham Young University. In that interview, Smith set forth lucidly an issue that we now recognize separates the feminist perspective from the more "traditional" scientific perspectives. The issue is whether isolating component parts enables or distorts greater understanding of the whole.

> In general it appears that the biochemists have been able to isolate the protein manufacturing part of the cell and have been able to study this under a whole series of varied conditions. It is fascinating that one process is isolable out of this complex process; however, it has not been possible to make this isolated system really work as efficiently as a natural system (Bergin & Strupp, 1972, p. 388).

The differences between the feminist and the more traditional scientific perspectives represent fundamental differences in assumptions about reality. At the very least, the differences between these perspectives signify what Kuhn meant by a battle over paradigms.

The feminist interpretation of science involves assumptions about the **influence of values, epistemology** (the study of the origin, nature, and limits of human knowledge), and the **role of the scientist as a social activist** (Ricketts, 1989). Unlike some scientists who argue that research occurs without reference to values, feminists argue that all human endeavors are value-laden. Philosophers and historians of science have made this very argument since they began attacking and demolishing logical positivism (Feyerabend, 1975; Hanson, 1972; Holton, 1978; Suppe, 1977; Toulmin, 1961).

Feminists argue that isolating human phenomena into discrete components alters the phenomena. Whereas the more traditional paradigm assumes that focusing upon an isolated component provides knowledge generalizable to a larger context, feminists argue that once isolated from their contexts, phenomena about humanity cease being meaningful (Grimshaw, 1986; Harding, 1987; Ricketts, 1989).

Feminists maintain that researchers and research subjects interact and are involved in an egalitarian learning relationship. The more traditional perspective maintains that researchers are independent of research subjects who are fundamentally passive (Gergen, 1988). The conflict of **interconnectedness versus isolation** comes through clearly in this distinction between the paradigms.

Feminists contend that reality is a **social construct** strongly influenced by language (Gergen, 1989; Guba & Lincoln, 1989; Lincoln & Guba, 1985). That is, language is used to create reality. Adherents of the more traditional approach maintain that reality exists independent of human construction and that language enables reality to be represented as observed. From this perspective, scientific language is believed to be more precise and to represent reality more reliably than ordinary language.

According to the feminist perspective, science is a product of culture, pressures from social institutions, and the interests of individual scientists (Longino & Doell, 1983). Adherents of the more traditional paradigm insist that science blocks out the influence of culture and any other contaminants and pursues scientific truth through value-free, logically rigorous methods.

Feminists take an avowedly social activist stance, maintaining that the more traditional approach has legitimized gender discrimination and diminished scientific understanding by enshrining interpretations of reality that overlook alternative viewpoints and emphasize a male-dominated construction of reality (Grimshaw, 1986; Harding, 1987; Ricketts, 1989). From the more traditional approach, social activism is believed to contaminate objective scientific endeavors. Adherents maintain that an abstract, detached method of viewing reality provides clarity, certainty, and greater control.

One of the themes that I have attempted to weave throughout this book is the interconnectedness of adolescence to other ages in the human life span. The theme of interconnectedness is a hardy feminist notion.

Feminists endorse social activism. While this book has not gone so far as to endorse specific social agendas, I think I have done something more radical. I have posed questions and asked readers to think about dilemmas (those human experiences that leave many of us "clueless" about what is the right thing to do). What could be more activist in essence than to foster independent, critical thinking?

The robust, feminist theme regarding the influence of social and cultural values on human thought has particular salience for a book on adolescent development. It causes us to question how many assertions about adolescence are the product of particular cultural frames of reference. Feminists would caution us that all efforts to think are not only influenced by culture but are, in their very essence, social constructs. Thus, we might readily see the ideas of G. Stanley Hall or Sigmund Freud as social constructs developed by men of late 19th and early 20th century mores. A pressing question is, How do I detect the cultural influences on my thoughts?

The feminist call for appreciation of diversity has influenced the emerging sensitivity of many social scientists to cultural differences. It is incumbent that a textbook on adolescent development include cross-cultural comparisons if it is to represent in any way the diversity of human experience and development.

Cross-Cultural Comparisons

A perusal of English language research literature about human development quickly indicates that most of our understandings are based on studies of white, middle-class Americans. Many of the studies are normed on males and then generalized to females.

A hue and cry has been raised for greater sensitivity to diverse racial, cultural, and ethnic groups as well as to females. It is paradoxical that studies purporting to be rigorous and to provide generalizable results so seldom include sufficient numbers (if any at all) of individuals from divergent racial, cultural, or ethnic groups. Other than the study of human bereavement reactions, which have been normed on female responses (Balk, 1990a, 1991a; Rando, 1988), our studies on human development have focused first on males, compared females to males, and often decided females are "inadequate" when they respond unlike their male counterparts. In terms of adolescent research, you would expect investigators at the very least to study adolescents; in some cases, however, investigators rely on secondary sources of information (parents, teachers, school records).

Robert Munroe, Ruth Munore, and Beatrice Whiting noted:

> most of the research on human development has been undertaken by European and American psychologists. The subjects of their research have been predominantly parents and children native to the United States and the Continent. The findings, however, are presented as relevant to the human race. When challenged, all are quick to add the phrase 'in our culture.' Until recently, however, few have had the motivation or the opportunity to consider the implications of this phrase (1981, p. ix).

These authors identify the misunderstandings that accrue due to cultural blindness and, perhaps, due to ethnocentric attitudes (that is, assumptions that one's ethnic group is superior to all others).

One test of cultural differences is whether adolescence exists as a universal phase of human development or is specific to some cultures. This issue is the *stage of development versus cultural artifact* debate, and we take it up next.

Stage of Development or Cultural Artifact?

Blos (1976/1979j) drew attention to the definition of *adolescence* given in the *Oxford English Dictionary* (OED). The OED traced the term back to the 15th century and noted that the word referred then to the span of life between childhood and adulthood. In other words, for at least six centuries, adolescence has been recognized as a distinct period of development by English-speaking people.

You might be surprised to learn that some 20th-century scholars considered adolescence to be the invention of Western industrialized societies (Church & Sedlack, 1976; Frank, 1938). They argued that the requirements for survival in preindustrial

In the 20th century, adolescents in indus-trialized soceities are expected to be in school to prepare for a more complex tech-nological world.

societies forced individuals into adulthood without any moratorium between child-hood and adolescence. Historical documents from the 18th and 19th centuries make clear that, by the age of seven, many children had assumed work burdens that strike us as not only unusual but inhumane.

One study on how American psychologists view adolescents during times of eco-nomic hardship and economic prosperity concluded that when American society needed more workers (in times of economic prosperity), adolescents were depicted as resourceful, mature, and independent, and when American society needed to pro-tect the scarce jobs available for adults (in times of economic hardship), adolescents were viewed as unaccomplished, immature, and dependent (Enright, Levy, Harris, & Lapsley, 1987). Kurt Lewin (1939/1951) remarked that modern society keeps ado-lescents from participating fully and thereby relegates adolescents to a marginal sta-tus. Similarly, Paul Goodman (1960) argued that adolescents feel alienated from society because they are prevented from contributing meaningfully.

The increasingly complex nature of our technological society requires much more extensive education and training before an individual can compete in and contribute to the work force. For example, computer literacy has become a necessity for get-ting ahead in this society, whereas only 20 years ago, computers were luxuries and handheld calculators were intricate, expensive pieces of equipment. It is not difficult to see why society-imposed delays in taking on adult roles lead to practices that extend the adolescent years and provide evidence that adolescence is a product of the Western postindustrial world.

Although some societies rush children past adolescence and into adult roles while others prevent adolescents from engaging in adult activities, it is critical to remem-ber the developmental changes that occur during the adolescent years. Is it likely that the physical changes of puberty were absent in preindustrial societies? If anything, evidence indicates that these societies ritualize the transition from childhood to adulthood once puberty ensues. Furthermore, historical records indicate that for Western children, the onset of puberty has been occurring earlier consistently for over the past 160 years (Chumlea, 1982).

Is it possible that "adolescent" changes in cognitive operations, social perspective taking, or identity formation also took place in individuals from earlier times during their second decade of life? Perhaps these changes are influenced by environmental expectations; thus, some of the developments we consider signs of adolescence may have occurred prior to the adolescent years, particularly in a society that admitted individuals into adulthood earlier than does American society. I remain skeptical, however, that a person could be forced to achieve the social perspectives that rely on abstract thinking prior to individual readiness. Whereas we may have institutional-ized and extended adolescence through the high school and college years, I do not believe we have created the developments that mark adolescence. It is possible that we attribute them to adolescence, whereas other societies attribute them to adult-hood. This issue provides a starting point for deciding how expectations influence your understanding of the adolescent years.

Textbook Structures and Paradigms

Kuhn (1962, 1970) wrote that textbooks signify that a paradigm has taken hold in a scientific field of inquiry when the textbooks in that field are structured in the same manner; the authors discuss the same subjects, raise the same issues, make the same conclusions, identify the same puzzles to be solved, and lead the student to a grasp of the accepted views in that field.

Implicit in Kuhn's idea is the gatekeeping function that publishers and college faculty provide on behalf of the paradigm. They dictate, for example, what college textbooks on adolescent development must contain. According to the current para-digm, the book must contain chapters on physical development, cognitive develop-ment, peer relations, family relations, school, work, self-concept, and psychological disturbances. Other topics may be covered, but these eight are essential.

CHAPTER SUMMARY

The adolescent years extend from age 10 to age 22. Adolescent development involves three age periods: early (10–14), middle (15–17), and late (18–22). Twentieth-century scholars have offered divergent views about adolescent develop-ment, including:

- G. Stanley Hall's recapitulation theory and his storm and stress theory of adolescence;
- The extremely influential views of the psychoanalysts, particularly the ideas propagated about adolescent turmoil, the second individuation process, and the crisis of identity formation;
- The social learning view of adolescence as primarily a time of relative calm and stability;

- The cultural anthropological view that adolescents in nonindustrialized societies have a fairly idyllic, untroubled development in contrast to the turbulent adolescence of modern society.

Researchers debate the value of quantitative versus qualitative methods, and many now see the value of combining both methods in their work. Three methods characteristic of quantitative developmental research are the cross-sectional, longitudinal, and sequential approaches. Some scholars are calling for greater use of the case study approach as a means to increase understanding about issues and questions peculiar to specific situations, although case study research limitations must be recognized.

Thomas Kuhn applied the notion of a paradigm to describe the work of scientists. He argued that during a period of normal science, scientists work out answers to puzzles within an overall framework (a paradigm) accepted by scientists in that field. This overall framework is a model for conducting scientific inquiry. A paradigm shift occurs when some significant puzzles cannot be solved in the reigning model, and a new framework, which can resolve the dilemmas, wins the allegiance of scientists.

The concept of a paradigm can help explain two things about research into adolescence. First, it explains the prominence of certain assumptions for investigating and interpreting adolescent development. Second, it explains the common structure of textbooks written about adolescent development.

Feminist interpretations of science offer a clear illustration of a struggle over paradigms. Feminists emphasize, among other things, that reality is a social construct and that science, as part of the social construction of reality, is a product of cultural values and influences.

The growing interest in cross-cultural comparisons also fits into a discussion of paradigms. Much of psychology has emerged from studies of white males in middle-class society. A hue and cry has been raised for greater sensitivity to racial, ethnic, and cultural diversity. A similar interest has emerged for reliable studies of female experiences.

The textbooks written about adolescent development signify that a paradigm exists about the study of adolescence. The structure of these textbooks invariably includes sections on the same topics. Investigators have increasingly adopted a cognitive view of these topics.

In the next chapter, we turn to a topic of singular importance in any study of adolescent development. We will examine the physical changes that mark the transition from childhood, and we open with the story of a 14-year-old female who has matured early.

INDISPUTABLE EVIDENCE:
Physical Changes in Ever-Living Color

Looking Older than She Really Is

Juliet celebrated her fourteenth birthday two weeks ago. Because her birthday is in August, she is younger than most of her school classmates. She is, however, taller than most children her age and has been since she was born—at birth she was 22 inches long, about 4 inches longer than most newborns.

When she was 4, Juliet looked about 7. Nearly everyone who has seen a photograph of her standing before a Christmas tree at the age of 4 guesses that she is 7, maybe 8 years old. A series of photographs showing her at ages 12 and 13 illustrates how she has consistently looked older to most people.

Looking older has its advantages and disadvantages or, as Juliet puts it, an upside and a downside:

At the age of 4, Juliet looked like a child of 7.

The upside is that when I go into the college area, college guys will talk to me. College students and older high school students will talk to me and be more willing to be friends, as long as I don't tell them my age. Sometimes, I can get into places a lot easier, like into R-rated movies. If I have my hair done up right and dress right, people believe I'm 17.

I remember coming out of a movie when I was in seventh grade and some college guy looked at me and said, 'Boy, is she a babe.' And when I was in eighth grade, I remember getting whistled at and told I'm sexy. It's kind of nice to hear sometimes. Also, it's fun to fool older guys, just to see their looks of surprise when I tell them how old I am.

On the downside, people think I'm older and ask me what grade I'm in. And when I tell them, they think I must be really stupid to only be a freshman in high school. When I was younger, there were times when I wanted a meal at a restaurant that had kid's prices, but I couldn't get the kid's price because the people in the restaurant wouldn't believe me when I told them my age. They'd go, 'Yeah, right!' When I was younger, I couldn't get into movies for children's prices, even though I was the right age. Also, people look at me really strange when I go see a Disney film, like 'Why would someone your age want to see Cinderella?' There have been times when people won't believe me about my age when I want them to. Like when a

Age 12   *Age 13*   *Age 13*

A series of photographs of Juliet at age 12 and 13 illustrates how she has looked older to most people.

guy is being raunchy and I want him to back off. Sometimes, it isn't good enough just to tell him how old I really am.

Juliet summed it up for herself, "All things considered, I prefer looking older than looking younger."

Her mother shares some of Juliet's views, but she did note that

> . . . things Juliet sees as advantages, I don't see that way. Having college guys hit on my 14-year-old daughter I do not see as an advantage. Another problem is people expect her to act like a grown-up because of her size, but she's not.
>
> Most of my reactions are like Juliet's. It goes back to when she was a child. People would assume she'd been held back when, in reality, she was one of the youngest in her class.
>
> I don't like the hassles when trying to get Juliet into movies or amusement parks for children's prices. People make it clear that they don't believe me and think I'm trying to cheat them.
>
> I remember when she was younger, less than 5, and we were at Disneyland, and the people dressed up like characters were ignoring her and not giving her hugs but giving them to other kids smaller than her who were her age.
>
> Once when Juliet was 3, she and I were in a grocery store and a woman asked me (a bit indignantly) why my child was not in school. Not that it was any of the woman's business, but Juliet was only 3.
>
> There have been good things for her because she looks older than she is. Because of her size, she's been modeling clothes since she was 12. All the other models were in their late teens or were adults. People picking the models at the tryout expressed amazement that she wasn't at least 16.

Time of physical maturation is an important topic in adolescent development. Physical changes in a young girl can elicit reactions from family members and from others. As noted in the case study, family issues also emerge during this time of physical maturation, issues that signify an adolescent's struggle to be independent of his or her parents. Juliet's story synthesizes the reality of early physical maturation for a daughter and her mother, and accents familial and cultural involvement in gender socialization (social pressures to act in a manner considered appropriate for members of one's sex).

This chapter covers physical development during adolescence. The change from childhood to adolescence is marked initially by a series of physical changes. These physical changes provide the most obvious evidence that a person is maturing.

Physical maturation is linked inextricably with sexual development. Social concerns over gender differences intensify when the sexual aspects of physical maturation begin. These concerns involve individual psychological reactions to the changes that are occurring, as well as an intensification of pressures to adopt socially accepted, sex-linked behaviors.

Physical development also involves health and nutrition. In this chapter, I discuss the nutritional needs of adolescents as well as a variety of factors affecting physical health. Extremes in nutritional intake can lead to three abnormal developments that affect physical health negatively—anorexia nervosa, bulimia nervosa, and obesity. These eating disorders are discussed under the heading of nutrition extremes, along with their psychological effects. We will also review an important link between physical exercise and health throughout the life span.

PUBERTY, HORMONES, AND PHYSICAL CHANGES

Before we turn to the topics of puberty, hormones, and physical changes, it is important to distinguish between adolescence and puberty (Beiser, 1991; Chumlea, 1982; Malina, 1978; Roche, 1976; Sklansky, 1991). **Puberty** is a distinct event marked by the achievement of reproductive maturity. **Reproductive maturity** refers to the completion of sexual development, when females can conceive a child and males can impregnate females. The beginning of **menstruation** signals the completion of reproductive maturity for females, whereas the **ejaculation of mobile sperm** heralds reproductive maturity for males.

Scientists do not currently agree on the defining event of adolescence. For **ethologists** (scientists who study the biological basis of behavior), reaching reproductive maturity is the hallmark event of adolescence (Savin-Williams & Weisfeld, 1989). Over the past 40 years, however, many psychologists have considered cognitive development and identity formation to be the most important adolescent achievements. Ethologists argue that cognitive development and identity formation are notions most cultures do not apply to adolescent development. In most cultures, say ethologists, adolescence ends when the individual reaches reproductive maturity.

In addition to reaching reproductive maturity, adolescence is marked by many other physical changes, including *bone growth, changes in body composition*, and *changes in motor performance*. **Physical maturation** comprises all the physical changes of adolescence, including reaching reproductive maturity.

While achieving physical maturation provides a clear benchmark for assessing the completion of adolescence, it is important to note that adolescent development consists of more than physical changes. These other changes do not necessarily cease once an individual becomes physically mature. Would you consider that either achieving reproductive maturity or completing other physical growth provides a reliable and valid criterion signaling the completion of adolescence? Some investigators do adopt one of those two positions; however, my position is that adolescence is marked indisputably by pronounced physical changes as well as by psychosocial changes. These psychosocial changes are discussed later in this chapter as well as in several following chapters.

The Role of the Central Nervous System

Physical development is controlled by the central nervous system (CNS) and is regulated, for the most part, by the endocrine system (Chumlea, 1982; Kreipe & Strauss, 1989). The endocrine system includes the thyroid gland, the pituitary body, and other endocrine glands that produce **biochemical agents** called **hormones**. Hormones affect behavior and physical development when released into the blood system in sufficient quantities.

Neuroreceptors keep hormone levels low prior to puberty, but permit higher levels as puberty approaches, much as a thermostat increases a furnace's output when the temperature setting is raised. Both genetic and environmental factors influence the time at which the settings of these neuroreceptors change (Grumbach, 1978).

As puberty approaches, the set points of the neuroreceptors reach higher adult settings, thereby allowing an increase of sex hormones to a level that far exceeds prepubescent levels (Chumlea, 1982). Increased levels of sex hormones initiate the onset of puberty.[1]

An analysis of longitudinal studies of twins suggests that genetics determines, to a great extent, how quickly the physical events of puberty occur and how quickly physical maturation is achieved (Fischbein, 1977; Rowe & Rodgers, 1989; Wilson, 1976). However, studies of the **secular trend** (the tendency for succeeding generations to reach physical maturation earlier) indicate that environmental factors also play a significant part in the physical development of adolescents. The secular trend is reviewed later in this chapter.

The role of the central nervous system in physical development involves several biochemical changes that begin during middle childhood. Researchers are only beginning to understand these changes and the mechanisms whereby they occur (Paikoff & Brooks-Gunn, 1989), but most agree that the changes occur because of the production of sex hormones and the growth hormone (Chumlea, 1982).

Sex Hormones

The primary **sex hormones** are **estrogen** and **testosterone**, which are produced by two stimulating hormones—the follicle stimulating hormone (FSH) and the luteinizing hormone (LH). When the levels of FSH and LH increase, an individual's **gonads** (primary sex glands—the ovaries and testes) are stimulated to mature. Gonad stimulation increases production of estrogen in females and testosterone in males.

---

[1]The psychoanalysts attributed the transformation of sexual instincts at puberty to hormonal changes. G. Stanley Hall said the physical changes of puberty create inevitable psychological conflict and result in a period of life marked by storm and stress. See Chapter 1.

Both estrogen and testosterone affect physical development and maturation. Males and females produce both estrogen and testosterone; however, the amounts differ significantly for each gender. Each sex hormone is closely associated with increases in physical stature, lean body mass, and total body fat. Estrogen stimulates bone development and maturation, while testosterone stimulates muscle development. Because males produce greater amounts of testosterone, their muscles develop more than females'. Both estrogen and testosterone play significant roles in the development of **primary sex characteristics** (reproductive capabilities) and **secondary sex characteristics** (such as pubic hair and enlarged genital organs) (Chumlea, 1982).

The Growth Hormone

The human body also produces a biochemical agent called the **growth hormone**. In combination with **somatomedin**, a byproduct of the liver and the kidneys, the growth hormone stimulates physical growth. Evidence seems clear that skeletal growth depends on somatomedin. However, the exact mechanisms whereby the growth hormone and somatomedin work remain to be disclosed (Chumlea, 1982). Researchers are puzzled, for instance, by the fact that anencephalic fetuses (fetuses lacking a brain) grow despite the absence of the growth hormone in their systems.

The level of the growth hormone in children does not differ significantly from the level found in adults. Fatigue, exercise, diet, rest, and stress affect the level of the growth hormone in an individual. Alterations in blood glucose and fatty acid levels also affect levels of the growth hormone (Bryson & Reichlin, 1966; Chumlea, 1982; Winter, 1978).

Skeletal Growth and the Growth Spurt

Many bones grow rapidly during adolescence. For example, during physical maturation, the female pelvis widens in order to allow passage of a fetus during labor. Leg bones typically reach their peak lengths before shoulder and chest bones reach their peak growth. We call this rapid skeletal growth the **growth spurt**.

The growth spurt is marked by rapid changes in height as well as in body weight. Adolescents frequently "shoot up" nine or ten inches in a short period of time. While changes in body weight vary considerably and are influenced by heredity, life style, and diet; on average, boys' weight increases about 42 pounds and girls' about 38 pounds during the growth spurt (Malina, 1990; Sinclair, 1978; Thissen, Bock, Wainer, & Roche, 1976). Gender differences in the growth spurt are illustrated in Figure 2-1.

On average, the growth spurt begins about two years earlier for girls than for boys. For North American and Western European girls, the growth spurt begins between 8.7 and 10.3 years of age, and for boys, between 10.3 and 12.1 years of age (Chumlea, 1982; Malina, 1990). However, the growth spurt lasts longer for boys, thereby producing larger skeletons and thus, larger statures for males. Girls begin their growth spurt when about 54 inches tall, while boys begin their spurt at about 59 inches tall. Since each gender gains around 10 inches in height during the growth spurt, we can see the reason for gender differences in adult stature.

The human skeleton is composed of three types of bones: long bones, irregular bones, and flat bones. The arms and legs are made up of long bones. Irregular bones

FIGURE 2-1
Growth Spurt
Gender Differences

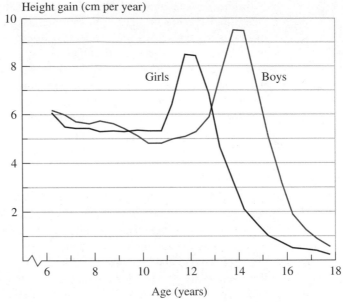

SOURCE: From *Growth at Adolescence* by J. M. Tanner, Copyright © 1962 by Blackwell Scientific Publications Ltd. Reprinted by permission.

are found in the wrists and ankles, while flat bones are found in the pelvis and the skull. Most skull bones do not grow much during adolescence because the skull grows to accommodate the growth of the brain: by the age of 10, the human brain has nearly reached its full size.

Changes in Body Composition

Certain components of body composition that change during adolescence have been identified—**lean body mass (LBM)**, **total body fat (TBF)**, and **free-fat weight (FFW)**. Only LBM and TBF concern us here, because FFW, which is body weight minus all fat, can be determined only during analysis of a cadaver (Chumlea, 1982).

LBM is primarily muscle; it is calculated by subtracting TBF from body weight (Chumlea, 1982; Siri, 1956). TBF is stored primarily as subcutaneous fat—that is, beneath the skin. Changes in LBM and TBF during adolescence are different for boys and girls.

For girls, TBF and LBM increase earlier than for boys. This increase is attributed to their earlier onset of puberty (Chumlea, 1982; Malina, 1990). However, by the age of 15, LBM stabilizes and changes very little for girls until later in life.

Female adolescents experience increased levels of TBF primarily because of higher levels of estrogen. Contemporary understanding of female puberty has begun to focus on the important role of the female body fat in maintaining the abilities to **gestate** (carry a fetus in the uterus) and to **lactate** (secrete breast milk) (Savin-Williams & Weisfeld, 1989).

For boys, the increase in LBM begins in early adolescence (around the age of 13) but, unlike the pattern for girls, continues increasing until late adolescence or even young adulthood. By the end of their LBM growth spurt, boys have three to five times more LBM than girls (Chumlea, 1982). An increase in muscle mass in adolescent boys helps to explain the increase in LBM during adolescence. This increase of muscle mass also leads to changes in motor performance.

Adolescent Physical Growth and Motor Performance

Throughout adolescence, boys demonstrate greater performance gains than girls on several measures of strength, aerobic, and other motor tasks (Haubenstricker & Seefeldt, 1986; Malina, 1990). Similar findings are mentioned in a longitudinal study of adolescent growth and motor performance in Belgian boys (Beunen, Malina, Van't Hof, Simons, Ostyn, Renson, & Gerner, 1988). According to some writers, girls reach their peak on tasks of speed, agility, and balance by the age of 14, whereas boys continue to improve noticeably in these areas throughout adolescence (Chumlea, 1978; Malina, 1990).

William C. Chumlea (1982) and Robert M. Malina (1990) contend that girls reach a plateau in motor performance, with Chumlea asserting, "a few girls will perform as well as the average boy after age 16, but only a few boys will perform as low as the average girl" (1982, p. 478). However, little, if any mention is given to the role of experience and socialization in producing these outcomes. Boys are often expected and given opportunities to participate in physical activities that girls are denied. Other than strength due to muscle mass and overall running speed, what inherent advantage do adolescent males have over females in tasks requiring agility, balance, and speed? Some investigators have noted that girls who continue to engage in physical activity during adolescence extend their performance (Dyer, 1977; Herkowitz, 1978). In fact, female marathon runners in the 1980s set running marks that would have beaten males who competed in the Olympic Games during the 1930s and 1940s (Shaffer, 1989).

We have looked at several important features of physical maturation, including the growth spurt, changes in body composition, and changes in motor performance. Another integral part of physical maturation is developing the ability to reproduce sexually.

Sexual Development

In boys, the first change directly related to **sexual development** is growth of the testes and scrotum (Chumlea, 1982; Tanner, 1962). During puberty, cells in the testicles (called *leydig cells*) produce greater amounts of testosterone, thereby inducing sperm production. The age when sperm production starts is uncertain, although several studies indicate that by age 15, a majority of boys are producing sperm (Chumlea, 1982; Richardson & Short, 1978).

Approximately one year following the growth of the testes and scrotum, and shortly after the start of the growth spurt, a boy's penis begins to increase in length. This is accompanied by the appearance of pubic hair, first at the base of the penis, then surrounding the penis and scrotum, and eventually, forming an inverse pyramid that extends from the genitals onto the thighs (Chumlea, 1982; Tanner, 1962).

About two years after the growth of male pubic hair, hair appears in the armpits and on the face. Heredity greatly affects the amount as well as the distribution of hair on male bodies (Chumlea, 1982; Reynolds, 1951; Tanner, 1962).

While uncommon, the breasts may enlarge temporarily for some boys during sexual development. The process is called *gynecomastia* and can produce anxiety in boys who wonder if they are going to have a chest like a woman's. However, gynecomastia lasts only a short time and leaves no visible trace once the boy's breasts reduce in size. Estimates of the frequency of gynecomastia vary, but the incidence is small, between 1.6% and 8% (Chumlea, 1982).

Whereas enlargement of the breasts is an uncommon occurrence in males, the appearance of breast buds is the first sign that puberty is approaching for females. At about the same time as the start of breast enlargement, the female's vagina and uterus begin to grow—the vagina lengthens, the vaginal epithelium thickens, and the vaginal mucous membranes become more acidic (Chumlea, 1982; Stuart, 1946).

Menstruation begins about two years after the start of breast, uterine, and vaginal development. The first menstruation is called **menarche.** Why menarche occurs when it does is debated. R.E. Frisch and his associates proposed that menstruation occurs once a girl's body reaches sufficient weight to trigger hormonal changes (Frisch, 1974; Frisch & Revelle, 1970, 1971; Frisch, Revelle, & Cook, 1973). It is known that menstruation ceases for anorexic females (American Psychiatric Association, 1987; Rees & Trahms, 1989), a fact that lends credence to Frisch's views. While the rate of the growth spurt offers a good predictor of menarche, the increase in body fat offers a better prediction of ovulation and the ability to reproduce than it does for the onset of menstruation (Lancaster, 1984).

Girls begin developing pubic hair as the breasts begin to enlarge. Male and female pubic hair is alike in both texture and appearance, but not in distribution over the body (Chumlea, 1982). Estrogen keeps a girl's body hair (as well as her skin) more childlike than a male's; ethologists surmise that this feature makes females more attractive than males to children (Savin-Williams & Weisfeld, 1989).

Assessment of Sexual Maturity

Sexual development does not necessarily coincide with chronological age. Thus, children who are the same age chronologically may be quite different in terms of **sexual maturity.** Given the variance in sexual development, researchers have produced systems to rate sexual development according to different levels. Male sexual maturation is typically ranked according to genital and pubic hair development, whereas female maturation is ranked according to breast and pubic hair development (Chumlea, 1982; Tanner, 1962).

James Tanner (1962) produced the system most commonly used to rate levels of sexual maturation. **Tanner's system** divides levels of sexual maturity into five grades based on the development of secondary sex characteristics:

Grade 1. The absence of any secondary sex characteristics

Grade 2. The first appearance of a secondary sex characteristic

Grade 3. The further development of a secondary sex characteristic

Grade 4. More mature stages of a secondary sex characteristic

Grade 5. The arrival of full adult development in a secondary sex characteristic

Tanner's system uses four measures to chart sexual development in females—breast development, pubic hair development, menarche, and peak height velocity. **Peak height velocity** refers to that point during the growth spurt when the maximum annual increase in stature occurs (Roche, 1976). Sexual development in males is

charted according to three developments—genital development, pubic hair development, and peak height velocity.

Use of Tanner's system illustrates clearly the variance within each sex in the
attainment of sexual maturity. For instance, if we examine genital development,
between ages 9 and 10, 97% of males are in grade 1 and 3% are in grade 2. Between
12 and 13 years of age, 32% of males are in grade 1, 47% are in grade 2, 16% are in
grade 3, and 5% are in grade 4. By age 16, 97% of males have reached grade 4 genital development and 3% have reached grade 5. By 18 years of age, 25% of males
are in grade 4 and 75% have entered grade 5. By 18.5 years of age, all males have
achieved full sexual maturity (Chumlea, 1982).

Female sexual development reflects variability similar to that displayed in males.
For instance, females enter grade 2 breast development between the ages of 9 and
14, grade 3 between ages 10 and 15, grade 4 between ages 11 and 15.5, and grade 5
between ages 12 and 19. When male genital development and female breast development are compared, it becomes clear that most males reach grade 5 genital development before most females reach grade 5 breast development. The order in which
stages of puberty appear also varies, both between the sexes and within each sex.
These variations in sexual maturation across the adolescent years are illustrated in
Figure 2-2.

FIGURE 2-2
Sexual Maturation
Across Adolescence

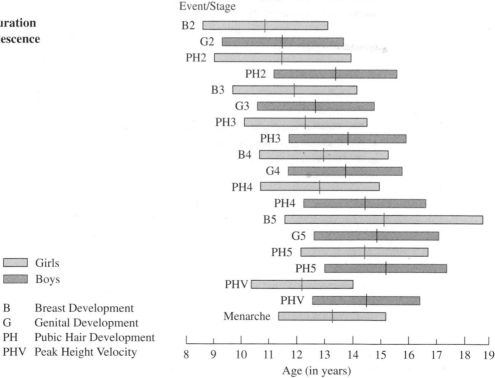

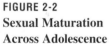

Girls
Boys

B   Breast Development
G   Genital Development
PH   Pubic Hair Development
PHV   Peak Height Velocity

SOURCE: From *Handbook of Developmental Psychology* by W. C. Chumlea, pp. 471–485. Copyright
© 1982 by Prentice-Hall, Inc. Reprinted by permission.

Individual sexual development can also vary. As an example, a boy can attain grade 4 genital development while remaining in grade 3 pubic hair development. Furthermore, while some children pass quickly from one level of sexual development to the next, other children pass quickly through some stages only to stay much longer in others (Chumlea, 1982; Roche, 1976). Marshall and Tanner (1969) reported that the age at which a pubertal event occurs is not influenced by the length of time between events. They did note, however, that pubertal events are positively related. They reported a very high correlation (.82) between Grade 2 breast development and peak height velocity in girls, and a similarly high correlation (.78) for grade 2 genital development and peak height velocity in boys.

Variability in sexual maturation is also found within and between racial and ethnic groups, but a chief influence appears to be socioeconomic class. For instance, menarche occurs in middle-class Western European, North American, and Chinese girls at about the age of 13, while for Mexican girls, the onset of menstruation occurs around 14 years of age. For girls in New Guinea, menarche occurs considerably later, between the ages of 15.5 and 18.4 (Chumlea, 1982).

The next section discusses the trend over the past several generations of earlier physical maturation, including sexual development, among youths in industrialized countries.

The Secular Trend

Researchers have noticed a trend in physical maturation over the past 150 years—individuals mature more rapidly than persons from the previous generation. As previously mentioned, this trend toward earlier physical maturation is called the **secular trend**. While this trend has been documented in industrialized Western societies, researchers have also reported an earlier onset of puberty in some Nigerian and Bangladeshi children. These children came from affluent families, indicating a probable association between better nutrition and health care and earlier physical maturation (Haq, 1984; Imobekhai, 1986).

The chief pieces of evidence of the secular trend are (a) noticeable increases in average height, (b) earlier start of the growth spurt, (c) earlier attainment of maximum height, (d) earlier onset of menstruation, and (e) earlier changes in vocal quality for boys. Since 1900, the average height of children growing up in Western Europe and North America has increased approximately one inch every ten years; by the time children who were born in 1980 reach their maximum height, they will be about nine inches taller than their 1900 counterparts.

Of seemingly greater significance than gains in stature is the earlier onset of menstruation. Since 1830, girls in Western Europe and North America have started menstruation three to four months earlier each decade; by 1990, the average age of menarche was approximately 13, whereas in 1850, the average age was around 16. Menarche used to occur in the years we ascribe to middle adolescence but now occurs in early adolescence (Birren, Kinney, Schaie, & Woodruff, 1981; Chumlea, 1982).

The secular trend toward earlier maturation explains why adolescence in industrial societies stretches over a longer period of time than in less developed countries—individuals enter adolescence earlier in industrialized societies and thus have

Affluent socioeconomic conditions can stimulate physical growth, whereas poverty can retard physical growth.

a longer period of time between childhood and adulthood. In less developed countries, such as New Guinea, menarche is still a fairly late phenomenon, occuring just before a girl enters adulthood (Chumlea, 1982). Distinctions between early, middle, and late adolescence may be an outgrowth of the secular trend.

Poverty inhibits the secular trend. For children of poverty, the secular trend of gains in height lags behind by a generation. For example, 10-year-old children raised in poverty in the United States during the 1970s were approximately two inches shorter than children from families above the poverty line. The inhibiting effects of poverty on physical growth are not influenced by racial or ethnic membership. Impoverished white children in the United States during the 1970s were shorter than black children whose families had the same income, but all these children were shorter than children from middle-class families. Furthermore, impoverished children in the United States of the 19th century were smaller than children alive today in impoverished developing countries (Birren et al., 1981). The secular trend is not limited to the United States.

It is too simplistic to assert that wealth is solely responsible for stimulating the secular trend. However, societal affluence does translate into better health care, better living conditions, and better nutrition. Such conditions characterize developed countries and are closely associated with the secular trend. Even when these signs of a higher standard of living characterize a society, they frequently are not available to the impoverished members of that society. The differences in physical stature for children above and below the poverty line testify to the role of health, nutrition, and living conditions in stimulating or retarding physical development (Birren, et al., 1981; Chumlea, 1982).

We have looked at the physical aspects of adolescent development, including the growth spurt, changes in body composition, changes in motor performance, sexual development, and the overall tendency for successive generations to mature more quickly. We now turn to a review of the psychological reactions to these physical changes.

PSYCHOLOGICAL REACTIONS TO PUBERTY

The physical changes that mark adolescence produce psychological reactions within the individual and within others. Anne Petersen and Brandon Taylor (1980) criticized cross-cultural research for its lack of in-depth studies of adolescents' psychological reactions to the varied cultural norms, values, and practices employed to teach youth about puberty. Gwen Broude (1981) made more sweeping criticisms that cross-cultural anthropological findings about socialization and puberty are questionable due to serious methodological problems (for example, unrepresentative samples, small samples, and invalid measures). In the following section, we look at psychological reactions to the timing of pubertal development.

Effects of Early, On-Time, and Delayed Puberty

An important characteristic of anticipated life events is whether they occur when expected. The differences in pubertal development from individual to individual—as well as variation within the same individual—produce distinct personal and social perceptions, depending on whether puberty is early, on time, or delayed. Perceiving oneself as early, on time, or late in terms of physical development, and fielding the reactions of others to this changing physical status, can influence one's self-concept and self-esteem.

Studies of the timing of puberty for boys have concluded that early-maturing boys gain a lasting psychological and social edge over their peers. Early-maturing boys have greater self-confidence, are more independent, are more attractive to adults and other adolescents, and are considered to be leaders (Tobin Richards, Boxer, & Petersen, 1983). Earlier physical maturity gives boys an advantage in athletics, and being a star athlete offers a definite edge in adolescent culture. Physically, the early-maturing boy appears to be more like an adult than like his peers.

Initial male gains due to early pubertal maturation are balanced by developmental losses. Early-maturing males are more somber, less spontaneous, more submissive, and less flexible than other adolescent boys. Early maturers seem less willing or even interested in exploring options, and more willing and interested in accepting the values of adults (Brooks-Gunn, 1987; Peskin, 1967). One hypothesis is that boys respond to early maturation with rigid attempts to be in control of what is happening to them, and they acquiesce more readily to goals and choices carrying adult approval. Another explanation is that having gained early acceptance by the adult world, the early-maturing boy has no motive to try alternatives, whereas later-maturing boys must develop their own style of handling the choices they meet during adolescence.

During the onset of puberty, early-maturing girls consider themselves to be less attractive than do girls who mature on time. In fact, early-maturing girls report greater tension and anxiety and poorer self-concepts than do other girls. Increases in weight and body fat strongly influence the early-maturing girl's feelings about what is happening to her (Tobin-Richards et al., 1983). In contrast, weight gain is not a significant factor in the self-perceptions of boys during puberty.

Petersen (1983) suggested that early-maturing girls lack support from their same-age peers, making the experience of physical maturation even more difficult. Early-maturing girls with older friends engage in more delinquent behaviors than early maturers without older friends (Magnusson, Stratton, & Allen, 1985). Related findings of sexual and aggressive behaviors were found in early-maturing girls who had been sexually abused (Weinstein, Trickett, & Putnam, 1989).

Maryse Tobin-Richards and her associates (1983) suggest that early-maturing girls do not have the same social advantages offered early-maturing boys—athletic prowess, expectations of career success, and leadership. They contend that a female's early maturation is explicitly sexual in meaning and generates ambivalent reactions from adults and peers.

An early-maturing girl's life may also be upset by the transition from a self-contained, elementary school classroom to a larger, more bustling middle school or junior high school. There is some evidence that early-maturing girls who are able to stay in an eight-grade elementary school respond less negatively to their bodily changes than girls who must cope with both early physical maturation and transition to a new school (Crockett, Petersen, Graber, Schulenberg, & Ebata, 1989).

Over the course of adolescence, however, early-maturing girls develop increased social competence, prestige, and self-confidence (Tobin-Richards et al., 1983). One hypothesis to explain this outcome is that girls who mature early must learn to cope with new social circumstances (for example, dating), which place greater pressures on them than on their peers who are the same age chronologically but not biologically.

On-time boys and girls also perceive their pubertal changes differently. On-time boys feel less attractive than do early-maturing boys, but more attractive than do later maturers. These comparative data suggest that the physical approach to adulthood, with the concomitant advantages that adulthood offers, is what boys perceive as positive, not simply that they are ahead of others or are on time (Tobin-Richards et al., 1983).

During puberty, on-time girls have greater positive body images and perceptions of social attractiveness than early- or later-maturing female adolescents. Girls whose physical maturation occurs later than their same-sex peers' still feel better about themselves than early maturers (Tobin-Richards et al., 1983).

Other researchers, however, indicate that by late adolescence, late-maturing girls are less popular, have less sophisticated coping skills, and are less self-directed than early maturers. One hypothesis is that delays in puberty create barriers that cause late-maturing girls to lose social prestige and to adjust poorly, whereas the early onset of puberty causes early-maturing girls to find new resources for dealing with their peers and with adults (Sprinthall & Collins, 1988).

The overall findings regarding reactions to the timing of pubertal change are presented in Table 2-1. As the table indicates, initial and later reactions vary. There are gains and losses for early maturers, but in different directions for boys and girls. Whereas early-maturing girls initially experience distress and early-maturing boys initially experience increases in confidence and social prestige, the females show gains in coping in later adolescence and adulthood not clearly matched by the males. On-time maturing is a positive experience for boys and girls, while late maturing causes distress. Late-maturing boys eventually demonstrate social and internal competencies not experienced by early-maturing boys. Late-maturing girls, however,

TABLE 2-1   **Adolescents' Reactions to the Onset of Puberty by Age at Onset and Gender**

Time of Onset of Maturation	Reaction	Male*	Female*
EARLY	Initial	+ +	− −
	Later	− +	+ +
ON-TIME	Initial	+ +	+ +
	Later	+ +	+ +
LATE	Initial	− −	− −
	Later	+ +	− −

* Positive reactions are marked by +, and negative reactions are marked by −. The first mark indicates the reactions of others, and the second mark, personal reactions.

SOURCE: From *Life Span Nutrition: Conception through Life,* by S. R. Rolfes and L. K. DeBruyne. Copyright © 1990 by West Publishing Co. Reprinted by permission.

seem to continue to have difficulties due to loss of prestige and delayed social skill development. Table 2-1 suggests that early-maturing girls and late-maturing boys mirror each other in terms of turning distress into competencies.

Preparations for Puberty   While many of the physical changes that characterize adolescence are outwardly obvious, societal taboos about human sexuality have inhibited the traditional societal institutions (family, school, church) from preparing youths for the bodily changes they will experience during puberty. In fact, evidence suggests that the onset of puberty leads to increased conflict and distance between adolescents and their parents, rather than to closer communication (L. Steinberg, 1981, 1988, 1989).

In the United States and several other countries, little evidence can be found that any societal group pays more than lip service to preparation for puberty. Several cross-cultural researchers have noted that the theme of "sex anxiety" pervades education about sexuality in many cultures (Broude, 1981). The development of school-based health-care curricula to teach about human sexuality may be evidence of a change in this pattern.

Because menarche is so dramatic and potentially frightening for an unprepared child, one would think particular attention would be paid to preparing a girl for menarche. Research about the practices in many countries indicates that most information for girls prior to menarche comes from conversations with friends or with their mothers. The same research indicates that a girl is most likely to tell her mother once menstruation begins, and mothers then inform their husbands (Logan, 1980). There is little evidence that these conversations, however, prepare a girl for menstruation.

Prior to the recent changes in school curricula in the United States, hardly any males obtained accurate information on the physical changes that were going to occur in their lives. It is estimated that up to 90% of all boys receive no formal information about nocturnal emissions or spontaneous erections; what information they do receive does not come from mothers or fathers but from poorly informed peers.

Howard Barnes, David Wright, and their graduate students conducted a four-year study of parents' and adolescents' attitudes toward human sexuality (Barnes, 1991; Retter, 1991; Russo, 1991; Russo, Barnes, & Wright, 1991; Wright & Barnes, 1986,

FIGURE 2-3
Sexual Knowledge
of Parents and
Adolescents

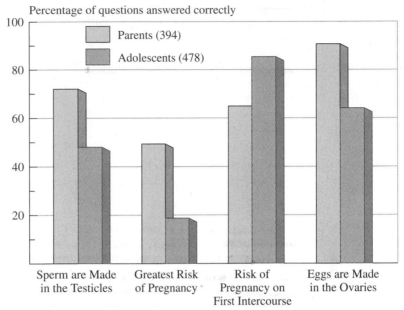

Percentage of questions answered correctly

SOURCE: Adapted from *Teenage Sexual Behavior and Pregnancy: A Needs Assessment for a Rural Kansas Community* by D. W. Wright and H. L. Barnes, 1986, Kansas State University: unpublished report.

1989). In surveys conducted with 394 parents and 478 adolescents, these researchers used seven multiple-choice and true–false items to assess knowledge about such fundamental facts as (*a*) where sperm are made, (*b*) when a woman's risk of getting pregnant is the greatest, (*c*) whether a female who has started having menstrual periods and does not use birth control can get pregnant the first time she has intercourse, and (*d*) where the female's eggs come from. Results of this survey are provided in Figure 2-3. Note that only 72% of the parents and 48% of the adolescents knew that sperm are made in the testicles. Forty-nine percent of the parents and 19% of the adolescents knew that a woman's risk of getting pregant is greatest two weeks after her period. Sixty-five percent of the parents and 86% of the adolescents knew that a female who is menstruating can get pregnant the first time she has intercourse. Ninety-one percent of the parents and 64% of the adolescents knew that eggs come from the ovaries.

The findings shown in Figure 2-3 provide some sobering conclusions about parental preparedness to educate children about human sexuality. It is startling that the adolescents were much better informed than their parents about the risk of pregnancy at first intercourse, and nearly as troubling, that less than half the parents knew that a woman's risk of getting pregnant is greatest two weeks after her period. In some cases, parents acknowledged their ignorance, but in most cases, the parents expressed confidence their mistaken understandings were correct. The adolescents also expressed conviction that their incorrect answers were correct.

Invoking parents as the ones to educate their children about human sexuality assumes that parents have correct information to impart and that they feel comfortable teaching their children about sexuality. Wright and Barnes (1989) suggest some strategies to educate parents in these matters. Their approach depends on involving the community in discussions of adolescent sexual activity, sources of sexual knowledge, and development of community goals.

Effects of Puberty on Parent-Adolescent Relations

Pubertal changes affect family relations. The extent to which researchers claim family relations change seems to depend on the perspective from which they view the adolescent vis-à-vis the family. Psychoanalysts, for example, accentuate the conflict that young adolescents introduce into a family, whereas other researchers contend this appeal to turmoil slavishly repeats the storm and stress view with no empirical backing (Bandura, 1964/1980; Blos, 1971/1979d; A. Freud, 1958/1969; Offer, 1969).

Lawrence Steinberg (1981, 1988, 1989) found that adolescents, their mothers, and their fathers all report an increase in family conflict coinciding with pubertal changes. This rise in conflict seems more true during the child's early adolescent years than during later periods of adolescent development.

Daughters report significantly less cohesion with their parents, fewer calm communications with their parents, and less acceptance by their parents during pubertal changes. Daughters also report a significant increase in the intensity of conflict with their mothers. Sons report significantly less cohesion with their mothers, fewer calm communications with their fathers, and less acceptance by their fathers during this time. Mothers and fathers report that they often resort to authoritative decision making with their adolescent children, a phenomenon viewed by girls as maternal efforts to exert control.

Adolescents report more conflict with their mothers than with their fathers. Conflict often occurs within a family in which the parents and child have developed strong attachments for each other. This conflict seems to serve a functional purpose by forcing adolescents to develop more mature relations outside the family and to attain greater emotional autonomy. Physical maturation, in other words, is a trigger that stimulates a quest for autonomy and independence.

Steinberg (1988) proposed that the parent-child conflict associated with pubertal changes actually speeds a girls' maturation. This view is called the **accelerating**

Steinberg proposed that conflict with her mother speeds up a girl's physical development.

hypothesis. In short, Steinberg argues that physical maturity occurs more quickly for girls who experience a significant decrease in calm communications with their mothers and a significant increase in conflict with their mothers. One explanation for this accelerated maturation is that stress causes greater hormonal secretions into the girl's blood stream.

A study of the accelerating hypothesis confirmed that pubertal maturation proceeds more rapidly for girls in intact families, but only when emotional closeness is maintained and the girl is able to engage in some autonomous behavior (Ellis, 1991). Nancy B. Ellis studied 709 adolescents and 707 parents over a two-year period, and asked them questions about emotional closeness, peer versus parental influence, and self versus parental rule making. Seventy percent of the adolescents lived with their biological mothers and fathers (intact families), while the others lived either in blended families or with their mothers (nonintact families). Girls in intact families proceeded into puberty more quickly if certain signs of child-parent distance were present; however, contrary to the Steinberg acceleration hypothesis, girls in intact families who reported feeling more emotionally distant from their parents had slower rates of pubertal maturation. Furthermore, girls in nonintact families who reported greater self-governance had slower, rather than accelerated, pubertal maturation. While partially confirming Steinberg's hypothesis, the Ellis study raises important questions about the influences of family structure and emotional relations on accelerating or retarding a girl's physical maturation.

In this section, we have looked at the effects of physical maturation on parent-child relations. We now turn to societal efforts to impose gender-appropriate roles and behaviors once an individual enters puberty.

INTENSIFICATION OF GENDER DIFFERENCES AT PUBERTY

Social rules and cultural patterns to behave in ways deemed appropriate for members of one's gender are pervasive influences during puberty. This kind of pressure is present early in a child's life, when a boy is told not to show his emotions (for example, "Big boys don't cry") and a girl is discouraged from being aggressive ("Girls don't hit"). These pressures intensify during puberty. We call such social rules and cultural patterns **gender-related role expectations. Gender intensification** is the term used to denote differentiation of gender roles during adolescence. Although ethologists emphasize that the biological events of puberty promote sexual dimorphism (that is, gender identity differentiation) and gender-specific behavior and roles (Savin-Williams & Weisfeld, 1989), other researchers have proposed that social pressures enforce and shape gender-related role differences (Douvan & Adelson, 1966; Hill & Lynch, 1983; Huston, 1983; Huston & Alvarez, 1990). Self-image, motivation, and achievement become tied to traditional gender-related role expectations which clearly favor males over females (Benenson & Dweck, 1986; Dweck, 1986; Dweck & Elliott 1983; Roberts, Sarigiani, & Petersen, 1990).

Rhoda Unger, professor of psychology at Montclair State College, has argued that *sex* is determined by biology, whereas *gender* is a **social construct** (Unger & Crawford, 1992). Belief that reality is formed by producing social constructs is called **constructivism** (Guba & Lincoln, 1989; Unger, 1989). Unger has argued that the construct of gender differs from one social context to another, as well as from one personal relationship to another, and she asserts that socialization produces norms about and reinforcements for responding in ways appropriate to one's gender (Unger, 1990).

Unger's views echo the wide-spread acceptance in scholarly literature that socialization, rather than heredity, accounts for gender-related role expectations. Over the past 30 years, developmental psychologists have increasingly rejected the assertion that traditional patterns of gender-role typing are desirable and, instead, have asserted that such patterns both discriminate against females and restrict personal fulfillment by limiting acceptable options for both males and females.

It is necessary to point out that the new views of gender-related role expectations are the result of values and assumptions that have been embraced by scholars and by much of society at large. In short, the new and the traditional views about gender roles are value-laden. Earlier developmental psychologists evaluated traditional gender socialization as desirable for healthy development and personal adjustment, and they would have expressed grave concern over sexual identity confusion should the traditional role differences not be maintained.

Some of the effects of traditional gender intensification seem to be harmful, particularly for females who, during adolescence, face restrictions that eventually limit their adult opportunities. The intensification of gender-related role expectations operates for females in at least five ways:

1. Girls are seldom adequately prepared for menstruation. Not only does menarche prove stressful for many girls, but adaptation to recurrent menstrual cramps can also be distressing. One girl was overheard saying that she was ready to move right into menopause now that she'd experienced menstrual cramps for the fourth month in a row.

2. For girls, changes in physical appearance often coincide with entry into a school environment that is less personal. Older boys may pressure early-maturing girls to date. Changed physical appearance, lower self-esteem, a new and less personal social environment, and pressure to date result in stress for the girl at a time when she is feeling increasingly unsure of herself.

3. Changes in a girl's physical appearance leads peers to have different expectations. On a positive note, after the onset of puberty, girls seem to develop intimacy skills with friends that far surpass what boys learn.

4. By high school, relations with boys tend to increase the importance of being attractive and to decrease the importance of academic achievement. Girls typically have higher grades than boys and express aspirations equal to those of boys, but parents and teachers give them less positive reinforcement for academic accomplishments and personal goals.

5. Parents contribute to intensifying gender-related role differences by encouraging their daughters to behave in feminine ways, which include being less assertive than boys, less confident, more dependent, and more devoted to others.

John Hill and Mary Ellen Lynch (1983) reviewed research in six separate areas that suggest gender intensification increases with age, thereby giving support to the gender intensification hypothesis. One of these areas is susceptibility to anxiety. In early adolescence, girls show much more anxiety than boys over self-identity: girls at this age are more self-conscious than are boys.

As boys and girls become older, standards for achievement become more sex-typed. A continuum of achievement has been demonstrated to exist in children's minds regarding what is feminine and what is masculine. This continuum extends from social and artistic skills at one end to spatial and mechanical skills at the other. By late adolescence, boys demonstrate clear gains in spatial skills. Girls used to demonstrate better verbal skills than boys, but some researchers say boys have caught up with girls or even passed them in verbal abilities as measured by standardized tests (Feingold, 1988; Hyde & Linn, 1986; Jacklin, 1989).

During early adolescence, girls develop more intimate friendships than boys and use more sophisticated (that is, more adultlike) bases for friendship. Girls become skilled at self-disclosure, sharing their own feelings and ideas, and accepting and understanding the feelings and ideas of others. Boys tend to be involved in friendships that center on doing things, rather than on sharing thoughts and feelings (Hill & Lynch, 1983).

Adolescent girls adopt less active and more compliant ways of responding to others than do boys, while boys are much more likely than girls to take risks. Hill and Lynch (1983) suggested parental protectiveness of adolescent daughters helps to account for girls' behaviors.

From an early age, boys typically manifest more aggressive behavior than girls; however, from a very early age, aggression in girls in much less tolerated than is aggression in boys. Parents have been noted to increase their discouragement of aggression when their daughters reach adolescence (Hill & Lynch, 1983).

The family is one of the most significant means whereby gender intensification is imparted. As stated earlier, adolescent-parent relations change markedly with the onset of puberty; conflict and emotional distance increase. These effects seem particularly true in the relationships between adolescent girls and their mothers.

Parents value intellectual achievement for their sons and daughters, but typically consider the completion of college more important for boys than for girls. Whether this parental expectation is a cohort issue, tied to an earlier generation that younger parents will supplant, remains to be seen. Current research indicates that parents value mathematics achievement more for boys, expect their sons to be competent in math, and consider math achievement less important for their daughters' futures.

Parents encourage daughters to be dependent, affectionate, submissive, and gentle. They encourage sons to be independent, competent, assertive, and competitive. When giving help to girls, parents have been overheard to mention that girls are less capable than boys. In short, parents are likely to expect and demand that their sons achieve more than their daughters (Hill & Lynch, 1983; Huston, 1983; Huston & Alvarez, 1990).

Parents in lower socioeconomic homes openly verbalize these sex-typed expectations. Observations of middle-class homes indicate socialization of daughters and sons also follows these same sex-typed patterns (Eccles, Adler, & Kaczala, 1982; Hill & Lynch, 1983; Huston, 1983; Huston & Alvarez, 1990).

Effects of Parental Employment on Gender-Related Role Expectations

The changing role of women in Western Europe and North America has been brought about particularly by economic demands that mothers and fathers must both work to support a family. This change in roles has pervasive and subtle influences on children's ideas about gender-related role expectations. The traditional notion of appropriate behavior for a mother is to stay at home while her husband works outside the home. A comparison of television shows depicting families in the 1950s and 1960s with similar shows from the 1980s and 1990s makes apparent the changing role of married mothers. The mothers on *Ozzie and Harriet*, *The Donna Reed Show*, *Father Knows Best*, and *The Brady Bunch* were very unlike the mothers on *Roseanne*, *Murphy Brown*, *Family Ties*, *The Cosby Show*, and *Growing Pains*. In short, recent shows portray the mothers working outside the home, especially in shows that depict single-parent homes.

Lois Hoffman (1979, 1989) conducted two reviews, ten years apart, on the effects of maternal employment in two-parent families. In her 1979 study, she noted that women increasingly were working outside the home as their children grew older: 33% of mothers with children under 3, 42% with preschoolers, and over 50% with school-age children were working. By her 1989 study, these figures had increased— of mothers with school-age children, 71% were employed outside the home (Hoffman, 1989).

Children in two-parent families where the mother works outside the home hold less traditional sex-role beliefs than other children (Hoffman, 1979, 1989). These children live in homes in which their fathers help with the housework, and their mothers emphasize greater childhood independence than do mothers who are not employed. Maternal employment seems to fit the needs of adolescent sons particularly well, but both "the sons and daughters of working mothers showed better social and personality adjustment, had a greater sense of personal worth, more sense of belonging, better family relations, and better interpersonal relations at school" (Hoffman, 1979, p. 864).

Daughters of working mothers frequently adopt flexible sex-role attitudes. Called **androgyny,** such attitudes encourage males and females to integrate behaviors traditionally ascribed to only one gender. Thus, androgynous girls and boys can be assertive and gentle, independent and compliant, expressive and task-oriented, empathic and competitive (Bem 1974, 1981; Spence & Helmreich, 1978). Girls with working mothers develop greater educational, career, and achievement aspirations and higher self-esteem than girls whose mothers stay home (Hoffman, 1979). A related study in the Netherlands found that adolescents whose mothers work outside the home perform as well in school as adolescents whose mothers are full-time homemakers (Donkers, 1989).

Women typically find that working outside the home boosts their morale and bolsters them against anxieties. Although working mothers find combining the dual roles of mother and worker to be stressful, full-time homemakers are more likely than working mothers to transfer frustration to their children (Hoffman, 1989).

For fathers, the effects of maternal employment outside the home are mixed. Marital conflict often erupts in homes with fathers who espouse the traditional gender role of being the breadwinner. Other men find their participation in household chores and child care enhances their self-esteem and has positive effects on their children (Hoffman, 1989).

One effect of both parents working outside the home is that the child is unsupervised after school. Such children are called **latchkey children** because they must carry a key to unlock the house. This issue will be discussed, along with other effects on children when both parents work, in Chapter 6.

Social learning theory provides a plausible means of explaining gender socialization and current efforts to break down traditional forms of gender intensification. The explanation appeals to *modeling*, the procedure whereby a person learns a behavior by observing someone else. In many homes with working mothers, both the mother and father tend to behave in more androgynous ways, and to display nontraditional attitudes toward sex-typed behaviors. Children see their dads vacuuming, doing dishes, and cooking meals, and their moms mowing the lawn, filling the car's gas tank, and balancing the checkbook. They also see both parents going to work. As a result, the children learn to be more flexible in their sex-role expectations.

Personality traits may also interact with a child's social learning to produce less traditional sex typing. For example, women employed in professional capacities are generally more assertive, more independent, more achievement oriented, and as feminine as married mothers who are not employed outside the home (Huston, 1983). These personality traits probably influence children in terms of parent-child interactions, in terms of what children observe as acceptable behaviors for men and women, and in terms of the interactions they observe between adults.

THE NUTRITIONAL NEEDS OF ADOLESCENTS

In the previous section, we looked at gender intensification, which increases noticeably when puberty begins. We now turn to another set of issues in adolescent physical development—adolescents' nutritional needs. We begin with the effect of improved nutrition on physical growth.

Improved nutrition contributes to earlier maturation (the secular trend) and increased physical size. Essays on the nutrition requirements of adolescents discuss explicitly or refer implicitly to the rapid physical changes adolescents experience (Heald, 1976; Rees & Trahms, 1989; Rolfes & DeBruyne, 1990; Whitney & Hamilton, 1987).

Nutrient Requirements of Adolescents

Except for periods of pregnancy and lactation, the adolescent growth spurt demands greater total nutrient intake than any other time of life (Rolfes & DeBruyne, 1990). Estimates of the nutrients—vitamins and minerals—that are necessary for adolescents are based on the **recommended dietary allowance (RDA)** of adults (Food and Nutrition Board, 1989). The RDA for individuals of ages 11 to 14, 15 to 18, and 19 to 24 are provided in Table 2-2.

Experts in food and nutrition sciences acknowledge that difficulties plague their efforts to determine nutrient requirements. A common method is to survey what people eat and infer the influence of dietary habits on growth and the presence of disorders. This approach produces imprecise results that cannot distinguish between

TABLE 2-2 **Recommended Dietary Allowances for Adolescents by Age-Group and Gender**

	AGE-GROUP						
	11–14		15–18		19–24		
	M	F	M	F	M	F	
VITAMIN*							**SOURCES**
Vitamin A	1,000	800	1,000	800	1,000	800	Butter, eggs
Vitamin D	10	10	10	10	10	10	Sunlight, fish
Vitamin E**	10	8	10	8	10	8	Leafy green vegetables
Vitamin K	45	45	65	55	70	65	Liver, milk
Thiamin**	1.3	1.1	1.5	1.1	1.5	1.1	Pork, nuts
Riboflavin**	1.5	1.3	1.8	1.3	1.7	1.3	Milk, yogurt
Niacin**	17	15	20	15	19	15	Leafy green vegetables
Vitamin B_6**	1.7	1.4	2.0	1.5	2.0	1.6	Milk, poultry
Folate	150	150	200	180	200	180	Fruits, fish
Vitamin B_{12}	2.0	2.0	2.0	2.0	2.0	2.0	Leafy green vegetables
Vitamin C**	50	50	60	60	60	60	Meat, fish, milk, cheese
MINERAL							**SOURCES**
Calcium**	1200	1,200	1200	1,200	1,200	1,200	Milk, broccoli
Phosphorous**	1,200	1,200	1,200	1,2000	1,200	1,200	Animal tissues
Magnesium**	270	280	400	300	350	280	Nuts, seafood
Iron**	12	15	12	15	10	15	Red meats, fish
Zinc**	15	12	15	12	15	12	Grains, poultry
Iodine	150	150	150	150	150	150	Iodized salt, seafood
Selenium	40	45	50	50	70	55	Meat, grains, seafood

*Allowance given in micrograms unless otherwise noted.
**Allowance given in milligrams.

SOURCE: From *Life Span Nutrition: Conception through Life,* by S. R. Rolfes and L. K. DeBruyne. Copyright © 1990 by West Publishing Co. Reprinted by permission.

what people eat and what their growth requires (Heald, 1976). Because of potential error in determining nutrient requirements, each RDA incorporates a margin of error in order to avoid disorders that nutrition deficiencies produce.

The Food and Nutrition Board groups adolescents into two time blocks of four years each, ages of 11 to 14 and 15 to 18, and includes late adolescents with young

Some adolescent groups typically suffer from nutritional deficiencies: females need iron, Hispanic females need Vitamin A, and black males need energy-yielding nutrients.

adults. Adolescents age 19 to 22 are included in a block that extends through age 24 because, in most cases, bones continue to grow until age 25 (Food and Nutrition Board, 1989).

People need energy-yielding nutrients, vitamins, and minerals. **Energy-yielding nutrients** (proteins, carbohydrates, and fat) are measured in terms of **kcalories (kcal)**. The energy-yielding RDA for 11- to 14-year-old adolescents is 2,500 kcal for males and 2,200 kcal for females; for 15- to 18-year-old adolescents, 3,000 kcal for males and 2,200 kcal for females; and for 19- to 24-year-olds, 2,900 kcal for males and 2,200 kcal for females (Food and Nutrition Board, 1989).

An individual adolescent's actual nutrient needs depend on four greatly varying aspects of physical development: age when puberty begins, velocity of growth, level of activity, and length of time to achieve maturation (Rolfes & DeBruyne, 1990). This variability in physical development is further complicated by the known fact that adolescents in affluent societies engage in irregular eating habits (in other words, they snack on food a lot) (Rolfes & DeBruyne, 1990; Whitney & Hamilton, 1987).

Certain **nutrition deficiencies** are characteristic of specific adolescent groups. For example, young women are often deficient in iron, and young black males are often deficient in energy-yielding nutrients. Young Hispanic women frequently lack sufficient levels of vitamin A. (Whitney & Hamilton, 1987).

Vitamin requirements increase during early and middle adolescence. Most of the adolescent RDAs for vitamins resemble the adult requirements; however, all three age-groups (11–14, 15–18, and 19–24) require twice as much vitamin D as adults (Food and Nutrition Board, 1989). Although nutrition experts indicate that higher amounts of vitamin D are needed to support the rapid pace of skeletal growth during adolescence (Rolfes & DeBruyne, 1990), in fact, the RDA for vitamin D remains constant (10 micrograms) from age 6 months through 24 years. Vitamin D provides minerals, primarily calcium, for the bones. More vitamin D is needed in childhood, adolescence, and early young adulthood because skeletal growth continues from childhood until about age 25.

Minerals on the RDA table include calcium, phosphorus, magnesium, iron, zinc, iodine, and selenium. The RDA for each mineral increases during adolescence, and in the cases of calcium and phosphorus, dramatically so. Both calcium and phosphorus are essential components of bones, and all adolescents need 1,200 milligrams (mg) of each mineral daily. An excellent source of both calcium and phosphorus is cow's milk. Lack of proper amounts of calcium has been linked to loss of bone density, particularly for adult females. Reduced bone density (called **osteoporosis**) leads to crippling disorders and fractured bones in adulthood that can speed the onset of death (Food and Nutrition Board, 1989; Rolfes & DeBruyne, 1990).

Iron is an essential part of hemoglobin, a protein that carries oxygen in the blood stream, and of myoglobin, a protein that provides oxygen for muscle contractions. Sources of iron include red meat, fish, and eggs. Females lose iron during menstruation, and therefore require greater amounts of iron than males—15 mg per day compared to 12 mg for males. This RDA for iron remains the same for females until they reach their fifties and then decreases to 10 mg (Food and Nutrition Board, 1989; Rolfes & Debruyne, 1990).

Adolescents in the United States love to eat hamburgers, shakes, and french fries (as I heard one teenager exclaim, "The three basic food groups, man!"). How does a meal of a hamburger, shake, and fries compare in terms of the RDA for a 16-year-old adolescent male and female? Table 2-3 provides a comparison of seven nutrients.

As shown in the table, such a meal provides a female nearly all the riboflavin, over half the protein, and nearly half the calcium needed. The meal is clearly deficient in iron, thiamin, vitamin C, and vitamin A. This meal meets even less of the male's nutrient requirements. Perhaps we should all breathe a sigh of relief. How many 16-year-old adolescent males do you know who eat a meal of only one hamburger, a shake, and some fries? However, unless adolescents increase their vitamins A and C intake (for instance, by eating fruits and vegetables) and eat more sources

TABLE 2-3   **Nutrients in a Hamburger, Shake, and French Fries: RDA Proportion Met for 16-Year-Old Male and Female**

NUTRIENT	RDA PROPORTION	
	Male	Female
Calcium	47%	47%
Iron	31%	25%
Protein	40%	53%
Riboflavin	54%	75%
Thiamin	23%	32%
Vitamin A	3%	3%
Vitamin C	21%	21%

SOURCE: Adapted from *Understanding Nutrition* (p. 481) by E. N. Whitney and E. M. N. Hamilton, 1987, St. Paul, MN: West. Updated using more recent RDA pronouncements from *Recommended Dietary Allowances* by the Food and Nutrition Board, 1989, Washington, DC: National Academy Press.

of iron and thiamin (green beans, for example), other meals may not make up for deficiencies in these nutrients (Whitney & Hamilton, 1987). Sharon Rolfes and Linda DeBruyne (1990) also call attention to the lack of fiber and the amount of fat in this fast-food meal. They encourage adolescents to supplement such food with salads, fruits, and generous portions of dark green vegetables.

We close this section on adolescent nutritional needs by looking at the differing nutritional needs of pregnant and nonpregnant adolescent females. Figure 2-4 shows that in 15 out of 20 categories, pregnant adolescents need more nutrients than non-

FIGURE 2-4
**Nutrient Require-
ments for Pregnant
and Nonpregnant
Adolescent Females**

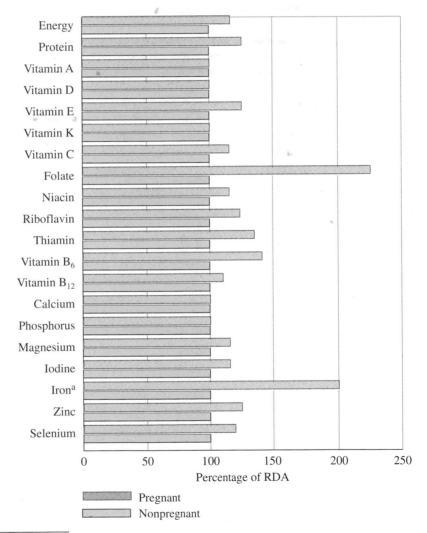

aSince the increased iron requirement cannot be met by typical diets or by iron stores, supplements are recommended.

SOURCE: Adapted from *Life Span Nutrition: Conception through Life* by S. R. Rolfes and L. K. DeBruyne, 1990, St. Paul, MN: West.

pregnant adolescents. In no case do they need less, and in two categories, pregnant adolescents need at least twice as much of a nutrient as nonpregnant adolescents. The energy needs for a pregnant female are increased 300 kcal in the second and third trimesters, and 500 kcal in the first 12 months of lactation (Food and Nutrition Board, 1989). What do you suppose happens to a pregnant adolescent and her fetus if she does not meet her RDA needs?

Nutrition Extremes   Three extreme disorders that result from improper nutrition are anorexia nervosa, bulimia nervosa, and obesity. Anorexia nervosa and obesity are at opposite ends of a continuum in terms of food intake.

Anorexia nervosa is an eating disorder of individuals—primarily females in affluent societies—obsessed with looking thin and fearful of gaining weight. The term *anorexia* refers to loss of appetite, but victims of anorexia nervosa engage in practices that can result in serious health ramifications brought on by malnutrition. **Bulimia nervosa** involves eating large amounts of food at one sitting and then purging the food by vomiting or taking laxatives. **Obesity** is the term given to individuals 20% or more over the weight considered normal for their age, height, and body frame.

Each of these eating disorders involves complicated psychological and physical problems, but all involve both disordered nutritional habits and disordered views of food, which severely affect an individual's physical health. Treatment programs that minimize or ignore nutritional behaviors do not appear to be effective for victims of any of these disorders. However, these disorders involve more than improper nutrition.

Certain social variables are associated with vulnerability to anorexia nervosa and bulimia nervosa. Of particular relevance are gender (female), age (adolescence and young adulthood), socioeconomic class (affluent), and a family history of eating disorders (Attie & Brooks-Gunn, 1992). Individuals suffering from anorexia nervosa or bulimia nervosa often come from families that emphasize appearance, status, and achievement (Levine & Smolak, 1992).

Key transitional events in an individual's life also present risk factors for developing an eating disorder (Rutter, 1990). One such event is the transition from elementary to middle school, particularly when girls who have entered puberty become sensitive to cultural values about desirable feminine body weight and appearance. There is some speculation that increases in mother-daughter conflict during middle adolescence, when teenagers intensify their struggles for autonomy, present risk factors as well (Attie & Brooks-Gunn, 1992). Linking these social risk factors to the development of eating disorders does not occur without difficulty. Many females who come from affluent homes, engage in conflict with their parents, and invest in achievement, pass through these transitions without developing anorexia nervosa or bulimia nervosa.

Another serious issue in identifying risk factors for eating disorders centers on the vulnerability of female adolescents in contrast to the apparent immunity of male adolescents. Males are vulnerable to other complicated affective and addictive behaviors, but incidence and prevalence data indicate they are generally resistant to anorexia nervosa and bulimia nervosa (Attie & Brooks-Gunn, 1992).

Anorexia Nervosa

Cases of anorexia nervosa have been documented since medieval times, and several women declared to be saints by the Roman Catholic Church were clearly anorexic (Bell, 1985). They engaged in self-starvation, and some died from the complications of malnutrition. Victims of this eating disorder are called **anorectics** or **anorexics**; these terms are used interchangeably.

The typical anorectic is a white adolescent female from a middle- or upper-class family (Farley, 1986). Anorexia nervosa is found much more often in females than in males. One estimate is that females outnumber males 10:1 (D. Steinberg, 1983), whereas a more recent publication places the ratio at 20:1 (Noshpitz, 1991).

Anorexia nervosa typically begins in early or middle adolescence and is thought to affect less than 1 in every 200 individuals (.5%) in the general population. However, prevalence estimates vary according to which population groups are studied. The .5% rate was found in a study of middle- and upper-middle-class adolescent girls in British high schools (Crisp, Palmer, & Kalucy, 1976), but studies of other groups reveal a much higher prevalence of the problem: a 9% rate among female ballet dancers and a 6% rate among female diabetics (Rodin, Daneman, Johnson, Kenshole, & Garfinkel, 1985; Eisler, Gillies, & Hayward, 1985). One study of college students estimated 4 of every 100 females are anorexic (Pope, Hudson, Yurgelun-Todd, & Hudson, 1984). David Schlundt and William Johnson (1990) explain these varying rates as a matter of sampling, that is, some groups in the general population have a greater risk of anorexia than the general population as a whole.

The profile of the anorectic is filled with complexity and seeming contradictions. Typically, she excels in all activities and strives for perfection, primarily to receive praise and acceptance. However, she rebels internally at the compliance she feels others force upon her and, to gain some sense of personal control, severely regulates what she eats. As she begins to lose weight, she receives praise for being so thin. What others would consider signs of hunger, she interprets as a normal state of her body.

Even before beginning her self-starvation diet, the anoretic typically shows signs of depression and feelings of helplessness. Being out of control frightens her; weight gain is seen as the ultimate loss of control, and staying thin means being perfect.

The increases in weight, stature, and body fat that accompany puberty frighten the girl who becomes anorectic. She starts a weight loss program and, soon, dieting becomes an obsession as well as a compulsion. The media encourages her notion that thin is beautiful and desirable.

The anorectic's family typically relates poorly with each other. She depends inordinately on attention from her father as a source of self-worth; however, her father is emotionally distant. Desiring so desperately to please her parents, the anorectic loses contact with her own identity and feelings and learns subtle, covert means to get others to tell her what she should do to please them (Garfinkel, 1981; Rolfes & DeBruyne, 1990; Rutter & Garmezy, 1983; Whitney & Hamilton, 1987).

Anorectics refuse to maintain body weight normal for their age and height, fear obesity intensely, have distorted perceptions of their body shapes, and stop menstruating (American Psychiatric Association, 1987). They also commonly engage in strenuous, even excessive daily exercise (Rolfes & DeBruyne, 1990).

While refusing to eat, anorectics think obsessively about food, its caloric content, and what it will take to get even thinner. They engage in peculiar behaviors, such as spending a great deal of time cutting food into tiny pieces, rearranging food on their plates, and attempting to dispose of food unobtrusively rather than eating it. They hoard and hide carbohydrate-rich foods, but do not eat any. Despite excessive weight loss, which leads to emaciated appearances, anorectics typically deny they have an eating problem and continue to express worry that they are fat (American College of Physicians, 1986; Halmi, 1987; Rolfes & DeBruyne, 1990; Warren, 1983). I heard one anorexic female say she recalled thinking how lucky Karen Carpenter—a popular singer during the 1970s who was also anorexic—had been to die looking so thin.

The compulsive hyperactivity displayed by anorectics runs counter to the apathy displayed by other malnourished persons. Strenuous daily exercise becomes routine. A typical day for an anorexic may involve swimming up to 100 laps, running five or more miles, doing aerobics for an hour, and lifting weights (Rolfes & DeBruyne, 1990). The unusual alertness and physical activity of anorectics may provide some evidence that their hypothalamus is functioning improperly (Rees & Trahms, 1989). The hypothalamus is the part of the brain involved with emotional expression as well as reactions in the stomach, intestines, heart, lungs, and brain.

The physical effects of anorexia nervosa are widespread; they are similar, if not identical, to problems associated with starvation, affecting almost every organ in the body. Anorexia apparently alters the way the hypothalamus operates, produces difficulties in regulating body temperature, reduces estrogen levels, and delays puberty. Anorectics who have already reached puberty stop menstruating. They also suffer cardiovascular problems, kidney dysfunctions, and electrolyte imbalances (electrolytes help conduct electrical charges across cells). Anorexia contributes to osteoporosis, which becomes a significant health problem for females as they grow older. The malnutrition associated with anorexia can permanently retard breast development and growth in stature, although some victims of anorexia nervosa do not suffer lasting physical harm and develop normally when properly nourished (Palla & Litt, 1988; Rees & Trahms, 1989).

Some researchers suspect that anorexia nervosa occurs due to a dysfunction in the hypothalamus, although considerable evidence also points to deep-seated adjustment difficulties and bouts of depression (Garfinkel, 1981; Warren, 1983). Until long-term, longitudinal studies follow anorectics before the onset of serious weight loss, we will not know whether hypothalamic malfunctions produce or are caused by the starved condition of the body. We will also not know whether psychological disorders, hypothalamic malfunctions, and self-starvation interact to produce an anorexic disorder.

Investigators have begun examining the role of nutrition in anorexia nervosa. Because their estrogen levels remain low, anorectics disrupt their calcium metabolism and become vulnerable to osteoporosis. Lack of zinc in the anorectic's body has also gained attention. Zinc affects genetic material, immune reactions, healing of wounds, fetal development, and perceptions of taste (Rees & Trahms, 1989; Rolfes & DeBruyne, 1990).

Anorectics have an unusual perception of the role of nourishment. Rather than seeing nourishment as fundamental in maintaining life and health, anorectics consider all food threatening and do not realize (or perhaps believe) that the body requires food (Rees & Trahms, 1989). When several anorexic patients were asked to fill out a questionnaire on eating attitudes for themselves and as they imagined other people would complete it, not only did the anorectics deny having any problems but they expressed a very idealized view of how "normal people" view food. Their expectations of normality were so high that the investigators surmised that anorectics consider normality to be beyond their reach (Furnham & Kramers, 1989).

As their malnutrition deepens, anorectics' emotional difficulties increase and reinforce the eating disorder. The chief affective disturbances typical of anorexia nervosa are depression, anger, and anxiety. Because clinically depressed individuals and anorectics have similar endocrine abnormalities, researchers have begun to investigate whether depression causes the eating disorder. Studies are thus far inconclusive (Rees & Trahms, 1989).

Treatment programs to help anorectics have become increasingly effective; however, as in other addictive behaviors, anorexia nervosa never seems completely cured. A "recovering anorectic" seems a more realistic hope than a "cured anorectic." Effective treatment programs focus on enabling individuals to alter their views on nourishment, to become sensitive to body messages that signal hunger, and to adopt nutritional eating patterns. Successful treatment programs also involve families so that everyone in the anorectic's home environment stops reinforcing the girl's anorexic habits. Evidence suggests that residential, rather than outpatient programs, have greater success in altering the anorectic's maladaptive behavior, but success in maintaining treatment gains depends on behavior once the anoretic leaves the residential program. A considerable, subtle challenge for treatment programs revolves around issues of control; tight regimens imposed on anorectics by others actually undermine chances for long-term success (Rees & Trahms, 1989; Rolfes & Debruyne, 1990; Whitney & Hamilton, 1987). Katherine Halmi (1987) reports that anorectics are tempted to engage in binge eating and purging once their weight is restored.

Bulimia Nervosa

Bulimia means "binge eating," the rapid consumption of a great quantity of food. The term **bulimia nervosa** was coined recently for a psychiatric disorder marked by (*a*) binge-eating episodes at least twice a week, (*b*) feeling out of control during a binge, (*c*) purging the food consumed during a binge by vomiting, using laxatives, or using diuretics, (*d*) feeling ashamed of purging behaviors, and (*e*) preoccupation with body shape and weight (Russell, 1979; American Psychiatric Association, 1987).

It is difficult to get clear indications of the prevalence of bulimia nervosa for several reasons. Unlike the anorectic, who looks unusually thin and avoids eating if at all possible, the bulimic appears normal physically, and eats in public, hiding her binge-and-purge episodes. As a rule, we learn about bulimics when they seek help, or when someone observes them in a binge-and-purge frenzy.

Several studies with different samples suggest bulimia is more prevalent than anorexia. For instance, 10.3% of shoppers surveyed at a mall, 15.2% of ballet dancers, 21.6% of college students, and 12.5% of high school students indicated they were bulimic (Hamilton, Brooks-Gunn, & Warren, 1985; Pertschuk, Collins, Kreisberg, & Fager, 1986; Pope, Hudson, & Yergelun-Todd, 1984; Williams, Schaefer, Shisslak, Gronwaldt, & Comerci, 1986). By averaging findings from over 20 studies, Schlundt and Johnson (1990) estimated that 7% to 8% of the total population suffers from bulimia. They noted that this estimate is too high for older populations and too low for younger groups at special risk, such as ballet dancers. The estimate of 7% to 8% does not seem to present a reliable picture of the prevalence of bulimia in young female college students.

Some data suggest new cases of bulimia nervosa are occurring more rapidly than previously reported (Pope et al., 1984). However, all incidence and prevalence studies of bulimia nervosa are plagued by problems, such as failing to distinguish between occassional binge eaters and true bulimics (Halmi, 1987).

More males suffer from bulimia nervosa than from anorexia nervosa. Evidence suggests that up to 10% of all bulimics are male, whereas, at most, 1% of all anorexics are male. Males in certain occupations requiring strict weight control, such as jockeys, as well as homosexual men appear to be more vulnerable to bulimia than other males (Scott, 1988).

Despite the greater number of male bulimics, the typical bulimic is a white female under 30 years of age; her eating disorder began in late adolescence following a series of unsuccessful diets (Rolfes & DeBruyne, 1990; Whitney & Hamilton, 1987). Unlike the extremely thin bodies of anorectics, bulimics look normal in stature, making their eating disorder much more difficult to spot. Whereas an anorectic does not believe she has a problem despite her physical condition, the bulimic recognizes her binge-and-purge behavior as a problem and attempts to hide it from others. Bulimics typically maintain normal body weight but think of themselves as fat. Like anorexics, bulimics have serious misunderstandings about the role of food and nourishment (Halmi, 1987; Rees & Trahms, 1989).

Gerald Russell (1979) considered bulimia nervosa to be the aftermath of chronic anorexia nervosa. However, a very small percentage of bulimic individuals (perhaps 5%) fit the criteria developed to diagnose anorexia, and an even smaller percentage are actively anorexic (Whitney & Hamilton, 1987). Some medical researchers, however, report that 50% of their bulimic patients were anorexic at some point (Scalf-McIver & Thompson, 1989).

Bulimics often experience difficulties in interpersonal relationships, possess low self-esteem, experience high levels of anxiety, and engage in compulsive behavior. Their binge-and-purge episodes induce feelings of self-reproach and guilt. Bulimics typically suffer from depression, which affects their cognitive processes. Despite the clear association between depression and bulimia nervosa, researchers are unsure about the origin of depression in bulimics' lives (Halmi, 1987; Rees & Trahms, 1989).

In addition to bingeing and purging, bulimics typically engage in other behaviors that endanger their health and safety. Alcohol and amphetamine abuse are common among bulimics, and their rate of cigarette smoking is high. Many bulimics also steal impulsively (Halmi, 1987; Rolfes & DeBruyne, 1990). The addictive behaviors, such as alcohol and drug abuse and cigarette smoking, seem to fit with the compulsive, even addictive, binge-and-purge pattern, but why might bulimics steal impulsively? Do they take things in stores in much the same manner that they stuff themselves with food—that is, realizing they are out of control but overcome by a desire of "wanting more"?

Purging behaviors have direct and very nasty physical effects. Efforts to purge food produce damaged teeth and gums, lacerated hands, reddened eyes, cracked and damaged lips, and an irritated or even ruptured esophagus (Rees & Trahms, 1989; Whitney & Hamilton, 1987). While not considered life-threatening, these physical problems form part of a more comprehensive and serious set of physical dangers.

Bulimic behaviors lead to fluid and electrolyte imbalances (electrolytes conduct electrical charges in the human body). These imbalances can produce serious medical problems, such as heart disorders, kidney injuries, bladder infections, and renal failure. Excessive use of laxatives can damage the lower intestinal tract. Osteoporosis is also an outcome of long-term bulimia nervosa (Whitney & Hamilton, 1987).

Treatment programs using cognitive behavioral techniques have reported success in changing bulimics' beliefs about food. Cognitive behavioral techniques emphasize altering an individual's beliefs, thoughts, and behaviors through rational argument, role playing, classical conditioning techniques, and homework, such as reading. Because bulimics agree that their behavior is abnormal, they are often more cooperative during treatment than anorexics (Halmi, 1987; Rees & Trahms, 1989).

The greatest obstacle to developing treatment programs for bulimia nervosa has been identifying what triggers binge-eating episodes. Bulimics must gain personal control over this triggering mechanism to overcome the disorder. Rolfes and Debruyne (1990) note that binge episodes are preceded by extreme efforts to control eating carbohydrate-rich food. They have developed a rigid dietary program that empowers bulimics to eat no less than 1500 kcal daily while eliminating potential anxiety over decisions about food. Foods that the bulimic likes to binge on are kept out of the diet until the individual achieves control over her eating habits.

Another term used to denote the binge-and-purge cycle seen in bulimia nervosa is **bulimarexia**, coined in the mid-1970s by Marlene Boskind-Lodahl (1976), with subsequent writings under the name Boskind-White (1985; Boskind-White & White, 1986, 1987). Bulimarexia refers to a pattern of binge eating and purging engaged in by women of normal weight who are obsessed with thinness and weight loss. Bulimarexia shares some features with anorexia nervosa and some with bulimia nervosa.

Boskind-White was greatly interested in highlighting the social and cultural influences behind a woman's binge-and-purge behavior. She wanted to establish that the pattern is a learned behavior, rather than a disease or mental illness (Boskind-White & White, 1987).

The term *bulimarexia* has not received widespread use, at least partially due to confusion with *bulimia nervosa*, a widely accepted term. Also, the criteria for diagnosing bulimarexia are unclear, whereas diagnostic criteria for bulimia nervosa are both clear and detailed (Schlundt & Johnson, 1990).

We have discussed two eating disorders, anorexia nervosa and bulimia. We turn now to a third, obesity.

Obesity

Obesity is customarily defined as being 20% heavier than one's ideal weight, although several complicating issues, such as body frame, activity level, and location of body fat, make the exact definition of obesity more difficult to determine (Whitney & Hamilton, 1987). As a working definition, however, nutritionists begin with the criterion that obesity is being at least 20% above one's ideal weight.

The causes of obesity have proven elusive, and researchers believe that several causes are at work simultaneously in most instances. They also believe that different obese individuals may have different sets of causes (Rolfes & DeBruyne, 1990). Uncertainties about its causes hamper programs to treat obesity.

Between 10% and 25% of the adolescents in the United States are at least 20% heavier than their ideal body weight (Whitney & Hamilton, 1987). Obese adolescents suffer profound physical, intellectual, emotional, and behavioral consequences. Not the least of these is death at a younger age than their nonobese peers.

Obesity's most damaging effect on adolescent physical development is greater storage of energy (primarily fat) than a person requires. Greater energy storage is damaging because it is irreversible and has permanent, abnormal effects on metabolism. As a result, it is much more difficult for obese individuals to decrease energy storage through exercise. Obese children are likely to be obese adolescents and obese adults. Obesity has considerable effects on physical and psychological health.

Physical health problems of obesity include vulnerability to diseases of the heart and blood vessels. These diseases are referred to as **cardiovascular disease (CVD)**. One CVD caused by obesity is **atherosclerosis**, or hardening of the arteries. Obese adolescents are at particular risk for developing **coronary heart disease**, a specific type of atherosclerosis that affects the heart muscle (Rolfes & DeBruyne, 1990).

In addition to physical problems, adolescent obesity produces psychological problems as well. For instance, obese adolescents usually have distorted body images, but not always about themselves. Whereas some obese individuals believe they are even fatter than they actually are, others consider themselves normal and other people skinny (Rees & Trahms, 1989). Hilda Bruch (1981) noted that obesity also restricts adolescents from participating in many social activities that promote intellectual development, such as working with peers on projects. These restrictions are often self-imposed due to a lack of inner security and low self-confidence fostered since childhood.

Obese adolescents often feel helpless in overcoming social prejudice and rejection. Their difficulty in losing weight due to greater energy storage reinforces these feelings of helplessness. Jane Rees and Christine Trahms (1989) point out that obese adolescents respond to social prejudice by succumbing to increased feelings of helplessness about themselves and life in general.

Food provides a source of comfort and gratification for some obese adolescents. They find exercise and activity uncomfortable and unsatisfying. Obese adolescents tend to withdraw from people and to rely on eating as a means of coping, thereby maintaining or increasing their obesity (Rees & Trahms, 1989).

Weight loss is governed by one intransigent rule—body fat decreases only when stored energy decreases. For reasons discussed earlier, decreasing energy storage is not a realistic goal in a treatment program for the obese adolescent. The initial treatment goal should be to stop weight gain (Rolfes & DeBruyne, 1990). Once the adolescent achieves some semblance of control over his or her weight, the idea of losing weight will not seem totally hopeless. Treatment of obesity should focus on attainable goals and realistic actions whereby the obese adolescent can change attitudes and behaviors toward food consumption and toward oneself. A focus on reaching a "normal" weight may simply reinforce helplessness since such an outcome may be physically impossible (Rees & Trahms, 1989).

Treatment programs for obese adolescents must take a comprehensive approach. Families should be involved because their encouragement of overeating must be curtailed, and their support of proper eating must be improved. Successful treatment programs emphasize social support and health, and teach the adolescent self-management methods to control the intake of high energy foods.

In this section we have reviewed the nutritional needs of adolescents, and three nutrition extremes: anorexia nervosa, bulimia nervosa, and obesity. We have seen that these eating disorders affect an adolescent's physical health. We now turn to a wider review of the physical health of adolescents.

PHYSICAL HEALTH OF ADOLESCENTS

Most individuals consider adolescence to be the healthiest period of life and yet, since 1960, individuals aged 15 to 24 (primarily middle and late adolescents) have been the only age-group in the United States to experience a consistent increase in death rates (Daniel, 1991; Hendee 1991). Some of these deaths are caused by **chronic illnesses** (illnesses with constantly recurring symptoms).

Chronic Illnesses   Between 3% and 5% of children under the age of 18 have a chronic illness that severely restricts their activities. If they live in a single-parent family, children with chronic illnesses experience greater limitations than children from two-parent homes (Geber & Okinow, 1991). A plausible hypothesis for this disparity is the lack of adequate health insurance in single-parent homes.

In surveys conducted in the mid-1980s, asthma, heart diseases, bone deformities, and hearing impairment were the most prevalent chronic conditions reported for children in the United States (Bureau of the Census, 1990; Geber & Okinow, 1991).

TABLE 2-4   Annual Rates of Children with Selected Chronic Conditions in the United States

	RATE PER 1,000 CHILDREN	
CONDITION	1983–1985	1988
Asthma	45.1	52.5
Bone Deformity	34.9	35.8
Heart Disease	21.4	22.2
Hearing Impairments	20.6	16.0
Speech Impairments	17.2	*
Visual Impairments	10.1	10.1
Mental Retardation	9.9	*
Anemias	9.6	*
Epilepsy	5.0	*
Arthritis	2.3	2.8
Hypertension	2.3	3.2
Diabetes	1.7	2.0

*Not reported in 1988 data.

SOURCE: Adapted from *Statistical Abstract of the United States*: 1990 by the Bureau of the Census, 1990, Washington, DC: U. S. Government Printing Office and "Chronic Illness and Disability" by G. Geber and N. A. Okinow in *The Health of Adolescents*: *Understanding and Facilitating Biological, Behavioral, and Social Development* edited by W. R. Hendee, 1991, San Francisco: Jossey-Bass.

Table 2-4 shows the average annual rate per 1,000 children in the United States for specific chronic illnesses.

By averaging the rates for each time period, we can surmise that approximately 48 of every 1,000 children suffer from asthma, 35 from some form of bone deformity, 18 from a hearing impairment, and 21.5 from heart disease. The 1988 data did not include information on speech impairment, mental retardation, anemia, and epilepsy. However, in 1983–1985, 17.2 of every 1,000 children suffered from a speech impairment, 9.9 from mental retardation, 9.6 from anemia, and 5 from epilepsy.

Although the incidence of severe chronic illness in adolescents increased between 1960 and 1981, experts have concluded that the prevalence of these conditions has peaked, and that further significant increases are unlikely (Geber & Okinow, 1991). The 1988 data give some credence to this claim.

There is considerable variance in the severity and noticeable symptoms of the chronic illnesses suffered by adolescents. Adolescent adjustment to these conditions varies as well. At a time when body image is a serious preoccupation, physical disabilities can compound the adjustment difficulties of an adolescent. Some disabilities, such as cystic fibrosis—a crippling disease involving severe respiratory problems—can delay puberty. Such a delay causes emotional pain, complicates peer relations, and adversely affects how the individual perceives and copes with the illness (Geber & Okinow, 1991).

Wellness and College Students: Gender, Race, and Year in School

Wellness is a concept that means more than self-protective measures aimed at preventing disease or disability. Wellness encompasses physiological, emotional, and social dimensions (such as personal responsibility for health, exercise, nutrition), interpersonal support, stress management, and self-actualization. Self-actualization refers to personal development and the fulfillment of one's potential.

William Oleckno and Michael Blacconiere (1990) studied the wellness of 1,077 college students by administering the Health-Promoting Lifestyle Profile (HPLP). The HPLP uses 48 items to measure the 6 aspects of wellness given above, plus it provides an overall measure of wellness. Each person receives an individual score. Each item asks how frequently the individual engages in behaviors that promote wellness, with responses ranging from "never" to "routinely." The HPLP is highly reliable—people respond to items consistently—and valid—the instrument measures what it claims to measure. A test of an instrument's reliability and validity is called a *test of its psychometric properties*.

The 1,077 participants in Oleckno and Blacconiere's study were primarily female (59%), and nearly all (93%) were between 17 and 22 years of age. Of the participants, 38% were freshmen, 34.6% were sophomores, 19.9% were juniors, 6.7% were seniors, and 0.8% were graduate students. Racially, the sample was 86.7% white, 5.4% black, 4.3% Hispanic, and less than 1% other. Given the small percentage of participants from racial and ethnic groups other than white, the researchers grouped the students into two categories, white and non-white. Nearly 96% of the sample had never been married, 3.3% were married, and the rest were either divorced, separated, or widowed.

The students' overall wellness score was considered about average; that is, on average, they engaged in behaviors promoting wellness. Their highest wellness scores were in the areas of interpersonal support and self-actualization. They had lower levels for exercise, stress management, and nutrition. Their lowest wellness scores came in personal responsibility for health. Note that they had below-average wellness scores for areas directly related to physical development: exercise, nutrition, and health.

Group differences emerged for gender, race, and year in school. Females demonstrated a significantly higher overall level of wellness than males ($p < .009$), with particularly higher wellness scores in the social/emotional dimension of interpersonal support. While females had significantly higher wellness scores for health responsibility than males, they both scored well below average in this category.

White students reported significantly higher levels of wellness than nonwhites ($p = .04$). Whites specifically had higher wellness scores for interpersonal support, exercise, and self-actualization, while nonwhites had higher wellness scores for health responsibility. Of concern was the fact that both whites and nonwhites had below-average wellness scores for three areas directly related to physical development: health responsibility, exercise, and nutrition.

Wellness scores increased according to year in school. For instance, the seniors had higher self-actualization and interpersonal support scores than freshmen or sophomores. The juniors and seniors had higher nutrition scores than the underclassmen, and the seniors had higher stress management scores than any of the other students.

Death During Adolescence

The major cause of death for adolescents is some form of violence—an accident, suicide, or murder. Motor vehicle accidents are the single greatest cause of adolescent death in the United States, accounting for approximately 37% of all adolescent deaths in 1988 (National Center for Health Statistics, 1990).

Violence accounts for 59% of early adolescent deaths, 80% of middle adolescent deaths, and 76% of late adolescent deaths. As individuals move from early to middle adolescence, the causes of death change, with a shift toward more violent means. For example, there is a fivefold increase in deaths from motor vehicle accidents, a sevenfold increase in deaths from homicide, and an eightfold increase in deaths from suicide (National Center for Health Statistics, 1990).

Some of the violent adolescent deaths are due to taking risks (for example, drinking and driving). Placing oneself in danger of being killed is surely the most severe assault on one's physical health. We now turn to the tendency of adolescents to take risks that endanger their health.

Adolescent Risk Taking and Health

Health professionals consider **proclivity for risk taking** to be a major contributing factor in adolescent health problems (Daniel, 1991; Vernon, 1991). Adolescents who are serious risk-takers usually engage in more than one type of risk, thereby increasing their vulnerability to illness and injury. For example, adolescent substance abuse, sexual activity, and accidents cluster significantly (Daniel, 1991). Furthermore, social pressures to experiment with sex, drugs, tobacco, and alcoholic beverages prove difficult for some adolescents to resist (Hamburg, Mortimer, & Nightingale, 1991).

Although risk taking is seen in many cases to be "functional responses to the environment" (Daniel, 1991, p. 500), certain types of risk-taking behaviors often result in serious injury or illness. For example, sexual activity places adolescents at risk for contracting a plethora of sexually transmitted diseases. Alcohol use is involved in a significant proportion of motor vehicle accidents involving adolescents. One unexpected risk factor, now emphasized by health professionals, is the complicity of dysfunctional family systems in fostering denial of an adolescent's health risk, thereby contributing to the development of risky behavior (Bensinger & Natenshon, 1991).

It is important to eliminate barriers that get in the way of adolescents using health-care systems.

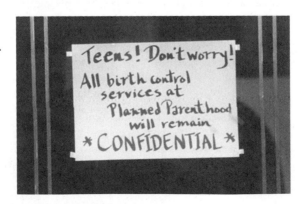

Exercise and the Health of School-Age Children, Adolescents, and Adults

Throughout the life span, physical exercise and health are clearly linked. Lack of exercise has cumulative, deteriorating effects on physical health, and individuals who engage in physical activity seem to live longer than those who are inactive (Shock, 1977; Woodruff, 1977). As demonstrated in Oleckno and Blacconiere's research (1990), college students have below average wellness scores for exercise, which means they do not engage in physical activity on a routine basis.

We know that individuals in affluent societies have access to better medical care, more food, and better hygiene than those in poorer countries. However, affluent societies also provide numerous alternatives to physical activity. For example, a chief alternative to exercise in the United States is watching television.

School-age children and adolescents in the United States spend at least 26 hours watching television. In previous generations, school-age children spent many hours playing outdoors with their friends and, in effect, exercising. Now children spend, at most, around 5 hours a week engaging in some form of physical exercise (Collins, 1984). Habits of physical inactivity are difficult to break, extend into later developmental periods, and impair health.

Adolescents in the United States spend less time exercising than school-age children, although middle school and high school physical education classes do promote some form of physical activity during the school year. A main concern about these programs, however, is the emphasis on competitive sports and the attention given to gifted athletes. Students with average or below-average athletic ability often get ignored. A welcome trend being provided in some schools is semester-long and year-long physical education courses in nontraditional activities, such as aerobics. Aerobics is a system of physical activity that causes exertion and thereby strengthens the body's power to carry oxygen in the blood.

A primary reason to be concerned about the patterns of inactivity developed during middle childhood and adolescence is the carryover into adulthood. As mentioned earlier, physical inactivity is a difficult habit to break. Lack of physical activity leads to serious physical health problems for many adults, including heart disease, the major cause of death for adults in the United States. Often the heart complications developed by adults are a direct result of inadequate exercise over several years, coupled with inadequate eating habits.

Adults benefit from physical exercise, particularly exercise that increases the body's capacity to take in oxygen (aerobics, for example) Longitudinal studies of adults from their early fifties to their late eighties showed that both males and females benefit markedly from exercise that produces aerobic effects (Adams & deVries, 1973; deVries, 1970; Stamford, 1972). Adults who undertake a regimen of physical exercise, especially if they have been inactive for a long period of time, should have a complete physical evaluation before beginning their exercise programs (deVries, 1975).

Health Concerns of Adolescents

What health concerns do adolescents bring to the attention of the medical profession? The most common reasons that adolescents consult a physician are (*a*) physical exams for extracurricular activities, (*b*) general medical exams, (*c*) throat problems, (*d*) cosmetic concerns (for example, acne or warts), (*e*) athletic injuries, and (*f*) allergies. Early adolescent females seek medical care primarily for coughs, throat

79

problems, general medical exams, and earaches, while early adolescent males seek medical care primarily for physical exams required for extracurricular activities, general medical exams, coughs, throat problems, and allergies. Females between the ages of 15 and 20 seek medical help primarily for prenatal care, throat problems, and acne, whereas males in that age-group seek medical help primarily for acne and throat problems. As they get older, adolescents seek preventive health care less often than do early adolescents (DuRant, 1991). What do you think accounts for this phenomenon?

Adolescent Use of Health-Care Services and Alternative Delivery Systems

Use of health-care providers decreases from early to late adolescence. Health-care professionals speculate that adolescents frequently encounter barriers from traditional health-care delivery systems. These barriers involve adolescents' perceptions that health-care providers are inappropriate, inaccessible, insensitive, or unavailable. Alternative approaches have been developed to overcome adolescent resistance to health care. These include providing peer counseling, placing health clinics in schools or shopping malls, and developing other innovative ways to deliver comprehensive health care (DuRant, 1991). Hurrelmann (1989) argues that providers of adolescent health care must understand that behaviors which place adolescents at risk are ways of coping with the life stress of adolescence. He contends that a singular focus on treating symptoms creates barriers that can be overcome only by combining and coordinating services to address the multiple social milieus of adolescence.

Successful alternative approaches emphasize social support systems, accentuate adolescent competence and healthy adolescent development, and offer family life education, such as parenting skill development. Examples of successful programs in New Jersey, New York, Massachusetts, North Carolina, and Texas deliver comprehensive medical, legal, recreational, mental health, and educational services. The emphasis is on the holistic aspect of the problems faced by adolescents (Daniel, 1991; DuRant, 1991; Vernon, 1991).

School Based Youth Services is a New Jersey program that focuses on 13- to 19-year-olds and seeks to increase their access to the state departments serving youths. Although the emphasis is on breaking down barriers between adolescents and state departments, the program provides additional services, such as employment counseling, family planning, day-care, and family life education for adolescent parents (Hamburg et al., 1991).

The Door is a New York City program that provides social, medical, nutritional, recreational, and psychological services for youths 12 to 21 years old. Over 90% of The Door's clients are poor, and the staff estimate that they serve at least 200 adolescents per day. Specialized services are offered to certain at-risk groups, such as pregnant adolescents, adolescent parents, and handicapped adolescents (DuRant, 1991; Hamburg et al., 1991).

Bridge over Troubled Water is a mobile medical van that serves 12- to 21-year-old runaways and street youths in Boston. The program offers comprehensive medical services, including dental care, laboratory screenings, and family counseling.

Bridge over Troubled Water, which has been running since 1970, reaches out to runaways with friendship and trust, and eliminates the barriers youths see in traditional health-care programs (DuRant, 1991).

Teen-Link serves 10- to 18-year-old inner-city adolescents in Durham, North Carolina. The program has developed extensive working relationships with private and public agencies, such as Duke University Medical Center, the county health department, the public housing authority, and local churches. In an attempt to interest adolescents in the comprehensive array of health-care services it provides, Teen-Link offers swimming lessons, martial arts instruction, and computer education courses. The American Medical Association has recognized Teen-Link as a model health-care program with proven strategies to reach at-risk youths (DuRant, 1991).

AVANCE is a program aimed at reducing family distress, improving parenting skills, and increasing parental nurturance of children in low-income Hispanic families in San Antonio, Texas. AVANCE seeks to empower parents to become educators of their children, and to help them overcome the severe family stressors that can place impoverished, minority children at risk for health problems (Hamburg et al., 1991).

We have looked at the physical health of adolescents, risk-taking behaviors that sometimes endanger their health, their health concerns, and their use of health-care delivery systems. To bring these issues closer to home, examine your county's health-care delivery systems. Do they create barriers to adolescent use, or do they offer accessible services? Can you find examples of alternative delivery systems that succeed in reaching adolescents?

CHAPTER SUMMARY

Adolescence involves physical changes. These changes are often dramatic, as when a 12-year-old boy gains 10 inches in height in half a year or when a 14-year-old girl looks like a young adult woman.

The event that marks the end of childhood and the beginning of adolescence is the onset of puberty. Puberty is a complex process involving the central nervous system, hormone secretions, changes in body height and weight, and sexual maturation. Physical maturity occurs at different rates, with girls typically entering puberty two years earlier than boys. Some individuals consider sexual maturation to be the focal point of adolescence, whereas most researchers view adolescent development as involving more than physical changes. Tanner (1962) developed a system for assessing the rate of sexual maturation. For the past 150 years, individuals in Western Europe and North America have been maturing more rapidly than individuals from previous generations; this secular trend seems tied to better nutrition, better living conditions, and better health care.

Reactions to the onset of puberty vary by gender. Early-maturing girls experience distress and self-consciousness, whereas early-maturing boys gain confidence and prestige, and become more attractive to peers and adults. By late adolescence, early-maturing girls develop greater social skills; both their prestige and their self-confidence increase. Early-maturing boys show some developmental losses in terms of being more somber, less spontaneous, more submissive, and less flexible than on-time and late-maturing boys.

On-time girls have more positive images of their bodies and feel more socially attractive than their early or late counterparts. By late adolescence, late-maturing girls are less popular, less sophisticated, and less self-directed than other girls. On-time boys feel less attractive than early maturers, but more attractive than late maturers. Late-maturing boys develop flexibility in problem solving and are less submissive to adult expectations than early maturers.

Adolescent-parent relations suffer during the early stages of puberty. Parents are often unwilling to educate their children about sexuality, and in many cases, parents are misinformed about sexuality. Conflicts between parents and adolescents increase as physical maturation occurs. Some speculation has linked female maturation to conflicts between mothers and their daughters.

Gender-related role differences intensify once a person enters puberty. Socialization seems most accountable for this phenomenon. Traditional gender-related role differences discriminate in favor of males, and show up in the academic, social, and interpersonal arenas. The family plays a significant role in intensifying gender differences. The growing number of working mothers in two-parent homes seems to be influencing children to develop more flexible attitudes about acceptable behaviors and roles.

Because of the growth spurt associated with puberty, adolescents require more nutrient intake than any other age-group. The recommended dietary allowance (RDA) groups adolescents into two age ranges: 11–14 and 15–18. The RDA age-group of 19- to 24-year-olds includes late adolescents and young adults. Several factors determine an adolescent's actual nutrient requirements: age at onset of puberty, velocity of growth, level of activity, and length of time to achieve maturation. The adolescent's love of snack foods—at least in the United States—complicates the nutrition picture.

Three nutrition extremes are seen in adolescents. Anorexia nervosa, an eating disorder much more common among females than males, involves an obsession with being thin, a disturbed body image, inability to acknowledge hunger signals, and difficulties with self-esteem and personal identity. If left unchecked, the serious medical consequences of malnutrition can result in death. Anorexics typically do not believe they have a problem and prefer "dying thin" to "living fat."

Bulimia nervosa is an eating disorder which is more common among females than males, although it does claim more male victims than anorexia. Bulimia nervosa refers to frequent bouts of binge eating followed by purging through self-induced vomiting or the use of laxatives. Bulimics feel out of control when they binge, feel ashamed of and guilty about their behavior, and try to hide it from others. Unlike anorexics, they admit they have a problem. There is controversy over whether bulimia is the aftermath of anorexia. The binge-and-purge behavior of bulimics can cause many physical problems, and bulimics also engage in other threatening behaviors, such as alcohol abuse and compulsive stealing.

Whether an individaul develops anorexia or bulimia is influenced by various social factors, including gender (female), age (adolescence and young adulthood), affluence, and a family history of eating disorders. Individuals suffering from anorexia or bulimia come from families that emphasize appearance, status, and achievement.

Obesity is an eating disorder marked by being 20% or more over one's ideal weight. Between 10% and 25% of adolescents in the United States are obese. The consequences of obesity involve feelings of helplessness, social rejection, cardiovascular disease, and death at an earlier age than nonobese individuals.

Adolescent health is generally quite good, and it is a common belief that adolescence is the healthiest time of life. Yet, 15- to 24-year-olds make up the only age-group whose death rate has consistently increased since 1960. Violence (automobile accidents, homicides, and suicides) is the major cause of adolescent death, a fact that many attribute to the propensity of adolescents to take serious risks, such as drinking and driving.

Another cause of adolescent death is chronic illness. Around 5% of children in the United States under the age of 18 suffer from chronic illnesses. The most prevalent conditions are asthma, heart disease, bone deformity, hearing and speech impairment, anemia, and mental retardation.

Adolescents consult physicians primarily for general medical exams, physical exams for extracurricular activities, throat problems, cosmetic concerns, athletic injuries, and allergies. Older adolescents obtain preventive health care less often than younger adolescents.

Adolescents seem less likely to seek medical care as they get older because of barriers that make traditional health-care delivery systems seem inaccessible. Health professionals have thus devised alternative approaches to overcome these barriers. These alternative approaches provide peer counseling, place health clinics in shopping malls and schools, and offer recreational, vocational, and educational activities as well as medical care.

In the next chapter, we move from the physical changes of adolescence to the cognitive changes. As always, we begin with a case study, this time, a story about an adolescent who is considered to be gifted.

COGNITIVE CHANGES AND INTELLECTUAL DEVELOPMENT

CASE STUDY

Deborah, A Gifted Adolescent

Michael and Elizabeth are members of the faculty at a southeastern university with a good reputation. Each was granted tenure and received promotion in the past year. Michael and Elizabeth are active in their community, particularly in their church, in the fine arts, and in their daughters' schooling. They have two daughters: Deborah, who is 14, and Susan, who is 9.

I became aware that Deborah is gifted while watching her play viola at middle school events. She was part of the orchestra and a member of a small ensemble and played marvelously. At the time, she was 12. Further evidence that she is gifted came on an evening of scholastic awards at her school when her name was called again and again.

I recently asked Michael, Elizabeth, and Deborah two questions: If you heard that an adolescent was gifted, what would that mean to you? and What would be your reaction if you were told that Deborah is gifted? I will present their answers to the first question and then the second.

MICHAEL   Do you want my honest answer? I'm naturally skeptical of these things. I taught seventh grade in a school system with a rigid tracking system. Two of my groups were "above average." Each group had roughly the same grades, but one group I called my "academic drones." They would do things well and thoroughly, but as ordered. Then there was my other group. I called them my "erratic geniuses." I could never predict what they would do. They did things just as well and thoroughly, but they were creative, divergent. I've always associated being gifted with the second group, the erratic geniuses.

Giftedness though may be as much a matter of focus and hard work—using your abilities—as of any inherent ability. I've always thought of gifted people as persons with a single ability or a set of related abilities that they develop at the expense of other abilities.

In my mind, gifted is a step below genius. Gifted is better than bright.

ELIZABETH   The term *gifted* calls up a whole complex of things: school criteria, considerable talent in one area or more. I remember being surprised that gifted to the schools means only academically gifted. It does here in our school system.

Some years ago I worked with a young boy, who was 7 or 8 at the time, who had special talents in drawing. He could do block designs on the WISC-R test at a twelfth-grade level, but had verbal skills of a 4- or 5-year-old. A school system would have identified him as retarded.

One potential problem is whether being identified [as] gifted is bad for the child. Socially, other kids could make the child an outcast. Also, the child could let the label go to her head.

I know one parent whose son is gifted in math, and is so far ahead of his peers that he has had an unhappy childhood. I think he's a risk for adolescent suicide.

DEBORAH   I'd think the person was a little smarter than average. That they'd been tested for it and done well on the IQ test. I'd think the teachers would have recognized the person as gifted and recommended the person be tested.

I'm not sure what all the parts of the IQ test do mean, or how the testers base their judgments to decide someone is gifted. My dad doesn't really like standardized tests very much.

But I guess a person could be gifted and not do well on an IQ test. Some people are not good test takers. Some people get really nervous. I guess you can not know things and really be intelligent . . . if you don't have access to books, but you really use your mind well. And then I suppose a person could be really good in something, like music, but not very good on IQ tests.

I know some gifted kids who hated being called gifted. The other kids considered them nerds and made them feel uncomfortable. And then I know one boy who is gifted but thinks only about school things and is not good at all socially.

On the second question, what their reactions would be if told Deborah is gifted, Michael began,

MICHAEL   I'm having to reconsider what I believe it means to be gifted. I don't think I thought of Deborah as gifted. I suspected she is very bright and knows a lot.

I think I am sensing a shift in my thinking, but I still consider gifted to be the erratic geniuses. The notion of the gifted program should be to catch the erratic genius the school system would overlook.

Deborah was identified as gifted in grade school. It surprised me when the school system identified her as gifted. She did very well on an IQ test, and she has done very well on other standardized tests. In seventh grade she took part in a program sponsored by Duke University to identify talented children in the United States through scores on the ACT or the SAT. She took the SAT, I think. I really don't remember. The middle school counselor informed us her scores were already good enough to get her into any good university in the country.

She fought playing viola early. It bored her at first. There weren't any large rewards other than what she could do on her own. She's been lucky since we arrived in this town to have a superb viola teacher, but I don't think he would consider her a gifted viola player. She's just been acquainted with the viola for a very long time, at least ten years.

In Deborah's case the real issue is whether her abilities are just a function of her life circumstances. She lives in a family that talks a lot, that places a premium on knowing a lot. Her abilities are a function of the way we live. We don't have a TV. People in our home have to make their own entertainment. People read a lot in our family, and three members play musical instruments.

ELIZABETH   My first reaction is "Well, of course she is." She's always been an exceptional kid in many ways.

I'd never thought of Deborah as gifted until the school asked us to test her. I knew she was bright. One of the first signs of how adept she was occurred in the social realm. At the three month reunion of our birthing class, I was holding Deborah on my lap. She kept eyeing another infant, and when I put Deborah on the floor, she moved herself across the floor—she hadn't begun crawling yet—to see the other child. No other infant was doing that.

Another sign from the social realm came when we began coming home on the bus from Deborah's day-care center. We did this for two years when she was 2 1/2 to 4 1/2 years old. She could work a bus like no one I'd ever seen—she knew everyone on the bus by name.

She started talking and walking at about ten months. I knew she was ahead of the game there. She didn't start reading though until she started elementary school.

One sign of her giftedness is a lively interest in nearly everything. She's always been a great reader, partly due to no TV in our home.

She's been interested in social justice for a long time. She's in debate now and eating up the question about federal intervention for the homeless.

Her interest in music waxes and wanes, but it's always there. I play viola, and I played with her during the first four years of her playing. She wanted to quit at the age of 9, and I told her she had to keep practicing until she was old enough to know how good she can be. I'm certain she won't spend her life playing viola, except as an avocation.

I think Deborah is going to go for a life of ideas. I think she would say she wants to be a scientist.

DEBORAH   I am considered gifted. I was tested in fourth grade—took an IQ test.

It's not that bad to be called gifted as long as it's not said in a derogatory way. I would feel uncomfortable in elementary school when taken out of the classroom or when kids would say, "Oh, she's the smart one." And I didn't like all of this group learning that became really big in my middle school. They put kids of different abilities together. I guess it's supposed to help the gifted kids reinforce all they know and help the other kids to learn. I disliked it intensely. I always felt embarrassed, felt like always having the answers made me condescending. So sometimes I wouldn't tell the answer.

Sometimes I wonder if I really am gifted. Like when I make stupid mistakes.

I'm a good test taker. I guess well. If answers aren't provided like on a multiple choice test, I still know a lot of things and if I don't know the answer right away sometimes it will come to me. But sometimes I'm not real good at thinking when there is time pressure. Sometimes my mind goes blank when I have to do things in a hurry.

I started playing viola about the age of 5. My parents let me pick which instrument I wanted to play. I like it more now. It's still hard to get time to practice, but I like more to practice now.

I like playing the viola because I enjoy the music, and because I can participate in orchestra and small ensembles. I don't think I could make the viola what I do for a living, thinking about the viola constantly.

We went to a concert by the Turtle Island String Quartet this year, and I really liked listening to them. They played jazz. I like playing more modern stuff. I like the music from the Kronos Quartet. I like rock and roll, U2. I don't like heavy metal a lot. Like some pop music. In fifth grade, I used to like Debbie Gibson, but don't like her much any more. I like Bette Midler.

Michael, Elizabeth, and Deborah made some additional comments.

ELIZABETH   I see Deborah as a lot like me. As a child, I was under a lot of pressure to do well in school. Plus, as the oldest child of eight children, I was given responsibilities to be a second mother to my four youngest sibs. Consciously, unconsciously, I strive not to put those pressures on Deborah.

MICHAEL   I think there's a cost in identifying someone as gifted through IQ tests and then having that label attached to the child. I'm thinking of my brother Henry. Early in school, he did very well on an IQ test and was told he was gifted. A few years later, his IQ score went down, and now he was no longer thought of as gifted. I think it has haunted him all his life that he is not as smart as he once thought he was.

DEBORAH   I guess my dad in particular doesn't like the term *gifted*. He considers it to be loaded down with presents.

I think my mom was probably considered gifted. My dad probably was too. Did they do tests for being gifted back then?

ELIZABETH   One thing Deborah is vulnerable for, from both sides of our families, is clinical depression. She's had a couple of three- to four-week episodes of depression. The first was when she was 4 years old. She became a child who didn't want us to leave her, especially at the day-care center. This went on for a couple of weeks. She'd cry all day after we'd leave her. It seemed to be in response to a complete change of staff and of children at the center.

The second episode occurred about four years ago. Just after moving to this new town, Deborah made close friends with the daughter of a woman in my department. Then the woman and her family moved away, and Deborah had another four-week bout of depression, this time with dreams and thoughts of hurting people—hurting adults, parent figures. The thoughts and dreams scared her sick. At the time, I was in therapy for clinical depression. My therapist advised me to spend time with her, to go on walks together. I tried to help her see these evil thoughts were the only way she could lash out at a situation she had no control over. She pulled out of her depression but took a long while, maybe a year, before she let herself get interested in someone else as a friend.

DEBORAH   I like reading, playing the viola, playing the piano, playing soccer. I'm taking debate this year.

We don't have a TV, and I read for entertainment. What I read depends on the mood I'm in. In fourth and fifth grade I read Agatha Christie a lot. In seventh and eighth grade I liked situational novels, the kind you'd find in the young adult section of the library. I don't like historical romance novels. I've read one or two of them and can live without them. I like reading about girls who make the football team and stuff like that.

During the past summer I read my dad's Elmore Leonard novels. And the Fletch books. But I haven't had time to read much for pleasure due to all I have to read for debate. I did read *Go Ask Alice*, a really sad, interesting book. It wasn't like a drug education teacher talking to you, but an actual person telling what it's like.

I have no idea what I want to do when I grow up. I'll probably do something connected with a university. I'm interested in a lot of different things, but not sure what I'm the most interested in.

The views of the individuals in this case study highlight the competing views about what it means to be gifted and, more generally, what it means to be intelligent. In this chapter, we address the phenomena of intelligence and cognitive development of adolescents. Specifically, this chapter is about cognitive theories of intelligence. We look at different views of intelligence, and focus much attention on two dominant theories of cognitive development: the ideas of Jean Piaget and the information-processing view. We begin with a discussion of what it means to be intelligent.

VIEWS ON COGNITIVE DEVELOPMENT AND INTELLIGENCE

When asked the signs of intelligence, most people refer to the ability to learn from experience and to adapt to environmental demands. These are implicit references to cognitive functions. Today, interest in intelligence emphasizes cognitive aspects, such as thinking, planning, and deciding.

The **cognitivist position** currently dominates the fields of psychology and human development. This position emphasizes intellectual processes and uses hypothetical constructs to understand and explain human psychology and development. **Hypothetical constructs** appeal to nonobservable events, such as thinking.

The triumph of the cognitivist position is evident in contemporary explanations of adolescence. Although physical changes mark the beginning of adolescent development, cognitive processes account for many of the adolescent changes in critical areas such as, social relations, moral reasoning, self-identity, career and occupational interests, coping skills, and intelligence. The extensive appeal of cognitive processes presents compelling evidence that the cognitive view has triumphed as a paradigm in the field of adolescent development.

Are intelligence and cognitive development the same? When a person studies cognitive development, is he or she really studying how intelligence changes over time? Most authors who write about cognitive development cover extensively ideas about intelligence. It is my view that cognitive development is distinct from intelligence: cognitive development refers to how a person's mental processes change as the person ages. How individuals use their intelligence as they age provides the data for studies of cognitive development.

Considerable debate about intellectual development surrounds the question "as to just what develops or whether the intelligence that develops is the same thing at different ages" (Sternberg & Powell, 1983, p. 341). This debate has involved sweeping differences, ranging from the view that it is too early to produce a comprehensive review of adolescent intelligence (Neimark, 1983), to the assertion that enough information is available to produce a plausible model of intellectual development during adolescence (Sternberg & Powell, 1983).

Neither cognitive development nor intelligence can be weighed or touched. Each is a process, and our views of these processes can be implicit as well as explicit. Implicit views of these processes guide researchers as they strive to devise explicit theories.

Implicit Notions about Intelligence and Cognitive Development

Implicit notions refer to common sense beliefs, attitudes, and ideas that people hold about intelligence and cognitive development (Sternberg & Powell, 1983). The implicit ideas that adolescents develop about intelligence profoundly impact their personal expectations of success, persistence, and motivation in academics (Dweck & Elliott, 1983).

What would you accept as signs that a person is intelligent? If you said a high IQ, then you are accepting that intelligence tests can provide valid signs to identify intelligent people. Intelligence tests take implicit notions about intelligence and place them in a structure that permits systematic study of these notions. For instance, if a researcher thinks good vocabulary is a sign of intelligence, he or she would construct an intelligence test carefully designed to measure a person's understanding of words.

If a person is intelligent in areas not measured by a given test, what can be inferred about the person's intelligence as indicated by that test? For example, what if a person is very adept in fine arts, and the test measures academic subjects, such as spelling and vocabulary? This issue highlights the concern that traditional intelligence tests are biased culturally and are exclusive of many types of intelligence. We will discuss intelligence tests in more detail in the section on psychometric views of intelligence.

If you could not make use of intelligence tests, how would you determine whether someone is intelligent or, conversely, not very bright? Whatever you consider to be signs of intelligence forms your implicit notions about intelligence. Studies of psy-

Verbal skills, problem solving, and common sense are three ideas that crop up in people's descriptions of intelligence.

chologists—who supposedly are experts on intelligence—and of people in various other occupations have turned up five ideas that characterize implicit notions about intelligence:

1. the ability to *learn from experience*,
2. the ability to *adapt to the environment*,
3. *verbal skills*,
4. *problem solving skills*, and
5. *common sense*

(Sternberg & Powell, 1983; Sternberg, Conway, Ketron, & Bernstein, 1981).

Individuals differ on what signs of intelligence they consider to be important. People questioned in a university library, for instance, give much higher marks to verbal ability than do people in a supermarket. The correlation is high (.85), however, between what psychologists and other people mention as the important signs of intelligence (Sternberg & Powell, 1983).

Implicit notions of intelligence change as children age. Older children consider intelligence to be much more malleable than do younger children. They also consider intelligence to be an internalized quality, whereas younger children point to observable behaviors as signs of intelligence (Sternberg & Powell, 1983). Carol Dweck and Elaine Elliott (1983) have indicated that gender differences are markedly evident in school-age children's implicit notions of intelligence, with boys much more likely to consider intelligence to be a repertoire of skills open to development. Girls are more likely to consider intelligence to be a fixed trait, one not open to modification.

Explicit notions are systematic efforts to investigate the data believed to be indicative of intelligence. Explicit notions build upon implicit understandings. We now look at several explicit notions of intelligence.

The Maturationist View of Learning

Arnold Gesell (1880–1961) studied child development in his Yale University laboratory. He compared children of different ages (cross-sectional research) and followed the same children over time (longitudinal research) to record the sequence and the timing of the appearance of specific skills, such as crawling, walking, climbing stairs, and running. His research produced child development norms that are widely accepted today.

Gesell asserted that **maturation**, or development, occurs due to a genetic plan that regulates the appearance of all behavioral and mental skills. He further asserted that the environment plays a negligible role in development. Thus, for Gesell, intelligence develops according to an **unfolding genetic blueprint**, which does not depend on environmental experience (Gesell, Halverson, Thompson, Ilg, Costner, & Amatruda, 1940; D. Kuhn, 1988).

To test his views, Gesell conducted an experiment on identical 11-month-old twin sisters. One girl was given the opportunity to climb stairs, while the other girl was denied this experience. After six weeks, the first girl was able to climb stairs, but her sister was not. However, in a few more weeks, both girls were climbing stairs.

While Gesell's study seems to challenge his assertion that genetics rather than environmental experiences influence development, Gesell concluded that practice merely enables an individual to perfect skills that emerge due to maturation (Gesell & Thompson, 1929; D. Kuhn, 1988; Shaffer, 1989). However, because Gesell's study did not control for the prospects of environmental influences outside the laboratory, either of the twins could have engaged in all kinds of motor activities relevant to climbing stairs without Gesell's knowledge (D. Kuhn, 1988; Shaffer, 1989). The "control" twin could have observed her sister climbing stairs at home and begun to imitate her. In addition, as Deanna Kuhn has noted, Gesell's research contained a logical flaw by maintaining that observations of children can occur in an experiential vacuum, whereas "a process of maturation can be observed only in the case of a living organism that is undergoing experience of some sort during the period of observation" (1988, p. 209).

Maturationists insist that biological changes enable cognitive skills to emerge. Researchers are currently exploring the mechanisms whereby cognitive skills develop, and neuroscientists have made vast strides in showing the influence of neural mechanisms on cognitive development (Siegler, 1989). Biological changes cannot explain how a child develops new complex behaviors, such as planning or reading; rather, biological changes provide "enabling conditions that make it possible for the behavioral developments to take place" (D. Kuhn, 1988, p. 209).

Applied to adolescent development, maturationism suggests that the events of puberty facilitate or enable new cognitive skills to develop. An example is the increasing ability of adolescents to understand the experiences of others. It is important to note, however, that new cognitive skills do not emerge simply because puberty ensues; there are plenty of adolescents insensitive to the ideas and experiences of others. The biological events of puberty are a necessary condition, but not the sole condition, for the emergence of new intellectual skills during adolescence.

The Empiricist View of Learning

Gesell's dismissal of environmental influences is countered by scientists strongly influenced by British empiricism. **Empiricism** contends that all knowledge derives from experience. Empiricists argue that the environment conditions all behaviors, and that all learning is attributable to environmental actions on the living organism. We discussed the chief American empiricist, B. F. Skinner, in Chapter 1.

Skinner and his colleagues developed an explicit notion of intelligence known as **stimulus-response (S-R) theory**, which greatly influenced studies of how organisms, including humans, learn. The notion was that learning is the pairing of S-R connections, and intelligence is demonstrated in the ease with which someone makes these S-R connections. For instance, as many people have learned, hearing a certain song can evoke the memory of someone special. The pairing of hearing a bell with food led Pavlov's dogs to salivate. Note that these connections are considered to be physiological, not mental.

The S-R investigators placed tight boundaries around the activities of scientists. They insisted that scientists must limit themselves to studying observable events, and must resist the allure of attributing causes to internal events, such as mental processes. From the late 1930s to the early 1970s, the S-R approach ruled psychological literature and theory. This approach slipped from prominence as researchers turned to cognitive constructs to study and explain human development.

Applied to adolescent development, the views of S-R learning theorists rightly draw our attention to the role of environmental experience in forming knowledge. The S-R theorists contend that new intellectual skills result from the increased connections the person has formed, and from increased skill at forming such connections. S-R theorists attribute an adolescent's increased ability to appreciate the perspectives of others to increased pairing of responses to interpersonal experiences (that is, environmental stimuli) and greater skill at forming such associations. Pairing the tone in a person's voice to how the person feels is an example of S-R associations linked to interpersonal experiences. This appeal to increased experience as an influence on greater sensitivity seems plausible, as far as it goes.

Critics have scoffed at the S-R focus on simple tasks, and have insisted that the interesting, demanding research issues in cognitive development exceed the grasp of S-R methods and are beyond the comprehension of S-R theory. It seems quite difficult to use S-R theory to make an adequate account for such varied human achievements as libraries, literature, acts of moral courage, social justice, computers, musical composition, reading, mathematics, astronomy, friendship, learning to communicate, or a person's sense of wonder at natural beauty.

The Psychometric View

The psychometric view of intelligence has the clearest relation to implicit notions of any explicit theories about intelligence and cognitive development. **Psychometry** refers to efforts to measure human mental functioning. Adherents of the psychometric view measure abilities in areas considered to signify intelligence. Sometimes they also measure individual achievement. The wide acceptance of this approach is evident in the pervasive reliance on intelligence tests as a means of measuring intellectual capability.

This approach differs from other theories of intelligence in its use of sophisticated statistical procedures to identify both the factors that make up intelligence and those elements in the test that address the different factors (Sternberg, 1988; Sternberg & Powell, 1983; Vernon, 1971). Scholars have suggested that intelligence is composed of up to 120 factors (Guilford, 1967; Spearman, 1904; Thurstone, 1938), and that these factors change as people age (Sternberg, 1988; Sternberg & Powell, 1983). Philip Vernon (1971) proposed two factors: verbal-educational ability and practical-mechanical ability.

You may be familiar with the psychometric approach to intelligence that produces **intelligence quotient (IQ)** scores. In order to obtain an IQ score, the researcher must know the person's chronological age (CA) and how people of different chronological ages perform on the intelligence test being used. The second bit of information enables the person's mental age (MA) to be calculated. For instance, if a child performs as well as most 10-year-olds on a test, then that child is said to have the MA of 10. Knowing that a child's MA is 10 and her CA is 8 could lead one to conclude that she is bright.

The IQ is a person's MA divided by CA and multiplied by 100. Using the previous example, let's calculate the girl's IQ. The formula is MA/CA $\times$ 100 = IQ. Thus 10/8 $\times$ 100 = 125. The girl's IQ is 125.

If the girl's MA and CA had been the same, her IQ would be 100. An IQ of 100 signifies average intelligence for people of the same chronological age. More precisely, an IQ of 100 "means that the child has passed all the items that age mates typically pass and none of the items at the next level higher" (Shaffer, 1989, p. 358).

Today, the method of determining IQ scores by calculating the person's MA has been replaced by the concept of a **deviation IQ**. A deviation IQ is determined by the percentage of same-age individuals whose performance on the intelligence test equals or exceeds the performance of the person being tested. A deviation IQ of 100, which still denotes average intelligence, indicates that 50% of the population equals or exceeds the performance of the person being tested.

A critical feature of intelligence tests is administration to large numbers of persons in order to obtain norms for different chronological ages. Because psychometricians have developed these norms, judgments can be made about individual performance on a test. The average IQ score on an intelligence test is 100, and scores spread out from 100 in a normal distribution. For instance, approximately 68% of all individuals tested receive IQ scores that fall between 85 and 115. How does the 8-year-old girl with an IQ of 125 compare to her same-age peers? Only 6% of all 8-year-old children have an IQ at least that high (Shaffer, 1989; Sternberg, 1988). Interpreted from the deviation IQ method, her score equals or exceeds the performance of 94% of the population (Conger, 1991; Shaffer, 1989). You would be correct to conclude that the girl is bright, at least on items measured by the test she took.

There are many intelligence tests on the market. Three of the most widely used are the Stanford-Binet, the Wechsler Intelligence Scale for Children—Revised (WISC-R), and the Wechsler Adult Intelligence Scale (WAIS).

The Stanford-Binet, which places emphasis on verbal skills, measures four general categories of intellectual performance: verbal reasoning, arithmetic reasoning, abstract/visual reasoning, and short-term memory. For instance, the Stanford-Binet expects 12-year-old children to be able to define the word *muzzle* (verbal reasoning) and to repeat in reverse order a series of five numbers spoken by the test administrator (short-term memory). Two-year-olds through adults can be examined using the Stanford-Binet.

The WISC-R can be used to test 6- to 16-year-olds, while the WAIS can be used to test individuals too old for the WISC-R. Each of these intelligence tests assesses verbal and nonverbal intellectual skills, such as verbal and arithmetic reasoning, and the ability to assemble puzzles, solve mazes, and arrange pictures into meaningful stories. The results of the WISC-R and the WAIS are used to calculate three IQ scores: a verbal IQ score, a performance IQ score, and a full IQ score combining the verbal and performance scores. The WISC-R and the WAIS provide a **qualitative interpretation** of intelligence, ranging from "Very Superior" for IQ scores of 130 and above to "Mentally Retarded" for IQ scores below 70.

The Stanford-Binet, the WISC-R, and the WAIS employ the deviation method for computing IQ scores. Table 3-1 provides a comparison of nine deviation IQ scores as they would be interpreted when calculated on the Stanford-Binet and the WISC-R.

The areas of intelligence measured on these tests are closely related to the general criteria for success in school, such as verbal comprehension, arithmetic reasoning, and memory. Some researchers are concerned, however, that the results are influ-

TABLE 3-1   Deviation IQ Scores as Interpreted on the Stanford-Binet and the WISC-R Intelligence Tests

DEVIATION IQ	STANFORD-BINET EQUALS OR EXCEEDS PERCENTAGE OF POPULATION	WISC-R QUALITATIVE INTERPRETATION
140	99.3	Very Superior
130	97	Very Superior
120	89	Superior
110	73	High Average
100	50	Average
90	27	Average
80	11	Low Average
70	3	Borderline
60	<2	Mentally Retarded

SOURCES: Adapted from *Adolescence and Youth: Psychological Development in a Changing World* by J. J. Conger, 1991, New York: Harper Collins, *Developmental Psychology: Childhood and Adolescence* by D. R. Shaffer, 1989, Pacific Grove, CA: Brooks/Cole, and *Wechsler Intelligence Scale for Children* by D. Wechsler, 1974, New York: Psychological Corporation.

enced by **cultural biases** built into standardized tests, particularly intelligence tests. Lack of familiarity with what is being tested may place individuals from a particular culture at a distinct disadvantage. For example, consider the performance prospects for a child who understands only Spanish on an English language intelligence test.

One response to issues of cultural bias was to develop **culture-free** tests. However, efforts to produce culture-free tests are now recognized as fundamentally in error because all experience and construction of meaning depend upon cultural influences. Because cross-cultural contacts permeate American society, test makers now attempt "to construct tests that presuppose only experiences that are *common* to different cultures" (Anastasi, 1988, p. 357). However, constructing a test that is equally fair to several cultural groups seems unlikely. "Every test tends to favor persons from the culture in which it was developed," and middle-class Americans "may be just as handicapped on tests prepared within other cultures as members of those cultures are on our tests" (Anastasi, 1988, pp. 357–358).

The psychometric view facilitates comparisons of the intellectual abilities (or, in the case of some tests, intellectual achievement) of adolescents. These comparisons could be used to predict academic achievement, although how individuals perform in school depends on more than their IQ scores. By the time an adolescent reaches high school, past academic performance gives a strong indication of likely future performance, and IQ scores suggest whether the adolescent is living up to his or her academic potential. (As indicated earlier, on the whole, the most widely used intelligence tests—Stanford-Binet, WISC-R, and WAIS—measure intelligence in domains closely related to academic criteria.)

There is growing awareness that standardized intelligence tests measure conventional academic abilities while ignoring other abilities that are distinct aspects of intelligent behavior, such as musical talent, athletic skill, and creative writing skill. The formulation of alternate models of intelligence has been hailed as an advance over tests that focus solely on scholastic ability (Silverman, 1986b; Sternberg, 1986). One such model refers to multiple intelligences.

Multiple Intelligences

Harvard psychologist Howard Gardner (1983, 1985, 1993; Hatch & Gardner, 1986) argues that the traditional view of intelligence favors knowledge of academic subjects. This view, which he considers restrictive, actually does a disservice to society because it overemphasizes rationality, ignores several intellectual processes valuable to every culture, and limits our understanding of intelligent behavior (Gardner, 1983; Hatch & Gardner, 1986).

Gardner incorporates ideas from diverse fields, such as genetics, cultural anthropology, neurobiology, information processing, and abnormal psychology, to make his case that the human mind engages several intellectual potentials that exist relatively independent of each other. Gardner likens the human mind to a computer, a metaphor agreeable to the current generation of psychologists. Earlier metaphors likened the mind to a blank slate or *tabula rasa* (popular in the 17th century); a muscle to be exercised (popular during the time of William James); and a telephone relay system (popular in the 1920s). Gardner qualifies his computer metaphor by pointing out that human intelligence surpasses the sum of the ignorant mechanisms it uses and involves an executive function of self-consciousness (Gardner, 1983). He acknowledges that the human mind is not a separate entity from the various functions that compose it but rather emphasizes that the human mind is the very intelligences whereby a person deals with reality.

Gardner identifies seven separate intellectual domains of human competence: (*a*) linguistic intelligence, (*b*) musical intelligence, (*c*) mathematical-logical intelligence, (*d*) visual-spatial intelligence, (*e*) bodily-kinesthetic intelligence, (*f*) intrapersonal intelligence, and (*g*) social-interpersonal intelligence. Humans typically use more than one intelligence when acting intelligently. For instance, a concert violinist engages linguistic intelligence (to read musical notation), musical intelligence (to respond to tone, pitch, and rhythm), and bodily-kinesthetic intelligence (to position both fingers and the violin bow to play the notes). We discuss each intelligence in turn.

Linguistic intelligence.   The domain of competence in which writers and public speakers excel is called **linguistic intelligence**. Gardner himself possesses highly crafted linguistic skills, as readers of his writings attest, including those who disagree with his argument about multiple intelligences.

All human beings possess the core operations needed to use linguistic intelligence, and all humans use language for the same fundamental purposes: to persuade, to remember information, to learn and impart information, and to be self-reflective (Gardner, 1983). Linguistic intelligence serves all other intelligences, which seem to be "know-how" capabilities, rather than "know-that" capabilities.

Cross-cultural data provide evidence for the universality of linguistic intelligence. For example, Gardner refers to the remarkable use of oral traditions in preliterate cultures (Gardner, 1983). Biblical scholars have noted with astonishment the reliable preservation over several thousand years of extensive oral traditions in what Christians call the Old Testament (B. Anderson, 1975; Gunkel, 1907; von Rad, 1962).

Musical intelligence.   The domain of competence in which composers and performers excel is called **musical intelligence**. Gardner refers to successful composers, such as Bach and Mozart, as individuals who exemplify musical intelligence. Gardner contends that musical talent appears earlier than all other talents, that it develops in a variety of fashions, and that it is available to all human beings in all cultures. In the United States, the existence of the Grammy Awards, the Country Music Awards, and the prodigiously successful musical recording industry attest to the value of musical intelligence in our society. Is there any culture in the world without an appreciation for musical talent? Can you imagine your own life without music?

The core operations of musical intelligence are sensitivity to pitch, rhythm, and timbre; that is, to melody, to groupings of certain auditory frequencies, and to characteristic qualities of tone. Musicians and composers often speak of the constant presence of music in their minds. Miles Davis, the extraordinary jazz trumpeter, said he *always* heard music, regardless of where he was or what he was doing. The jazz

Musical intelligence is present in all cultures.

saxophonist in the acclaimed film *'Round Midnight* said the same thing. Beethoven composed his greatest music after becoming profoundly deaf.

Mathematical-logical intelligence.   The domain of competence achieved by scientists, logicians, and mathematicians is known as **mathematical-logical intelligence.** When introducing this type of human intelligence, Gardner makes immediate reference to Jean Piaget, who investigated problem solving that requires mathematical-logical intelligence. Gardner acknowledges that Piaget's research has helped clarify skills that rely on mathematical-logical operations, but he considers Piaget's theory deficient because it gives no attention to the core operations whereby mathematical-logical reasoning occurs.

The core operations of mathematical-logical intelligence involve competence to deal with extended sequences of abstract ideas (Gardner, 1983). Abstraction and generalization are two operations central to mathematical-logical work. All great scientists possess intuition, and a powerful ability to explain reality by identifying rules or laws that govern the natural world.

These intellectual powers seem keenest before the age of 30, particularly for mathematicians. The personal tragedy of mathematical-logical geniuses, akin to a similar fate for great athletes, is being destined to live 30 or more years past the prime of their intellectual powers. In contrast, linguistic, visual-spatial, and musical intelligences are more enduring, and masters in the humanities continue to produce major works in their later years (Gardner, 1983).

The contrasts between the mathematical-logical intelligence of science and the intelligences of the humanities involve more than differences in onset of decay. A gulf separates the understanding, acceptance, and appreciation of the sciences by the humanities and vice versa. C. P. Snow (1963) elucidated brilliantly this gulf in his metaphor of "two cultures" that do not communicate due to arrogance, distorted images, and mutual incomprehension.

Scientists and literary intellectuals know practically nothing of the works and traditions produced by the other culture. The inability of a humanities scholar to describe the Second Law of Thermodynamics is "the scientific equivalent of: *Have you read a work of Shakespeare's?*" (Snow, 1963, p.14). While scientists receive little education in great works of literature, many literary intellectuals are even more deficient in grasping the fundamentals of science. Asking a person "What is the meaning of acceleration?" is for Snow "the scientific equivalent of saying, *Can you read?*" (Snow, 1963, p. 14).

Snow's assessment is a plea to educational systems to educe more than one type of intelligence in growing minds, and an indictment of contemporary Western societies' failure to educate the whole mind. The problem reveals itself when we accept as evidence of high intelligence being gifted in mathematics or in the natural sciences. A growing trend for educating well-rounded minds has emerged in several universities and is evident in concern that all undergraduates should gain a general education, enabling them to think critically about the sciences and the humanities (Boyer, 1987; Lacey, 1990; Nelson, 1990).

Visual-spatial intelligence.   The domain of intellectual competence found in architects and engineers is known as **visual-spatial intelligence**. Chess experts display this competence in their mastery of the layout of a chess board and of how the pieces will look should certain moves occur. Geometry requires visual-spatial intelligence. Sculptors and painters are also examples of humans who have developed their visual-spatial intelligence.

The core processes of visual-spatial intelligence involve accurately seeing the world, and then transforming these perceptions to "re-create aspects of one's visual experience, even in the absence of relevant physical stimuli" (Gardner, 1983, p. 173). Consider the skill of hunters and trackers, such as mystery writer Tony Hillerman's major characters, Navajo Tribal Policemen Joe Leaphorn and Jim Chee. In his stories, Hillerman (1970, 1978, 1984) points out that they have what seems to white men to be an uncanny sense of reading the terrain; they take for granted that their ability to track animals or men across desert landscape is a matter of patience, practice, and knowing how to distinguish marks on the ground.

Francis Crick and James Watson displayed an extraordinary use of visual-spatial intelligence when they demonstrated that the double helix solved the puzzle of the structure of the DNA molecule (Watson, 1968). Gardner (1983) contends that the theory of evolution began to take hold when Darwin imagined species development in terms of a tree with multiple branches. Sir Kenneth Clark (1970) recounts remarkable achievements that depended on visual-spatial intelligence: the Greek Parthenon, the Cathedral of Notre Dame in Paris, and Michelangelo's sculpture of David. The 20th-century achievements of Frank Lloyd Wright, I. M. Pei, Edward Hopper, and Andrew Wyeth have caught the attention of many admirers. On a less serious note, the cartoonists Gary Larson (creator of *The Far Side*) and Bill Watterson (creator of *Calvin and Hobbes*) entertain hundreds of thousands of people with their visual-spatial intelligence.

Many nonindustrialized cultures greatly value visual-spatial intelligence. Eskimos, South Sea Island natives, and Kalahari bushmen all have developed keen, but differing, uses of this competence. For example, the Eskimo ability to return safely over a seemingly invariant, white terrain is astounding. In fact, "at least 60 percent of Eskimo youngsters reach as high a score on tests of spatial ability as the top 10 percent of Caucasian children" (Gardner, 1983, p. 202).

Bodily-kinesthetic intelligence.   The intellectual domain of dancers, athletes, circus performers, actors, and mimes is called **bodily-kinesthetic intelligence**. Surgeons require this intelligence, as do musicians. Due to the philosophical influence of René Descartes, who persuaded Western cultures to divorce physical realities from mental realities, Americans commonly consider intelligence to be mental, and bodily actions to be reflexive, habitual, and not based on intelligence. By proposing a bodily-kinesthetic intelligence, Gardner argues against this deep-rooted, American belief. Do you think, for instance, that bowling or playing college football requires intelligence? Or do you restrict intelligence to more clearly mental operations, such as solving math problems and getting good grades?

Take the case of a batter in major league baseball. The ball moves from the pitcher's hand to home plate very quickly. In many cases, the ball is traveling over 90 miles an hour—and in all cases, the ball travels less than 61 feet to reach the batter. All major league pitchers can make the ball change direction abruptly, as when they throw a curve ball or a slider. How does a batter see the ball, determine whether to swing at it or let it go by, move the bat in time to meet the ball, and correct a swing when the pitch does the unexpected? Major league batters do all of those things regularly, and the better hitters actually have a good chance of getting on base.

The batter's rapid motor activity exemplifies bodily-kinesthetic intelligence. Other types of bodily-kinesthetic performance are illustrated by a keyboard operator reliably entering more than 100 words per minute, a violinist racing unerringly through a Mendelssohn concerto, a hospital emergency team working to stop a patient's massive bleeding, and a student feverishly taking lecture notes from a professor who speaks faster than the speed of light.

Involved in these highly coordinated bodily movements is a sequence of preprogrammed "overlearned, automatic, highly skilled, or involuntary activities" that enable the performance "to unfold as a seamless unit" (Gardner, 1983, p. 211). William James (1892/1967) called such behaviors *habits*.

We use bodily-kinesthetic intelligence every day. Imagine how confounding it would be if you had to concentrate on how to produce every letter of the alphabet as you write. Or if you had to focus on the distinct movements required to walk down a flight of stairs. This could result in a loss of control.

The personal intelligences.   The personal intelligences are the domains of competence for individuals who excel in self-understanding (intrapersonal intelligence) or in understanding others (social-interpersonal intelligence). While Gardner claims these are distinct forms of intellectual capacities, he emphasizes their common roots in attachment to caregivers, awareness of bodily sensations, and ability to distinguish one individual from another.

Intrapersonal intelligence is an inner-directed, information-processing capacity that, at its core, involves awareness of one's emotions. Although Gardner claims that the ability to distinguish pleasure from pain is the most primitive form of intrapersonal intelligence, it seems to me that such ability hardly distinguishes humans from other forms of life. In its most developed forms, intrapersonal intelligence enables humans to recognize and represent subtle, complicated emotional reactions. Novelists, psychotherapists, and wise elders are three examples of humans who achieve highly developed forms of intrapersonal intelligence.

In his intricate, eleven-volume novel sequence called *Strangers and Brothers*, C. P. Snow demonstrated repeatedly an understanding of his emotions. Take, for example, the following paragraph from Snow's (1970) final novel in the sequence. The narrator, a 60-year-old man who suffered cardiac arrest while undergoing an eye operation, is commenting on the dread and terror he feels at being alone after having found out he had died and been brought back to life only by the heroic efforts of the surgical team.

> I had learnt enough about anxiety all through my life. Worse, I had been frightened plenty of times—in London during the war, on air journeys, visits to doctors, or during my illness as a young man. But up to that night I hadn't known what it was like to be terrified. There was no alleviation, no complexity, nor, what had helped in bad times before, an observer just behind my mind, injecting into unhappiness and fear a kind of taunting irony, mixed up with hope. No, nothing of that. This was a pure state and apart from it I had, all through that night, no existence. All through that night? That wasn't how I lived it. The night went from moment to moment. There mightn't be another (Snow, 1970, pp. 132–133).

Social-interpersonal intelligence (hereafter referred to as "social intelligence") is an outward-directed, information-processing capacity that, at its core, involves skill at distinguishing other people's "moods, temperaments, motivations, and intentions" (Gardner, 1983, p. 239). Ability to differentiate individuals and their moods is the most primitive form of social intelligence. More developed forms enable individuals to understand what motivates others and to use that understanding to influence others. Religious leaders, politicians, parents, counselors, advertisers, and teachers all occupy positions requiring social intelligence.

One form of social intelligence is **empathy**, the ability to understand someone else's experiences. Skilled helpers possess finely tuned empathic skills, know how to communicate their empathic understanding, and actually gain greater understanding of someone else's situation than that person has attained (Egan, 1990). An example of this advanced empathic understanding is recognizing that a student's difficulty with his history professor is mirrored in the student's continual conflicts with other males in positions of authority.

Mark Barnett and Sandra McCoy (1989) reported that undergraduates who experienced a traumatic incident in childhood develop far more empathic understanding than unaffected students. Balk (1981, 1990a) noted that sibling death during adolescence as well as bereavement while in college leads to greater sensitivity to others' troubles and increased tolerance for others' emotional pain.

Both intrapersonal and social intelligence have their roots in evolution and, according to Gardner (1983), are the birthright of each human being. Over their life spans, individuals become more competent in using the personal intelligences. Early development involves attachment to caregivers, growing skill at using mental imagery, and increasing involvement in the world of one's peers. The personal intelligences continue to develop during adolescence, as evidenced by the growing capacity to take the perspectives of others and the push to produce a more coherent sense of self. Gardner asserts that the adolescent push for self-understanding and identity "is a project—and a process—of the utmost importance. The manner of its execution will determine whether the individual can function effectively within [his or her] social context" (Gardner, 1983, p. 251).

Gardner acknowledges that not all cultures value the inner-directed, individualistic orientation of intrapersonal intelligence. Some cultures consider a focus on individual development to be an aberration, endangering "a sense of community and . . . the virtue of selflessness" (Gardner, 1983, p. 253). The Chinese, in particular, exemplify adherence to group norms over individual goals.

Gardner's theory of multiple intelligences has clear applications to understanding and fostering adolescent development. It may contribute to the nurturing of talents and understandings as wide-ranging as scholastic skills, social intuition, intrapersonal growth, and musical virtuosity. The multiple intelligences framework calls for acceptance of individual differences based on more than IQ tests, and cries out for identifying and promoting diverse intellectual abilities. A chief application of Gardner's ideas to adolescents concerns the notion of being intellectually gifted.

GIFTED ADOLESCENTS

In the case study earlier in this chapter, we met Deborah, a gifted adolescent, and her parents. When you hear that an adolescent is gifted, what do you think that label means? Do you assume the adolescent gets good grades in school? Perhaps you consider being gifted as having an extraordinary IQ or a special talent in music or painting. Do you think a gifted adolescent appreciates or dislikes being considered gifted? Do you think a gifted adolescent has greater problems adjusting than other individuals of the same age? We look at all of these questions in this section.

First, we examine the more general issue of what it means to be gifted. One view is that the gifted are characterized by unique, special aptitudes and make up perhaps less than 2% of the total population. Another view is that all individuals in a democracy are gifted. Yet another view, related to these rival positions, is that no one is gifted in a generic sense, but rather in some specific way. For instance, Harry may be enormously talented in drawing, but is average in musical talent and quite weak in writing. According to educators, gifted individuals manifest special talent or aptitude in one of five areas: general intelligence, a specific academic area, creativity, leadership, or the visual or performing arts (Stake, Raths, Denny, Stenzel, & Hoke, 1986).

IQ Scores and Identifying the Gifted

Lewis Terman and Melita Oden (1947, 1959) conducted longitudinal studies of children who obtained unusually high scores on intelligence tests and found that most of the individuals made outstanding contributions to society as adults. A person could use data from the Terman and Oden studies to support policies that high IQ scores are a reliable and valid means for identifying gifted youths. Indeed, when school systems provide special programs for the gifted, they typically use IQ scores to identify students for the program.

Considerable controversy surrounds the use of IQ scores to identify the gifted (Silverman, 1986a; Sternberg, 1986). What are the arguments for and against IQ scores as demarcators of gifted individuals?

A multi-layered argument for using intelligence tests to identify the gifted contends that (*a*) a general cognitive ability is common to all special talents, (*b*) intelligence and creativity are not essentially different, and (*c*) reliable, valid measures of intelligence are available (Silverman, 1986a). According to this argument, intelligence tests measure general cognitive ability, thereby providing a clear indicator of giftedness.

Proponents of IQ scores as indicators of giftedness insist that relying solely on IQ scores is mistaken because "the identification should bring in other information such as motivation and values" (Silverman, 1986a, p. 169). You may recall that Gardner (1983) considers intelligence to be multi-dimensional. He specifically notes that identifying the gifted by means of IQ tests misses many of the strengths and cognitive styles of gifted individuals (Gardner, 1993).

Although John Feldhusen and Steven Hoover (1986) do not argue explicitly for or against using IQ scores to identify the gifted, they do emphasize that superior general cognitive ability marks many gifted youths. This general cognitive ability (sometimes called the *g* factor) correlates highly with scores on intelligence tests according to interview comments by Elizabeth Hagen, one of the developers of the current version of the Stanford-Binet Intelligence Scale (Silverman, 1986a). Other researchers express doubt that the g factor adequately represents the diversity in human intellectual talent (Hatch & Gardner, 1986).

Many—if not most—individuals do not equate traditional academic aptitude with being gifted. Robert J. Sternberg (1986) says using intelligence tests, which measure traditional academic aptitude, to identify the gifted provides modest success. He adds, however, that IQ tests fail to identify gifted individuals whose intelligence reveals itself when circumstances require them to synthesize information or to respond creatively to novel situations. In information-processing terms, IQ tests favor people who can store and retrieve a great amount of scholastic data, but such tests are incapable of assessing creative strategies people use to deal with ambiguous, nonacademic tasks. Gardner (1993) argues against the use of standardized tests to identify the gifted—or even to identify intelligence, for that matter—and supports identifying intelligent behavior by observing people in action.

Three of Sternberg's (1986) case studies illustrate the inability of IQ tests to identify all gifted individuals. These case studies present the stories of three college students with differing IQ scores and academic records. The first is an example of **componential learning**, which enables individuals to understand discrete aspects of information and to explain those aspects when required to do so. The second is an example of **experiential learning**, which enables individuals to analyze situations and apply information relevant to those situations. The third is an example of **contextual learning**, which enables individuals to evaluate environmental demands and respond appropriately.

A Case Study in Componential Learning

Alice was "the admissions officer's dream" (Sternberg, 1986, p. 143). She had superb aptitude scores, an excellent academic record, and handled traditional course work brilliantly until her graduate training in clinical psychology demanded her to use her knowledge to help resolve other people's problems (Sternberg, 1986). Alice faltered greatly once her studies demanded that she make decisions in ambiguous situations. While Alice had high IQ scores, and while she could store and retrieve great amounts of academic data, she was deficient in applying and synthesizing information.

A Case Study in Experiential Learning

Barbara was "the admissions officer's nightmare" (Sternberg, 1986, p. 144). While her grades were good, her aptitude scores were abysmal. People who knew her gave sterling letters of recommendation and stressed her independence, reliability, and exceptionally creative mind. Barbara was admitted to Yale University's clinical psychology program under unusual circumstances and performed well in her courses, though not quite as well as Alice. However, once the emphasis of the program shifted to creative syntheses of information, Barbara noticeably outperformed Alice. Had decisions about Barbara depended solely on intelligence test scores, which do not assess an individual's ability to use information creatively, she would have been denied admission to the program (Sternberg, 1986).

A Case Study in Contextual Learning

Celia was neither an admissions officer's dream nor nightmare, but rather a person whose ability measures and grades were good, but not outstanding. Expected to be an average student, Celia surprised everyone on the faculty by using her practical intelligence to determine what success at Yale University required and then acting consistently on that information. She was highly skilled in picking up and acting on cues important to succeeding in her environment. Sternberg notes that such intelligence is difficult to express in words and needs to be seen in action (Sternberg, 1986).

Multiple Intelligences and Gifted Adolescents

Given the previous discussion, it seems logical to return to Gardner's theory of multiple intelligences. The primary argument against overreliance on IQ scores as identifiers of the gifted is that they do not assess the many forms that intelligent behavior takes, and they certainly do not measure creativity. While psychometrically sound means do not yet exist to identify most of the intellectual domains in Gardner's scheme, traditional intelligence tests do focus on fairly specific forms of linguistic intelligence.

While Terman and Oden's (1947, 1959) subjects did excel in school as adolescents and in various careers as adults, Gardner (1983) notes that many great talents in literature, music, dance, and science were not outstanding students. For example, it is common knowledge that Albert Einstein's teachers considered him dull and most unlikely to succeed in life.

Acceptance of Gardner's formulation about multiple intelligences, however, still leaves us with the problem of identifying those who are gifted in nonacademic areas. Truly exceptional musical talent is noticed when individuals are given the opportunity to perform. Our society enables gifted athletes to show their talents and to develop under close tutelage. Observing performance can enable researchers to assess many of the intellectual domains that cannot be validly evaluated in a paper-and-pencil inventory. Ralph Tyler (1942) introduced this approach years ago when he developed assessment procedures pertinent to the behavior being evaluated. For instance, when assessing a person's skill in using a microscope, Tyler devised a checklist of behaviors that observers could identify when watching a person use the microscope.

Gifted Adolescents' Views of Themselves

Ann Robinson (1990) studied how comfortable adolescents feel about being labeled as "gifted." Whereas many earlier studies indicated that adolescents hold positive or neutral attitudes to being labeled gifted, Robinson notes the emergence of evidence which suggests that a significant proportion of adolescents feel unsure about or uncomfortable with the gifted label.

One study (Ziv & Gadish, 1990) has shown that peers perceive gifted adolescents to have either a good sense of humor or no sense of humor at all. The peers react in an either/or way, with no subtleties or qualifications. This extreme reaction by one's peers could pose problems for adolescents who dislike being seen as gifted.

Several researchers have focused attention on the risks presented by being gifted. The incidence of suicide by gifted adolescents is considered to be a matter of particular concern (Delisle, 1990; Hayes & Sloat, 1990). While acknowledging that accurate data on suicide and gifted adolescents is difficult to obtain, Marnell L. Hayes and Robert S. Sloat (1990) reported that nearly 20% of suicides in several Texas school districts during the 1986–1987 school year involved gifted adolescents.

Robinson (1990) studied the perceptions of and reactions to the gifted label of 396 high school seniors considered to be gifted on the basis of academic performance, school contributions, or juried decisions about fine arts talent. Over 70% of these students indicated they felt comfortable with being considered gifted, while nearly 30% reported feeling uncomfortable with the label. At the extreme poles on the comfort scale, 84 adolescents (21%) reported feeling extremely comfortable with the gifted label and 71 (18%) reported feeling extremely uncomfortable.

Adolescents who felt extremely comfortable with being labeled gifted were significantly more likely than their extremely uncomfortable counterparts to accept the label, to acknowledge that their parents identify them as gifted, and to admit that their close friends treat them differently because of the label. Adolescents extremely uncomfortable with the gifted label rejected it with noticeable anger; however, rejecting the label did not appear to help them cope with being treated differently despite their protestations. Unlike those gifted adolescents who felt extremely comfortable with the label, these adolescents strongly disliked being considered different from their peers (Robinson, 1990).

While the majority of Robinson's (1990) gifted adolescent sample felt positive with or were indifferent to being labeled gifted, a significant number expressed distress and difficulty coping with the label. Since approximately one in every six gifted adolescents has difficulty with the label, Robinson asserts that schools need to assist these students in adjusting. The schools are usually the source for being labeled gifted in the first place.

The family can also provide valuable assistance to adolescents who have difficulty coping with the gifted label. Carolyn Callahan, Dewey Cornell, and Brenda Loyd (1990) studied 60 adolescent females identified as gifted through their IQ scores and performance in a high school honors program. They examined the girls' self-concepts as well as their perceptions of self-competence and communication with parents.

The gifted females reported self-competence and self-concept scores significantly higher than "norms provided in the literature on average students" (Callahan et al., 1990, p. 262). Significant positive correlations were found between feelings of competence and perceptions of communication with parents; that is, girls who reported high levels of self-competence also perceived their communication with parents as healthy. The only exception was "a significant negative relationship between communication with father and perceptions of athletic competence" (Callahan et al., 1990, p. 264).

Callahan, Cornell, and Loyd (1990) concluded that healthy family communication benefits adolescent females in several areas of personal growth and intellectual performance. However, they acknowledge that their methodology raises questions about generalizing their findings, and they admit that self-concept and parental communication "are mutually influential and . . . should be regarded as bi-directional" (Callahan et al., 1990, p. 265).

So far, we have looked at several approaches to the study of intelligence and have reviewed some phenomena associated with gifted adolescents. We turn next to the current dominant views on cognitive development: the ideas of Jean Piaget and the information-processing view.

TWO DOMINANT VIEWS: GENETIC EPISTEMOLOGY AND INFORMATION PROCESSING

Jean Piaget's View: Genetic Epistemology

Developmental psychologists maintain that prior to Jean Piaget (1896–1980), the Swiss scholar who revolutionized the study of thinking, learning had been studied, but cognitive development had been ignored (D. Kuhn, 1988; Neimark, 1983). Piaget explained cognitive development in terms of biological changes and environmental pressures; human knowledge results from the interaction of genetic predispositions and responses to the world. His theory is called **genetic epistemology** to indicate that human knowledge (epistemology) unfolds in a developmental sequence determined by human biology (genetics).

Piaget's theory combines aspects of maturationism and empiricism; however, he did much more than produce an eclectic version of two opposing viewpoints. Piaget's theory offers a unique explanation of how human thought processes unfold in qualitatively distinct stages to produce abstract logical reasoning. In essence, his approach studies the development of mathematical-logical intelligence. His theory uses change mechanisms borrowed from biology (for instance, assimilation, adaptation, and accommodation) and uses hypothetical constructs, such as schemata, that are strongly disliked by strict behaviorists.

Piaget's adherents say S-R learning theorists ran pointless experiments, waged meaningless arguments, and produced a wasteland of data; they assert that since the arrival of Piaget's genetic epistemology, no serious challenge has been posed to his explanation of how conscious thought processes develop over time (Neimark, 1983). Other, more critical writers contend that Piaget's concepts inherently resist systematic study (Emerick & Easley, 1978; Ennis, 1975; Sternberg & Powell, 1983). Still other critics argue that investigators have designed and conducted poor research to test Piaget's theory (Nagy & Griffiths, 1982).

Fundamental Concepts of Piaget's Theory

The three fundamental concepts of Piaget's theory are structure, function, and content.

Cognitive structure.   Piaget considered **structure** to be the concept of central importance in his theory (Brainerd, 1978). Structure denotes the shape of cognitive development as a human being's reasoning capabilities change. Cognitive structures are inferred, abstract ideas, rather than directly observed entities. We infer the existence of cognitive structures by studying "what the various cognitive contents specific to a given stage of development have in common" (Brainerd, 1978, p. 19). Thus, the structures of reasoning are inferred to change when a person's intellectual activities change.

To cite a famous example from Piaget, a young child is unable to understand that water does not change in volume when it changes shape. However, for a child of 10, such an understanding is obvious. Another example is the ability of an adolescent to do algebra or trigonometry, which signifies that the cognitive structures have changed from the preadolescent cognitive stage of development. Piaget's expecta-

The ability of an adolescent to do algebra or trigonometry shows that cognitive structures have changed from the person's preadolescent cognitive stage of development.

tions about the advances in cognitive reasoning during adolescence indicate that he did not view adolescence as a time of turmoil and stress.

Cognitive structure serves the same purpose in Piaget's theory as hypothetical constructs in other branches of knowledge—the electron in physics, dark matter in astronomy, and the self in psychology, for example. "We infer their presence by measuring other things—notably the effects they have on physical and biological systems" (Brainerd, 1978, p. 19). Historians and philosophers of science make clear that scientists rely on inferred, abstract structures to advance their understandings of reality (Butterfield, 1957; Hanson, 1972; Holton, 1978; T. Kuhn, 1970; Toulmin & Goodfield, 1962).

How do cognitive structures change? Piaget used the biological ideas of **equilibrium**, **assimilation**, and **accommodation** to explain these leaps from one manner of thinking to a qualitatively new manner. A biological organism strives to keep its relationship with the environment in balance. As a thinking organism, the human being strives to keep its mental representations and experiences of the world in balance. To achieve cognitive equilibrium, the human first seeks to incorporate new experiences into an existing structure; this process is called assimilation. When assimilation fails to produce equilibrium, the person is forced to change the structure, thereby accommodating to new features of reality. Piaget would call structures *schemata*.

Cognitive structure changes because interaction with the environment requires an individual to act in intelligent ways that extend his or her current cognitive structure (Brainerd, 1978). For instance, a 12-year-old boy raised in a small, Catholic, rural community moves to a large town and meets several classmates whose ideas about religion differ from his own. Not only does the boy discover that a Methodist classmate has a picture of Jesus in his home, but he also learns that some of his classmates have no religious beliefs. This experience can lead to a mental struggle to balance his religious view of the world with the different perspectives of his peers. He must adjust his cognitive structure in order to handle this discrepant information. Learning to appreciate the different life experiences of one's peers—as in the case of the 12-year-old Catholic boy—is an example of cognitive structure undergoing change.

The processes of assimilation and accommodation interact and gradually enable an individual to think about reality in a completely different way. This change in cognitive structure is closely related to the second fundamental concept of Piaget's theory—cognitive function.

Cognitive function.   The goals of cognitive development are referred to as **cognitive functions**. One function of cognitive development is to think abstractly. This occurs gradually as an individual matures and interacts with the environment. A more specific example of function involves memory (for instance, the act of recalling a person's telephone number).

Cognitive development occurs because of two invariant activities, a person's organization of information and adaptation to experience. In short, cognitive development occurs because of an interaction between the individual's cognitive structure and the functions that the structure can perform.

Like structure, function is an inferred property of the human mind. According to Piaget, a person must organize information from the very beginning of life, which suggests that this functional aspect is innate or hereditary. Furthermore, Piaget asserted that cognitive functions occur because the human mind actively strives to achieve them.

Cognitive content.   The data contained in one's intellectual structure—that is, what a person knows and what a person is able to do to interpret reality—is referred to as **cognitive content**. Unlike structure and function, cognitive contents can be measured and observed. Piaget actually inferred that cognitive structures and functions must exist because of changes in cognitive contents. Cognitive contents are "the raw contents of cognition . . . the hard empirical facts without which the notions of structure and function would have no meaning" (Brainard, 1978, p. 26). The dramatic changes in the contents of an individual's intelligence as he or she develops led Piaget to postulate four qualitatively distinct stages in human cognitive development.

Stages of Cognitive Development

Piaget maintained that human intelligence proceeds in stages which provide increasing coherence between the mind and reality. In combination with biologically regulated physical changes and interactions with the environment, the individual incorporates new understandings of the world and develops new abilities to perform mental operations about external reality, abstract concepts, and thinking itself. The **stages of cognitive development** proposed by Piaget are listed in Table 3-2.

The **sensorimotor stage** occurs between birth and age 2. During this stage, remarkable advances occur as the infant's physical development enables increasing exploration and interaction with the environment, resulting in **behavioral schemata**. Behavioral schemata are patterns of behavior whereby infants respond to their worlds in an organized fashion. For example, a behavioral schema for one infant boy was to go into his family's kitchen every day, remove all the pots and pans from a cupboard, spread them out on the floor, and play with them. A behavioral schema for

TABLE 3-2   Piaget's Stages of Cognitive Development

STAGE	DESCRIPTION	APPROXIMATE AGE
Sensorimotor	Physically exploring the environment resulting in behavioral schemata	Birth to 2 years
Preoperational	Constructing mental symbols to understand reality	2 to 7 years
Concrete Operations	Using mental schemata to understand and act on reality	7 to 11 years
Formal Operations	Using more abstract, flexible mental schemata to understand and act on reality	11 years and beyond

my infant daughter was to climb out of her crib, flop onto an adjacent bed, and call for attention. In both cases, the youngsters experienced clear delight and a sense of accomplishment; the behaviors were repeated again and again until new ones took their places. Piaget emphasized that infants do not use symbols to represent reality, and that the production of symbolic schemata occurs in the next stage in cognitive development.

The **preoperational stage** emerges in the second year of life and lasts until around age 7. During this stage, a child begins to use mental representations to think about the world. The stage is called "preoperational" because children have not developed the cognitive schemata that permit them to perform logical operations about reality. Preoperational children engage in play and fantasy, and commit errors in logic that older children scoff at (for instance, believing that liquids change in volume when poured into containers of different shapes). Preoperational children become adept at focusing on conspicuous features of an object—for instance, the shape of a liquid—and thus, are influenced by appearances. Piaget acknowledged the qualitative gains of the preoperational over the sensorimotor stage, but he seemed to focus on the errors in logical thought that preoperational children are prone to make.

According to Piaget, the **concrete operations stage** emerges around the age of 7 and lasts until approximately the age of 11. During this stage, children develop mental schemata to represent the world and to perform mental operations about the world. If a concrete operational child sees liquid poured from a tall, thin glass into a squat container, the child understands that the volume has remained the same, despite a change in appearance. Piaget called this mental operation *reversibility*—that is, the ability to reverse in one's mind what has happened. Other mental operations acquired during the concrete operations stage include *seriation* (placing objects in the correct order), *conservation of number* (recognizing that the number of objects remains the same if they are arranged in a new shape), and *decentration* (considering more than one aspect of a problem, rather than focusing on the most conspicuous feature). Concrete operations are limited, on the whole, to real objects a person can observe or imagine, while more abstract concepts, such as algebraic equations, pose formidable challenges to concrete operators. Evidence indicates that how individuals acquire the mental operations that distinguish the concrete operations stage varies greatly (Case, 1985; D. Kuhn, 1988). Piaget referred to such variation as **decalage**; namely, the presence of cognitive operations in some tasks but their absence in apparently similar tasks. For instance, Piagetians invoke decalage to account for a child's ability to conserve mass, but not volume or weight. However, these findings challenge Piaget's assertion that simpler schemata must precede the acquisition of more complex schemata.

The **formal operations stage** emerges around age 11 and is the final stage in human cognitive development. Formal operators can reason about abstract concepts without visible representations. Whereas some commentators contend that formal operators can think about concepts that are neither real nor even imagined (Shaffer, 1989), it seems difficult to believe that even the most abstract concepts (for instance, gravity waves, black holes, or irrational numbers) are outside the imagination of the formal operators who ponder them. Einstein was famous for his thought experiments, such as imagining what the world would look like if he were riding on a beam of light (Bronowski, 1973; Holton, 1978).

Formal operators use schemata that enable systematic, logical, and analytic approaches to problem situations. A hallmark of formal operations is the use of logical hypotheses to deal with reality. Piaget's image of formal operators seems to be that of the scientist who uses the **hypothetical-deductive method** (systematic application of logic) to bring to light the secrets of nature. In a very real sense, Piaget's image of the formal operator is autobiographical; his whole approach to studying cognitive development employs the systematic, logical, and analytical operations in which he excelled. Furthermore, his intent was to uncover how reasoning changes over time until it culminates in the use of systematic, logical, and analytical operations.

Adolescents Using Formal Operations

What in adolescence illustrates the use of formal operations? If we are to understand formal operations only from the perspective of scientific thought, then few adults, let alone adolescents, could be shown to be engaging in formal operations. However, formal operations involve characteristics we see in many adolescents but do not see in school-age children.

One of the chief characteristics of formal operations is **systematic thinking**. An example is a 16-year-old's purchase of a car stereo. She read about car stereos in consumer magazines, talked to people about various models, listened to car stereos in friends' cars, and eventually, chose a model that was both affordable and had high consumer ratings. It was not the most popular model with many of her friends, but she had found out from her research that it performed as well as other models, was less expensive than these other models, had an excellent maintenance record, and could have components added fairly easily.

Closely related to systematic thinking is another characteristic of formal operations—the ability to **consider competing points of view** and to **keep these points in mind** while examining an issue. An example is the reflections of a 19-year-old college sophomore about lowering the legal drinking age to 18. He started out unsure of his position, listened to arguments about increased fatalities and injuries to adolescents due to drinking while driving, weighed arguments that equated the age to vote with the age to drink, and heard other arguments deploring drinking as immoral. He finally decided that he favored lowering the age to 18 because such a law would legalize what occurred extensively in practice. He also decided he favored linking a low legal drinking age with stricter laws about driving under the influence, applicable to both adults and adolescents.

It is now recognized that individuals who attain formal operations do not use such reasoning in all situations. For example, an 18-year-old boy who can design and carry out complicated chemistry experiments does not use his formal operations when shopping at the grocery store; although he checks his results carefully in a chemistry experiment, he does not apply simple mathematics to determine the best buys at the store. Recently, he bought a six-pack of 12-ounce cans of soda at $2.49 (3.5 cents per ounce) without realizing his better buy would have been a 67.6-ounce bottle at $1.25 (1.8 cents per ounce). He had been fooled into thinking the number of cans gave him more for his money. He also put things into his shopping cart impulsively, rather than working from a list made out before going to the store. When he got home he realized he had forgotten to buy bread and had four more cans of orange juice to go with the six others he had bought on his last trip to the store.

Some serious criticisms have been raised about Piaget's claims. We look at these criticisms next.

Criticisms of Piaget's Theory

Edith Neimark (1983) expressed conviction that Piaget's is the only coherent model of cognitive development worth consideration. Other writers are less sanguine. While they admire Piaget's achievement, and consider his theory to be elegant, they point out several logical and empirical problems in his work.

Robert Ennis (1975, 1976, 1978) has argued that Piaget (*a*) surprisingly offers no guidance regarding children's use of deduction, (*b*) presents a defective model of propositional logic, and (*c*) asserts mistakenly that children around 11 to 12 years of age can handle class logic but are unable to use propositional logic.

Propositional logic is a type of deductive reasoning that, in its basic form, uses the "if . . . then" argument—for instance, "If I don't return this library book on time, then I will get a fine." **Class logic** involves the concepts of inclusion and membership—for instance, "Dogs and cats are members of the class called animals." Class logic can also be stated in propositional form—"If this is a dog, then it is an animal."

Ennis (1978) expressed considerable puzzlement over the meaning of Piaget's claim that children 11 to 12 years of age can handle class but not propositional logic. He noted that teachers and researchers acquainted with young children maintain that children do reason using the principles of propositional logic.

Sternberg and Powell's (1983) criticisms of Piaget's theory of intellectual development focus on how Piagetians determine whether a child has successfully handled a cognitive task, how observations are interpreted, the validity of the theory, and the usefulness of the theory.

Some researchers consider Piaget's criteria for determining whether a child has successfully handled a cognitive task to be so stringent that younger children who complete a task are often overlooked. The criticism focuses especially on two criteria: (*a*) that children must resist the investigator's efforts to talk them out of successful performance of a task and (*b*) that children must explain clearly why their response is correct. For instance, imagine a child correctly identifies that the amount of clay is still the same regardless of its altered shape but begins to doubt her answer when the investigator starts questioning her. Critics claim that Piaget's method invalidly identifies the child as having failed when she actually had succeeded until the investigator interfered.

Critics also raise two issues interpreting what success or failure on a task indicates about a child's intelligence. The first concerns the validity of Piaget's method—do the Piagetian tasks actually measure what Piaget claimed? The second issue centers on the uniqueness of task performance—does success or failure on a task permit accurate conclusions about a child's developmental stage?

Equifinality is a concept some critics bring to bear on the validity of Piaget's method. This concept means individuals can arrive at the same outcome despite using different strategies. Sternberg and Powell (1983) cite empirical studies demonstrating that some preoperational children, who use strategies not recognized by Piagetians, successfully complete cognitive tasks supposedly limited to concrete operators. These studies question the validity of the tasks Piaget designed to assess cognitive performance.

Critics also question whether successful task performance accurately denotes the individual's stage of cognitive development. Piagetian adherents claim that task consistency identifies cognitive structures unique to specific stages of development, and suggest that transitional stages and decalage account for discrepancies in performance. However, research on this issue indicates that task performance depends on the content of the task one is given, rather than on any underlying structure. So many alternative and testable explanations can account for Piaget's data that Sternberg and Powell (1983) have recommend abandoning the notion of underlying unique structures and attending rather to how individual cognitive strategies develop.

The usefulness of Piaget's theory has also come under scrutiny. For instance, if an adolescent is identified as a concrete operator, what have we learned concerning how that individual reasons in daily situations? The Piagetian response is that Piaget was interested in competence, rather than specific performance, and that he wanted to determine if certain competencies are present, not the circumstances in which the person uses those competencies (Sternberg & Powell, 1983).

Another constraint on the usefulness of the theory is that it has little to say about individual differences in cognitive ability, other than acknowledging that individuals differ in their rates of intellectual development (Sternberg & Powell, 1983). While not considered a "necessarily damning" criticism of Piaget's theory, this limitation highlights the theory's constricted utility. Piaget's theory can neither explain nor predict differences in ability or performance of individuals whose cognitive functioning differs but whose stage of development is judged to be the same (Sternberg & Powell, 1983).

Deanna Kuhn (1988) criticizes Piaget's theory for its failure to recognize that variation in experience affects cognitive development and that social context influences cognitive development. Piaget's theory offers no means for predicting the effects of culture in enabling or retarding cognitive development. Furthermore, Piaget's theory does not take into account the interaction between children and their environments. As Kuhn notes, children internalize models of "all sorts of implicit or explicit examples of the higher level concepts" (1988, p. 229). Piaget's theory, however, ignores the social context in which cognitive development occurs. Kuhn concludes that "specific evidence is now accumulating to show that children attend to external models of higher level concepts in a sustained and deliberate manner" (1988, p. 229). Questioning how individuals attend to these external models has exposed a gap in the Piagetian theory.

Overview of Piaget's Contribution

Critics of Piaget's theory of cognitive development focus on his understanding of logic, difficulties in testing his ideas, and the influence of experience and social context on performing specific tasks Piaget designed to test cognitive operations. Although these criticisms do point out some flaws, it would be a mistake to conclude that Piaget's ideas have nothing to offer about cognitive development.

One of Piaget's major contributions is the identification of the changes in reasoning that mark the development of individuals as they mature. Another is his recognition that cognitive development seldom occurs in a smooth fashion, but rather in gaps called decalage.

Piaget's vision about intelligence, his method of studying reasoning, and his interpretation of his findings have inspired many researchers of adolescent development. Using Piaget's notions of formal operations, assimilation, and accommodation, these investigators have studied adolescents' expanded understanding of social reality. We will discuss in depth these uses of Piaget's theory in Chapter 5, which examines the new social perspectives adolescents attain.

Piaget's theory is not the only view on cognitive development with strong allegiances. Another view is information processing.

The Information-Processing View

The Computer Metaphor

Information-processing theorists develop and utilize concepts, models, and flow charts that demonstrate the power of the computer as a metaphor for human cognition. Fundamental concepts of the information-processing model include input, the human sensory register, short-term memory, long-term memory, control functions, and information retrieval and transfer strategies. In particular, Richard C. Atkinson and Richard M. Shiffrin's (1968) model of human memory has had considerable influence upon information-processing researchers and illustrates reliance upon the computer metaphor. This model is shown in Figure 3-1.

According to Atkinson and Shiffrin's (1968) model, environmental input feeds into the **human sensory register** and, if the person pays attention, flows into **short-term memory** (STM). Two features of STM are limited capacity and limited duration (approximately seven "chunks" of information retained for several seconds at best). Unless **executive control processes** focus on the STM information, it is soon forgotten. If operated on, STM information is transferred to **long-term memory** (LTM), an apparently infinite and permanent storage center from which the person can retrieve information when needed.

To illustrate, imagine that you are driving home in your car after having gone shopping at a mall across town. You are listening to the radio and thinking about a movie you have just seen. When you notice a car pulling out from a driveway, you slow down to avoid a collision. The traffic light changes from green to yellow just as you are entering an intersection, so you speed up to get through before the light changes to red. You notice but do not pay attention to several pedestrians on the sidewalk. The disc jockey plays a new song you have not heard before; it is by a singer you particularly like. The radio station interrupts its music to report that a coup has

FIGURE 3-1   **The Atkinson and Shiffrin Model of Human Memory**

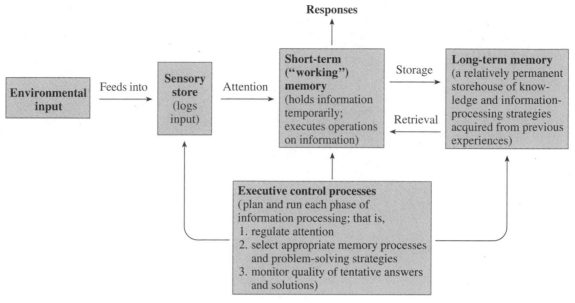

SOURCE: From *Developmental Psychology: Childhood and Adolescence* (2d ed.) by D. R. Shaffer. Copyright © 1989 by Brooks/Cole Publishing Company. Reprinted by permission.

toppled the president of Russia. The news is so startling and unexpected that you listen intently for the next ten minutes. You see your house, pull your car into the driveway, and go inside to tell your roommate about the news on the radio. You realize that you got home safely, but that for the past ten minutes, you did not pay much attention to anything but the news on the radio. You recall the song you were listening to just before the news of the coup because it was the latest release of one of your favorite singers.

In general, the environmental stimuli from your trip were not memorable—that is, you did not pay close attention to most of what you saw or heard. However, you recall vividly the news about the coup because you have been considering the implications of that event ever since the news report.

You automatically dealt with most of what occurred on your drive across town—it did not involve transfer from STM to LTM. Although you were literally bombarded by sensory stimuli, you paid attention to only a select few. You became absorbed in the news of the coup and focused much of your attention on its implications. To draw out these implications, you had to retrieve from LTM your knowledge of world events and apply that knowledge to this new situation.

"The guiding assumption underlying the model is that human cognitive functioning is composed of a set of individual processes that operate sequentially" (D. Kuhn, 1988, p. 231). As portrayed in Figure 3-1, the model suggests the human intellect works in linear fashion and is passive at the onset of any processing of information. In actuality, experimental studies emphasize that humans actively seek information

In contrast to younger children, college students make more exhaustive attempts to extract the main idea of what they read, to scan the text more completely, and to retrieve information about what they read.

and construct meaning, rather than merely waiting until stimuli reveal themselves (Gardner, 1985). Humans use organizing schemas to process information; these schemas involve active construction of meaning, rather than passive acceptance of data (Bransford & Johnson, 1972; Bransford & McCarrell, 1975). This active processing of information is characteristic of other primates as well; rhesus monkeys kept in laboratory cages do not wait passively; rather, they actively seek information about their environment and develop learning sets that produce insight about new information (Butler, 1953; Harlow & Mears, 1979).

LTM information is both factual and procedural. An example of factual LTM information is my view of information-processing as an important model of human intelligence. An example of procedural LTM information is my knowledge of how to outline a textbook chapter on cognitive development. To decide whether I have carried out this procedure well or poorly, you must engage several procedures and strategies; you must process the words I have written, use executive control processes to focus upon my ideas, retrieve information from your LTM about cognitive development, assess whether my explanations are clear and credible, and decide whether my approach meets your criteria of quality work.

Information-Processing Units of Behavior

Sternberg (1979, 1988; Sternberg & Powell, 1983) has suggested that the fundamental units of behavior whereby information processing operates comprise five elementary functions, or "components": metacomponents, performance components, acquisition components, retention components, and transfer components. Note that Sternberg's descriptions of these five components resemble executive control processes (Atkinson & Shiffrin, 1968).

Metacomponents are higher order processes whereby decision making and problem solving occur. These processes involve problem identification, strategy selection, and goal attainment. **Performance components** carry out the overall plans and decisions established by the metacomponents by encoding problem elements, combining elements to solve the problem, and assessing the applicability of the solution to possible solutions. **Acquisition components** enable a person to learn new information, **retention components** enable a person to retrieve stored information, and transfer components enable a person to apply stored information to new situations (Sternberg, 1988; Sternberg & Powell, 1983).

Intelligence develops as the five components interact by activating and giving each other feedback. However, the metacomponents control direct activation and feedback. "All control to the system passes directly from the metacomponents, and all information from the system passes directly to the metacomponents" (Sternberg & Powell, 1983, pp. 371–372). In Figure 3-1, these metacomponent functions are located in the executive function box, and the arrows in the figure indicate control and regulation of all phases of information processing.

Cognitive Development via Information Processing

Sternberg (1988) notes that several significant changes in cognitive development occur as people age. These changes include (*a*) more sophisticated control strategies, (*b*) more exhaustive processing of information, (*c*) greater ability to comprehend successively higher-order relationships, and (*d*) more flexibility and wisdom in using information.

More sophisticated control strategies.   Sternberg (1988) notes that as individuals age, they develop greater executive control processes. For example, in comparison to younger children, 10-year-olds more frequently use rehearsal strategies to remember information (Flavell, 1985). Older children (9- and 10-year-olds) organize information through semantic grouping strategies—such as placing "dogs," "cats," and "birds" into the category "animals"—more so than younger children, but less than adults (Liberty & Ornstein, 1973; Shaffer, 1989). Daniel Keating and Bruce Bobbitt (1978) noted that age differences favor 17-year-olds over 13-year-olds and 13-year-olds over 9-year-olds in both memory search rates and LTM retrieval efficiency. D. R. Shaffer (1989) summarizes studies on age differences in attending to relevant versus irrelevant information by noting that "older children are much better than younger ones at concentrating on relevant information and filtering out extraneous input that may interfere with task performance" (p. 332).

More exhaustive processing of information.   Sternberg (1988) notes that people process information more thoroughly as they age; they learn better encoding procedures and evaluation strategies, and they use these processes more exhaustively. In contrast to younger children, for instance, older children demonstrate consistently that they make more thorough attempts to (*a*) extract the main idea of what they read, (*b*) scan the text more completely while they read, and (*c*) retrieve information about what they have read.

Greater ability to comprehend successively higher-order relationships. Sternberg (1988; Sternberg & Rifkin, 1979) notes that the ability to comprehend relations of a successively higher order is due to increasing skill in abstract reasoning. For instance, understanding analogies, such as "a horse is to a rider as a car is to a driver," is a second-order relational skill that emerges in early adolescence (around the age of 12) according to Sternberg A more difficult order of abstract

Social Perception and Information Processing of Early and Middle Adolescents in Turkey

Hortascu (1990) studied 69 children in Turkey between the ages of 9 and 15 to examine whether social perception develops as information processing increases. The children read brief sentences about activities ("John went to the basketball game on Saturday"), sentiments ("Mary liked the book she read during vacation"), offers of help ("Tom helped Bob with the dishes"), and invitations ("Susan asked Mary home for her birthday") (Hortascu, 1990, p. 343). Hortascu used Turkish names in the sentences, such as Murat, Asli, and Mehmet. The researchers explained to them that the study involved asking good questions, and asked the children to write questions to help identify what or who caused things to happen in the various sentences.

Older children asked significantly more sophisticated questions to uncover causes than younger children. For example, 15-year-olds asked more questions about person-activity interactions ("Was it a game involving John's school team?"), about the general characteristics of activities ("Was it a particularly important game?"), and about specific personal attributes ("Does John play on the school team?"). Hortascu's (1990) study provided evidence that information processing is used outside of Euro-American cultures. Hortascu provided cross-cultural validation that Turkish children behaved consistently with the models developed from Western subjects.

reasoning, called third-order relations, emerges during adolescence and is exemplified in comprehending how separate analogies are analogous to each other.

Sternberg's example of a good higher-order analogy is: "(Happy : Sad :: Red : Courage) :: (Tall : Short :: Yellow : Cowardice)" (Sternberg & Downing, 1982, p. 214). To translate, happiness is the opposite of sadness and red symbolizes courage just as tall is the opposite of short and yellow symbolizes cowardice. The parallelism in the structure is critical—both happy/sad and tall/short are opposites; colors are used to represent opposite emotional states (courage and cowardice).

More flexibility and wisdom in using information. Sternberg (1988) notes that younger children are less flexible than older children in how they obtain information and in how they apply information to novel situations. Younger children fail to identify when they should change strategies. Sternberg suggests that flexibility in information use depends on developing "the ability to know when to change" (1988, p. 284).

An intriguing study of problem-solving strategies in young versus late adolescents provides support for Sternberg's hypothesis. Pitt (1983) analyzed the problem-solving strategies employed by tenth grade students and college undergraduates in solving basic chemistry problems (such as, "What would account for this color reaction?"). The high school students had not taken chemistry, and the college students were not chemistry majors; while there could have been some differences in the individuals' educational experiences with chemistry, the researchers claimed there were no differences of a substantial nature. In all cases, the tenth-graders were less flexible than the college students. The tenth-graders developed poorly stated hypotheses and poorly stated problem definitions, they demonstrated poor skills at synthesizing and organizing disparate information, and their planning was haphazard. Because the college students performed much better in all of these areas, Pitt concluded that their use of problem-solving strategies and their acquisition of information surpassed the ability of tenth-graders. As Sternberg notes, the college students had developed greater flexibility in knowing "when to change strategy or transfer information and when not to do so" (1988, p. 284).

Information-Processing Conclusions About Human Intelligence

Various conclusions can be drawn about the accomplishments, limitations, and future of information processing as a cognitive science. I now present some of these conclusions.

Changes in strategies and intellectual development.   Changes in intellectual strategy are associated with increasing age, and these changing strategies give us insights into the development of the mind (Sternberg, 1988; Sternberg & Powell, 1983). Older children and older adolescents use more information to solve problems, and they integrate the information more successfully than their younger counterparts (Pitt, 1983; Ryan, 1990). Sternberg (1988) urges researchers to study whether these changes in strategies suggest overall increases in cognitive capabilities.

Metacognition and changes in the knowledge base.   Information processes need content on which to operate, but the distinction between process and knowledge base is sometimes obscure (Sternberg, 1988). Sternberg takes it as given that a person's knowledge store—the content in LTM—increases as a person grows older. What he suggests to be less certain—but of considerable interest for cognitive development—is whether awareness of one's knowledge (**metacognition**) influences the acquisition of new knowledge.

Changes in how information is represented.   Access to one's knowledge base depends on skill in symbolizing and relating information to other aspects of one's knowledge base, or in information-processing terms, encoding and transforming information to serve new purposes. Chess experts, whether children or adults, represent information about the pieces on a chess board more thoroughly and efficiently than chess beginners (Chi, 1978). Encoding and transformation processes seem to improve with age and experience, although evidence is not conclusive.

Increased availability of processes.   Experience seems clearly connected to increased availability of cognitive processes (Sternberg, 1988). Using cross-sectional methods, Sandra Hale (1990) studied processing speed and component aspects of information processing in four age-groups: 10-year-olds, 12-year-olds, 15-year-olds, and 19-year-olds. Her results indicate that processing speed is fastest in older subjects and that older subjects use more component processes. Using cross-sequential methods, however, Ted Nettlebeck and C. Wilson (1985) found that processing speed levels off at about age 13, and they suggested the beginning of adolescence marks a leveling off of processing information as well.

Charles White (1987) demonstrated that early and middle adolescents can be taught to develop and use more cognitive processes, regardless of verbal ability or age. Junior and senior high school students were randomly assigned to participate in an experimental curriculum designed to increase the use of cognitive processes, such as identifying, retrieving, organizing, and evaluating information, needed to solve problems in social studies. Their scores on tests of information-processing skills were significantly higher than the scores of students who did not participate in the experimental curriculum.

Reductionism and the Lack of Self-Reflection

Deanna Kuhn (1988) notes that information processing's focus on analyses of specific cognitive tasks reintroduces the **reductionist approach** of behaviorism that Piaget's holistic constructivism had overcome. **Reductionism** is a term denoting breaking up some process or phenomenon (for instance, walking or a blood cell) into its constituent parts and analyzing these smaller components. At times, reductionism leads people to claim the process or phenomenon is *nothing but* the components. Such a view can lead to losing appreciation that a living cell or walking (or any other process or phenomena) is more than its component parts. Piaget's **holistic perspective** emphasizes the interrelationships between various aspects of development and emphasizes that human development cannot be reduced to isolated components.

While Kuhn commends the accomplishments of information-processing researchers in identifying the mechanisms whereby intelligence operates and changes, she laments the loss of a holistic perspective. The analysis of specific tasks produces no synthesis, and meticulous focus on tasks lures investigators "to maintain that the performance is *nothing but* the serial execution of a specified set of individual processes [rather than to invoke] some higher order organizing entity" (D. Kuhn, 1988, p. 236).

This concern over reductionism calls to attention a major difference between a computer and a human being. Computers are not self-reflective, whereas humans clearly are. Humans exercise voluntary control to "initiate, organize, and monitor our own cognitive processes . . . . decide what to attend to . . . . [and] choose the very problems that we will attempt to solve" (Shaffer, 1989, p. 331). As Kuhn says, "computers do not 'know' what they are doing" (D. Kuhn, 1988, p. 238).

Work in developing artificial intelligence may some day produce a self-reflective machine, but to date, our encounters with such computers come in imaginative literature, the cinema, and television. Consider the novel *When Harlie Was One* (Gerrold, 1988), the films *2001: A Space Odyssey*, *Alien*, and *Terminator*, and the television show *Star Trek: The Next Generation*. Should humans one day produce a self-reflective computer, there will be intellectual dilemmas over many issues, such as what it means to be a person.

The lack of a self-reflective mechanism, or metacognition, is considered a serious limitation of information processing (D. Kuhn, 1988). This criticism can be seen as merely what Gilbert Ryle (1949) called a logical error about the human mind. As Gardner (1983) points out, intellectual operations are not "self-aware" but provide the means for "self-awareness." Attention given to executive control processes appears to emphasize their metacognitive functions (Flavell, 1984; Sternberg, 1984, 1988). However, Sternberg and Powell, who conclude that allocating mental resources and adapting them to tasks is "the core of intelligence" (1983, p. 399), acknowledge that more attention must be given to executive control processes over intelligence.

So far, we have covered implicit and explicit notions of intelligence, what it means to be intellectually gifted during adolescence, and two dominant theories about cognitive development. We now turn to a review of the effects of college on intellectual growth.

THE INTELLECTUAL GROWTH OF COLLEGE STUDENTS

Do college students grow intellectually? If they do, are these changes the effects of college or can other explanations, such as maturation, plausibly account for the changes? As part of an exhaustive review of the effects of college on students, Ernest T. Pascarella and Patrick T. Terenzini (1991) investigated several areas in which college students are said to demonstrate intellectual growth: using writing skills, reasoning at a formal operational level, thinking critically, learning new concepts, engaging in reflective judgment, and handling conceptual complexity. They concluded that the net effects of college benefit students' cognitive development.

Using Writing Skills
Cross-sectional studies reported by Pascarella and Terenzini (1991) indicate that college seniors do considerably better on writing tests than freshmen. Analyses indicate these results cannot be attributed to differing academic aptitude or maturation. Because these studies were conducted in the late 1970s and middle 1980s, it seems unlikely that their results are due to cohort effects not found in college students in the 1990s. Thus, when measured on the standard of using writing skills, exposure to college accounts for changes in intellectual growth (Pascarella and Terenzini, 1991).

Reasoning at a Formal Operational Level
Despite claims that formal operations develop during adolescence, several studies indicate that only slightly more than half of all college students reason using formal operations. A synthesis of these studies can be found in Patricia King's (1986) review of the literature.

Some longitudinal work to assess whether college students show gains in formal reasoning has led to conclusions that (*a*) significant gains occur during the freshman year, (*b*) significant increases occur between the beginning of the freshman year and the end of the sophomore year, and (*c*) significant differences separate freshman from senior performance. Pascarella and Terenzini (1991) point out that students make these gains primarily in the first two years of college and that later gains are not significant.

Researchers have not paid much attention to the effects of college on the development of formal operational reasoning (Pascarella & Terenzini, 1991). One study that compared Canadian and black South African college students found that both groups showed mastery of Piagetian tasks of proportional reasoning, but that only the Canadian students showed mastery of propositional reasoning tasks

(Mwamwenda & Mwamwenda, 1989). The authors assert that cultural differences favored the Canadian students in the experiment.

Thinking Critically

Critical thinking involves the higher-order cognitive skills of interpreting, evaluating, and synthesizing information. It also involves basing judgments on evidence, rather than on personal preference. In addition, critical thinking involves making judgments about the logic and substance of arguments for or against a position.

Pascarella and Terenzini (1991) reported findings from studies conducted in the 1950s and 1960s that suggest college influences students to think more critically by the end of their freshman year. These studies are vulnerable to concerns over cohort differences; skepticism about the intellectual preparedness of current high school graduates (National Commission on Excellence in Education, 1984; Singal, 1991) raises the question of whether findings about an earlier generation of college students pertain to today's college students.

Longitudinal and cross-sectional investigations in the early and middle 1980s demonstrated gains in critical thinking during the college years. These studies were conducted at several different institutions, and all showed the same pattern of results: statistically significant gains in critical thinking, not only among late adolescents (18- to 22-year-olds), but also among adults who had returned to college as nontraditional students.

Pascarella (1989) reported a longitudinal quasiexperiment that tracked two matched samples of late adolescents following graduation from high school. The individuals were matched on academic aptitude, family socioeconomic status, and total scores on a test of critical thinking. One group attended college; the other did not.

Pascarella followed the samples for a full year. By the end of the freshman year of college, the college students scored significantly higher on the test of critical thinking than their counterparts who had not enrolled in college. Pascarella and Terenzini (1991) noted that the gains shown by the college students resembled the gains in critical thinking of college students in the 1950s.

College influences students to think critically.

Learning New Concepts

Pascarella and Terenzini (1991) reported that few studies have looked at changes in college students' abilities to acquire new ideas. They also noted that none of these studies supports the belief that a college education increases one's skill in learning new concepts. Comparisons between freshmen and seniors were statistically non-significant on this criterion.

Engaging in Reflective Judgment

An influential model of college students' cognitive development suggests that students perceive learning in one of three divergent ways: they adopt a dualist, relativist, or committed relativist position (Perry, 1970). **Dualists** are interested in facts, do not consider that shades of meaning exist, believe that facts are true or false, and understand answers to be correct or incorrect. Rather than a changing, evolving body of understanding, knowledge is seen as stable, unchanging, and true for dualists. Connections between ideas are difficult for dualists to comprehend, and synthesizing information to form theories is beyond their scope.

William Perry (1970) considered **relativists** to have reached a more advanced stage of intellectual development. They engage in a more critical, skeptical approach to claims about truth and to claims based on authority, rather than evidence. They appreciate that several sides can exist to a story and that alternative points of view compete for allegiance. They appreciate that some ideas explain reality more adequately than others, but that all ideas are open to revision. They can synthesize information to form theories and get beyond mere memorization of unconnected facts. Relativists see no basis for choosing one position over another. They are convinced that relativism is correct, can show the subtlety of arguments for and against a position, but make no commitment to a position other than relativism. In *The Paper Chase*, a novel about first-year law students at Harvard struggling in a course on contract law, John Osborn (1971) illustrated the difference between the dualist and the relativist: one student had a photographic memory but did not know how to synthesize or evaluate information he memorized; the other student critically analyzed and compared cases he studied, and organized this information into a larger whole that he called "Contract Law."

Committed relativists have achieved a level of cognitive development beyond that of relativism. In addition to being able to reason abstractly and to compare competing points of view, committed relativists make value judgments based on their reasoning. Unlike dualists, who consider facts to be right or wrong, committed relativists see the ambiguity in knowledge, the need to remain open to new information, and the strength of persuasive arguments. Unlike relativists, who accept that alternate views of reality are normative but choose none, committed relativists weigh evidence and choose a position; the pluralism in competing claims does not overwhelm committed relativists and persuade them to decide that no position has better claims than any other. Committed relativists take committed, but provisional, stands because new evidence may require reevaluating what they endorse. Committed relativists recognize that intellectual inquiry requires taking risks, and that these risks expose one to change.

Researchers have used both cross-sectional and longitudinal methods to investigate Perry's view about intellectual development. A theme common to all these studies is that college students demonstrate "significant gains in reflective judgment either from the beginning to the end of the freshman year, from the freshman year to the senior year, or from the freshman to upperclassman years in college" (Pascarella & Terenzini, 1991, p. 124). These gains are found particularly in reasoning about issues that possess no correct, verifiable answers. These are the sorts of problems one encounters as part of human existence (for instance, poverty, abortion, and the existence of God). Gains in reflective judgment do not seem attributable to academic aptitude or maturation (that is, age), but rather to the continued exposure to formal education in college. A six-year longitudinal study reported by Pascarella and Terenzini (1991) demonstrated that individuals who earn a bachelor's degree show greater gains in reflective judgment than individuals who have not attended college (Kitchener, King, Wood, & Davison, 1989); the researchers determined that the two groups were similar in academic aptitude.

Handling Conceptual Complexity

An overarching standard for assessing cognitive growth is the extent to which individuals "can generate their own criteria for organizing and evaluating their dichotomous distinctions, . . . can view more subtle relationships between elements in their environment, and . . . can synthesize these elements more fully" (Pascarella & Terenzini, 1991, p. 126). Evidence from longitudinal and cross-sectional research indicates that college enables individuals to handle conceptual complexity more proficiently. As Pascarella and Terenzini (1991) reported, gains occur from the freshman through the senior year, with the greatest gains seen between the beginning and end of the freshman year.

CHAPTER SUMMARY

Some scholars who have worked to make explicit their ideas about intelligence have staked out several well-known positions. The maturationists state that human intelligence emerges according to a developmental plan that is practically impervious to environmental influences. The empiricists argue that all intelligence is a matter of learning, and learning depends completely on environmental influences. The psychometricians consider intelligence to be a construct that can be measured accurately with standardized tests; these are the tests that produce IQ scores. And then there is the position of Howard Gardner, who believes that intelligence comprises seven distinct intellectual domains available, to some extent, to all human beings with normal brain development. Gardner is one of the leaders in the cognitivist approach to studying human behavior and development. The appeal to cognitive processes dominates contemporary psychology.

Intelligence tests are the typical means used to identify gifted adolescents. This practice is challenged by individuals who assert that intelligence tests cannot assess important cognitive operations, such as synthesizing information or applying information in real-life situations. Another challenge to using intelligence tests to identify the gifted is the realization that intelligence tests do not assess many domains of intelligence—for instance, musical intelligence—that characterize the gifted.

Gifted adolescents, on the whole, accept the label of being gifted, but a significant minority—up to 30%—feel uncomfortable with the label and angrily reject it. Gifted adolescents report good lines of communication with parents, above average self-concepts, and above average perceptions of personal competence. However, investigators are concerned about the rate of suicides among gifted adolescents.

The dominant views about human intelligence are the theory of genetic epistemology and the information-processing approach. Jean Piaget developed the genetic epistemology theory, in which he maintained the human mind is structured to comprehend reality according to fundamental categories. Piaget argued that human intelligence develops initially from complete reliance on physical sensation, and that humans eventually develop mature skill in using abstract thought. While Piaget has his adherents, several critiques of his theory have emerged; these critiques question Piaget's understanding of logic, his theory's resistance to scientific testing, and his failure to acknowledge the influence of experience and social context on performing tasks designed to assess cognitive development.

Information-processing theorists use the computer as a metaphor of the human mind. Concepts used in information processing include input, feedback, short-term memory, long-term memory, and retrieval strategies. Researchers in the information-processing tradition spend most of their efforts analyzing how individuals handle cognitive tasks, such as comprehending written and spoken language, remembering, and solving puzzles.

Human cognitive development is marked by increased processing of information, more sophisticated strategies to control processing, greater ability to understand higher-order relationships, and increased flexibility and wisdom in using information. Critics express concern that information processing has reintroduced reductionistic explanations of human behavior; they are concerned that information-processing theory's minute analyses of cognitive tasks bolster the notion that human thinking is *nothing but* complicated, essentially ignorant processes. Critics express concern that information processing cannot accept a self-reflective person who processes information.

College influences cognitive growth, and its net effects benefit students in several domains: (*a*) using writing skills, (*b*) reasoning at a formal operational level, (*c*) thinking critically, (*d*) engaging in reflective judgment, and (*e*) handling conceptual complexity.

Cognitive developments during adolescence provide the foundation for many of the other changes that occur in the adolescent years. In the next chapter, we review one of these developments, namely, the adolescent search for identity.

THE RELENTLESS PERSONAL JOURNEY:

Adolescence and the Search for Identity

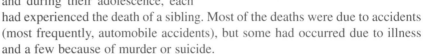

CASE STUDY

The Self-Concepts of Three Bereaved Adolescents

In 1980, I conducted extensive interviews with 42 adolescents who lived in middle- to upper-middle-income families in the midwestern United States. Most lived in urban areas (St. Louis, Chicago, Indianapolis, and Rockford, for instance), and during their adolescence, each had experienced the death of a sibling. Most of the deaths were due to accidents (most frequently, automobile accidents), but some had occurred due to illness and a few because of murder or suicide.

Each person I interviewed completed an instrument called the Offer Self-Image Questionnaire for Adolescents (OSIQ) prior to the interview. The OSIQ produces self-concept scores whereby individuals are identified as having high, average, or low self-concepts. High scores are 65 and above, average scores are around 50, and low scores are in the 30s. The OSIQ is discussed at considerable length later in this chapter.

The interview topics included noticeable changes in social relationships, emotional reactions to the sibling's death, effects on sleeping and eating, persistent thoughts of the dead sibling, thoughts of suicide, effects on grades and study habits, relations with family members, and perceptions of personal maturity. While complete write-ups of these findings can be found elsewhere (Balk, 1981, 1983a, 1990b, 1991b), here I present portraits of three adolescents whose OSIQ scores differed considerably. These portraits were first presented in the *Journal of Adolescent Research* (Balk, 1990b).

A Portrait of Ann Ann is an 18-year-old whose brother Sammy died in a fire nearly three years ago. She was close to Sammy. Ann is also very close to her mother and two sisters, but not to her two other brothers or her father, who she has seen very little of since her parents divorced when she was 10. Ann says that her mother took Sammy's death harder than anyone else in her family. She talks to her mother often, and finds that her mother confides in her a lot more than she did prior to Sammy's death.

Ann's study habits and grades were good to very good before Sammy died, then "they took a nose dive" before returning to normal after about 18 months. She finds talking about her brother's death "somewhat difficult" because of "conflicting feelings" and because "it is so confusing."

Ann says, "There is still grief I would say, and there seems some guilt has sunk in a little more as time went on. That is the hardest thing right there, just trying to get it to go through your mind and figure it all out seems to be harder."

Ann says she is interested in how her mom feels about Sammy's death because "it still affects her more than anyone else." She would like to talk to her brother Philip about Sammy's death but has never had the chance.

Ann briefly had trouble sleeping after Sammy died. She has not had any dreams associated with her brother and, to her dismay, has had no trouble eating. "I wish," she jokes. She has not considered suicide.

Ann has had difficulty because she and Sammy were not getting along when he died. "I think that's where some of the guilt comes from. I was very bothered by this, and it seems even more bothered these days." She thinks she would have been home to save him from the fire if they had been getting along at the time.

Besides guilt, Ann feels confused, sometimes depressed ("but not often"), and a bit angry at herself. Although her feelings about Sammy's death have become more intense over time, she no longer thinks about her brother as often as she once did. She considers that her maturity level has increased since Sammy's death. "I would say his death would have something to do with it. Experiencing loss and grief for the first time, and finding out how everyone feels, how it affects them, not just how it affects you."

Ann's overall OSIQ score was 68.72, an indication of high self-concept.

A Portrait of Regina

Regina is a 17-year-old whose brother James died of cancer nearly three years ago. As James's condition worsened, tension increased around the house. Regina said her parents "almost had a divorce" when James became ill; the tension rose, and there was "a lot of hostility." Toward the end of James's illness, her family became "close together," and today, she talks to all members of her family about things that matter and are personal.

Before James's death, Regina's grades were good, as were her study habits. After his death, her grades became excellent (straight As) and she studied much more. She has maintained these changes.

James died at a time when he and Regina were not getting along. She says it bothered James that she would not come to see him at the hospital. "I couldn't go there and see him lying there dying." To this day, she remains very bothered that she and James were not getting along when he died.

As things got worse for James, Regina began to think it would be better if he were to die. "I couldn't stand to see him suffer." When he did die, Regina felt relieved, angry, and guilty. "I was relieved that maybe our family could get back together because it was really tearing us apart. I was relieved he wouldn't have to lie there suffering. And I was relieved we could stop our medical bills that were at $60,000. I was guilty in the fact that I didn't spend enough time with him. I was angry that he looked so horrible, angry that the Lord let this gorgeous kid shrivel away to skin and bones."

She still feels relieved, still feels guilty, and still feels angry. The intensity of the feelings has remained constant. She finds herself thinking about James, and expresses some surprise that his absence "has been easy to get used to."

Regina has had no difficulties eating or sleeping, reports no dreams associated with James, and has not considered suicide. "No, I'm selfish," she said when asked about suicide.

She rated herself as mature before James's death, and now considers herself very mature. She says that "now I think of other people more than I do of myself, and I think about the future." Her brother's death enabled her "to learn a lot about myself, like how I would push important things to the back of my mind. It has helped me to try not to do that because I should deal with a problem firsthand and not let it ride. James's death also taught me the importance of a close family."

Regina's overall OSIQ score was 50.99, an indication of average self-concept, much like the majority of her peers.

A Portrait of Elizabeth   Elizabeth is a 16-year-old whose brother Tim died of a brain tumor a little over four years ago. She knew he had a brain tumor for nearly a year before he died. As Tim became increasingly ill, she spent more time with him inside their house. She says her family "stuck basically together. Tim's illness bound us more together." However, once Tim died, Elizabeth reports that she "started getting really distant. I wouldn't even talk to friends about it sometimes."

She feels close to her parents these days, and talks to her mom about personal matters. She says that her parents took the death hard, but it is difficult to know if anybody in her family took the death harder than others. "I don't really know how bad my parents felt, but I'd say it hit me very hard."

Elizabeth's study habits were "probably average" before Tim's death, and her grades were good. After his death, her study habits slipped, and her grades became a bit worse. Although she studies more now, her grades fluctuate because she gets moody.

Her relationships with other students changed after Tim died. "If they would say, 'I know how you feel', I'd get very mad. The kids avoided me most of the time, but if they did come up to say anything, they didn't know what to say. I just wanted to be alone, with nobody to bug me, but I had no choice but to go to school."

Her relationships with students are better these days "because some people, as they grow older, can deal with it more . . . . They're not little sixth-graders that don't know how to handle the situation."

After Tim died, Elizabeth says she felt shocked, numb, confused, guilty, depressed, scared, and alone, but also relieved "because Tim was so sick and in so much pain but yet he never hardly ever expressed it." She explains, "I didn't know how to deal with the situation at first. I knew he was going to die, but I didn't know why he had to. I felt so alone, which is sometimes how I feel now. It was sometimes too much for me. When my parents would leave me alone, sometimes I felt very scared. Every noise would make me jump. Tim and I were the only children, so there was no one left except me, and it seemed like my other part was missing."

Elizabeth still feels a little shocked, mostly because she has dreams that Tim has returned. She no longer feels numb or guilty or scared or relieved, but she does feel angry, confused, depressed, and lonely. Her feelings have lessened in their intensity, although at first Elizabeth says she thought the feelings would never go away. After Tim's death, she "sort of thought about committing suicide so that [she] wouldn't have to worry about anything anymore," and says she has thought about suicide since, "but not too often."

She rated herself as mature before Tim's death and now considers herself very mature. She says signs of her increased maturity are her dislike for gossip and her disapproval of how some other students make fun of a student with epileptic seizures. Elizabeth says she grew up due to her brother's sickness and death.

Elizabeth's overall OSIQ score was 39.61, an indication of a lower self-concept than the self-concepts of most of her peers.

These three cases highlight the influence of the crisis of sibling death on identity formation. For the adolescents in these case studies, the deaths of their siblings are likely to have lasting effects on how they view themselves. These three cases help illuminate that identity formation involves facing dangers, resolving crises, and making decisions in the face of unexpected life events.

This chapter deals with the adolescent search for identity, meaning, and an understanding of self. In many ways, this search is the overarching theme of adolescent development, for personal identity encompasses so much of experience—physical change, cognitive growth, interpersonal relations, employment, and schooling.

Two researchers have been particularly influential in the study of adolescent identity. James Marcia (1964, 1980) worked with the ideas of Erik Erikson (1963, 1968) on the role of crisis and commitment in adolescent identity formation. Daniel Offer (1969) investigated the self-concepts of adolescents and gathered data on adolescents in several cultures, countries, and ethnic/racial groups. A clear link can be seen between identity formation in adolescence and self-concept development over the life span.

One of the factors influencing identity formation is coping with stressful life events. Research emphasizes that adolescents' personal development is enhanced by coping with life crises (Offer, 1969).

ADOLESCENCE VIEWED AS A CRISIS OVER IDENTITY FORMATION

The theme of identity formation as an encounter with the unexpected fills the traditions of cultures around the world and across time. A chief example comes from mythology, which portrays identity formation as a journey filled with dangers and risks (Campbell, 1949). This metaphor has influenced 20th-century scholars of adolescent development. Erikson (1963, 1968), Blos (1967/1979i), and Hall (1904) all asserted that this journey becomes increasingly salient during one's adolescent years. Erikson is probably the scholar most responsible for the contemporary notions that adolescents face a crisis over identity, that this crisis occurs due to changes in one's internal and external environments, and that successful resolution of this crisis is not guaranteed.

Developing a clear sense of personal identity is a task that continues throughout one's life (Erikson, Erikson, & Kivnick, 1986; Gould, 1978; Havighurst, Neugarten, & Tobin, 1968; Levinson, Darrow, Klein, Levinson, & McKee, 1978; Maas &

Kuypers, 1974; Vaillant, 1977; Woodruff & Birren, 1972). Harold Grotevant (1987) has noted that the lifelong task of identity formation is multidimensional and encompasses four dynamic components: individual characteristics (such as one's cognitive ability), the contexts within which development occurs (such as one's family or one's culture), specific domains about which one makes personal choices (such as one's occupation or one's political views), and interaction between the specific domains.

One of the most prominent shapers of contemporary thought about adolescent identity formation was Erik Erikson. We turn to his ideas on these matters next.

Erikson on Identity Formation During Adolescence

Erik Erikson (1963, 1968) has made a singular contribution to our thinking about adolescent identity formation. We discussed Erikson's views on adolescence in Chapter 1; here, I recap his ideas and summarize his notions of crisis and commitment.

Erikson considers identity formation to be a lifelong task or—to use the journey metaphor—an excursion prolonged over one's life course. At certain times in our journeys, we come to forks in the road, where we must make decisions. These forks are the developmental crises that facilitate identity formation. In choosing which way to proceed, we make commitments about our journeys. Thus, for Erikson, the lifelong journey of identity formation involves meeting crises and making commitments.

The sense of crisis during adolescence centers on the process of self-discovery, with the ultimate stake being either the formation of a clear identity or the malformation of a vague sense of self (that is, a confused identity). For the adolescent, developing a sense of identity is filled with tension for it carries not only the possibility of failure (Erikson, et al., 1986) but also the need to make choices. The tensions surrounding making choices about one's identity involve renouncing a host of possible selves, all of which cannot exist in the same person. An example is the

Tensions surrounding making choices about one's self involve selecting among a host of sometimes incompatible possibilities.

tension felt by a late adolescent who is debating some choices he sees as incompatible: whether to enter a religious order, to become a criminal lawyer, or to get a college education in agricultural science and return to manage his family's farm. No matter which choice he makes, the boy must give up the others.

The pitfalls facing an adolescent in the crisis over identity formation are twofold. First, by selecting too quickly, the adolescent may settle on a path approved by others, rather than one the adolescent has personally chosen. Erikson called this pitfall **identity foreclosure**, a premature resolution to the crisis over identity. Adolescents in identity foreclosure no longer experiment with possible roles, and thus do not gain the experiences necessary to make a personal commitment to the self they want to be.

The second pitfall is that the adolescent may avoid making any decision and may drift without lasting commitments to anyone or any values. Erikson called this pitfall **identity confusion** (also called *identity diffusion*). Adolescents in identity confusion do not experiment with possible roles because they make no extended commitments. They are usually self-centered, emotionally immature, and lack any roots of friendship.

Erikson said the adolescent's journey to identity must include a **psychological moratorium**—that is, an extended time allowing the adolescent to experiment with possible roles without the pressure to fulfill excessive obligations. Erikson's views on this moratorium are that it is adaptive and should be supported. In short, he maintained that a moratorium enables an individual to explore options and gain the basis for a fulfilled identity.

The desired end results of a moratorium are a sense of purpose and a sense of continuity in one's life. Erikson called this continuity **fidelity**—that is, faithfulness to the person of one's past, one's present, and one's future. Fidelity to one's sense of self is particularly threatened during adolescence because of the physical, cognitive, emotional, and social changes the individual experiences.

Adolescents whose journeys toward identity result in a clear sense of self become **achieved identities**. According to Erikson, adolescents with achieved identities possess several important personal traits; they feel confident about their values, live independent, autonomous lives, and form intimate relations with others. Unlike individuals whose identities are confused, foreclosed, or in moratorium, individuals with achieved identities have come to terms with several domains of social life (specifically, religion, politics, and occupation), and their choices in these domains enhance their abilities to contribute to society. Furthermore, individuals with achieved identities gain the skills to manage the next developmental crisis in identity formation, the crisis over intimacy with others versus isolation from others (Erikson, 1963, 1968; Erikson et al., 1986).

IDENTITY STATUS: THE WORK OF JAMES MARCIA AND RESEARCHERS WHO FOLLOWED

A considerable portion of this chapter looks at adolescent identity formation research built on the Erikson framework. A key figure in this research is James Marcia, a scholar at Simon Fraser University in Canada. Building on the work of

Erikson, his research has inspired several attempts at mapping the journey adolescents undertake to form an identity.

Marcia (1964, 1966, 1980) postulates that identity takes four qualitatively distinct forms, or **identity statuses**. Each status is defined in terms of the presence or absence of a sense of crisis and the presence or absence of a sense of commitment. Marcia's four identity statuses are (*a*) identity diffusion, (*b*) identity foreclosure, (*c*) identity moratorium, and (*d*) identity achievement.

Marcia's theory of identity formation rests on the assumption that a person attains the identity achieved status only because of a sense of psychological crisis. For Marcia, the journey to an autonomous identity is marked by anxiety, moments of feeling lost, desire to find one's way, and hope of establishing meaningful choices about such fundamental aspects of life as the role of work, the role of political ideas, and the role of spirituality. In short, each status is defined in terms of (*a*) the presence or absence of personal decisions regarding occupation, political ideas, and religious beliefs—that is, the experience of commitment—and (*b*) the presence or absence of decision making—that is, the presence or absence of a sense of crisis. Marcia's use of the term *crisis* refers strictly to whether the individual has struggled over making personal decisions. His concern is that decisions are self-chosen, rather than externally imposed. These aspects of crisis and commitment are portrayed in Table 4-1.

The Four Identity Statuses in Marcia's Theory

A person in **identity diffusion** makes no commitments, appears to be drifting through life, and reports no sense of needing to search for answers to questions about existence. For instance, a diffuse individual would say, "When it comes to religion, I just haven't seen any need to make any decisions. What does it matter?"

A person in **identity foreclosure** has accepted the values espoused by others—particularly parents—but has accepted these values without any sense of struggle over personal choice. A person with a foreclosed identity would say, "I've really never questioned my religion. If it's right for my parents, it must be right for me."

A person in **identity moratorium** is searching for persuasive answers to questions about personal and communal existence. Individuals in moratorium are struggling over issues of commitment and existential meaning. Their searches often lead them to grapple with seemingly unresolvable questions, such as why is there evil in

TABLE 4-1   Crisis and Commitment in Marcia's Theory of Identity Status

	IDENTITY STATUS			
	Diffusion	Foreclosure	Moratorium	Achieved
CRISIS	Present or Absent	Absent	In Crisis	Present
COMMITMENT	Absent	Present	Vaguely present	Present

SOURCE: Adapted from *Handbook of Adolescent Psychology* by J. E. Marcia, 1980, New York: John Wiley & Sons.

the world? On religion, a person in moratorium would say, "There are so many religious faiths and so many questions about the existence of God. I can't decide if I should follow any specific religion until I answer a lot more questions."

Individuals considered to have developed an **achieved identity** status have come through the moratorium period of struggle. They have explored many significant matters, such as careers, politics, and religion, and have reached meaningful closure in these matters. Because they have found personally satisfying answers to these matters, it is going to take unusual circumstances—probably highly distressing times of intense personal crisis—to change their commitments or to entertain the notion that their commitments were poorly chosen. The individual with achieved identity would say when asked about religion, "A person's religious beliefs are unique to each individual. I've considered these matters and know what I believe and what I don't believe."

Marcia's Research Design   Marcia's initial work on identity status appeared in his doctoral dissertation written at The Ohio State University (1964). He published an abridged version of this research in 1966. This part of the chapter is based on his dissertation.

Marcia's (1964) sample comprised 86 undergraduate males enrolled in introductory psychology (76%) or in history or religion courses (24%). He trained 10 students to administer the battery of tests used in his dissertation research, which included measures of IQ, self-esteem, submission to authority, levels of goal setting, concept attainment under stressful conditions, and reactions to definitions of self challenged by the test administrators (called **invalidated self-definitions**). Invalidated self-definitions (ISDs) involve falsely informing subjects that test data indicated they were more (or less) mature than they believed and more (or less) mature than other individuals in the study. ISDs provide an assessment of susceptibility to external sources of information about oneself.

Deceiving research participants is a serious ethical issue, and looking back on Marcia's research, one wonders how he would justify deliberately deceiving people about the information they had given him. A significant concern is whether deceiving participants involves risks they are not clearly informed about before they consented to participate. Today, Marcia would be required, at the very least, to (*a*) convince reviewers of his project that deceiving participants was of overriding importance and (*b*) explain to his research participants the truth of what had happened once their participation was complete.

Marcia developed two instruments to assess identity status. The first instrument required each subject to complete 23 phrases in his own words. Examples of these incomplete phrases include (*a*) "When I consider my goals in the light of my family's goals _____," (*b*) "I am really convinced that _____," and (*c*) "Ten years from now I _____" (Marcia, 1964, pp. 157-159). Marcia called this instrument the Ego Identity Incomplete Sentences Blank (EI-ISB). He developed scoring criteria to assess the relationship of the participants' responses to their identity statuses.

Three independent raters achieved 74.3% agreement on the subjects' identity statuses revealed through completed sentence blanks. Each rater analyzed the content of the participants' sentences. High inter-rater agreement (at least 70%) indicates reliable results. Marcia resolved cases of disagreement by reviewing the material and determining which identity status was associated with the participant's response.

The second instrument Marcia developed was an interview called the Identity Status Interview. Each interview took about 30 minutes to complete, was tape recorded for content analysis, and focused on three topics: occupation, religion, and politics. Marcia combined religion and politics into a measure of ideology.

Whereas Marcia intended the EI-ISB to determine how well an individual meets criteria associated with establishing ego identity, he designed his interview to identify the style whereby the person handles issues of identity. These styles correspond with the four identity statuses—diffusion, foreclosure, moratorium, and achievement.

Marcia developed scoring procedures for analyzing interview data and assigning identity status. These procedures required determining whether the person had resolved crises over identity and whether the person was committed to an occupation, religious ideas, and/or political views. Three independent raters achieved 75% agreement on assigning identity status from interview content, and Marcia resolved cases of disagreement. All but 2 of the 86 students could be assigned a specific identity status from their interview responses. No status was overrepresented. There were 21 diffused, 24 foreclosed, 23 moratorium, and 18 achieved identities.

Marcia conducted several analyses to assess whether identity status relates significantly to other variables. Neither IQ nor self-esteem nor year in college related significantly to identity status. Marcia found that foreclosed subjects were significantly more likely than the other subjects to defer to authority and to maintain high goals, despite evidence of failure to complete tasks successfully. While results were not significant, moratorium and diffused subjects accepted ISDs more than foreclosed and achieved subjects. Identity achieved individuals performed better on the concept attainment task than other individuals; foreclosed subjects performed more poorly than all other subjects, and moratorium individuals had the most in-group variance of all subjects on this measure.

Summary of Marcia's Contributions

Marcia's work has had a seminal impact on research into adolescent identity formation. He established a systematic procedure to investigate Erikson's concepts of identity, and he demonstrated a reliable means to differentiate the various outcomes of handling the crises and commitments integral to adolescent identity formation. The ramifications of such an achievement have not escaped other researchers who have since built on Marcia's work.

Not all of Marcia's efforts, however, have gone without criticism. A chief issue is his exclusive sampling of males, all of whom were college students, and all of whom were white. Thus, the validity of his results may be narrow. However, the composition of his sample is not a critical failure since he had to start with some base from which other studies could expand should his more homogeneous sample provide significant outcomes.

A second limitation to Marcia's research is its cross-sectional approach. Rather than providing a view of the journey toward identity formation, cross-sectional methodology renders a static picture of identity at one point in time. Cross-sectional research cannot determine how individuals arrived at their current identity statuses, nor determine the trajectory involved in movement toward an identity status. This shortcoming can only be overcome by using longitudinal or sequential methodologies. Some investigators of identity formation have recognized this need for research methods that follow the same individuals over time.

Finally, Marcia's interview method struck some researchers as more time-consuming, more expensive, and less reliable than using a standardized instrument with strong validity and reliability. Marcia's interview procedure does provide a richness of detail available only with qualitative data, but research programs aimed at obtaining generalizable results need measures that can be administered to several subjects at one time, computed quickly, analyzed with sophisticated statistical procedures, and compared to norms about specific groups in the overall population.

We now turn to work inspired by Marcia's research, starting with the efforts of one team of investigators to develop a standardized instrument that captures identity status information more efficiently than one-on-one interviews. Such an instrument, if proven valid, would enhance comparisons of the identity status of different groups.

Development of a Standardized Measure of Identity Status

Gerald Adams, a scholar at the University of Guelph, and Harold Grotevant, a scholar at the University of Minnesota (1984), have developed a standardized instrument to measure identity status, which consists of 64 items and uses a 6-point scale, ranging from "strongly disagree" to "strongly agree." Their goal was to produce an instrument that would reliably, validly, and quickly provide a measure of Marcia's (1964) four identity statuses. They call their instrument the Extended Objective Measure of Ego Identity Status (EOM-EIS). An earlier version, called the Objective Measure of Ego Identity Status (OM-EIS), had 24 items and covered the domains included in Marcia's interview: occupation, politics, and religion (Adams, Shea, & Fitch, 1979).

The EOM-EIS measures psychosocial identity in terms of occupation, politics, and religion as well as friendship, dating, sex roles, philosophical life-style, and recreation. Examples of items from the EOM-EIS include (a) "My parents know what's best for me in terms of how to choose my friends," (b) "I'm not sure what religion means to me. I'd like to make up my mind, but I'm not done looking yet," and (c) "My preferences about dating are still in the process of developing. I haven't fully decided yet" (Bennion & Adams, 1986).

Grotevant and Adams wrote two items for each identity status. They also had participants indicate how much they were thinking about these issues. This last part is used to access what Marcia (1964) called the "period of decision making," or crisis.

Grotevant and Adams have tested the reliability of the EOM-EIS using measures of internal consistency (alpha coefficients) and test-retest correlations. They tested the instrument's validity using several statistical measures. Reliability levels appear acceptable on both internal consistency and test-retest measures. A later study reported analyses of 14 studies using the EOM-EIS; the median alpha value was .66 and the median test-retest correlation was .76 (Adams, Bennion, & Huh, 1989). These reliability estimates are considered acceptable.

Ten independent raters reached 96.5% agreement about which status is associated with each EOM-EIS item. Several factor analyses made clear that the EOM-EIS items load on the identity statuses they are intended to identify. Very low correlations were found between identity status and variables that are not supposed to be associated with identity status. These include verbal ability, academic achievement, and social desirability.

Social desirability denotes faking one's answers in order to make a favorable impression on others. Examples of socially desirable responses are affirmative responses to "I never lose my temper," "I never lie," or "I pray every day." Motives for giving socially desirable answers are complex (Anastasi, 1988). An answer to some items intended to identify socially desirable responses could not necessarily be interpreted as faking. For example, you would expect a monk to answer the item "I pray every day" affirmatively; such an answer would be true, not an effort to impress the researchers.

Grotevant and Adams found that accurate predictions could be made regarding identity status and individual styles of coping using the EOM-EIS. A more recent analysis confirmed these validity findings (Adams et al., 1989). In short, the EOM-EIS assesses identity status consistently and measures what it purports to measure. The significance of this achievement is that other researchers now have available a reliable and valid measure with which to economically gather data about identity status.

Studies of Marcia's Theory   Several researchers have investigated adolescents using Marcia's theory of identity formation. I have divided these studies into two broad categories: identity status of early and middle adolescents and identity status of late adolescents. The reason for including the studies on early and middle adolescents is that identity formation is a dynamic process that impacts the early and middle years of adolescence. Adolescents are struggling with the issues of crisis and commitment before they reach their late adolescent years, when, if all is going well, their experimenting with various roles will consolidate into an achieved identity. Although it is common to focus on the late adolescent years when discussing identity formation, such an approach can misguide readers by overlooking the identity formation process already underway.

As you think about identity formation during early and middle adolescence, consider whether it is plausible that adolescents can reach an achieved identity status before the age of 18. If you think it is plausible, what portion of early and middle adolescents do you think might reach an achieved identity status?

Identity Status of Early and Middle Adolescents

Investigations of identity status of early adolescents have covered such topics as academic achievement, perception of parents' child-rearing practices, self-consciousness, reflections on personal ethnicity, and ethnic diversity. These studies all use the

Marcia framework and confirm the role of environmental pressures in the formation of identity. We begin with an investigation of academic achievement and early adolescent identity formation.

Academic achievement and early adolescent identity formation.   Janice Streitmatter (1989) investigated 208 early adolescents (sixth-, seventh-, and eighth-graders) to determine whether academic achievement and identity status are related. Over half of her 208 participants (54.3%) were female. One-third were in sixth grade, one-fifth in seventh grade, and nearly one-half (47%) in eighth grade. Most of the students (68.8%) were black, while about one quarter (23%) were white. Streitmatter rejected using racial/ethnic membership as a variable because the ratio of minority to nonminority students was so disparate.

Streitmatter used the EOM-EIS to obtain measures of identity formation. She used school records to obtain attendance information and used results from annually administered standardized achievement tests to obtain achievement data. She found significant results for identity statuses, school attendance, and academic achievement.

Early adolescents identified as diffuse attended school more frequently than their peers but performed much more poorly in math. Foreclosed students attended school often but had low achievement scores in math. Moratorium students had higher absentee rates than the other students but also had higher math achievement scores than their peers. Achieved students had high math achievement scores. Streitmatter pointed out that in math, the diffuse and foreclosed students were **underachievers**, whereas the moratorium and achieved students were **overachievers**.

Underachievement denotes accomplishing less than one's aptitude, but such determinations are fraught with error because tests of aptitude and tests of achievement rarely correlate perfectly (Anastasi, 1988). For example, by calling the moratorium and achieved students overachievers, is Streitmatter suggesting they were not really as smart as their work indicated? Or is she simply saying the overachievers did significantly better than the diffuse and foreclosed students on a standardized math achievement test?

Let's focus on one significant finding in Streitmatter's study—academic performance in math was clearly associated with moratorium and achieved identity statuses. These statuses are most indicative of resolution of the crises and commitments of adolescent identity formation. What is the significance of such a finding? The answer is probably not to attribute mathematical potential to identity but, rather, to consider the link between achievement and identity. One explanation is that students in moratorium and achieved identity statuses focus more on environmental cues (in this case, mathematics curriculum) than students who are diffuse or foreclosed. Another explanation is that students in achieved and moratorium statuses use formal operations more readily than other students. Thus, they perform better in mathematics in middle school and high school, which is more abstract than the arithmetic in elementary school.

Cognitive prejudice and early adolescent identity status.   Streitmatter and Glen Pate (1989) used a questionnaire to determine whether identity status is associated with forms of cognitive prejudice. By **cognitive prejudice**, the authors meant accepting stereotypes about racial, ethnic, or religious groups. Examples are endorsing such statements as "On the average, blacks have less intelligence than whites" or "Jews have more power and influence in the United States than any other group" (Streitmatter & Pate, 1989, p. 147).

Streitmatter and Pate (1989) randomly selected 270 students, with equal numbers of sixth-, seventh-, and eighth-graders, from a school in Arizona. Seventy-three percent of the student body were white, 16% Hispanic, 8.1% black, 1.8% Asian, and 0.6% Native American. Approximately two-thirds of the students completed the research instruments, which included the EOM-EIS, a self-esteem scale (Rosenberg, 1965), and a measure of social desirability (Reynolds, 1982). The final sample was 54% male, with a disproportionate ratio of whites to other ethnic/racial groups (74% to 26%). The investigators decided that the ethnic/racial distribution precluded using ethnicity as more than a descriptor of the subjects (Streitmatter & Pate, 1989).

Diffuse and foreclosed students demonstrated more cognitive prejudice than moratorium and achieved youths. Social desirability was significantly associated only with foreclosed students, and socially desirable responses correlated positively with cognitive prejudice.

What do these findings mean? First, they suggest that efforts to increase sensitivity to ethnic/racial diversity will likely succeed only with students open to reviewing alternatives. Students who are diffuse or foreclosed do not want to consider alternatives. Second, the findings indicate that a middle school curriculum designed to build ethnic/racial sensitivity cannot stretch a good portion of the students beyond the prejudices they already have picked up. There appears to be a gap between the experimentation by youths exercising formal operations (namely, achieved and moratorium students) and the lack of possibility testing by youths working on a concrete operational level. Third, the legacy of cognitive prejudice will spill over into adulthood for these early adolescents if they remain diffuse or foreclosed. They will not change their opinions by looking at new information or challenging experiences.

Middle adolescent identity status and perceptions about parents.   Adams and Randy Jones (1983) studied 82 females in middle adolescence (tenth-, eleventh-, and twelfth-grade students). They examined whether significant associations existed between the girls' identity statuses and their perceptions of their parents' child-rearing practices. The researchers used the OM-EIS to measure identity status and used five items to measure perceptions of parents' child-rearing practices. Examples of these items are "How free and independent do your parents allow you to be?" and "How often do your parents show their warmth, love, and affection toward you?" (Adams & Jones, 1983, p. 251)

Adams and Jones (1983) found all four identity statuses present in their sample. Identity achieved and moratorium youths reported their parents encourage independence and exert less control. Diffuse youths particularly reported their parents use inconsistent child-rearing practices—they exert control but encourage independence; they offer praise but discipline unfairly. Foreclosed youths indicated their parents exert more control over them and encourage less independence than the parents of achieved and moratorium adolescents.

These findings indicate that parenting practices most likely influence the type of resolution adolescents give to the crises and commitments of identity formation. The findings emphasize that identity formation occurs within a social environment, not in isolation from one's family. Experimentation is fostered by parents who encourage independence, while failure to invest in alternative selves is fostered by parents who give mixed messages about independence and control, or who inhibit the shaping of independence by exerting control.

Middle adolescent identity status and self-consciousness. Adams, Kitty Abraham, and Carol Markstrom (1987) wanted to determine if self-consciousness is associated with certain identity statuses more than others. **Self-consciousness** denotes exaggerated concern that other people constantly notice what one says or does. The researchers hypothesized that adolescents in identity achievement would feel assured about their identities, would expect other people to respect their choices, and would willingly talk about themselves. The researchers also predicted striking contrasts between achieved and diffuse youths (Adams et al., 1987).

The investigators studied 870 high school students in a city in the Southwestern United States. Slightly more than half of the sample (51.1%) were male; 82% were white, and 18% were Hispanic. Grade levels were fairly evenly distributed: 26.6% ninth-graders, 29.3% tenth-graders, 27.1% eleventh-graders, and 17% twelfth-graders.

To gather data on identity status, the researchers used the EOM-EIS. To gather data on self-consciousness, they used the 12-item self-report instrument called the Imaginary Audience Scale (IAS) (Elkind & Bowen, 1979). The IAS measures the **imaginary audience** construct developed by David Elkind (1967); this construct postulates that adolescents believe other people are preoccupied with the adolescents' appearance and behavior, and are constantly scrutinizing and criticizing them. We discuss the imaginary audience construct further in Chapter 5.

Nearly 90% of the 870 students could be classified into one of the four identity statuses; the remainder of the adolescents gave responses on the EOM-EIS that defied clear classification. For the 779 classified students, 82 (10.5%) were diffuse, 84 (10.8%) foreclosed, 514 (66%) moratorium, and 99 (12.7%) achieved. Achieved youths were more willing than diffuse, foreclosed, or moratorium adolescents to disclose their ideas and beliefs. In nearly all cases, these differences reached significant levels of less than .01.

The significance of these findings is that they confirm what one would predict should occur in each of the four identity statuses. Achieved identity students had confidence in their beliefs and ideas, whereas other identity statuses (particularly diffuse students) lacked this assurance. Foreclosed adolescents felt uneasy discussing beliefs and ideas adults might criticize. Moratorium students were experimenting with possibilities but felt less sure of their opinions than the achieved identity students. They were therefore likely to be uneasy about disclosing their views.

Ethnic identity and middle adolescence. Jean Phinney (1989) used an interview format to measure the extent to which reflections about ethnicity influence identity formation. Their sample included 91 tenth-grade adolescents; 14 were Asian, 25 were black, 25 were Hispanic, and 27 were white. Marcia's (1966, 1980) theory formed the crux of Phinney's understanding, and she developed her interview to measure ethnic identity development in terms of diffuse, foreclosed, moratorium, and achieved statuses.

Identity Differences, Cultural Values, and Ethnic Diversity

The issues of cultural differences, cultural values, and researcher assumptions about desirable identity formation may need to be reexamined. Many researchers who have investigated adolescent identity status and ethnic diversity have concurred with Marcia (1966, 1980) that identity achievement is the optimal state of identity formation (Abraham, 1986; Adams et al., 1987; Adams & Jones, 1983; Phinney, 1989; Streitmatter, 1989; Streitmatter & Pate, 1989). Could this conclusion be based on white, middle-class values?

Abraham (1986) investigated identity differences in 826 adolescents grouped according to ethnic membership; 83% were white and 17% were Hispanic. You may recall that Streitmatter (1989; Streitmatter & Pate, 1989) said such disproportionate ethnic ratios precluded using ethnicity as an independent variable in her studies.

Abraham wanted to determine whether ethnicity is associated with identity status as measured by occupational, interpersonal, and ideological beliefs. She analyzed whether the educational level of parents influences the identity formation of their children using the EOM-EIS as her measure of identity formation. She concluded that Hispanic adolescents are more likely than whites to adopt "their parents' commitments to occupational and ideological choices and activities" (Abraham, 1986, p. 162) She also concluded that parents' educational level does not influence these results. She suggested that her results can be explained by Adams and Jones' (1983) conclusions regarding foreclosure among minority youths. Adams and Jones asserted that minority culture parents consistently enforce

Is the construct of identity achievement the product of an Anglo-American culture that prizes independence and individuation over communal investment and fidelity to traditions?

socialization about values and ideas, whereas white parents are more likely to encourage exploration of alternatives.

Because many Hispanic and Native American families place a high value on tradition, to them foreclosed identities are ideal for child development and responsible parenting; the other three statuses are considered aberrations. Should we reexamine our notions of identity achievement in the developmental psychology literature? Is this construct the product of an ethnocentric white culture that prizes independence and individuality over communal investment and fidelity? These are questions to keep in mind as you read such studies.

Phinney (1989) reported that independent coders reliably categorized the identity statuses of 94% of the minority adolescents in terms of ethnic/racial identity; 56% were diffuse or foreclosed, 23% were moratorium, and 21% were achieved. However, the inability of her coders to distinguish diffuse from foreclosed youths raises other questions about her interview format's power to assess identity status in terms of ethnicity.

141

Phinney (1989) concluded that none of the white students reflected about their ethnic/racial group membership. She asserted that white American youths are unaware of and insensitive to the growing ethnic/racial pluralism in the United States "and [are] frequently unaware of their own ethnicity apart from being Americans" (Phinney, 1989, p. 45). It must be noted that when Hispanic, black, and Asian youths did not endorse ethnic identity issues, these students were classified as diffuse, whereas white students who did not endorse ethnic/racial issues were judged insensitive. For instance, one Hispanic adolescent said, "My past is back there (in Mexico); I have no reason to worry about it. I'm American now." This adolescent was considered diffuse, rather than insensitive to ethnic/racial group membership.

The criteria whereby these judgments were made are unclear. After all, insensitivity to ethnic/racial diversity is not an identity status, whereas diffusion is. Why are the Hispanic, black, and Asian youths considered diffuse, rather than insensitive? In terms of identity formation theory, it is worse to be diffuse than to be any other status; *in terms of this theory*, there are no ramifications for being insensitive to ethnic/racial diversity. There are, of course, ramifications in terms of one's dealings with others in this pluralistic society if one is insensitive to ethnic/racial differences. You may recall Streitmatter and Pate's (1989) work with early adolescents regarding cognitive prejudice. Diffuse and foreclosed identities are unlikely to overcome insensitivity to ethnic/racial diversity.

Identity Status of Late Adolescents

We now turn to studies of identity status in late adolescent youths. These studies have investigated self-reflection, socioeconomic class influences, the timing of marriage, female decision making, overall gender differences associated with identity formation, and patterns in the sequencing of identity statuses.

Marcia (1980) noted that most of the research into identity formation has been conducted on college students, and he suggested that college encourages adolescents to extend their identity quests by prolonging a state of moratorium. We now look at five studies that used Marcia's theory to investigate identity development in 18- to 22-year-olds, some in college and some not.

Identity status, female college students, and self-reflective ability.   Lee Shain and Barry Farber (1989) accepted the contention that achieving a mature identity requires reflection on personal experience (Adams, 1976; Adams & Shea, 1979) in their examination of whether female college students in achieved or moratorium statuses demonstrate more self-reflective capacity than their foreclosed or diffuse peers. Their sample included 85 students who were, on average, 18 to 19 years old, primarily in the freshman or sophomore year of college, and ethnically diverse (44% white, 27% Hispanic, 20% black, and 9% Asian). The students were enrolled in college in New York.

Shain and Farber (1989) used the EOM-EIS to assess identity status and used 23 items from the Self-Consciousness Scale (SCS) (Fenigstein, Scheier, & Buss, 1975) to assess self-reflective capacity. The SCS possesses strong psychometric properties and is not prone to socially desirable responses.

The identity statuses of less than 40% of the 85 students could be categorized reliably; 9 were achieved, 10 were moratorium, 6 were foreclosed, and 7 were diffuse.

Tests indicated that neither age nor year in college was associated with identity status for these categorized students. For analysis purposes, Shain and Farber grouped these 32 students into two categories: an advanced identity development group for the moratorium and achieved students and a less advanced group for the diffuse and foreclosed students. The advanced group demonstrated significantly higher ($p < .05$) self-reflective scores than the less advanced group.

Shain and Farber (1989) concluded that these results support the belief that self-reflection plays an important role during identity formation in late adolescence. They cautioned, however, that self-reflection should not be mistaken for identity development. They identified two possible processes: (*a*) self-reflection significantly influences identity formation or (*b*) identity formation stimulates self-reflective capabilities. There is also the possibility that identity formation and self-reflection interact to produce mutual gains.

As you think about Shain and Farber's research, (1989) do not lose sight of the fact that over 60% of their sample defied reliable categorization regarding the very topic to be studied. This study helps illustrate the care needed when extending the meaning of results to people not in the sample. In this case, there is even concern over extending the results to the individuals in the sample.

Identity formation of working-class late adolescents. Working-class youths form a frequently overlooked group of late adolescents, particularly when compared to college students (William T. Grant Foundation, 1988). There are two reasons that the great share of studies of late adolescent identity formation has investigated college students: (*a*) traditional college students are in the desired age range, and (*b*) because they are so readily available, they are easy for college professors to study. The unfortunate result is the identity formation of a large portion of late adolescents is thereby overlooked. Any review of identity formation during late adolescence should include some mention of working-class adolescents.

Merry Morash (1980) studied 34 late adolescent, working-class males who were attending night classes for steamfitters' and electricians' apprentices. Morash used Marcia's (1966) semi-structured interview format, and compared her identity status results with data Marcia (1966, 1967) reported for middle-class college students. Morash found that significantly more middle-class college students were in foreclosed or moratorium statuses, whereas significantly more working-class youths were in achieved or diffuse statuses.

These results led Morash (1980) to conclude that working-class youths are less likely than middle-class youths to be in a state of crisis over decision making and to accept unquestioningly their parents' values. Morash suggested that environmental demands to earn a living preclude working-class youths from living in an extended moratorium about values and beliefs; environmental demands lead working-class youths to quickly assess what they need to succeed in the working world. Her interview data supported her contention that experiences outside the family influence identity formation for working-class late adolescents whose peer groups encourage discussion of ideas and participation in politics (Morash, 1980).

Late adolescent college students, intimacy, and identity status. Erikson (1963, 1968) maintained that establishing a firm sense of identity is a necessary precondition to entering into lasting intimate relations. Given the roots of Marcia's theory in Eriksonian concepts, it is understandable why researchers attempt to link Marcia's identity statuses with intimacy. Erikson maintained that forming intimate relationships is a developmental task for late adolescents and young adults, and that resolving this task depends on achieving a clear sense of identity.

Marcia along with Jacob Orlofsky and I. M. Lesser (1973) identified five intimacy categories based on depth versus superficiality of interpersonal relations, mutuality versus self-centeredness in relationships, and presence versus absence of close friendships. The five intimacy categories are intimate, preintimate, stereotyped, pseudointimate, and isolate individuals.

Intimate individuals form enduring, mutual, and close relationships, and enter into commitment with a heterosexual partner. **Preintimate individuals** resemble the intimate individuals except they have not entered into an enduring heterosexual love relationship. **Stereotyped individuals** have relationships that involve a minimum of self-disclosure and sharing, while **pseudointimate individuals** offer little open communication or depth of sharing but have entered into a heterosexual relationship of apparent permanency. **Isolate individuals** lack personal relationships, withdraw from social situations, and have casual acquaintances at best. Apparently, the identity status theorists excluded the possibility that homosexual partners could develop intimate relationships.

For data analysis purposes, Orlofsky, Marcia, and Lesser (1973) collapsed the five intimacy categories into three: intimates, stereotypes, and isolates. They found intimates enter into relationships characterized by stability, sociability, and warmth; stereotypes have relationships marked by formality, lack of warmth, and absence of spontaneity; and isolates are self-centered, self-doubting, and distrustful of others.

The researchers established links between identity statuses and the three condensed intimacy categories. Diffuse youths tend to be isolates, foreclosed youths tend to be stereotyped, and moratorium and achieved youths tend to be intimates. This link is predictable, since there are associations between identity status and such traits as willingness to engage in self-disclosure, self-esteem, and sense of personal direction.

One way to test these ideas about intimacy and identity status is to examine the lives of married and single college students. We look at one such study next.

Early marriage and late adolescents.   Candida Lutes (1981) studied 96 college students to examine whether early marriage is related to identity foreclosure. Her sample averaged 20.1 years of age and was divided into four groups, each comprising 24 students: single males, single females, married males, and married females. The students completed four questionnaires: an open-ended set of questions adapted from Marcia (1964), 50 true-false questions assessing temperament, the Bem Sex Role Inventory (Bem, 1974), and three problems whose solutions require formal operations.

The married students in the study were significantly more likely to be foreclosed than single adolescents. The single students were typically in moratorium. Lutes (1981) confirmed her hypothesis that early marriage and foreclosure are significantly associated. The married students seemed significantly more impulsive, appeared significantly more concerned about social desirability, and provided significantly less numbers of solutions to the formal operations tasks. Foreclosure, impulsivity, socially desirable appearances, and less abstract skills seemed to Lutes to have been present in these students long before they had gotten married.

Lutes's results conform to Marcia's expectations about foreclosed identities; the early married students expressed anxiety over uncertainty, made decisions impulsively, rather than after reflection, and seemed constrained from seeking alternatives. Data from Orlofsky, Marcia, and Lesser (1973) indicate that individuals with foreclosed identities develop meager skills in sharing intimate friendships, whereas college students in moratorium or achievement develop skills that promote intimacy.

Although data indicate that early marriage and high divorce rates are linked, Lutes (1981) thought that postponing marriage would not ensure better marriages for her foreclosed late adolescent subjects. They had a long history of avoiding self-disclosure and intimate friendships, and of acting impulsively in uncertain situations. A successful marriage needs self-disclosing, intimate partners who can weather ambiguities in their relationship. Lutes predicted that her foreclosed married students would probably divorce in the years ahead.

Lutes's (1981) findings support the notion that identity formation is not merely the work of late adolescence. One can speculate that patterns developed earlier in life—for instance, anxiety over doubt and uncertainty—led a good portion of her sample to foreclose their identity searches before they entered late adolescence. These patterns emerge again and again for the youths as they face other moments of doubt and uncertainty. They are ill-prepared for the developmental tasks of adulthood.

Sequencing of identity formation.   Alan Waterman (1985) concluded from analysis of cross-sectional data that several patterns of identity formation are possible. While all people begin identity formation in the diffuse status, individual development thereafter follows complicated sequences.

Waterman (1985) accepted that the achieved status is the desired end of identity formation, but added that data indicate the pursuit of identity among late adolescent college students is ongoing, even for individuals in the achieved status. People may shift their identity statuses, in other words, as life experiences alter, and they may simultaneously be in various identity statuses depending on the personal domain under consideration (for instance, in diffusion about political beliefs, in moratorium about religious beliefs, and in achievement about a career).

The major identity crisis for late adolescents in college centers on the domain of vocational commitment; about 50% of college students struggle with this crisis. Around 33% of college students experience identity shifts regarding the domain of religious choice and commitment, and at most, 25% of college students report identity concerns related to political beliefs. It is very uncommon, according to Waterman's (1985) analyses, for late adolescent crises to occur in multiple domains at the same time. That is, adolescents are able to focus on resolving one identity crisis at a time.

John Coleman (1978) provided a framework to explain how this sequencing of identity patterns occurs. Coleman has argued that the majority of adolescents deal with the many changes of adolescence—for example, changes in physical development, family relations, and emotional understanding—by facing one issue at a time.

Adolescents spread out the process of coping with issues by concentrating their efforts on resolving one issue before focusing attention on another. By maintaining such focus, adolescents can deal with what otherwise would be turmoil. Coleman called this view of adolescent coping **focal theory**.

Waterman's (1985) notions about the sequencing of identity statuses fit Coleman's focal theory description of adolescent coping. Late adolescents deal with one domain of identity formation at a time and then, if necessary, move on to another.

Waterman (1985) reported four sets of **identity sequences**. Each is described below.

- **Movement from diffusion to foreclosure or moratorium, or remaining diffuse**. Movement from diffusion to foreclosure occurs when the adolescent selects the first clear alternative found and forgoes exploration of other options. As an example, consider the dilemma of a student who, uncertain about which major to choose, selects accounting because the student newspaper reported it is the most popular major on campus. Movement from diffusion to moratorium occurs when social expectations are nonspecific but cover areas of personal concern to the adolescent. As an example, consider the case of another student who realizes the importance of selecting a career that suits her talents but is told the decision is totally up to her. She delays making any career decision so she can consider various possibilities. In some cases, a person may remain diffuse because an area important to identity formation (for instance, views about politics) never attains significance for the individual.

- **Movement from foreclosure to diffusion or moratorium, or remaining foreclosed**. Movement from foreclosure to diffusion can occur when an individual's commitments become obstructed, and the individual decides that examining other options is not worth the effort. For example, consider a person who decided getting married and having children was the right thing to do for personal fulfillment. An abusive husband, a divorce, and lack of opportunities led to a radical revision of those ideas, but she had no sense of a plausible alternative set of choices. Movement from foreclosure to moratorium occurs when an adolescent's early commitments are challenged and new explorations become necessary. An example is an adolescent who rethinks his political views when his political role models were exposed as criminals. In some domains, a person may remain foreclosed, especially when early commitments lead to success.

- **Movement from moratorium to achievement or diffusion**. Movement from moratorium to achievement occurs when a person's exploration leads to synthesis of his or her potential, and social supports exist for expressing these potentials. An example is an adolescent searching for answers about the meaning of human existence who finds resolution to her quest in the choice to become a medical doctor treating childhood trauma. Movement from moratorium to diffusion occurs when the adolescent relinquishes efforts to choose and decides no persuasive options are available. As an example, imagine another adolescent searching for the meaning of human existence; when his girlfriend is stricken with cancer and dies, he decides it's absurd to think existence has any meaning. Because of the elements of crisis experienced in moratorium and the desire to find resolution, Waterman (1985) maintained it is highly improbable to remain in moratorium for an indefinite period of time.

- **Movement from achievement to moratorium or diffusion, or remaining achieved**. Movement from achievement to moratorium occurs when the pursuit of important personal concerns is obstructed, and the individual is forced to review alternatives. As an example, consider the situation of a young woman who chose law as a career but, upon graduation from law school, finds the practice of law itself unrewarding. Movement from achievement to diffusion occurs when a person's ideals are deeply shattered, and the individual begins to question fundamental beliefs. While for some people, such an identity crisis precipitates reentering the moratorium status, Waterman (1985) said for others, their sense of commitment and interest in exploring alternatives abandons them. In a sense, they lose hope. People committed to a cause can sometimes become disillusioned and burned out after heroic efforts on behalf of that cause. Imagine, for instance, the case of the person who entered medical service to treat childhood trauma, worked herself to exhaustion while providing the best possible care, and eventually began to lose hope because of constant, grisly encounters with childhood victims of parental abuse.

Gender Differences and Identity Formation

Erikson's emphasis on the link between identity formation and commitments toward politics, religion, and occupations is clearly biased for earlier generations of males, who were expected to settle on a career and enter the world of decision making. Females were expected to center their identities on marriage, raising children, and managing a home.

Times have changed. Both males and females have career aspirations, interests in politics, and ideas about the meaning of human existence. We now realize that societal and cultural patterns shape expectations and opportunities regarding the potential roles and possible selves males and females may consider.

A telling critique of the identity status framework borrows from this notion of societal and cultural patterns of expectations and opportunities. Carol Gilligan (1982, 1986) says males and females face decisions about commitments in a different order. Gilligan contends that males must first establish independence and personal achievement, whereas females must first establish emotional bonds of interpersonal attachment. The criticism says that Erikson's views, taken up by Marcia, only acknowledge male patterns of identity formation. In short, this critique asserts that Erikson's theory and Marcia's approach to investigating identity status are gender-biased against females.

Waterman (1985) acknowledged that most research on identity formation has concentrated on areas assumed to be of more interest to males. He drew attention, however, to several studies that demonstrated males and females are more alike than different in the decisions they make about politics, religion, and occupations. These studies are summarized in the following paragraphs.

- Studies of vocational choice by sixth- through twelfth-graders found no gender differences in identity status, and only one of six studies of college students indicated males were more represented in the achieved status and females more in the diffuse or foreclosed status (Adams & Fitch, 1982; Archer, 1982,1985; Meilman, 1979; Poppen, 1974; Waterman, Geary, & Waterman, 1974; Waterman & Goldman, 1976; Waterman & Waterman, 1971).

- Studies of early and middle adolescents found no gender differences regarding religious choices and identity status, whereas studies of religious choice and identity status among college populations were not consistent; some placed males, but not females, in achieved status, while others placed females, but not males, in achieved status. Still other studies reported no gender differences (Adams & Fitch, 1982; Archer, 1982, 1985; Meilman, 1979; Poppen, 1974; Waterman et al., 1974; Waterman & Goldman, 1976; Waterman & Waterman, 1971).

- Studies of sixth- through twelfth-graders reported no gender differences regarding political ideology and identity status. Two studies reported males were significantly more likely to be identity achieved and females foreclosed around political ideas, although four studies of college students reported no gender differences (Adams & Fitch, 1982; Archer, 1982, 1985; Meilman, 1979; Poppen, 1974; Waterman et al., 1974; Waterman & Goldman, 1976; Waterman & Waterman, 1971).

Waterman (1985) concluded that both genders are fully capable of making decisions about the important domains of occupations, politics, and religion.

As we continue our examination of issues of gender and identity formation, let's turn to a study that seems to support Gilligan's (1982, 1986) ideas that female identity formation follows a pattern separate from the pattern of male identity formation.

Female college students and uneven decision making about identity. Dennis Raphael (1979) applied the Piagetian concept of decalage to explain female adolescents' uneven decision making about occupation, religion, and politics. As you may recall, *decalage* in Piaget's cognitive development theory denotes uneven ability to solve problems of the same type; for instance, a child may conserve quantity but not volume. Raphael used decalage to explain his female subjects' needs to fully resolve one aspect of identity formation before they could explore alternatives in another.

Raphael (1979) studied 69 female college undergraduates, mostly freshman and sophomores, all of whom were enrolled in psychology courses. His findings indicated that females follow a pattern of decalage in forming decisions regarding occupation, religion, and politics. Raphael conjectured that "society has set up the world of the adolescent so that in most cases occupations or vocational matters should be of major and most immediate (and perhaps concrete concern) . . . . A female who was unable to explore occupational alternatives, due to either cognitive or attitudinal factors, could not be expected to do so in the religious area" (1979, p. 79).

Raphael concluded that exploration of politics could only follow after the female had fully explored occupations and religion.

Raphael's study is intriguing in its findings and provocative in its conclusions. Does the sequence of occupation, then religion, then politics seem a plausible generalization regarding late adolescent female identity formation? Has Raphael established evidence that warrants talk of a female identity response to societal demands?

According to Waterman (1982), other investigators have found few gender differences in identity status for vocational choice, but for religious beliefs, males tend to be foreclosed and females tend to be diffuse. Other researchers disagreed about which identity status fit males and females in their explorations of religious beliefs, but one study identified males as achieved and females as moratorium, while a second study placed males in the foreclosed status and females in diffusion (Waterman, 1982). In each area of decision making, the sequence suggests Raphael's identity formation decalage and also implies females lag at least one status behind males. These interpretations are controversial. Do you think they are accurate? What evidence would you use to support your argument?

Late adolescent gender differences regarding success.   Orlofsky (1978) did report some telling gender differences in college students' identity statuses, achievement orientations, and attitudes toward success. Orlofsky's study formed part of a series of investigations that indicated identity achieved females score high on self-esteem tests and on measures of anxiety (Howard, 1975; Marcia & Friedman, 1970). Marcia (1980) evaluated Orlofsky's (1978) research as the most definitive study he had read on identity status, achievement orientation, and fear of success in females.

Orlofsky (1978) studied 55 male and 56 female college undergraduates at a state university in Missouri. He used Marcia's (1964, 1966) interview format to assess identity status, a 20-item instrument to measure fear of failure, an instrument to measure self-esteem, and Thematic Apperception Test (TAT) stories (McClelland, Atkinson, Clark, & Lowell, 1953) to assess achievement and fear of success. In research using TAT procedures, subjects are asked to make up stories about pictures on the TAT cards. The subjects describe what happened before the picture, what people in the picture are thinking and feeling, and how things will turn out.

Orlofsky (1978) found all four identity statuses present in his sample, with both males and females in each status. However, over half of the females were either achieved (28.6%) or moratorium (23.1%), whereas nearly two-thirds of the males were either foreclosed (40%) or diffuse (25.4%). Achievement motivation was highest for achieved identities of either gender; moratoriums had slightly lower achievement scores than achieved students, and foreclosure and diffuse students had significantly lower scores than moratorium or achieved identities. Fear of success varied by gender and identity status; achieved and moratorium females along with diffuse and foreclosed males feared success the most. Table 4-2 on the following page presents these data regarding gender, identity status, fear of success, and desire to achieve. Self-esteem scores were not associated with identity status for either gender.

These findings regarding gender differences, identity status, fear of success, and desire to achieve follow different patterns for males and females. The data indicate that females, in general, seem more fearful of success than males, despite similar

TABLE 4-2   Gender, Identity Status, Fear of Success, and Desire to Achieve Among College Students

	FEAR OF SUCCESS		
Identity Status	Males	Females
Diffusion	Highest	Low
Foreclosure	Next highest	Low
Moratorium	Next lowest	Highest
Achieved	Lowest	Next highest

	DESIRE TO ACHIEVE		
Identity Status	Males	Females
Diffusion	Lowest	Lowest
Foreclosure	Next lowest	Next lowest
Moratorium	Next highest	Next highest
Achieved	Highest	Highest

SOURCE: Adapted from "Identity Formation, Achievement, and Fear of Success," by J. L. Orlofsky, 1978, *Journal of Youth and Adolescence, 7.*

gender patterns in desire to achieve. What do you think can plausibly account for these gender differences and gender similarities?

Orlofsky (1978) concluded that females interpret success differently than males. The women in his study believed success led to interpersonal rejection and loss of femininity. The men who feared success placed less importance on accomplishing material goals and achieving than the women. Orlofsky also noted that men with high fear of success feared the responsibilities attached to being an achiever. Women did not demonstrate any fear of added responsibilities.

Whereas autonomy, independence, and serious exploration of alternatives are considered desirable attributes in males, these qualities traditionally have been discouraged in females. Females who pursue nontraditional goals implicitly or explicitly understand they will pay a price for their efforts; social support will be absent, pressures to conform will be present, and a protracted conflict over values and needs may ensue. Given these factors, Orlofsky (1978) suggested fear of success in moratorium and achieved women is understandable.

An important issue in Orlofsky's research is the possible influence of cohort effects. Are his results applicable to an earlier generation of females, for whom societal options held open less opportunities and for whom success in the working world involved constant battles over then-dominant expectations about gender-appropriate roles? Examine your own reactions to both males and females who are independent and who succeed in the working world. Is it still a greater struggle for women— externally against cultural expectations and internally with personal ideals?

Several studies we have examined look at pieces of the female identity formation process. None of these studies, however, have had a longitudinal base. We now turn to a longitudinal research project that used Marcia's concepts to study identity formation in females from late adolescence into adulthood. You may recall that one of the criticisms raised earlier in this chapter was Marcia's lack of longitudinal results.

Ruthellen Josselson's Research Portraits of Females

Ruthellen Josselson, a scholar in the Department of Psychology at Towson State University in Maryland, has conducted longitudinal studies to produce research portraits of women whose identity statuses she first assessed during their senior year of college. She completed her first study as her doctoral dissertation (Josselson, 1972). She published those findings in 1973 and produced follow-up data in her popular book *Finding Herself: Pathways to Identity Development in Women* (Josselson, 1987).

Josselson's dissertation research involved in-depth interviews with college seniors, all females in their early 20s, randomly selected from three universities in Boston. The actual number of individuals in the study is hard to pin down. In one source, Josselson (1973) says 48 college seniors from three separate universities made up her sample, and in another source, she indicates "I intensively interviewed sixty female college students, chosen randomly from college lists, at four quite different colleges and universities" (Josselson, 1987, p. 33). In her dissertation, Josselson (1972) indicated that of 102 women actually invited to take part in her study, 58 came to the interview and 10 of them were screened out because she had already identified enough people considered to be in the achieved status (she needed 12 people per identity status). In a footnote to her dissertation, Josselson (1972) said every person in her study was a member of Susi Schenkel's companion research project. Schenkel (1975) reported that her study included 55 subjects, but she did not explain any screening procedures.

Josselson used Marcia's (1964) interview schedule to gather data on identity status; a clinical psychologist interviewed each woman for about 90 minutes and gathered biographical information about relations with family members, management of conflict, significant interpersonal relationships, and life dreams. Josselson developed portraits in terms of the identity statuses her research subjects had attained. Twelve years later she published follow-up information on 34 of these women (Josselson, 1987).

Diffusion

The individuals in identity diffusion were the hardest for Josselson to understand. Their lack of commitment and lack of decision making made their identities difficult to comprehend. Josselson found four subgroups among the diffuse subjects in her study: two women were severely disturbed psychologically, three women had been traumatized due to extreme neglect in childhood, three women moved between moratorium and diffusion, and four women vacillated between diffusion and foreclosure.

All of the diffuse females lacked personal integration, and, desiring to erase their pasts, they existed only from moment to moment. What seemed real to them were emotions, and Josselson summed up their position, "I feel; therefore, I am" (1973, p. 35).

At the end of their college years, Josselson's diffuse subjects were characterized by fear of losing their identities if they made any commitments. Rather than becoming involved in real-life events, they preferred to use fantasy to bolster self-esteem. They escaped from difficulties and challenges, and had not developed coping skills that lead to mastery of events. They led lives marked by fear, fantasy, and flight (Josselson, 1973).

Twelve years later, her diffuse subjects showed variant patterns. Some remained diffuse despite attempts to gain a more definite identity. One individual, while still diffuse, was trying to establish some roots and stability. Two of the women died before they reached age 30, one by her own hand after entering an ever-worsening depression. Three of the women had established life goals based on someone else in their lives; one cared for her widowed mother, one centered her life on relationships with her husband and children, and one based her actions on directions from a spiritual leader of an Eastern religion.

The trajectory of these diffuse women's lives since college had led most to function in mentally healthy ways. However, for half of them, their identities remained as unsettled as they had been in the early 1970s. Josselson (1987) concluded that, rather than a temporary development, diffuse identities during college indicate a person in serious psychological distress.

Foreclosure

The central theme in the lives of the foreclosed women was the closeness and security their families had provided during childhood. The main criterion for their self-esteem was approval from their parents. Whereas other people typically develop meaningful relationships outside their families during adolescence, these foreclosed women seemed incapable of trusting anyone other than family members. Their fears of events and people outside their families were noticeable. They judged all things in terms of dichotomies; things were either all good or all bad. In Josselson's terms, these foreclosed women could not tolerate ambiguity or ambivalence. You may recall that anxiety over doubt and uncertainty marks the foreclosed personality.

These foreclosed women were self-centered, materialistic, and unreflective. Their descriptions of reality had a "Pollyanna" quality. Any struggles were projected onto external sources that could not be trusted. While young adults chronologically, these college students had remained children psychologically. Rather than offering adaptive outcomes, becoming foreclosed had exacted a cost in terms of limited personal strengths and limited relationships with others. Josselson summed up their position, "I am loved and cared for; therefore, I am" (1973, p. 12).

At the end of their college years, Josselson's foreclosed subjects were characterized by three prominent life developments: (*a*) in their interpersonal relationships, they attempted to recreate the closeness they treasured in their families of origin, (*b*) they remained tied to parental values and norms, and (*c*) they generally inhibited spontaneous expression of ideas or emotions. In short, these foreclosed students carried forward into adulthood childhood-based definitions of self (Josselson, 1973).

Twelve years later, her foreclosed subjects were still living out decisions they had chosen during childhood. They had adapted well, maintained their senses of self-worth, and did not vacillate in their convictions. None of the women had entered a new identity status; still foreclosures, they showed few, if any, signs of personal development. The one foreclosed woman who seemed to have grown personally had her dream of a perfect marriage shattered when her husband divorced her; however, this life event did not lead her to change her beliefs or commitments.

Moratorium

Several complicated themes interweaved in the lives of Josselson's moratorium college students: guilt over disappointing their parents, strong identification with their fathers, idealization of a friend or peer, daydreams and fantasies of remarkable achievements, dedication to right answers, intense devotion to interpersonal relationships, conflicts in late adolescence over separating from parents, and acute insight and sensitivity to personal and social concerns (Josselson, 1973).

All the moratorium students felt guilty for having disappointed or betrayed their parents. However, none of these females emulated their mothers; rather, each one rejected identification with her mother and resisted dependency lest she turn out to be trapped as she perceived her mother to be. The moratoriums idealized their fathers and, in this respect, had something in common with their foreclosed peers. They attributed strength, warmth, success, and love to their fathers. Rejecting identification with their mothers and holding tightly to identifications with their fathers led moratoriums to conclude they had betrayed their mothers twice.

For each moratorium student, a peer had emerged as the embodiment of perfection and competence. None of the females in the other identity statuses fell under the spell of a peer. To illustrate, Josselson quoted two of her moratorium subjects, one who said she wanted to be like "my roommate who has no problems" and one who said she wanted to be like "my friend who does everything right" (1973, pp. 31–32).

The moratorium females fantasized about accomplishing remarkable feats: becoming a foreign ambassador, a Supreme Court justice, or the discoverer of a cure for cancer. From their childhoods, they had also placed great stress on being correct, and this conviction had stayed with them through adolescence. They experienced a crisis when they discovered several competing values and other people with compelling arguments against what they believed. The moratorium female was faced with deciding which competing values to choose, and until she made her choice, her identity seemed insecure.

Interpersonal relationships had taken on considerable import in these females' lives. Their self-definitions always seemed a reflection of their relationships, not of their actions or their accomplishments. Josselson (1973) noted that this need for relationships was unlike the quest of the foreclosed females to recover the security their parents had given them. For moratoriums, the need for relationships was fueled by a craving for new encounters with reality. The moratoriums alone sought feedback from the research interviewers and expressed particular curiosity over what topics had been mentioned in other interviews.

Josselson (1973) said that of all the identity statuses, the moratoriums possessed the greatest personal and social insights and expressed interest in the great questions that have intrigued philosophers, such as "What is the meaning of life?" and "Why is there evil in the world if there is a God?"

The moratoriums did resemble other identity statuses in some respects. Josselson likened them to diffuse females because they were anxious, expressed emotion intensely, and had low self-esteems. However, they were more energetic and less depressed than their diffuse peers. Unlike the diffuse subjects, the moratoriums fought to maintain control over their episodes of conflict and feelings of depression. Josselson summed up the moratoriums' position, "I am right; therefore, I am" (1973, p. 27).

At the end of their college years, Josselson's moratorium subjects were personally sensitive, insightful, and likable. They were in conflict over rejecting dependency on their mothers while trying to fulfill their fathers' ambitions. They engaged in considerable daydreaming and had an excessive need to be correct in their ideas. Their interpersonal relationships were intense and ambivalent.

Twelve years later, Josselson found it difficult to categorize the identity statuses of many of the women who had been moratoriums in college. She developed a new category—**foreclosure/achievement**—that fit six of the moratoriums who seemed to have reverted to the foreclosure status after careful consideration of their options (Josselson, 1987).

Three members of the sample had resolved their identity crises and entered the identity achievement status after several years of integrating experiences into their lives. For the moratorium women who became foreclosed/achieved or entered true identity achievement, they made such changes only because of a relationship with someone who cared about them.

One moratorium woman continued to struggle over commitments and remained unresolved about issues central to identity foreclosure or identity achievement. This woman was marked by ambivalence and perpetual conflict. Even for the women who had resolved their identity crises, most were still troubled by self-doubts and regretted decisions they had not made (Josselson, 1987).

Achievement

While heterogeneity marked the identities of Josselson's achieved status subjects, she also discerned certain common traits in these females. Chief among these was autonomy; other traits were attraction to males who promote their independence, learning to rely on personal efforts, ambivalence to one parent and fairly smooth relations with the other, sibling rivalries, preference for action rather than introspection, and fantasies tempered by experiences with reality (Josselson, 1973).

These females had discovered from experience that they were competent, could make it on their own, and could achieve independence by skillfully handling the world outside their families. Their male friends supported their struggles to separate from parents and to achieve independence. In contrast to foreclosed females, who sought substitute father figures, the achieved females selected men who cared about, rather than took care, of them. Their male companions helped them accomplish separation from their parents and retain self-esteem in the process (Josselson, 1973).

The achieved females had learned from experience that personal efforts produce a sense of accomplishment, a feeling of mastery, and belief in their self-worth. In short, they had developed a clear internal sense of personal control and efficacy.

These late adolescent females frequently described their relationships with one parent as untroubled, but emotional ambivalence colored their relationships with the other parent. Usually, the unconflicted relationships were with their fathers and the ambivalent relationships with their mothers. The ambivalence generally centered on the parent who had been the enforcer of rules; separation from that parent was difficult and provoked guilt in the adolescent (Josselson, 1973).

Sibling rivalries marked many of the childhoods of the achieved females. In most cases, these rivalries were with a brother whose accomplishments they attempted to outdo. Struggling against the standards achieved by a brother had provided personal goals and even energy to get ahead.

Most of the achieved females showed a preference for action over introspection and did not demonstrate self-reflective skills. The achieved identities who did demonstrate insight and emotional awareness had overcome self-doubts experienced during moratorium phases of their identities. The achieved women who exerted greater control over their emotions resembled the foreclosed students in this regard.

While her achieved subjects did engage in daydreams and fantasy, Josselson noted they had tempered these aspirations with clear evaluations of their capabilities. She summed up the achieved identities' position, "I have an effect on the world and on others; therefore, I am" (Josselson, 1973, p. 19).

At the end of their college years, Josselson's achieved subjects were marked by an internal locus of control, tempered by the realization that some things were not in their powers to effect. They invested in establishing personal goals, rather than winning the love and approval of parents. They trusted their abilities. They chose men who would be cooperative partners, rather than protective parents. They expressed more concern over who they might be than over who might love them (Josselson, 1973).

Twelve years later, Josselson found all but one of the achieved subjects still in the identity achievement status. One woman had reverted to the moratorium status because she was unsure of the choices she had made and was struggling to make new choices (Josselson, 1987).

In her 12-year follow-up, Josselson stressed the differences separating the achieved women from their foreclosed peers. While their daily lives seemed quite similar, psychologically, the achieveds differed fundamentally from the foreclosures. These psychological differences included greater flexibility, more openness to experience, more security in knowing their identities, and less dependence on outside validations of self-worth. The achieved women had gained a subtle personal freedom that Josselson noticed the more she grew to know them, a freedom others might easily overlook in day-to-day behaviors.

While no more intelligent or talented than women in any of the other identity statuses, the achieved women placed value on intrinsic rewards or, as Josselson said, "what matters is not making others proud of them but feeling proud of themselves" (1987, p. 97). All of the achieved women had occupations, but they were not necessarily career successes; they worked but did not identify with their careers.

The achieved subjects exhibited tolerance for ambiguity and believed in their abilities to make a difference. Josselson (1987) speculated these women would continue to grow personally because they were open to the future and willing to learn more about themselves.

Summary of Josselson's Contribution

Josselson's study was unique. She studied changes in the identity formation of late adolescent females into their adult lives. You may recall that a great deal of psychological research has focused solely on males and only on identity status at a specific point in time.

Her study did note some movement in identity formation, but almost exclusively for the women who had been in moratorium during their senior year of college. The foreclosed identities clearly seemed resistant to change, a resistance grounded in a confidence about the ideas and beliefs the women held. The diffuse identities were in psychological distress and remained unsure of commitments, while the achieved identities had developed a balance between convictions about their beliefs and openness to other viewpoints.

Josselson's work has at least two limitations. First, she studied only a small number of women, and, while her information is rich in detail, one can question whether these patterns of identity formation apply to women from other cultural niches, either in this country or in other countries. To test this limitation, you might consider how the stories she tells about these women compare with your own experiences, either as a woman yourself or as a man whose learning includes becoming friends with women.

Second, the individuals Josselson studied were of a different cohort than most college students today. In most cases, all of Josselson's research subjects had reached young adulthood before most of today's college students were born. There may be cohort effects, but we would need to examine comparative information about different cohorts to know if such effects are present.

We now turn from the influence of James Marcia's ideas on identity formation during adolescence to another prominent line of adolescent research. Daniel Offer's research on adolescent self-concept has contributed to our understanding identity and adolescence.

SELF-CONCEPT OF ADOLESCENTS: THE WORK OF DANIEL OFFER AND RESEARCHERS WHO FOLLOWED

Daniel Offer's Research Program

Daniel Offer, a psychiatrist who holds appointments in the Department of Psychiatry at the University of Chicago and at Michael Reese Hospital and Medical Center, is also the editor of *Journal of Youth and Adolescence.* Since the middle 1960s, Offer and his colleagues have been studying the psychological world of normal adolescents (Offer, 1969, 1984; Offer & Franzen, 1979; Offer & Howard, 1972; Offer & Offer, 1975; Offer, Ostrov, & Howard, 1977a, 1977b; Offer, Ostrov, Howard, & Atkinson, 1988; Offer & Sabshin, 1974).

Offer (1969) noted that few, if any, studies about adolescents had actually collected information from adolescents; most had obtained information from secondary sources, such as probation officers or clinical psychologists, who often see only deviant teenagers. Unfortunately, generalizations to all adolescents have been made on the basis of these secondary reports. Offer, however, has focused on adolescents as primary sources in his studies on the self-concepts of adolescents.

The Offer Self-Image Questionnaire for Adolescents

Offer developed an instrument to measure the self-concepts of adolescents called the Offer Self-Image Questionnaire for Adolescents (OSIQ). Several other well-known instruments are inappropriate for measuring the self-concepts of adolescents. Chief among these instruments are those designed for use with children (Piers-Harris Children's Self-Concept Scale), those which measure a single dimension of self-concept, such as self-acceptance (Rosenberg's Self Esteem Scale), and those designed for clinical populations (the Minnesota Multiphasic Personality Inventory) (Wylie, 1989).

Since 1962, the OSIQ has been used with over 30,000 adolescent subjects to gain self-descriptive data regarding psychological well-being and adjustment (Offer et al., 1988). One hundred thirty items were written to measure 11 areas that theory, clinical experience, and empirical findings from other studies indicated are important to an adolescent's internal psychological life (Offer & Howard, 1972). The OSIQ asks respondents to indicate on a six-point scale how well each item describes them. Norms have been developed for interpreting OSIQ results vis-à-vis other individuals of the same sex, same race, and similar age. The answers range from "does not describe me very well" to "describes me very well." Placing answers along such a continuum is called a **Likert format**. A score of 50 on the OSIQ indicates average or normal self-concept for members of one's norm group. The standard deviation for OSIQ scores is 15, and scores one standard deviation or more above 50 indicate better adjustment than adolescents in one's norm group.

The 11 areas of the OSIQ are impulse control, emotional tone, body and self-image, social relationships, moral values, sexual attitudes, family relations, mastery of the external world, vocational-educational goals, psychopathology, and superior adjustment. Through the 1970s, all but the sexual attitudes scale consistently distinguished between normal, emotionally disturbed, and delinquent adolescents (Offer et al., 1977a, 1977b). More recent evidence indicates the sexual attitudes scale has gained greater discriminatory power (Chen & Yang, 1986; Koenig, Howard, Offer, & Cremerius, 1984; Offer et al., 1988; Ostrov, Offer, & Howard, 1986).

A total self-concept score can be obtained from the OSIQ as an indicator of psychological well-being. Measures of individual scales can be obtained as well (Offer & Howard, 1972; Offer et al., 1977a, 1977b). Descriptions of each OSIQ scale, plus a sample item from the instrument, are given below.

- The **impulse control scale** measures the extent to which the ego can ward off stress. "I get violent if I don't get my way."

- The **emotional tone scale** measures affective harmony, or the extent to which some emotions fluctuate in contrast to others that remain stable. "Most of the time I am happy."

- The **body and self-image scale** measures attitudes toward one's body and feelings of security or doubt about oneself. "The recent changes in my body have given me some satisfaction."

- The **social relationships scale** measures the strength of relationships with people outside one's family. "I find it extremely hard to make friends."
- The **morals scale** measures the extent to which the conscience has developed. "I do not care how my actions affect others as long as I gain something."
- The **sexual attitudes scale** measures attitudes, feelings, and behavior toward the opposite sex. "I do not attend sexy shows."
- The **family relationships scale** measures how the adolescent relates to his or her parents, the type of parent-child relationship, and the emotional atmosphere in the home. "Understanding my parents is beyond me."
- The **mastery of the external world scale** measures how well the adolescent adapts to his or her immediate environment. "When I decide to do something, I do it."
- The **vocational-educational goals scale** measures how well the adolescent is learning and planning for a vocational future. "I am sure that I will be proud about my future profession."
- The **psychopathology scale** measures the extent to which the adolescent manifests overt or severe symptomatology. "When I am with people, I am bothered by hearing strange voices."
- The **superior adjustment scale** measures the extent to which the adolescent copes with self, significant others, and his or her world. "If I know that I will have to face a new situation, I will try in advance to find out as much as is possible about it."

A series of studies conducted between 1962 and 1981 indicated the OSIQ possesses satisfactory reliability and validity (Offer et al., 1977a, 1977b, 1982). The internal consistency of the scales was moderate to high, indicating that individuals' responses to the items in each scale were consistent and trustworthy.

Reviews of the OSIQ have been mixed. Robert Hogan (1985) considered the instrument to be well-developed and one of the best instruments for people interested in normal adolescent populations. He added that the OSIQ manual contains abundant information about the construction of the OSIQ scales, about the various normative samples, and about the instrument's validity and internal consistency. Roy P. Martin (1985) commended several aspects of the OSIQ, particularly its focus on self-concept and adjustment of normal teenagers as well as the multi-dimensionality of the instrument. However, he expressed concern with the manual, saying that it has left unanswered basic questions about the construction of the instrument. He was also concerned about insufficient information regarding the normative samples and variant internal consistency scores for the eleven scales.

Offer and his colleagues produced norms based on 3,817 adolescents grouped according to gender and age and ethnic/racial membership (Offer et al., 1977a). The authors also reported significant differences in the OSIQ responses of normal, delinquent, and disturbed adolescents on 7 of the 11 scales: impulse control, emotional tone, body and self-image, family relationships, vocational-educational goals, psychopathology, and superior adjustment. In fact, the responses of normal adolescents

Self-Concept Across the Life Cycle: Links Between Middle Childhood, Adolescence, and Adulthood

There are continuities and discontinuities in self-concept development for people in their middle childhood, adolescent, and adult years. We all have an intuitive grasp of this sense of continuity and discontinuity with our pasts. You are the same person you were at the age of 10; yet, since then, many experiences and biological changes have worked to make you different.

What do we know about the concepts of self held by school-age children? Raymond Montemayor and Marvin Eisen (1977) asked 262 fourth-through twelfth-graders (51.9% male; 48.1% female) to give 20 answers to the question "Who am I?" School-age children (fourth- and sixth-graders) gave more concrete answers, listing their names, ages, genders, addresses of their homes, and favorite activities. Older youths used more abstract descriptions, such as their beliefs, relationships, motives, and personal traits (for example, being kind, loyal, or short-tempered). A clear difference in the responses of school-age and high school youths was the skill in selecting psychological factors as self-descriptors. In short, the adolescents showed greater use of self-reflective operations than school-age children.

Some age differences in self-concept awareness have been explained by Harvard psychologist Robert Selman (1980), who noted that school-age children are much less capable than adolescents of reflecting on who they are. Selman said younger children are essentially incapable of distinguishing between their private and public selves (**private self** is one's inner thoughts and feelings, whereas **public self** is one's behavior others can observe). We discuss Selman at length in Chapter 5.

Both adolescents and adults have acquired the self-reflective capacity to deepen their self-understandings. By old-age, people frequently use such reflective capacities as they reminisce about their lives. Erikson's (1963, 1968; Erikson et al., 1986) model of identity formation places reminiscing about one's life as the preeminent psychological task of older adults.

Erikson noted certain changes in self-concept perceptions occur in the lives of older adults. He interviewed several people, now in their 80s, who had been studied since they were adolescents (Bayley, 1955, 1968; Jones, 1967; Macfarlane, 1938) and found they had a different understanding of who they are since becoming the oldest living members of their families. In some cases, they were three or more generations removed from the youngest family members. Reflecting on this singular fact of their existence, they sized up what they mean to younger generations in their families. They reassessed the choices and behaviors of their lives. One motive for their reflections was to determine how faithful they had been to their senses of self over the years.

Erikson also noted that these elderly people described themselves in terms of abstract personal characteristics that accented their senses of continuity. Some of these characteristics were optimism, fairness, and a sense of humor. For many, the sense of personal continuity centered on friends and associates they had selected over the years.

The common threads in these studies of self-concept are continuity and self-reflective skill. School-age children are beginning to use this skill, but it emerges more fully in adolescence and remains with people through their adult years, unless they fail to retain their mental faculties.

differ from the responses of both delinquent and disturbed adolescents at a remarkably high significance level ($p < .0001$). The pattern is always the same—the normal adolescents demonstrate better psychological adjustment than delinquent and/or disturbed adolescents.

Significant other differences between samples have been determined by complex statistical analyses of OSIQ responses. OSIQ responses can distinguish younger from older adolescents, males from females, and rural from urban adolescents. The inventory also distinguishes between American, Australian, and Irish adolescents; between American, Irish, and Israeli adolescents grouped by age and gender; and between white and black adolescents grouped by age and gender (Offer et al., 1977a). The significant OSIQ differences between culturally, socially, ethnically, racially, or otherwise distinct groups of teenagers provide evidence of the validity of the OSIQ, and of its potential in studying self-concept cross-culturally.

Offer's work is particularly relevant to the study of identity formation during adolescence. An important theme in identity formation is experimenting with potential roles and selves. Offer understands that these potential roles and selves vary across several social contexts. His work is particularly important in this regard because (*a*) he has provided longitudinal data on the increasing differentiation in adolescent self-concept across various social contexts and (*b*) his research instrument, the OSIQ, has been administered to thousands of adolescents in different ethnic/racial groups and in different countries providing valuable cross-cultural data.

Offer's Longitudinal Study   In 1962, Offer administered the OSIQ to 326 male high school freshmen in two Chicago suburbs. Boys whose scores on nine out of ten scales (excluding the scale of sexual attitudes, which proved unreliable) fell within one standard deviation from the mean were chosen as normal subjects; from this pool, 84 boys were identified for in-depth interviewing over the next several years. During the four years of high school, neither the boys' parents nor their teachers indicated that any of these adolescents responded deviantly to school, family, peers, or any other aspects of their environments. All but 11 of the boys completed the four-year longitudinal project, and by the age of 21, 61 of the original 84 subjects had participated in follow-up studies (Offer & Offer, 1975).

Offer and Melvin Sabshin (1974) noted that these male adolescents had achieved independence with little devaluation of their parents. They considered their fathers to be reliable and their mothers to be understanding. During high school, their emotional ties were closer to their mothers than their fathers. After high school, most of the boys identified more with their fathers and entered into a brief period of conflict with their mothers, due to growing emotional investment in girlfriends. These 84 adolescents managed to cope well with severe stressors, such as the death of a parent or the severe injury of a sibling, first by denying the emotional impact of the event then by immersing themselves in time-consuming activities, such as studies. The adolescents gradually permitted themselves to feel the distress of their losses.

Offer (1969) was encouraged with the capacity of normal adolescents to respond adaptively to stressful situations. At most, only 20% of his subjects viewed stress as a major tragedy, and few experienced their adolescence as times of turmoil, stress, and strain. Like researchers before him (Bandura, 1964/1980; Douvan & Adelson, 1966), Offer (1969) found the great majority of adolescents to be relatively stable and well-adjusted. Offer commonly found adolescents in his study profited developmentally from situational crises, using these experiences as opportunities to help them mature.

Offer (1969) was also impressed with the ability of adolescents to master special crises. It was not that his subjects did not experience anxiety.

> On the contrary, they experienced a considerable degree of anxiety. They coped with the situations by attending to manageable details first, concentrating on them and thereby minimizing the threat (or even repressing it altogether). They were able to keep shifting gears and to concentrate on different aspects of the same problem. They could also leave one topic of conversation and follow to another, even though they still felt that there was unfinished business to take up. The subjects adapted to traumatic situations, such as a death of a parent, with initial overconcern about the reality of the situation. (Examples: Will Mother have enough money to support me? Should I still plan to go to the college of my choice?) The subjects tended initially to deny the emotional loss, isolate it, and handle it intellectually. At the same time the teenagers began to utilize the experience as a crisis that helped them grow. They had been shaken and now had to expedite the process of adolescence, which before had seemed less urgent. They would proceed a little more quickly into adulthood than their contemporaries, who had been left in a world where dependency-independency issues needed no immediate resolutions (Excerpt from page 221 from *The Psychological World of the Teenager* by Daniel Offer. Copyright © 1969 by Daniel Offer. Reprinted by permission of HarperCollins Publishers, Inc).

Offer (1969) noted that his subjects acted in the face of severe stress by seeking information regarding new behaviors, new roles, and potential future problems. They seemed unable to imagine hindrances to their goals, but did respond well when new behaviors or new roles were demanded of them.

Offer's subjects also impressed him with their self-reflective capabilities. These adolescents had noticeably accurate senses of reality and could talk about themselves with detachment.

Offer also studied the self-concepts of adolescents in various countries around the world. Before looking at his multi-national study, let's discuss the importance and limitations of cross-cultural research.

Importance and Limitations of Cross-Cultural Research

Anthropologists (for instance, Margaret Mead) study other cultures, partly to learn more about their own cultures through vicarious comparison. You may recall from the discussion in Chapter 1 that Mead argued that adolescent turmoil is the result of Western cultural problems not present in Samoan society.

Other disciplines, such as psychology, have become interested in cross-cultural research. Cross-cultural psychology stresses techniques to compare different cultures directly, not vicariously. Cross-cultural research is important because we cannot assume findings based on people in one culture apply to people in other cultures.

However, studying people in other cultures is not as simple as some may assume. What appears to be a valid finding may be invalid, due to limitations in the gathering or interpretation of data.

Threats to the validity of cross-cultural research boil down to a few issues. Two of the most prominent are biases and incongruent communication (that is, terms mean different things from one culture to the next or may even lack translation in another language) (Berry, 1980).

The concern about biases is grounded in the realization that observations taken in a culture foreign to the researcher may be inherently ambiguous to that individual. The observations may be part of the other culture but may be distorted by the researcher because of what he or she expects to see. In short, an observer may impose a biased interpretation on another culture, the bias being what the observer expects to find because of his or her cultural upbringing. Earlier, I addressed the possibility that this sort of bias occurs in identity status research when researchers expect the optimal outcome of identity formation to be an achieved identity, whereas for some cultures, a foreclosed identity is valued because it promotes the survival of its traditions.

Incongruent communication affects the validity of a study. This problem emerges because researchers and members of another culture may misunderstand what the other is saying. This issue can involve informal interaction between people. For instance, touching someone from a Middle-Eastern culture with one's left hand may seem innocent to a Westerner, but it can be an insult to the other person because Middle Easterners use the left hand for wiping themselves after going to the bathroom.

Incongruent communication can also occur in translations of standardized instruments from one language to another; subtle phrasings may convey unintended meanings. As an example, consider the problem when a mental health clinic attempted to translate a questionnaire from English to Spanish. The purpose of the questionnaire was to get a sense of the effectiveness of the clinic's therapy programs, but when the clinic translated the question, "Are you satisfied with your sexual relations?" protests emerged from the Hispanic clients. The translated question used terms that suggested the women were engaged in prostitution. The lesson here is that seemingly accurate translations may create serious miscommunication.

Now that we have discussed the importance and limitations of cross-cultural research, let us look at the efforts of Offer and several colleagues to study adolescent self-concept cross-culturally.

Cross-National Studies of Adolescent Self-Concept

Offer and his colleagues (1988) collaborated with scholars from ten nations to make cross-cultural assessments of adolescents' reflections on their self-concepts. Besides the United States, the study included Australia, Bangladesh, Hungary, Israel, Italy, Japan, Taiwan, Turkey, and West Germany. Successful translations of the OSIQ into the languages of these countries were completed in the early 1980s.

A total of 5,938 adolescents participated in this multinational study, with nearly equal numbers of younger males and females (1,270 and 1,303, respectively) and nearly equal numbers of older males and females (1,625 and 1,730, respectively).

Younger adolescents were age 13 through 15, and older adolescents were age 16 through 19 (Offer et al., 1988).

Most of the adolescents were middle-class, high school students from one or two specific schools in each country. All indicated they could read and understand the OSIQ in their own languages.

The results of these studies are aggregate findings. While internal differences abound in each culture, these studies present the data from one country as though the findings represent all members of that culture. As you read the results of these studies, think about the implications of basing national findings on data from high school students in one or two schools. What would your response be, for instance, to generalizations made about American adolescents if data came from two high schools in the Midwest (or anywhere else in this diverse country)? Thus, take these aggregate findings with some caution.

We will begin with what OSIQ data revealed about the universal aspects of adolescence.

Common Findings About Adolescence Across Nations

The overwhelming majority of adolescents in the studies held similar views about relations with their families, vocational-educational goals, superior adjustment, social relationships, and moral values. For instance, 93% denied their parents are ashamed of them, 91% denied they carry a grudge against their parents, 89% denied their parents would be disappointed with them in the future, and the overwhelming majority denied their mothers or fathers are no good (91% and 89%, respectively). Over four-fifths (82%) said their parents get along well with each other. Offer and his colleagues (1988) interpreted these data as evidence that adolescents around the world approve of their parents, feel accepted by their parents, and are not alienated from their parents.

The teenagers endorsed gaining financial independence, having career goals, and accomplishing tasks. Offer and his colleagues (1988) interpreted these cross-national data as strong challenges to beliefs that adolescence is a time of self-centered, directionless experiences.

The adolescents reported coping skills that indicated mastery of situations. For instance, nearly 90% said they use failure as a cue to obtain more information in order to avoid future failures, and nearly 90% denied they would be unable to accept responsibilities when adults. Their self-images indicated confidence and a desire for challenges, and confirmed again for Offer that teenagers do not perceive themselves to be driven by impulse, incapable of delaying gratification, or confused.

The great majority (over 87%) reported they like other people, enjoy being with them, and like helping friends when able to do so. Telling the truth was considered important by 85% of the adolescents. These results question beliefs that adolescents are self-centered and insensitive to others.

Despite areas of strong agreement in terms of goals, relationships, and values, the cross-national data did highlight differences influenced by gender and age. Rather than suggesting differences between cultures, these data indicate similar age and gender differences across the different cultures. We look at these differences next, starting with gender differences.

OSIQ Gender Differences Across Nations

Gender differences favored boys over girls in many self-image dimensions: impulse control, emotional tone, superior adjustment, and body image. As examples, 71% of the boys, versus 53% of the girls, said they can control emotional reactions, such as crying or laughing; 67% of the boys, versus 52% of the girls, expressed pride in their bodies; and 68% of the boys, versus 57% of the girls, expressed confidence in living in a competitive world. In addition, 62% of the girls, versus 44% of the boys, said their feelings are easily hurt; 35% of the girls, versus 27% of the boys, said they are confused most of the time; and 24% of the girls, versus 18% of the boys, indicated they often feel they would rather die than continue living (Offer et al., 1988).

However, some findings clearly favored girls over boys. These results had to do with social awareness and interpersonal commitments. As we will study in the chapter on peer relations, evidence consistently indicates that females develop greater skills in sharing personal information, in developing intimate friendships, and in acquiring empathic understanding.

In the ten-nation study, females reported greater sociability and empathy than boys. For instance, whereas the great majority of all subjects reported feeling sad when friends experience tragedies, significantly more girls than boys (94% versus 83%) said that particular OSIQ item describes them. In addition, 22% of the boys, compared to only 14% of the girls, said whether they gain something they want is more important than how their actions affect other people. Finally, more boys than girls (21% versus 15%) said school and studies are not important to them.

The researchers found the gender differences were not influenced by age differences. In other words, these responses cannot be attributed to psychological reactions to early, on-time, or late physical maturation.

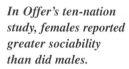

In Offer's ten-nation study, females reported greater sociability than did males.

Two critical issues regarding the OSIQ interpretations of cross-cultural gender differences need discussion: (*a*) the influence of social desirability and (*b*) assumptions about what is good and what is bad. These issues are not restricted to the interpretations of the gender differences, of course.

Social desirability and the OSIQ.   Self-report measures, such as the OSIQ, are vulnerable to social desirability. Offer and his colleagues (1988) argued that their data-gathering procedures emphasized anonymity and, therefore, fostered disclosure of actual feelings.

Actually, Offer and his colleagues (1988) seemed to argue both sides of this issue. They maintained that sorting out socially desirable from genuine responses was irrelevant, since people's "perceptions of what is socially desirable and their true underlying feelings and attitudes will be determinative of their behavior" (Offer et al., 1988, p. 72). Does that argument strike you as persuasive? It would be more persuasive to me were Offer and his colleagues able to identify which OSIQ results are genuine; one step in this direction would be to provide independent measures of social desirability on the subjects who completed the OSIQ.

Assumptions about what is good and what is bad.   Researchers using the OSIQ make conclusions about the health of an adolescent's self-concept by comparing scores to OSIQ norms. Some potentially ethnocentric assumptions influence these decisions. For instance, on the sexual attitudes scale, youths who indicate that they do not attend sexy shows, do not like dirty jokes, and do not find sexual experiences pleasurable would be considered less well-adjusted than adolescents who answered differently.

Whose cultural views are being imposed here? If an adolescent with a Chinese upbringing does not attend sexy shows, tell dirty jokes, or engage in sexual activity, is that youth less healthy than a middle-class American adolescent whose imagination is being bombarded by explicit portrayals of sex on TV, in popular music, and in the cinema? If American adolescents raised in Amish communities say the items on the sexual attitudes scale do not describe them, are we to say their sexual self-concepts are less well-developed or less healthy than the self-concepts of Offer's norm groups? Decisions about normal and abnormal adjustment should not be made without critical examination of the assumptions guiding those decisions and examination of the sociocultural environment in which the adolescent lives.

OSIQ Age Differences Across Nations

Older adolescents' responses to the OSIQ suggested increasing maturity and self-confidence. In contrast to 13- to 15-year-olds, older adolescents reported they could learn from other people and could hear criticism without becoming resentful. Younger adolescents—the majority of whom had begun puberty—were more likely than 16- to 19-year-olds to be self-conscious about their bodies, to fear others would make fun of them, and to expect their parents to side against them and with someone else (Offer et al., 1988). These age differences confirm David Elkind's (1967) views that early adolescents are practically overwhelmed with preoccupation with self, whereas such interests fade as adolescents grow older. Elkind's views will be taken up in greater detail in Chapter 5.

It is important to understand that none of the multinational data are longitudinal. That is to say, they do not demonstrate changes over time. The theme of greater maturity in middle adolescence is strong, but you cannot use these cross-cultural data to discuss development (change over time).

Cross-National Differences

We have thus far looked at findings that indicate the self-concepts of adolescents in the ten study countries are remarkably alike in terms of the OSIQ scales. However, some differences in self-concept did emerge. These differences were associated with the standard of living available in each country. In countries with similar standards of living, the adolescents' self-concepts were more alike than the self-concepts of adolescents in countries whose standards of living were considerably higher or lower.

In no instance did adolescents from one country describe themselves better or worse off than all other adolescents on every OSIQ scale. Adolescents from each country showed self-concept strengths as well as weaknesses. However, given the overall lower quality of life of Bangladesh and the higher quality of life of Israel, West Germany, and the United States, marked national differences on OSIQ subscales point to the influence of pervasive, variant social conditions in the development of adolescent self-concept. Quality of life indices considered by Offer and his colleagues (1988) were life expectancy, infant mortality, and literacy. On a scale of 1 to 100, Bangladesh received an overall quality of life score of 36, whereas Israel had a 92, West Germany a 94, and the United States a 96. Of the ten nations in the study, only Bangladesh and Turkey received quality of life scores below 88 (36 and 62, respectively).

National differences did emerge on all OSIQ scales except the moral values scale. These differences are highlighted in Table 4-3.

Adolescents from Bangladesh and Taiwan had lower self-concept scores on more subscales than adolescents from any of the other countries. For instance, in comparison to other adolescents in the study, a very high percentage of Bengali youths reported having uncontrollable fits of crying and laughing; in addition, they reported feeling tense most of the time, feeling worried about their health, feeling inferior to others, feeling very lonely, and frequently feeling sad (Offer et al., 1988).

Israeli, West German, and American youths reported more favorable self-concepts on several OSIQ scales than adolescents from other countries. American and West German adolescents had the most favorable perceptions of their physical appearances, Americans had the highest vocational-educational goals, Israeli youths reported more positive family relationships, and American and Israeli youths had the highest self-concept scores in coping with their environments. Both West German and Hungarian adolescents had the lowest signs of psychopathology, whereas Bengali and Taiwanese youths had the highest scores on the psychopathology scale.

Despite their poor self-concepts on several OSIQ subscales, Bengali and Taiwanese youths indicated they have relatively high levels of adjustment; their scores indicated they plan ahead despite fearing their futures. Israeli, West German, and American youths had the highest scores on the superior adjustment scale; they

TABLE 4-3 ■ **Cross-National Differences on OSIQ Scales**

OSIQ SCALE	SELF-CONCEPT SCORE COMPARISONS									
	Australia	Bangladesh	Hungary	Israel	Italy	Japan	Taiwan	Turkey	USA	W.Germany
Impulse Control		Low			Low					
Emotional Tone		Low	High							
Body Image		Low					Low		High	High
Social Relations		Low	High							
Vocational-Educational Goals			Low	Low					High	
Sexual Attitudes							Low	Low		
Family Relations	Low			High						
Mastery				High			Low		High	
Psychopathology		High	Low				High			Low
Superior Adjustment	Low	High		High			High		High	High
Moral Values	(mixed results across all countries on moral values items)									

SOURCE: Adapted from *The Teenage World: Adolescents' Self-Image in Ten Countries* by D. Offer, E. Ostrov, K. I. Howard, and R. Atkinson, 1988, New York: Plenum Medical Book Company.

all felt confident of their talents, their futures, and their decision making (Offer et al., 1988).

Adolescent Disturbance and Turmoil

Since the late 1960s, Offer has presented data that, at most, 20% of the adolescent population in the U.S. are in psychological turmoil and need professional help (Offer, 1969; Offer & Offer, 1975; Offer et al., 1988; Ostrov et al., 1984). As we will see in Chapter 15, which is devoted to psychological disturbances during adolescence, other researchers report findings that mirror Offer's (Rutter, Graham, Chadwick, & Yule, 1976).

Offer does not deny that some adolescents suffer from psychiatric disturbances. In fact, he maintains that the self-concepts of disturbed adolescents, as revealed by the OSIQ, differ from the self-concepts of other adolescents.

Next, we look at what Offer's research says about the self-concepts of disturbed adolescents. Then, we take up a companion topic—the evidence of turmoil in the lives of adolescents.

Self-Concepts of Psychiatrically Disturbed Adolescents

Offer and three colleagues (Koenig, Howard, Offer, & Cremerius, 1984) studied 366 adolescents hospitalized with a psychiatric diagnosis of psychopathology. The adolescents fell into one of four diagnostic groups (DG); the majority (58.2%) were suffering from clinical depression, 19.3% from eating disorders, 18.6% from conduct disorders, and 3.8% from a psychosis.

Clinical depression is marked by extremely negative thoughts about oneself, feelings of guilt and shame, ideas about suicide, and eating and sleep disturbances. Eating disorders primarily include anorexia nervosa and bulimia nervosa. Conduct disorders involve physical aggression, property destruction, truancy, running away from home, cruelty to animals, and stealing, while psychoses involve extremely disturbed thoughts and affects, such as experienced in adolescent schizophrenia.

In Offer's study, each DG produced its own distinct self-concept pattern. Depressed adolescents had OSIQ scores similar to Offer's norm groups on six scales (body image, peer relations, vocational-educational goals, sexual attitudes, psychopathology, and superior adjustment) and lower OSIQ scores on five scales (impulse control, emotional tone, moral values, family relations, and mastery of the external world). Very low family relations scores particularly characterized depressed adolescents and indicated that problems getting along with their parents are their most significant difficulties (Koenig et al., 1984). The OSIQ scores on the psychopathology scale indicated depressed adolescents and those with conduct disorders are less distressed than psychotic adolescents and those with eating disorders.

Conduct disorder adolescents had OSIQ scores similar to Offer's norm groups on five scales (body image, peer relations, sexual attitudes, mastery of the external world, and psychopathology) and lower scores on six scales (family relations, impulse control, emotional tone, moral values, vocational-educational goals, and superior adjustment). The conduct disorder adolescents' family relations scores, by far the lowest of the four groups studied, indicated severe communication problems, defiance of parents, and dysfunctional family relations (Koenig et al., 1984).

The adolescents with eating disorders resembled Offer's norm groups on four OSIQ scales (family relations, vocational-educational goals, moral values, and superior adjustment). In fact, the eating disordered adolescents were the only group that had good scores on the family relations scale. However, these adolescents had significantly low scores on seven of the scales (impulse control, body image, emotional tone, peer relations, mastery of the external world, psychopathology, and sexual attitudes). Only these adolescents had abnormal scores on body image and sexual

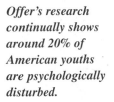

Offer's research continually shows around 20% of American youths are psychologically disturbed.

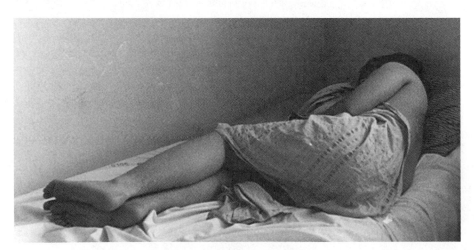

Cross-National Evidence of Turmoil in the Lives of Adolescents

Offer argues that a significant minority of youths in his ten-nation sample experienced difficulty coping, had poor self-concepts, and described themselves as depressed. Offer called this aspect "the dark side of adolescence" and noted that most endure their depression as a "quiet disturbance"—that is, "emotional disturbance that is not shown through acting-out behavior or other highly visible symptomatology" (Offer et al., 1988, p. 93).

To gather data about depression, the authors used five OSIQ items: (*a*) "I feel empty emotionally most of the time," (*b*) "I often feel that I would rather die than go on living," (*c*) "I feel so very lonely," (*d*) "I find life an endless series of problems—without solution in sight," and (*e*) "I frequently feel sad" (Offer et al., 1988, p. 99). High internal consistency scores were found for responses to these five items by adolescents from all countries.

The most positive finding was that the great majority of adolescents indicated these five items do not accurately describe them. Table 4-4 provides the percentage of youths in each country's sample that described themselves as depressed. As the table indicates, the percentage of youths who described themselves as depressed ranged from 14% in West Germany to 48% in Bangladesh. The average rate across the ten countries was 28.2%.

As Offer has consistently argued elsewhere (1969; Offer & Offer, 1975; Ostrov et al., 1984), "these results cast a heavy shadow of doubt upon those developmental theories that describe unusual and especially marked disturbance among adolescents" (Offer et al., 1988, p. 100). Offer and his colleagues used the OSIQ in a follow-up of adolescents studied during the 1960s, 1970s, and 1980s, and found that, no more than 20% of the individuals were emotionally disturbed (Offer, Ostrov, Howard, & Atkinson, 1990). However, cohort differences were found in two areas: individuals from the 1960s had significantly higher scores on the moral values scale, and individuals from the 1980s

TABLE 4-4 ■ Percentage of Depressed Adolescents by Country (According to OSIQ Data)

	MALES	FEMALES	AVERAGE
AUSTRALIA	25.0	34.5	29.75
BANGLADESH	42.0	54.0	48.00
HUNGARY	14.0	15.5	14.75
ISRAEL	18.0	23.5	20.75
ITALY	16.5	28.5	22.50
JAPAN	45.0	44.0	44.50
TAIWAN	30.5	32.5	31.50
TURKEY	35.0	37.5	36.25
USA	17.0	22.5	19.75
WEST GERMANY	14.0	14.0	14.00
TOTAL PERCENTAGE	25.7	30.7	28.2

SOURCE: Adapted from *The Teenage World: Adolescents' Self-Image in Ten Countries* (p. .99) by D. Offer, E. Ostrov, K. I. Howard, and R. Atkinson, 1988, New York: Plenum Medical Book Company.

were significantly more concerned for their personal welfare.

The cross-national data indicated females are more depressed than their male counterparts. Offer argued that these gender differences could be due to female adolescents' sensitivity to body image (Offer et al., 1988). The role of gender socialization may also help explain these gender differences regarding depression. Girls may internalize expectations about affiliation with others; that is, they may adopt social expectations that they should form connections with others. Gilligan (1982, 1986) has argued that affiliation motives do separate females from males. Data from a study of affiliation motives of 170 adolescents indicated that those females with high affiliation have better OSIQ emotional tone scores than less affiliative girls (Wong & Csikszentmihalyi, 1991). The highly affiliative girls prefer to be with friends, rather than to be alone or by themselves. The authors suggested that gender-role expectations about affiliation moderate the girls' emotional experiences.

attitudes, showed poor self-concepts in terms of coping, and "displayed by far the most deviant profile both in terms of the number of deviant scales and the magnitude of deviation on these scales" (Koenig et al., 1984, p. 65).

The psychotic individuals were similar to Offer's norm groups on seven of the eleven OSIQ scales (impulse control, body image, moral values, vocational-educational goals, sexual attitudes, mastery of the external world, and superior adjustment). They had low scores on four scales (emotional tone, peer relations, family relations, and psychopathology). What characterized these disturbed adolescents was distress over social isolation and lack of emotional control. The psychosis DG contained only 14 subjects, and the authors caution that conclusions based on this small sample are fraught with risk (Koenig et al., 1984).

Quietly Disturbed Adolescents

Offer has also turned his research to a group of adolescents who do not come to the attention of mental health professionals but who are **quietly disturbed** (Ostrov et al., 1984). A quietly disturbed adolescent is distressed emotionally but gives no outward indication of any difficulties.

Consistent findings, as we have already seen, identify around 20% of the adolescent population to be in turmoil and distress. According to Offer's data, of this 20%, many more females than males are quietly disturbed. This finding fits other gender-role expectations regarding male versus female socialization; girls are raised to be more quiet and less aggressive than boys.

Quietly disturbed females had OSIQ scores lower than Offer's norm groups on all 11 scales, with markedly low scores on emotional tone, mastery of the external world, peer relations, psychopathology, impulse control, and body image. The quietly disturbed males, who keep their distress hidden from view, resembled Offer's norm groups on four OSIQ scales (impulse control, moral values, vocational-educational goals, and superior adjustment). They were especially low, however, on the other six OSIQ scales (body image, mastery of the external world, emotional tone, sexual attitudes, peer relations, and psychopathology) (Ostrov et al., 1984).

Of concern to Offer and his colleagues is the fact that at least half of the disturbed youths had not received any professional help, or even become known to mental health professionals. These adolescents "have OSIQ profiles resembling those of youths who have been hospitalized for psychiatric illness" and therefore "have serious psychiatric problems" (Ostrov et al., 1984, p. 80).

Summary of Offer's Contribution

Offer's achievements in the study of adolescent development are unparalleled for several reasons. He developed a valid, reliable measure of adolescent self-concept—a measure normed specifically on adolescents. This instrument is grounded in a multidimensional understanding of self-concept, and provides information on a variety of significant perceptions of self.

The OSIQ enables researchers to gather self-concept information in an efficient, economical manner. Norms have been developed for interpreting OSIQ responses in terms of the adolescent's age, gender, and ethnic/racial group. The OSIQ has been used successfully with males and females in several countries.

Offer conducted longitudinal research over eight years to chart the development of identity from early adolescence through late adolescence. The changes he observed gave him his first set of empirical data to challenge the storm and stress version of adolescent development. Multiple studies in several cultures and nations have confirmed that the great majority of youths experience adolescence as a time of relative calm and stability, not a time of turmoil. To rephrase Anna Freud (1946), the one thing normal about adolescence is normality.

Offer has also helped researchers grasp the true extent of adolescent turmoil. Individuals in turmoil make up about 20% of American teenagers and, on average, less than 30% of the adolescents in other countries. These individuals do experience their adolescent years as a time of storm and stress; their lives do not mirror the typical adolescent experience.

In addition, Offer gathered empirical data on a group of adolescents whose turmoil goes unnoticed by the people around them. He called these youths quietly disturbed adolescents. The irony of their situation is that, while in turmoil, they do not appear to be undergoing storm and stress.

Offer's research program does have limitations. While he conducted a major longitudinal study in the 1960s to chart the trajectory of adolescent psychological development, the study focused solely on males. Gilligan (1986), in particular, has concentrated attention on this gender bias not only in Offer's work but also in Erikson's and Marcia's.

The extensive use of the OSIQ has produced data about adolescents' self-concept perceptions; however, without in-depth qualitative information, a rich understanding of the world of adolescents cannot be obtained. Marcia and Josselson provided a model for gathering rich, detailed interview data. With the OSIQ, we obtain a broad sweep of several aspects relevant to adolescent self-concept, but no grasp of the meaning of adolescent experiences. We need a combination of qualitative and quantitative approaches in the study of adolescent self-concept. You may recall that this call for multiplism was discussed in Chapter 1.

Since Offer's initial longitudinal study, use of the OSIQ has concentrated almost exclusively, if not completely, on gathering cross-sectional data. While such an approach enables us to see age differences, any questions about development (that is, changes over time) are left unanswered.

We now turn to other studies that have used Offer's approach. In particular, we will look at three topics: self-concepts of early adolescents, self-concepts of ethnic minority adolescents, and self-concepts of bereaved adolescents.

Changes in Self-Concept During Early Adolescence

As part of an overall interest in the impact of life transitions on early adolescent development, Anne Petersen and her colleagues investigated whether multiple transitions produce negative consequences on early adolescent self-concept (Abramowitz, Petersen, & Schulenberg, 1984). For these authors, multiple transitions refer to the number of times a young adolescent changes schools between sixth grade and high school. Part of the overall context of such transitions are the changes in physical development that mark early adolescence and any concomitant events requiring adaptation, such as parental divorce or moving to a new town.

To investigate the effects of multiple transitions on early adolescent self-concept, Petersen and her colleagues (Abramowitz et al., 1984) developed an abridged form of the OSIQ. This new version, which they called the Self-Image Questionnaire for Young Adolescents (SIQYA), has nine scales and 98 self-report items to be answered in the same six-point Likert format used in the OSIQ. The SIQYA scales are emotional tone, impulse control, body image, social relationships, family relationships, mastery, vocational-educational goals, psychopathology, and superior adjustment. The authors reported high reliability and validity data for the instrument.

Petersen and her colleagues gathered SIQYA data on 254 early adolescents (sixth-, seventh- and eighth-grade students) in a three-year, longitudinal study. Some significant gender differences emerged. Boys had higher overall self-concept scores than girls, and, over the three years of the study, girls maintained higher family relationship and vocational-educational scores than boys.

The SIQYA findings indicated that early adolescent self-concept develops in a complicated fashion for boys and girls, and is influenced by the transitions early adolescents face as they leave elementary school and enter junior high or middle school. This complex pattern of development was demonstrated by the fact that males' and females' scores that changed over time on seven of the nine scales. Males' and females' self-concepts improved on emotional tone, peer relations, mastery, impulse control, and psychopathology, but declined on body image and superior adjustment. In two areas—family relations and vocational-educational goals—the scores remained stable over the course of the study, with the girls' scores remaining higher than the boys'.

Given their increases in five self-concept areas and stability in two others, the self-concept development of early adolescents appears to occur in relatively calm, steady progress, rather than in tumult, storm, and stress (Abramowitz et al., 1984). The authors did note that students who experienced the greatest self-concept difficulties were early adolescents whose parents were divorced or separated and those who were depressed, anxious, fearful, or caused problems at school. Middle school administrators can use such information to provide needed outreach programs to early adolescents at risk.

Self-Concepts of Ethnic Minority Adolescents

Offer's ten-nation study provided glimpses of the psychological worlds of teenagers from various countries. What about the self-concept perceptions of American adolescents who are members of ethnic minorities? We now look at two studies on this question. The first investigated the self-concepts of Chinese-American adolescents, and the second studied the psychosocial adjustment of black adolescent females.

Self-Concepts of Chinese-American Adolescents

Clarence Chen and Dorothy Yang (1986) used the OSIQ to investigate the self-concepts of 67 Chinese-American teenagers. Chen and Yang compared the overall self-concept profiles of their sample with the profiles of normal American and Taiwanese adolescents obtained in previous studies (Offer et al., 1982; Turner & Mo, 1984).

The Chinese-American adolescents had low sexual attitudes scores, particularly in comparison to the scores of American norm groups presented in the OSIQ manual

Except for differences on sexual attitudes, Chinese-American adolescents' self-concept scores resembled the OSIQ scores of other American adolescents.

(Offer et al., 1982). These low scores, which were considered very conservative, resembled the self-descriptions of Taiwanese adolescents about their sexual attitudes (Turner & Mo, 1984). Other than the very significant differences on sexual attitudes ($p < .001$), the Chinese-American adolescents' OSIQ scores resembled the scores of other normal American adolescents; body image scores were slightly lower, while moral values and psychopathology scores were slightly higher. Although the Chinese-American and Taiwanese groups had nearly the same scores on three scales (morals, family relationships, and superior adjustment), Chen and Yang (1986) concluded that the Chinese-American adolescents resembled American teenagers more than they resembled Taiwanese for two reasons. First, on eight OSIQ scales, the Chinese-American and Taiwanese adolescents differed significantly. Second, on ten OSIQ scales, the Chinese-American and American adolescents had similar scores.

These findings are significant because they suggest self-concept perceptions of American adolescents are more alike than different. This similarity does not rule out cultural and ethnic differences, but it does suggest that many sociocultural experiences in American life have broadly similar ramifications for adolescents in this country.

Psychosocial Adjustment of Urban Black Adolescent Females

Jewelle Gibbs (1985) examined the psychosocial adjustment of urban black adolescent females. From a larger study of nearly 400 early adolescent girls, Gibbs pulled data on 204 black and 116 white females. Her focus was psychosocial adjustment and psychological functioning as measured by the OSIQ and an instrument she designed, the Adolescent Biographical Questionnaire (ABQ) (Gibbs, 1985). The ABQ gathers self-report data on demographics, psychosocial functioning, and educational and vocational aspirations by asking adolescents to answer each ABQ item in terms of a five-point scale, ranging from "very satisfied with myself" to "very dissatisfied with myself." Gibbs used answers to the ABQ as a measure of adolescent self-esteem.

The adolescents in Gibbs's (1985) study were enrolled in San Francisco area public middle schools and junior high schools, with the largest portion (39%) in eighth grade. The girls ranged in age from 12 to 16, with 14 being the average age.

In Gibbs's (1985) study, the black adolescent females demonstrated psychosocial adjustment similar to or better than the white females on emotional tone and body image, but slightly lower adjustment on the impulse control scale. Both groups' peer relations and vocational-educational scores hovered around the norm, but the blacks' moral values scores were significantly lower than the whites', and significantly below the mean. Gibbs suggested the differences on the morals scale indicated the black adolescents' alienation from middle-class values "and/or their cynicism about the way these values are differentially applied to them" (1985, p. 30). Gibbs found no differences between the black and white females on sexual attitudes; both groups scored a bit below the mean for their norm groups. The black adolescents had significantly lower scores than the whites on the family relations scale and, unlike the whites, expressed anger toward their parents, negative attitudes about their fathers, and concern that their parents are ashamed of them. Their scores on the mastery scale suggested that the black teenagers have more problems than the white teenagers in dealing with environmental demands, but their above-average scores on the psychopathology and superior adjustment scales indicated they are free from psychological disturbances and have positive attitudes about the world. When Gibbs adjusted OSIQ findings for socioeconomic status (SES), she found that scores within the group of black adolescents were highly associated with SES: girls from higher SES families were much better adjusted than girls from lower SES families on all but the emotional tone scale.

Over half of the blacks (58%) and over half of the whites (64%) said they are moderately to very satisfied with themselves. The black and white females showed similar attitudes and aspirations, while significant differences in educational expectations followed SES lines both for the black and white adolescents. The blacks indicated general satisfaction with themselves as measured by the ABQ; however, while the blacks' vocational goals were higher than the whites' on the ABQ, their career aspirations did not match the levels of education they considered likely for themselves.

At times, Gibbs (1985) seems determined to explain away blacks' scores that fell below the norm and to praise their scores above the norm. For instance, when her black subjects scored significantly below the mean on the moral values scale, Gibbs attributed such responses to alienation from middle-class values. But when they scored significantly higher than Offer's norm groups on superior adjustment and psychopathology, she praised the blacks for being "relatively free of psychological symptoms" and exhibiting "an overall positive adjustment to their world" (Gibbs, 1985, p. 31).

What seems more relevant is to consider the influence of social class upon values and adjustment. When Gibbs (1985) considered SES, blacks and whites from similar SES backgrounds looked very much alike on the OSIQ and the ABQ. These results suggest ethnic/racial group membership has less influence on adolescents' self-concepts than SES. Other studies have confirmed the influence of SES. For instance, in the area of educational attainment, higher SES correlates positively with greater educational attainment, and in the area of employment, higher SES correlates positively with the likelihood of having a job (Applebee, Langer, & Mullis, 1986; Bachman, O'Malley, & Johnston, 1978; Fine, Mortimer, & Roberts, 1990; Jencks, Smith, Acland, Bane, Cohen, Gintis, Heyns, & Michelsen, 1972).

Self-Concepts of Adolescents Coping with Bereavement

We began this chapter with case study information about the self-concepts of three adolescents grieving the deaths of siblings. We have now come full circle and will examine in-depth research on bereaved adolescents' self-concepts.

A paradoxical aspect of life crises is that they can promote growth and maturity while at the same time threatening dysfunction and dissolution. Since the early 1980s, several researchers have studied the impact of one type of life crisis—death and bereavement—on adolescent self-concept (Balk, 1981, 1983a, 1990b, 1991a, 1991b; Guerriero, 1983; Guerriero-Austrom & Fleming, 1990; Hogan, 1987; Hogan & Balk, 1990; Hogan & Greenfield, 1991). These researchers have taken their cues from crisis intervention authors (Baldwin, 1978; Moos, 1986), who emphasize the significant influence of self-concept in coping with a life crisis, and from Offer (1969), who was impressed not only with the resiliency of adolescents in the face of family traumas but also with their capacities to use life crises as catalysts for growth and maturation.

Studies using the OSIQ, as well as studies using other measures of self-concept, have noted that bereaved adolescents either resemble normal adolescents (Balk, 1981, 1983a, 1990b; Hogan, 1987; Hogan & Balk, 1990; Morawetz, 1982) or have self-concept scores significantly higher than nonbereaved adolescents (Guerriero, 1983; Martinson, Davies, & McClowry, 1987). Mary Guerriero-Austrom and Stephen Fleming (1990) conducted a longitudinal study of adolescents whose siblings had died and found that in their first year of grief, the self-concepts of bereaved adolescents were higher than the self-concepts of their nonbereaved peers. Balk (1981, 1983a) found his bereaved adolescent subjects scored significantly higher on the OSIQ moral values scale than adolescents in Offer's norm groups. Nancy Hogan (1988) studied 144 bereaved adolescents and found their OSIQ scores resembled the scores of Offer's norm groups, with the moral values scale being the adolescents' highest self-concept dimension.

Balk (1990) studied 42 adolescents grieving the death of a sibling and found that their OSIQ responses could be grouped into high, average, and low self-concept scores. These groupings significantly differentiated the adolescents' emotional reactions to a sibling's death. Profiles of three of these adolescents are given in the case studies at the beginning of this chapter.

Of all the bereaved adolescents, those with high self-concepts reported having trouble eating and feeling confused in the first few weeks after their siblings died; as time passed, they were less likely than the other adolescents to feel confused, lonely, afraid, or depressed. In the time immediately surrounding the death, adolescents with average self-concepts were angrier than the other bereaved youths, but had less trouble eating; with the passage of time, they reported even more anger, loneliness, and depression than the other adolescents in the study. Youths with low self-concepts were fearful and depressed after their siblings' deaths, thought about suicide, experienced trouble sleeping, and often thought about their dead siblings; with time, they reported more confusion, but much less anger, than the other adolescents. They continued to think about suicide, to be fearful, and to have trouble eating.

Nancy Hogan and Daryl Greenfield (1991) found that OSIQ profiles of 165 adolescents significantly changed depending on the intensity of their grief following a sibling's death. They measured intensity of grief by calculating the number of items on a 39-item inventory that the adolescents said portrayed their present feelings of grief. Intensity scores were grouped into three categories: 0–9 (mild intensity), 10–18 (moderate intensity), and 19–39 (severe intensity).

While intensity of grief was similar for the 165 adolescents during the first 18 months following the siblings' deaths, variations in intensity emerged after 18 months. Furthermore, while OSIQ scores for all the subjects were within the normal range of Offer's norm groups, intensity of grief after 18 months was associated with three distinct OSIQ patterns: (a) above-average OSIQ scores were associated with mild grief intensity, (b) average OSIQ scores were associated with moderate grief intensity, and (c) below-average OSIQ scores were associated with severe grief intensity. After inspecting the three OSIQ profiles, Hogan and Greenfield (1991) concluded that enduring grief symptoms are associated with poor self-concept.

Hogan and Greenfield's (1991) results, along with Balk's (1990b) findings about distinct clusters of adolescent self-concept and grief reactions, strengthen our understanding of the mediating influence of self-concept on coping with bereavement during adolescence. Adolescents with above-average self-concepts seem to fare better over time in resolving grief. There may be interactive effects, however. Handling grief may increase a person's self-concept.

CHAPTER SUMMARY

The search for personal identity has become a chief concept influencing our understanding of development during the adolescent years. The scholar most associated with this view is Erik Erikson, who considered the primary developmental task of adolescence is to obtain a clear sense of self in terms of occupation, politics, and religious ideas. Erikson viewed identity formation as a journey, and this metaphor permeates his writings. Erikson has had a profound influence on scholars investigating the adolescent search for identity. Two of the most important are James Marcia and Daniel Offer.

Marcia constructed the Identity Status Interview to assess identity formation in terms of Erikson's ideas. Marcia proposed that identity has four qualitatively distinct forms, and each form is a separate ego identity status marked by the presence or absence of personal choice of and commitment to values and goals. The four ego identity statuses are identity diffusion, identity foreclosure, identity moratorium, and identity achievement. Marcia was clear that achievement is the goal of identity formation, that moratorium and achievement are preferable to diffusion and foreclosure, and that a person can become identity achieved only through a struggle over personal decisions.

Marcia has spawned a considerable amount of research. Some investigators, such as Ruthellen Josselson, have used his interview format to study identity formation in late adolescents. Other researchers, notably Gerald Adams, have looked for a reliable, valid, and quick alternative for obtaining data about ego identity status; Adams and his colleagues have produced a 64-item self-report instrument, the Extended Objective Measure of Ego Identity Status (EOM-EIS), that researchers have used successfully with early, middle, and late adolescents. Some of the ego identity topics investigators have studied include academic achievement, racial and ethnic prejudice, adolescents' perceptions of their parents' child-rearing practices, gender differences, ethnic differences, working-class versus college identity formation, and intimacy in relationships.

Daniel Offer has studied the psychological world of normal adolescents since the middle 1960s. He has concentrated on adolescent self-concept, which he understands to be multidimensional. Some of the self-concept dimensions he has identified are body image, family relationships, and moral values. Prominent features of Offer's research are his longitudinal focus on normal adolescents, his use of adolescents as the primary source of his information about adolescents, and his insistence that empirical data indicate that most adolescents develop in a relative calm, stable fashion. Offer also constructed a standardized instrument to investigate adolescent self-concept, the Offer Self-Image Questionnaire for Adolescents (OSIQ). While a plethora of instruments has been developed to study self-concept, only the OSIQ was designed specifically with normal adolescents in mind.

Like Marcia, Offer inspired considerable research into the adolescent search for identity. By the late 1980s, over 30,000 adolescents had completed the OSIQ, and norm groups had been developed to judge an individual adolescent's responses on the instrument.

An impressive ten-nation study using the OSIQ produced self-concept findings on 5,938 adolescents. Results included common findings across nations, gender differences, age differences, and cross-national differences. A constant finding from Offer's work is that, on average, 20% of the adolescent population, not the majority, experience turmoil and stress during their adolescent years. Offer has expressed particular concern for those adolescents whom he calls "quietly disturbed."

Many American researchers have used the OSIQ to investigate various aspects of adolescent self-concept. Their research topics include changes in self-concept during early adolescence, the self-concepts of Chinese-American adolescents and of urban black adolescent females, and the self-concepts of adolescents faced with a sibling's death.

In the next chapter, we turn to developments linked to self-concept dimensions of interpersonal relations and moral values. In Chapter 5, we investigate the changing social perceptions that occur from early through late adolescence. We begin with a case study on caring.

THE ENTRY OF NEW PERSPECTIVES:

Social Reasoning During Adolescence

A Profile in Caring

Gail is a 22-year-old who graduated last month with a bachelor of science degree in life-span human development. She had a secondary emphasis in gerontology and recently passed a rigorous exam to be a licensed nursing-home administrator. The faculty selected her as the outstanding graduating senior in her major and had the following remarks to share when they announced the award.

> In addition to being a very good student, Gail is a leader in her peer group, and a young adult willing to become involved in situations that extend herself. She applies herself well and sees into issues and events with insight. Her work consistently shows her stretching her understanding into such educational objectives as applying and analyzing material and ideas.
>
> Her level of maturity impresses us. She is caring and empathic. She has demonstrated her commitment to social, personal, and institutional issues by becoming involved in several matters of concern on our campus: teaching students learning skills, working with our university's Center for Aging to link elderly citizens with programs meeting their needs, and being a leader in the Student Interest Group in our department.
>
> She combines very good academic skills with a strong sense of social commitment. She is a thoughtful, secure young woman. Her quiet resolve is a theme that has come back to us constantly as we have written these remarks. Combined with her social and academic intelligence and her involvement in issues larger than her own welfare, this quiet resolve marks her as an individual whose contributions will be of value and importance.

Gail's immediate career goal is to be a lawyer. She did very well on the Law School Admission Test (LSAT) and applied to about nine schools of law for admission. She was accepted by several good schools, including University of Houston, University of Iowa, Kansas University, and University of Minnesota. She accepted the offer from Kansas University and began studying to be an attorney last fall.

She knows all the lawyer jokes and will even tell some and laugh. She says, "What have you got if you have 10,000 lawyers on the bottom of the ocean? A good start." Her friend adds, "If you could lay end-to-end all the lawyers in the world, this would be a good thing." They both laugh.

Gail acknowledges that the lawyer jokes convey skepticism about the morals of attorneys. She looks beyond the question of lawyers' lack of moral integrity and sees the opportunity to provide assistance to underrepresented populations. She sees law as a helping profession. However, she notes, "People think I'm drawn to law because of big bucks. That's not it at all for me. For me, it's more the opportunity to empower people. To give people the benefit of the doubt. Just because I don't believe in what someone else believes doesn't mean that person doesn't deserve assistance—my assistance.

"I think of older adults—for example, in health care, particularly those who have used all their resources and are struggling to survive. These are people struggling just to get by, with no family support and no means of economic security. What it comes down to with any underrepresented population is, 'What do we owe them?' The 'we' are the ones in positions of power or privilege who have advanced because of oppression of others.

"I'm not sure I agree with the concept of owing. In this sense, owing puts both parties at a disadvantage. When starting off on 'owing', you aren't looking at a cooperative effort but more of a one-up position that places people in superior/inferior relationships."

When pressed on how being an attorney will help her work on her goals, Gail says, "The law will help by enabling me to understand society and policy—and from this understanding, help to create change through policy. As an example, let's talk about making changes in the policies that currently regulate interaction between elderly adult day-care clients and children in day-care centers; I want to increase the frequency of interaction. Currently, the policy says children and elderly cannot have a common area for interaction. I'm not saying separate areas are wrong, but I think common interaction would produce wonderful benefits, such as breaking down stereotypical barriers about older people and even preventing such barriers from developing. More frequent interaction would break down obvious barriers against these generations knowing each other. I suspect a case could be made in court that policies prohibiting intergenerational interaction are discriminatory. I just don't know now how to argue such a case."

Gail thinks another "policy need" concerns affordable and accessible day-care for children raised by "parents struggling to keep above the poverty line. Often parents can only afford day-care by quitting their jobs and becoming dependent on government welfare. Policies should promote independence, not dependence."

When asked about what she considers to be a significant moral dilemma, Gail reflected and then talked about abortion. "A moral dilemma I've struggled with is the abortion issue. My dilemma is that pro-lifers equate abortion with killing babies. No one wants to be for killing babies. People are not in favor of killing babies.

"When I think about an abortion, I'm not sure I could have one. I'd struggle with that decision. I think that life is precious, but I'd never condemn someone for making the decision to have an abortion. For some people, that is the right decision. "I can't conceive of conditions when I would be able to judge that someone else having an abortion is making the wrong decision. I would not tell the person she is wrong, but I might tell her that I disagree.

"If a person had had a series of abortions, I'd have to sit down with her and discuss her need to learn about birth control. I'd have to tell her I'd think what she is doing is not morally correct (at least in my view of morality)."

Gail was asked to say more about what makes abortion a dilemma for her. "Personally, it is not something I could do. But I'm not saying it is wrong for someone else to have an abortion. I find the absolute black-and-white positions wrong. It's a big, deep shade of gray.

"If someone were to ask me would I be pro-choice, I'd have to say that the tactics of the pro-life, antiabortion protestors disgust me. I watched the protests in Wichita this summer [1992], watched the protestors pushing kids in front of cars, condemning and judging people in the name of Christ, blocking any efforts to provide birth control. I'd have to say those tactics disgust me.

"I'm not an advocate of pro-choice, but I would have to say that now I am pro-choice because I think the pro-choice viewpoints are more along my line of thinking. They advocate nonviolent means and advocate protecting the right to an abortion, but are not fanatical and hateful. That's not to say there are not people in the pro-choice movement who are hateful. But the pro-choice people are logical, and the pro-life supporters preach guilt and sin without alternatives.

"Earlier in my life—like in high school—I'd have been more drawn to the pro-life position, due to the guilt tactics used and the scare tactics used by showing films of aborted fetuses. But since those days, I think I've overall developed cognitively. Thousands of things have helped me grow on my own. There have been deaths in my family, I've developed leadership skills, and I've learned to speak independently and have my views listened to. College gave me a broadened educational background. All of that has helped me to gain a different perspective on the pro-choice versus pro-life positions."

When asked if she has any heroes or heroines, Gail said, "The most obvious people who are heroes to me are my parents. Not to say they are perfect, but they are heroes because they are imperfect. I've seen them grow through mistakes, and deal with those mistakes, and admit those mistakes. They've shown me the kind of person I'd like to become, as far as being involved and committed. Not that I always agree with them.

"I've seen how they are genuine and sincere in dealing with people. They do live by the Golden Rule, and it is amazing the results that occur—friendship and respect.

"Growing up in Topeka, Kansas during the 1950s, they developed prejudices. This was the time of the famous Supreme Court case *Brown* v. *Topeka Board of Education* that did away with segregated schools. It is frustrating for me but enlightening to see them struggle with their prejudices and work to overcome them. To say, 'It's always what I'd accepted, but I need to think that over again.' They have shown me the importance of being open-minded and of growing."

This case study highlights several topics uncovered by research on moral reasoning during adolescence. For example, Gail has learned to differentiate her ideas from the ideas held by others. As witnessed by her discussions of health care and abortion, she sees moral issues in terms of both personal and societal outcomes. She places considerable emphasis on treating others fairly, or what Lawrence Kohlberg (1969, 1976) would consider the principle of justice. But she also embodies Gilligan's (1982) theme of attachment and care; in her decision to accept the Kansas University School of Law's offer, she said major factors were (a) the quality of the school, (b) the offer of a full scholarship, and (c) the intangibles, such as how people treat each other. She turned down a school with a prestigious reputation—the school that had been her number one choice prior to visiting its campus—because she felt very uncomfortable with the indifferent manner whereby people at the school interacted during her visit.

Gail did not always have her moral vision or her ability to reason about moral issues. Her ideas developed over time, as she had experiences that challenged her viewpoints and provided her opportunities to make decisions. We turn now to the contemporary thinking about how changes in moral and social reasoning occur.

THE INFLUENCE OF COGNITIVE CHANGES AND EXPERIENCES

This chapter explores the developing ability of adolescents to think about moral questions in a more complicated fashion, to understand viewpoints of others, and to overcome self-consciousness. In this chapter, we also look at the link between changes in cognitive operations and the development of political reasoning and social awareness. New social awareness produces increased sensitivity to other people's experiences. There is also evidence that changes in reasoning about the meaning of existence mark adolescent development.

The cognitivist paradigm has been influential in the study of moral and social reasoning. The cognitivist revolution in psychology enables us to explain how adolescent understanding of social realities develops. The cognitive view explains how adolescents' reflect on their social experiences. Piaget (1929) maintained that advances in formal reasoning enable adolescents to engage in such reflections. The information-processing viewpoint emphasizes that greater facility to process and use increasing amounts of information allows adolescents to go beyond the constraints of childhood when thinking about their experiences and interactions. The work on social reasoning has a definite Piagetian flavor.

Cognitivists have offered radically new theories to explain the changes observed in adolescents' thinking about social realities. The leading theories adopt a stage approach, accentuating that changes in intellectual skill—what many call *reasoning*—and increased experiences in a world beyond their families enable adolescents to understand social relationships in ways that go beyond the capabilities of children.

It is crucial to understand that these changes in social reasoning occur because adolescents reflect on what they do, what they observe, and what happens to them. The adolescents' new reasoning skills would not by themselves produce the changes, nor would new experiences. The theorists maintain that by using formal operations, adolescents reason about experiences and extend their understandings of themselves. We begin with the current thinking about moral reasoning, primarily the ideas of Lawrence Kohlberg.

MORAL REASONING

The Views of Lawrence Kohlberg

Lawrence Kohlberg (1927–1987) was a professor in the Graduate School of Education at Harvard University from the late 1960s until his death in early 1987. While at Harvard, Kohlberg established the Center for Moral Education. His influence on our understanding of developmental changes in moral reasoning has been profound, extensive, and controversial. Kohlberg's contribution can be seen not only in his theory about moral reasoning but also in his prominent association with and influence on such key cognitive-developmental figures as Robert Selman, Carol Gilligan, James Fowler, Anne Colby, James Rest, and John Snarey.

The main influence in Kohlberg's thinking has to have been Piaget. While acknowledging his debt to John Dewey (1909), James Baldwin (1906), and George Herbert Mead (1934), it is Piaget to whom Kohlberg more often refers. Kohlberg was impressed with Piaget's reasoning about stages of development, his portrait of children as philosophers, and his work to provide a theoretical structure explaining moral development.

Kohlberg's 1969 Essay on Stage and Sequence

In 1969, Kohlberg wrote an extensive essay about the development of moral reasoning. The purpose of this lengthy essay was to present the cognitive-developmental explanation of socialization, to contrast this approach with social learning theory and psychoanalysis, and to discuss the critical place of role taking, imitation, and identification in human social development. Friends said he later referred to this essay as perhaps too optimistic, but he believed it offered an attractive alternative to behaviorism and psychoanalysis to explain both social and moral development (Rest, Power, & Brabeck, 1988).

Two concepts central to Kohlberg's essay are important for an understanding of what cognitive-developmental theorists mean by social and moral reasoning. The first is **structure and structural change**. The second is **role taking and experience**.

Structure and structural change.   A key debate in research on learning and development centers on whether some changes are **reversible** (that is, the old behavior returns) while others are **irreversible** (that is, they transform earlier stages of development). An illustration of reversible change is an adolescent who ignores the curfew his parents have imposed until they take away his driving privileges, but he eventually resumes staying out beyond his curfew when he finds his parents do not intend to enforce rules against curfew violations any longer. An example of irreversible change is children's beliefs about dreams. Until around age 5, children believe that dreams are real events, but between the ages of 5 and 7, they come to recognize that dreams are not visible to other people, are not events in the real world, and are produced by people when they sleep (Kohlberg, 1969). Children do not resume their earlier opinions about dreams after developing this new understanding.

Another debate in research on learning and development is whether changes parallel other developments or transform earlier stages of development. **Parallel**

change is exhibited by a child's going through an oral stage and an anal stage of development simultaneously; the emergence of pleasure in anal behaviors does not preclude continuing pleasure in oral behaviors. **Transformed development** is exhibited by children's mastery of the concept of conservation of volume.

You may recall conservation of volume means the amount of a substance (for example, water) does not change when its shape changes. Thus, when you pour water from a tall, thin glass to a short, fat cup, the volume of water remains the same. A preoperational child is fooled by the appearances, but a concrete operational child is not. If you want a vivid example, give two four-year-old children drinks of Kool-Aid and use a tall, thin glass for one child and a short, fat cup for the other child. Even if you pour the first drink to the top of the glass and then transfer the drink to the cup, and then refill the glass, the children will not think they have the same amount; they will be convinced the child with the tall glass has more to drink. Try this experiment on concrete operational children. Having mastered conservation of volume, children do not use preoperational principles to understand what happens to the amount of liquid when liquid is poured from a tall, thin glass to a short, fat cup.

Structural changes in reasoning are irreversible and reintegrate earlier forms of reasoning; that is, they are **hierarchically integrated**. Something is hierarchically integrated if later developments are dependent on the completion of earlier stages. As an example, consider this notion from the field of curriculum development: there are different levels of educational objectives, including knowledge of facts at the lowest level to evaluation of information at the highest level (Bloom, Madaus, & Hastings, 1981). A student must know facts in order to evaluate what those facts are about. It is a fact that Abraham Lincoln was President of the United States during the Civil War. Students could not evaluate the impact of the Civil War unless they know facts about Lincoln as well as many other facts.

Structural change also involves **qualitative differences in reasoning**, which always occur in the same sequence and result in a **structured whole** (that is, an underlying organization that determines responses). All of these properties of structural change are what we understand to be the cognitive-developmental theory about cognitive stages of development (Kohlberg, 1969).

Rather than a maturational understanding of development, the cognitive-developmental doctrine of cognitive stages emphasizes that experience plays a necessary role in the form reasoning takes in the person's life. Gesell would have disagreed with this position. You may recall Gesell's position that experience has no role in promoting development. Cognitive-developmental theorists assert that experience plays a major role in development.

The doctrine of cognitive stages also asserts that individuals in richly diverse and stimulating environments advance through the stage sequence more rapidly than those in environments lacking variety. In other words, structural change emphasizes that development depends on personal interaction with one's physical, internal, and interpersonal environments. In later thinking about moral reasoning, these personal interactions became known as **sociomoral experiences** and produced some bitter debate over whether Kohlberg's theory is biased against females. This debate is discussed later in the chapter.

The doctrine of cognitive stages asserts that advances through the stage sequence occur more rapidly for individuals in richly diverse environments than for individuals in environments lacking variety and challenge.

Role taking and experience.   Kohlberg (1969) said that sharing lies behind all ideas of what is social. The fundamental form whereby sharing leads to changes in sociomoral reasoning involves **role-taking opportunities**. An example of a role-taking opportunity that involves sharing is working with a team on a school project.

Some role-taking opportunities are universal because they emerge from basic institutional features found in all cultures. Examples of such social institutions are laws, social class distinctions, and government (Kohlberg, 1969). These institutions provide all human beings, regardless of cultural differences, the experience of knowing who they are in relationship to others and of knowing how to behave.

Moral reasoning emerges and develops as individuals discover that their claims conflict with others' claims. Conflicting claims lead individuals to reevaluate their moral understandings and to even change their moral judgments. Changing one's moral judgment involves gaining a different *sociomoral perspective*. Your sociomoral perspective is the framework you use to make moral decisions. It is the most basic, defining feature in the development of reasoning about moral matters (Colby & Kohlberg, 1984).

The transformation of your principles of moral reasoning occurs because of the role-taking opportunities—the sociomoral experiences—you have had. Whereas some researchers stress the role of the family in moral development, Kohlberg considered the family to be of negligible influence in the individual's development of moral reasoning. He stated unequivocally that groups outside the family (for instance, peers) provide the necessary sociomoral experiences to stimulate changes in moral reasoning (Kohlberg, 1969).

For Kohlberg, the critical issues in development are (*a*) the extent and the variety of role-taking opportunities available to the individual and (*b*) the ability of the person to incorporate new social stimulation into current levels of understanding. The second point is what Kohlberg called the *problem of structural match,* or the **one stage up or down principle**. By this distinction, Kohlberg meant an individual is incapable of assimilating information that greatly exceeds his or her current grasp of moral principles. Kohlberg gave an excellent example to illustrate this point by noting how a stage 2 juvenile delinquent perceives remarks from a counselor: ". . . a stage 2 delinquent is offered 'role taking opportunities' by an understanding psychotherapist, but these opportunities are perceived as opportunities to 'con a sucker' and do not stimulate development beyond stage 2" (1969, p. 402). In other words, an opportunity to engage in mutual understanding is overlooked as the adolescent focuses on what will serve his own interests.

Empirical studies have established that humans do operate on this one stage up or down principle (Rest, 1968, 1986; Rest, Turiel, & Kohlberg, 1969). We saw some likely examples of the limits imposed by the one stage up or down principle in Chapter 4 when we looked at the difficulties for schools trying to develop students' sensitivities to cultural differences. Some students seem incapable of appreciating the value of cultural differences, probably because the idea requires reasoning more than one stage above their stages of moral reasoning. If this hypothesis is true, then it suggests a link between identity formation and moral reasoning development. In one study, adolescents who refused to accept other cultural values as worth knowing were in the diffuse and foreclosed statuses of identity formation, whereas moratorium and achieved identities were open to cultural diversity (Streitmatter & Pate, 1989).

An example of an adolescent assimilating information and extending her understanding of moral principles is offered by the case of Juliet (the early-maturing girl presented in the case study at the beginning of Chapter 2). Juliet had thought teachers would always be fair, but several experiences from fifth grade into ninth grade led her to see some teachers do or say things that are not fair. Finally, in her sophomore year of high school, she was placed in a classroom in which the teacher incorrectly accused her of not following directions on more than one occasion. The final straw for Juliet came, though, when the teacher ridiculed a classmate from another country because the girl did not know American Christmas customs. Juliet placed herself in the other girl's shoes, explained her outrage to her parents and to the school principal, and demanded to be placed with a different teacher. The principal gave Juliet her wish and also discussed with the offending teacher his concern over "culturally insensitive remarks."

Kohlberg's Stage Theory

Like Piaget, Kohlberg (1976, 1980, 1981) developed a stage theory of the development of moral reasoning. His theory involves six stages grouped into three levels. These stages and levels are presented in Table 5-1. Later, after a review of considerable empirical data, Kohlberg revised his position and said moral reasoning actually moves through five stages. We look at this change in Kohlberg's thinking later in the chapter.

TABLE 5-1   **Kohlberg's Stages and Levels of Moral Reasoning**

LEVELS AND STAGES	PRINCIPLES FOLLOWED
PRECONVENTIONAL LEVEL	
Stage 1 Obey authority and avoid punishment	Obedience to enforcers of punishment
Stage 2 Serve one's own interest's	Individualism and fairness
CONVENTIONAL LEVEL	
Stage 3 Protect shared feelings, agreements, expectations	Mutuality, interpersonal connections, conformity
Stage 4 Maintain the social order	Social system and conscience
POSTCONVENTIONAL LEVEL	
Stage 5 Mutually agreed upon standards that provide the greatest benefit to all	Utilitarianism
Stage 6 Self-chosen, consistent principles that all humans should follow	Universal ethical principles

SOURCE: Adapted from "Moral Stages and Moralization: The Conitive-Developmental Approach" by L. Kohlberg, *Moral Development and Behavior: Theory, Research, and Social Issues* (pp. 34–35) edited by T. Lickona, 1976, New York: Holt, Rinehart & Winston.

Kohlberg's levels of moral reasoning.   Most children under the age of 9 operate at the **preconventional level** of moral reasoning. At the preconventional level, individuals understand morality means either to obey authority and avoid punishment or to serve one's own interests. An example of a child reasoning at the preconventional level is presented by Robin, a 7-year-old girl who, when asked to explain why a person should tell the truth, said, "You will be spanked if you lie." Kohlberg (1976) also noted this level of moral reasoning applies to some adolescents and to many criminal offenders.

Conventional moral reasoning is the level at which most adolescents and adults operate. By *conventional,* Kohlberg (1976) meant complying with and upholding societal rules and expectations. On the surface, at least, there appears a link between Kohlberg's conventional moral reasoning and Marcia's (1964, 1966) concept of foreclosed identity. Preconventional individuals reason it is right to conform to society's rules when it is in their interests, whereas conventional individuals reason one should uphold these rules because the rules are in society's interest.

Postconventional moral reasoning—considered to involve a minority of adults—bases moral behavior on personal formulation of and commitment to the principles upon which societal rules are grounded. One would predict an association between postconventional moral reasoning and Marcia's achieved identity status, although I have never seen a research piece exploring the possibility.

Kohlberg suggested an individual's level of moral reasoning indicates the type of relationship the person has established with society. Preconventional individuals perceive rules and social expectations to be externally imposed, conventional individuals have internalized society's rules and expectations, and postconventional individuals distinguish their identities from the rules of society and work from self-chosen principles that are grounded in the concept of justice.

Kohlberg's moral orientations.   Kohlberg identified four **moral orientations** whereby people reason about moral issues: normative, fairness, utilitarianism, and perfectionism. By *normative,* he meant reasoning in terms of blaming or approving, obeying or consulting authorities, and having rights and duties. By *fairness,* Kohlberg meant reasoning in terms of maintaining equity and reciprocity, weighing different perspectives, and sustaining free agreement among individuals. By *utilitarianism,* he meant reasoning in terms of good versus bad consequences for individuals and groups. By *perfectionist,* he meant reasoning in terms of ideals, such as upholding self-respect, serving human dignity, or promoting human autonomy (Colby et al., 1983).

Kohlberg's levels of moral reasoning and moral orientations may seem very abstract and removed from the dilemmas people grapple with in their everyday lives. Some scholars have argued that people reason differently about real moral problems they face compared to hypothetical dilemmas they are asked to discuss (Ford & Lowery, 1986; Gilligan, 1977, 1982; Lyons, 1982, 1983). Examples may help illustrate the distinct application of Kohlberg's ideas to actual people.

Preconventional adolescents and adults lack a conscience; using psychological terms, we call them "antisocial personalities." In short, preconventional adults are individuals who uphold social rules and expectations only when it fits their interests. They may be quite shrewd at avoiding getting caught in criminal activities, and express remorse only because they did get caught. They may even be able to mimic in a discussion of moral issues what a postconventional person would say. A chilling example of a preconventional adult who could mimic postconventional moral reasoning is the serial killer Ted Bundy (Rule, 1980).

The majority of adolescents and adults use conventional moral reasoning principles. Their moral development has culminated in an acceptance of the social order. In Kohlberg's terms, at stage 3, the conventional person desires to live by the Golden Rule (do unto others as you would have them do unto you), and at stage 4, the individual suppresses personal desires for the good of social institutions and follows his or her conscience to keep society going. An example of such a person is a National Guard soldier who accepted orders to fight in the Persian Gulf War because it was his duty to his country.

Postconventional individuals are less common than the majority who use conventional moral reasoning. In fact, John Snarey (1985) indicates that Kohlberg stopped talking of stage 6 and accepted the likelihood that people do not proceed beyond stage 5 moral reasoning. In a telephone conversation, Ann Higgins, who worked very closely with Kohlberg at the Center for Moral Development and Education, said Kohlberg's revised system (Colby & Kohlberg, 1987) considered stage 5 to be the final unfolding of moral reasoning (A. Higgins, personal communication, February 6, 1992).

Whereas a preconventional person might question following social rules because they interfere with his or her self-interests, a postconventional person would question following social rules that conflict with the principles of human rights. An example of postconventional moral reasoning is the rationale of civil rights workers who used nonviolent protest during the 1950s and 1960s to stop racial segregation in the United States. At the time, of course, many people considered civil rights workers to be trouble makers who should be thrown in jail.

Let us consider the deep divisions in our country over abortion as another example of differing uses of moral principles. An entire movement called Operation Rescue has mounted vigorous campaigns to stop abortions. The members of Operation Rescue staged several weeks of protest in the summer of 1992 to shut down Wichita, Kansas medical facilities in which abortions are performed (Fusco, 1992; Hull, 1991). Apparently working from their reasoning about moral principles, some antiabortion protestors have placed bombs in clinics that conduct abortions (Schneider, 1986), and the TV program "60 Minutes" indicated on its February 2, 1992 broadcast that tactics in North Dakota have included threats of violence against doctors who practice abortion. In March 1993, an abortion protestor carried out one of these threats when he shot and killed David Gunn, a physician who performed abortions in Florida (Warner, 1993). In August of 1993, another protestor shot in both arms a physician who performs abortions and later said the doctor's practice justified murdering him (Perry, 1993).

Current demonstrations against abortion clinics may involve a wide set of moral reasoning. Within this group of antiabortion protestors, you will probably find preconventional individuals, who consider it acceptable to endanger the lives of others by bombing clinics or encouraging children to lie in front of moving cars to block the entrance to clinics; conventional individuals, who protest out of acceptance of what religious authorities say is the right thing to do and who harass the children of doctors who perform abortions; and postconventional individuals, who are moved to action because they consider abortion a violation of justice and are willing to use nonviolent means to protest abortions. I am sure that defenders of abortion rights also range across the same moral reasoning continuum. We will return to the example of abortion when considering Gilligan's views on moral development.

Kohlberg (1980) insisted that, at its core, moral development is cognitive, and argued that the sequence of moral development is invariant and universal. The concept of an invariant, universal sequence is a staple of cognitive-developmental stage theories.

By a **cognitive core**, Kohlberg meant the structure of principles whereby a person reasons about what is the right thing to do and why it is the right thing to do. Because Kohlberg asserted that moral development is cognitive, he denied that emotions form the foundation for morality. Akin to Piaget's ideas about the mechanisms of change in cognitive development, Kohlberg said experiences lead people to reason about social behavior, assimilate new information, and thus restructure the principles that govern their moral behaviors. Longitudinal research has indicated that people restructure these principles only gradually and do not make dramatic shifts to a new stage of moral reasoning (Colby et al., 1983).

Kohlberg's Method

Kohlberg studied moral development by asking his subjects to respond to stories in which **moral dilemmas** trouble characters. The dilemmas involved various types of conflict: the preservation of life versus the demands of the law, the demands of conscience versus the societal need to punish misdeeds, and agreements between people and the demands of individuals in authority. The moral dilemmas involved competing demands about what is the right thing to do.

Kohlberg's assumption was that in reflecting on the moral dilemmas in these stories, a person discloses the cognitive structure that underlies his or her present stage of moral development (Gibbs & Widaman, 1982). Keep in mind that Kohlberg was interested in the rationale a person provided, not in how a person behaved.

Kohlberg's dilemmas were hypothetical, and evidence suggests individuals reason about real-life problems differently than about hypothetical problems. For instance, one study found that high school students reason at a higher level of moral reasoning about hypothetical problems than about their own sexuality (Sprinthall & Collins, 1989).

Probably the most famous of the stories crafted by Kohlberg concerns Heinz, a man whose wife is dying of an illness for which a drug is available; however, Heinz cannot afford to buy the drug and the sole person who possesses it will not give it to him. The dilemma Kohlberg poses is whether Heinz should steal the drug in order to save his wife's life (Colby, Kohlberg, Speicher, Hewer, Candee, Gibbs, & Power, 1987).

Another story regarding the moral dilemma of life versus law is found in Kohlberg's vignette about Dr. Jefferson. The story goes as follows:

> There was a woman who had very bad cancer, and there was no treatment known to medicine that would save her. Her doctor, Dr. Jefferson, knew that she had only about six months to live. She was in terrible pain, but she was so weak that a good dose of a painkiller like ether or morphine would make her die sooner. She was delirious and almost crazy with pain, and in her calm periods she would ask Dr. Jefferson to give her enough ether to kill her. She said she couldn't stand the pain and she was going to die in a few months anyway. Although he knows that mercy killing is against the law, the doctor thinks about granting her request (From *The Measurement of Moral Judgment. Volume 2. Standard Issue Scoring Manual,* by A. Colby, L. Kohlberg, B. Speicher, A. Hewer, D. Candee, J. Gibbs, and C. Power, p. 279. Copyright © 1987 by Cambridge University Press. Reprinted with the permission of Cambridge University Press.).

Once the story has been presented, the researcher directs the conversation by asking specific questions. Some of the questions accompanying the story about Dr. Jefferson are, "Should Dr. Jefferson give her the drug that would make her die? Why or why not?" "Should the woman have the right to make the final decision?" and "Is there any way a person has a duty or obligation to live when he or she does not want to, when the person wants to commit suicide?" (Colby et al., 1987, p. 279). As you would expect from the questions, responses to the stories are open-ended and divergent.

In his 1969 essay, Kohlberg presented 25 aspects he considered present in all societies as (*a*) the means whereby individuals reason about what is the moral thing to do in a situation and (*b*) the means to assess the stage of a person's moral reasoning. Some of these aspects are motives, consequences, punishment of law breakers,

Kohlberg claimed all societies use the same aspects to reason about what is the moral thing to do.

responsibility to enforce social rules, and the disruption of personal relationships. Kohlberg (1971) studied the 25 aspects carefully and developed criteria for identifying which aspect a person is invoking when responding to a given situation. However, as early as his 1969 essay, Kohlberg said that all of the aspects reduce to principles about justice; by *justice,* Kohlberg meant **reciprocity** (that is, mutual give-and-take) and **equality**. He argued that justice defines social regulations and social expectations. This focus on justice has not gone unchallenged, as we shall see in the section about Carol Gilligan's views.

Kohlberg considered how an individual reasons about an aspect to be indicative of a specific stage of moral reasoning. For example, by arguing that Heinz should be punished for stealing the drug because judges are supposed to punish people who break the law, a person would be invoking "a stage 3 punishment issue criterion" unless the subject elaborated "his or her conception of the judge's role in stage 4 terms (the judge should punish because he has accepted a responsibility to uphold the laws of society)" (Colby et al., 1983, p. 90).

Cross-cultural research in Tibet, Israel, and India has indicated that certain cultures place some values, such as community or life, in a very different perspective from Kohlberg's (Snarey, 1985). The conclusion is that not all of the aspects used to make or assess moral judgments are present in Kohlberg's 1969 article and that some aspects present in one culture may be absent in another.

At each interview, the researcher gives the subject three stories to discuss. Each story involves two of the three conflicts: life versus law, conscience versus punishment, and contracts versus demands of authority. The researcher scores responses to all six issues according to the 25 aspects that Kohlberg identified. When one of the aspects is mentioned, it provides the criterion needed to match the subject's ideas with a stage of moral reasoning. Whenever a subject's discussion does not match an issue to one of the 25 aspects, Kohlberg instructed raters to make an educated guess about what stage of moral reasoning is involved. Guess scores are given half the value of criterion matches. The researcher combines the scores for each of the six issues and derives both a global score and a more refined weighted average score (Colby et al., 1983).

How to Calculate a Weighted Average Score

The weighted average score is calculated in four steps. (1) Multiply each stage by the number of criteria matches noted for that stage. (2) Add up the total of all stages. (3) Divide the total by the number of matches. (4) Multiply the quotient by 100. Perhaps an example will make the method's simplicity clear.

Imagine that during an interview, a person mentioned moral aspects associated with separate stages, and each stage had the following set of criterion matches: stage 1 had one match, stage 2 had two matches, stage 3 had seven matches, and stage 4 had one match. First, multiply each stage by its number of criterion matches: $1 \times 1 = 1$, $2 \times 2 = 4$, $3 \times 7 = 21$, and $4 \times 1 = 4$. Second, add up the total products: $1 + 4 + 21 + 4 = 30$. Third, divide the total by the number of matches: $30/11 = 2.73$. Fourth, multiply the quotient by 100: $2.73 \times 100 = 273$. The person's weighted average score is 273, which suggests the person is in transition to stage 3 moral reasoning.

Global scores consist of the stage of moral reasoning most often mentioned plus any other stage of moral reasoning with at least one-fourth of the points given by the researchers. Global scores can result in one of three outcomes: (a) the person reasons purely at one stage, (b) the person reasons mostly at one stage but also at another stage at least 25% of the time, or (c) the person uses principles from two stages more than 25% of the time and is thus in transition from one stage to the next (Colby et al., 1983).

A **weighted average score** (**WAS**) can range from 100, stage 1 moral reasoning, to 500, stage 5 moral reasoning. The WAS is given different names in the literature, such as **moral maturity scores** (**MMS**) and **moral maturity quotients** (**MMQ**) (Rest, 1986). The calculation steps for the WAS, MMQ, and MMS are identical, as are the explanations of what each score denotes.

A WAS of 100–199 indicates an individual is in stage 1 moral reasoning, 200–299 indicates stage 2, 300–399 indicates stage 3, 400–499 indicates stage 4, and 500 indicates stage 5. There is no WAS above 500. Transitions from one stage to the next are highlighted by scores that lie one-quarter to three-quarters above the starting score for that stage; for example, scores ranging from 225–275 indicate a person in transition from stage 2 to stage 3. Scores above 275 indicate that the person has moved into stage 3 (A. Higgins, personal communication, February 6, 1992).

Kohlberg and his colleagues (Colby & Kohlberg, 1987; Colby et al., 1987) produced a two-volume manual that revised earlier versions of his scoring system (Kohlberg, 1971). Kohlberg claimed the impetus for the revision came, in part, because he evaluated research findings and realized changes to the scoring system were needed. He recognized that appeals to interpersonal connecions can involve moral reasoning principles beyond stage 3. Lawrence Walker (1984) indicates that Kohlberg undertook the revision in response to heralded challenges that the scoring system was biased against females (Gilligan, 1977, 1982).

We have covered Kohlberg's understanding about changes in moral reasoning. We now turn to how he studied the stage of moral reasoning a person used and how he assigned numerical values in assessing a person's stage of moral reasoning.

Research Investigating Development of Moral Reasoning From Kohlberg's Perspective

While there are several volumes of research using Kohlberg's approach, I will focus on a 20-year longitudinal study of males' moral development from early adolescence into young adulthood and present a summary of research on the effects of college on moral reasoning. The box on page 194 presents information from a 10-year longitudinal study of adolescent moral development in an Israeli kibbutz. Each of these investigations involved longitudinal methods. According to Snarey (1985), longitudinal studies provide the only valid means of determining whether moral development occurs in an invariant sequence.

It can be argued that a valid variation on strictly longitudinal methods would be to use sequential methods, whereby cross-sectional and longitudinal approaches are combined. The major issue would be to ensure that the longitudinal sections of the study involve enough time to permit change in moral reasoning to occur and be identified. The following 20-year study is an example of a sequential investigation. It involved three age-groups, rather than a single age-group as in a purely longitudinal study.

A 20-year study of American male moral development.   Along with three colleagues, Kohlberg studied changes over time in the moral reasoning of 58 males from the Chicago area (Colby et al., 1983). The boys were interviewed up to six times over a 20-year period. Interviews began in 1955 and occurred every 3 to 4 years. All interviews were evaluated using the most current version of Kohlberg's scoring method (Colby & Kohlberg, 1987; Colby et al., 1987).

The project started with 84 subjects. However, some of the boys dropped out before the six interviews were completed. In their analysis, the researchers used only the responses of the 58 boys who had been interviewed at least twice. To compensate for the greater loss of boys from working-class families (compared to boys from upper-middle-class families), the researchers added 5 boys from working-class families at the time of the third interview.

Dropouts can seriously affect interpretation of results in a longitudinal study. If, by the end of the project, all individuals with low moral reasoning scores had left the study, the researchers might have erroneously concluded much higher gains over time than actually were the case. To test this possibility, the researchers compared the first mean scores of the boys who dropped out with first mean scores of boys who remained in the project. Because these first mean scores did not differ, the authors judged that average increase in moral maturity scores had not been artificially inflated by the loss of some subjects (Colby et al., 1983).

An important question in this study was whether development occurred in the stage pattern Kohlberg's theory predicted. The results showed a positive relationship between the ages of the subjects and their stages of moral reasoning, demonstrated

John Snarey, a student of Kohlberg and currently a faculty member at Emory University, completed his doctoral dissertation on the social and moral development of members of kibbutz communities. Kibbutzim (the plural form of the word *kibbutz*) are "intentionally created collective communities in Israel characterized by communal child rearing, collective economic production, and direct participatory democracy" (Snarey, Reimer, & Kohlberg, 1985, p. 5). A member of a kibbutz is called a *kibbutznik*.

Snarey's original sample included 92 adolescents. Over a nine-year period, he interviewed 64 of them at least twice; the second interviews occurred between one and two years after the initial interviews. The third set of interviews, which involved 32 adolescents, occurred at least five years after the second.

Nearly half of the subjects (45) entered the study during their early adolescence (12 to 14 years of age), and a significant proportion (38) entered during their middle adolescent years (15–17). The remaining 9 persons were between the ages of 13 and 15 when they entered the study. All 92 adolescents lived in the same kibbutz. Interviews were conducted in Hebrew and analyzed using Kohlberg's standardized scoring system (Colby & Kohlberg, 1987; Colby et al., 1987). At the time of the final interviews, the average subject was in late adolescence (18–22).

Snarey was interested in answering questions about stage sequence, structural wholeness, and age norms for moral development. He wanted to determine if moral reasoning of kibbutz adolescents develops in the same form as research with other groups of adolescents had demonstrated.

Snarey was also interested in answering questions about culturally defined gender differences, culturally defined moral issues, and culturally defined moral structures. In addition to assessing cultural similarities in moral reasoning, he also wished to determine if kibbutz adolescents reason about morality differently than adolescents in other cultures.

The adolescents were asked to respond to stories with moral dilemmas over life versus law, conscience versus punishment, and contracts versus demands of authority. The interviewers used several standard questions to help the adolescents illuminate why they reasoned as they did. Frequently, for instance, they asked people to tell why they had made a certain moral decision.

Sixty out of the 64 adolescents (94%) either progressed to a new stage of development (66%) or showed no stage change (28%) over the course of the study. The fact that 6% regressed to an earlier stage of moral reasoning seemed attributable to measurement error caused by testing some individuals more than once (Colby & Kohlberg, 1987; Snarey et al., 1985). Of great significance to Kohlberg's developmental sequence thesis, none of the 64 adolescents skipped a stage in moral reasoning.

At each interview, the great majority of the adolescents used reasoning principles consistent with a specific moral stage. Most other adolescents used principles that indicated their reasoning was in transition to the next highest stage. These findings support the thesis that moral reasoning involves structural wholeness.

In Snarey's sample, progression in moral reasoning clearly was linked to the age of the subjects. For instance, no one scored lower than the transition between stages 2 and 3 (all 12-year-old subjects), nobody between the ages of 13 and 17 scored higher than the transition between stages 3 and 4, and nobody began the transition from stage 4 to stage 5 prior to late adolescence (18–19).

The average stage of moral reasoning for kibbutz adolescents consistently surpassed the moral reasoning of the American adolescents studied by Kohlberg and his colleagues (Colby et al., 1983). Furthermore, after an extensive review of cross-cultural research that had used Kohlberg's methods, Snarey (1985) reported American subjects seldom, if ever, equal the stage of moral reasoning shown by comparable age-groups from Taiwan, India, Turkey, or Israel. Using Kohlberg's own ideas, one would speculate that adolescents in these other countries engage in sociomoral experiences (which provide opportunities for decision making and conflict resolution) American adolescents do not experience.

Snarey (1985) found no significant gender differences in the moral reasoning of kibbutz adolescents. This finding is particularly pertinent because of the accusations made that Kohlberg's method discriminates against females (Baumrind, 1986; Gilligan, 1977, 1982; Walker, 1984, 1986).

Snarey (1985) also investigated whether what Kohlberg identified as universal moral principles are more salient in one culture than in another. As an example, the value humans attribute to life may extend to animals in some cultures but be restricted to human life in others. Nisan and Kohlberg (1982) acknowledged the possibility that some cultures may use moral principles distinctively unlike the principles used in Western societies. If this is true, then the moral structures explained by Kohlberg would have narrower applicability than he claimed.

Culturally specific outcomes did emerge in the kibbutz adolescents' use of advanced moral reasoning principles. Snarey (1985) found his subjects made use of postconventional principles advocating community equality and happiness, principles missing in Kohlberg's updated scoring system. Because such an oversight in the scoring manual would lead to failure to identify elements of kibbutz moral reasoning, the prospect lies open for oversights with other cultures or, as Gilligan (1977, 1982) has claimed, with female moral reasoning.

Finally, Snarey and his collegues (1985) reported some clear differences between the responses of the

TABLE 5-2 ■ Cultural Differences Between American and Kibbutz-Born Adolescents: The Percentages in Each Sample Endorsing Moral Issues

ISSUES	AMERICAN (N = 58)		KIBBUTZ-BORN (N = 64)	
	Number	%	Number	%
Law	19	33	3	5
Life	39	67	61	95
Conscience	26	45	35	55
Punishment	32	55	29	45
Contract	35	61	60	93
Authority	23	39	4	7

SOURCE: "Development of Social-Moral Reasoning Among Kibbutz Adolescents: A Longitudinal Cross-Cultural Study" by J. R. Snarey, J. Reimer, and L. Kohlberg, 1985, *Developmental Psychology, 21.*

64 adolescent kibbutzniks and 58 adolescent urban Americans studied in Kohlberg's 20-year study (Colby et al., 1983). For instance, 67% of the Americans argued for life over law in the moral dilemma facing Heinz, who can save his wife only if he steals an expensive drug. However, 95% of the kibbutzniks said life should take precedence over the law. In the case of conscience versus punishment, less than half (45%) of the American adolescents argued that a policeman should not arrest Heinz for stealing the drug, whereas more than half (55%) of the adolescent kibbutzniks argued for leniency. In the case of a contract versus authority (in this case, a father promises his son that he may spend some money and later demands his son return the money), 61% of the Americans argued the father should keep his promise compared to 93% of the kibbutz-born adolescents. These results are presented in Table 5-2.

that subjects did not skip a stage, and demonstrated that subjects did not regress to an earlier stage of moral reasoning (Colby et al., 1983).

At the beginning of the study, most of the 10-year-olds were in transition between stage 1 and stage 2 or were already using stage 2 reasoning; 10-year-olds had a mean WAS of 189. The majority of 13- and 14-year-olds were in transition from stage 2 to stage 3, with a mean WAS of 246. The majority of 16- to 18-year-olds were in stage 3 or in transition to stage 4, with a mean WAS of 290. Ninety percent of 20- to 22-year-olds were either in stage 3, in transition to stage 4, or in stage 4 already; their mean WAS was 327 (Colby et al., 1983).

There were positive correlations between WAS and age, with particularly high correlations between scores of early adolescents (13- and 14-year-olds) and their scores as young adults. Changes over time were gradual, with periods of stabilization in both early and late adolescence. Positive correlations were also found between WAS and (a) socioeconomic status, (b) intelligence, and (c) educational experience (Colby et al., 1983).

The scores of the three age-groups showed the same developmental pattern across time. Not only did they proceed in the same sequence—that is, none of the groups regressed or skipped a stage—but, at each testing period, the reasoning of each group demonstrated movement toward the next higher stage of moral development (Colby et al., 1983).

This longitudinal study provided notably clear answers to three critical questions: (a) whether moral development follows an invariant sequence, (b) whether individuals use moral reasoning principles consistently, and (c) how development proceeds. As Kurt Fischer (1983) remarked, the study not only confirmed a stage sequence to moral development but also demonstrated that sociomoral experiences play a significant role in a person's slow but gradual adoption of new perspectives on moral concerns and issues.

Moral reasoning and the effects of college.   College students show noticeable gains in cognitive abilities, such as thinking critically, engaging in reflective judgment, and using formal operations (see Chapter 3). Other evidence, which Pascarella and Terenzini (1991) characterized as substantial, indicates that college also produces more open-mindedness about differing values.

Evidence from a multitude of studies confirms that an increase in use of postconventional moral reasoning occurs during the undergraduate years. Pascarella and Terenzini (1991) expressed concern that most studies are not longitudinal and do not contain control groups of noncollege individuals. However, they did favorably cite Kohlberg and his colleagues' (1983) 20-year study for using statistical procedures to control for possibly competing explanations of results, such as socioeconomic status or intelligence. In that study, increased WAS correlated positively with the amount of formal education, confirming the positive effect of college on moral reasoning.

We have finished our formal look at the research regarding moral reasoning during adolescence. The evidence clearly points to an increase in principled reasoning as individuals encounter more experiences allowing for decision making and resolving conflicts. Adolescents in several cultures seem more principled in their reasoning than adolescents in the United States. There is also evidence linking college education with higher levels of moral reasoning.

We now turn to an issue that has divided several investigators regarding Kohlberg's methods and his theory of moral reasoning. Researchers have debated whether Kohlberg's method and system treats female moral reasoning unfairly. I have already mentioned Gilligan's argument with Kohlberg over how his system calculated female moral reasoning. We now turn to a review of her challenge to Kohlberg.

Carol Gilligan's Challenge to Kohlberg

Carol Gilligan is on the faculty at Harvard University and worked closely with Kohlberg on several projects (Gilligan, Kohlberg, Lerner, & Belenky, 1971; Kohlberg & Gilligan, 1971). For several years, she had an office in the Center for Moral Development and Moral Education, which was directed by Kohlberg.

In the late 1970s and early 1980s, Gilligan (1977, 1982) began to question in print the pertinence to females of Kohlberg's theory of moral development. She became particularly concerned that (*a*) people respond quite differently about real dilemmas than about hypothetical dilemmas, (*b*) women use different reasoning principles (care and compassion, rather than justice) when reasoning about moral issues, and (*c*) Kohlberg's scoring system relegates females to, at best, stage 3 moral development. We will look at each of these points in turn.

Hypothetical versus Real Dilemmas

Gilligan (1977) emphasized that the significant difference between **hypothetical** and **real dilemmas** is that people only face real consequences when reasoning about real dilemmas. Hypothetical dilemmas present abstract conditions unrelated to life and segregated from truth.

Gilligan's challenge to Kohlberg on this issue began with the evidence she obtained from a study of pregnant women's reasoning about a real dilemma they faced—whether to have an abortion. This sociomoral dilemma forced pregnant women to face real consequences and to consider the conflict regarding self and the needs of others. By bringing this conflict into sharp focus, abortion made females come to terms with their own femininity and with responsibility for their own actions.

Male and Female Principles of Reasoning

Gilligan contended that Kohlberg's notions of the higher stages of moral reasoning exclusively emphasize values traditionally considered masculine (for example, detachment, abstraction, and impersonality); and relegate to stage 3 values traditionally considered feminine (such as caring for the welfare of others, compassion, and attachment). Gilligan believed that Kohlberg undervalued the **interpersonal component** in women's moral judgments, thereby preventing the **feminine voice** in moral reasoning from being heard (Gilligan, 1977).

This issue was highlighted for Gilligan in her study of women's reasoning about abortion. Of course, abortion is a sociomoral experience men cannot have, one unique to women. It challenges women to reconcile the competing demands of compassion and autonomy, and of virtue and power. In Gilligan's frame of reference, the sociomoral experiences of pregnancy and abortion provide a new perspective whereby a female faces the fundamental moral dilemma of hurting another.

The dilemma for women, said Gilligan, is feminine traits, such as compassion, attachment, and caring for the welfare of others are considered in Kohlberg's system to be deficits for mature moral reasoning based on the principles of justice. However, Gilligan acknowledged that Kohlberg was open to females' achieving higher stages of moral development, as long as they got beyond relying on compassion and care as moral principles.

A Scoring System Unfair to Females

Gilligan (1977) reserved special criticism for Kohlberg's scoring system, specifically its undervaluing interpersonal understanding of what is moral and its ignoring the sociomoral interpersonal experiences that enable females to make a transition from stage 3 to stage 4. She admitted that in a study she conducted with Kohlberg and two other colleagues (Gilligan et al., 1971), high school girls gave moral responses at the stage 3 level, whereas the boys usually gave responses one stage higher (Gilligan, 1977). However, she attributed these findings to a flaw in the method of scoring female responses, a flaw that made researchers deaf to the special language females use when reasoning about morality. In short, Gilligan maintained Kohlberg's system was insensitive to the **different voice** women use in moral reasoning and classified their reasoning as immature (Kohlberg, 1977).

Gilligan conducted three studies in her efforts to differentiate the masculine and feminine voices that speak about morality. One study dealt with college students' images of violence, another study dealt with notions of rights and responsibilities across the life span, and a third study dealt with reasoning about abortion. I will give brief synopses of the first two mentioned and detailed discussion of the abortion decision study.

In the study of college students' images of violence, Gilligan and a colleague (Pollak & Gilligan, 1982) noted significant gender differences in stories males and females wrote about a picture of a man and a woman sitting by a river. A total of 138 students participated in the study—88 males and 50 females. Whereas more than 20% of the males wrote stories depicting violence—physical or sexual assault, murder, or suicide—none of the females wrote stories with any violent themes. Gilligan and her colleague wondered whether the picture represented danger to males because it suggested intimacy. Subsequent analyses intimated males project violence into scenes of interpersonal attachments, whereas females depict violence in scenes of competition and achievement. These gender differences suggest male and female voices speak differently about issues of attachment and competition.

In the study about rights and responsibilities, Gilligan (1982) studied 72 males and 72 females who were matched on several demographic variables, such as age, education level, and socioeconomic status. The design was cross-sectional; there were 8 males and 8 females at each of the nine points in the life arc: ages 6–9, 11, 15, 19, 22, 25–27, 33, 45, and 60. She collected data on her subjects' ideas about morality, life experiences with moral dilemmas, and reasoning about hypothetical dilemmas. The females indicated situational conditions influenced how to decide when there were conflicts between individual rights and personal responsibilities.

Whereas males expressed concern over interfering with the rights of other people, females expressed that the responsibility of helping others takes precedence over the chance of failing to prevent harm.

Gilligan's (1977) study of abortion decisions involved 29 women who were referred to her by agencies providing pregnancy counseling and abortion services. The women participated in Gilligan's study for various reasons; some came to gain more understanding about whether to keep or abort their fetuses, some came to help researchers interested in how women reason about abortion, and some came in response to their counselors' concerns over multiple abortions.

It was from the responses to the abortion study that Gilligan (1977) first suggested women's moral reasoning develops using a different voice and separate language than used by men. The women's language involved conflicting themes of selfishness and responsibility. Such themes indicate moral concerns about caring for others and avoiding hurting others.

With themes of selfishness and responsibility heard over and over in the reasoning of her 29 female subjects, Gilligan believed she had the key to solve the puzzle of why Kohlberg's system typically placed adult women at stage 3 moral development. Kohlberg simply did not recognize that men and women approach moral reasoning differently and that members of each gender achieve fulfillment in their moral development, but in a different sequence.

Gilligan proposed a separate sequence of female moral development. Gilligan's female sequence is cognitive-developmental in nature and follows a stage format. However, in no way does it substantively match Kohlberg's understanding of the development of moral reasoning.

In Gilligan's system, female moral reasoning extends over three levels, with two transition periods. This sequence is presented in Table 5-3. At level 1, the woman's

TABLE 5-3 ■ Comparison of Gilligan's and Kohlberg's Models for the Development of Female Moral Reasoning

GILLIGAN		KOHLBERG	
Level 1	Orientation to individual survival	**Stage 1**	Obey authority and avoid punishment
1st Transition	From selfishness to responsibility	**Stage 2**	Serve one's own interests
Level 2	Goodness as self-sacrifice	**Stage 3**	Protect shared feelings, agreements, and expectations
2nd Transition	From goodness to truth	**Stage 4**	Maintain the social order
Level 3	The morality of nonviolence	**Stage 5**	Arrive at mutually agreed upon standards that provide the greatest benefit to all
		Stage 6*	Live by self-chosen, logically consistent principles all humanity should follow

*Stage 6 is no longer part of the Kohlberg system except as a hypothesis.

SOURCE: Reprinted by permission of the publishers from *In a Different Voice: Psychological Theory and Women's Development,* by Carol Gilligan, Cambridge, Mass.: Harvard University Press. Copyright © 1982 by Carol Gilligan.

Voices in Gilligan's Model of Moral Reasoning

Gilligan (1977, 1982) provides glimpses into the decision making of women considering abortion. Short excerpts of their responses at each level and transition phase in Gilligan's model will illustrate what Gilligan meant about the qualitative differences in their moral reasoning and her ideas about a progression in the development of the feminine voice.

LEVEL 1:
Orientation to Individual Survival
"An eighteen-year-old, asked what she thought when she found herself pregnant, replies: 'I really didn't think anything except that I didn't want it . . . . I wasn't ready for it, and next year will be my last year and I want to go to school'" (Gilligan, 1977, p. 492; 1982, p.75).

FIRST TRANSITION:
From Selfishness to Responsibility
"What I want to do is to have the baby, but what I feel I should do which is what I need to do, is have an abortion right now, because sometimes what you want isn't right. Sometimes what is necessary comes before what you want, because it might not always lead to the right thing" (Gilligan, 1977, p. 494; 1982, p. 77).

LEVEL 2:
Goodness as Self-Sacrifice
"I don't know what choices are open to me; it is either to have it or the abortion; these are the choices open to me. . . . I think what confuses me is it is a choice of either hurting myself or hurting other people around me. What is more important? If there could be a happy medium, it would be fine, but there isn't. It is either hurting someone on this side or hurting myself" (Gilligan, 1977, p. 496; 1982, p. 80).

SECOND TRANSITION:
From Goodness to Truth
"I think in a way I am selfish for one thing, and very emotional, very . . . and I think that I am a very real person and an understanding person and I can handle life situations fairly well, so I am basing a lot of it on my ability to do the things that I feel are right and best for me and whoever I am involved with. I

moral judgments are completely self-centered and oriented to personal survival. Prior to entering level 2, a woman makes a transition by discovering the salience of the principles of responsibility; that is, a woman moves from self-centered attachment to attachment to others. At level 2, the woman becomes concerned for others' needs and equates goodness with self-sacrifice. Caring for others and protecting them become clear themes in female moral reasoning at this point. Prior to entering level 3, a woman begins linking responsibility for self to responsibility for others, and bases her notion of responsibility on principles of honesty and fairness. At level 3, the woman begins to use principles of nonviolence to reason about moral dilemmas and views caring as a universal, ethical obligation.

Responses to Gilligan

Gilligan's manifesto on the different voice females use in moral reasoning has attracted attention, praise and support. Female college students have told me they recognize themselves in Gilligan's 1982 book, *In a Different Voice: Psychological* think I was very fair to myself about the decision, and I really think that I have been truthful, not hiding anything, bringing out all the feelings involved. I feel it is a good decision and an honest one, a real decision" (Gilligan, 1977, p. 500).

LEVEL 3:
The Morality of Nonviolence
"Well, the pros for having the baby are all the admiration that you would get from being a single woman, alone, martyr, struggling, having the adoring love of the beautiful Gerber baby. Just more of a home life than I have had in a long time, and that basically was it, which is pretty fantasyland. It is not very realistic. Cons against having the baby: it was going to hasten what is looking to be the inevitable end of the relationship with the man I am presently with. I was going to have to go on welfare, my parents were going to hate me for the rest of my life, I was going to lose a really good job that I have, I would lose a lot of independence. Solitude. And I would have to be put in a position of asking help from a lot of people a lot of the time. Cons against having the abortion is having to face up to the guilt.

And pros for having the abortion are I would be able to handle my deteriorating relationship with [the father] with a lot more capability and a lot more responsibility for him and for myself. And I would not have to go through the realization that for the next twenty-five years of my life I would be punishing myself for being foolish enough to get pregnant again and forcing myself to bring up a kid just because I did this. Having to face the guilt of a second abortion seemed like, not exactly, well, exactly the lesser of the two evils but also the one that would pay off for me personally in the long run because by looking at why I am pregnant again and subsequently have decided to have a second abortion, I have to face up to some things about myself" (Gilligan, 1977, p. 505).

(Excerpted from Gilligan, Carol, "In a Different Voice: Women's Conception of the Self and Morality," *Harvard Educational Review,* 47:4, pp. 481–517. Copyright © 1977 by the President and Fellows of Harvard College. All rights reserved. Reprinted by permission).

Theory and Women's Development. There is a power to such intuitive recognition, and I take writings able to evoke self-recognition seriously.

Gilligan's views have also attracted skepticism. A major criticism is that she conducted no carefully designed tests of her hypothesis that females employ a different voice in moral reasoning. She presented enlightening case studies but never carried out longitudinal research to test her views. Unlike Kohlberg, for instance, Gilligan identifies no time lines or age norms for the appearance of the levels and transitions she suggested mark the development of feminine reasoning in moral matters.

In response to Gilligan's criticism that Kohlberg's approach is biased against females, I would point out that gender bias could stem from the characteristics of Kohlberg's initial sample, which was exclusively male. Results from an all male sample cannot be generalized to females without some problems of misrepresentation. Unless investigators include females in moral reasoning research, inferences regarding female moral development are not valid. Ironically, because Gilligan has almost exclusively studied only females, she has no real means of concluding males reason differently than females about real dilemmas. We now look at an assessment of 79 studies that included both males and females.

Walker's review of gender bias in studies using Kohlberg's system. Lawrence Walker (1984) analyzed 79 studies that looked at the moral reasoning of males and females in three age-groups: (*a*) childhood and early adolescence, (*b*) late adolescence and young adulthood, and (*c*) adulthood. Each study used Kohlberg's approach and scoring system. Walker wished to determine if gender differences in moral reasoning are consistent across age-groups.

Walker (1984) found 31 studies dealing with moral reasoning in childhood and early adolescence that included both males and females. Upon analyzing these studies, he concluded that gender differences in moral reasoning at this stage of life are rare. He noted that when investigators did report differences, females were considered more mature in their moral reasoning than males (Walker, 1984).

Walker found 35 studies dealing with moral reasoning in late adolescence and young adulthood. While gender differences were reported in some studies, Walker (1984) contended such findings were confounded by cultural barriers that hindered females from decision-making role opportunities; Walker referred specifically to studies conducted in Islamic cultures. He attributed the findings of gender differences to impoverished sociomoral experiences, not to inherent sex differences. Overall, however, Walker said it was rare to find studies that reported gender differences in moral reasoning during late adolescence and young adulthood.

Thirteen studies examined moral reasoning of adults. The majority of these studies found similar numbers of men and women operating with stage 3 or stage 4 reasoning principles. Although gender differences were mentioned in some of the studies, Walker (1984) again noted that other factors intervened to produce these results. For instance, males in business careers had significantly different sociomoral experiences due to educational and work opportunities not available to homemakers. Additionally, cohort issues were clearly at play; older adults' responses were much more gender specific than the responses of younger adults (Walker, 1984).

When studies included adult men and women from similar occupational and educational backgrounds, Walker (1984) said no differences in moral reasoning could be found between males and females. An issue here is how society impedes women from advancing in education and careers, and this issue speaks directly to Kohlberg's contention that moral development depends on sociomoral role-taking opportunities. Impoverished sociomoral experiences produce lower stages of moral reasoning, whereas qualitatively rich sociomoral experiences produce higher stages of moral reasoning in both males and females (Walker, 1984).

Walker (1984) found no support for the assertion that Kohlberg's system relegates females to stage 3 moral reasoning while men proceed to higher stages. He also commented on the difficulty of publishing in major journals when a study reports non-significant findings. He wondered how many researchers had filed away studies that found no gender differences in moral reasoning.

Walker (1984) asked some intriguing questions, such as why people continue to believe that Kohlberg's system discriminates against females when so little evidence supports such a position. He also wondered what sociomoral experiences are needed to facilitate moral development and whether these experiences could be made part of an education program.

Baumrind's response to Walker.   Walker's (1984) study did not go unchallenged. Diana Baumrind (1986) criticized him on four counts: (*a*) he used age periods other than adulthood, (*b*) his statistical methods were improper, (*c*) he accorded the concept sociomoral experiences practical meaning without acknowledging the logical implications of the concept, and (*d*) her own data refuted Walker's conclusions. We take up each criticism in turn.

Baumrind (1986) asserted that only data on adults are relevant to a study of gender bias in Kohlberg's method because the accusation against Kohlberg stemmed from disproportionate numbers of males at the higher stages of moral reasoning. The higher stages (4 and 5) are considered open only to adults, due to cognitive and experiential factors beyond the capabilities of children and adolescents.

Baumrind (1986) noted that data from children and adolescents that indicate girls are more advanced than boys in moral reasoning can easily be explained. According to Baumrind, females develop more quickly than males during middle childhood and adolescence, and this accelerated development would produce higher moral reasoning scores for females.

Baumrind (1986) also criticized Walker for using statistics incorrectly. Such a charge, if true, sends shudders through researchers. What can be more embarrassing than commiting fundamental errors with basic tools?

Basically, Baumrind (1986) said Walker took ordinal data and used statistical procedures that require interval data. Let me give an example to explain her criticism. **Ordinal data** are ranked. Our nation has institutionalized the use of ordinal data in polls that rank college football and basketball teams. **Interval data** have equal distances between units of measure. Our nation has institutionalized the use of interval data in daily stock market reports.

To illustrate the difference between ordinal and interval data, consider the following examples. The ordinal data of one poll might identify the top five college football teams as Washington, Colorado, Miami, Notre Dame, and Texas, but the difference between the first and second rank is not the same as the difference between the second and the third rank, the third and fourth rank, etc. You cannot conclude that the team ranked number three is twice as good as the team ranked number six. The data used to report on the Dow Jones Industrial Index are interval data. The interval between 2000 and 2001 is the same as the interval between 2001 and 2002. You can conclude that a Dow Jones Industrial Index of 3000 is three times as much as an Index of 1000.

Baumrind (1986) said Walker had ordinal data, similar to a college football poll, but treated the data as though they were as precise as interval data, as in the Dow Jones Index. She said his conclusions were based on statistics that are valid with interval data but invalid with ordinal data.

Baumrind (1986) criticized both Walker and Kohlberg for not comprehending the serious challenge to the theory of moral reasoning presented by the notion of sociomoral experiences. The challenge came in identifying a critical test of the theory.

A **critical test of a theory** is a set of circumstances that, if they do not occur as predicted, indicate the theory is false. The most famous critical test in modern physics is Einstein's prediction of how a star would influence light passing near it. When photographs of a solar eclipse of the sun indicated that light was bent as Einstein had predicted, his theory of relativity was considered to have been established as true.

Baumrind (1986) contended that the idea of sociomoral experiences should enable Kohlberg to identify how much experience is needed to reach a new stage of moral reasoning. She noted that a person in postconventional morality needs to have attained formal operations and to have incorporated sufficient sociomoral experiences. Baumrind's criticism is that neither Kohlberg nor Walker spell out the nature of the relationship between cognitive development and sociomoral experiences. Baumrind contends that they must specify what threshold is required to achieve a new stage of moral reasoning.

I fail to see the power of this criticism. The assertion that a critical mass of development and experience is necessary for changes in moral reasoning to occur is Baumrind's idea. Neither Kohlberg nor Walker believe some critical mass of cognitive development and sociomoral experience pushes one to a new stage of moral reasoning. They do refer to types of experiences, specifically, those that require the person to make decisions. Kohlberg also indicates that there is a one stage up phenomenon, which dictates that a person cannot incorporate new perspectives that exceed current use of moral principles by more than one stage of reasoning.

Finally, Baumrind (1986) challenged Walker using data from one of her own studies conducted with 164 nine-year-olds (78 girls, 86 boys) and their parents. There were 158 mothers, who averaged 38 years of age, and 145 fathers, who averaged 41 years of age. The study used Kohlberg's method for gathering data and used a version of Kohlberg's scoring system that preceded the revised system.

Baumrind (1986) reported that adult males were significantly more often in postconventional moral reasoning stages than the females. However, unlike Gilligan (1977, 1982), who charged Kohlberg's system with limiting females to stage 3 reasoning, Baumrind said her adult female subjects were placed more often in stage 4 than any other stage. She considered this finding an argument against Kohlberg's (1969) notion that women fixate at stage 3, but did not discuss how her findings relate to Gilligan's charges.

In her study, Baumrind did not control for educational differences that have greatly favored males over females. Baumrind (1986) said it begged the question to control for education. Controlling for educational differences, in her eyes, would leave out a significant factor whereby discrimination functions against females and for males.

Walker's response to Baumrind.   Walker (1986) could hardly be expected to ignore Baumrind's charges. First, he noted that she had misrepresented the very intent of his article. Rather than an attempt to confirm that gender differences are nonexistent in moral reasoning, Walker's study was an attempt to see whether empirical data from a variety of sources indicated moral reasoning develops differently for males and females.

Baumrind challenged the very notion of sociomoral experiences, but Walker considered these experiences stretch a person to consider new perspectives and to rethink what is morally correct.

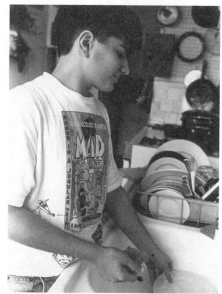

Second, Walker challenged Baumrind's accusation that his use of a specific statistical test was invalid. He claimed that the test he had used was more powerful than the one Baumrind proposed, but also said he recalculated his data using the test she suggested and found only a minor, nonsignificant change resulted.

Third, Walker (1986) commented on the criticism that the only valid age period to investigate when studying sex differences in moral reasoning is adulthood. He asked why gender bias at younger age periods would not matter. If Baumrind argues that Kohlberg's theory is pervasively biased against how females reason about moral issues, Walker wondered why findings of gender differences would not occur before adulthood and why there would be no interest in showing whether such biases do exist.

Fourth, he took up Baumrind's challenge about sociomoral experiences. Rather than a serious challenge to the theory of the development of moral reasoning, in Walker's estimation, the relationship between cognitive development and sociomoral exposure was one of the most compelling aspects of Kohlberg's position. Walker (1986) emphasized that one of the major factors promoting change is being exposed to emotional and personal experiences involving personal responsibility and decision making, which enable a person to appreciate new perspectives, and which induce a person to rethink what is the morally correct thing to do. In Walker's assessment, it is not the amount or quantity of exposure but, rather, the quality of the experience that matters. In short, what matters is whether exposure to life experiences encourages an individual to reflect on and discuss moral conflicts and issues. The keys to development are opportunities to make decisions, take new perspectives, share in responsibility, and engage in self-reflection. The key does not seem to be to reach a threshold magnitude in cognitive operations and sociomoral exposure.

Personal reactions to the Baumrind-Walker debate.   I think the evidence supports Walker's analysis. I find him persuasive in his arguments that both males and females achieve similar levels of complexity in moral reasoning.

The appeal to sociomoral experiences that stretch one's reasoning strikes me as very convincing. It fits well with the work of other researchers whom we have studied (Erikson, 1963; Marcia, 1964, 1966, 1980; Offer, 1969; Piaget, 1972) and with researchers coming up later in this chapter. However, evidence suggests that sociomoral experiences differ for males and females. The gender intensification hypothesis and personal beliefs about intelligence could readily restrict females from role-taking opportunities made available for males.

The Walker (1984, 1986) and Baumrind (1986) essays were indirect assessments of Gilligan's view that Kohlberg's method is biased against females, not frontal attacks on her position or defenses of it. The target is Kohlberg's theory and whether it is gender-biased. To the extent that I accept Walker's reasoning, I consider Gilligan's views to be suspect.

Personal reaction to Gilligan's position.   I believe Gilligan's argument strikes to the heart of feminism, a worldview I wish to uphold. My concern, however, is that by intimating that there are different voices of male and female moral reasoning, Gilligan's argument actually concedes that men and women reason using different principles in other areas as well. Following Gilligan's ideas, we would conclude that because men and women use different reasoning principles, men and women develop qualitatively different cognitive skills. What would be the logical outcome of such an argument? In short, I think Gilligan's views provide unintended, but powerful, positions to support prejudices against feminine competencies and potential in mathematics, logic, analysis, and science. If females' different voice engages reasoning principles so different than the principles males use, perhaps counseling girls against taking advanced mathematics and science courses is prudent. I consider such counsel to be preposterous, and I rebel at such a notion not only as injurious and prejudiced against my own daughter but as insidious against the development of all females.

Other scholars have let me know they consider my views on this matter untenable or, to use one person's characterization, "absurd." Arguments raised against my assessment of Gilligan's different voices emphasize that Gilligan considered women gain their different voices through socialization.

Frankly, this reference to socialization strikes me as a shaky foundation for a rebuttal to my concerns. We could turn the socialization argument around and say that socialization of males gives them an advantage in the use of reasoning principles needed to succeed in the analytic worlds of science and mathematics. Are we to rail against socialization that gives males an edge in the analytic skills of math and science, but revel in the socialization that gives females an edge in the interpersonal skills of nurturance and empathy? We need more balanced development in male and female socialization, not the dichotomy of Gilligan's different voices, regardless of the source of the different voices.

We have looked at other people's reactions to Gilligan on Kohlberg's theory and method. What did Kohlberg think of her arguments?

Kohlberg's reactions to Gilligan.   Kohlberg insisted that empirical evidence from several studies has demonstrated female responses to his traditional hypothetical dilemmas could be scored by his revised system (1987) without sex differences emerging in stage assignment. He also noted that moral dilemmas involving interpersonal relations and social justice tap the fundamental issues underlying moral reasoning (Colby & Kohlberg, 1987).

Kohlberg also noted Gilligan's central concern that by focusing on the fundamental importance of justice, he had overlooked the principles of compassion and responsibility. While it is true, Kohlberg said, that his interview format used hypothetical dilemmas posing conflicts over rights, people's responses to these dilemmas can concentrate on justice or on a variety of other principles, including compassion and responsibility. All these concepts define what is moral, and Kohlberg saw them as part of the breadth his concept of morality possessed. He emphasized that reasoning about morality incorporates more than the principle of justice (Colby & Kohlberg, 1987).

The Importance of the Kohlberg-Gilligan Debate   The extensiveness of the debate over Kohlberg's and Gilligan's claims about moral reasoning may strike you as puzzling. You may be wondering, what are the issues at stake here? Why would people care so much about how moral reasoning develops? As one student questioned, "Does any of this really matter?" Let's review what is at stake.

First, a major issue at stake is the very notion of whose explanation of moral reasoning corresponds to the actual development noticed in people. Does Kohlberg's approach adequately portray both male and female development, or is his position biased against females? If his system is biased, then actions people take on the basis of Kohlberg's ideas can damage the notion of equal opportunity for men and women.

Does Gilligan's approach adequately portray female development, or is her position biased as well? If her system is biased, it could mistakenly lead people to overlook aspects of moral reasoning in which males and females do engage.

Second, there is the difference between hypothetical and actual moral decision making. Many people intuitively understand that individuals give different answers when they have something personally at stake (as in a real-life dilemma). In fact, when adolescents were asked to identify the moral dilemmas in their lives, their stories went beyond Kohlberg's focus on issues of authority and obeying the law (Yussen, 1977). Results obtained on actual moral situations, along with Gilligan's emphasis on real versus hypothetical dilemmas, provide some compelling reasons to question the applicability of the very data Kohlberg's system obtains.

Third, a point linked to the second issue, is the realization that moral reasoning in Kohlberg's system may have little connection to moral action. A college student may know the postconventional principles that come to bear when faced with a real situation (for instance, deciding whether to leave the scene of an accident), but may act out of self-interest when actually confronted with that situation. For instance, he may know it is morally wrong to leave the scene of an accident, but he leaves anyway in order to avoid being given a ticket or, worse, arrested. Whether Gilligan's system offers a solution to this quandary is not clear. A woman may reason about abortion using what Gilligan's system calls level 3 principles but act out of level 1 or 2 principles.

Fourth, an issue that made Gilligan's system popular in many circles was her rationale for differences between male and female experiences. As mentioned earlier, several female college students who have read Gilligan's writings remark that they find themselves portrayed there. She has spoken eloquently to many females (and to some males as well), and because of this support, her views have to be taken seriously and evaluated. Thus, her criticisms of Kohlberg have to be evaluated as well.

Although the debate between Kohlberg and Gilligan could stay at a philosophical level, Walker decided to test empirically their ideas about moral reasoning. We look at this study next.

A Longitudinal Study Comparing Kohlberg and Gilligan

Walker (1989) conducted a longitudinal study that examined both Gilligan's and Kohlberg's constructs about moral reasoning. Walker's project studied 80 family triads (mother, father, and child)—a total of 240 individuals—over a two-year period. When the youths entered the project, they were in either first, fourth, seventh, or tenth grade. At the conclusion, they were in third, seventh, tenth, or twelfth grade. Only 7 individuals failed to complete the study: 2 family triads and 1 twelfth grade boy. Thus, Walker had longitudinal data on 233 people to analyze. The very high retention rate (97.1%) was remarkable. Longitudinal studies commonly report a loss of between 10% and 20% of the subjects by the end of the studies.

Walker's (1989) intent was to examine age trends and sex differences in (a) Gilligan's two proposed moral orientations (for males, justice and rights and for females, caring and responsiveness), (b) Kohlberg's four proposed moral orientations (normative, fairness, utilitarianism, and perfectionist), (c) individual reasoning about hypothetical versus real dilemmas, and (d) relations between Gilligan's and Kohlberg's orientations.

Walker (1989) used three hypothetical dilemmas from Kohlberg's structured interview. Once the individuals responded to the hypothetical dilemmas, they were asked to select and review a dilemma from their own lives. Highly reliable content analyses (94% inter-rater agreement) of each real-life dilemma identified whether it revolved around a personal or impersonal moral conflict. Personal dilemmas involve relationships of a sustained nature with one or more individuals, while impersonal dilemmas involve issues unique to the person being interviewed, people whom the subject did not know well, or social institutions.

Scoring procedures for the hypothetical dilemmas came from Kohlberg's revised system (Colby & Kohlberg, 1987). Walker (1989) slightly modified the system for the reviews of the real-life dilemmas. He calculated weighted average scores (WAS) for reasoning about hypothetical and real dilemmas. He consulted the Kohlberg manual to calculate Kohlberg's moral orientations. He calculated Gilligan's moral orientations by using procedures developed by Nona Lyons (1982, 1983) who had written a doctoral dissertation on the subject.

Walker's (1989) findings supported Kohlberg's theory of an invariant stage sequence in the development of moral reasoning. Not a single person skipped a stage, and only 14 (6%) reverted to an earlier stage of moral reasoning. A nearly equal number of males (8) and females (6) regressed to an earlier stage of moral reasoning.

All age-groups significantly increased their use of moral reasoning principles. However, while there were highly significant effects for age as well as effects for time, there were no gender differences in moral reasoning.

Walker's (1989) data did not support Gilligan's claim that males and females reason from different moral orientations. The people in his study used multiple orientations—regardless of age or gender. In fact, at the second interview, subjects were prone to reason about their real-life dilemmas with a different orientation than the one they had used initially.

Males and females equally used both of Gilligan's proposed moral orientations on the hypothetical dilemmas. At the follow-up interviews, the ninth grade boys and girls used the caring and response orientation when reasoning about the hypothetical dilemmas but not the real-life dilemmas. Adults demonstrated gender differences on the real-life dilemmas, with females using the caring and response orientation more than males (59.6% to 50.2%). However, these data indicate that half of the males used a moral orientation that Gilligan claimed identifies the unique female voice in moral matters. Males used Kohlberg's moral orientations to the same extent that the females did. Such a finding undermines assertions about gender differences and moral orientation.

In addition, Walker (1989) found a clear association between Kohlberg's moral orientations and stages of moral reasoning. Specifically, both normative and utilitarian orientations were characteristic of lower stage reasoning, and fairness and perfectionism were more typical of higher stage reasoning.

One irony in Walker's (1989) study is the finding about the different approaches taken to hypothetical and real dilemmas. Gilligan (1977, 1982) had predicted that real-life dilemmas would allow the different voice of a woman to speak, particularly when the woman had to make a choice effecting her sense of self. However, it was not Gilligan's typology of moral orientations that distinguished how Walker's subjects handled either hypothetical or real-life dilemmas. Rather, it was Kohlberg's typology of four orientations that supported Gilligan's prediction regarding reasoning about real versus hypothetical dilemmas. In other words, Gilligan's justice and rights orientation and her caring and response orientation were used by all subjects in Walker's study, regardless of the kind of dilemma, whereas Kohlberg's normative and fairness orientations were applied to hypothetical dilemmas, and his utilitarianism and perfectionism orientations were used to reason about real-life dilemmas. Walker emphasized that Kohlberg's moral orientations seemed clearly influenced by context, while Gilligan's orientations seemed both context-free and gender-blind.

Walker's (1989) final conclusions about orientations and moral reasoning are intriguing. Gilligan had argued that females, oriented more toward caring and responsiveness, are consistently placed at stage 3 in Kohlberg's system. She also argued the male orientation of moral reasoning, which leans toward justice and rights, enabled them to be placed at higher stages in Kohlberg's system. However, in his analysis of his longitudinal data, Walker found that individuals who used the responsiveness orientation were judged to be reasoning at higher stages of moral development.

Another study confirmed Walker's (1989) findings regarding Gilligan's assertions about male and female orientations to moral reasoning. Maureen Ford and Carol Lowery (1986) studied the moral reasoning of over 200 college students (101 males, 101 females). The students described three moral conflicts in their lives and then, using a seven-point Likert-scale version of Lyons's (1982) coding scheme, Ford and Lowery assessed the extent to which students used justice or care when they reasoned about these conflicts. They said their results gave support to Gilligan; women used the principle of caring more often than the men, and men used the justice principle more frequently than the women. However, later in their article, they acknowledged that the gender differences were statistically nonsignificant. In research terms, "statistically nonsignificant" differences are the equivalent of no differences at all. In Chapter 1, I referred to inferences based on nonsignificant findings as **wishful thinking**.

We now turn to another facet of changing social reasoning during adolescence—the transformation of self-consciousness, which increases in early adolescence, into greater self-assurance and awareness of others. We turn to the ideas of David Elkind.

EGOCENTRISM AS AN ADOLESCENT CHARACTERISTIC: THE VIEWS OF DAVID ELKIND

David Elkind, a professor at Tufts University, has written several scholarly and some popular books on children and adolesents. He has called attention to the damages inflicted on children who are forced to grow up quickly (Elkind, 1981, 1984). He predicts that the next generation of parents will become less involved with their children and that an incorrect image of children will emerge; they will be falsely seen to possess competency beyond their means, an image that will be used to defend parental neglect (Elkind, 1987).

Elkind was instrumental in making Piaget accessible to Americans, who found Piaget's essays presented formidable challenges. Of chief interest to this chapter on social and moral reasoning is Elkind's extension of Piaget's notion of egocentrism (Piaget, 1929). By **egocentrism**, Piaget meant children lack the cognitive ability to understand someone else's viewpoint or to picture a situation from any perspective but their own.

Elkind (1979) noted that egocentrism takes on progressively new forms as youths outgrow earlier forms of thought invalidated by social experiences. To paraphrase Elkind, individuals form egocentric concepts because their abilities to think about themselves and the world outstrip their abilities to evaluate their thoughts. As an example, young children in a moving car watch the moon and think it is following them.

Elkind proposes that the emergence of formal operations produces a new type of egocentric thinking. These new mental powers enable adolescents to think about what they and other people think and feel about their feelings. And yet, early adolescents typically fail to act on these powers because, preoccupied with changes in their physical appearances and emotions, they are not interested in testing whether they are correct about other people's thoughts and feelings.

Two categories of egocentric assumptions dominate an early adolescent's views about self and other people. The first is an assumption about the adolescent's role in the world; Elkind (1967) called this assumption the imaginary audience. The second assumption has to do with the early adolescent's extreme notions of uniqueness; Elkind called this assumption the adolescent's personal fable. Elkind said adolescents tend to form exaggerated beliefs about their uniqueness. They begin to formulate a personal fable and consider their experiences to be totally unlike what anyone else has experienced or can understand.

The Imaginary Audience

Elkind's **imaginary audience** concept refers to early adolescents' tendency to think they are the center of everyone else's world. They go through a period of time operating as if they are on stage, with people constantly observing and judging them. Elkind maintained that early adolescents continually construct such audiences in their imaginations, whether they expect others to admire or to criticize them. Consider this example: upon moving over 1,000 miles to a new town, an adolescent boy believed that everyone in his new school of over 1,200 students noticed him (while at the same time, he felt dreadfully alone) and that some boys would so want to be his friend that they would even follow him home to see where he lived.

Elkind (1967) suggested the imaginary audience assumption contributes to the self-consciousness noticed in early adolescents, who seem to believe that private thoughts are transferred to the consciousness of everyone else. For this reason, adolescents are concerned with feeling ashamed, exposed to the gaze and ridicule of others. The irony is that early adolescents assume peers are concentrating on them, while their peers place their age-mates in the same imaginary audience role.

The Personal Fable

The assumption of an imaginary audience occurs because early adolescents do not distinguish their thoughts and feelings from what others think and feel. At the same time, they begin to form exaggerated beliefs about their uniqueness, reaching almost mythical stature in their own minds. This conviction of special uniqueness becomes a **personal fable**, a story which [the adolescent] tells himself and which is not true" (Elkind, 1967, p. 1031).

Two common experiences of the personal fable are (a) the adolescent belief in immortality and (b) the idea that emotional experiences are totally unlike those felt by anyone else. Others have picked up on the immortality theme to describe adolescent risk taking as an expression of feeling invulnerable (Noppe & Noppe, 1991).

Note the difficult situation for the early adolescent who assumes an imaginary audience and a personal fable: no one understands, but everyone is paying attention, probably to criticize.

Adolescents grow out of this egocentrism. Elkind (1967) attributes this leaving egocentrism behind to the emergence of firmly established formal operations. First to go is the belief in an imaginary audience. Rather than an assumed reality, the imaginary audience becomes a hypothesis that the middle adolescent tests against social experience. These tests lead adolescents gradually to grasp that their concerns and interests differ from other people's.

It takes longer for a person to dismiss the assumption of utter uniqueness encompassed by the personal fable. Elkind thinks people get beyond their personal fable mythologies only when they establish intimacy with someone else. Thus, for Elkind, overcoming the assumption of a personal fable requires forming an identity and forming an intimate relation with another person.

Elkind uses Erikson's (1963) theory to explain how someone grows out of adolescent egocentrism. Specifically, by confronting the developmental task of intimacy, the adolescent deals with egocentric blocks to growth. By learning what is important to someone else—and understanding the importance in terms of the other person's experience—the adolescent overcomes the prison of a personal fable and the self-consciousness of always feeling the center of everyone else's attention.

We look next at an elaboration of adolescents' growing awareness of other people. Robert Selman claimed understanding the perspective of someone else is a matter of increased levels of social cognition.

INTERPERSONAL UNDERSTANDING AND LEVELS OF SOCIAL COGNITION: THE THEORY OF ROBERT SELMAN

Imagine a 12-year-old boy, called Fred, who has been getting into verbal and physical fights with classmates. These fights have escalated over the semester, and seem to occur with little or no provocation. What other boys accept as unintentional (for example, being bumped in the cafeteria line), Fred considers a deliberate assault when it happens to him.

Robert Selman, a psychologist at Harvard University, posed such a situation to introduce his theory of changes over time in interpersonal understanding (Selman, 1976). He said some theorists influenced by psychoanalysis would try to understand Fred's reactions by analyzing his defense mechanisms—for instance, displacing anger toward his father onto others.

Selman did not mention the plausible explanations social learning theorists would provide for aggressive behavior. This omission seemed unusual to me. Selman could have explained Fred's aggression by noting whether Fred had observed others whom he admired acting aggressively.

TABLE 5-4   **Domains and Issues in Selman's Interpersonal Understanding Interview**

FIRST DOMAIN: CONCEPTS ABOUT INDIVIDUALS	
Issues	Subjectivity, Self-Awareness, Personality, and Personality Change
Example	How and why do people change?
SECOND DOMAIN: CONCEPTS ABOUT FRIENDSHIP	
Issues	Formation of Friendships, Intimacy, Trust and Reciprocity, Jealousy, Resolving Conflicts, and theTermination of Friendships
Example	How do friends resolve problems?
THIRD DOMAIN: CONCEPTS ABOUT PEER-GROUP RELATIONS	
Issues	Formation of Peer Groups, Cohesion, Conformity, Rules, Decision Making and Organization, Leadership, and the Termination of Peer Groups
Example	What are the qualities of leadership in a group and the functions of leadership to a group?
FOURTH DOMAIN: CONCEPTS ABOUT PARENT-CHILD RELATIONS	
Issues	Formation of Parent-Child Relations, Emotional Ties, Obedience, Punishment, and Conflict Resolution
Example	What are the ideal qualities of parents?

SOURCE: From *The Growth of Interpersonal Understanding: Develomental and Clinical Analyses,* by R. L. Selman. Copyright © 1980 by Academic Press. Reprinted by permission.

As an alternative approach to understanding Fred, Selman suggested cognitive-developmental theory. This approach begins by attempting to understand Fred's perspective on the world, inquiring whether Fred can distinguish between intentional and unintentional behavior. In short, this approach assesses **social cognition**, or how the individual perceives social reality, determines the stage of interpersonal understanding the individual has achieved, and identifies the next stage in interpersonal understanding a person can achieve.

Similar to Kohlberg's assertions about issues around which moral reasoning is organized, Selman believes that interpersonal reasoning is organized basically in terms of 25 issues. Certain issues pertain to specific domains. These issues and the domains to which they pertain are identified in Table 5-4.

Selman's Means of Studying Social Cognition and Interpersonal Understanding

Selman studies social cognition and interpersonal understanding by interviewing children and adolescents about four **domains of interpersonal relations**: individuals, friendship, peer-group relations, and parent-child relations. Selman presents vignettes and uses open-ended questions to learn what the youths think about each domain. He instructs interviewers to elicit the youths' ideas about interpersonal relations by having them reflect on issues pertinent to the four domains.

Selman's vignettes always contain dilemmas. To better understand his approach, let's look at one of Selman's vignettes.

Charlene and Joanne have been good friends since they were five. Now they were in high school and Joanne was trying out for the school play. As usual she was nervous about how she had done, but Charlene was there to tell her she was very good and give her moral support. Still Joanne was worried that a new-comer in school would get the part. The new girl, Tina, came over to congratulate Joanne on her performance and then asked if she could join the girls for a snack. Right away Charlene and Tina seemed to hit it off very well. They talked about where Tina was from and the kinds of things she could do in her new school. Joanne, on the other hand, didn't seem to like Tina very well. She thought Tina was a little pushy, and maybe she was a bit jealous over all the attention Charlene was giving Tina.

When Tina left the other two alone, Joanne and Charlene arranged to get together on Saturday, because Joanne had a problem that she would like to talk over with Charlene. But later that day, Tina called Charlene and asked her to go to see a play on Saturday.

Charlene had a dilemma. She would have jumped at the chance to go with Tina, but she had already promised to see Joanne. Joanne might have understood and been happy that Charlene had the chance to go, or she might feel like she was losing her best friend when she really needed her (From *The Growth of Interpersonal Understanding: Developmental and Clinical Analyses,* by R. L. Selman., p. 332. Copyright © 1980 by Academic Press. Reprinted by permission).

Following this vignette, interviewers ask several questions to understand the adolescent's views on the six issues pertaining to the domain of friendship. For example, to discover what adolescents think about motives, Selman asks, "Why are friends important? Why does a person need a good friend?" To find out their ideas about closeness and intimacy, Selman asks, "What kinds of things can good friends talk about that other friends sometimes can't? What kinds of problems can they talk over?" To discover adolescents' perspectives on trust and reciprocity, Selman asks, "Is it important to do things for each other for a good friendship? Why?" and "What is trust anyway? Is it something more that just keeping secrets and paying back? Is there something more, something deeper to trust?" (Selman, 1980, pp. 323–324).

Selman also asks open-ended questions to help adolescents articulate their understandings of jealousy, conflict resolution, and the end of friendships. A question about jealousy is, "What does it mean to be jealous in a friendship?" A question about conflict resolution is, "Can people be friends, even if they are having arguments? How is that possible?" Finally, a question about the end of friendships is, "What does a person lose when they lose a good friend?" (Selman, 1980, p. 324).

Using vignettes that contain interpersonal dilemmas is reminiscent of Kohlberg's (1969, 1976, 1979; Colby & Kohlberg, 1987) method of using stories with moral dilemmas. The link is not coincidental. Selman worked closely with Kohlberg, acknowledged the influence of Kohlberg's thinking on his ideas, and modeled his approach on Kohlberg's interview method (Selman, 1980).

Piaget also had a significant influence on Selman. This influence is hardly surprising considering Kohlberg's heavy debt to Piaget and considering Selman's open advocacy of a cognitive developmental framework.

Selman appealed to Piaget's ideas of accommodation and assimilation to account for how change occurs in interpersonal understanding. Selman considered that adolescents change their social perspectives for one of two reasons: either the individual comes across external evidence that contradicts personal understanding of social reality, or the person becomes aware that his or her own values or beliefs are deficient. For the person to undergo change, however, the conceptual conflict cannot require thinking far above his or her current level of interpersonal understanding. In this regard, Selman seems to be working from a notion similar to Kohlberg's (1969) one stage up idea.

To clarify Selman's understanding of how social cognition changes, I will relate some stories adolescents told me about events that led them to change their social perspectives.

- A girl changed her sweeping belief that all teachers are to be trusted when a teacher began singling her our for criticism and ridicule in front of her classmates after she had dared to express opinions the teacher disliked.

- After his sister died in an accident, a boy learned who his real friends were when several classmates stopped talking to him while other individuals offered him their support and an attentive ear.

- A girl learned the importance of being careful when confiding in other people when someone she thought was her friend began to gossip about some very private information she had told the other girl in confidence.

- A boy who firmly believed that poor and homeless people are at fault for their troubles did some wrenching reappraisals when his family became homeless after his parents lost their jobs in the aerospace industry and could not find other work to pay their bills.

In these examples, the individuals encountered evidence that required a change in their perspectives. The evidence could not be ignored or denied, and the adolescents progressed to a level of social cognition that permitted them to assimilate the new information.

We now turn from how Selman studies social cognition and interpersonal understanding to what he says his findings indicate. We turn next to his notion of levels of interpersonal understanding.

Five Levels of Interpersonal Understanding

Selman postulates that the ability to understand the perspectives of others develops from fairly primitive understandings to complex, abstract, symbolic representations of social reality. This development comprises five qualitatively distinct levels of understanding people and relations between people.

The first level (what Selman terms level 0) is characterized by a youngster's confusion over physical appearances and psychological realities. This level is typical of children between the ages of 3 and 6, and seems strongly influenced by the Piagetian notion of preoperational thought. In level 0, a child might not understand a smiling stranger could mean to harm her. While a level 0 child understands the physical difference between herself and others, she is not able to understand that other people could interpret the same event differently than she (Selman, 1976, 1980).

The second level (what Selman calls level 1) is characterized by a child's clarity about the difference between physical and psychological realities. Selman attributes level 1 thinking to children between ages 5 and 9. According to Piaget, children enter concrete operations during these years. At level 1, a child should be able to dis-

Level 4 adolescents can realize interactions with friends involve "filler" conversations about trivial matters as well as empathic sharing of personal thoughts and ambitions.

tinguish between purposive and unintentional behavior, and understand that other people have hidden psychological lives as private as his or her own inner thoughts and feelings. Furthermore, while a level 1 child understands that others have subjective lives, he or she is limited in appreciating how people will react. As an example, a level 1 boy will choose a present because he likes it and assumes another child will feel the same way about the gift (Selman, 1976, 1980).

The third level (what Selman calls level 2) is characterized by a child's ability to mentally step outside oneself and take a look at his or her own thoughts and behavior. A level 2 child also realizes that other people reflect about their own thoughts and actions. Selman says children enter level 2 between the ages of 7 and 12. Level 2 requires concrete operational thinking. Level 2 children recognize that they and other people possess the ability to put themselves in someone else's shoes. At this level of perspective taking, children understand there is imprecision and ambiguity in knowing another person's thoughts and feelings (Selman, 1976, 1980).

The fourth level (what Selman calls level 3) is characterized by "a true third-person perspective" whereby individuals "simultaneously see themselves as both actors and objects, simultaneously acting and reflecting upon the effect s of action on themselves, reflecting upon the self in interaction with the self" (Selman, 1980, p. 39). This level emerges during early adolescence and may continue until age 15. An adolescent would have to reach formal operations to be in level 3. The level 3 adolescent knows that a complex mutuality marks social relationships. Using level 3 thinking, adolescent girls and boys can mentally step outside interpersonal interactions, consider the perspectives they have of others and the perspectives others have of them, and "see the need to coordinate reciprocal perspectives" if interpersonal relations are to be mutually satisfying (Selman, 1980, p. 39).

At the fifth level (what Selman calls level 4) individuals understand they and others are more complex than they can sometimes understand. Level 4 individuals recognize—at least tacitly—unconscious motives, attitudes, and reactions exist. Level 4 social understanding requires formal operations and emerges as early as age 12. Level 4 individuals possess in-depth beliefs about people; their concepts of interpersonal relations are abstract, complex, symbolic representations. Relationships are understood to extend from the superficial to the multidimensional. For example, a level 4 adolescent can realize interactions with friends involve "filler" conversations about trivial matters as well as intimate, empathic sharing of personal thoughts and ambitions. In addition, level 4 adolescents recognize that multiple factors, such as politics, the legal system, the economy, international affairs, and cultural customs, influence their social worlds.

Real-World Concerns and Applications   The real test of Selman's theory is whether it can be used in real-life settings, not only in controlled laboratory investigations. Selman has worked to extend his theory into real-life situations; going into the real world provides a means to apply his ideas and test their usefulness.

One application of Selman's ideas was a year-long study of eight early adolescents in a special program for youths with learning difficulties and severe emotional or behavioral problems, such as physical aggression and extreme anxiety (Jaquette, 1980). Daniel Jaquette (1980) observed the adolescents in 32 weekly class meetings. He focused on their social reasoning in three of the four interpersonal domains identified by Selman: individuals, friendship, and peer-group organization. Had he observed the adolescents with their families, he could have included the fourth domain, parent-child relations. He developed a complex system for recording and assessing data obtained in the class observations (Jaquette, 1980).

A methodological concern for Jaquette (1980) was how to identify when Selman's issues were at play. He decided to refer to the context within which responses were being made. The most frequently identified issues were self-awareness, group cohesion, conflict resolution, leadership, decision making, and organization.

The eight students showed a clear progression in interpersonal understanding over the first two-thirds of the school year and a marked regression over the final one-third. The growth in social reasoning was slow at first, probably due to the students' lack of familiarity with the methods used in the special school. The regression to earlier levels of social reasoning was strikingly attributable to the students' realization they would lose their special class once the school year ended (Jaquette, 1980).

The experiences of two students, Gary and Debbie, illustrate Jaquette's (1980) research findings. Gary was very intelligent and aware of social reality, but had difficulty with anger, which interfered with his progress. His level of social reasoning began to decline in the final third of the school year until, by the end, his reasoning was no different than it had been at the beginning of the year. Over the first 22 meetings, Debbie showed growth in social reasoning about individuals, friendship, and peer-group issues. However, her eventual decline was by far the most pronounced

One important aspect of social intelligence is **empathy** (the ability to understand the experiences of someone else from that person's point of view). Gerard Egan (1990) has distinguished between empathic understanding and empathic communication. **Empathic understanding** occurs when you comprehend how someone else is responding to an experience. For example, imagine you comprehend how an acquaintance feels after breaking up with her boyfriend. **Empathic communication** occurs when you express that comprehension to your friend. There are times when we appreciate how someone else feels but are at a loss for what to say to communicate that understanding.

The transition from empathic understanding to empathic communication is what several writers call the arousal of **prosocial behavior** (Aronfreed, 1968; Barnett, 1982; Hoffman, 1981, 1982) or **altruism** (Kanfer, 1979). Prosocial behavior, or altruism, involves actions taken on behalf of someone else. We recognize the truly exceptional feats of altruism in public figures who devote their lives to the service of others (a contemporary example is Mother Teresa, who works with the poor of Calcutta in India) and in the extraordinary, singular acts of heroism performed by individuals who endanger their lives to save others (fire fighters, for instance).

Selman's theory of interpersonal understanding postulates that social cognition occurs in an invariant, irreversible, universal sequence that leads to increased ability to understand how others perceive the world. Selman's ideas on interpersonal understanding help explain differences in empathic understanding and, perhaps, differences in assessing motives behind someone else's altruistic behavior (Barnett, 1987).

Unless a person has developed at least level 2 perspectives, even the most rudimentary empathic responses are impossible (Selman, 1980). Empathy requires an individual to differentiate between his or her thoughts and feelings and another person's thoughts and feelings. Empathy means I can put myself in someone else's shoes without losing sight of the difference between my experience and someone else's (Rogers, 1961).

Altruism is behavior generated by empathic understanding, but empathic understanding does not always lead to altruistic behavior. While people may accurately perceive how someone else feels, they will not transform their empathic understanding into helping behavior if they (*a*) do not perceive any personal responsibility to help, (*b*) feel incapable of doing anything effective, (*c*) become overwhelmed by **empathic distress** (incapacitation over someone else's problems), or (*d*) lack skills to communicate their empathy (Aronfreed, 1968; Barnett, 1982, 1987; Barnett, Thompson, & Pfeiffer, 1985; Egan, 1990; Hoffman, 1981, 1982).

Mark Barnett, a psychologist at Kansas State University, has conducted a set of inquiries into empathy and prosocial behavior. One of these studies was an investigation of how adolescents evaluate peers' motives for helping (Barnett, McMinimy, Flouer, & Masbad, 1987).

In this study, Barnett and his colleagues studied whether the gender of the helper influences how high

and dramatic. Her social reasoning began to decline steeply in the final ten class meetings. Jaquette speculated that Debbie became profoundly disturbed when she realized the special classes were ending and she would be returning to a regular classroom. Her self-esteem deflated, and Debbie attempted suicide two days after the special classes ended.

school juniors and seniors evaluate motives for helping. Certain sex-related role expectations suggest that females will emphasize caring for others and should express empathic understanding when they explain altruistic actions. Males, on the other hand, are not expected to express caring for others as a reason for engaging in altruistic behaviors. Given these sex-role socialization patterns, Barnett and his colleagues wondered whether high school students also base their perceptions of motives for helping on the gender of the helper (Barnett et al., 1987).

Ninety-two adolescents around 17 years of age participated in the study. Like their cognitive-developmental colleagues, the researchers used stories to elicit responses from research participants. They presented a fictional newspaper account about an adolescent hospitalized after an accident caused by a drunk driver. The newspaper article indicated two high school students, strangers to each other, learned about and visited the injured teenager, even though neither had ever met this individual before going to the hospital.

The 92 research participants were divided into four groups of 23 individuals each. The researchers systematically varied the gender of the injured teenager and the gender of the helper (the visitor). They produced extensive comments supposedly given by the helpers. Some comments attributed to the visiting teenagers were clearly empathic ("I was emotionally moved by the person's situation") while others were not ("I would have felt guilty if I did not help").

The four groups of high school students were asked to assess the motives of and make five separate judgments about the teenagers who visited the injured adolescent. Specifically, the students were asked to indicate how much they (a) would like the person who visited the hospital, (b) would want the person who visited the hospital as a friend, (c) liked the person's motives for helping, (d) considered the motives similar to their own in comparable situations, and (e) considered certain adjectives described the helpers (emotional, attractive, masculine, feminine, friendly, kind, honest, sensitive).

Results clearly favored empathic motives for helping. The high school students liked helpers with empathic motives more than the others, expressed more interest in being friends with empathic helpers, and considered them "friendlier, more emotional, more feminine, kinder, and more sensitive" (Barnett et al., 1987, p. 583). However, the adolescents did not consider empathic helpers more masculine, honest, or attractive than nonempathic helpers.

Gender of the helper was strongly associated with evaluation of motives. The students indicated they liked female helpers whose reasons were empathic but harshly judged females whose reasons were not empathic. They equally liked males who offered empathic and those who offered nonempathic reasons.

The students were also more interested in opposite-sex helpers and wanted them as friends more often than same-sex helpers. They rated the opposite-sex helpers more attractive than same-sex helpers. Barnett and his colleagues suggested these opposite-sex preferences reflect adolescent interests in dating and intimacy (Barnett et al., 1987).

Jaquette (1980) attempted to understand how all eight of the young adolescents viewed the end of their special school program. Each viewed the end of the special program with alarm, and their resulting anxiety produced considerable strain on their self-control and their abilities to interact well with others. Such insight about regression to earlier forms of behavior provides potential leverage for individuals working with these adolescents. Their gains in social reasoning are vulnerable to impending changes in their life circumstances, particularly the loss of support from trusted adults. The practitioner is alerted to look for the meanings that the youths attribute to both interpersonal and intrapersonal happenings.

We have now looked at contemporary ideas about moral reasoning, egocentrism, and interpersonal understanding. Another form of social reasoning involves political realities. Let's review adolescents' thinking about politics.

POLITICS AND SOCIAL COGNITION: THE VIEWS OF JOSEPH ADELSON

Exploration about and commitment to personally chosen political ideas are considered the mark of an achieved identity (Marcia, 1964, 1966, 1980). Reasoning about politics is part of the developments of adolescents as they expand their understanding of their place in society. In short, changes in reasoning about politics is part of the overall development of social cognition. One scholar who has studied adolescents' reasoning about politics is Joseph Adelson.

Adelson's views fall into the cognitive developmental school inspired by Piaget. His research looked at 120 adolescents in the Ann Arbor, Michigan area. He had an equal number of males and females. He divided the adolescents into four groups of 30 subjects each according to grade level: fifth, seventh, ninth, and twelfth. The average age of the adolescents by group were 11, 13, 15, and 18, respectively. He also examined subjects according to IQ scores on the California Test of Mental Maturity; 67% had average IQ scores of 95 to 110 and 33% had superior scores of 125 and above. The study was thus an age by gender by intelligence design (Adelson, Green, & O'Neil, 1969; Adelson & O'Neil, 1966).

To Adelson's surprise, neither gender nor intelligence separated adolescent thinking about politics, government, community, or laws. He also found no impact of social class on adolescent political understanding. What did significantly influence responses, however, was age of the respondent. As Adelson said, "What does count, and count heavily, is age. There is a profound shift in the character of political thought, one which seems to begin at the onset of adolescence—twelve to thirteen—and which is essentially completed by the time the child is fifteen or sixteen"(1971, p. 107).

The principle invoked by Adelson to explain this shift is Piagetian cognitive development, particularly the shift from concrete operations to formal operations. Whereas younger adolescents are restricted to concrete examples and simpler appreciation of the world, around the age of 15, adolescents show increased cognitive sophistication and realization about the ambiguity of social reality (Adelson, 1971).

Adelson's Method of Studying Adolescent Political Reasoning

Adelson's method of inquiry involved telling a brief vignette and asking the adolescent to comment on the scene presented and on a dilemma for people in the story. (Does this method sound familiar?) His vignettes always began with this opening context: "Imagine that a thousand men and women, dissatisfied with the way things are going in this country, decide to purchase and move to an island in the Pacific once there, they must devise laws and modes of government" (Adelson & O'Neil, 1966, p. 295).

The interviewers asked the adolescent subjects about several hypothetical issues confronting the men and women on the island. They stayed away from current political issues because pilot studies had indicated adolescents' underlying ideas about politics are often clouded by current issues being debated in society. During Adelson's research, Americans were deeply divided over the Vietnam War and racial desegregation.

Rather than drawing on topics currently dividing Americans, Adelson used hypothetical issues and dilemmas as the substance of the interview. Each adolescent was asked about the merits and shortcomings of several forms of government (democracy and dictatorship, for instance) and about the purpose and enforcement of laws. One dilemma concerned the intent of the island government to build a road from one side of the island to the other. However, one person who owned land along the proposed path for the road refused to sell his land. The adolescents were asked, "Many people thought he was selfish, but others thought he was in the right. What do you think?" (Adelson & O'Neil, 1966, p. 301).

Other dilemmas presented were how to respond to a landowner's threat to shoot individuals who tried to force him from his land and what to do when an established law was not being obeyed (Adelson et al., 1969; Adelson & O'Neil, 1966). The adolescents were asked not only the purpose of laws but also whether a law should be passed to forbid smoking, what to do if people refused to follow such a law, and how to deal with the rights of minority citizens (Adelson, 1971; Adelson et al., 1969; Adelson & O'Neil, 1966).

For Adelson's subjects, the shift to formal operations proved decisive in prompting a qualitatively new understanding of the political community, social institutions, and the purpose of laws. Whereas younger adolescents' political ideas were limited to concrete examples, by about age 15, adolescents invoked abstract principles and moved with ease between concrete examples and principles.

Adelson identified several differences between the political understanding of younger adolescents and that of older adolescents. Three of these differences involve (*a*) whether laws can be changed, (*b*) personalistic understandings of government, and (*c*) notions of history.

The Mutability of Laws

Prior to entering formal operations, Adelson's subjects neither knew nor grasped that laws could be changed; they viewed law in an either/or fashion. Rather than revising laws that are not achieving their aims, adolescents in concrete operations suggested such laws should be more energetically enforced. For instance, if a law prohibiting cigarette smoking does not produce compliance, younger adolescents solemnly suggested using organized physical force to insure people do not smoke (Adelson et al., 1969).

Adolescents develop more pragmatic and functional ideas about laws around the age of 15. Adelson noted these changed views about laws are the outcome of gaining formal operations and thereby being able to reason that laws must reflect the needs of the people being governed.

Early adolescents favor using organized physical force to make people comply with laws against smoking.

Personalistic Understandings of Government

Adelson saw two related tendencies in younger adolescents. First, they used their experiences with people to understand governments. Second, the younger adolescents considered political decisions have only personal consequences, rather than social consequences. In contrast, adolescents 15 years of age and older comprehended that the abstract ideas of government, community, and society represent community networks, which link people together. In other words, older adolescents developed a sociocentric understanding that transcends the personalistic; with a sociocentric understanding, older adolescents realized politics circumscribes the entire society, not just individuals in that society, and that society accomplishes things beyond the ability of individuals (Adelson & O'Neil, 1966).

Notions of History

Adelson's younger adolescents showed little sense of history, rarely considered how the past influenced the present, and considered the future only in the most constricted terms. Adelson judged that early adolescents are constrained by immediate experiences, and that neither a sense of tradition nor a consideration of alternate possibilities influences the younger adolescent's ideas about time.

Adelsons' older adolescents began to look beyond short-term concerns, to consider long-term impacts, and to entertain multiple possibilities. For instance, when considering a proposed law, the older adolescents discussed its short-run impact and its potential long-run consequences (Adelson, 1971). Understanding that human beings devise laws and that human beings make mistakes, older adolescents asked whether there could be more to a proposed law than immediately apparent. For instance, the older adolescents predicted widespread disobedience if a law were passed to forbid cigarette smoking, and they disavowed any trust—as had been expressed by younger adolescents—that passing laws could change human tendencies (Adelson et al., 1969).

So far, we have looked at changes in moral reasoning, interpersonal understanding, and political reasoning. All these points of view are guided by cognitive assumptions and methods. We now look at the adolescent's development of religious understanding. This area of inquiry, as carried out by James Fowler, also assumes a cognitive approach.

THE QUEST FOR MEANING: THE VIEWS OF JAMES FOWLER

As you may recall, Marcia (1964, 1966, 1980) explored religious ideas and considered commitment to one's ideas about religion a mark of an achieved identity. A scholar who has studied cognitive development of faith and religious understanding is James Fowler, a professor at Emory University and a former student of Kohlberg. Fowler has credentials as both a theologian and a psychologist. For several years, he has been Director of the Center for Faith Development at Emory University.

Fowler explicitly acknowledges his dependence on three key figures in developmental psychology. In his book *Stages of Faith* (Fowler, 1981), he created a fictional conversation between Erikson, Piaget, and Kohlberg on the subject of human development. In this conversation, he presented the substantive ideas of these three thinkers, their points of agreement and dispute, and their influence on his views.

Fowler has been interested in developing a theory about the development of faith consciousness across the life arc. He makes clear that faith need not be religious in content or expression. Rather than a matter of religious commitment, **faith** is the term he gives to the universal human quest to identify what is of ultimate value, what gives meaning to existence, and what enables a person to be connected to others. Given the importance of religion in Marcia's theory, and given both Marcia's and Fowler's close ties to Erikson, it surprises me that Fowler mentions no connection between his ideas and Marcia's.

Faith encompasses, but, is not limited to religion or religious beliefs. Atheists and agnostics can have faith. Albert Camus (1948, 1954, 1955), the French author, is a supreme example of an atheist with very strong convictions and beliefs about the ultimate meaning of human existence. Another example is offered by adherents of Buddhism, a very influential philosophy of life that seems to deny the existence of God (Smith, 1989).

Beliefs are how one expresses his or her faith. Because faith encompasses not only conscious beliefs but also unconscious motivations, much about faith is inexpressible (Fowler, 1981). Something that is inexpressible is *ineffable;* that is, it defies verbal communication.

It may come as no surprise to readers that Fowler presents a stage theory of faith development. Look at the work of the thinkers who most influenced him: Erikson's stages of psychosocial development, Piaget's stages of cognitive development, and Kohlberg's stages of moral reasoning. Not only is Fowler committed to developing a stage theory of faith development, he is committed to investigating the structural components in the development of faith. An emphasis upon structural components characterizes the cognitive developmental approach to theory building.

Fowler's Method of Inquiry

The cognitive developmentalists we have studied thus far have used stories containing dilemmas and asked their research subjects to answer open-ended questions about those stories. Fowler also collects vast amounts of qualitative data from his research subjects, but, rather than giving them a story to analyze, he encourages individuals to tell their own life stories.

The interviews last two hours or more and cover four basic areas: (*a*) the person's life and family history as well as what and who have been or are valuable to the person; (*b*) experiences and relationships that shaped the person's life; (*c*) the person's current values, beliefs and commitments; and (*d*) religion. Table 5-5 presents some questions used in the interview and identifies where they occur in the interview.

TABLE 5-5   Fowler's Faith Development Interview Guide: Representative Questions

PART 1   LIFE REVIEW

In order for me to understand the flow and movement of your life and your way of feeling and thinking about it, what other persons and experiences would be important for me to know about?

Thinking about yourself at present, what gives your life meaning?

PART 2   LIFE SHAPING EXPERIENCES AND RELATIONSHIPS

Have you experienced losses, crises, or suffering that have changed or "colored" your life in special ways?

Have you had moments of joy, ecstacy, peak experiences, or breakthrough that have shaped or changed your life?

PART 3   PRESENT VALUES AND COMMITMENTS

What is the purpose of human life?

What does death mean to you? What becomes of us when we die?

PART 4   RELIGION

If you pray, what do you feel is going on when you pray?

Where do you feel that you are changing, growing, struggling, or wrestling with doubt in your life at the present time? Where is your growing edge?

SOURCE: Adapted from *Stages of Faith: The Psychology of Human Development and the Quest for Meaning* by James W. Fowler, pp. 310, 312, Copyright © 1981, by James W. Fowler. Reprinted by permission of HaperCollins Publishers, Inc.

Stages of Faith Consciousness

Since the early 1970s, Fowler and his colleagues have interviewed over 500 people. The interviews have included nearly the same number of males and females, involved individuals age 4 to 84, and consisted of representative numbers of Protestants, Catholics, and Jews (Fowler, 1991). Analyses of the interviews have led Fowler to propose seven stages in the development of faith across the life arc: (*a*) primal faith, (*b*) intuitive-projective faith, (*c*) mythic-literal faith, (*d*) synthetic-conventional faith, (*e*) individuative-reflective faith, (*f*) conjuctive faith, and (g) universalizing faith. Fowler calls these stages of faith "evolving patterns of constructive knowing" (1991, p. 34).

Primal faith is a rudimentary, emotional response that focuses on trust offsetting mistrust—you may see Erikson's influence here—and enables each human being to experience separation without anxiety or fear for one's safety (Fowler, 1991). According to Fowler, humans are born with a structural predisposition to find meaning. That is to say, humans are innately a meaning-making species. Primal faith, which occurs in infancy, lays the foundation on which a person's faith grows and is nurtured in the family. Fowler (1991) speaks of the family as the incubator of human faith development.

Fowler appears to have modified his views on faith and infancy since he wrote *Stages of Faith.* While he wrote that infants are involved in "undifferentiated faith," he did not consider this starting point a stage in faith development. Fowler has transformed his thinking about the initial structure to faith understanding. It would be helpful for Fowler to present the evidence that led him to change his mind. However, I have not seen any discussion of empirical data on the matter.

The second stage of faith development, *intuitive-projective faith,* emerges in early childhood and is present in all children by the age of 3. It grows out of childhood imagination and is related to the child's growing awareness of moral standards—that is, conscience.

The third stage, *mythic-literal faith,* occurs during middle childhood and lasts for some people into early adolescence (Fowler, 1991). This stage depends on the development of concrete operations and on the ability to understand the perspectives of others. Fowler sees the rise in mythic-literal faith in the ability of youths to use narratives to share their experiences and to make meaning out of the stories they tell. There is, thus, a clear element of Selman's growth of interpersonal understanding in the rise of mythic-literal faith; both Selman and Fowler emphasize the role of the person as a meaning maker.

Interest in building interpersonal relationships during early adolescence is complemented by the task of forming personal beliefs and making commitments (Fowler, 1991). This aspect of developing consciousness is Fowler's fourth stage of faith development, *synthetic-conventional faith.* During this transformation in cognition, adolescents shape their worldviews as they meet people and have experiences that enable them to gain orientations about human existence and about searching for truth.

Fowler calls the fifth stage of faith development *individuative-reflective faith.* He ascribes this stage to the years of late adolescence and young adulthood, although he noted that some individuals have entered this stage as early as age 13 (Fowler, 1981).

People reach individuative-reflective faith only when they engage in two important changes in self-identity (Fowler, 1991).

The first important change involves examining, evaluating, and restructuring one's values and beliefs. In terms of faith understanding, the person makes conscious, personal choices, rather than accepting unexamined commitments. This change seems closely related to what Marcia (1964, 1966, 1980) identified as identity achievement. The movement into this stage of faith can only occur after a period of crisis or decision making during the moratorium stage of identity formation.

The second important change in self-understanding, on which individuative-reflective faith depends, is also a characteristic of an achieved identity. Rather than having choices imposed because of one's roles and relationships, the person makes choices about the roles and responsibilities he or she will assume. In the individuative-reflective stage of faith, people seek foundations that underlie the roles and relationships in their lives. The psychodynamic literature refers to these foundations as the "executive ego," and Marcia (1980) would see in such movement the formation of an autonomous identity.

The sixth stage of faith development occurs around a person's midlife years, typically around age 40, although Fowler (1981) said a very small proportion of his sample entered before age 30. Fowler called this stage of faith understanding *conjunctive faith*. In this stage, the individual accepts, and even embraces, paradox as part of the human condition.

The ineffability of conjunctive faith frustrates Fowler, who wrote, "I cannot communicate the features of this stage clearly" (1981, p. 184). He used rich, descriptive metaphors to convey the structural features of this sixth stage in faith development. For example, he said moving into conjunctive faith resembles "discovering that one's parents are remakable not just because they are one's parents" (Fowler, 1981, p. 185).

Rather than seeing reality in either/or disjunctive terms, the individual with conjunctive faith accepts and knows that reality is filled with seeming contradictions. As an example, the person knows that someone is no less admirable because of character flaws. This realization occurred for me when I understood that an adult role model from my adolescence was still worthwhile despite his prejudice against blacks.

In stage six, the person overcomes the temptation to impose meaning on the world and lets the world disclose itself. Perhaps that attribute explains the frustration Fowler experiences in attempting to impose his meaning on an aspect of existence that is revelatory, rather than controlled.

The seventh stage, *universalizing faith*, eludes most people. Fowler found less than one-half of 1% of all individuals interviewed were in this stage of faith understanding. That is less than five people out of his total sample. Over 65% of his sample were either in stage three or four (Fowler, 1981). No one had entered this seventh stage earlier than their 60s.

Universalizing faith emerges once people have escaped seeing themselves as the center of value, have completed an ever widening involvement in empathic understanding of other perspectives, and "have identified with or . . . participate in the perspective of God" (Fowler, 1991, p. 41). This process is captured primarily in the great religious literature, such as the Buddhist understanding of freedom from desire and absorption into the One, the Hindu scriptures, which say, "One is forever free who has broken out of the ego-cage of I and mine to be united with the Lord of Love. This is the supreme state. Attain thou this and pass from death to immortality" (Easwaron, 1978, cited in Fowler, 1991), and the Christian scriptures, which say, "anyone who wants to save his life will lose it, but anyone who loses his life for my sake will find it" (Matthew 16:25; Mark 8:25; Luke 9:24; John 12:25).

Are there any models of universalizing faith in our times? Fowler suggests Mahatma Gandhi, Mother Teresa, and Martin Luther King, Jr. embody universalizing faith. Other figures he proposes are Dag Hammarskjold, the leader of the United Nations who died in the 1960s attempting to end civil war in Africa, and Dietrich Bonhoeffer, the Lutheran minister executed by the Nazis because of his involvement in the attempt to assassinate Hitler.

People in stage seven become dedicated to fighting oppression and violence and promoting love and justice. These individuals elicit anxiety and dread in many, and many people who reach stage seven are assassinated. Why? Because they challenge the powerful to end injustice and share power with the powerless.

In summary, Fowler's position shows many of the same features seen in the other theorists discussed in this chapter. He proposes a stage theory of development, relies on Piaget's view of cognitive development, and uses a variant on the story-telling technique of Kohlberg, Selman, and Adelson. More similar to Gilligan, who had her research participants discuss a real issue in their lives, Fowler has his participants tell their own life stories.

CHAPTER SUMMARY

During the adolescent years, individuals begin to think about relationships with others in ways that differ from childhood reasoning. Researchers attribute these changes in social reasoning to changes in cognition that occur in adolescence. All the leading work today regarding social reasoning is conducted by researchers who accept a cognitivist approach to understanding human development.

One type of social reasoning has to do with reasoning about morality. Moral reasoning has captured the interest of many researchers since the work of Lawrence Kohlberg. He modeled his thinking and theories on Piaget's explanations of cognitive development. Kohlberg produced a stage theory of moral reasoning in which he maintained that people use distinctly different reasoning principles at different stages of their thinking about moral dilemmas.

Kohlberg argued that the stages of moral reasoning occur in an invariant, universal, hierarchical sequence. Kohlberg's method for studying moral reasoning was to present stories with moral dilemmas and ask his research participants to comment on the stories.

Kohlberg's theory has produced both staunch advocates and staunch critics. One criticism raised by Carol Gilligan, who collaborated at one time with Kohlberg, is that his model is biased against females. She has produced her own stage and sequence description of female moral reasoning. One of her fundamental concerns is that individuals reason differently when dealing with a real-life issue as opposed to a hypothetical situation.

Gilligan claims that males and females use different principles when reasoning about morality. She says that men and women have different voices and that Kohlberg's method relegates the feminine voice to less than adult status. Longitudinal studies and meta-analyses of several projects using Kohlberg's and Gilligan's schemes fail to support charges that Kohlberg's method assigns adult females to a moral reasoning level lower than adult males. Studies have been unable to confirm Gilligan's stage and sequence claims.

One of the cognitive changes in social reasoning involves what David Elkind termed adolescent egocentrism. He said early adolescents, in particular, seem to think other people are constantly observing and judging them. In other words, adolescents go through a period of time operating as if they are on stage before an imaginary audience. Elkind also said adolescents tend to form exaggerated beliefs about their uniqueness. They begin to formulate a personal fable and consider their experiences to be totally unlike what anyone else has experienced or can understand. Elkind says these forms of adolescent egocentrism pass due to the emergence of firmly established formal operations.

Another cognitive psychologist has studied the changes that occur in interpersonal understanding during adolescence. Robert Selman considers it vitally important to determine what an individual perceives social reality to be. Selman argued that human interpersonal understanding occurs in an invariant sequence of stages. These stages extend from fairly primitive understandings to complex, abstract representations of social reality. He used stories containing interpersonal dilemmas about such issues as jealousy, conflict resolution, and the end of friendships. Selman appealed to Piaget's theory to explain how interpersonal understanding changes.

Adolescents' views about political realities became an interest of Joseph Adelson. He too was strongly influenced by Piaget. Like Kohlberg and Selman, Adelson used stories containing dilemmas in order to enable adolescents to disclose their political understandings. His most famous story sets 1,000 people on an island, and has the islanders face dilemmas regarding the establishment of rules for maintaining social order. One dilemma, for example, involves conflict between the island government, which wants to build a road, and a landowner who refuses to sell the land. Adelson noted responses to his dilemmas were clearly age-related, with older adolescents more sophisticated in the principles they applied in reasoning about political concerns.

Another aspect of social reasoning is the quest for meaning. James Fowler has developed a complex set of interview questions to help individuals articulate their ultimate beliefs. Beliefs may take the form of traditional religious views, although this is not necessarily so. Fowler proposes a stage theory of faith development, with development occuring in an invariant, universal sequence. Rather than giving his research participants a story to analyze, Fowler asks them to tell him their life stories. Fowler explicitly acknowledges his intellectual debt to Piaget, Kohlberg, and Erikson.

This chapter focused on gains in social perspective taking during adolescence. In the next chapter, we turn to an ecological niche important in the development of adolescents. An *ecological niche* is an environment whose features may nourish optimal growth but—should the environment contain features toxic to growth—may prove detrimental to the individual. The ecological niche examined in the next chapter is the family.

THE DRAMA PLAYED OUT ON THE FAMILY STAGE

"We're Not as Close as My Parents Think"

Rachel is a 22-year-old college senior majoring in family studies and prelaw. She will graduate in about six weeks. About a month after graduation, she and her fiancé will marry and move to a city in the eastern United States where he has been offered a good job.

Rachel comes from an intact family. Her father is a hospital administrator and her mother is a homemaker. Both have college degrees. Rachel has a 17-year-old brother, Brett, and a 6-year-old sister, Melanie.

"We're a pretty average family I guess. I think my mom tends to be the domineering person in the family. Mom tends to be the one who will have things go her way, to have the last say on important decisions. She was an only child, so I wonder if that's why. She is much more outspoken than my dad.

"Dad comes from a very big family—nine brothers and sisters. My dad's father was married twice, so dad has stepbrothers and stepsisters too.

"I think I am a happy medium of my mom and dad. I can be really outspoken or shut up and not say anything. Of course, I have my own traits that come from I don't know where.

"My brother, Brett, is your typical teenager. Apparently, he is very outspoken at school about controversial issues. He's also very outspoken with my parents. He rebels a lot, especially with my mom. He gets in a lot of arguments with my mom. I did that when I was his age," Rachel says almost in an aside.

"Brett didn't used to get in arguments with my dad. But now, he looks less to my Dad to back him up against Mom. Now, since I left for college, he seems to talk to me more.

"We used to have this major sibling rivalry. We used to argue a lot, mostly over little petty stuff. Just screamed and hollered at one another, never hit each other.

"We had really good times too, especially when one of us had gotten in trouble with Mom or Dad. Then we'd sort of band together.

"My brother is a lot like I was. I like knowing that I wasn't the only one acting like that. He used to be so shy and timid, and now he stands up for what he thinks is right. I really admire that in him. I know to an extent I don't have that quality.

"What don't I like about him? If you'd asked me five years ago, I would have thought of lots of stuff. The only things I can think of are he has a lot more freedom than I did. He has his own car. Mom and Dad are letting him skim by without having a job.

"I think he gets all this freedom because he's a boy. But I don't think my parents play favorites. He gets away with a lot more than I did, but I don't know why. When I used to live at the house, he still got away with a lot more. I think because I was the oldest and he was the young one and wasn't supposed to know better.

"My sister, Melanie, is only 6. She thinks she's a lot older. She's a very hyper child. She likes to attract attention. She is spoiled. At one point she had every person in the family catering to her every whim. She can get real annoying when she starts nagging at people.

"She's funny. She laughs on purpose, just like Ernie on Sesame Street, when company is around. She's smart, really very smart.

"It's hard to know her. I've been away from her so much. All I hear about her growing up is stuff I hear over the phone. I see her a lot more lately than I used to.

"It's still odd for me to say I have a sister. At times it's really weird to think I have another sibling besides my brother. It is difficult to be close because I haven't been with her much and because of our age difference. She knows who I am. Whenever I used to go home for a visit, she would cry when I left. She doesn't do that anymore.

"My folks were really strict with me. I guess I was difficult at times for them. Mom used to say, 'I hope you have a teenager just like yourself some day. Then you'll understand.' And I think, 'I sure hope I don't have a teenager like I was.'

"They used to ground me a lot. I didn't get spanked a lot. Mom enforced the rules. She hardly ever used the phrase, 'Wait until your Dad gets home.' She'd inform Dad when he got home, and then that would make things worse if I'd done something bad.

"The only thing Dad ever lectured me on, pushed me on, was academics. He really stressed school. Mom was more pushing me on my behavior.

"I always went to my dad when I got into trouble with Mom. He was the softie— well, most of the time.

"I was never really close with my Dad until about two years ago when I started working over one summer at the same place he works. I used to ride in with him, and we talked a lot in the car about things that matter. We've talked a lot about my upcoming marriage.

"I really feel that now I can talk to my Dad about a lot more stuff. I've grown out of the stage where I felt the only person I could talk to was Mom. I talk to him, rather than Mom, about getting married, about starting a family, my going to work or staying at home when Tom and I start a family. Over the past year, Dad and I have talked about all the things to do with my wedding and my marriage.

"I've found out Dad listens and seldom gives advice. He doesn't lecture me and tell me what I am supposed to do. He treats me like I'm an adult and he's interested in me.

"Mom and I get along better now that I am in college. When I was in high school, we had those mother-daughter quarrels over my friends, boys I was dating, that sort of stuff. Mom felt I was too nice and let my friends use me. At the time, it felt like she was trying to butt in and run my life. Now, when I look back on it, I think a lot she said made sense. She told me I didn't have to listen then, but when I was older, I'd understand. I guess she was right, but I've never told her. Guess I don't want to give her that satisfaction. If I told her, she'd be sarcastic with an 'I told you so.' But inside, she would feel differently. She just doesn't let on how she really feels.

"She jokes around a lot about things I don't like to joke about. We got into a religion thing when Tom and I went home recently. Mom was real sarcastic about him joining our church. She wasn't trying to be mean. She was just teasing him. But a lot of people, including me, take offense when she says these things."

Rachel hesitated when asked if she feels close to her mom. After some reflection, she replied, "For our relationship, yes, I'd say we're close." When asked what that statement meant, Rachel said, "I've seen worse mother-daughter relationships. I know some daughters who don't even talk to their mothers. I feel fortunate my mom and I are as close as we are, particularly considering how we got along in the past. In the past, I had just such a troubling relationship with her that I feel fortunate we are as close as we are. Mom has said she thinks we were close in the past. I just sat there dumbfounded to hear her say that. I never really felt close to her just because I talked to her."

When asked to rate on a scale from 0 to 100 how close she is to her mom and her dad, Rachel said, "With my mom, just on the short side of 50. Mom would probably put it higher than that. With Dad, it depends on the situation. I am probably a little closer to my dad, so I'd put it above 50 on this scale. Dad would put it the same as I did." (When asked how close she feels to her fiancé, she lights up and says, "Very close to the 100 side of the scale.")

"I really hope I don't become my mother in my new family. I can see a lot of things in my mom coming out in me. Around Tom, I can be a real cold fish if we have an argument. I can just leave and refuse to discuss it. My mom does that a lot when she has an argument. But she leaves because she is convinced she's right. I leave because I know I'm wrong.

"Tom definitely does not remind me of my mom. There's a tender nature in Tom that I see in my dad."

Rachel talks about her upcoming separation from her parents and says, "I don't think it's really quite hit me yet that I'm going to be on my own, and that I won't be calling Dad to tell him I need money. And I won't be calling Mom when I am upset about things. While I don't do that excessively, I do it even less since I met Tom. I turn to him when things go wrong. I think I'll feel able to rely on myself after Tom's company moves him to his second job in about ten months. I could hardly believe my ears when Mom and Dad agreed with the decision Tom and I made to buy a car. I thought they would be finding fault. But they just treated us like we were adults and had the right to make such a decision."

Rachel's comments about her nuclear family mirror most of what is presented in this chapter. She loves her family but says communication with her parents (particularly with her mother) is strained. Notice how she describes her relationship with her father—distant for the most part until recently. Her relationship with her teenage brother is mixed with care and exasperation. She barely knows her younger sister, who has grown up while Rachel was in college and living away from home.

Rachel is on the cusp of young adulthood, and her conversation indicates her awareness of the transition she is experiencing. Her feelings about this transition into young adulthood are marked primarily by eagerness, but there is also a wistfulness for earlier days of childhood. She seems to have given up on establishing a closer relationship with her mother, has gnawing concerns that she has undesirable traits she associates with her mother, and has found a way to talk personally with her father in the past several months. She is extending her loyalties to her fiancé, and together, they are rehearsing the independence they soon will adopt as a young, married couple without children.

This chapter is about families and adolescents. One means of studying families is to view their development in terms of a family life cycle. The dominant perspective on family functioning is called a *systems perspective*. In this chapter, we look at three systems models that provide explanations of family functioning. We also discuss a tool that family therapists have developed to study families called the *genogram*. We study what genograms are and how they can be used to understand family influences that span generations.

In this chapter, we also examine the multiple forms of the family. In American society, the traditional family model consists of a mother, father, and their children. However, the divorce rate and the rise in single-parent families make the traditional model only one of several types of families in the United States.

A major task of families, regardless of their form, is to raise children to become independent and to go out into the world on their own. The ability of a family to perform this task is influenced by adolescent-parent perceptions and by parenting style. In this chapter, we investigate whether there is a generation gap separating adolescents from their parents. We also look at adolescent respones to varying parental styles of child rearing.

This chapter also examines other important issues, such as the relationship between siblings and alternatives to family maltreatment of children. However, we begin by studying some of the prominent theoretical viewpoints about development in the life of a family followed by some viewpoints about family functioning.

FAMILIES AND THEIR LIFE CYCLES

One influential theme in the study of family life is the **family life cycle** comprising specific stages of development. When applied to a family, the notion of stages of development is a system of qualitative changes occurring to a family over time (McGoldrick & Carter, 1982). Concepts related to the family life cycle are part of a larger field of study that investigates **normative life transitions** (Cowan, 1991; Cowan & Hetherington, 1991; Danish & D'Augelli, 1980; Datan & Ginsberg, 1975; Elder, 1991). A normative life transition is anticipated, can be prepared for, and is expected to happen to the great majority of people. The birth of a child to a newly married couple, the onset of puberty for an early adolescent, and the time when a late adolescent leaves home are examples of normative life transitions that affect both individuals and the family.

Sociologists have criticized the idea that there is a cycle to family life. They offer, instead, the notion of a **family life course** (Germain, 1990; Hagestad, 1988). The idea of a cycle is that everything starts all over again, much like the seasons of the year. Sociologists argue that a family does not go through its life cycle then start the cycle anew. Whereas the same stages are found in different families, a course is completed, not to be run again by the same people.

Although researchers in the family studies field agree that developmental stages characterize family life, there is no agreement on the number of stages families experience. This lack of agreement indicates the field is in ferment and provides a clear example of what Thomas Kuhn (1970) called a *search for normal science* (see Chapter 1). Let's look at three models of the family life cycle.

One model of the family life cycle proposes that families develop over time in six stages (McGoldrick & Carter, 1982). These stages begin with unattached young adults (stage 1) and end with later life after children move on (stage 6).

Another approach to the family life cycle suggests eight stages (Strong & DeVault, 1989). These stages begin with young married couples without children (stage 1) and end with elderly married couples in retirement (stage 8).

Using the work of Reuben Hill and Roy Rodgers (1964), researchers at the University of Minnesota have proposed a seven stage model for the family life cycle. I will refer to this perspective as the *Minnesota Model*. Criteria for the model were based on the belief that a family's needs change as its children develop (Olson, McCubbin, Barnes, Larsen, Muxen, & Wilson, 1983). We will discuss the Minnesota Model in greater detail later in this chapter.

The stages of these three models of the family life cycle are presented in Table 6-1. Despite differences in the number and names of stages, there is extensive agree-

TABLE 6-1   Three Models of the Family Life Cycle

McGoldrick and Carter	Minnesota Model	Strong and DeVault
Stage 1 Unattached Young Adults	**Stage 1** Young Couples without Children	**Stage 1** Beginning Families
Stage 2 The Newly Married Couple	**Stage 2** Childbearing Families and Families with Children in the Preschool Years	**Stage 2** Childbearing Families
Stage 3 The Family with Young Children		**Stage 3** Families with Preschool Children
Stage 4 The Family with Adolescents	**Stage 3** Families with School-Age Children	**Stage 4** Families with School Children
Stage 5 Launching Children and Moving On	**Stage 4** Families with Adolescents in the Home	**Stage 5** Families with Teenagers
Stage 6 The Family in Later Life	**Stage 5** Launching Families	**Stage 6** Families as Launching Centers
	Stage 6 Empty Nest Families	**Stage 7** Families in the Middle Years
	Stage 7 Families in Retirement	**Stage 8** Aging Families

SOURCES: The data in column 1 are from "The Family Life Cycle" by M. McGoldrick and E. A. Carter, *Normal Family Processes* (p. 176) edited by F. Walsh, 1982, New York: The Guilford Press. The data in column 2 are from *Families: What Makes Them Work?* (p. 23) by D. H. Olson, H. I. McCubbin, H. L. Barnes, A. Larsen, M. J. Muxen, and M. Wilson, 1983, Beverly Hills: Sage. The data in column 3 are from *The Marriage and Family Experience* by B. Strong and C. DeVault, 1989, St. Paul, MN: West.

ment among the models. Each of these models identifies the beginning stage in a family's life and refers to stages linked to the developmental ages of the children. Each specifically refers to the launching stage, when late adolescents and young adults separate from their families of origin. Each model also focuses on the lives of middle-aged and elderly parents who no longer have children under their care. The idea of stages of individual development over the life span influences the descriptions given to the stages in a family's life cycle.

The Minnesota Model of the Family Life Cycle

Stage 1 in the Minnesota Model deals with **young couples without children**. At this beginning stage of family life, couples are interested in establishing individual and couple goals. They work on developing mutually acceptable lifestyles. At this stage, the couple does not face the demands of raising children. In their national study of family life, which included 1,140 families, the Minnesota researchers reported 40% of the spouses expressed they were very satisfied with married life in this beginning stage (Olson et al., 1983).

Couples in stage 1 face four types of strains: (*a*) work pressures versus family demands, (*b*) tensions over finances, (*c*) marital relationship strains, and (*d*) medical and health concerns. Families that cope well with these demands promote family harmony, feel satisfied with financial decisions, communicate clearly and directly, enjoy each other's personality, enjoy leisure time, and engage in healthy behaviors (for instance, exercise) (Olson et al., 1983).

The second and third stages center on **families with young children** and **families with school-age children**. While some demands carry over from stage 1, the couple also faces a new set of pressures. For example, they daily lose what used to be free time. They also find their patience, even their senses of self-esteem, under attack daily. Children not only present demands for attention but also introduce financial pressures because they need food, clothing, medical care, shelter, and an education.

Families with young children and school-age children use a broad array of social supports to cope with pressures. Examples of social supports are grandparents, school, clubs, neighbors, and religious groups. Families that cope inadequately with these stages in the life cycle communicate poorly, dislike each other and their acquaintances, and argue over finances (Olson et al., 1983).

Stage 4 centers on **families with adolescents in the home**. This stage imposes new demands because the children are gaining greater independence from their parents. The primary family focus in stage 4 is preparing adolescent children to eventually strike out on their own.

Stage 4 is markedly stressful for most families. Financial strains are the primary pressures families at this stage face; other strains come from intrafamily conflict, work-related pressures, and problems managing adolescent children.

Families that cope well with stage 4 pressures rely on intrafamily strengths, such as clear communication and satisfaction with relationships. What seems to help especially cushion stage 4 families are positive feelings about financial management, about the personalities of family members, and about friends.

Stage 5 in the Minnesota Model deals with **launching families**. During this stage, the late adolescent works on establishing independence from the family, while the parents develop new family roles and rules. This phase of the family cycle involves many pivotal transitions, primarily, grown children leaving the home, the spouses of grown children entering the extended family, and the parents' establishing meaningful life activities aside from rearing children. Monica McGoldrick and Elizabeth Carter (1982) refer to this stage as "Launching Children and Moving On," thereby including empty nest families, which the Minnesota Model considers a separate stage.

Intrafamily strengths that help families with adolescents in the home to manage pressures are also used in the launching families stage of the family cycle. In addition, the married couples in stage 5 families who cope well enjoy each other, like being married to each other, and feel satisfied with their lives (Olson et al., 1983).

While the Minnesota Model poses other stages to the family life cycle, they are of less importance to this book than stages 1 through 5. What runs through the tapestry of these first five stages are multicolored threads of parallel changes: changes in children are matched by changes in their parents. The life cycle tapestry emphasizes mutual interaction and reaction across time. What we sometimes overlook is that developments in children and adolescents promote changes in parents—and that sometimes changes in parents influence the children. The family life cycle perspective takes such developments in a family into account.

The family life cycle perspective assumes that stages in families involve interaction between family members. Other researchers have developed models to understand such family functioning. We now turn to some of these models. All of them adopt a systems perspective.

SYSTEMS THEORY AND FAMILY FUNCTIONING

A Systems Perspective   Researchers of family functioning have been greatly impressed by the contribution of the systems perspetive in understanding and explaining human interaction. The critical assertion of a systems perspective on family functioning is that families are sets of mutually influential, interconnected relationships. Rather than a mixture of discrete individuals, a family is considered to be greater than the sum of its individual members. In systems terms, the whole is greater than the sum of its parts.

Some family systems theorists go so far as to maintain, "one part of the family cannot be understood in isolation from the rest of the system" (Epstein, Bishop, & Baldwin, 1982, p. 117). I for one consider that position to be extreme and simplistic. Individuals come into contact with many systems other than their families. Examples of other systems that influence adolescents are schools, peers, the world of work, and television. I do concur, however, that families greatly influence individual development. I believe that disregarding the role of the family in a person's life is sheer ignorance, and I accept that family functioning is more clearly understood by applying systems theory ideas.

Systems Models   Various models based on systems theory have captured the interests of family researchers as means to describe family functioning. Three of these models are (*a*) the Circumplex Model, (*b*) the McMaster Model of Family Functioning, and (*c*) the Beavers-Timberlawn Model.

The Circumplex Model

The **Circumplex Model** is the work of David Olson, Candyce Russell, and Douglas Sprenkle (1983; 1979; Russell, 1979). Olson and his associates use the term *circumplex* to mean their model encompasses the complexity of the issues that surround family life.

The Circumplex Model expects family functioning to change over time. In this regard, the model is dynamic because it assumes families respond to changes in their environments or in family members (Olson et al., 1979). The authors propose communication as the means whereby families accomplish these changes and remain stable. In effect, the quality of communication enables or prevents families to deal with internal and external pressures. Examples of internal pressures are the birth of a child or an adolescent's demand for a change in restrictions. Examples of external pressures are the father's loss of his job, the mother's job offer that demands relocating, or a fire that damages the family's home.

Of considerable importance in the Circumplex Model are the concepts of family cohesion and family adaptability. **Family cohesion** refers to how emotionally attached family members are to one another and how much individual autonomy families encourage in their members. Two cohesion extremes can develop. At one extreme, called **enmeshment**, overidentifying with one's family produces excessive attachment and confined autonomy; at the other extreme, called **disengagement**, extreme indifference to one's family produces little, if any, attachment and unlimited autonomy. The authors of the Circumplex Model believe effective families develop attachments that foster individual development and promote individual autonomy. Such family functioning is referred to as **balanced cohesion** (Olson et al., 1979).

Family adaptability is the capacity of a family to respond positively to stressors. Adaptability involves the capacity to change as well as the capacity to resist change. As with family cohesion, there are bi-polar extremes of family adaptability. At one extreme is the family that resists all demands for change, while at the other extreme is the family that maintains no stability, but rather shifts constantly when pressured. For example, in a family resisting all demands for change, the parents refuse to discuss discipline with their adolescent children, whereas in a family maintaining no stability, the parents constantly revise rules at the insistence of their children.

Effective families seek to maintain balance in their adaptability. Such families engage in open communication and work with explicit, rather than implicit, rules of behavior. Families with balanced adaptability have flexible parental leadership, successfully negotiate expectations of individuals, and trust each other about family rules to be followed and roles to be accepted.

Balanced adaptability emerges from the family's self-correcting change processes and its self-directing stabilizing processes. **Self-correcting change processes** are analogous to the target-seeking properties of "smart bombs," which change course in response to feedback from the environment. **Self-directing stabilizing processes** are analogous to the balancing functions of a gyroscope, which enables the smart bomb to maintain equilibrium throughout its course.

Family adaptability is considered to exist along a continuum, with one pole marked by rigidity, the other pole marked by chaos, and the midpoint marked by a balance between these extremes. Balanced adaptability can involve either flexible or structured processes. In conjunction with family cohesion, balanced family adaptability is considered to promote healthy individual development and harmonious family relationships (Olson et al., 1979).

Using adaptability and cohesion as the fundamental dimensions of family functioning, the Circumplex Model identifies 16 types of family systems. There are 4 balanced types of family functioning, 4 extreme types of family functioning, and 8 mixed types (called *midrange families*). These 16 types are presented in Table 6-2.

The most common types of family functioning are considered to be the 4 balanced and 4 extreme types. While it is possible for a family to be balanced on one dimension and extreme on the other (for instance, to be flexible but enmeshed), Olson and his colleagues (1979) suggest the eight midrange family types are less likely outcomes because extremes in one dimension tend to accompany extremes in the other.

Balanced family functioning enables individuals to gain independence from and to remain connected with other family members. In balanced families, there is a healthy relativism regarding independence from and connectedness to the family. Individuals may spend time alone or time with others without incurring suspicion or guilt. In short, a balanced family encourages autonomy in members, fosters attachment between members, and promotes interpersonal relationships outside the family. Let's look at an example of a balanced family.

Example of a balanced family.   John and Helen Black have been married for 17 years. They have three children, two adolescents and one school-age boy. The

TABLE 6-2   Sixteen Types of Family Functioning According to the Circumplex Model

Four Balanced Types	Four Extreme Types
Flexibly Separated	Chaotically Disengaged
Flexibly Connected	Chaotically Enmeshed
Structurally Separated	Rigidly Disengaged
Structurally Connected	Rigidly Enmeshed

Eight Mixed (Midrange) Types	
Chaotically Separated	Rigidly Separated
Chaotically Connected	Rigidly Connected
Flexibly Disengaged	Structurally Disengaged
Flexibly Enmeshed	Structurally Enmeshed

SOURCE: Adapted from "Circumplex Model of Marital and Family Systems: VI. Theoretical Update" by D. H. Olson, C. S. Russell, and D. H. Sprenkle, 1983, *Family Process, 22,* p. 71.

adolescents are Sally, a 16-year-old high school junior, and Jim, a 14-year-old high school freshman. Mark is a 9-year-old fourth-grader.

John and Helen both have professional careers. He is a loan officer at a large bank, and she is a dentist in a private practice. As you might guess given the parents' careers, the Black family is well-off financially.

Rules have been getting more liberal for Sally. Two years ago, her curfew was 10 P.M. on weekends, and she was not allowed to date. Sally disliked these rules and pressured her parents to change them, but they stayed firm and told Sally it was important for her to become more grown up emotionally. Once, Sally tested her parents' curfew rule and found herself grounded for two weeks. Now at 16, she can stay out until midnight on either Friday or Saturday and go out twice during the school week with her boyfriend if her homework is done and if she is home by 9:30 P.M.

Jim's curfew is what it was for Sally when she was his age. Jim is more interested in cars and sports than in girls, so he is not bothered about the rule about having to wait until he is a sophomore to date. Both he and Sally are encouraged to bring friends over to the house, and each can spend the night at friends' homes once John or Helen talks with the parents. Jim has been pushing his parents to let him get a car when he turns 16. Their response has been that Jim must show them in the next two years that he can handle such a big responsibility.

Mark is the youngest member of the family. There is enough of an age difference between Mark and his other siblings that they have little in common. Mark looks up to his brother. They often play sports together when Jim has to take care of Mark.

The children in the Black family talk fairly easily with their mother about matters that concern them. Their dad keeps most of his feelings to himself, but Jim and Sally have been talking with him about possible adult careers.

Sally and Jim would both say they respect and trust their parents and think their parents are fair. They like their parents' willingness to tell them the reasons for rules, and they clearly know what the rules are. While they sometimes don't like having to stay home and look after Mark, they accept it as part of their jobs in the family.

Both Sally and Jim expect to go to college. Sally wants to become a surgeon, and Jim is thinking of being an architect. Jim wants to study architecture at the university in his hometown, but Sally intends to go out of state. Their parents feel encouraged by the sense of direction each of their older children has. They think one of their major tasks as parents is to help their children grow up to be independent.

Extreme family types are found at the **cohesion-adaptability poles**. While balanced families sometimes engage in extreme functioning for limited times, the extreme family types maintain excessively high or low cohesion and adaptability as their standard functioning modes. Each of the four extreme types of family functioning endangers individual development by constraining the shaping of personal freedom and by inhibiting the formation of interpersonal ties.

The Circumplex Model of family functioning emphasizes both the individual and the family system. Changes in one person produce changes in other family members and in the family rules. As an example, consider the changes presented by an early adolescent female who asks her parents to allow her to date. If she is a persistent teenager, the request will resemble a demand, rather than a request. In a balanced family system, the girl's desire for a change in dating rules will lead to an open discussion and may lead to the establishment of revised rules. As in the Black family, parents in a balanced family may review the matter with their daughter and inform her that they consider her still too young to date.

In a rigidly enmeshed family system, a daughter's request to change rules about dating would be met with severe restrictions on her freedom and probably with questions about her loyalty to the family. In the case of a chaotically disengaged family system, the girl would make no request because there are no family rules for her to follow regarding relations outside the family.

We have reviewed the central ideas about family functioning proposed by the Circumplex Model. Let's now look at what research says about the usefulness of this model for understanding adolescents and their families.

Research about families, adolescents, and the Circumplex Model.   As a first step in looking at research using the Circumplex Model, let us consider the serious methodological problem posed for researchers who study families. You cannot give a psychological instrument to "a family," but only to the individual members of the family. The typical solution is to average the scores of all the members and to call that average the family's score. Do you think such a procedure produces a score about the family system (where the whole is greater than the sum of its parts) or a score that reflects a focus on the sum of the individuals, not on the system itself?

Howard Barnes and David Olson (1985) applied the Circumplex Model to a study of communication between parents and adolescents. They noted that researchers had tended to focus on extreme family types in clinical treatment. Barnes and Olson tested whether communication in balanced families with adolescents is more positive than communication in extreme families.

The Barnes and Olson (1985) sample consisted of 452 families that were part of a larger national study with a randomly selected sample of 1,140 intact families (Olson et al., 1983). The 452 families were selected because each had an adolescent—57.8% ($n = 261$) were in the family life cycle stage of families with adolescents in the home, and 42.3% ($n = 191$) were in the family life cycle stage of launching families. Equal numbers of male and female adolescents participated in the study. They ranged in age from 12 to 20, and averaged 16.4 years of age. Parents were in their mid-40s and made, on average, $25,000–35,000 a year. Most of the families were from cities with a population of at least 25,000.

To determine family type, Barnes and Olson (1985) used an instrument called the Family Adaptability and Cohesion Evaluation Scales, Version II (FACES II). This self-report instrument includes 30 items scaled on a five-point Likert scale; 14 items assess family cohesion and 16 assess family adaptability. Reliability tests indicate the instrument's internal consistency is quite high (Olson, Portner, & Bell, 1982).

Balanced and extreme families differ significantly in their responses to FACES II, thereby providing some evidence for the instrument's validity. However, individuals do not always agree about their families, an issue that raises questions over whose perceptions to use when family members disagree (Jacob & Tennenbaum, 1988).

To deal with the problem of differing individual scores, Barnes and Olson (1985) obtained mean scores for each family by averaging the scores of all family members.

While this strategy can work, it runs the risk of washing out differences between widely discrepant individual scores, thereby misidentifying an extreme family as balanced due to the process of averaging.

To illustrate this problem, imagine that balanced scores are close to 100 and extreme scores are at least 40 points higher or lower than 100. Consider the following hypothetical scores from two families, each considered balanced due to the average family score each received.

- The Johnsons had an average family score of 102: Dad's score was 104, Mom's score was 102, and the adolescent twins' scores were 99 and 103. These four scores add up to 408, and divided by 4, they average 102.

- The Richardsons had an average family score of 102. Dad's score was 141, Mom's score was 147, and the adolescent twins' scores were 62 and 58. These four scores also add up to 408, leading to an average of 102.

In the Richardson's case, the mother and father's scores are extremes at one end, while the twins' scores are extremes at the opposite end. Are the Richardsons a balanced family or an extreme family?

Results in Barnes and Olson's (1985) study indicated that differences exist in perceptions about communication in families. Adolescents do not think communication with their parents is as open as the parents believe. Mothers and adolescents perceive communication with each other as more open and positive than communication between fathers and adolescents. The real discrepancies in parent-adolescent opinions occurred in perceptions about problems in communicating. Parents consider communication with their adolescents to be significantly less problematic than do the adolescents.

In the Barnes and Olson (1985) study, parents' responses about communication tended to support the hypothesis that balanced families have more positive communication than extreme families. However, adolescent responses suggested that all types of families have communication problems. The adolescents strongly disagreed with their parents' views.

While these parent-adolescent differences may suggest what other authors have labeled a *generation gap* (Noller & Callan, 1991), Barnes and Olson (1985) wisely noted that we have yet to understand why such intergenerational differences occur. One answer may be that parents who score higher than their adolescents in cohesion and adaptability will report more positive levels of communication than their children. However, this answer suggests that these parents are blind to adolescent dissatisfaction with the major means whereby family process occurs—namely, communication between family members—and, thus, causes one to wonder about the accuracy of assigning a family functioning type when family members perceive their families in such divergent ways.

The Barnes and Olson (1985) findings suggest the Circumplex Model provides a useful overall assessment of family functioning. However, the model does not capture tensions between parental and sibling subsystems, or the differing perceptions that subsystems have regarding intercommunication. We now look at an alternative model, the McMaster Model of Family Functioning.

The McMaster Model of Family Functioning

The **McMaster Model of Family Functioning** (**MMFF**) is based on systems theory and assumes five crucial aspects characterize any family. The MMFF assumes:

- interrelationships exist between family members,
- isolated from the family system, no family member can be understood,
- an understanding of individual family members does not produce an understanding of family functioning,
- family structure and organization significantly influence behavior of family members, and
- adaptability and stability of a family system significantly influence how family members behave (Epstein, Bishop, & Baldwin, 1982).

The MMFF was developed my Nathan Epstein, Duane Bishop, and Lawrence Baldwin (1982). Epstein and his colleagues propose that family functioning involves six dimensions: problem solving, communication, roles, affective responsiveness, affective involvement, and behavior control. The MMFF authors prefer the term *healthy* to the term *normal*. By healthy, they mean a family whose functioning is characterized by positive features of the six dimensions in the MMFF model (Epstein et al., 1982). I will briefly describe each of these six dimensions.

In the MMFF, **problem solving** refers to a family's ability to resolve problems that affect its functioning as a family. Families face two types of problems: *instrumental problems*, which include finances, food, shelter, transportation, and clothing, and *affective problems*, which involve emotions.

It is absolutely essential for a family to deal effectively with instrumental problems if it is to handle affective problems. Epstein and his colleagues (1982) do not consider the reverse to be true; a family may cope poorly with affective issues while still taking care of ongoing instrumental needs. As an example, imagine a family that provides for food, shelter, clothing, transportation, and the children's education but does not permit the expression of affection.

Communication provides the linkage between problem solving, role acceptance, and role execution in families. Families characterized by open communication engage in problem solving more consistently acceptable to members, and open communication enables family members to understand, carry out, and revise their various family roles.

Family roles are the repetitive behavior patterns whereby families fulfill necessary functions, such as providing food and giving nurturance and support. Facilitating personal development is another necessary family role. Several miscellaneous functions are included under family roles: decision making, paying bills, and maintaining discipline, for example. The need to deal with instrumental and affective problems shapes family roles.

Affective responsiveness involves the ability of family members to respond with feelings that fit a situation. Responsiveness is not the expression of emotion per se, but, rather, is measured by (*a*) whether specific emotions are present or absent,

(b) whether the emotions are congruent to the situation, and (c) whether family members are allowed to express how they feel (Epstein et al., 1982).

The MMFF distinguishes between two categories of affect. *Welfare emotions* include support, affection, and tenderness. *Emergency emotions* include depression, anger, and fear.

Affective involvement, which refers to interpersonal attachment and empathy, designates the amount of family interest in and appreciation for the activities of individual family members. Affective involvement ranges along a continuum from total lack of involvement at one pole (disengagement) to extensive involvement at the other (enmeshment). Interpersonal attachment and empathy are critical for healthy family functioning; disengagement or enmeshment progressively incapacitates families.

Behavior control refers to how families handle three types of situations: physical danger, the fulfillment of psychobiological needs, and interpersonal relationships. *Physical danger* refers to issues of security. *Fulfillment of psychobiological needs* refers to such varying issues as nutrition and sexual fulfillment. *Interpersonal relationships* refer to communication and association with other people. The MMFF examines family standards and rules for handling these situations and flexibility in changing standards and rules.

Epstein and his colleagues (1982) have identified four patterns of behavior control: chaotic, flexible, laissez-faire, and rigid. Chaotic behavior control, which is marked by standards enforced unpredictably, is considered the least effective style. Flexible styles, which are marked by negotiation and reasonable change to meet situational demands, are considered the most effective forms of behavior control. Laissez-faire and rigid forms of control are the opposite of each other. Laissez-faire control is inconsistent and easily manipulated, whereas rigid control is marked by inflexibile enforcement of standards and no consideration of circumstances.

We have now reviewed the central ideas about family functioning proposed by the MMFF. Let's turn to what research says about the usefulness of this model for understanding adolescents and their families.

Research about families, adolescents, and the McMaster Model.   The McMaster Model has been used to investigate how families solve problems, how the emotional health of children relates to parental relationships, and how effective are programs to place emotionally disturbed children with families (Epstein et al., 1982). While the one extensive study of adolescents and families that Epstein, Bishop, and Baldwin (1982) cite is dated (Westley & Epstein, 1969), they note certain findings remain germane. Adolescents in this study were all college students at McGill University in Canada. One impressive finding was that the emotional health of these late adolescents was correlated significantly with the feelings their parents had for each other and did not depend on the emotional state either parent achieved as an individual. When the parents had a good marital relationship, their children were emotionally healthy, even if one of the parents was individually disturbed.

The Beavers-Timberlawn Model   Another systems model of family functioning is advocated by W. R. Beavers (1977, 1982). The **Beavers-Timberlawn Model** emerged from his interest in uncovering what makes some families healthy and others severely dysfunctional. Beavers has refined his notion of healthy families into a two-tier system of optimal and adequate family types.

Optimal families do four things: (*a*) they nourish interpersonal relationships, both in the family and outside, (*b*) they recognize that individual members affect everyone else in the family, (*c*) they realize that simple explanations frequently misrepresent complex events, and (*d*) they promote self-efficacy while acknowledging some things lie beyond human control. Beavers (1982) said these characteristics of optimal families are fundamental hypotheses not only of his model but also of a systems orientation.

In addition to these four characteristics, optimal families develop clear boundaries, distinguish between parent and child roles, and promote respect for individual privacy. Beavers (1982) likens the notion of clear family boundaries to the functions of a living cell, which interacts with the external world while it retains individuality.

Parents, not children, lead optimal families, and the parents work as equals. While children are not in charge, parents listen to them and promote increased decision making as they grow older. This hierarchical power arrangement in optimal families attains expression in investment in each other and in the success of each member outside their families.

Compared to optimal families, **adequate families** possess weaker parent bonds, express less intimacy, negotiate problems with greater strain and tension, and emphasize control, rather than love. However, like optimal families, adequate families establish clear boundaries, respect individual privacy, and promote individual responsibility and self-efficacy.

Parents in adequate families are in charge, but there is less intimacy and attachment between the parents. Disagreements between children and their parents involve emotional upset and blaming. Parents seem less sure of their authority, and compensate for this uncertainty by appealing to their positions of power, rather than to reasons why they have made rules and decisions.

Severely dysfunctional families establish either vague or rigid boundaries. Vague boundaries promote a sense of confusion within the family and, to borrow a term from the Circumplex Model, enmeshment. Rigid boundaries promote a sense of alienation from the external world and foster feelings of persecution.

Severely dysfunctional families resist change and develop poorly defined systems of control. Communication within these families occurs infrequently and is unsatisfying. The atmosphere in these families is "pervasively depressed or cynical," and children in severely dysfunctional families engage in continual conflict with parents and siblings because family members routinely ignore the individual's right to make choices (Beavers, 1982, p. 63).

The Beavers-Timberlawn Family Evaluation Scale.   Beavers (1977, 1982) developed an evaluation instrument to assess family functioning called the Beavers-Timberlawn Family Evaluation Scale. This scale is valid only when applied to a family the researcher has observed in action. In other words, a person is not supposed to apply the instrument to someone else's account of a family.

How could a researcher observe a family in action? One way is to spend time with a family in its home, observing family interaction in a natural setting. Another is to watch a family in therapy through a two-way mirror. Another method is to be in the room when the therapy is underway, although, unless the researcher is part of the family therapy team, the family may object to the researcher's presence and/or in some way become inhibited. In all these methods for observing a family in action, the researcher would be required to obtain explicit permission from the family to conduct the research. In the case of family therapy, it would be straightforward to explain the data being gathered are part of the clinical procedure.

The Beavers-Timberlawn Family Evaluation Scale measures five dimensions of family functioning: family structure, family mythology, goal-directed negotiation, autonomy, and family affect. I will describe each dimension in turn.

Family structure is measured by three subscales. *Overt power* ranges from chaos to shared leadership. *Parental coalitions* range from parent-child coalitions to a strong parental coalition. Closeness ranges from vague, indistinct interpersonal boundaries to close relationships with distinct boundaries.

Family mythology has only one scale. Family mythology refers to the family members' senses of each other's traits and skills. Optimal families share a mythology that outsiders agree is congruent with reality. A family mythology congruent with reality is that individual initiavive and talent bring rewards, as demonstrated in the case of an adolescent who earns recognition for scholastic and academic achievements. Severely dysfunctional families share a mythology at odds with reality. A family mythology incongruent with reality is that the outside world is against everyone in the family, as demonstrated in the case of a family who blames the authorities when an adolescent is arrested for car theft. Thus, the continuum on which family mythology is assessed ranges from very congruent with reality to very incongruent.

Goal-directed negotiation refers to a family's capacity to resolve difficulties efficiently and to involve all members of the family in negotiation. Families that resolve difficulties efficiently do so with little wasted time and emotional energy. The Beavers-Timberlawn instrument measures efficiency along a continuum ranging from extremely efficient to extremely inefficient.

Autonomy comprises clarity of expression, responsibility, invasiveness, and permeability. The Beavers-Timberlawn Family Evaluation Scale assesses each. *Clarity of expression* refers to whether family members disclose feelings and ideas intelligibly. The continuum for this element of autonomy ranges from very clear to hardly anyone in the family is ever clear. *Responsibility* means the extent to which individual family members acknowledge accountability for their behaviors; this element of autonomy ranges from consistent acceptance of responsibility to consistent avoidance of responsibility. To avoid responsibility, disturbed families exercise a variety of mechanisms, including denial, forgetting, and blaming and attacking others. *Invasiveness* refers to the degree to which family members speak as though they can read someone else's mind, and is assessed on a continuum ranging from many examples of invasiveness to none. *Permeability* is how receptive individuals are to other family members' ideas, and this construct is measured along a continuum ranging from very open to members unreceptive.

The **family affect** scale has four subscales: range of feelings, mood and tone, unresolvable conflict, and empathy. The family's range of feelings is measured on a continuum extending from direct expression of a wide range of feelings to little or no expression of feelings. Mood and tone is measured along a continuum ranging from usually warm, affectionate, and optimistic to cynical, hopeless, and pessimistic. Unresolvable conflict is measured along a continuum ranging from severe conflict and impairment of family functioning to little or no unresolvable conflict. Finally, empathy, which is the extent to which family members understand each other's feelings, is measured along a continuum ranging from consistent empathy to grossly inappropriate responses to feelings.

After assessing these five dimensions, an evaluator using the Beavers-Timberlawn instrument must rate the family's overall health. This scale ranges from 1 to 10, with lower scores indicative of healthier families.

Now that we have looked at the central ideas about family functioning proposed by the Beavers-Timberlawn Model, what does research say about the usefulness of this model for understanding adolescents and their families?

Research about families, adolescents, and the Beavers-Timberlawn Model. J. M. Lewis (1978) applied the Beavers-Timberlawn Family Evaluation Scale in a study of adolescents and families. He wanted to see how families distribute power in the family.

Lewis videotaped 150 families. Fifty were families that volunteered to be part of the study, and 100 were families with an adolescent admitted to a psychiatric hospital's adolescent unit. Using the Beavers-Timberlawn Family Evaluation Scale, Lewis assessed family structure, family mythology, goal-directed negotiation, autonomy, and family affect.

Lewis identified four levels of family functioning: optimal families, competent but pained families, midrange dysfunctional families, and severely dysfunctional families. It would have been instructive if he had provided at least some descriptive statistics on the proportion of the 150 families that fell into each category. It would also have been useful to know the number of adolescents involved in the study, their ages, and their gender breakdown. He did describe each of the families as white, middle-class, and intact. Let's look at his discussion of adolescents in the two healthy family types—Lewis did not discuss adolescent development in the dysfunctional family types.

Adolescents in the optimal families tended to trust others and to communicate openly. The parents agreed with one another in their assessments of their adolescents' personalities. The adolescents did well in school, were involved in a variety of activities, had close friends, and demonstrated motivation to succeed. The parents worked cooperatively, were very satisfied with their marriages, and did not look to their children for companionship not provided by their spouses.

Adolescents in the competent but pained families tended to trust others less and to constrict their communication more than adolescents in optimal families. They seemed to carry a burden of fulfilling parental needs not met in the marriage; these needs were particularly expressed by their mothers.

On the whole, adolescents in competent but pained families seemed similar to adolescents in optimal families. While an optimal level of functioning may be desirable, the findings suggest that healthy children can develop in pained families. In fact, even when one parent suffered significant psychological distress, the adolescents seemed unaffected because their parents' marital relationship was, on the whole, satisfying. These findings recall the conclusions of the McMaster study that a good marital relationship protects children from developing the emotional difficulties that plague one or both parents as individuals (Westley & Epstein, 1969, cited in Epstein et al., 1982).

Lewis (1978) concluded that healthy families' competencies positively correlate with the health of the children. Lewis likened adolescents in healthy families to the normal adolescents Offer had reported in his research (Offer, Sabshin, & Marcus, 1965) (see Chapter 4).

Systems models of family functioning emphasize the significant role parents play in the development of children. The three systems models discussed here each focus on different aspects of family functioning. The Circumplex Model emphasizes adaptability, cohesion, and communication. The McMaster Model emphasizes the multiple dimensions of family functioning: problem solving, communication, roles, affective responsiveness, affective involvement, and behavior control. The Beavers-Timberlawn Model distinguishes healthy families from dysfunctional families.

According to the systems perspective, individual development is influenced not only by one's immediate family but also by previous generations. We now turn to a tool developed by family therapists to better understand the impact of several generations on a family. The tool is called a *genogram*.

USING GENOGRAMS TO UNDERSTAND PAST AND CURRENT FAMILY INFLUENCES

Family therapists have produced an intriguing tool, called a **genogram**, to increase understanding about the history of a problem in a family. The genogram particularly casts light on emotional relationships across generations. Using the genogram depends on understanding each generation in a family as a system that influences later generations and has been influenced by earlier generations. Another way of looking at genograms is to liken them to a family tree of interrelationships (Strong & DeVault, 1989).

Genograms can disclose how certain patterns of conduct emerge in successive generations. For instance, some families teach their children to negotiate interpersonal difficulties and to develop close bonds of attachment. A genogram may reveal that this style of interaction was present in earlier generations as well.

Another pattern that marks some families is pretending conflict or distress has not happened. The film *The Prince of Tides*, adapted from the novel by Pat Conroy (1986), depicted just such a family. The devastating effects of the imposition of silence remained with the children in their adult lives. This pattern of avoiding any discussion of distress was likely present in earlier generations as well. Research suggests that child abuse is also passed on from one generation to the next, with the child victim becoming the adult perpetrator (Garbarino & Guttman, 1986; Sebes, 1986).

What might a genogram disclose about the family's interactions over significant developmental tasks? A significant developmental task for any family is to shape its children so that by late adolescence they are ready to launch out into the world on their own. Seeing how earlier generations have prepared their late adolescents to be independent adults can provide clues to what is going on in a current generation. Monica McGoldrick and Randy Gerson (1985) provide genograms for several famous American families, including the Kennedys, the Adams, and the O'Neills, that illustrate patterns of success and failure over several generations in launching late adolescents.

Genograms use symbols to identify individuals and indicate relationships. These symbols are presented in the key of Figure 6-1 on page 250.

Figure 6-1 presents a hypothetical family, George and Joanna Mitchell and their two living adolescent children, Phyllis and James. Both George and Joanna were raised on family farms. Our interpretation of the Mitchell family genogram focuses primarily on their 18-year-old son, James.

The first lesson we can learn concerns rules about intimacy. Males in the Mitchell family have close, but, conflictual relations with females. This pattern covers the past three generations. Through years of interacting within his family and observing others interact, James has learned that relationships with females are risky. He has learned males and females protect themselves by mixing intimacy with conflict. Like many adolescent sons, James perceives his father as distant; James also sees that his father and paternal grandfather are emotionally distant with each other.

The farm has been in James's family for five generations. Each oldest son has inherited the farm and improved it—this tradition dates back to his great-great-grandfather's family. James is expected to take over the farm from his father. The mantle of inheritance was passed to him when his older brother, Henry, died in an automobile accident six years ago.

There are problems for James and his family over this family tradition. James, first of all, wants to go to college and become a history teacher like his uncle John. Communication between James and his uncle is open, and the two feel close to each other. Second, the family farm is in serious economic crisis, and his father might lose it before the end of the year unless arrangements can be made with creditors. The level of distress in the family over the potential loss of the farm has three generations of Mitchells deeply upset. James feels guilty about his desire for a college career at a time when his family is in such need.

A third dynamic has entered the picture and might provide James and his family an outlet if they can get beyond gender the 20-year-old sister of James, has expressed a desire to take over the farm and keep it in the family. She began to express her interests a few years after Henry's death. James and Phyllis are close but argue a lot, particularly over the future of the farm.

James's father is also close with Phyllis, but like other males in the Mitchell family, tempers this closeness with conflict. He is, however, beginning to say to others in the family that perhaps his daughter can help to save the family's inheritance. He particularly respects Phyliss's fiancé, a young man who knows a good deal about farming and who has a college degree in agricultural economics.

James is feeling confused about what is appropriate for men and women to do now that he knows his father's opinions about his sister. James is suspicious of Phyliss's fiancé, whom he thinks is an outsider more interested in getting the farm than in marrying his sister. While he wants to follow in the footsteps of his uncle

FIGURE 6-1   A Genogram of James Mitchell's Family*

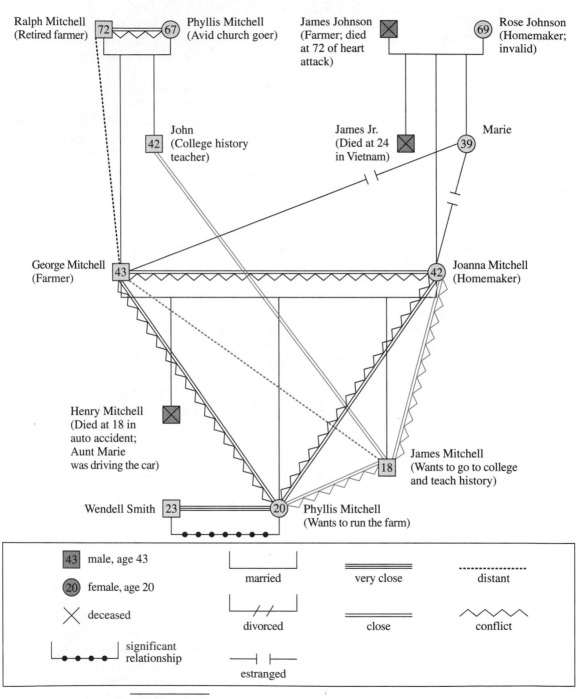

John, James is confused about his duty to his family. Were it not for Henry's death, he would not have assumed the role of inheritor and could, without any distress, have been given his family's blessing to become a college teacher.

John feels very torn about what advice to give his nephew. While he thinks James would make a very good college teacher, he feels hesitant to interfere in an issue that is so emotionally charged for his brother's family.

James would like to talk to his aunt Marie about his confusion. For some reason James cannot understand, he is relaxed around his aunt; however, the Mitchells have a family rule not to share family secrets with anyone the parents do not approve of. Relations between James's parents and his aunt are very bad. They blame her for Henry's death; she was driving the car when it was hit by a sudden gust of wind, went out of control, turned over, and caused Henry to die of massive internal injuries. Marie suffered some cuts and bruises but was practically unscathed.

James definitely believes his parents are blaming Marie for something that was not her fault. James knows that Marie and her brother, who was killed in Vietnam and after whom James was named, were very close. James reminds everyone in the family of his uncle James.

Unresolved grief seems to haunt the Mitchells, preventing any closure to the death of the older son, Henry. The estrangement with Marie over his death has made unwelcome one relative James feels at ease with. One wonders how Marie and her sister Joanna dealt with the death of James Johnson, Jr. when he was killed in Vietnam.

The genogram in Figure 6-1 helps concisely portray these family dynamics. A key example is the presence of so many close, but, conflictual relationships between males and females. It is little wonder that separation from his parents is a matter of difficulty for James given the family dynamics illustrated in Figure 6-1. James feels he can achieve separation from his parents only by maintaining emotional distance from them.

The genogram makes clear that communication in the Mitchell family is fraught with risk. These risks extend across generations. James and his father feel emotionally distant from each other, a pattern found between George and his father. Given the gravity of the family farm's economic situation and given James's plans for himself, one would think James and his father would discuss these matters. However, when his son hinted at leaving the farm and becoming a college teacher like his uncle John, George became very autocratic, gave him a lecture about family responsibility and duty, and refused to listen to his son's ideas.

Opening up to his family now about his wishes leaves James vulnerable to conflict and to being influenced by his parents at a time when he wants to be his own person. He is beginning to become emotionally isolated from his mom and dad as a means to keep his independence.

THE CHANGING STRUCTURE OF THE AMERICAN FAMILY

The structure of the family in American society is changing. The standard of the nuclear family is less normative for many people. How do these changing structures affect adolescents?

Since the 1960s, an increasing proportion of children are part of single-parent families.

Some writers have taken a strongly relativistic position to the changing structure of the family. Jaber Gubrium and James Holstein (1990) assert that a family is a **social construction** (that is, a family is given meaning through the communication of its members). In other words, while there may be biological and legal definitions of families, these researchers say families take form in the patterns of interactions between members.

Family life is unsettled territory being explored and mapped by contemporary thinkers. In this section, we focus on family processes and outcomes, rather than discuss whose definition of family is most persuasive. Despite some changes occurring in family structure in American society, the intact, **nuclear family** is the norm in research literature unless the intent is to study effects of growing up in other types of families (for instance, families without fathers).

A challenge to the nuclear family is presented by the dramatic increase of **single-parent families**. Other alternatives to the nuclear family include **blended families**—families with children from different marriages—and couple-run group homes for youths who have been abandoned by their parents or taken from them due to neglect and/or abuse.

A family is commonly believed to include a father, mother, and their children living together in the same dwelling until the children are old enough to live on their own and start their own families. This is the image of the nuclear family. Within the past 30 years, anthropologists have portrayed the nuclear family as a universal human phenomenon (Murdock, 1967, as cited by Strong & DeVault, 1989). However, census data over the same 30 years cast doubt about applying such an assertion to American families (Bureau of the Census, 1991a, 1991b).

Census data provide sobering news about changing family structures in the United States. Since the 1960s, the proportion of children who are part of single-parent families has been increasing. The data indicate that the American nuclear family is an endangered species.

Between 1960 and 1990, the proportion of children in single-parent households (usually headed by a divorced or never married mother) increased dramatically. In 1960, 23% of American children lived with a single parent who was divorced, and 4.2% with a never married parent. (Widowed parents account for about 5% of parents with children at home.) Thus, in 1960, around 27% of American children lived with a single parent. By 1990, a total of 69.2% of American children were living with either a divorced parent (38.6%) or a never married parent (30.6%) (Bureau of the Census, 1991b). Nearly all of these single-parent families were headed by a female.

Such data have alarming implications for child development. In 1990, nearly 40% of one-parent families made less than $10,000 a year, and nearly 27% made between $10,000 and 20,000. Two-parent households, however, present a distinctly different picture—nearly 50% make more than $40,000 a year, and less than 17% make under $20,000 (Bureau of the Census, 1991a).

The financial hardships imposed on single-parent households, particularly those with a female head, are anything but negligible. Between 1983 and 1986, the Bureau of the Census (1991a) investigated the immediate consequences for children when a parent abandoned the family. The study was longitudinal, lasting a total of 32 months. Participants included two-parent and single-parent families. Children in two-parent families remained economically advantaged throughout the course of the investigation. But for children whose fathers left the family, the family's income decreased 23% over the 32 months of the study, and was less than 60% of the income in stable, two-parent families (Bureau of the Census, 1991a). Furthermore, once these single-parent families headed by mothers experienced their dramatic declines in income, they seldom could recoup their losses.

This plunge toward poverty in single-parent families affects adolescents differently according to age. Early adolescents have less appreciation for financial realities than their older adolescent siblings and are much more insistent on having material possessions (designer clothes, for instance) in order to gain peer acceptance. Middle and late adolescents are more able to comprehend the financial straits their families experience and are more able to contribute to meeting the families' financial needs by getting a job. Producing income for the family provides a sense of accomplishment for these adolescents. However, financial pressures can lead older adolescents to cut short educational plans and even to drop out of high school to help meet the family's expenses.

Binuclear Families   A **binuclear family** is the aftermath of a nuclear family sundered by divorce (Strong & DeVault, 1989). Two forms of the binuclear family are (*a*) the single-parent family and (*b*) the blended family.

We have looked at some of the impacts, primarily financial, on single-parent households headed by women. A blended family produces its own variety of impacts. In a blended family, relationships can become particularly complicated. Take the following example, which is a true story, as an illustration.

Rhonda and Catherine Phillips were 16 and 14 years old, respectively, when their father, Edward, died. About a year following the death, their mother, Helen, began seeing Ralph Jones, who had custody of his three teenage children, Matt, Sarah, and John, following his divorce from his former wife, Elizabeth. Ralph's parents were still living; Edward's and Helen's parents were still living as well.

About six months after Helen and Ralph began to see each other, they married. Rhonda found it difficult to accept her mother's decision to date Ralph and even more difficult to accept her decision to marry him.

Ralph and his three children moved into what had been the Phillips' home. The children from each family got along warily at best. Two years after Helen and Ralph's marriage, they had a daughter. Thus, in less than four years following their father's death, Rhonda and Catherine had a stepparent, two stepbrothers, one stepsister, and one halfsister. Their family also included two sets of biological grandparents and one set of stepgrandparents.

Similar permutations could be derived for other members of this blended family. Of course, what is only hinted at is the quality and strain in the various relationships these people have with each other now that they are joined in a blended family.

Constance Ahrons and Roy Rodgers (1987) identified several relationship subsystems in a blended family. These relationships involve (a) the former spouses, (b) the remarried couple, (c) the biological parents and their children, (d) the stepsiblings and halfsiblings, and (e) former spouses vis-à-vis the remarried spouses. Ahrons and Rodgers need to account also for the continued relationship of biological siblings to each other as well as to extended family members on both sides of each remarried spouse's former nuclear family. These multiple permutations in subsystems within a blended family highlight Strong and DeVault's comment that "the binuclear family may be the most complex in America today" (1989, p. 485).

A distressing aspect of blended families is the prospect that family problems, especially marital conflicts, will be blamed on a specific child. This child serves as the scapegoat for disturbed functioning in the family and as a means for the marital couple to defend themselves against self-blame for another failed marriage (Ransom, Schlesinger, & Derdeyn, 1979).

Adolescents in Blended Families

As we have mentioned, blended families produce complicated relationships involving stepparents, biological parents, stepsiblings, and biological siblings. James Mikesell and James Garbarino (1986) note that many participants experience negative feelings when a stepfamily forms. Some of these negative feelings interact with the developmental changes adolescents normally experience and affect the adolescent's adjustment.

However, not all is gloomy for an adolescent entering a blended family. There are opportunities as well as risks. Mikesell and Garbarino (1986) identify three opportunities for adolescents in a blended family: (a) a secure family, (b) increased autonomy and personal development, and (c) help in cognitive development.

The loss of a father due to death or divorce may be so traumatic for an adolescent that he or she finds it difficult to cope. When the mother remarries, the adolescent may find the new family affords security, money, and a sense of family unity (Mikesell & Garbarino, 1986). Gaining a more secure, stable environment is surely a gain in the life of a troubled youth.

Stepfamilies can provide adolescents opportunities to take on greater responsibility for care of younger family members. Such responsibility increases personal autonomy and promotes growth in self-esteem and maturity.

Cognitive development in adolescent males seems particularly to benefit when an accepted replacement father enters the boy's life. One reason for such gains may be that the stepfather helps alleviate the boy's grief over the loss of his natural father. The stepfather may also provide a needed role model. Girls do not appear to make similar cognitive gains when a stepfather enters their lives (Mikesell & Garbarino, 1986).

Adolescents may also be at risk in stepfamilies. Mikesell and Garbarino (1986) report several studies indicate adolescents experience difficult psychological adjustments in blended families. For instance, the adolescents typically possess lower self-esteem, experience greater stress that increases, rather than decreases, over time, and become more at risk for abuse. Mikesell and Garbarino particularly were concerned that several social indicators (for instance, family income, education level of parents, parental attitudes toward child mistreatment, and parental attitudes toward discipline) signify the potential of being abused is greater for adolescents in stepfamilies than it is for adolescents in nuclear families.

Combining adopted children with biological children may also cause problems in a family. Adolescent siblings typically react poorly to adopted older children (Ward & Lewko, 1987, 1988). In several studies, adopted children were viewed as creating more problems than biological siblings, and adolescents reported more frequent problems with the adopted siblings than with their biological siblings.

We have looked at typical structures of American families, and reviewed evidence that, for the most part, suggests blended families put adolescents at risk. We now turn to a major task for all types of families; namely, to nurture separation as the children become adults.

ACHIEVING SEPARATION FROM ONE'S PARENTS

Separation from parents is closely linked to identity formation. Adolescents whose identities are marked by foreclosure (see Chapter 4) have a considerably different perspective on separating from parents than adolescents whose identities are achieved or are in moratorium. Research indicates adolescents who have attained some emotional autonomy from their parents fare better in living away from home (Campbell, Adams, & Dobson, 1984).

A substantial body of literature categorizes adolescent separation from parents as a matter of **individuation** (Blos, 1967/19791; Collins, 1990; Cooper, Grotevant, & Condon, 1983; Grotevant & Cooper, 1986; Hauser & Greene, 1991; Quintana &

Kerr, 1993; Steinberg & Silverberg, 1986; Youniss & Smollar, 1985). W. Andrew Collins (1990), for instance, has noted that most parents and their late adolescents work out a process that leads the adolescents to assume more equality as well as obligations vis-à-vis their parents. You may recall from discussions in Chapter 1 that Blos (1967/1979i) depicts adolescence as a second individuation process. For Blos, this individuation involves a greater sense of autonomy and an increased sense of competency and responsibility for one's life. James Youniss and Jacqueline Smollar (1985) portrayed individuation as a process with dual aspects; on one hand, late adolescents gain a greater sense of autonomy and independence while, on the other hand, they relate to their parents with attachments based on personal respect, rather than on authority and servility. Nga Anh Nguyen (1992) used the concept of individuation to understand the development of Asian-American youths and efforts of therapists to work with Asian-American adolescents and their families.

These notions of individuation emphasize that most adolescents achieve separation from their parents while retaining emotionally warm and close relationships with them. Several studies indicate distinct features mark late adolescents who separate with relative ease from parents (Bell, Avery, Jenkins, Feld, & Schoenrock, 1985; Campbell et al., 1984; Moore, 1984, 1987; Sullivan & Sullivan, 1980). This body of research indicates that (*a*) the way in which adolescents interpret separation from parents is directly associated with the adolescents' psychological well-being and with ongoing ties to their families; and (*b*) that males and females experience separation from parents differently. Gender differences especially emerge when separation issues involve self-governance and emotional detachment.

Adolescent separation from parents involves several multidimensional issues:

- functional independence—managing one's personal and practical affairs with little assistance from parents;
- attitudinal independence—seeing oneself as unique from one's parents and possessing a personal set of beliefs, values, and ideas about life;
- emotional independence—being free from excessive need for parental approval, closeness, and emotional support; and
- conflictual independence—being free from excessive guilt, anxiety, resentment, responsibility, and anger in relation to one's parents (Moore, 1984, 1987; Sullivan & Sullivan, 1980).

In addition to these four independence issues, adolescents themselves have identified several kinds of evidence that signify having achieved separation from parents. Among the items on their lists are gaining economic independence, establishing a separate residence, graduating from school, making independent choices, and achieving emotional detachment (Moore, 1987).

The effects of gaining separation from one's parents are mediated through the adolescent's interpretation of the meaning and character of this task. Family systems theory says intricate family interactions over several years, even over several generations, combine to instruct an adolescent how to construe what it means to seek independence.

Another model for understanding how adolescents manage the transition from dependence on their parents to living on their own is life-span developmental psychology's understanding of normative life transitions. One aspect of such thinking is that how a person appraises a developmental task influences how the person copes with that task (Moos, 1986). We discuss this approach in detail in Chapter 11. By studying how peopele cope with life crises, researchers have inferred that the meaning attributed to a critical life event significantly affects resolution of the crisis. As applied to the normative life crisis of gaining independence, the meaning attributed to separation from one's parents influences whether adolescents maintain or cut off ongoing relations with them.

The most important aspect of parent-adolescent separation appears to be **self-governance**. Self-governance is the acquisition of autonomy and is demonstrated by an adolescent's responses to such questions as:

- Who do you consider to be an adult and how much are you like that person?
- How mature are you?
- How much do you feel like an adult?
- How much do you do things for yourself?
- How independent are you?
- How often do you make your own decisions?
- How much do you take care of yourself?

Adolescents who successfully live on their own and become self-governing have positive relations with their families (Campbell et al., 1984; Sullivan & Sullivan, 1980). You may recall that positive relations with family members is one of the distinguishing features of healthy families in the launching adolescents stage of the family life cycle (Olson et al., 1983).

Late adolescents who become successful in their self-governance also display positive personal characteristics, such as high self-esteem. They value themselves and, in addition, appear to view separation from their parents as an important achievement. In terms of coping, they view separation as a matter of acquired competency (Campbell et al., 1984; Sullivan & Sullivan, 1980). Most adolescents, in fact, downgrade the importance of emotional detachment in gaining separation from their parents.

However, adolescents who report poor relationships with their parents often consider separation a matter of getting away from problematic family interaction. For these adolescents, the key characteristic of separation is emotional detachment from their parents (Moore, 1984). Features of emotional detachment include feeling distant from one's family, breaking ties and communication upon separation, feeling out of place when at one's parents' home, and seeing the family infrequently, at best. While emotional detachment may become most visible when the adolescent leaves home, family systems theory has taught us to understand that interactions between family members laid the seeds for emotional detachment long before the separation took place.

TABLE 6-3   When Separation from Parents Is Associated With Emotional Detachment: Gender Differences

	MALES	FEMALES
LONELINESS	More	Less
SELF-ESTEEM	Lower	Higher
LIFE SATISFACTION	Less	More
DIFFICULTIES LEAVING HOME	More	Less
ACHIEVING SEPARATE IDENTITY	More Difficult	Less Difficult

SOURCES: Adapted from "Parent-Adolescent Separation: Intrafamilial Perceptions and Difficulty Separating from Parents" by D. Moore, 1984, *Personality and Social Psychology Bulletin, 10* and "Parent-Adolescent Separation: The Constriction of Adulthood by Late Adolescents" by D. Moore, 1987, *Developmental Psychology, 23.*

Gender differences have been found in late adolescent separations marked by emotional detachment. In contrast to their peers who remain engaged with families after achieving independent lives, males who disengage from their families report greater loneliness, lower self-esteem, less achievement of an identity separate from their parents, less satisfaction with life, and greater difficulties leaving home (Moore, 1984, 1987).

Compared to males, females who associate separation with emotional detachment are marked by less loneliness, greater self-esteem, greater life satisfaction, less difficulty leaving home, and greater achievement of an identity separate from their parents. The contrasts between males and females on separation and emotional detachment are presented in Table 6-3.

One hypothesis about why females whose separation is marked by emotional detachment are more effective than males at coping with separation from home is that males are less effective at coping with emotional intimacy and with relationships in general. It has been argued that females internalize richer emotional relationships with other people than do males. Therefore, reserves of internalized personal relationships insulate late adolescent females during times of separation and make them less emotionally dependent on their parents.

ADOLESCENT-PARENT PERCEPTIONS: A GENERATION GAP?

Adolescents and their parents perceive interaction with each other differently (Olson et al., 1983). Because these differences are widespread and prominent, Patricia Noller and Victor Callan (1991) maintain they constitute a **generation gap**.

A fairly common belief is that a generation gap separates adolescents from their parents. The image is of a tug-of-war between parents and peer groups for the loyalties of adolescent sons and daughters. Few people (if any) question that during their adolescence, individuals move from parents to peer groups as important frames of reference. Anna Freud (1958/1969) and Blos (1965/1979e) portrayed this reorienta-

Separating from Parents and Becoming an Adult

Notions of self-governance and feelings of attachment or detachment are important aspects of adolescent views of separation. Males, in particular, seem to view separation as a journey over one of two distinctly separate roads: either a road of self-governance or a road of emotional detachment. According to researchers, more choose the road of self-governance (Campbell et al., 1984; Moore, 1984, 1987; Pascarella & Terenzini, 1991; Sullivan & Sullivan, 1980).

The less-travelled road, that of emotional detachment, is considered less optimal for late adolescent males. In choosing this path, they are believed to be less likely to achieve well-being as an adult. I seriously doubt, however, that problems in life satisfaction as an adult are caused solely by construing separation from one's parents in terms of emotional detachment. By the time late adolescent males define separation in these terms, several years of personal development and family interactions have shaped them.

Viewing separation in terms of emotional detachment may signify that these late adolescent males have difficulty becoming attached to other people and have difficulty giving and receiving nurturance. They may find it inconceivable that separation could be anything other than a form of emotional isolation, and inconceivable that independence can be achieved if one retains ties.

If nothing else, the data on adolescents' achieving separation and becoming self-governing adults indicate that family relationships influence the adolescent transition toward achieving independence and a separate identity. A history of detachment between parents and adolescents produces particular risks for males seeking to establish autonomous identities.

Another influence on gaining independence from parents is college. In addition to having a liberalizing influence on values and an enriching effect on cognitive development, college produces changes in relating to others and to the world outside one's family. One measure of these changes is an increased sense of internal responsibility and control (or autonomy). Persuasive evidence marshalled by Pascarella and Terenzini (1991) suggests that college positively effects increases in an internal locus of control. An internal locus of control indicates the individual believes he or she has a significant effect on producing desired outcomes. An external locus of control suggests beliefs that the individual's life is mostly influenced by forces outside his or her control (Rotter, 1966).

In addition to increasing a person's internal locus of control, college also seems to lead students to be less dependent on their families. Pascarella and Terenzini (1991) caution that studies of the effects of college on increasing independence have not used nationally representative samples. Yet, they suggest the evidence indicates that during college, students increase their independence from parents. They are not as certain that college, attendance promotes increased autonomy from peer influence because the research in this area has been flawed by using small samples, not obtaining measures of the students' levels of independence prior to college, and gathering data from students at a single institution.

tion as part of a new struggle over oedipal conflicts brought on by puberty. Erikson (1963, 1968), who gave more emphasis than Sigmund Freud to social factors in the search for ego identity, agreed that puberty catalyzes adolescents to seek identity independent of parents and to pursue feedback about identity from peers.

One way to study whether a generation gap exists is to look at value differences in three generations: adolescents, their parents, and their grandparents. Sam Payne, David Summers, and Thomas Stewart (1973) investigated (*a*) whether a generation gap exists between adolescents and their parents, (*b*) whether a generation gap influences development across the life span, and (*c*) whether younger generations are more permissive than older generations. Their sample included 95 college undergraduates, 68 parents around 48 years of age, and 59 grandparents around 72 years of age. Payne and his colleagues (1973) asked questions related to conventional morality, attributions of personal failure, and embarrassment.

The grandparents in the study were stricter in their self-punishments over violations of conventional morality than parents or late adolescents. In fact, as the generations became younger, self-punishment over violations of conventional morality declined. Examples of conventional morality examined in the study were attitudes toward trying marijuana, lying about one's past in order to get a job, and having sexual relations with someone you are not married to and for whom you do not feel strong attachment.

The parents were harder on themselves when they faced personal failure than either their adolescent children or their children's grandparents. Examples of personal failures are cheating on an exam and getting caught, losing your temper and threatening to strike one of your parents, and not speaking up for a friend when other people are being critical.

The parents and grandparents were more likely to become embarrassed than the college students. Examples of potentially embarrassing situations were practicing birth control even when your partner considers birth control wrong, forgetting a parent's birthday, having unexpected guests drop in when your home is a mess, and being with someone of the opposite sex who shows too much affection in public.

While gaps were present between these generations, Payne and his colleagues (1973) did not detect a singular pattern to these gaps. The differences in values depended on the situation presented to each generation. One finding, however, is noticeable—the late adolescents were never less permissive than their parents or their grandparents. Furthermore, the results suggest that changes in values are attributable to changes in society.

The cross-sectional nature of Payne and his colleagues' study did not enable the researchers to truly test developmental trends. While there were generational differences, we cannot conclude whether the differences were static (that is, individuals from the differnt generations did not change as time elapsed) or dynamic (changes occured as cohorts aged).

Given the date of Payne and his colleagues' study, one can only surmise how the current generation of college undergraduates, their parents, and their grandparents would respond. Since the early 1970s, technology has dramatically altered American society. To take one example, consider the inventions of cable television and the video cassette recorder (VCR). Youths in the 1990s have access to adult-oriented films of varying quality and subject matter that, when their parents were adolescents, they could not view because theater owners would not sell them a ticket. Children today can easily see these films because of video rental stores and the ubiquity of cable television. One might infer viewing these films gives today's younger generation attitudes toward violence, sexuality, and language that earlier generations of adolescents did not share.

Fathers and the Generation gap

Of some interest, given our earlier discussion of gender socialization in families, is the finding that fathers are less willing than mothers to share power with their adolescent children (Weinmann & Newcombe, 1990; Youniss & Smollar, 1985). More than a matter of misperception, actual differences regarding roles and rules in the family, particularly as expressed by adolescent children and their fathers, create a generation gap in families. Lance Weinmann and Nora Newcombe (1990) demonstrated that this gap extends to feelings of intimacy and affection. In their study, college students reported love between themselves and their mothers increased during their adolescence, whereas their relations with their fathers remained distant.

Research conducted by Youniss and Smollar (1985) helps throw light on adolescent perceptions of the father's role in maintaining this generation gap. These investigators conducted several studies of adolescents during the early 1980s. They sampled over 1,000 adolescents between 12 and 19 years of age, with nearly equal numbers of males and females. The focus of their research was adolescent perceptions of relations with parents and friends. Most of the adolescents were white, most came from middle-class families, and all lived in the eastern United States.

Adolescent females perceived their fathers as supportive, but emotionally distant. They did not report their fathers understand or accept them. Although conflicts with their fathers seemed to occur infrequently, adolescent females said they lack a relationship with their fathers. Few reported having a negative relationship (Youniss & Smollar, 1985).

Adolescent males shared work and recreational activities with their fathers, but did not see their relationships with their fathers as close or intimate. (I recall one adolescent who expressed utter astonishment when his mother told him that his father loved him deeply.) Conflicts arose when fathers or sons failed to treat each other with respect. Adolescents looked to their fathers for advice about practical matters, such as where to apply for work or where to get a car fixed.

Adolescent females developed intricate, complicated relationships with their mothers involving intimacy and conflict. They viewed their mothers as authority figures in whom they could confide. However, they quarreled with their mothers, not with their fathers. Mothers and their adolescent daughters talked about many topics, and the daughters considered themselves able to give their mothers advice as well as seek it from them.

Adolescent males developed close relationships with their mothers. They confided in their mothers about personal matters. Mothers made rules and demanded obedience and respect, and mother-son conflicts predominately involved the mother's role in making rules and enforcing discipline. However, regardless of conflicts about discipline, the males acknowledged that their mothers care about them (Youniss & Smollar, 1985).

Conflicts between parents and adolescents seem to involve, for the most part, day-to-day squabbles over chores, curfews, and friends (Olson et al., 1983). In Olson

Australian Adolescents' Perceptions of Their Parents

An extensive, well-designed survey of adolescents in Australia investigated the values adolescents place on parents and peers (Connell, Stroobant, Sinclair, Connell, & Rogers, 1975). In this study, 10,000 adolescents between the ages of 12 and 20 were chosen by strictly random sampling techniques. The adolescents were asked several questions about their relations with parents and peers.

One question aksed who adolescents prefer to spend time with. The great majority—70%—preferred their friends over their parents.

Another question asked whether the adolescent would choose to go on a picnic with friends or with family. Early adolescents (up to age 14) preferred their parents, middle adolescents (14–17) preferred their friends, and older adolescents (age 18 and above) preferred their parents. These results suggest parents are important at different times during the adolescent years.

Another question in the study dealt with whose disapproval counted most—parents, teachers, or peers. Around 70% of the adolescents said the disapproval of parents was the hardest to take, around 20% said the disapproval of friends, and the remaining 10% said teachers' disapproval counted the most.

The Australian researchers also asked the adoles-cents who they discuss personal problems with. There were gender differences in these answers. For males, 27% said they confide in their fathers, 44% in their mothers, 17% in their friends, and 12% in their siblings. For females, only 3% said they confide in their fathers, 62% in their mothers, 24% in their friends, and 11% in their siblings. These results indicate that parents—particularly mothers—remain far more important as confidants than might typically be believed. However, the father's place as a confidant seems much less important overall to these adolescents than their friends.

The researchers concluded that a generation gap exists, though not as exaggerated as some would argue (Connell et al., 1975). In particular, they said the clash of values between parents and peer groups was much less pronounced than has been commonly asserted. Only on some behaviors (such as length of hair and curfews) did adolescents ally with peers rather than with parents. On several issues related to peer relations, parents, peers, and the adolescents fundamentally agreed. These issues include dancing, dating, using makeup, and kissing. Adolescents were more likely to side with their parents' views, rather than their peers' views, about drinking alcoholic beverages, smoking tobacco, and gambling.

and his colleagues' (1983) study, adolescents conceded that they add to the level of conflict in their families when they use drugs, smoke cigarettes, drink alcoholic beverages, or engage in sexual intercourse.

Parental distress,such as changes in employment, family medical problems, and the infirmity of grandparents, affects adolescents. Thus, it cannot be said that adolescents affect parents but remain immune from events that affect their parents. Family systems theory would, of course, say such immunity is impossible in a family.

PARENTAL STYLES OF CHILD REARING AND ADOLESCENT RESPONSES

Another familial influence on adolescent development is parental style of child rearing. Diana Baumrind (1967, 1968, 1972, 1977, 1978, 1991) has studied effects of parental discipline and child-rearing styles on child development, and from her studies, she has identified three patterns of parental interaction with children: authoritarian, permissive, and authoritative.

Initially, Baumrind (1967) conducted a longitudinal study of 134 preschool children and their parents. Members of her research team observed each child many times in both the preschool and home environments, and produced ratings on several dimensions, including sociability, self-reliance, moodiness, and self-control. They also observed parent-child interactions in the home on several occasions. From these observations, Baumrind identified her three patterns of parental interaction with children.

Authoritarian parents use restrictions, imposing rules on their children, seldom with an explanation for the purpose of the rules. Authoritarians expect strict compliance with the letter of the law. They often rely on physical punishment and force to gain compliance.

Permissive parents enforce rules inconsistently at best. They have a laissez-faire attitude about disciplining their children. They make relatively few demands on their children, permit free expression of feelings and impulses, and do not monitor their children's behavior. They seldom exert firm control over their children, and children's wishes become law in the family. Parental inconsistency with rules leads to unpredictable occasions when parents insist on compliance in matters they often tolerate.

Authoritative parents provide more flexible controls than authoritarian parents, and firmer, more consistent controls than permissive parents. They explain their reasons for rules and ensure that children follow the rules. While breaking rules can lead to punishments, authoritative parents are willing to listen to their children's explanations for behavior and adjust responses to fit the occasion. Authoritative parents teach children that freedom has boundaries, and they gauge children's exercise of freedom by children's developmental levels. They respond to their children's needs and listen to their points of view while still remaining in charge.

Baumrind's three parenting styles can be imagined to exist along a continuum measuring exertion of power. At one end is the authoritarian style that insists on rigid, total exercise of power, while at the other end is the permissive style that abdicates power. The authoritative style exists as a balanced, moderate use of power in children's lives.

Children of authoritarian, permissive, and authoritative parents display distinct behavior patterns. These patterns are presented in Table 6-4 on the following page.

Baumrind's (1967) findings about parenting styles and the behaviors of preschool children strongly suggest that children develop optimally with authoritative parents. Behavior problems were distinctive of children whose parents employed authoritarian or permissive child-rearing approaches.

TABLE 6-4   Parental Style and Children's Behavior

AUTHORITARIAN	PERMISSIVE	AUTHORITATIVE
Fearful	Rebellious	Self-reliant
Apprehensive	Low self-control	Self-controlled
Moody	Low self-reliance	Cheerful
Unhappy	Impulsive	Cooperative with adults
Easily annoyed	Aggressive	Curious
Aimless	Domineering	Purposeful
Unfriendly	Aimless	Achievement-oriented
Vulnerable to stress	Low achievement	Copes well with stress

SOURCES: Adapted from "Child Care Practices Anteceding Three Patterns of Preschool Behavior" by D. Baumrind, 1967, *Genetic Psychology Monographs, 75* and *Developmental Psychology: Childhood and Adolescence* (p. 572) by D. Shaffer, 1989, Pacific Grove, CA: Brooks/Cole.

Baumrind (1972) indicated one exception to her conclusions about the effects of parenting styles on the development of preschool children. She noted that black parents appear authoritarian when viewed from white, middle-class norms. She also noted that black children who were assertive and self-reliant were reared by parents who seemed the most authoritarian of all the parents in her study. However, Baumrind also mentioned these same children were bossy and overbearing with peers and defiant with adults.

Baumrind and her associates wondered if preschool children raised by authoritarian or permissive parents would outgrow their preschool problems. They also wondered if children raised by authoritative parents would maintain the behavioral competencies they demonstrated in preschool. Baumrind (1977) did a follow-up study of these children at ages 8 and 9. The children with authoritative parents continued to demonstrate social and academic competencies, whereas children with permissive parents were stunted in their social and academic growth, and children of authoritarian parents were, at best, average in their social and academic development.

A review of these same children in their early adolescent years (Baumrind, 1991) again reported that the highly authoritarian and permissive parents hindered the development of autonomy. Authoritative parents, whom Baumrind now refers to as *responsive parents*, fostered their young adolescents to be independent and to form individual identities. Other researchers confirmed that individuals continue to display in their adolescence the types of academic and social competencies seen in their preschool and school-age years (Dornbusch, Ritter, Leiderman, Roberts, & Fraleigh, 1987).

A few years earlier than Baumrind, Glen Elder (1963) studied over 7,000 early and middle adolescents to see their perceptions of parental uses of power. From the adolescents' reports, Elder identified three categories of parental use of power. Although he used somewhat different terms, Elder's categories correspond exactly with Baumrind's three categories. Elder said parents use power autocratically, permissively, or democratically. Whereas Baumrind's categories are more well-known,

Elder's seem easier to understand, particularly his distinction between democratic and autocratic. Baumrind used nearly identical terms to identify these different parental styles: authoritative and authoritarian.

In Elder's (1963) study, adolescents said **autocratic parents** did not allow them to express views about behavior or allow them to exercise control over their behavior. Autocratic parents used coercion and disregarded their adolescent children's feelings.

Democratic parents encouraged adolescents to participate in discussion of issues, while reserving the rights of final decision making for themselves as parents. They became teachers as well as enforcers of rules. They showed respect for feelings and legitimated their power in the family by reasoned explanations for decisions and by empathic communication about feelings.

Permissive parents did not exercise power in their families. They modeled for their children a lack of concern and lack of involvement in their children's lives. They enforced rules inconsistently and unpredictably.

Elder (1963) found adolescents clearly favor democratic parents and are quite critical of autocratic or permissive parents. Adolescents from democratically run families are self-confident and more independent than adolescents from autocratic or permissive families. They say they want to grow up and be like their parents.

In addition to Baumrind's and Elder's research, other investigators have demonstrated that normal, healthy adolescents emerge from families with authoritative/ democratic parents (Hauser, Borman, Jacobson, Powers, & Noonan, 19991; Hill & Holmbeck, 1986). Do you have any speculations why such findings occur? One conjecture I have is that authoritative/democratic parents provide models of socially responsible, caring adults; in contrast, authoritarian/autocratic parents and permissive parents arbitrarily exercise discipline and ignore their children's individuality. Another guess is that democratic/authoritative parents provide multiple opportunities for their children to grow gradually in responsible decision making, and they provide constructive feedback about the decisions their children make; in contrast, autocratic/ authoritarian parents are less likely to provide opportunities for decision making and more likely to shame their children for making mistakes. Permissive parents avoid providing clear guidelines geared to their children's experiences and levels of maturity.

SIBLING RELATIONSHIPS DURING ADOLESCENCE

Another familial influence on adolescents is sibling relationships. We begin our discussion with the phenomena of *sibling rivalry*.

Sibling Rivalry   Psychoanalytic studies have indicated that unresolved sibling rivalries prevent some people from intelligently sizing up situations they face (White, 1976). Robert White noted that any interactions that produce such enduring effects cannot be ignored as unimportant in a person's early development.

White (1976) was loath to say sibling interactions inevitably produce emotional trauma; he identified, rather, conditions that increase rivalry between siblings. Chief among these conditions is the age of a child when a new sibling is born (18 to 42 months being an apparently vulnerable period). Poor marital relationships also tend to produce sibling jealousy toward the newborn child, especially if the newborn is male and/or if the other child is the first-born (White, 1976).

As children grow, circumstances continue to present occasions for jealousy and rivalry among siblings. Older children are given chores from which the younger children are exempted; sometimes, older children's play with their friends is ruined when younger brothers or sisters must be included because of parental demands. Younger children may resent having to take orders from older brothers or sisters and resent privileges that older children enjoy because of their ages.

White (1976) indicated that college-age males and females attest to the keenness with which sibling rivalry remains an important aspect of their lives.

> In autobiographical papers submitted by college students, sibling rivalry emerges as a fairly common theme, and it is by no means a dead issue at college age. The sharp sensitivity that may surround this problem during childhood is shown in the large variety of situations described. One student, much alienated from his family, remembered with bitterness that his older brother was warmly praised for grades of C on his report card whereas he himself was congratulated only for As. Perhaps the brother was scholastically handicapped, but this did not alter, especially from a child's point of view, the gross unfairness of parental expectations. In another case the situation was almost reversed: the less gifted of two brothers bitterly resented parental rejoicing over his brother's high grades and the unequal allocation of family resources to his higher education. In still another instance a girl described an earlier orthopedic handicap that had necessitated some months in a hospital; she experienced this period as an unfair desertion by her parents who were mostly home with the other children, but the siblings were miffed that their parents rushed to the hospital every day and lavished so much attention on the privileged invalid. Keenly sensitive as they are to their status in parental affection, children find evidence of injustice and favoritism in a great variety of situations (From *The Enterprise of Living: A View of Personal Growth*, 2d ed., by Robert W. White, p. 88. Copyright © 1976 by Holt, Rinehart, and Winston, Inc. Reprinted by permission).

White (1976) provided a case study of the effects of a sibling's death to illustrate the depth of feelings involved in sibling rivalry. The case, which involved bitter rivalry and even hatred, may not be typical. However, the responses of the surviving sibling to the death of his older brother bear notice. In short, he felt little sadness and did not miss his older brother, who had been his parents' favorite child. The brothers' rivalry had been openly harsh, the older boy's accomplishments consistently had exceeded the younger child's, and the parents often publicly compared the younger boy unfavorably to his older brother. When his parents turned their attentions to him after his brother died, the younger son rebelled, displayed minor delinquent acts, and refused to accept his parents' attention. He developed psychosomatic symptoms and, nine years later, displayed anger, violent outbursts, discouragement, depression, and had suicidal thoughts. He felt guilty and admitted that the death of his brother was singularly the most influential event in his life (White, 1976).

Sibling Alliance   While sibling rivalry needs to be recognized, sibling alliance is another possibility to consider when studying sibling relations. Rather than providing only rivalry and competition, siblings can offer each other love, support, nurturance, friendship, companionship, and admiration. Siblings may also be sources of refuge when parenting is grossly inadequate. Studies of development that only looked at sibling rivalry would be woefully incomplete and misleading (White, 1976).

Large age differences between siblings reduce the likelihood of rivalry and competition and increase the possibilities of alliance. Brothers and sisters seem more likely to become allies than same-sex siblings. Siblings may form an alliance in order to present a common front against a more favored child or against parents (White, 1976). Research on sibling alliance scarcely acknowledges that siblings may band together because they care for one another, not just because of self-interest.

Most recent studies of adolescents and siblings focus on the negative effects of sibling relationships. For instance, D. J. Huberty and C. E. Huberty (1986) describe siblings in family therapy as saboteurs of adolescent recovery from drug dependence, and they emphasize that attempts to change addicted adolescents must identify the roles siblings play in the family of a chemically dependent adolescent. One motive for siblings to sabotage another sibling's recovery from drug dependency is that family conflicts will no longer have an identified scapegoat should the therapy succeed.

Bruce Roscoe and his associates (Goodwin & Roscoe, 1990; Roscoe, Goodwin, & Kennedy, 1987) have examined sibling verbal conflict and physical violence during adolescence. They studied 244 junior high school students and 272 high school students. The results are startling. Early adolescents, in particular, reported many hostile exchanges with siblings closest to them in age. They were both the victims and perpetrators of attacks. Gender differences were absent, although males seemed more prone to resort to more severe uses of force. The researchers emphasized that parents seem ignorant of the extent to which early adolescents use physical force to resolve conflicts with a sibling (Roscoe et al., 1987).

These findings of sibling violence were replicated in a study of middle adolescents (Goodwin & Roscoe, 1990). In this study, 272 high school students responded to questions about physical violence and extreme verbal combativeness with siblings. While this study confirmed the earlier work with early adolescent siblings, the middle adolescents reported physical force with siblings is less common. Perhaps such findings indicate siblings engage less in combat with each other as they grow older.

Raymond Montemayor and Eric Hanson (1985) interviewed adolescents about conflicts with their parents and siblings. Their study involved 64 tenth grade students, all from white, middle-class families. The adolescents reported the most conflict with their mothers and their same-sex siblings, and much less conflict with their fathers. The cause of most quarrels was perceived interference; for instance, when a mother tells her adolescent daughter to get off the phone and clean her room or when a sibling "borrows" something from his brother without asking. Arguments between siblings occurred as frequently as arguments with mothers.

Adolescent siblings perceive their family experiences differently; they perceive that parents treat siblings differently. For instance, Denise Daniels, Judy Dunn,

Frank Furstenberg, and Robert Plomin (1985) studied 348 families, each with two adolescents between the ages of 11 and 17. Siblings reported differences in parental love, maternal and paternal closeness, use of discipline, parental favoritism, and permission to be involved in family decisions. Perceptions were associated with differences in emotional adjustment, but had little to do with birth order, gender, or age.

The authors cautioned that these differences in perception could not be seen as either the cause or the effect of the adolescents' emotional adjustment. What causes siblings' differential perceptions of family experiences could only be established by controlling for heredity or by carrying out a longitudinal study. They pointed out that adoption studies of adolescents and infants indicate that family environments, rather than heredity, account for markedly different sibling perceptions of family experiences (Daniels et al., 1985)

Some researchers report positive effects of sibling relationships. Brent Waters (1987) indicated that siblings in families disrupted by divorce may support and care for each other, provide role models, and contribute structure in an otherwise chaotic family.

Early adolescents often have positive relationships with disabled siblings (McHale & Gamble, 1987). The early adolescents spend time caring for their disabled brothers or sisters, and they seem more inclined to internalize difficulties, rather than to act them out. Researchers of adolescents bereaved over a sibling's death have also reported a maturing effect of increased empathy seen in adolescents as they work through their grief (Balk, 1981, 1990b, 1991a; Guerriero-Austrom & Fleming, 1990; Hogan, 1987).

Up to this point the chapter has focused on adolescents in nuclear, single-parent, or blended families. Some children and adolescents, however, grow up in other circumstances, specifically in foster homes or in residential settings for youths removed from their families. Why would youths be removed from their families? Some families so maltreat their children that legal authorities intervene to protect the child from further abuse or neglect.

Foster Care and Residential Homes: Alternatives to Family Maltreatment

One response to parental abuse and neglect is foster care. When a child is judged to be at risk of maltreatment, the state can intervene by placing an at-risk youth with a foster family or in a group home. Social workers will be instructed to study the problems besetting the child's birth family ("When foster care ends," 1991). As of 1991, the number of youths in foster care in the United States was over 400,000, and experts have estimated the numbers will top 550,000 by 1995 (Lemov, 1991). A high proportion of these youths have run away from their homes, have been thrown out, or have been abandoned (Finkelhor, Hotaling, & Sedlak, 1990).

Youths placed in foster care seldom stay in the same setting for long. Foster care is intended as a short-term solution until a permanent placement can be found. Reuniting the child and the family is considered the first goal and is to be pursued unless being placed back in the home subjects the youth to renewed risk. In physical and sexual abuse cases, evidence suggests the prospect of renewed risk is substantial (Burton, 1989).

If reunion with the family is not an option, the goal is to free the youth for adoption. Very few foster parents express interest in adopting children placed in their care (Thornton, 1991), and many youths in foster care are too old to be likely candidates for adoption (Lemov, 1991).

Multiple foster placements become a numbing reality for most youths removed from the custody of their parents. It is not uncommon for youths in foster care to have 20 or more placements as they grow up. Joel Elizur and Salvador Minuchin (1989) recount a case of a youth who had 65 placements, and they make clear that this startling case highlights the failure of permanency planning once children are taken from the custody of their parents.

Parental abuse and neglect make youths very hesitant to trust adults. Lack of trust presents formidable problems in adjusting well to foster care. Multiple placements teach the youths not to become attached to any adult in the foster care system. The following example illustrates the point. Valerie was a 17-year-old who ran away from her last group home and turned to using sex to get food and a place to sleep. She had been in seven foster care homes since her 13th birthday.

> Valerie, who was placed in foster care at the age of 13 after repeated sexual assaults by her stepfather, said she had reached the point where she did not want anyone telling her what to do. "So many placements try to act like parents," she said in a recent telephone interview, "and I refuse to let anyone tell me how to run my life." Valerie, who is now living in an abandoned housing project with her boyfriend, said she spends most days at the Larkin Street Youth Center, a private organization that provides food, medical care, and counseling for young people in need ("When foster care ends," 1991, p. 10).

An alarming trend is the high number of the homeless who were formerly children in foster care. Nearly all state child protective services stop foster care pay-

An alarming finding is the high number of the homeless who were formerly in foster care.

ments when youths reach 18, and effectively force these young people to fend for themselves before they have marketable skills ("When foster care ends," 1991). It seems very doubtful that many 18-year-old youths are prepared to live independently.

One response to overcoming the risks of multiple foster care placements is the **family preservation movement**. This approach makes reuniting children with their families as quickly as possible a top priority. This approach does have its critics. Many individuals consider such reunions endanger children by placing them back in abusive environments. R. Burton (1989) argues that the family preservation movement places victims of physical and sexual abuse in the hands of child-care workers who advocate in court for the perpetrators of the abuse, rather than for the best interests of the children. Family preservation may simply be an unrealistic goal in many circumstances because the families have not learned ways to nurture rather than harm their children (Lemov, 1991).

The Villages, another alternative to multiple foster care placements, provides separate group homes clustered together, each run by a husband and wife team who live in the home. Karl Menninger, the famous American psychiatrist, began The Villages in 1969 as a means of providing neglected, abused, and abandoned youths a caring home, a supportive family, a sense of belonging, and hope for the future (Menninger, 1973).

Each Villages home is comprised of married houseparents, their natural children, and up to ten children placed there by state authorities. By clustering the homes together, a "village" is formed. The homes are in open country because Menninger considered awareness of nature a key component of healthy maturation (Menninger, 1973).

The houseparents serve as adult role models, maintain a normal family routine, and live with all the children as a family. The youths attend regular schools, join clubs, and compete in sporting events. The basic idea of The Villages is to provide the youths with a normal, secure family atmosphere.

The Villages has eight group homes in Kansas. The model has inspired similar projects in Indiana and Michigan. The Kansas group home program has worked with over 400 youths since its inception.

In a study of the first 20 years of The Villages, researchers found the average age at admission was 14 (Balk, Murray, Nelson, & Johnson, 1993). Youths stayed slightly more than 2 years on average. Sixty-five percent of admissions were white adolescents, 19% black, and 10% Hispanic, Native American, and "other" ethnic/racial groups. More males (58%) than females (42%) have been admitted.

In the first 10 years of The Villages, the primary goal upon admission was reuniting the youths with their families. Since 1980, the primary goal has been to foster independent living skills because of the very dysfunctional family systems the children come from.

Forty-six percent of youths admitted to The Villages were victims of abuse, and 60% victims of neglect. Typically, youths had been placed up to four times in foster care prior to coming to The Villages. Ten percent of the youths had been in ten or more different foster care homes prior to their admission to The Villages. Over 93% of the youths were referrals from the state department concerned with protecting children from family maltreatment.

In 89% of the cases, at least one parent was missing from the home—the mother was absent in 7% of the cases, the father in 34.5%, and both parents in 47.5%. Divorce, separation, and abandonment most frequently accounted for absences of mothers and fathers. On average, the mothers had been absent for nearly six years and fathers for over eight years.

Approximately half of the youths were considered to have made an excellent or adequate adjustment to life at The Villages. Sixteen percent were judged to have adjusted less than adequately, and 26% were considered to have adjusted extremely poorly. In 11% of the cases, no data were available regarding how the youths had responded to living in the group home structure.

The houseparents stay in contact with many of the youths placed with them after the adolescents graduate from The Villages. House parents speak with pride that less than 3% of all Villages youths enter the welfare system as adults, despite the histories of having grown up in a welfare-subsidized family before coming to The Villages.

CHAPTER SUMMARY

The very definition of a family is undergoing change in the United States. More and more children grow up in single-parent, poverty-stricken families headed by women or in families comprising previously married adults and their children from an earlier marriage. This latter type of family, called a blended family, leads to complex interrelationships involving biological parents and their children, stepsiblings, half-siblings, and the new couple and the former spouses.

Adolescents in blended families face both risks and opportunities. The risks involve conflictual relationships and vulnerability to physical and sexual abuse. Opportunities involve security, increased autonomy and personal development, and—particularly for males—growth in cognitive development.

Researchers discuss anticipated family changes in terms of a family life cycle. Some writers prefer the term *family life course*. Each concept contains the notion of qualitative, normal changes across time. Proponents of family life cycle models adopt the idea of developmental stages to explain family unfolding; however, there is no agreement on the number of developmental stages.

The systems perspective dominates research on the family. The critical assertion of a systems perspective is that families are sets of interconnected, mutually influential relationships. Systems theorists maintain that every system is more than the mere aggregation of its parts. In other words, a family is greater than the sum of all its members.

Several systems models of family functioning have been proposed, including (*a*) the Circumplex Model, (*b*) the McMaster Model, and (*c*) the Beavers-Timberlawn Model. The Circumplex Model emphasizes adaptability, cohesion, and communication; the McMaster Model emphasizes multiple dimensions of family functioning; the Beavers-Timberlawn Model distinguishes healthy families from dysfunctional families.

One way to understand family interaction is to create a diagram of family relationships. Such a figure is called a genogram and extends over at least three generations. Genograms are quite useful in disclosing how patterns of conduct emerge in successive generations of a family.

A key developmental task for adolescents is to separate from parents and to live independently as a young adult. Family models include parent-adolescent separation as a distinct stage in the family's life cycle. Adolescent separation involves achieving functional independence, attitudinal independence, emotional independence, and conflictual independence. Adolescents who separate successfully from their parents still retain emotional ties with them. Some adolescents equate separation with emotional detachment. Males who construe separation in this way adjust poorly to independent living, whereas females adapt quite well.

College helps individuals achieve separation from parents. On the whole, college students become more assured of their capabilities to produce outcomes they desire. There is less certain evidence that college promotes independence from peer influence.

For several years, people have talked of a generation gap separating parents from their adolescents. Research paradoxically shows the gap to be both less and more than has been supposed. There seems to be less of a clash of values between parents and adolescents than has been commonly asserted; however, adolescents express much more dissatisfaction with family communication than their parents realize or express themselves. Parents consider communication with their adolescents to be more open and less troublesome than their adolescents believe.

Consistent data indicate that adolescent boys and girls feel closer to their mothers than to their fathers, feel love between them and their mothers actually increases after high school, and report that relationships remain distant with their fathers. At the same time, adolescents quarrel much more with their mothers than with their fathers. Squabbles usually involve day-to-day hassles over such things as using the car, getting chores done, and coming home at set times.

Parental styles of child rearing have long-term effects on individual development. Three different parenting styles have been identified: authoritative or democratic, authoritarian or autocratic, and permissive. Developmental outcomes indicate authoritative/democratic parenting styles have optimal long-term effects on child development, whereas other parenting styles raise children with social and academic deficiencies. Ranking parenting styles in terms of outcomes for child development, the permissive style is clearly the worst. The authoritative style is best, followed by the authoritarian style. One exception has been found in black families. Preschool children of black, authoritarian parents develop self-reliance and assertiveness.

Sibling relationships during adolescence are packed with emotion. Most studies have focused on negative aspects, such as sibling rivalry. Much more physical conflict occurs between early adolescent siblings than earlier research recognized. However, some research has disclosed positive effects of sibling relationships, such as friendship, loyalty facing common difficulties, and nurturance and support during times of family conflict. Siblings seldom perceive their families the same.

Some families so maltreat their children that state authorities remove the children from the home and place them in foster care. A primary goal of foster care is rapid solution of family strife and reunification of the child with the family. In many cases, child experts consider the goal of reunification to be against the best interests of the child.

Foster care frequently results in multiple placements and in children who grow into late adolescents poorly prepared to live on their own. A high proportion of homeless individuals were in the country's foster care system as youths.

One innovative response to multiple placements and an alternative to placing a youth back in an abusive family is the parent-run set of group homes in Kansas called The Villages. Started in 1969 by Karl Menninger, the internationally famous American psychiatrist, these homes provide a surrogate family for the youths. To date, over 400 adolescents have lived in The Villages. The average stay is slightly over two years. Very few graduates of The Villages enter the welfare system as adults despite coming from families replete with welfare recipients.

In this chapter, we have focused on the important role of the family in adolescent development. We have hinted that adolescents are also influenced by their peers. In the next chapter, we explore the role of peers in adolescent development.

PEERS, FRIENDS, AND ONGOING INTERPERSONAL SOCIALIZATION

"Phyllis Is My Best Friend"

Lindsey is a 22-year-old college senior majoring in life-span human development. Until her junior year, she had been studying to be an elementary school teacher but reports, "[I] didn't feel I was learning what I should be learning. I couldn't see myself being a teacher. Took some human development courses, liked them, talked to my advisor, and switched over."

Lindsey has two brothers, one younger and one older. Her father, an insurance salesman, died of a heart attack in his mid-40s—Lindsey was 15. After her husband died, Lindsey's mother, to whom Lindsey feels very close, went to work as an assistant to the administrator of a residence for the physically and mentally disabled. Now, her mother is an administrative assistant for a large construction company that builds highways and bridges. From what Lindsey says, her mom is independent and full of grit.

Lindsey and I talked about friendship; we talked about her friends, what makes them close friends, and problems that can develop between people who become friends. She distinguishes between acquaintances, friends, and close friends.

"An acquaintance is someone I know, perhaps because I met the person in a class. It is someone I say 'hi' to and engage in small talk. Someone I recognize when I see.

"A friend is someone who knows me and someone I can be myself around. We can be comfortable to just sit there and not have to talk all the time.

"A close friend is someone I would confide in about anything. Someone who understands me, who would be there for me, and I would be there for them. Close friends share a mutual respect for one another."

When asked what people do if they are close friends, Lindsey answered, "I spend a lot of time together with my friends. Their names are Phyllis, Beth, Doris, and Chris. I don't have just one best friend but have different friends I go to for different things.

"One person who stands out in my mind as my close friend is Phyllis. I've known of Phyllis for eight years, but did not meet her until coming to college. We are from the same hometown but went to different high schools.

"Phyllis's always been there for me if I need advice. She's real stable, cares, and is honest. She would tell me what I should do no matter what. Her ideas always seem the right thing to do. So, I always go to her for advice. Never any big, huge deal I went to her with, but just some dilemma at the time. An example would be problems with school or with a guy. For instance, I had dated a guy Phyllis also knew. After the date, he kept calling me—real aggressively. It was a real turnoff for me. So, I kept trying to ignore him and that wasn't working. I talked with Phyllis about what to do, and she told me I had to phone him and break things off. She made me make the call. She even took a picture of me and labeled it 'Lindsey before the phone call' and, after I phoned, took another picture and labeled it 'Lindsey after the call.' Everything turned out great. He was glad I was honest with him, and, once again, Phyllis proved right.

"Now, Phyllis is married and is no longer available. That's bothered me ever since I knew she was getting married. I can't any longer just call her and get together like we did a month ago. She's my age, and she made a lifelong commitment. She's happy, and I'm happy for her—very happy. I can tell this is what she wants. She found someone good enough for her. Our friendship won't be less, as far as emotions go, but I won't be able to see her as much.

"I consider my mom to be a close friend. She and Phyllis rank right up there. Mom knows everything about me there is to know. Mom doesn't open up to me like I do to her. She keeps a lot inside because she wouldn't want to bother me. She'll say, 'There's a lot going on right now that I can't talk about.' So I share a lot with her, but she doesn't do the same with me.

"Actually, a lot of my friends keep a lot inside. Keep a lot to themselves. It has to do with individual differences in how each of us handles difficulties. Some of us have to talk immediately, and others need to wait.

"Last week Phyllis, Beth, Doris, Chris, and I were talking about how lucky we were that we support each other, don't talk behind each other's backs, and don't interfere even though we do get a little overprotective of each other. We confront each other with our opinions and take such statements well. I would do anything for any of them and feel it would be given in return too.

"What makes us close friends is that we know each other so well. For instance, I know when Doris's in a bad mood not to try to get her out of how she feels.

"Misunderstandings are what create the biggest problems between close friends. With Beth recently, she was upset about something and pulled me aside and said, 'Lindsey, this has been bothering me for some time. I feel we are competing for our friends. I don't think you put me as high on your list as you do other people. When I think of a best friend, I think of you, but you don't think of me in that way.'

"I didn't want to say she was right, but I guess it's true. When I think of a best friend, I think of Phyllis. Phyllis is my best friend. Also, Beth has a boyfriend she spends a lot of time with. She does not share a lot of the little things which we experience together, and I guess she feels left out."

Lindsey spent some time talking about being betrayed by someone she had thought was her friend. "A lot of people might not think this was so bad. Let me give you the background.

"My family moved when I was going into eighth grade. I met this girl who I was friends with through our sophomore year in college. I think we became good friends because we were part of the same church, but I don't think we were a lot alike. She was the first person who became a friend when I moved to our new hometown, and we tried to build on that. Now, when I look back on it, I see we had less in common than I realized at the time. For example, I am really close to my mom, and she is not close to hers. She doesn't feel good about herself, and I feel good about me.

"In college, I started dating a guy who became real abusive verbally and emotionally with me. My 'friend'—her name is Mary—knew everything this guy had done to me that hurt me, and she had even been telling me to break up with him. She even told me she hated him. And then, I did break up with him, and two months later, they started going out. She even called me to tell me it was true. Just seeing him on campus hurt me, and she knew all about what had bothered me with him. I felt she betrayed me. I feel she could have placed our friendship ahead of going out with this guy. Any time I see her now, our conversations are forced. I think she must feel pretty low about herself to get with this guy.

"The whole experience with this guy and Mary makes me wonder what I had missed about her that now I know. I think she's always been insecure and never has felt good about herself. When my friends found out all this had happened, they said, 'That doesn't surprise me.' I guess they saw a selfish side of her I hadn't thought would go so far as hurting our relationship.

"I don't see any need to reconcile with her. Right now, I have so much resentment I can't imagine things ever being the same. I suspect our friendship had started to fade away, even up to six months before all this happened. We didn't talk as much, or see each other as much.

"What did I learn about friendship from this experience with Mary? I don't take my friendships for granted. My mom always used to say, 'You have to nurture a relationship if it is going to grow.' If Phyllis had done what Mary had done—but of course Phyllis wouldn't—I would be upset. But knowing Phyllis the way I do, it is impossible to think it could happen."

We discussed that betrayal by a friend can shake a person's confidence in evaluating other people's characters—even in trusting one's own character. Lindsey said, "The reason it didn't affect my trust in myself is that I didn't care a lot about Mary. If it happened with a close friend, it would really bother me. I'd start to doubt my ability to pick friends. I doubted myself a lot when I broke up with the guy Mary is now with. I was bothered I could be that bad a judge of character. My friends could see flaws, but I couldn't.

"If one of my close friends were to betray me, I would be deeply hurt. I respect my four friends more than I respect Mary. I just let it go with Mary, but I'd try to talk with my friend to understand why it happened and how it happened. Like my mom said, 'You have to nurture a relationship if it is going to grow.'"

As a final topic, I asked Lindsey how her view of friendship has changed since high school. She jotted down the question, went home, and returned with a short essay in which she wrote, "My mom has always told me that I am mature for my age. Therefore, I feel that I did value some of the close friendships I had in high school. (Because I think it takes maturity to value a relationship of any kind.) However, I am able to notice a change in myself as far as close friends in college go.

"Because I am more mature now, I realize what it means to have a genuine friend and what it means to be a genuine friend. I depend more on my college friends than I did on my high school friends. I'm not too dependent though because I don't think that's healthy. I guess I'm trying to stress the point that the friends I have made in college will be lifetime friends. One reason is that we all have a lot in common, be it the same values, morals, or opinions. That's probably why we can relate so well to each other."

Lindsey's conversation indicates she has placed increasing value on her friends and has spent increasingly less time with her family. Her cognitive development and a wider range of experiences than were available in middle childhood (or even middle adolescence) have helped her understand more clearly the place of interpersonal relationships in her life.

This chapter takes up these themes, plus several others of importance in the interpersonal socialization of early, middle, and late adolescents. In this chapter, we look at adolescent-parent struggles over peer influences, the role of peers in the development of adolescents, issues surrounding rejection and isolation from peers, and the place of friendship in adolescents' lives. We also look at loneliness in the lives of early, middle, and late adolescents.

PARENT-PEER STRUGGLES, CONFLICTS, AND PRESSURES

Parents often express interest in their adolescents' relations with peers. Parents may become concerned that a peer's behavior will be damaging to their adolescent son or daughter. These parental concerns can translate into struggles with their adolescents over regulations about peer associations.

Gary Ladd, Susan Profilet, and Craig Hart (1992) asked some fundamental questions about parental management of their children's peer associations. They asked whether parents consider their children's peer relations to be a parental responsibility and whether parents take an active role in managing these peer relations. From a review of research literature, Ladd and his colleagues (1992) determined that parents do take an active role in managing the peer relations of their children.

Parental involvement in children's peer associations takes on increasing significance as adolescents spend greater time away from the direct supervision of their parents (Cooper & Cooper, 1992). Persuasive evidence indicates inadequate parental regulation of adolescents' peer relationships is highly predictive of delinquent activity (Patterson, DeBaryshe, & Ramsey, 1989). Parents who maintain a consistent awareness of their adolescents' whereabouts help keep their children from falling prey to peer pressure (Steinberg, 1986).

Parental management and monitoring of adolescents' peer associations implies the parents make rules for the adolescents to follow. What do adolescents think about parental rules regarding their associations with peers?

Marie Tisak and her colleagues (Tisak, Tisak, & Rogers, 1989) have looked at how youths interpret parental rules about peer relations. Their particular interests have been (*a*) children's and adolescents' reasonings about parents' views concerning peer relations, (*b*) children's and adolescents' understandings of parental expectations about peer relations, and (c) children's and adolescents' reasonings about maintaining or abandoning relations with peers who violate parental rules. They conducted a series of studies to examine these issues.

School-Age Children's Views About Parental Regulation of Peer Associations

Tisak and her colleagues (1989) studied 120 children in the second, fourth, and sixth grades. The sixth-graders were significantly less likely ($p < .001$) than the younger students to agree that parents should make rules about peer relations when a peer's moral behavior is questionable. An example of morally questionable behavior is stealing. The sixth-graders were also less likely ($p < .001$) than the younger children to agree that parental regulation of peer relations is acceptable when parents feel concerned for their child's physical safety.

Ninth- and Twelfth-Graders' Views About Parental Regulation of Peer Associations

In a study of 82 adolescents (41 ninth-graders and 41 twelfth-graders), Tisak and her colleagues (1989) asked the subjects if they agree that parents could restrict associations with peers who use marijuana, cigarettes, or beer. Results were influenced by the age of the subjects and by the type of substance involved. Older adolescents agreed less than younger adolescents ($p < .001$) that parents should regulate peer relations when peers use marijuana, smoke cigarettes, or drink beer. The type of substance being used significantly affected adolescents' evaluations of parental rules ($p < .001$). Nearly 75% of the adolescents agreed parents would be correct in restricting associations with peers who use marijuana. Approximately 58% of the adolescents agreed that drinking beer is a legitimate reason for parents to regulate their relations with peers. However, less than half (38%) agreed parents should regulate associations with peers who smoke cigarettes.

Adolescents understood parental concern over the effects of drugs. The adolescents rarely mentioned legal consequences as reasons for agreeing with parental regulations but, rather, emphasized the negative personal consequences of associating with peers who use drugs.

Ninth- and Twelfth-Graders' Views About Discontinuing Association with a Peer

Tisak and her colleagues (1989) also examined ninth through twelfth grade students' thoughts about whether they would terminate peer relations with a peer who broke their parents' rules against smoking marijuana, drinking alcohol, and smoking cigarettes. Adolescents said they would be most likely to stop associating with peers who continued smoking marijuana, but not with friends who continued smoking cigarettes or drinking beer ($p < .001$). They agreed that associating with someone who drinks alcohol would induce them to drink also, regardless of their parents' rules.

Tisak's (Tisak et al., 1989) findings made clear that youths—particularly adolescents—assess the overall **social context** when considering peer behavior, violation of parental rules, and continued friendships. Some social contexts (or what some refer to as **social domains**) are clearly more important to adolescents than others. Of course, Tisak's results pertain to self-reported attitudes, and are not observations of actual behavior.

The studies we have looked at so far talk about adolescents' acceptance and rejection of peers, and the extent of their understanding and acceptance of parental regulations about unacceptable peer behaviors. Let us turn next to the role of peers in adolescent development.

PEERS AND ADOLESCENTS

As school-age children mature into early adolescents they spend increasingly less time with their families and increasingly more time by themselves and with peers. Reed Larson and Maryse Richards (1991) devised an elegant means to determine whether age and gender influence the time school-age children and early adolescents spend with their families, friends, and by themselves. The investigators provided 483 fifth-, seventh-, and ninth-graders (241 males; 242 females) electronic pagers for a week. When signalled, the youths wrote down who they were with, where they were, and how they felt. The youths were signalled on a random basis. The school-age children (fifth-graders) spent twice as much time with their families as did early adolescents (seventh- and ninth-graders). Early adolescent boys spent more time alone than with friends, whereas girls more equally divided their time between friends and being alone.

Joyce Benenson (1990) has documented that both social context and gender play significant roles in peer relations during middle childhood and adolescence. In work with 154 nine- and eleven-year-old children, she found that males have as many best friends as females, but interact with more people than females. She also discovered that males consider a person's status within a peer group more important for peer acceptance than do females. Lastly, she demonstrated that males and females notice different attributes in same-sex peers. Whereas males are more likely to describe boys in terms of attitudes toward authority, quality of work habits, athletic ability, and interests, females are more likely to notice girls who engage in reciprocity (mutual give-and-take) and who are nice. Benenson (1990) concluded researchers need to examine more closely gender differences in interpersonal relationships.

Early and middle adolescents place more importance on being members of a popular group of peers than late adolescents. Their peer groups also expect greater conformity than peer groups in either middle childhood or late adolescence. Conflict with and antagonism toward peers outside the group are common experiences for early and middle adolescents. Girls are particularly bothered when in conflict with members of their peer groups, but the boundaries of girls' peer groups are more flexible than the boundaries of boys' groups (Gavin & Furman, 1989).

On the whole, adolescent development and maturation benefit from peer relationships. This assessment of peer relations runs counter to the popular belief that peers negatively influence adolescent development. A popular notion is that during adolescence, peers undo the positive effects of parents on their children. In fact, several investigators emphasize that peers promote drug use, alcohol consumption, cigarette smoking, and delinquency in general (Bailey & Hubbard, 1991; Brownfield & Thompson, 1991; Coombs, Paulson, & Richardson, 1991; Kaplan, Johnson, & Bailey, 1987; Urberg, Cheng, & Shyu, 1991; Wills & Vaughan, 1989). These studies do demonstrate a link between some adolescent peer relations and deviant behavior; however, peer relations more frequently have a positive impact on adolescent development.

Relations with peers provide a base for developing independence from parents and learning early forms of intimacy with people outside one's family. Some researchers emphasize that early adolescents are more often directed by peers to conform to social norms and become socially involved than to engage in misconduct (Brown, Lohr, & McClenahan, 1986). Saul Scheidlinger (1984) even concluded that belief in peer groups' negative influences stems from the misguided notion that turmoil, rather than healthy adaptation, marks the adolescent years.

Not uncommonly, when researchers investigate the role peer relationships play in development, they more frequently concentrate on peer interaction than on peer relations (Berndt, 1989). For instance, investigators study conflict between peers (Eisenberg & Garvey, 1981; Shantz & Hobart, 1989), the manner whereby youths interact in structured group activities (Furman & Gavin, 1989; Johnson & Johnson, 1985) and compare adolescent behavior with peers and with friends (Hartup, 1989; Hinde, Titmus, Easton, & Templin, 1985). A study of peer relations would focus on issues, such as intimacy, self-disclosure, attachment, and rejection.

One body of research, however, has examined qualities and outcomes of peer relationships, such as intimacy, acceptance or rejection, attachment, respect, pressure to conform, and empathy (Berndt, 1989). This chapter includes studies of peer interactions as well as studies of the more abstract qualities of peer relationships. These studies help us understand the developmental changes in peer relations as youths move out of middle childhood and through the adolescent years.

Social Acceptance and Social Rejection

The phenomena of **social acceptance** and **social rejection** are important concepts in our discussion of the influence of peers on adolescents. To illustrate these concepts, let's begin with some memories of your fifth grade classroom. Close your eyes and recall your teacher's face, features of the classroom, where your desk was placed, who sat near you, and the faces and names of other children in the class. Who in this classroom was popular with the students? What made this person popular? Who was someone the students disliked? Why was this person disliked?

Social acceptance is personified by a very popular student, someone that all, or nearly all, the other students pick out as someone they like. These students are called "stars" because of their universal appeal to other students. **Social rejection** can be seen in students that others actively dislike. These students are singled out as individuals most, or even all, the other students do not want to be around. There are usually some students who are neither popular nor disliked but, rather, ignored or neglected. These students may be shy or strangers to the other students; sometimes they possess poorly developed understandings of social interaction.

When you recalled your fifth grade classroom, you may have recalled someone who was a star and someone who was actively disliked. Could you recall other students who were simply ignored? When college students use this exercise, they inevitably recall vividly someone who was a star and someone whom they particularly disliked. In fact, they often disliked the person so much that they could never consider giving that person's name to a child of their own. In many cases, often because their families had just moved to a new town and they were new to a school, the college students placed themselves among the individuals whom others neglected.

Educators have devised a means to determine social acceptance and rejection within a group of peers. The method, called **sociometry**, is a technique to assess how well peers accept others and to ascertain a group's internal social structure. Since the introduction of this method into public-school classrooms in the 1930s, sociometry has spread to a wide variety of settings, including prisons, work situations, and youth camps. Investigators use sociometry to identify the attitudes of individuals toward other people in their surroundings (Gronlund, 1959). Contemporary researchers have used sociometry to identify the extent to which children accept, reject, and ignore other children (Bichard, Alden, Walker, & McMahon, 1988; Coie & Dodge, 1983; Newcomb & Bukowski, 1983; Parkhurst & Asher, 1992).

An easy way to conduct a **sociometric rating** is to give students the names or photographs of all individuals in their classroom. The students are asked to identify classmates they like or with whom they would prefer to do something, such as work on a project or play. Once they complete the first task, the students are asked to identify classmates they do not like or with whom they would not like to do something.

Sociometric results are sometimes grouped into five distinct categories:

- **Stars**—individuals chosen by everyone or nearly everyone as someone they like.

- **Overchosen individuals**—individuals chosen by a majority, but not all, as someone they like.

- **Underchosen individuals**—individuals chosen by a plurality as someone they like.

- **Neglected individuals**—individuals chosen by only a few people at most as someone they like.

- **Rejected individuals**—individuals specifically singled out as someone not desired as an associate.

More frequently, individuals in the first three categories are simply labeled "popular" or "accepted." Individuals in the fourth category are often referred to as "isolated."

Sociometry has shown that peer acceptance comprises two distinct characteristics: popularity and status. **Popularity** refers to likability—that is, the extent to which others seek out a person for interaction and association. **Status** refers to prestige or standing in the group—that is, the extent to which other members of a group value an individual's membership. Some people confuse popularity with status. Let's look at this distinction in terms of the particular **frame of reference** (the circumstances a person considers when looking at a situation) people use when making their sociometric choices.

Frame of reference is a limiting factor for social acceptance or rejection. Consider these three very different frames of reference: Who do you want as your friend? Who would you select to be on your basketball team? and Who would you prefer to be in your algebra study group? Usually, students do not name the same person for all three frames of reference. The first frame of reference involves popularity, whereas the latter two refer to status. Of course, there can be individuals chosen because their prestige invests the person who chooses them with status. However, this notion contradicts the mutuality and commitment that characterize friendship.

The stability of sociometric choices has been demonstrated as children grow older. Over a year's time, 16- to 19-year-olds are less likely to change their preferences than 11- to 15-year-olds. Advanced techniques of assessment have demonstrated that sociometric status also remains stable across settings, particularly for children rejected by their peers (Coie, Dodge, & Kupersmidt, 1990; Gottman and Parkhurst, 1980).

The extent of one's knowledge and familiarity with the people in the sociometric exercise directly affects choices. The less I know someone at the beginning, the more likely I am to change my preferences as I get to know the person better. However, once I know the person fairly well, my preferences are more likely to remain stable.

What makes some youths popular and others actively disliked? Five characteristics have been found to be associated with peer acceptance and rejection: name, physical appearance, self-esteem, social skills, and perceptions about the person's academic intelligence.

Name

Peers consider some names attractive, and others odd or funny. You may be able to generate a list of first names you consider attractive and a corresponding list of names you consider unattractive. Names reflect cultures as well as changing times. A list of favored names among Salvadoran, Pakistani, Saudi Arabian, or Vietnamese parents probably would not match a list produced by American parents. Currently, Jessica and Jennifer are popular names for daughters of white middle-class American parents, while the names Jason and Joshua have gained popularity for boys. Among earlier white American generations, Violet, Mabel, Ralph, and Henry were popular names.

Studies have shown that popularity among peers is associated with perceived attractiveness of someone's name. In one study, 10- to 12-year-old children were shown a long list of names that included the names of everyone in their classes. The students were asked to rate the attractiveness of names; then, using sociometric procedures, the investigators obtained popularity ratings for all the students in the classes. They found a positive relationship between peer popularity and name attractiveness. Furthermore, when 10- to 12-year-olds who did not know any of the children in the classes were asked to rate the attractiveness of the names on the list, they rated the names in a very similar fashion as the first group of children (McDavid & Harari, 1966).

What remains uncertain is whether individuals with names considered odd are ridiculed and teased, thereby affecting their self-esteem and how they interact with other children. It could be the case that children with odd-sounding names have parents who behave in peculiar ways and model eccentric social skills (Hartup, 1983).

An odd name does not necessarily doom someone to be unpopular, nor does a highly attractive name guarantee popularity. A child with a very unusual name may emerge as a star among classmates, and one with an attractive name may become someone who is actively disliked. However, data suggest the significance of the effect on peers of a child's first name should not be discounted.

Physical Appearance

The importance of physical appearance is accentuated during adolescence, particularly for early-maturing adolescent males. You may recall some of the gender-specific consequences of early, on-time, and late physical maturation presented in Chapter 2.

In contrast to late-maturing boys, early-maturing adolescent males are typically more popular among their peers (and among adults) and seem more socially mature. They are usually more poised, more self-confident, and are considered more masculine. These gains seem to be maintained, even into their early 40s.

Among girls, the relation between rate of maturation and social acceptance is more complicated. Early-maturing girls seem to experience some adjustment problems but demonstrate considerable competencies in terms of social maturity by late adolescence.

An influential socialization stereotype in the United States is that physical beauty is desired. Self-fulfilling prophecies about physical beauty can influence a child's social relations from an early age. For instance, consider the numerous research findings indicating that both parents and teachers have different expectations of children based on the children's physical appearances. Adults respond more positively to physically attractive children than to physically unattractive children (Adams, 1978; Adams & Crane, 1980; Allgozzine, 1977; Clifford & Walster, 1973; Corter, Trehub, Boukydis, Ford, Celhofer, & Minde, 1978; Stcyznski & Langlois, 1977).

Self-Esteem

A plausible hypothesis is that self-esteem correlates positively with peer acceptance. However, the relation between self-esteem and peer acceptance is not as straightforward as might be anticipated. Although not completely understood, the relationship between self-esteem and peer acceptance takes a curvilinear path. That is to say, individuals with moderate self-esteem are more accepted by their peers than individuals with very high or very low self-esteem.

A possible explanation for this trend is that individuals with inordinate self-esteem behave in ways that annoy others. An example is the arrogance shown by a teenager who thinks he is superior to everyone else. At the other end of the self-esteem spectrum is the continual abasement shown by a teenager who thinks he is inferior to everyone else. It is, of course, possible that some high self-esteem individuals are less interested in gaining others' acceptance and, thus, act tactlessly.

Social Skills

Howard Gardner (1983) proposed a form of intelligence that manifests itself interpersonally. He called it *social intelligence* (see Chapter 3). Popular adolescents demonstrate social intelligence.

Popular adolescents are described by their peers as cooperative, helpful, and friendly. In information-processing terms, they retrieve and enact a **reliable script** about what it means to be friendly. Other people respond to stars in supportive, reinforcing ways.

On the other hand, rejected children—youths who are actively disliked—seem to be victims of their reputations. Other people expect them to behave in unfriendly ways. For instance, if they accidentally bump someone, their actions will be seen as intentional. Rejected children, as well as neglected and isolated children, often have ineffective social skills; that is, they do not have a reliable script about what it means to be friendly. Others respond to them in negative and unsupportive ways that reinforce a continuation of their ineffective interpersonal behaviors.

Perceptions of Academic Intelligence

Outstanding academic performance is positively associated with status, but not necessarily with popularity. Thus, grades may provide some degree of standing among peers, but may endanger popularity when the individual does not possess social intelligence. Several adolescents—particularly females—have told me they decided to sacrifice academic success in high school in order to achieve and maintain popularity. Being labeled a "brain" or a "nerd" is undesirable in most adolescent circles.

An Overview of Peer Acceptance and Rejection

In summary, the following aspects are associated with peer acceptance and rejection:

- it is an advantage to be physically attractive;
- having an ordinary name, rather than an odd name, increases the likelihood of being accepted;
- popular individuals have mastered socially accepted behaviors and are skilled at identifying when these behaviors are appropriate;
- academic achievement contributes to social status but can be considered a threat to popularity.

The fact that some people are very popular, while others are less so, and some are rejected altogether by peers is no great insight. The importance lies in the practical consequences associated with one's social status among peers. Do you think there are reasons to be concerned about the development of rejected youths?

Peer Rejection as a Harbinger of Other Problems

A child with chronically poor peer relationships warrants concern that later social problems will emerge in adolescence and adulthood. Research indicates that rejected children are more likely than others to drop out of school, to engage in criminal behavior as juveniles, and to experience mental health problems (Cowen, Pederson, Babaijian, Izzo, & Trost, 1973; Parker & Asher, 1987; Roff, Sells, & Golden, 1972). Note that the research identifies associated phenomena of rejection, not causes.

One reason for the development of these problems is that children without friends do not have opportunities to fulfill several social needs. For instance, during difficult times, rejected children do not gain needed ego support from peers. Rejected children are bereft of social standards against which to compare their behaviors. They lack companionship, affection, and intimacy. They neither provide nor receive the stimulation available in informal social interaction with peers around whom they feel at ease.

A longitudinal study of aggressive youths rejected by their peers in third grade indicated that peer rejection and social aggression strongly predicted poor adjustment in early adolescence (Coie, Lochman, Terry, & Hyman, 1992). Social rejection in third grade correlated significantly with troubles four and five years later in middle school as reported by parents and teachers. Aggressive behavior in third grade also correlated significantly with interpersonal difficulties with early adolescent peers. These youths continued to be disruptive, aggressive, low academic achievers, and rejected. In short, as early as third grade, these individuals' future difficulties could be reliably foreseen (Coie et al., 1992). The need for intervention with these rejected youths clearly emerges. Can anything be done to help such youths learn competent social skills and, thereby, transform their social development?

Programs to Help Isolated and Rejected Children and Adolescents

We can identify isolated and rejected youths with some reliability; using sociometric techniques, we need only survey the students in a class to find out who is ignored and who is rejected. However, once we identify these children, can we do anything to help them improve their relationships with peers?

Steven Asher is a prominent figure in efforts to help neglected and rejected children improve their peer relations. Asher is a faculty member in the College of Education at the University of Illinois at Urbana-Champaign. For several years, Asher and his colleagues have been perfecting procedures to coach children in friendship-making skills (Asher & Coie, 1990; Asher & Dodge, 1986; Asher & Hymel, 1981; Asher, Markell, & Hymel, 1981; Asher & Renshaw, 1981; Asher & Wheeler, 1986; Oden & Asher, 1977; Parker & Asher, 1987).

One issue that Asher has investigated involves appropriate methods to use when teaching children skills in making friends. He has concluded that methods that increase the frequency of interaction between children but do not attend to how the children interact cannot succeed in increasing a child's acceptance by peers (Asher et al., 1981).

A second issue involves what children should be taught to do when they interact. Asher coaches children about certain **interpersonal rules of behavior** and about specific **interpersonal strategies**. The focus of Asher's coaching is teaching youths to associate rules with actual behavior in specific social situations. Because isolated children lack **friendship scripts**, Asher introduces interpersonal rules of behavior and provides opportunities to rehearse behaviors linked to the rules. For instance, such behaviors as "take turns" and "share materials" are linked to rules about cooperating with others.

Asher believes in teaching children skills that correlate with social competencies and peer acceptance. This strategy is called a **competence-correlates approach**. Asher has identified four categories of behavior that correlate with social competencies and peer acceptance.

- **Participation**—for example, playing with others and paying attention.
- **Cooperation**—for example, taking turns and sharing materials.
- **Communication**—for example, talking with other children and listening to what others say.
- **Support**—for example, offering to help and giving encouragement or praise.

Asher's method is cognitive-based and is similar to Selman's (1980) emphasis on the importance of learning how someone construes a situation. Selman, whose research on the development of interpersonal understanding was discussed in Chapter 5, has focused attention on uncovering what youths think social realities require. Asher insists that it is crucial to assess what a child thinks during a social situation as well as to evaluate how the child behaves in the situation. Asher's method teaches youths to comprehend interpersonal rules, to identify social situations to which the rules apply, and to acquire interpersonal skills that fit the situations.

Asher's research has demonstrated that youths with low sociometric status are quick to respond to interpersonal conflicts with physical retaliation (Asher & Cole, 1990; Asher & Dodge, 1986; Asher et al., 1981). He has also found that when social situations lack conflict, low sociometric youths seem perplexed as to how to behave. When conflict is present, these children have a script for how to respond, but seem clueless when the situation is harmonious or neutral. Asher concludes that low sociometric status youths suffer from **social-cognitive deficits** that obstruct interpersonal problem solving during times of conflict and that sabotage efforts to build successful peer relationships.

Asher's research has direct implications for efforts to assist adolescents neglected or rejected by peers. Some of these efforts focus specifically on aggressive youths incarcerated or living in residential facilities (Guerra & Slaby, 1990; Hains, 1989; Hardwick, Pounds, & Brown, 1985), while most are conducted in regular school settings with socially deficient adolescents or in outpatient clinics with adolescents and their families (Bank, Patterson, & Reid, 1987; Bulkeley & Cramer, 1990; Jupp & Griffiths, 1990; Larson, 1989; Snyder & Patterson, 1986). We now look at two approaches to helping neglected and rejected youths, one with students in a school setting and one with incarcerated youths.

A Training Program for Students in a School

Richard Bulkeley and Duncan Cramer (1990) conducted social skills training with early adolescents in a school in the United Kingdom. Bulkeley and Cramer identified three major assumptions that influenced their approach.

- Early adolescents are more likely than middle or late adolescents to increase social skills by participating in a training program.
- A small group would prove effective because it makes use of peer group influence, provides a safe setting to practice social skills, and gets the adolescents out of social isolation.

▪ A school provides ideal conditions to teach social skills to early adolescents because it is more familiar to students than a clinic and because the school administration can help in selecting students, collecting data, and obtaining follow-up information (Bulkeley & Cramer, 1990).

Nine 12- and 13-year-old adolescents took part in Bulkeley and Cramer's training (six boys and three girls). They were selected because each had noticeable difficulty in interacting with peers and teachers. Nine other adolescents whose social skills were considered good were selected for a control group.

Adolescents in the training group participated in ten weekly sessions for 75 minutes each. A psychologist and two teachers ran the sessions. The sessions included instructional material, role playing, observation, group discussion, and practice in real settings. Topics for the sessions included verbal communication, nonverbal skills, and situations that caused the adolescents distress. In role playing, the adolescents dealt with such events as greeting a friend, joining a group, dealing with a bully, talking with a teacher, and coping with malicious teasing. Participants heard immediately from the trainers and other group members about their performances. Asher and Peter Renshaw (1981) had concluded that immediate feedback is valuable for isolated and rejected children.

Bulkeley and Cramer (1990) obtained data about the participants in the study from several sources. They used a social skills questionnaire that assessed particular areas of difficulty the adolescents experienced with peers and adults. Data included the frequency with which the difficulties occurred, the severity of each difficulty, and the setting in which the difficulties emerged. They also used a self-report instrument and sociometric procedures. The self-report questionnaire asked about 60 interpersonal situations (for example, "Do you feel shy with strangers?"). Subjects responded to each situation by answering yes or no. The sociometric procedure was administered to all 12- and 13-year-old students at the school. The students were asked to identify which peer they would choose as a partner in two work and two play activities.

Training sessions to teach social skills often use role playing.

All pretest scores indicated the students in the training sessions had social skills significantly lower than their peers in the control group ($p = .05$). By the posttest, the training group members had social skills comparable to the control group members. Furthermore, when pretest scores were compared to posttest and follow-up scores, the students in the training group showed significant change for the better at the posttest ($p < .05$) and even greater improvement at the follow-up ($p < .01$). The teachers in the school also reported marked improvements in the training group students' social skills.

What was not seen was any change in the sociometric statuses of the students in the training sessions. Bulkeley and Cramer (1990) suggest that their sociometric procedure was too imprecise to detect changes in social status or popularity. It is also possible that increasing a youth's friendship-making skills will not be sufficient to raise the person's reputation among peers, especially when nothing is done to change the peers' expectations about this person (Hymel, Wagner, & Butler, 1990).

The problems of the early adolescents in Bulkely and Cramer's (1990) study were much less serious than those of adolescents incarcerated for their aggressive, anti-social behaviors. We turn next to an examination of an effort to teach new social understandings and interpersonal behaviors to confined adolescent offenders.

A Training Program for Incarcerated Adolescents

Nancy Guerra and Ronald Slaby (1990) designed a 12-session program to assist aggressive adolescent offenders to reduce their aggression by altering what they think about interpersonal conflict. The training involved 120 adolescents (60 males and 60 females) between 15 and 18 years of age. All of the youths were incarcerated in a juvenile offender facility in California. They had committed such crimes as murder, attempted murder, rape, and assault (Guerra & Slaby, 1990).

The researchers randomly assigned the youths to one of three groups: one training group and two control groups. Data were gathered in five areas of interest: (a) social-problem solving, (b) beliefs about aggression, (c) aggressive, impulsive, and inflexible behavior, (d) participant assessments of the intervention, and (e) 12 to 24 month recidivism rates (that is, a return to crime).

The intervention, which was called **cognitive mediation training** (CMT), involved 12 sessions devoted to teaching social information-processing skills in four basic areas:

- paying attention to pertinent and nonhostile cues;
- seeking more information;
- identifying different ways to respond and the likely consequences attending each response; and
- ranking responses in terms of achieving legal and nonviolent goals.

One control group participated in 12 sessions devoted to basic skills, such as reading, math, and career planning. The other control group simply filled out the data instruments at the pretest and posttest times.

While the groups did not differ in their pretest scores, results favored the CMT participants in nearly all the outcome data. At the posttest data collection, the CMT participants showed significantly better social-problem-solving skills; were much less likely to endorse beliefs that support aggression; demonstrated greater behavioral adjustment in impulsivity, aggression, and inflexibility; and endorsed the intervention significantly more than control group participants.

Guerra and Slaby (1990) said the participants in the intervention appeared not as likely as adolescents in the other two groups to commit offenses after being released from jail. However, follow-up data discovered the three groups did not differ in parole violations. Thus, to claim the training group participants were less likely to commit violations when they returned to society overstates the case. Recidivism rates suggested that work needs to be done to prevent juvenile offenders from losing all the gains made in CMT once they are released from detention.

The studies reported so far have been based on the assumption that neglected and rejected youths have poor or immature ideas about social interaction. However, not all research on interpersonal understanding substantiates that, in contrast to their peers, rejected or neglected adolescents have developmentally immature concepts about social interaction. Sandra Bichard, Lynn Alden, Lawrence Walker, and Robert McMahon (1988) compared Selman's (1980, 1981) theories of interpersonal understanding in second and seventh grade children. The children had been identified through sociometric procedures as accepted, rejected, or neglected. Analysis indicated that the seventh-graders, regardless of their sociometric statuses, had developmentally higher levels of interpersonal understanding than the second-graders ($p = .001$). There was no support for the belief that youths who are rejected or neglected have less mature understandings about friendship than accepted youths, nor was there support for the belief that rejected and neglected children lag behind socially accepted peers' understanding that resolving conflict is important to friendship.

Differences probably exist between reasoning about friendship and engaging in satisfying interpersonal relationships, that is, the differences may extend to applying knowledge. Children may understand what friendship is but lack skills in making or keeping friends. Renshaw and Asher (1983) have demonstrated that, compared to popular children, rejected and neglected children exhibit subtle differences in their understandings of peer relations, and they use markedly less effective strategies for making friends and for resolving conflicts.

Making new friends is a challenge many adolescents face each year as their families leave familiar surroundings and the youths enter a new school where everyone is a stranger to them. Rejected and isolated adolescents lack a reliable script for behaving as a friend in their new surroundings. Analysis of social skill training programs highlights that cooperating, sharing, helping, manifesting loyalty, initiating activities, and developing intimacy are critical skills for peer acceptance (Asher & Gottman, 1981; Inderbitzen-Pisaruk & Foster, 1990). Unfortunately, training programs often fail to address behaviors that lead to peer rejection. Heidi Inderbitzen-Pisaruk and Sharon Foster (1990) suggest that actually making and keeping friends should be standards applied for determining the success of social skills training with rejected youth.

The influence of peers on adolescent development does not end in high school. Peers continue to play important roles in the lives of college students. In some ways, peers wield uncommon influence on late adolescents in their college years.

College Students and Interpersonal Relationships

Once late adolescents experience the freedom from parental controls that college affords, some find the temptations intoxicating. For many of these students, intoxication literally becomes a way of life. Some evidence suggests that peers strongly influence college students to engage in problem drinking as well as drug usage (Lo, 1991). Several studies raise concerns about the negative influences of peers on early and middle adolescents (Bailey & Hubbard, 1991; Brownfield & Thompson, 1991; Coombs, Paulson, & Richardson, 1991; Kaplan, Johnson, & Bailey, 1987; Urberg, Cheng, & Shyu, 1991; Wills & Vaughan, 1989), and the findings about peer influences on late adolescents in college only extend these concerns. Specifically, Pascarella and Terenzini (1991) noticed that college students seem more influenced by peer opinions than one would expect given the noticeable growth in self-concept that occurs over the four-year college experience.

Many studies on the effects of college on peer relations are faulty. Some investigators who have studied the net effects of college on students' growth in interpersonal maturity have used methodologically weak designs and have produced mixed and inconclusive results (Pascarella & Terenzini, 1991). Either the studies included relatively small samples, or the researchers involved only one institution in their investigations. Many researchers have also failed to control for possible **maturation effects** (changes that are due to development). Given these considerations, there are some findings worth discussion.

One large-scale study investigated changes over a four-year period in college students' **social introversion** and **social extraversion** (Chickering, 1974, as cited by Pascarella & Terenzini, 1991). Social extroverts prefer to be with people, and they seek out social activities, whereas introverts withdraw from social gatherings. The data from this study showed no change from the freshman through the senior year in students' interests in social events and interpersonal activities.

Pascarella and Terenzini (1991) report other studies indicate college students' extraversion mildly declines over a four-year undergraduate experience. This con-

Over the course of their undergraduate years, college students become more interested in a select group of friends, and may spend most of their time with one close friend.

clusion is not based on evidence of an increase in social introversion, but, rather, on developmental expectations regarding intimacy and isolation (Erikson, 1963, 1968). That is, students become more interested in a select group of friends and spend more time in intimate activities with a few people or one person who has become a close friend.

Peer relations actually require various types of competencies which vary according to specific social domains. We now turn to these domains and the interpersonal competencies involved.

Domains of Interpersonal Competence in Late Adolescent College Students

Duane Buhrmester, Wyndol Furman, Mitchell Wittenberg, and Harry Reis (1988) collaborated to investigate **domains of interpersonal competence** in college students' peer relations. They conducted three studies and identified five domains: initiating relationships, disclosing personal thoughts and feelings, expressing displeasure with someone else's behavior, giving emotional support, and handling interpersonal conflicts.

A total of 453 undergraduates (219 males; 234 females) participated in the first study, which established that the five domains of interpersonal competence are distinct and can be measured. In the second study, the researchers used 138 undergraduates (74 males; 64 females) to examine the association between self-perceptions and peer perceptions of the five domains of interpersonal competence. In the third study, 151 undergraduates (82 males; 69 females) participated in an examination of changes in interpersonal competencies as relationships with peers develop. We will focus on the results of the second and third studies.

Self-Perceptions and Peer Perceptions of Interpersonal Competencies

To study the association between self- and peer perceptions of the domains of interpersonal competence, Buhrmester and his colleagues (1988) had students complete a battery of research instruments, including the Interpersonal Competency Questionnaire (ICQ), an inventory that was successfully tested in the first study the researchers completed. Other instruments included the Personal Attributes Questionnaire (PAQ), which measures perceptions of masculinity and femininity; the Texas Social Behavior Inventory (TSBI), which measures self-esteem; and the UCLA Loneliness Scale, which is a frequently used self-report instrument to assess loneliness.

The 138 participants in this study were roommates (37 male roommate pairs and 32 female pairs), all in their first year of college. At the time they completed the instruments, the students had known their roommates for about eight months. Students first filled out the instruments about themselves, and two weeks later, filled out the instruments about their roommates.

The self-ratings and roommate ratings on all five domains of interpersonal competence correlated significantly ($p < .01$). Students considered their roommates more competent than themselves in initiating relationships ($p < .01$), but rated themselves as more competent than their roommates in disclosing thoughts and feelings ($p < .05$) and in providing emotional support ($p < .01$).

Other findings from this study included significant correlations (all at $p < .01$) between sex-role orientation (measured by the PAQ) and interpersonal competence. Self-ratings of masculinity correlated with self-ratings on initiating relationships, handling interpersonal conflicts, and expressing displeasure with someone else's behavior. Self-ratings of femininity correlated with self-ratings on disclosing personal thoughts and feelings, giving emotional support, and handling interpersonal conflicts.

Self-esteem (measured by the TSBI) correlated significantly (all at $p < .01$) with each of the five domains of interpersonal competence. However, upon further analysis, the researchers determined that self-esteem accounted most for initiating relationships.

Self-reported loneliness experienced over the past few days, sometimes called **state loneliness**, negatively correlated with roommate ratings of interpersonal competencies for four domains (initiating relationships, giving emotional support, handling interpersonal conflicts, and disclosing personal thoughts and feelings). Self-reported **trait loneliness**, loneliness that is pervasive, negatively correlated with roommate ratings for handling interpersonal conflicts and for giving emotional support.

The significance of these studies is multifold. First, the high correlation between self-ratings and roommate ratings indicates that college students have achieved very reliable, mutual understandings of one another; their ideas of their own interpersonal competencies match what their roommates think is true about them. Second, gender stereotypes emerge for specific types of interpersonal competencies, a result that has practical implications regarding loneliness in this age-group. People who had skills in both masculine and feminine domains of interpersonal competence were less likely to have felt lonely just prior to the study; people who could handle interpersonal conflicts and give emotional support (the former a masculine domain and the latter a feminine domain) were less likely to be chronically lonely (Buhrmester, Furman, Wittenberg, & Reis, 1988).

Perceptions of Changes Needed in Interpersonal Competencies as a Relationship Develops

Buhrmester and his colleagues (1988) also investigated whether college students need different types of interpersonal skills for an acquaintanceship to become a friendship. They examined college students' perceptions of interpersonal competencies needed with someone just met and with an established friend. They expected certain trends to emerge. For instance, they expected ratings of interpersonal competencies by a close friend would correlate more with self-ratings than would ratings by a new acquaintance. Second, they predicted new acquaintances could, at best, form reliable impressions of another person's competence in initiating relations, but could not be expected to form credible impressions of the other four interpersonal competence domains. Third, they predicted judgments of another's interpersonal competencies would associate with level of satisfaction with the relationship.

The sample for this project consisted of 151 students (82 males; 69 females). Each person was introduced to another student of the same sex, and the two were told to get acquainted. After about seven minutes, the researchers separated the new acquaintances and had each person complete the ICQ, first on his or her own interpersonal competencies and then on the competencies of the new acquaintance. Each student was then given an ICQ inventory and asked to have a close friend of the same sex rate him or her on interpersonal competencies. The friend completed the questionnaire in private and returned the form in an envelope provided for that purpose (Buhrmester et al., 1988). The response rate of friends—95%—was quite remarkable.

The researchers' predictions held up. New acquaintances' ratings of initiating relationships correlated positively ($p < .01$) with self-ratings. Acquaintances' ratings of the other person's self-disclosure also correlated positively, but at a lower significance level ($p < .05$). Close friends' ratings positively correlated ($p < .01$) with self-ratings on all five domains of interpersonal competence.

Satisfaction with the relationship correlated positively with new acquaintances' ratings of the other person's competency in initiating relationships ($p < .01$). Close friends' satisfaction with relationships correlated positively ($p < .01$) with their ratings of the other person's competency in providing emotional support, disclosing personal thoughts and feelings, handling interpersonal conflicts, and initiating relationships.

Viewed as a whole, Buhrmester and his colleagues' (1988) three studies demonstrated the importance of distinguishing among domains of interpersonal competence. The findings indicate that college students make these distinctions with some accuracy. Buhrmester and his colleagues (1988) suspected additional studies would confirm skills at beginning relationships and opening up about oneself are especially important early in a relationship, and skills at providing emotional support and managing conflict enable people to keep and enrich relationships.

The distinctions between these domains of interpersonal competence and their relative importance in the life of a relationship provide directions for social skills training programs for shy, isolated, or rejected adolescents. They give the person designing the training program a clear idea about the types of competencies the participants need to learn. Taking a cue from Asher and his colleagues (Asher & Hymel, 1981; Asher et al., 1981; Asher & Renshaw, 1981; Oden & Asher, 1977; Parkhurst & Asher, 1992), social skills interventions with adolescents can focus on the behaviors that match specific interpersonal domains and on the rules that coincide with using those behaviors.

In their studies, Buhrmester and his colleagues (1988) distinguished between acquaintances and friends. Friendship is a special type of relationship that emerges for some adolescents. We turn next to a discussion of friendship.

FRIENDSHIP

Chaim Potok (1967) wrote a rich, evocative novel, *The Chosen*, about the friendship of two adolescent boys, Reuven Malter and Danny Saunders, who lived in Brooklyn, New York during the 1940s. Each boy was Jewish, religious, and very intelligent. Danny, who was probably a genius, had a father who was a rabbi in a very conservative Jewish sect. Reuven and his father, who was a teacher and biblical scholar, belonged to a more liberal sect of Judaism. The boys became friends despite grave misgivings on the part of Danny's father.

In one scene, the rabbi, who was poignantly aware of the torment his son Daniel was experiencing as he neared adulthood, embraced Reuven but warned that friendship is fraught with risk.

> 'I am happy you are friends. It is good Danny has a friend. I have many responsibilities, I am not always able to talk to him.' I saw Danny stare down at the floor, his face hardening. 'It is good he has acquired a friend.'.
> . . . Reb Saunders looked at me, his eyes dark and brooding. 'You think a friend is an easy thing to be? If you are truly his friend, you will discover otherwise' (Potok, 1967, p. 144).

A friend is someone very special, and it is uncommon to have many friends. We may have many acquaintances, but few people to whom we disclose our private hopes, thoughts, and feelings. As Reb Saunders advised Reuven, friendship places obligations on the individuals involved. Friends are present when times are rough, such as following a sibling's death.

Friendship and Healthy Adjustment

Friendship is closely linked to healthy adjustment. It would be very unlikely to find a psychologist or personality theorist who would claim that the complete absence of friends is a desirable condition or who would assert that friendships play an insignificant role in healthy psychological development. Friendship is understood to be valuable in developing social competencies and maintaining mental health. Friends are considered a sign that a person is both socially competent and mentally healthy.

On the other side of the coin, having no friends is an indicator of some psychiatric disorders, such as schizophrenia and autism. However, there are times when having no friends occurs through no fault of a youth—that is, it does not result from a psychiatric disorder or from poor social skills. Lack of friends may ensue because of bigotry and exclusion. I recall the torment a 12-year-old girl endured throughout sixth grade because she lived in a housing project while her peers lived in an exclusive section of the city. They wore designer jeans; she wore clothing bought at discount stores.

Evidence also suggests exceptionally gifted children choose to limit their relations with peers because of their uncommon, superior skills and abilities. For example, a 12-year-old boy who works easily with calculus and is absorbed with contemporary problems in astrophysics may find conversations with his same-age peers of little interest. Whether he is lonely is not a question to be easily dismissed or glibly answered. He probably lacks the emotional maturity and personal experience to develop mutuality with adults. However, the boy may have older friends who provide him a sense of belonging and a sense of importance.

Friendship as Considered by Researchers

Let's turn from these overall comments on the link between friendship and healthy adjustment to a discussion of the place researchers have given to the study of friendship. Friendship has only begun to be studied extensively in the psychological literature. However, certain developmental aspects of friendship have become clear.

- With increasing age, youths change their expectations about friendship. As an example, emphasis on playing together diminishes, while accent on reciprocity increases.

- While prefigured in earlier associations with peers, intimacy and physical support are two attributes of friendship that noticeably emerge in the adolescent years.

- Mutuality can be seen in younger ages, but this phenomenon takes on increasingly complex content in adolescence due to the cognitive changes that promote self-disclosure and perspective taking (Asher & Gottman, 1981).

Harry Stack Sullivan's Ideas About Friendship

Harry Stack Sullivan (1953), an American psychiatrist whose views on psychological development are still attractive to some people today, said the major task of preadolescence is to become invested in someone else's security and satisfaction as though that person's concerns are one's own. Sullivan noted that the preadolescent is capable of distinguishing between personal satisfaction and security and what matters to others. Thus, investing in someone else's concerns does not stem from a lack of perspective taking or a failure to differentiate one's identity from the personality of someone else.

Sullivan's notion suggests that the Golden Rule ("Do unto others as you would have them do unto you") takes on a special meaning around the age of 10. The child becomes specifically invested "in a *particular* member of the same sex who becomes a **chum** or a close friend" (Sullivan, 1953, p. 245). The youth becomes sensitive to things the close friend cares about, primarily because the other person's happiness becomes important to the youth.

Sullivan said friends are important during preadolescence and early adolescence because they help shape socially competent behaviors in ways not amenable to adult influence. Sullivan saw this socialization occurring in four ways:

- chums provide candid, even brutal evaluations and responses of disagreeable attributes;

- chums reinforce favorable traits;

- chums provide exposure to a broader range of standards than exists in the youth's family; and

- chums bolster self-concept and self-esteem by providing interactions with a variety of personalities and stimuli that expand and deepen one's knowledge of self and of the external world (Sullivan, 1953).

In Sullivan's framework, the acquisition of a chum in the preadolescent years provides a significant marker in individual human development. Caring for someone else enhances the means to develop capacities for intimacy that emerge in adolescence and adulthood.

Selman's Explanation for Adolescent Development of Friendships

Robert Selman, whose views on interpersonal understanding we looked at in Chapter 5, explains how adolescents develop friendships in ways unavailable to school-age children (Selman, 1979; Selman & Schultz, 1990). These ideas extend his views about interpersonal understanding (Selman, 1980, 1981). Selman argues that changes in cognitive development enable young adolescents to engage increasingly in empathic understanding. Young adolescents can appreciate and understand the situation of someone else by seeing things from that person's perspective.

Selman hypothesizes that this change in empathic understanding typically leads early adolescents to seek exclusive friendships, to engage in intimate communication, and to cooperate with someone else on long-range, mutual goals. He maintains that increased empathic abilities enable young adolescents to value friendships, both relationships with particular individuals and the phenomenon of friendship itself.

Selman explains his argument about developmental differences in friendship by contrasting what a typical 5-year-old and typical 15-year-old would say about friendship. When asked What makes two people good friends? Selman suggests each would be "as likely as the other to respond spontaneously, 'If they are close to each other.' These words ('being close') can look and sound the same and still mean different things—that is, have different 'conceptual structures' and meaning" (Selman & Schultz, 1990, pp. 9–10).

Selman (1981) has built a developmental scheme similar to his model of interpersonal understanding in order to explain changes over time in how youths construe the meaning of friendship. His developmental scheme is a model extending across five stages. This model is presented in Table 7-1 on the following page.

Each stage combines a distinct understanding of friendship and a corresponding ability to make distinctions about other people. In early adolescence, individuals enter stage 3, which is characterized by a **mutual commitment between peers** that replaces the school-age child's notion that friendship involves reciprocity. Stage 3 emerges as youths become strongly attached to a particular person (Selman & Schultz, 1990). Sullivan (1953) would call these attachments *chumships*.

Youths who have achieved stage 3 understandings about friendship are also able to adopt a **third-person perspective** in which they step outside a situation, as it were, to consider their behavior and the behavior of others. By means of the cognitive advance over stage 2 understanding, third-person perspective taking in stage 3 enables adolescents to comprehend that friendship requires mutual security, understanding, and conflict resolution.

Selman acknowledges that his description of stages of social perspective coordination seems detached from real life (Selman & Schultz, 1990). Do these stages of understanding about friendship actually make a difference in how people behave with one another? That is, does the cognitive processing peculiar to each stage result in actions that differ across stages?

Selman (1976) and other researchers (Bichard et al., 1988; Dodge, Pettit, McClaskey, & Brown, 1986; Pellegrini, 1985) have noted that developmentally mature stages of interpersonal understanding do not automatically lead to satisfying

TABLE 7-1 ■ Selman's Model of the Development of Understanding About Friendship

STAGE 0 **MOMENTARY PLAYMATES**	Friendship is based on physical proximity. A close friend lives nearby and the child just happens to be playing with the other child at the moment.
STAGE 1 **ONE-WAY ASSISTANCE**	A close friend is someone who does things that the other person wants to have accomplished. The friend's actions must match what the other person wants.
STAGE 2 **FAIR-WEATHER COOPERATION**	Close friendship is based on awareness that each partner has likes and dislikes, and friends coordinate their activities to accommodate each other. However, arguments can break off the relationship even if the parties still like each other.
STAGE 3 **INTIMATE AND MUTUALLY SHARED RELATIONSHIPS**	Friendships are seen as a fundamental way to develop support and intimacy. Arguments do not mean the relationship is over because the partners in the friendship are aware their affection for each other provides an underlying continuity to the relationship. Friendships are exclusive, and jealousy arises when a friend enters into a relationship with someone else.
STAGE 4 **AUTONOMOUS INTERDEPENDENT FRIENDSHIPS**	Friends realize they rely on each other for support and that they gain senses of identity from their close relationship with each other. Partners accept that a friend needs to relate to other people in order to continue to grow.

SOURCE: From "The Child as a Friendship Philosopher," by R. L. Selman. In S. R. Asher and J. M. Gottman (Eds.), *The Development of Children's Friendships*, pp. 242–272. Copyright © 1981 by Cambridge University Press. Reprinted by permission.

relations with peers. While necessary for such relations, mature understanding about relations is not sufficient to produce friendship. Having the mental understanding of what friendship requires is no guarantee that a person can behave like a friend. People need social skills to match their mental understandings; they need what earlier was called "a friendship script."

While Selman's model of interpersonal understanding helps to explain developmental changes in social reasoning, there is no compelling evidence that attaining these cognitive stages will lead to behaviors which peers find attractive. It seems plausible, however—as Asher's coaching strategies convincingly demonstrate—that enabling rejected and isolated children to see the connections between rules about interpersonal behavior and strategies that make and keep friends depends on the children's having achieved a normal stage of understanding about interpersonal interaction.

Gottman's Generalizations About Interactions Between Adolescent Friends

John Gottman has been studying friendship interactions of young children, school-age youths, and adolescents to determine what actually occurs between friends. Gottman has set out to overcome limitations in current studies about friendship and youths. First, he pointed out that researchers commonly have mistaken acceptable peer-group behaviors for what is required in a friendship. Second, he questioned the validity of inferring that responses youths give about their expectations concerning friendship indicate how these youths behave with friends. Third, he noted that a youth's lack of fluency in answering a researcher's question may camouflage the youth's sophisticated understanding of what friendship entails (Parker & Gottman, 1989).

To overcome these limitations, Gottman and his associates (Gottman & Parker, 1986; Gottman & Parkhurst, 1980; Parker & Gottman, 1989) have conducted a series of studies using extensive observations of how friends—from preschoolers to adolescents—behave with each other. We focus here on Gottman's findings about friendship behaviors in adolescence.

Gottman asserted that as children develop into adolescents they gain more sophisticated friendship skills. For instance, adolescents engage in self-disclosure much more often than preschool and school-age children.

Gottman's observations led him to posit **four generalizations about interactions between friends**. These generalizations are presented below. They assert that friendship provides mechanisms for coping with the social concerns of a specific developmental period.

- As a result of periodic upheavals and reorganization, development is parsed into three major periods: early childhood, middle childhood, and adolescence.

- Friendship interaction during any given (developmental) period has a characteristic organization and content with respect to conversational processes, giving each period a distinct signature or theme.

- The themes of each period and their developmental progression are normative insofar as they reflect children's attempts to adapt to demands of the social-ecological niche in which children in our society operate, and these demands change with development.

- Through interaction with their friends, children (acquire) unique information about their own affective experiences and the probable responses of others to their overt displays of these experiences (From "Social and Emotional Development in a Relational Context: Friendship Interaction from Early Childhood to Adolescence," by J. G. Parker and J. M. Gottman. In T. J. Berndt and G. W. Ladd (Eds.), *Peer Relationships in Child Development*, pp. 102–103. Copyright © 1989 by John Wiley & Sons. Reprinted by permission).

Let's explore the topic of adolescent friendship interaction from the vantage point of Gottman's four generalizations. The first and second generalizations deal with the underlying theme of forming an identity, and forming an identity during adolescence is closely bound to friendship.

Increasing **cognitive complexity** and increasingly **heterogeneous friendship groups**, particularly mixed-gender groups, lead the adolescent to reflect on diverse issues involving themselves and others. Because adolescents achieve more mature perspective taking (Selman, 1980; Selman & Schultz, 1991), they can work on identity formation from different viewpoints and can consider that part of their identities involves being empathic and caring for friends. Adolescents, in fact, consider that friendship imposes obligations, such as being available when needed, being trustworthy, and being protective (Youniss & Smollar, 1985).

Gottman's third and fourth generalizations about friendship interaction involve the **conversational processes** salient to a developmental stage and the types of **affective learning** taking place during the stage. Adolescents engage in self-disclosure and listen to what their friends have to say.

Gottman found adolescent friends discuss the psychological ramifications of behavior, confront friends about their behavior, and talk about their friendships. Consider this example of two friends discussing psychological ramifications of behavior—when discussing a proposed family vacation, one adolescent mused to a friend it would be better to stay home "and get away from my parents for a while because I really need to." The adolescent's friend asked, "When you go on vacations with them, do you get along with them very well?" When the response was yes, the friend suggested going on the vacation "might be good for you," and the adolescent agreed (Parker & Gottman, 1989, p. 121).

Gottman's fourth generalization deals with **affective development**. Gottman observed adolescent friends analyze at great length the effects of relationships and of life events on emotions. Some of these discussions become quite emotional (for instance, discussions about the breakup of a friendship or the divorce of parents). In other discussions, adolescent friends reflect on the kinds of interpersonal events that arouse their emotions. A third common topic involves disclosing and investigating feelings for someone else, particularly someone of the opposite sex. In all these situations, adolescents turn to friends to help them understand their emotions. The differences between adolescent conversations with friends and school-age children's friendship interactions are noticeable partly because adolescents can reflect on their behaviors but also because adolescents can appreciate what their friends are experiencing (examples of formal operations and empathic perspective taking).

Adolescent Reasoning About Friendship

Early adolescents' understandings of what friendship requires change over time. For instance, between sixth and seventh grade, **commonality** (thinking friends should be like one another and do all of the same things together) becomes less important. By seventh grade, boys consider providing help or support less important for friendship, whereas girls continue to think friendship requires providing help or support. **Intimacy** (thinking friends should share secrets and be able to tell each other anything) remains important for both boys and girls, with girls considering it even more important than do boys (Bukowski, Newcomb, & Hoza, 1987).

Sources of interpersonal support for adolescents differ according to age. These differences mirror the changes one expects to see as youths' interpersonal worlds expand from middle childhood through late adolescence and as youths enter into deeper relationships. For instance, 9-year-olds identify their parents as their most frequent sources of interpersonal support, while early adolescents say parents and same-sex friends equally provide support. Middle adolescents say same-sex friends are their primary sources of interpersonal support. Late adolescents identify people with whom they are involved romantically as their main sources of interpersonal support, but also mention other friends and their mothers (Furman & Buhrmester, 1992).

Adolescents' Advice for Making Friends

Early adolescents who are accepted by peers have very clear understandings of what people who want to make friends should and should not do. These findings came in a survey of 440 middle school students (224 boys; 216 girls; 68% white, 23% black, 5% Hispanic, and 7% members of other ethnic/racial groups) who were asked what advice they would give people their age who want to make friends (Wentzel & Erdley, 1993).

These 440 youths offered the following advice: initiate interaction; be considerate, honest, and cooperative; show respect for oneself and for others; and be helpful. They knew it is important not to be rude or hurt someone's feelings, not to be physically or verbally aggressive, and not to be selfish or self-centered. Thus, we know that early adolescents have reflected on interpersonal relations and are in touch with what are fundamentally important strategies in making and keeping friends. You may recall the domains of interpersonal competence discussed earlier in this chapter. These early adolescents know from personal experience what research with college students has confirmed regarding interpersonal skills needed in late adolescence (Youniss & Smollar, 1985).

Interviews with Adolescents About Friendship

James Youniss and Jacqueline Smollar (1985) investigated activities and communication of close adolescent friends, as well as the problems and obligations close friendships present to adolescents. They asked adolescents to answer questions about activities they enjoy with close friends, topics they discuss with close friends, problems close friendships can produce, and obligations that close friendship imposes. We take up each of these questions in turn.

Activities adolescents enjoy with close friends.   A majority of females (64%) said they most enjoy going out with their friends, whereas 28% mentioned talking together. Because going out together involves talking as well, the researchers restricted "going out together" to specific mention of activities other than talking, such as going to the movies (Youniss & Smollar, 1985). One percent of the females said they most enjoy activities involving alcohol or drug use with their friends.

Males gave a somewhat different picture of activities they most enjoy with friends. Going out together was mentioned by 36% of the males, 24% mentioned recreational activities, such as sports, and 20% mentioned activities involving drugs or alcohol. Note the significant difference ($p < .01$) between males and females in the enjoyment of drug and alcohol activities with their friends. Males and females also greatly differed in their enjoyment of talking together with their friends. Whereas 28% of the females mentioned they most enjoy talking with a close friend, only 10% of the males picked that activity.

Gender differences marked the activities adolescents most typically engage in with close friends. With their close friends, 60% of the females said they typically engage in intimate conversations, 25% mentioned going places together, 7% mentioned nonintimate discussions, and another 7% mentioned fulfilling obligations of friendship, such as keeping secrets and sticking up for each other.

For adolescent males, the problems causing most difficulties with friends are disloyalty, disrespect, insufficient attention, and unacceptable behavior.

Many of the typical activities with close friends singled out by the females were also mentioned by the males, but not to the same extent. For instance, 30% of the males mentioned intimate conversations; 27%, nonintimate discussions; 23%, going places together; and 15%, fulfilling obligations of friendship.

Topics of discussion for adolescent close friends.   What do close adolescent friends talk about according to the Youniss and Smollar (1985) study? The topics most often mentioned by both males and females were relationships, future plans, schoolwork, religious beliefs, and dating. Males and females selected the same set of topics in practically identical fashion, except for the topic of their families. Eighty percent of the females discuss their families with close friends, while only 54% of the males said they do so. Fewer younger adolescents than older adolescents said they discuss social issues with a close friend. In addition, more girls than boys (70% versus 50%) identified their same-sex close friend as the person they most prefer to tell their intimate feelings and to discuss their problems with the opposite sex.

Problems and obligations presented by adolescent close friendships. Youniss and Smollar (1985) also investigated the problems and obligations adolescents experience in close friendships. The problems girls mentioned most frequently were acts of disloyalty (59%), insufficient attention (28%), unacceptable behavior (18%), and disrespect (17%). Examples illustrating each problem are given below, and these examples mirror the findings reported earlier in the book from research with early adolescents (Wentzel & Erdley, 1993).

- **Disloyalty**—not keeping secrets, lying, breaking promises.

- **Insufficient Attention**—being ignored, not calling, spending time with other people.

- **Unacceptable Behavior**—drinking too much, smoking pot, quitting school.

- **Disrespect**—being rude or bossy, making fun of others.

Children's understandings of friendship develop from a sense around age 7 that friends are companions who play together to a sense around age 9 that friends share and stick up for each other to a sense around age 10 or 11 that friends share similar interests and tell each other personal information (Bigelow, 1977; Furman & Bierman, 1983; Rotenberg & Mann, 1986). Selman (1981) theorizes that children's understandings of friendship progress from a self-centered, egocentric focus to a relationship based on reciprocity and intimate sharing. Sharing fun diminishes in importance during middle childhood. By age 11, over 25% of youths emphasize friends make you feel special and 10% mention friends share personal information about each other and friends understand each other (Goodnow & Burns, 1985).

One significant aspect of friendship is that friends reveal personal, private information to each other but not to acquaintances or to strangers. Ken Rotenberg and Dave Sliz (1988) have demonstrated that such **selective disclosure** is found even in kindergarten children and that older children increase the frequency of selective disclosure to friends.

A developmental advance seen in adolescence is the growing understanding of what friendship entails. Adolescents attach importance to personal qualities, such as loyalty and intimacy. Breaking trusts leads to serious conflicts between adolescent friends and, if not resolved, will end in disruption of the friendship. Adolescents see that friendship imposes obligations of support, although girls identify this obligation much more than boys.

Adolescent friendship promotes increased understanding of one's identity. This development occurs as adolescents' increased cognitive complexity and widening social exposure promote learning more about people unlike themselves. Such learning occurs because adolescents engage in more self-disclosure and listen to what friends disclose about themselves.

Adolescents with close friends possess positive self-esteem, develop empathic understandings of other people's experiences and feelings, and seem buffered from loneliness. Adolescents with close friends tend to be popular with other adolescents because their social skills are advanced and, apparently, because their positive self-esteem generalizes to positive views of peers.

Selman (1981) theorizes that adolescents progress from sharing intimacy to an awareness that friendships require promoting the autonomy of the other person. In Selman's model, adolescents begin to realize that friends need freedom to interact with other people.

The demands of adulthood lead adults to spend more time with their families and, although they interact with a diverse assortment of people, adults are not able to socialize with friends to the same extent as college students (Blieszner & Adams, 1992). Thus, as compared to college students, adults have fewer friends. According to two separate estimates, adults regularly interact with between three and seven people they consider friends (Fischer, 1982; Weiss & Lowenthal, 1975). Women report more friendships than men (Lowenthal, Thurnher, & Chiriboga, 1975; Maas & Kuypers, 1974).

For many adults, their friendships depend on work associations or are actually relationships formed between married couples. Such friendships prove vulnerable to various life events, such as death of a spouse, retirement, or divorce.

Older adults are more restricted in their mobility, particularly when their health begins to fail, and other events of old-age, such as widowhood, retirement, and relocation, lead to smaller friendship networks, especially as compared to the number of friendships present in middle adulthood (Blieszner & Adams, 1992). Older adults most vulnerable to suicide are individuals who lose meaningful interpersonal contacts and find their lives filled with social isolation (Cook & Oltjenbruns, 1989). As they do for children, adolescents, and adults, friends provide the elderly a sense of self-worth and a buffer against the stressors of life.

For males, the behaviors causing most problems with close friends were disloyalty (43%), disrespect (39%), unacceptable behavior (14%), and insufficient attention (13%). Gender differences about problems with close friends were significant ($p < .01$) in two categories: disrespect and insufficient attention. Both males and females mentioned serious conflict occurs most often when a friend breaks a trust.

Close friendships impose obligations on adolescents. These obligations were seen to emerge from the very intimacy that close friendship promotes. For 70% of the females, the primary obligation of friendship is to be available when a friend is in need, whereas only 38% of the males identified this as the primary obligation of friendship. There was no majority opinion among the males about the primary obligation of friendship. A plurality (40%) selected being loyal and protective. Youniss and Smollar (1985) concluded that the very basis of friendship between females is helping each other during times of trouble, whereas for males, being loyal and protective forms the basis of friendship.

LONELINESS AND ADOLESCENTS

Some adolescents do not fare as well as their age-mates who develop close friendships. Some adolescents feel isolated from others—they are lonely.

Loneliness is a painful feeling of separation from others. Sullivan portrayed loneliness as an intimidating experience "ordinarily encountered only in preadolescence and afterward," but with roots in a child's developmental history of emerging individuality (1953, p. 261). In contrast to **solitude**, which healthy individuals seek for a variety of reasons, such as creativity and peace (Storr, 1988), loneliness is a consequence of being separate from others with whom one desires intimacy and friendship. Furthermore, the very process of individuation, which adolescence has as a fundamental task, produces loneliness. Thus, forming a personal identity includes the possibility of experiencing loneliness, and loneliness is thrust upon adolescents because of the many cognitive, physical, and social changes that mark their development. While loneliness does not appear more prevalent during adolescence than in other stages of life, the adolescent's developmental tasks of identity formation, separation from home and parents, and the overall push toward autonomy make loneliness a particularly poignant experience, particularly for early adolescents (Ostrov & Offer, 1978).

Early Adolescents and Loneliness — Jennifer Parkhurst (1989), along with her colleague Steven Asher (Parkhurst & Asher, 1992), has studied loneliness in early adolescents who are rejected by their peers. Her work involved 450 seventh and eighth grade students in a Champaign, Illinois middle school. There were 219 girls and 231 boys in the study, most of whom were white (72%) or black (25%); the remaining students were Hispanic, Asian, or from another racial/ethnic group. The middle school organized the students into three teams of seventh-graders, averaging 75 students each, and two teams of eighth-graders, averaging 117 students each. Students took classes only with the members of their own teams (Parkhurst & Asher, 1992).

Gifted adolescents in rural isolation can be particularly vulnerable to feeling apart from others.

Parkhurst and Asher (1992) used sociometric procedures to identify popular, rejected, and neglected youths. Each student was also given an instrument to assess the behavior of classmates. The instrument contained eight descriptions of behavior, each placed on a separate page along with a list of 25 classmates. The class mates were the same sex as the student completing the instrument. The researchers asked the students "to circle the names of *any* teammates who fit (any of) the descriptions 'cooperates in a group,' 'starts fights,' 'someone you can trust,' 'shy,' 'can't take teasing,' 'disrupts things in a group,' 'kind,' and 'easy to push around'" (Parkhurst & Asher, 1992, p. 233).

Parkhurst and Asher (1992) were primarily interested in studying the emotional experience of loneliness as it relates to a young adolescent's peer-group status. They used a questionnaire designed by Asher and Wheeler (1985) to measure dissatisfaction with peer relations and feelings of loneliness. They assessed whether loneliness differs according to sociometric status and determined "that rejected students are significantly lonelier than popular students" ($p < .001$) (Parkhurst & Asher, 1992, p. 237).

One expects that popular early adolescents would be significantly less lonely than early adolescents rejected by their peers. Parkhurst and Asher (1992) did some intricate analyses of subgroupings of rejected students and found that early adolescents who were both rejected and submissive (in contrast to rejected youths who were aggressive) were significantly lonelier than popular students ($p < .001$). However, there was no difference in the loneliness reported by rejected-aggressive students and by popular students. These results are consistent with other research that has reported (*a*) depression is more common among socially withdrawn children and (*b*) lower self-esteem is more common among youths who submit to victimization (Alasker, 1989; Rubin, Hymel, & Mills, 1989).

Middle Adolescents and Loneliness

Randy Page (1991) surveyed nearly 1,300 high school students to assess the relationship between feelings of loneliness and lack of hope. Four distinct groups of adolescents emerged in terms of the extent of their hopelessness: high hopelessness, hopelessness, low hopelessness, and no hopelessness. **Hopelessness** is a belief that outcomes one desires are not going to occur. Feelings of loneliness distinguished these groups—adolescents with more hope had less loneliness. Page (1991) noted that identifying and treating loneliness in its early stages would prevent the debilitating effects of hopelessness on personality development.

Rural conditions can produce feelings of loneliness, and gifted adolescents in rural isolation can be particularly vulnerable to feeling apart from others. Two researchers at the University of Nebraska studied how 49 gifted rural adolescents (between 16 and 18 years old) cope with loneliness (Woodward & Kaylan-Masih, 1990).

The researchers used the Woodward Loneliness Inventory, which has been used since the late 1960s to measure feelings of loneliness in different Nebraska populations. The inventory contains 75 items with a five-point scale ranging from never lonely to almost always lonely. Psychometric properties of the instrument are good. Groups in Nebraska that have completed the inventory include divorced people, homemakers, older adults, college students, high school students, alcoholics, and single mothers. The rural gifted adolescents had the third highest mean scores seen on the inventory; they followed urban senior high school girls and rural adolescents.

Fifteen of the gifted adolescents (31%) reported they often feel lonely, 29 (59%) reported they sometimes feel lonely, and the remaining 5 students (10%) reported they rarely or never feel lonely. The adolescents reported feeling most lonely when situations are out of their control and when they feel isolated, rejected, or alienated from others. They admitted feeling less lonely when with other people and when celebrating special days, such as birthdays or Christmas. However, a significant minority of the adolescents found special occasions enhance their feelings of isolation and loneliness (Woodward & Kaylan-Masih, 1990).

To cope with their loneliness, the gifted adolescents used several strategies. The more common strategies were to gain a more positive perspective about their situation and to become absorbed in personal pursuits, such as reading or listening to music. Adolescents who seemed less self-reliant sought **external resources**, for example, religion, other people, physical labor or exercise, and counselors. The more self-reliant gifted adolescents looked to **internal resources** to cope with loneliness, such as imagination, hopes and creative outlets.

Late Adolescents and Loneliness

According to Larson (1990), when early and middle adolescents describe how they feel when by themselves, they frequently say they feel lonely. However, as adolescents mature, they experience time alone more positively, and the better adjusted adolescents actively seek time by themselves. Larson (1990) surmises that this solitude promotes individuality in the better adjusted adolescents.

R. Rogers Kobak and Amy Sceery (1988) have demonstrated that three types of attachment differentiate college freshmen: one group of students dismisses the importance of peer attachments, a second group feels secure in peer attachments, and a third group seems obsessed with peer attachments. Of the three groups, the students who dismiss attachments report feeling most lonely. In addition, they have little self-confidence, and their peers consider them hostile. The students obsessed with peer attachments are low in self-confidence, and peers consider them nervous or anxious. The secure group has more self-confidence than the dismissive or obsessive students. They report other students give them support, and their peers see them as amicable or calm.

Australian college students seem as vulnerable to loneliness as American college students. Jennifer Boldero and Susan Moore (1990) studied 138 first-year Australian college students (78% were females) to see whether intimacy, disclosure of feelings, and the extent of a person's social network predict loneliness. The best predictors for males were having few close male friends and not sharing feelings with a specific close male friend. For females the best predictors of loneliness were inability to give and receive support from a close female friend and living alone or with family.

Judy Jackson and Susan Cochran (1991) studied 293 college students (147 females; 146 males) to assess associations between loneliness and psychological distress. They found a significant correlation ($p < .01$) between low self-esteem and loneliness for both males and females. They also found a significant correlation ($p < .01$) between depression and loneliness for females. They concluded that loneliness in late adolescents correlates strongly with feelings of guilt, particularly with self-blaming thoughts and self-devaluation.

Gerald Adams and his colleagues (Adams, Openshaw, Bennion, Mills, & Noble, 1988) developed a social skills training program to help lonely college students with poor social skills. They developed the training program from a **social deficit model** that emphasizes loneliness in late adolescence is significantly associated with **interpersonal ineptness**. Adams and his colleagues (1988) noted that, in contrast to other students, lonely college students are less perceptive about nonverbal behaviors, take fewer risks in interpersonal relations, are ineffective in efforts to influence other people, have poor listening skills, and share little about themselves with others.

Adams and his colleagues (1988) designed their social skills training program to increase proficiency in social behavior and intimacy in personal relationships among college students. Participants in the program reported they were very lonely, said their social competencies were poor, and desired to improve their social skills. Twenty females participated in the study; 10 were randomly placed in the training program and 10 were randomly placed in a control group. The researchers informed all control group subjects they would become part of the training program once the study ended (Adams et al., 1988).

The researchers used a training program called Adolescent Social Skills Effectiveness Training (ASSET) (Hazel, Schumaker, Sherman, & Sheldon-Wildgen, 1981). This program focuses on eight social skills: giving positive feedback, giving negative feedback, accepting negative feedback, resisting peer pressure, solving problems, resolving conflicts, initiating and carrying on conversations, and following instructions. During training, the program staff describe these skills to the participants, outline their appropriate uses, model the skills, and offer feedback to students when they practice the skills. In addition, students get homework assignments to apply the skills.

aniel Offer and his colleague Eric Ostrov have used the Offer Self-Image Questionnaire for Adolescents (OSIQ, see Chapter 4) to study loneliness during the adolescent years. One item in the OSIQ is phrased, "I am so very lonely." As with all other items in the inventory, this item is answered on a six-point scale ranging from describes me very well to does not describe me at all. In his study of loneliness, Offer grouped responses into one of two categories—lonely and not lonely (Ostrov & Offer, 1978; also see Offer & Offer, 1975).

In all, Offer studied 2,939 adolescents—1,513 males and 1,426 females. The participants were Australian (46%), American (43%), and Irish (11%). Some of the American teenagers ($n = 365$; 12.4% of the total sample) were delinquents or psychiatrically disturbed. Ostrov and Offer (1978) described the great majority (87.6%) of the adolescents as normal youths.

Ostrov and Offer (1978) also predicted that younger adolescents would report more loneliness than older adolescents, who would have developed closer friendships with peers of the opposite sex. As predicted, younger boys were lonelier than older boys, and younger girls were lonelier than older girls ($p < .05$).

Ostrov and Offer (1978) also predicted females would feel lonelier than males. They reasoned that females are socialized into passivity and into desiring intimacy with a male, whereas males are encouraged to develop autonomy and independence. Adolescent girls have fewer occasions to seek close relationships with people outside their families, thereby making the task of achieving separation from the family more difficult. Comparison of boys' and girls' responses, however, indicated there are no gender differences related to loneliness.

Ostrov and Offer (1978) also predicted that mobility and rapid social change in the United States would leave American youths feeling lonelier than Australian and Irish adolescents. The researchers considered American adolescents to be more vulnerable to generational differences, value confusion, and identity bewilderment than Australian and Irish adolescents. The prediction held true when boys were compared ($p < .025$), but not when the girls from the three countries were compared. An average of 20.5% of the girls in each of the three groups said they were lonely, whereas 22% of the American boys, 16.4% of the Australian boys, and 12.6% of the Irish boys said they were lonely.

Ostrov and Offer (1978) had no explanation for their findings that American, Australian, and Irish males, but not females, differ regarding loneliness. The researchers did note that cultural factors they did not understand might have produced the differences among males.

What is intriguing is that the percentage of American boys who reported they were lonely matched the percentage of girls from all three countries who reported feeling lonely. Had Ostrov and Offer compared gender differences only among

The ASSET program lasted five days. Adams and his colleagues (1988) gathered assessment data at three points: a week before the program began, three days after the program ended, and three months after the program ended. Assessments included measures of loneliness, social competencies, and social inhibitions. The researchers also videotaped all the students acting out hypothetical social situations and had independent raters—who were unaware whether a student was a member of the

the Australian and Irish adolescents, their prediction that females would report more loneliness than males would have been confirmed.

Ostrov and Offer (1978) predicted disturbed and delinquent adolescents would report more loneliness than normal teenagers. Several features that contrast normal from pathological adjustments led the researchers to this prediction. Normally adjusted adolescents can be alone without a sense of dread or helplessness because they have developed a clear sense of their identities and they trust other people. Poorly adjusted adolescents find being alone threatening and experience human relationships as continuously disappointing and painful. You may recall Bandura's (1964/1980) assertion that troubled adolescents had been troubled children and likely would be troubled adults. Ostrov and Offer remarked that teenagers who find "adolescence to be a painfully poignant and lonely time would be, or will be, at risk at every stage of life" (1978, p. 35).

The changes demanded during adolescence because of heightened cognitive, physical, and social capacities (a) require modifying coping skills that were effective in middle childhood, (b) increase feelings of alienation, particularly among disturbed youths, and (c) lead both delinquent and disturbed adolescents to view adolescence as a threat (Ostrov & Offer, 1978, p. 42). While normal adolescents will feel lonely at times, their loneliness will be subdued by support from parents and friends and by trust in themselves.

The prediction about delinquent and disturbed youths experiencing more loneliness than normal adolescents held up for both males and females. Disturbed girls and boys reported greater loneliness than their normal and delinquent counterparts. Furthermore, delinquent males and females reported more loneliness than normal adolescents. Thus, Ostrov and Offer (1978) concluded that disturbed adolescents are lonelier than delinquent youths who are lonelier than normally adjusted youths. The differences between the responses of delinquent, disturbed, and normal boys were highly significant ($p < .005$). The differences between the responses of delinquent, disturbed, and normal girls were even more significant ($p < .001$).

In summary, Ostrov and Offer's (1978) study demonstrated that early adolescent boys and girls are more vulnerable to loneliness than late adolescents and American boys are lonelier than Australian or Irish boys. The researchers were surprised to discover that American, Australian, and Irish adolescent girls' reports of loneliness did not differ. They expressed fascination with the finding that American adolescent males report as much loneliness as Irish, Australian, and American adolescent females. Finally, emotionally disturbed and delinquent youths in all these countries reported more loneliness than their well adjusted adolescent counterparts.

training or control group—judge the students' proficiencies in performing the eight social skills. The raters had been trained to make their assessments according to carefully defined criteria.

The training and control group students did not differ on any of the measures taken before the training began. Three days and three months after the program, however, significant changes (all $p < .05$) were found in terms of social skill proficiency, feelings of being included in social situations, and feelings of being close to others. In all cases, the students who participated in the training program increased and maintained their social skills, their feelings of being included in social situations, and their feelings of being close to others.

Summary Remarks About Adolescent Loneliness

As this section has indicated, early, middle, and late adolescents experience loneliness. Some adolescents who are lonely have endured peer rejection, and, not uncommonly, adolescents who are both inordinately submissive and rejected by peers feel lonelier than other adolescents. However, some loneliness is due to geographical isolation, as found in rural areas. Late adolescents who are lonely commonly feel distressed by feelings of guilt, low self-esteem, and self-blame. Training programs have been designed to assist late adolescents, particularly college students, in dealing with loneliness and ineffective social skills.

We saw earlier in this chapter that college students seem paradoxically vulnerable to peer influence, but for many students a close friendship emerges and they become insulated from the undue influence of peers in general and from loneliness in particular.

CHAPTER SUMMARY

As youths develop from early through late adolescence, they spend increasingly less time with their families and increasingly more time with peers and by themselves. Both gender and age influence these changes. It is widely held that peers play a significant role in adolescent understanding of interpersonal relations. This chapter addresses the role of acquaintances and friends as adolescents' understandings of social behavior change.

Controversy surrounds the question of whether peers negatively influence adolescents. A popular belief is that peers undo the positive effects of parents on their children. Research does suggest a link between deviant behavior and some peer relations, but there is considerable evidence that peers provide a base for developing independence, learning forms of intimacy outside one's family, and becoming involved with the wider world.

Peer acceptance and rejection noticeably affect adolescent development. Rejected youths are particularly vulnerable to serious emotional and behavioral problems during adolescence and adulthood. Psychologists have developed methods to help isolated and rejected youths gain peer acceptance. A major component of these programs is teaching youths to link rules about acceptable behavior to pertinent social situations.

Adolescents reason differently than school-age children about parents' rules governing peer relations. For instance, early adolescents are significantly less likely than younger children to agree that a peer's moral behavior provides valid reasons for parental restrictions. In addition, younger children are more likely than adolescents to agree that parents have the right to regulate relations with peers who use marijuana, smoke cigarettes, or drink alcohol. Adolescents agree, however, that peers' marijuana use warrants parental concern.

Many studies of the effects of college on the development of interpersonal relations have been flawed. The studies seldom control for maturation effects, usually work with relatively small samples, and rarely involve students from more than one institution. There is some evidence that over a four-year college experience, students become more invested in specific individuals.

Friendship is a special type of relationship. Adolescents understand the importance of friendship and value their friends. The early stages of friendship are seen in school-age children's becoming invested in peers of the same gender.

Cognitive development enables adolescents to form friendships unavailable to school-age children. Unlike school-age youths, adolescents gain increased empathic understandings and appreciate the perspectives of others. Mutual commitments with specific friends develop for many adolescents.

Friendship provides adolescents the means to understand and explore the specific emotional tensions that characterize their development. Most importantly, the adolescent task of forming an identity constitutes the underlying theme of adolescent friendship interactions.

Adolescent friends understand that their relationship poses mutual obligations. Chief among these obligations for females is being available when a friend is in need. For males, the chief obligations of friendship are remaining loyal to and protective of each other.

The struggle to form an identity makes loneliness a particularly poignant experience, especially during early adolescence. Loneliness is an outgrowth of the adolescent push for individuation. In this sense, adolescent loneliness is part of becoming an adult. However, peer rejection produces a form of loneliness that can impede personality development. Some researchers have begun efforts to understand the type of loneliness that rejected adolescents experience.

Adolescents in many cultures report feeling lonely. Younger adolescents report more loneliness than older adolescents. American adolescent males report greater loneliness than Irish and Australian boys, but American adolescent females seem neither more nor less lonely than Irish and Australian girls.

The adolescent groups most vulnerable to loneliness are emotionally disturbed youths and delinquents. Emotionally disturbed youths report more loneliness than delinquents, and delinquents report significantly more loneliness than normal adolescents. Disturbed and delinquent girls seem particularly vulnerable to feeling lonely.

Interpersonal relations have been traced to five specific domains of competence. These domains are competency in initiating relationships, managing conflict, providing emotional support, expressing dislike for another person's actions, and disclosing personal thoughts and feelings. As relationships develop, certain domains increase in importance and others decrease. These findings have implications for developing programs to help shy, isolated, and rejected adolescents.

A prime location where American adolescents interact with peers is school. We turn to a discussion of schooling and adolescents in the next chapter.

CHAPTER

8

SCHOOLING AND ADOLESCENCE

Interview with a High School Student—The High School Caste System

High school students group individuals into a variety of categories. Consider the following description provided by a midwestern high school sophomore of the different types of students in her school of about 1,800 students.

"In our school, we have *preppies*, *ropers*, *punks*, *thespians*, *nerds*, blacks, and regular people. Do you really want me to describe each one? It's easier just to spot them when you see them.

"Preppies wear brand name clothing and are snobs. They usually run the student government. A lot of them, boys and girls, are in sports. I can't think of any cheerleader who isn't a prep. They think they're better than anyone else.

"Ropers are the cowboys. They listen to country western music. The girls wear Rocky Mountain jeans. The boys wear Wranglers and boots called ropers. They wear cowboy hats.

"Punks have mohawk hair styles, brightly dyed hair. The girls wear fishnet stockings and combat boots. The guys wear cutoff fatigues and combat boots. They're radical liberals and talk about anarchy and stuff.

"Thespians are in the school clubs that deal with acting. If you belong to the thespian club, you have a much better chance to be in school plays. A lot of thespians are also punks.

"Most of the nerds are guys. They belong to the computer club and the chess club. They give up their lunch period to go to the library to play chess. Some seem to wear the same clothing all year. It's so gross.

"There's a racial slur many people use to describe the blacks, but I'm not going to use it. The blacks listen to rap music, wear big old baggy pants that hang down to their knees, and wear Cross Colors a lot.

"There are students who don't belong to any group. I'm one of them. I call us regular people. Preppies would say we are all dorks. Punks would say we are just conforming to society. Blacks probably call us honkies, but I don't think they consider themselves better than others. Nerds think they are smarter than us; nerds think they're smarter than everyone. I don't know what ropers would say 'cause I don't hang around any of them."

In describing the social groups at her school, this girl demonstrates an ability to consider what various groups think about the regular people, the group in which she places herself. Such reflective ability is a sign of the maturing social perspective taking that marks adolescent reasoning (see Chapter 5).

In her descriptions, we can also see the girl's value judgments, especially her sense of indignation over students who think they're better and smarter than others. Whether her judgements are correct, the girl indicates scorn for arrogance and elitism and signifies a polarization between groups of students in her school.

Her description of the school's caste system has direct bearing for this chapter on schooling and adolescence. In addition to an examination of social groupings in high schools, this chapter addresses the transitions involved when early adolescents enter middle school or junior high, and the current state of American secondary education. We look at studies of some successful high schools in the United States. Because of the long-term adverse consequences for adolescents who continually perform below their potential in school, we look at the issue of high school underachievement. As a final topic, we continue our look at the effects of college on the development of late adolescents. We begin with the early adolescent transitions into the middle grades.

THE MIDDLE GRADES

Herschel Thornburg (1980), the founding editor of both the *Journal of Early Adolescence* and *Journal of Adolescent Research*, identified a set of developmental tasks (tasks that individuals in a specific culture are expected to accomplish at a certain age) early adolescents need to complete. These tasks are listed below.

- Become aware of their physical changes
- Assimilate knowledge into problem-solving strategies
- Learn new sex roles and social roles
- Develop friendships
- Achieve increasing independence
- Realize their proclivity to identify with stereotypes

Matching these developmental tasks to a special school setting formed the basis of the **middle school** (Staton & Oseroff-Varnell, 1990).

The middle school was introduced in the late 1950s to ease the transition between the elementary grades and high school (Noblit, 1987). By 1965, the demand increased for schools organized along middle school lines (George, Stevenson, Thomason, & Beane, 1992; Lounsbury, 1992). Educators wanted early adolescents to be in an environment that would foster their learning, permit them to develop their desires for independence, and prepare them for high school (Staton & Oseroff-Varnell, 1990). As we will see later in this chapter, research indicates the middle school has not provided the easy transitions that were intended and may, in fact, have increased some stressors for youths.

Middle schools are not uniformly structured. Some span from sixth grade to seventh or eighth grade, while others include only seventh- and eighth-graders. In the vein of traditional junior high schools, some middle schools encompass seventh, eighth, and ninth grades.

Early adolescent middle school students seek more independence, gain greater freedom from adult supervision, and place more reliance on their peers. In addition to their noticeable physical changes, early adolescent middle school students develop social and cognitive interests unlike the interests of elementary school children. Clear examples are the growing interest by a majority of early adolescents in heterosexual relations and the increasing ability of early adolescents to reflect on their own identities. In America, these social and cognitive interests emerge as early adolescents engage in two transitions, one developmental (puberty) and one socially planned (going to a new school). We discussed the transition of puberty earlier in this book. We now turn to the effects of school transitions on adolescents.

School Transitions and Early Adolescence

Nearly every adolescent studied in school transitions research says going to a new school produces stress and is problematic (Aneshensel & Gore, 1991; Crockett, Petersen, Graber, Schulenberg, & Ebata, 1989; Eccles, Midgeley, Wigfield, Buchanan, Reuman, Flanagan, & MacIver, 1993; Simmons & Blyth, 1987). Some of the stress involves general fear of change itself, while some involves concern over drug use, loss of friends, and the need to adjust to new teachers and unknown expectations about schoolwork. We begin our look at the impact of these transitions on adolescent adjustment with a description of what school transitions entail.

Many youths study in elementary schools made up of kindergarten through sixth grade (K–6) students, then move to a middle school comprising grades seven and eight followed by a four-year high school. Other youths leave the K–6 school environment, go to a junior high school of grades seven, eight, and nine, and then go to a three-year high school. These youths have two school transitions—from elementary to middle school or junior high school and then to high school.

Some youths make only one transition—from grade school to high school. These students attend a K–8 elementary school and then go on to a four-year high school. Many parochial schools (that is, church-related) follow this one transition pattern. Let's look at some studies on the impact of school transitions on adolescent development.

Timing of School Transitions

Roberta Simmons and Dale Blyth (1987) conducted a five-year study of 621 youths in Milwaukee, Wisconsin. They tracked these youths from sixth through tenth grade. They conducted interviews once each year with the students and school principals; they obtained annual standardized achievement test scores; and each year, they obtained an assessment from a school nurse of each student's physical maturation.

The objective of this longitudinal study was to assess the impact of developmental transitions on adolescent adjustment. The transitions of particular interest to Simmons and Blyth (1987) were the timing of puberty and the timing of entering a middle school and/or a high school. Simmons and Blyth used self-esteem and self-image as key indicators of adjustment. In addition, they identified other outcomes, such as interacting with peers, establishing independence, making future plans, and coping with conformity and deviance. They referred to all these adjustment measures as *developmental tasks of adolescence* (Simmons & Blyth, 1987).

The researchers lost only 11% of their subjects over the course of their five-year study. The students who left the study differed from those who remained in two ways: the ones who remained in the study came from intact homes ($p < .001$) and had less problem behaviors at school during sixth grade ($p < .01$) (the first year of the study).

Less than half of the youths (42.4%) attended K–8 schools, whereas the majority (57.6%) attended K–6 elementary schools. The transition from sixth to seventh grade was different for each group. The K–8 students stayed in the same building for seventh grade and had to adjust to a new classroom and a new teacher. The K–6 students, however, had to adjust to a new building with three separate grades (seventh, eighth, and ninth) and to becoming "small frogs in a much larger pond" (Simmons & Blyth, 1987, p. 30).

At the beginning of the study, many more students were enrolled in junior high schools than in K–8 or K–6 elementary schools. But going to a junior high school involved more than entering a new building with many more students. For example, the seventh grade junior high students moved continually from one classroom to another throughout the day and seldom attended any class with the same group of students or the same teacher. In contrast, the seventh grade elementary school students remained in the same classroom with the same teacher and classmates for the entire school day. In short, the seventh-graders in each type of school setting were required to adjust to very different environmental circumstances as they made their transitions from childhood into early adolescence.

What did Simmons and Blyth (1987) discover? In terms of their key indicators of adjustment—self-image and self-esteem—they found little evidence of negative effects for either group of students. In fact, for all the outcome variables (relating with peers, establishing independence, making future plans, and coping with conformity and deviance), they found no pattern of negative effects for the majority of students. Negative reactions were thus not the common outcome, but were noticeable for some early adolescents making the transition from sixth grade to a junior high school. Such negative reactions were not evident for youths making the transition from eighth grade to a high school.

For some students, the transition to a junior high school was marked by a decrease in self-image and self-esteem, with associated problems in other outcome variables as well. These students shared certain characteristics; they entered puberty early, began dating early, and gained early independence from parental supervision.

One adjustment difficulty faced by the students who went to junior high schools involved status at the school. Becoming the youngest group in the junior high school placed the seventh-graders at a disadvantage not felt by the youths who remained in a K–8 school. As sixth-graders, the K–6 youths had been "top dogs" in their schools, but as seventh-graders, they were "bottom dogs," low-ranking strangers in a new milieu.

Of considerable interest are the changes over time as the K–6 and the K–8 students made the transition to high school. Even though the entrance to high school placed the K–8 students as bottom dogs for the first time, they seemed to adjust fairly well. However, the K–6 students experienced the same negative reactions to being bottom dogs in high school as they had demonstrated as seventh-graders.

The most severe reactions occurred in early-maturing girls and extremely early-maturing boys who entered junior high school following a K–6 education. Simmons and Blyth (1987) explained the negative reactions of these early-maturing girls and extremely early-maturing boys as a matter of being developmentally unprepared. Physical maturation did not equip them emotionally to cope well with the new environment of a junior high school. While flattering to many early maturers, being "hit on" by older youths was not something they were prepared to handle. They were certainly not mature enough for greatly relaxed supervision from parents. They would have benefited had their environment not heightened expectations that they would behave like older adolescents.

The significance of these findings are fourfold. First, in their self-concept, self-image, and other measures of adjustment the youths in the study were coping well. School transitions did not produce evidence to support the storm and stress view of adolescence but, on the contrary, provided evidence that the majority of adolescents adjust well.

Second, the timing of school transitions did appear to be crucial. Developmental readiness for the adjustment demanded by the transitions was a factor, and entrance to a large junior high school seemed more difficult for seventh-graders than entrance to high school for adolescents who remained in a K–8 school.

Third, gender was a significant factor in adjustment to early transitions, with girls particularly vulnerable to declines in self-esteem and boys vulnerable to being victimized by older students. Boys and girls who entered junior high school showed declines in academic success and in extracurricular activity.

Fourth, despite evidence of some negative effects attributable to early transitions, on the whole, the adolescents did not suffer long-lasting damage. The difficulties some adolescents expressed involved a combination of the individual's coping styles, the changes demanded, and what aspect of adolescent adjustment was at stake (Simmons & Blyth, 1987).

Number and Timing of School Transitions

Anne Petersen and her colleagues (Crockett, Petersen, Graber, Schulenberg, & Ebata, 1989) studied three distinct groups of early adolescents to identify what impact the number and timing of school transitions has on the adjustment of the youths. The groups made very different transitions. One group ($n = 38$) made a double transition—first from a fifth grade elementary classroom to sixth grade in middle school and then to seventh grade in junior high school. The second group ($n = 34$) made a single transition from a fifth grade in an elementary school to sixth grade in a middle school. The third group ($n = 181$) made a single transition from sixth grade elementary classrooms to seventh grade in junior high school.

Petersen and her colleagues (Crockett et al., 1989) looked at (*a*) whether early transitions (in fifth grade) or late transitions (in sixth grade) had an effect on the adolescents and (*b*) whether the number of transitions had an effect. In all, 253 early

TABLE 8-1   Sample Characteristics in a Study of the Effect of Single or Double School Transitions on Early Adolescents

NUMBER OF TRANSITIONS	MALES	FEMALES	TOTAL
One—5th to 6th grade[a]	20	14	34
One—6th to 7th grade[b]	77	104	181
Two—5th to 6th[a], 6th to 7th grade[b]	16	22	38
Total	**113**	**140**	**253**

[a] Early transition
[b] Late transition

SOURCE: Adapted from "School Transitions and Adjustment During Early Adolescence" by L. J. Crockett, A. C. Petersen, J. A. Graber, J. E. Schulenberg, and A. Ebata, 1989, *Journal of Early Adolescence, 9*, p. 180.

adolescents took part in the study—113 boys and 140 girls. The composition of the sample is presented in Table 8-1. As the table indicates, 72 students were involved in early transitions, and only 38 students were involved in a double transition.

The students were followed for three years and were interviewed in the fall and spring of each year. The researchers gathered data about self-image and grades. Self-image data were obtained by using a modified version of the Offer Self-Image Questionnaire (OSIQ) (see Chapter 4). School officials allowed the researchers to obtain grades from annual school records.

The students who made two transitions consistently did poorer academically than students who made one. This was true in a variety of academic subjects, including language arts, literature, math, science, and social studies. These differences held for marks received in sixth, seventh, and eighth grade.

The self-image concepts tested included such areas as impulse control, body image, sense of personal adjustment, peer relations, and feelings of mastery over one's environment. Students who made two transitions had significantly lower over-all self-concepts as measured by the OSIQ and were significantly lower on two particular scales: mastery of the environment and sense of personal adjustment. By eighth grade, some changes had emerged in self-concept scores related to peers; boys who had made two transitions had the highest self-concept scores of any group regarding peer relations, whereas girls who had made two transitions had the lowest self-concept scores of any group in the study.

The significance of these findings are both practical and theoretical. On a practical level, the clearly adverse effects of double transitions and of early transitions provide important information to consider when planning children's educations. School systems that force children to make multiple and early transitions produce a very difficult set of circumstances for these youths to manage well.

On a theoretical level, we know that early physical maturation favors male adjustment but poses significant problems for females. Girls who made early transitions and who made double transitions were much more seriously affected, especially in their school work, than boys. It is more likely, given the earlier onset of puberty for females, that these gender effects are associated with pubertal changes (Crockett et al., 1989). Other longitudinal research confirms that girls experience greater stress in adjusting to a junior high school or middle school environment than boys (Fenzel, 1989; Simmons & Blyth, 1987).

These studies on the impact of school transitions have looked at the outcomes of transitions. We have not, however, examined the characteristics of a school that might contribute to adolescent coping. We now turn to such a study.

Junior High School and Adolescent Development

Jacquelynne Eccles and her colleagues (Eccles, Midgley, Wigfield, Buchanan, Reuman, Flanagan, & MacIver, 1993) examined whether changes seen in early adolescents' motivation, interests, performance, and behaviors can be explained as negative aspects of the junior high school environment. Specifically, the researchers wanted to know if the developmental changes of early adolescence—for instance, changes in cognition, identity, and desire for greater autonomy—are frustrated by the structure of junior high schools.

How do junior high schools typically operate, particularly in relation to the developmental needs of early adolescents and compared to how elementary schools typically operate? Eccles and her colleagues (1993) noted six characteristics of junior high schools.

- Junior high school teachers exert more control over students than elementary school teachers.

- Teacher-student relationships in junior high school are more impersonal and negative than in elementary school.

- In junior high school, greater emphasis is placed on large group instruction, public evaluations of performance, and ability grouping across classes.

- Junior high school teachers consider themselves less effective with students than do elementary school teachers.

- Seventh grade work in junior high school demands less of students' cognitive skills than sixth grade elementary work.

- Junior high school teachers enforce more demanding standards of performance than elementary school teachers.

Do these differences encountered by early adolescents in junior high school affect their development? To answer this question, Eccles and her colleagues (1993) conducted a two-year longitudinal investigation involving nearly 1,500 early adolescents. The study looked at the effect of the transition from elementary school to junior high school on the adolescents' behavior, values, motives, and beliefs about achievement. The researchers gathered data during the fall and spring of two separate school years.

The students were divided into four groups based on their experiences with math teachers in sixth and seventh grades. The transition from sixth to seventh grade differed for each group. These transitions are presented on the following page.

- From a sixth grade math teacher who felt ineffective with students to a seventh grade math teacher who also felt ineffective.
- From a sixth grade math teacher who felt effective with students to a seventh grade math teacher who felt ineffective.
- From a sixth grade math teacher who felt ineffective with students to a seventh grade math teacher who felt effective.
- From a sixth grade math teacher who felt effective with students to a seventh grade math teacher who also felt effective.

Adolescents who went from high-efficacy to low-efficacy math teachers developed lower personal expectations about math performance, perceptions of lower personal skills in math, beliefs in the greater difficulty of math, and poorer grades in math. In all of these changes, these students fared much more poorly than adolescents whose sixth and seventh grade teachers had similar beliefs about teaching effectiveness. Students who moved from low- to high-efficacy teachers, however, showed no such downward spiral in personal attributions and academic performance. Eccles and her colleagues (1993) concluded any decline could not be attributed to early adolescent development but, rather, to the school environment of junior high schools, particularly the school's learning environment.

In addition to these marked impacts on math, the transition from elementary to junior high school also adversely affected early-maturing females who experienced seventh grade as an environment that frustrated decision making. Late-maturing females in the same classrooms reported an increased involvement in decision making. Eccles and her colleagues (1993) were puzzled over how seventh grade girls in the same classrooms could have such dissimilar experiences. They suggested that early- and late-maturing females have markedly different desires for autonomy and concluded that the early-maturing girls find the junior high school environment to be controlling and inhibiting (Eccles et al., 1993). Frustrated over lack of opportunities for participation in decision making places early-maturing females at particular risk for increased truancy and misconduct in school.

Conclusions About School Transitions

These studies strongly suggest that early adolescents encounter difficulties in the transition from a K–6 elementary school setting to a junior high school setting. The effects are worse for students who make multiple transitions.

Negative effects can partly be explained by the restrictive environments of junior high schools. This is particularly true for early-maturing adolescents. One wonders if the restrictions are put into place because of the greater numbers of students in junior high schools as compared to elementary schools. The social pressures placed on early-maturing girls and very early-maturing boys influence negative outcomes for self-image and self-esteem. The early adolescents' demands for greater autonomy run into environmental constraints from junior high school teachers but, paradoxically, extract increased liberties from parental supervision. The evidence does not support any belief that the early-maturing adolescent is emotionally prepared for these increased liberties.

Simmons and Blyth (1987) did notice that the size of the junior high school is an important factor. Smaller schools promote self-esteem in seventh-graders, whereas larger schools impair seventh-graders' self-esteem. David Hamburg noted that this outcome "may well be because (smaller schools) tend to provide a niche for every-one, along with individual attention" (1992, p. 20).

Being a Middle School Student

What do early adolescents believe it means to be a middle school student? What information do they use to succeed in the middle school setting? What communica-tion strategies do they use to cope well in middle school? Are there critical aspects to succeeding as a middle school student?

In this section, we look at a study that addressed those four questions. Ann Staton and Dee Oseroff-Varnell (1990) wanted to learn what adolescents understand about their identities as middle school students and how they use communication in mak-ing the transition to a middle school.

Their data came from two public middle schools in a large city on the Pacific Coast of the United States. Enrollment at the schools was 886 students and 639 stu-dents, respectively. Entering students made up 29% of the student body for both schools. The schools were in a middle-class neighborhood, and busing had been used to integrate the schools. Minorities accounted for about 44% of the total enrollment.

Staton and Oseroff-Varnell (1990) used observations and interviews to collect data. They also had the sixth-graders write a letter to a hypothetical fifth grade stu-dent. In the letter, the sixth-grader was to tell the fifth-grader what to do to be happy and succeed at the middle school.

Observations occurred in classrooms, lunchrooms, assemblies, and hallways. The researchers also observed an orientation session for parents and incoming students. In addition, they interviewed 96 students twice—once during the first few weeks of school and then during the tenth week of the school year. Interviews took about 15 minutes. Fifty-three percent of the students in the interviews were male, 47% were female, 72% were white, and 28% were from minority groups.

What Does It Mean to be a Middle School Student?

According to students who were interviewed early in the school year, being a middle school student is dominated by a new physical and social setting, by changes in social status, and by new responsibilities. By the second interview, they continued to emphasize the social and personal dimensions but de-emphasized the physical setting.

The physical and social setting.   Examples of early interview responses were, "It's a huge school," "Classes are bigger," and "You have to move from class to class and stop at your locker to get your books and put your stuff back" (Staton & Oseroff-Varnell, 1990, p. 80). By the second interview, concerns over the physical environ-ment had diminished. A typical second interview response was, "There are lots of rooms and lockers, but don't worry (because) you get a schedule and a locker num-ber. Your schedule gives room numbers and teachers' names. The lunchroom, office, counselor, nurse, and auditorium are located on the first floor. There are three boys' bathrooms located on the first, second, and third floor" (Staton & Oseroff-Varnell, 1990, p. 80).

Gaining confidence about the physical layout of the school came with time, but the students did not forget the apprehensions they felt upon entering the middle school (Staton & Oseroff-Varnell, 1990). Hamburg (1992) noted that youths find their initial apprehensions about junior high schools or middle schools are not borne out by what they experience once in school.

The students also commented on the changed social structure in the middle school. There are new teachers, new students, and varying views. Some quotes from students were, "There's a lot of older kids around," "You can beat up elementary school kids," and "I'm not too crazy about boys. The other girls are always talking about what they do with their boyfriends" (Staton & Oseroff-Varnell, 1990, p. 80). Whereas one student was enthused over being able to meet other people from diverse ethnic and racial backgrounds, another simply thought school discipline was poor and "lots of people goof off" (Staton & Oseroff-Varnell, 1990, p. 80).

Changes in social status.   Upon entering middle school, students find themselves at the bottom of the social ladder. They are the underdogs, even though being in the middle school means they are more mature than elementary school students. The older students threaten them, both verbally and physically. One comment from an entering sixth-grader was, "You get pushed around by the seventh- and eighth-graders. They call you 'little sixth-graders,' bump into you in the hall, don't do anything to go out of their way for you." Another entering student said, "Expect that some of the seventh- and eighth-graders will pick on you" (Staton & Oseroff-Varnell, 1990, p. 81).

The perception of being more important than elementary school students, but vulnerable to verbal and physical bullying, did not leave the sixth-graders. They acknowledged that teachers did not always treat them like little kids and that some even treated them as more mature than elementary school students. The predatory behavior of older students led sixth-graders to advise incoming students how to deal with bullying. Thus, the researchers heard different comments about social status, such as, "We are growing up and becoming young adults" and "The first thing you need to know is never to mess with anyone" (Staton & Oseroff-Varnell, 1990, p. 81).

New responsibilities.   The new responsibilities of middle school involve academics and emerge from the new status of greater maturity signalled by being in middle school. The course work is more difficult than in elementary school, and teachers expect greater student responsibility in accomplishing work on one's own. Student comments included, "You have to rely on yourself to do everything. The teachers in fifth grade help you through the year—they went around with you. In sixth grade they just said, 'Go'" (Staton & Oseroff-Varnell, 1990, p. 82). Another student said, "You have to pay attention or you miss out. You could miss a day in elementary school, but now if you miss a day, you get behind and have to make up work from all your classes" (Staton & Oseroff-Varnell, 1990, p. 82).

Besides new responsibilities in academics, middle school students encounter new social responsibilities, particularly in following rules and behaving independently. The following two quotes convey these perceptions: "They're really strict on notices and being late—everything has to be with the rules. You have to be on time a lot" and "They don't watch you, don't have to walk in lines, get to do stuff on your own, but I also don't like that because if you mess up, it's all your fault" (Staton & Oseroff-Varnell, 1990, p. 82).

Observations of teachers indicated that they perceive being a middle school student means reaching both the academic and social expectations articulated by specific classroom teachers and formulated for the school building as a whole. The teachers did recognize and talk about the physical changes occurring in the lives of the students. They linked their expectations of students directly to the fact that the students were now in middle school. Teachers were heard to make such comments to students as, "You are not fifth-graders. You are in sixth grade now," "Verbal abuse is not allowed in your homes, and we have the same standards here," and "You are savvy and quick to adapt. You follow directions well. This week seems to be going well. How many of you like changing classes?" (Staton & Oseroff-Varnell, 1990, p. 84).

What Information do Students Use to Succeed in Middle School?

Staton & Oseroff-Varnell (1990) identified two types of information pertinent to student success. The first is information the students seek, and the second is information teachers provide without being asked.

Information students seek.   Students seek three types of information: procedural, content, and reassurance. Students want procedural information such as, "Can we use notes on the exam?" and "When will the first semester report cards come out?" Content information is particularly sought about academics. Examples are "What topics are OK to write about?" and "What does it mean to round a number to three decimal places?" Students also seek reassurance information, which ensures them that they will do well in middle school and will enjoy it. Parents and siblings are common sources of reassurance information.

Information teachers provide.   Teachers provide general information and information about expectations. They also provide information that serves as encouragement and praise. General information includes daily announcements of school activities and reviews of school policies, such as "Here is what to do during a fire drill." Information about expectations covers academic and social rules, such as, "When I call your name, answer 'Here'." Encouragement and praise "paralleled the students' category of seeking reassurance and focused on the students' success in their new school" (Staton & Oseroff-Varnell, 1990, p. 89). An example is "This is a great school, and that's because you are here."

What Communication Strategies do Students Use to Cope Well in Middle School?

Staton & Oseroff-Varnell (1990) found that students engage in seven basic communication strategies. Some are direct and involve an element of risk, such as asking someone how to do a math problem, thereby, letting others know you lack certain knowledge. Other approaches are covert and involve little, if any, risk; an example is watching what other people do in order to model their behavior.

TABLE 8-2   Communication Strategies Used to Succeed in Middle School

STRATEGY	DESCRIPTION
Overt	Asking someone directly for help.
	EXAMPLE: "How do you do this algebra problem?"
Being Interpersonal	Being friendly with others.
	EXAMPLE: "I've tried to be helpful and make sure the teacher knows my name."
Indirect & Rhetorical Questions	Using implied questions or asking questions of no one in particular.
	EXAMPLE: "Does anyone here really believe we have to do this by tomorrow?"
Testing Limits	Deliberately violating a rule to discover if it will be enforced.
	EXAMPLE: Turning in an assignment late to see the teacher's response.
Observing Others	Watching what other people do.
	EXAMPLE: Seeing what clothes students who are popular wear.
Getting Around in the School	Wandering through the hall
	EXAMPLE: Spotting landmarks in the building to find one's way around.
Letting Things Happen	Passively getting a feel for the school.
	EXAMPLE: "I just be myself and see what happens."

SOURCE: From "Becoming a Middle School Student," by A. Q. Staton and D. Oseroff-Varnell. In A. Q. Staton, *Communication and Student Socialization*, pp. 72–99. Copyright © 1990 by Ablex. Reprinted by permission.

The seven basic communication strategies are being overt, being interpersonal, asking indirect and rhetorical questions, testing limits, observing others' behaviors, getting around in the school building, and letting things happen. These strategies are presented in Table 8-2, along with examples of each.

Critical Aspects of Succeeding as a Middle School Student

Staton & Oseroff-Varnell (1990) identified several aspects of successful transitions. Successful students consider the transition to middle school a regular event that is supposed to happen. In addition, students who succeed consider the transition to be desirable and important to growing up. Students seek signs that the transition has occurred, such as changing classes, attending special assemblies, and taking on increased responsibilities. Successful students also recognize they are in transition together with other students, and they talk with one another about it.

Despite the collective aspect of the transition into middle school, it is critical for each student not to remain isolated from other individuals. When students have the support of a "chum" or "buddy," their fears and uncertainties about handling the new school diminish.

Transforming Middle School Education

Earlier, we briefly reviewed the developmental tasks early adolescents encounter and for which middle schools were instituted. Contemporary analyses have led many experts to assert that middle schools cannot accomplish these objectives unless they fundamentally change to meet the needs of today's students (Hamburg, 1992). In this section, we focus on recommendations from a national task force that called for "transforming the education of young adolescents" (Task Force, 1989, p. 35).

The task force made eight recommendations based on what were termed *essential principles* for change in the typical middle school. Chief among the principles is that the middle school "should be a place where close, trusting relationships with adults and peers create a climate for personal growth and intellectual development" (Task Force, 1989, 37). The task force recommended that middle schools should do the following:

- create a community for learning by dividing large middle schools into smaller communities;
- teach a common core of substantive knowledge that evokes learner curiosity, problem solving, and critical thinking;
- organize the school to ensure all students succeed "regardless of previous achievement or the pace at which they learn" (Task Force, 1989, p. 49);
- make local principals and teachers in charge of decision-making at the school;
- prepare teachers to work in middle schools;
- link education with improved health and fitness;
- create alliances between middle schools and families of students; and
- establish cooperative partnerships between the school and community organizations.

Let's look at each of these eight recommendations more closely.

Create a Community for Learning

This recommendation advocates dividing large middle schools into smaller communities of learning. To accomplish this objective, the school needs (*a*) to make each student part of a self-contained **house arrangement** (a small community of adults and students within the school); (*b*) to coordinate curricula by placing all subject matter preparation for the small community into the hands of a team of teachers who teach the 200 to 300 students in the house; and (*c*) to match each student with a specific adult whose task is to get to know the student well, to relate to the student as an individual, and to enable the student to succeed (Task Force, 1989).

Teach a Core of Common, Substantive Knowledge

To carry out this recommendation, schools need to challenge students to use critical-thinking skills. Students should be encouraged to reason, question, and challenge evidence. Such critical thinking will be fostered by integrating curricula across disciplines and by helping students connect ideas from different disciplines. In addition, this recommendation depends on teaching students to develop healthy lifestyles and the values of involved citizens (Task Force, 1989).

Organize the School to Ensure the Success of all Students

To accomplish this objective, schools must shape their educational programs to fit student needs. The task force (1989) suggested three methods. First, group students with diverse abilities and use teaching strategies such as cooperative learning and having older students tutor younger students. Second, provide flexible scheduling in order to ensure students have enough time to learn material in-depth. Third, provide expanded opportunities for learning, such as longer school days, special summer or weekend classes, individualized help, and parental involvement in the adolescent's learning (Hamburg, 1992).

Make Local Principals and Teachers in Charge of Decision Making

To accomplish this objective, schools must do three things. They must give teams of teachers greater influence in the classroom, particularly over matters of reaching academic goals, scheduling classes, allocating money, and choosing interdisciplinary themes. Schools must also establish school governance committees that involve all house arrangements and include parents, administrators, community members, and school support staff. Finally, schools need to designate a house leader and identify new roles for the school principal. The house leader will work with teaching teams to help them achieve their goals. The principal will ensure the building functions well and will communicate with the external community.

Prepare Teachers to Work in Middle Schools

The education of middle school teachers needs to include courses in adolescent development, exposure to cultural diversity, understanding of guidance principles, a paid internship or apprenticeship in a middle school, and certification followed by continuing education.

Link Education With Improved Health and Fitness

The task force(1989) emphasized every middle school "should have a health coordinator competent to provide limited medical assessment and treatment" and able to make appropriate referrals (Hamburg, 1992, p. 216). In addition, the school environment should model healthy living.

Create Alliances Between Middle Schools and Families of Students

To accomplish this recommendation, schools need to offer parents meaningful roles in the governance of schools by including them on the school governance committees. Schools should also keep parents directly informed of the school's rules and expectations and seek parents' ideas and expressions of concern. Finally, schools need to offer parents opportunities to support their adolescents' learning, both at school and at home. Coordination between parents and teachers could lead to homework assignments with which parents help their children. Of most importance, parents need to monitor that their children complete homework assignments, provide ongoing praise, and help in dealing with obstacles.

Establish Cooperative Partnerships Between Schools and Communities

To accomplish this objective, the task force (1989) identified five strategies whereby communities can be engaged with schools.

- Place students in community service, such as volunteer work in day-care or senior citizen centers.

- Ensure students have access to health and social services, such as youth service bureaus and family planning clinics.

- Support the middle school curriculum by providing places to study, alternative education offerings, and scholarships.

- Augment resources by providing computer equipment and furnishing "mentors from the community for students.

- Widen career guidance for students through such diverse groups as Junior Achievement, Career Explorers, and 4-H. One method that was especially recommended is to pair teenagers with successful members of the community.

We have now finished our discussion of the effects of middle school on early adolescents. As we have seen, middle school presents certain challenges to early adolescents. We turn next to high school and its influence on middle adolescents.

HIGH SCHOOL

The American secondary school system is under attack. Continually, reports indicate American adolescents fare poorly when compared to high school students in other industrialized countries (National Commission, 1983). In fact, American youths are considered especially ill-prepared in mathematics and the natural sciences when compared to Japanese and German students. Ernest Boyer (1983) noted the steady decline in Scholastic Aptitude Test (SAT) scores between 1970 and 1982; these declines continued into the 1980s; however, SAT scores have begun to climb again (Ogle, Alsalom, & Rogers, 1991).

There is considerable debate whether declining or increasing SAT scores say anything of merit about the quality of American education. For instance, alarm was raised when SAT scores dropped steadily between 1973 and 1981, and some relief expressed when scores climbed between 1982 and 1990. Robert Zajonc (1986) used demographic data to predict SAT scores would rise during the 1980s because family size had begun to decrease. Zajonc's model said larger families dampened SAT scores between 1963 and 1980 (scores did decline over this period), and predicted smaller families would enhance SAT scores through the year 2000.

Whatever the cause for the decline in SAT scores, the fact that they did decline led to public alarm over the state of our nation's high school education system (Astin, 1991). This alarm found public expression in a widely read document called *A Nation at Risk* (National Commission, 1983).

A major problem in using SAT scores to judge educational outcome is the unproven assumption that SAT scores validly measure what a student has learned. Furthermore, declining test scores do not provide an explanation for the decline or a possible remedy. As one educational researcher pointed out in the 1960s, standardized outcome measures do not provide information that classroom teachers and program developers can use to make changes (Hastings, 1966).

For the authors of *A Nation at Risk*, however, the fault lay in our high schools and the remedy lay in strengthening a core curriculum for every high school student (National Commission, 1983). Alexander Astin (1991) questioned how the authors of *A Nation at Risk* could know the problem was with the high schools.

In a sense, the issue of the quality of American secondary education involves the expectations that different groups have regarding high school. In the United States, there is not unanimous agreement that secondary schooling should focus on cognitive achievement. Evidence suggests that cognitive development occurs much less in high school than it does in the elementary grades (Jencks, 1985).

According to Doris Entwisle (1990), the major effect of high schools is to influence every phase of adolescent development, not just cognitive development. For Entwisle, every phase of adolescent development involves physical, social, personal, emotional, moral, prevocational, academic, and political changes. From this broad and diverse catalog of aims for secondary education, it is not difficult to see why debates emerge regarding what it means to provide a quality educational experience for every high school student.

13-year-olds in Spain, Korea, the United Kingdom, and Canada do noticeably better in science than 13-year-olds in the United States.

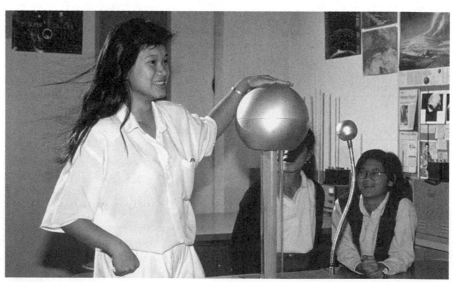

Some Issues in American Secondary Schools over the Past Several Decades

The issues facing American secondary schools have changed. Discipline issues during the 1950s involved chewing gum, talking out of turn, making noise, and running in school corridors. In the 1980s and 1990s, problems in schools involved much more serious issues, such as substance abuse, sexual assault, pregnancy, guns, gangs, robbery, and suicide. Teachers have identified drug use as the number one problem for schools.

Most people surveyed in Gallup polls believe American schools are in trouble and are not getting better. However, these ratings vary according to whether adults are rating their children's schools or the public-school system in general. People give their local school high marks, but many rate the overall public-school system as mediocre.

A major concern about school performance is dropouts. These concerns are tempered by evidence that many dropouts complete high school in late adolescence or early adulthood. Over the past 25 years, the percentages of 18- and 19-year-old blacks and whites completing high school have become nearly equal (77% of whites and 65% of blacks) and are nearly the same for 20- to 24-year-olds (85% of whites and 81% of blacks). Hispanic youths, however, are much less likely than blacks or whites to complete high school.

Other concerns involve American secondary students' achievement in math and science. American 13-year-olds rank lowest in mathematics proficiency when compared to early adolescents from Ireland, the United Kingdom, Spain, Canada, and Korea. The typical 13-year-old Americans are still limited to basic arithmetic operations, whereas 13-year-olds in the other countries are clearly at more advanced levels of mathematics proficiency (Van Scotter, 1991).

In the United States, reading achievement is particularly low for black and Hispanic adolescents. However, the average American high school student, regardless of race or ethnicity, struggles when asked to analyze or even to give basic explanations of what he or she has read.

Since the 1970s, American high school students have slipped most noticeably in science proficiency. When compared to students from foreign countries, American students do better than only Irish adolescents, and do noticeably worse than students in Spain, Canada, the United Kingdom, and Korea. The students who do better than the average American students apply scientific procedures and analyze scientific data; American proficiency is limited to understanding simple scientific principles but does not extend to using that understanding (Van Scotter, 1991).

Several years ago, Charles Silberman (1971) concluded that American secondary and college education was in crisis. He attributed the crisis in American education to several factors: gross inequalities in the achievements of white and nonwhite students, an education fostering docility, rather than critical thinking and a broad understanding of reality, and disheartening failures in attempts to reform education. Of great concern to Silberman was the attention given in high schools to authoritarian, repressive control of adolescents without any attention to academic accomplishment—to what Silberman called "a good education." Silberman concluded that "mindlessness affects the high school curriculum every bit as much as the elementary curriculum. And the junior high school, by about unanimous agreement, is the wasteland—one is tempted to say cesspool—of American education" (Silberman, 1971, p. 324).

Silberman's is a bleak assessment. Could it be true? Is it enough to dismiss his evaluation as "trash" as a previous reader wrote in the margin of the library copy of Silberman's work I used in my research on this chapter? Does such stern resolve in the face of Silberman's convictions accomplish anything? Perhaps we should look for evidence of "good" high schools and look at the reality of being a high school student.

Good High Schools

In this section, we look at two separate studies of high schools considered to be good. By a *good school*, the authors mean the educational outcomes for the students are exemplary. One striking feature of these good schools is diversity—both when compared to each other and when looked at individually.

Boyer's Report on American High Schools

In 1983, Ernest Boyer published the results of a lengthy study of secondary education in the United States. He emphasized that quality schools differ from other schools because they emphasize high academic standards, promote a core curriculum, provide for some electives, and have a vision of what it means to be an educated person. The good schools emphasize language literacy, math competency, social science understanding, and natural science comprehension. Such characteristics are what the authors of *A Nation at Risk* (National Commission, 1983) seemed to have in mind in their recommendations to reform secondary education.

In Boyer's (1983) assessment, mediocre high schools graduate students who are seldom, if ever, challenged to reach their potentials. Very bad schools are beset with daunting social problems, hold few academic goals for their students, and are plagued by violence and threats of violence.

Boyer (1983) did not sweep all secondary education into a trash heap, as some might claim Silberman (1971) wanted to do. In fact, Boyer showed what happens at schools he considered good. He called one of these schools Garfield High School, "a school that works" (Boyer, 1983, p. 66).

Garfield High School is located in the inner city of a large metropolitan area. Of the 2,000 students at Garfield, 80% are black or Hispanic. The majority of the students live in public-housing projects.

Garfield students consistently obtain high SAT scores, and graduates enroll in very good universities and colleges. Daily attendance is close to 100%. The students produce a newspaper, which is recognized nationally as one of the best high school papers. The school's mathematics team regularly trounces suburban teams in math tournaments.

Why does Garfield succeed? A primary reason is that the students, parents, and teachers consider the school special. Parental involvement in school affairs is noticeable. Teachers are interested in and care about student learning. Boyer (1983) said the teachers, students, and parents share the same goals and have clearly spelled out objectives. Teachers, students, and parents at Garfield High School express commitment to four central objectives:

- developing critical thinking;
- enabling students to continue learning;
- increasing career options for students; and
- building community spirit.

When Boyer (1983) visited other high schools, the students, parents, and faculty seemed amused at the notion of shared objectives. These other schools had such diverse objectives that no vision of education or rationale for the school emerged.

Lightfoot's Portraits of Good High Schools

In 1983, Sara Lawrence Lightfoot published naturalistic studies of six high schools considered exemplary for their attainment of educational success. **Naturalistic studies** rely on observing behaviors in the actual social settings where the behaviors occur. The six schools included two urban public schools, two suburban public schools, and two private schools. Lightfoot (1983) admitted that these six schools are not representative of high schools in the United States, but reported that colleagues did conclude the schools represent the diversity in educational choices offered in the United States, are geographically dispersed, and have noticeable contrasts in the students and teachers.

Here, we focus on one of Lightfoot's (1983) portraits of suburban high schools. Brookline High School (BHS) is located in Brookline, Massachusetts, a suburb of Boston. A common misperception of Brookline is that it is a community of affluence. The 55,000 residents include mostly whites, but the minority population includes "Asians, blacks, Hispanics, Israelis, Russians, Irish, and East Indian" (Lightfoot, 1983, p. 153). Lightfoot said everyone she talked to initially emphasized the ethnic and socioeconomic diversity at BHS. It struck her that everyone seemed intent on correcting the idea that Brookline is an elitist suburban retreat.

At the time of Lightfoot's (1983) study, BHS had 2,100 students; 30% were from minority groups. Twelve percent of the student body were black. Many of the Brookline students came from professional, upper-middle-class homes, whereas most of the black students came from Boston working-class homes.

While some hostilities separated various groups of students, particularly working-class students from Brookline and blacks from Boston, the differences had diminished each year. A social worker saw BHS as a milieu in which stereotypes, hostilities, and barriers were confronted and set aside, at least within the school.

Students at BHS were placed in one of four levels of instruction: basic, standard, honors, and advanced placement. Assignment to any level of instruction involved multiple factors, such as counselor evaluation, student choice, test scores, grades, and parental preferences. From what Lightfoot (1983) could determine, entering and leaving any level of instruction was done with ease. Shifting to a lower level was not marked by shame or humiliation. However, most teachers acknowledged that grouping students by ability had divisive effects on the school, and they admitted a much higher proportion of lower SES and minority adolescents were placed in the lower groups.

The BHS curriculum offered 300 courses. Course offerings emphasized the school's reputation for academic excellence. However, as a broader ranger of courses entered the catalog, some faculty became concerned over diluting the quality of education available at BHS. Observations led Lightfoot (1983) to conclude that academic engagement in the school is impressive.

> There is visible evidence of educational commitment. When you walk through the halls of the school during class periods and peer through open doors, students tend to be attentive and busy. A typing class is energetically engaged in pounding the keys, working against a stopwatch. In a physics laboratory, small groups of students work collectively on an experiment while the teacher circulates around the room offering encouragement and clarification. It is very quiet and all eyes face forward in a U.S. history course . . . . A quick, passing gaze finds things going on in the classrooms, minimal chaos, and directed attention . . . . Despite the absence of bells, all the classes I visited started easily on time and without much fanfare....Beyond these immediate signs of educational engagement, there is a great deal of evidence of the seriousness attached to schooling as one enters classrooms. The seriousness of purpose is not limited to courses for bright, academic students. In a reading class for students with major learning disabilities, the room is noiseless as the students work individually at their seats . . . . The same seriousness is attached to nonacademic courses. In an advanced dance class, the teacher has a friendly but no-nonsense approach . . . . Even in courses that tend to attract noncollege-bound students, there is attention to pedagogy and curriculum, and a commitment to good form (Selections from pages 200–202 from *The Good High School* by Sara Lawrence Lightfoot. Copyright © 1982 by Sara Lawrence Lightfoot. Reprinted by permission of BasicBooks, a division of HarperCollins Publishers, Inc. Reprinted by permission).

Lightfoot (1983) ended her book with some thoughts on what it means for a high school to achieve goodness. Openness to criticism and recognition of limitations and imperfections mark the good schools. These schools anticipate change, and they nurture all participants. She suggested that schools should work to become "good enough," rather than flounder after unattainable ideals. By valuing good enough, Lightfoot did not promote mediocrity but, rather, "a view that welcomes change and anticipates imperfections" (1983, p. 311). By confronting and articulating dimensions of wholeness, change, and imperfections, the good schools foster "the institutional support of good education" (Lightfoot, 1983, p. 311).

Social Grouping and Social Polarization in High School

James Coleman (1961), a professor of sociology at the University of Chicago, argued that adolescents in an industrial society form a subculture He meant that industrial societies require specialized and lengthy training if individuals are to contribute in the working world. These requirements result in segregating adolescents from adult society. The structure and pressures of industrial societies dictate that adolescent preparation take place in institutions that force the adolescents inward toward their peers and force them to carry out social lives almost solely with their peers. As a result, adolescents form a subculture with a language, symbols, and values that often differ from those known to adults. The gap between the adolescent subculture and the larger society was becoming more pronounced, and Coleman expressed concern over the effects such disparities would have on the adolescent transitions to adulthood. Other authors have argued that the lengthened moratorium forced on adolescents before they are permitted to act as adults promotes alienation and places adolescents in the position of being marginal members of society, denied opportunity to contribute to society, and denied constructive means to achieve their own potential (Adelson, 1986; Cloward & Ohlin, 1960; Friedenberg, 1959; Goodman, 1960; Lewin, 1939/1951).

Several factors maintain and reinforce the adolescent subculture. While the subculture may take various forms, depending on the communities in which the adolescents live, it is promoted chiefly by a prominent social institution; namely, the high school. High schools effectively segregate adolescents from the larger adult world and have replaced the family as the principal means of educating youths for the transition to adulthood.

Coleman (1961) studied the patterns and forms that the adolescent subculture takes in the high school. Ten schools were selected from a cross-section of American society (from rural to large metropolitan areas, from public to private schools, from affluent to lower-socioeconomic groups). The portrait Coleman painted seems to represent high school youths today, more than three decades after his study was published.

Coleman (1961) identified a caste system that prevails in the adolescent subculture. The effects of this caste system are so significant that he focused almost all of his book on interpreting how the caste system influences the development of values, aspirations, and self-understanding.

Certain individuals are members of an elite group that Coleman (1961) termed "the leading crowd." To be a member of the leading crowd requires several attributes held in high regard: a good personality, attractive looks, the right clothing, the right neighborhood, and the right reputation. Particularly for girls, a major influence on being a member of the leading crowd is having affluent parents. Male success in athletics is universally held in high esteem; it helps boys gain not only membership in the leading crowd but also wide popularity among the students.

Although members of the leading crowd often deny these membership criteria are true, outsiders note them consistently. Coleman quoted one male outsider, who said when a member of his school's leading crowd denied a leading crowd even existed, "You don't see it because you're in it" (1961, p. 34). There is thus an inclusive aspect to the leading crowd, but—even more apparent to observers—there is an exclusive aspect as well.

Only a small proportion of adolescents mention that getting good grades is a means to gain membership in the leading crowd. Coleman (1961) did identify some schools in which scholastic achievement was held in esteem, and in those schools, good grades became another criterion for entrance to the leading crowd. On the whole, however, good grades are not held in high regard by the leading crowds at most schools; what is of significance is that the leading crowd sets the trends that nearly all of the other students follow. Becoming educated is not considered very important.

Whereas academic achievement varies in importance, male athletic success always holds an extremely important position in the adolescent subculture. Successful male athletes are popular; they are stars. In Coleman's study, girls did not have an opportunity for athletic success; being popular with boys provided "the nearest equivalent for girls" (1961, p. 90).

The psychological effects of the adolescent subculture became apparent to Coleman. Being a member of the leading crowd produces in its members a strong sense of self-affirmation. Outsiders who want to be part of the leading crowd are more likely to feel negative about themselves. Coleman (1961) discovered that over one-third of all outsiders express a desire to be members of the leading crowd. Only a small proportion of outsiders is satisfied with not being members of the leading crowd. The psychological effects of the adolescent subculture are thus significant, particularly on individuals excluded from this elite group who desire its acceptance.

The adolescent subculture has a powerful and negative impact on females' perceptions of personal competence, particularly in scholastic achievement. Girls with good grades are very unlikely to value a reputation for academic brilliance. Coleman (1961) noted that over their four years of high school, the girls who are the best students grow to devalue the importance of academic excellence; they camouflage their true abilities. However, the importance the best boy students place on being recognized as smart increases over their high school years, and they strive to become even smarter. Coleman was convinced that the adolescent subculture damages girls with high scholastic promise by placing them "under a constraint . . . . not to be 'brilliant students'" (1961, p. 251).

A Study of Social Grouping in Detroit High Schools

Penelope Eckert (1990) conducted a three-year ethnographic study of social groupings in Detroit high schools. The students were mostly white. She found students fit into one of two social groups: the "jocks" or the "burnouts." The jocks came from upper-socioeconomic families, took school seriously, got good grades, and participated in school events. The burnouts came from lower-socioeconomic families, felt alienated from school activities, and expressed hostility to the academic curriculum.

An important note about Eckert's (1990) study—coming from a working-class family did not automatically mean a student was a burnout, and coming from an upper-income family did not guarantee a student would take school seriously. On the whole, however, the division of Eckert's subjects did follow social class lines. The problem with her assertion is its sense of determinism. It is as though she is postulating working-class backgrounds lead to alienation from education. The good high schools Boyer (1983) and Lightfoot (1983) studied indicate that working-class students in good high schools are highly invested in their educations.

The terms *jocks* and *burnouts* used in the Detroit high schools are far more inclusive than their normal usages in other parts of the United States. For many people

TABLE 8-3   **How Jocks and Burnouts Differ**

Variables	Jocks	Burnouts
High school courses	College Prep	Vocational
Drug use	Alcohol	Alcohol, hard drugs
School activities	Means to advance	Irrelevant
Clothing	Preppy	Fatigues, rock concert
Music	Mellow rock	Heavy metal
Attitudes to school	Accept school	Reject school
Career expectations	Professional	Blue collar
Use of information	Power	Autonomy
Attitude to adults	Valued	Considered obstacles

SOURCE: From "Adolescent Social Categories—Information and Science Learning," by P. Eckert. In M. Gardner, J. G. Greeno, F. Reif, A. H. Schoenfeld, A. Diseau, and E. Stage (Eds.), *Toward a Scientific Practice of Science Education*, p. 208. Copyright © 1990 by Lawrence Erlbaum & Associates. Reprinted by permission.

outside of Detroit, *jocks* are high school students who play athletics, particularly varsity sports. In many places, the term *burnout* refers to a drug user. In the Detroit schools, jocks were any students involved in school activities, and burnouts were students "who reject the school as a basis for social identity" (Eckert, 1990, p. 205).

Eckert (1990) considered the polarization between jocks and burnouts mirrors the polarization found in adult society between members of upper- and lower-socioeconomic groups. She considered this opposition fundamental and "close to universal in our culture" (Eckert, 1990, p. 205), regardless of the labels used to identify the opposing sides. One of the best fictional portrayals of these opposing socioeconomic groups among high school students is S. E. Hinton's (1967) novel *The Outsiders* with its antagonism between the "Socs" and the "Greasers." I have identified differences between jocks and burnouts in Table 8-3.

In Eckert's (1990) study, jocks pursued college preparatory work, such as foreign languages, natural sciences, and mathematics. Burnouts selected (or were directed toward by school counselors) vocational training such as metal shop. The polarization dividing jocks and burnouts extended to courses seen as the turf of one group. For instance,

> It requires great daring for a burnout to go into a science or math classroom other than the few designated for vocational students. They do not know anything about the teachers, the teachers do not know them, and they do not know any of the other students. And clearly the latter is the most important. A burnout going into a jock class will be isolated from the other students, will sit on the edge of the room, and will have no one to talk to or study with (Eckert, 1990, p. 208).

Feeling isolated from other students in a classroom produces anxiety, not only over feeling unwanted and unaccepted but also over difficulties getting help should the material become demanding. Eckert mentioned a burnout who dropped advanced algebra even though he liked the material and the teacher because the boy "had no one to talk to and feared he would have no one to work with when the going got tough" (1990, p. 208).

The social polarization dividing jocks and burnouts could also be seen in the culture of the high schools. Faculty and staff viewed jocks as "good kids" and burnouts as "bad kids." Jocks were seen to value things important to school personnel, whereas burnouts were perceived as adolescents who did not care. Jocks represented the promise of future success, and burnouts the prospect of future failure; jocks represented intelligence, and burnouts stupidity; jocks represented cooperation, burnouts rebellion.

Because of these labels, jocks and burnouts come into the high school carrying a legacy imposed on them by adults. While the burnouts do not simply accept the negative evaluation adults give them, "the power of the opposition and the school's acceptance of it ultimately leads to resignation. Rather than asking themselves how they can succeed in spite of the school, burnouts discard goals along with the available means to achieve them" (Eckert, 1990, p. 216).

Parental Influences on Adolescent Social Grouping

The studies of social grouping and social polarization in high school imply that the groupings are the work of adolescents alone, and while these groupings mirror socioeconomic class differences, they exist independently of parental influence. We look next at a study of how parents exert influence on the social groupings adolescents form in school.

Bradford Brown, Nina Mounts, Susie Lamborn, and Laurence Steinberg (1993) tested parental versus peer influence by examining whether parents have control over their adolescents' peer affiliations. (Perhaps you recall the discussion in Chapter 7 about parental management of peer associations.) The researchers looked at 3,781 15- to 19-year-olds in four-year public high schools: three in the Midwest and three on the Pacific Coast. The gender of the participants was nearly evenly divided—48% male, 52% female. Sixty-one percent of the students were white, 12% were black, 12% were Asian, and 13% were Hispanic.

Six types of adolescent social groups in the high schools were identified—*populars*, *jocks*, *normals*, *brains*, *druggies*, and *outcasts*. The outcasts combined both individuals whom adolescents considered loners and those considered nerds. These six groupings suggest that many high school students use greater differentiation than Eckert (1990) reported in Detroit high schools.

Brown and his colleagues (1993) had adolescents identify two boys and two girls in their classes who were considered prominent members of each of the six social groups. These lists of names were then shown to other students, who were asked to place the students in one of the six groups. The researchers identified an individual's group membership by accepting the group assignment given the person by a majority of his or her peers.

The researchers asked each adolescent about his or her parents' child-rearing practices. Specifically, the adolescents answered questions about parental emphasis on their school achievement, parental monitoring of their behavior, and parental inclusion of the adolescent in decision making.

The adolescents also answered questions about their behavior. Brown and his colleagues (1983) were interested in the adolescents' grade point averages (GPA), drug use, and self-reliance.

The adolescents provided information about their family's structures. The researchers labeled the families as "intact," "single-parent," "stepparent," or "other."

Certain family and parental characteristics were strongly associated with adolescent affiliation with specific social crowds. For example, adolescents from intact families were much more likely to be brains and much less likely to be druggies or outcasts. Adolescents from stepparent families were much more likely to be druggies and less likely to be jocks or brains. Brown and his colleagues (1993) hypothesized that hostility for stepparents colors the relationships these students have with adults at school and presents obstacles to participation in peer groups closely affiliated with teachers and other school personnel. (You may recall from the discussion about stepfamilies in Chapter 5 that adolescent stepchildren frequently fare poorly in their blended families.)

The druggies were much more likely to be white adolescents than adolescents from any other ethnic/racial group. However, other group membership rates mirrored the stereotype many Americans have formed of certain ethnic groups: whites in the populars, Asians in the brains, and blacks in the jocks (Brown et al., 1993).

Parental emphasis on school achievement did positively affect adolescents' GPAs and feelings of self-reliance, and led adolescents to seek affiliation with the popular crowds. When parental emphasis on achievement was linked with close parental monitoring of adolescent behavior, the youths tended to be brains. Parents who did not monitor their adolescents' behavior or who discouraged adolescent involvement in decision making tended to have adolescent children who pursued membership in either the popular or druggie crowds (Brown et al., 1993).

Brown and his colleagues (1993) cautioned readers not to overgeneralize these results or to think all the influences on adolescent peer group affiliation occur during a youth's teenage years. Some parenting behaviors prior to adolescence foster social skills whereas other parenting behaviors foster antisocial behaviors. More research is needed to determine what influences, besides parents' relationships with their adolescents, affect adolescent choices about peer affiliations in high school.

Underachievement in High School

Eckert's (1990) portrait of jocks and burnouts suggests the burnouts are at-risk students doomed to underachievement in school. What do we know about underachievement in general and about underachievers in high school?

Underachievement is considered to be school performance that falls below an individual's identified ability. However, this definition begs for greater precision. A student may be gifted musically, but failure to practice leads to performance below her potential for superior achievement.

A student's underachievement may be influenced by situational stress, such as family conflict or personal illness; once the stressful circumstances change, the student will likely correct his or her **situational underachievement**. In contrast to a situational underachiever, the **chronic underachiever** performs below ability for a long time (McCall, Evahn, & Kratzer, 1992). What a long period of time entails is unclear. There are also **hidden underachievers**; namely, students whose performances fall below the informed assessment of people who know the students well. Hidden underachievers are individuals whose underachievement extends to all school subjects, rather than to specific courses, such as math or English.

Researchers speculate that specific underachievement may occur for motivational reasons (McCall et al., 1992). We can make one other distinction between nonlearners and nonproducers. An individual with a learning disability (a **nonlearner**) may underachieve due to correctable problems, such as a poor attention span or impulse control problems. A **nonproducer** is an individual whose underachievement seems attributable to motivation.

Robert McCall, Cynthia Evahn, and Lynn Kratzer (1992) reported on a follow-up study of 6,720 males and females 13 years following high school. Considerable data were available to the researchers about the individuals' activities, estimates of ability, and academic performances in high school. Using sophisticated statistical procedures, the researchers identified a group of students whose high school grades were significantly lower than one would expect from standardized measures of their mental abilities (for instance, SAT scores, IQ tests, and the Iowa Test of Educational Development). In other words, they were underachievers. There were 649 underachievers (9.7% of the total sample)—444 males and 205 females. Taking care to match people in terms of gender and size of high school, the researchers grouped each underachiever with three other individuals in the rest of the population:

- An individual who had the same GPA as the underachiever but whose ability was considered below normal. We will refer to these individuals as *same GPA individuals*.

- An individual who had the same ability as the underachiever but whose GPA matched this ability. We will refer to these individuals as *same ability individuals*.

- An individual who had the same ability as the underachiever but whose grades exceeded expectations. We will refer to these individuals as *overachievers*.

Thus, the researchers were able to compare four groups: underachievers, individuals with the same GPA as the underachievers, individuals with the same ability as the underachievers, and overachievers.

During their high school years, significant differences separated the overachievers and same ability individuals from the underachievers and the same GPA individuals. All these differences were significant at either $p < .001$ or $p < .01$. In all cases, the differences indicated greater commitment to school by the overachievers and the same ability students. The significant differences were found in eight areas: interest in schoolwork, school offices held, satisfaction with school, involvement in school activities, educational aspirations, educational expectations, status of desired occupation, and academic versus nonacademic courses taken. Gender differences were not found. The data indicated underachieving high school performance reflected lack of motivation, not lack of capability (McCall et al., 1992).

What were high school underachievers like 13 years following high school? Differences seen between the underachievers, the overachievers, and the same ability peers in high school continued into adult life. For instance, underachievers held lower status jobs, had lower incomes, and expressed less job satisfaction than their overachieving and same ability peers. Underachievers were much more likely to change jobs frequently (McCall et al., 1992)

On several educational matters following high school, underachievers had records distinctly different from overachievers and same ability peers.

- Underachievers were twice as likely to attend a vocational school.

- Underachievers were much less likely to participate in professional training.

- Underachievers were more likely to attend a junior college or community college and much less likely to attend a four-year college or university.

- Underachievers were twice as likely to drop out of a four-year college or university.

- Underachievers were half as likely to graduate from a four-year college or university.

Underachievers reported less satisfaction with their social lives than overachievers, peers with the same ability, and peers with the same GPA but less ability. The underachievers were much more likely to divorce than overachievers ($p < .001$), same ability peers ($p < .001$), and same GPA peers ($p < .01$). Of greater alarm, there were also gender differences found in these results. Underachieving females were twice as likely as underachieving males to divorce. Because these divorce rates were definitely not seen in peers with the same GPA, the inference is strong that underachievement during high school is an indicator of serious psychological difficulties (McCall et al., 1992).

In summary, as adults, the underachievers fared poorly in both work and in love. For many interpreters of the human experience, the domains of work and love are the most critical for adult happiness (S. Freud, as cited in Allport, 1961; May, 1969; Super, 1957a, 1957). Because underachievers failed in both work and love, one can understand why McCall, Evahn, and Kratzer (1992) labeled high school underachievement a **syndrome** (a set of symptoms which occur together and characterize a serious problem).

We have looked at the influences of middle school/junior high school and high school on adolescent development. Now, we turn attention to the adolescent experience of college.

COLLEGE

Interspersed throughout each chapter are discussions of late adolescence, and much of the material pertains to **traditional college students** (students between the ages of 18 and 22). In this section, we look at the current thinking about the role and effects of college as an institution of higher learning. We look at two sources: the Boyer (1987) report on college, and the Astin (1977, 1993) longitudinal studies of college impact.

The Boyer Report

Ernest Boyer (1987) wrote a companion piece to his influential study (1983) of high school education in the United States. We looked at that study earlier in this chapter in the section on high schools.

The Boyer (1987) analysis of the undergraduate experience was commissioned by the Carnegie Foundation for the Advancement of Teaching. He looked at four-year colleges and universities that granted baccalaureate degrees. "This decision was made not because the other sectors (e.g., two-year community colleges and professional schools) are less important, but rather because the uniqueness of American higher education is rooted in preparation for the baccalaureate degree" (Boyer, 1987, p. xii).

Boyer and several other researchers visited 29 college campuses, both public and private, in all areas of the United States. Among the 29 institutions visited were "a church-related college in a sparsely settled area of the Northwest," "a sprawling campus in New England, part of a state university system," and "a highly selective private college in the East" (Boyer, 1987, pp. xii–xiii).

General education links students to the larger community and promotes students to make connections across diverse areas of knowledge.

Boyer (1987) contended that the American undergraduate experience has two critical goals: a commitment to individual development and a commitment to community involvement. The first goal is to enable individuals "to pursue their own goals, to follow their own aptitudes, to become productive, self-reliant human beings and, with new knowledge, to continue learning after college days are over" (Boyer, 1987, p. 67). Separate surveys conducted in 1969, 1976, and 1984 affirm that students consider "the personal utility of education" to be the most important goal of higher education (Boyer, 1987, p. 67).

The second goal of higher education is to enable individuals to see their places in the larger community. In this sense, an important function of the undergraduate experience is to help "students go beyond their own private interests, learn about the world around them, develop a sense of civic and social responsibility, and discover how they, as individuals, can contribute to the larger society of which they are a part" (Boyer, 1987, pp. 67–68).

Successful colleges have a clear vision regarding academic requirements. The essential components of the undergraduate program are specialization in a major field of study, proficiency in language skills, and general education that promotes breadth of understanding, connections across ideas, and application of knowledge to the world outside the college (Boyer, 1987).

The Place of General Education in the Undergraduate Years

Most college students consider the main, if not the sole, reason to go to college is to major in a special field of study that leads to a career. The yardstick against which they measure the other components of an academic program is how well requirements for proficiency in language skills and for general education promote or frustrate completing their majors. Not uncommonly, the students attempt to get all the language and general education requirements out of the way before their junior year of study. Of considerable interest are the reports from employers about two aspects of the college graduates they have hired. First, these graduates are very well prepared in their specialization; second, they are unable to carry on an educated conversation about matters outside their professions or careers.

Many American college faculty—but certainly not all—have seen the need to provide an integrated general education in order to endow educated people with an appreciation of the world beyond their areas of specialization. College administrators and faculty significantly increased their commitment to general education during the 1980s, whereas student commitment was, at best, lukewarm (Boyer, 1987).

Boyer (1987) proposed an integrated core for general education. He asserted that general education serves the essential goal of linking individuals to the larger community. As an integrated core, general education would introduce essential knowledge and connections across ideas to students. With this integrated core, students would apply knowledge to life beyond the college. General education would give students perspectives on what they know (Boyer, 1987).

Boyer (1987) recommended seven areas of inquiry he considered part of the common human experience—language, art, heritage, institutions, science, work, and identity. Faculty would be free to develop courses and experiences—for instance, volunteer work in another country—that capture the essential theme of each area of inquiry. As examples, Boyer pointed to a course offered at Wellesley College entitled "Technology and Society in the Third World" that fit the science theme, and a course offered at the University of Southern Maine, "Three Crises in Western Culture: Civilization on Trial," that fit the heritage theme.

Several institutions around the United States, including the University of California at San Diego and Kansas State University, have begun efforts to promote an integrated general education program in each undergraduate's curriculum. In neither case has the Boyer (1987) report been adopted at face value, but, rather, the principles embodied in the report have guided the efforts at each institution.

How Students Spend Their Time

Boyer (1987) contracted an extensive, national survey of college students to learn how they spend their time. The survey was administered to 4,500 undergraduates selected randomly. The findings were broken into hours spent in activities per week. Here is Boyer's introduction to the findings:

> There are 168 hours in a week. If the student takes 16 credit hours, and spends 2 hours in study for each credit hour of instruction (a generous estimate!), that means 48 hours of the week are assigned to academics. If 50 hours are assigned to sleep, that leaves 70 hours in the student's life unaccounted for, a block of time greater than either sleep or academics (From *College: The Undergraduate Experience in America*, by Earnest L. Boyer, p. 180. Copyright © 1987 by Tthe Carnegie Foundation for the Advancement of Teaching. Reprinted by permission of HarperCollins Publishers, Inc.).

What did the survey reveal about how students spend their time apart from sleep and academics? Nearly all the students spent part of their time working. Nearly 30% of full-time students and 84% of part-time students worked in excess of 20 hours a week. Work hours are likely to increase as the costs of higher education increase.

Besides attending class, working, and sleeping, what do students do? Forty percent spend ten or more hours a week talking with other students. Twenty-two percent watch television at least nine hours a week. Less than 50% spend even three hours a week studying in the library. At best, 25% spend three or more hours a week in leisure reading. Less than 20% talk with a faculty member even one hour a week.

The Astin Reports   Alexander Astin conducted a longitudinal study in 1977 on the impact of different college experiences on undergraduate students. He revisited his topic in a study several years later (Astin, 1993). We look at both of these studies in this section.

The 1977 Study

Astins' (1977) first study was multi-institutional, involving over 1,000 colleges and universities and containing data on over three million students in the 1960s and

1970s. The longitudinal study focused "not only on differences among different types of institutions, but also on differences among students' experiences at these institutions" (Astin, 1984, p. 65).

Astin (1977) reported college produces several affective and cognitive outcomes. For instance, his findings refuted the long standing opinion that the self-concepts of able students is negatively impacted when the students attend highly selective schools and must compete much more to obtain good grades. He found positive correlations between self-concept and extent of involvement in college activities and between self-concept and persistence (staying in college rather than dropping out). These changes were not considered plausibly explained as simply a maturation effect because self-concept and age were not correlated (Astin, 1977).

College had a significant impact on the values of undergraduates. Between their freshman and senior years, college students consistently showed an increased interest in art and culture. Between freshman and senior year, students also showed declining interest in being economically well-off and an increasing commitment to intrinsic over extrinsic rewards. Other value shifts noted were greater interest in liberal political views and decreasing interest in religious practices (Astin, 1977).

For many students, college was a means to implement a career. While more than half of all students changed their choices of a career during college, these changes seemed attributable to the students' increasing awareness of what their choices would entail as well as increasing awareness of current developments in other career fields (Astin, 1977). Considerable evidence suggests that college enables students to refine and refocus their ideas about a career (Cebula & Lopes, 1982; Florito & Dauffenbach, 1982; Freeman, 1971; Koch, 1972; Pascarella & Terenzini, 1991).

An institution with student-oriented faculty has very positive effects on undergraduates' satisfaction and their cognitive and affective development.

Astin's 1993 Report

Astin's 1993 report focused on 18- to 22-year-olds who went to college immediately after high school graduation. He obtained longitudinal data on approximately 500,000 students in more than 1,300 colleges and universities. He organized his outcome measures into two general categories. One was *college environment*, which contained 192 separate measures. The other was *student involvement*, which contained 57 separate measures.

The measures of college environment included institutional characteristics: size, emphasis on graduate study, student-faculty ratio, expenditures for student services, curriculum, faculty characteristics, and the qualities of the student body. The measures of student involvement included the first-year student's place of residence, financial aid, and choice of major field of study. Involvement measures also included involvement with studies, faculty, peers, work, and a variety of other involvements (such as student government and cultural productions) (Astin, 1993).

Summary of Environmental Effects

The most sweeping environmental effect on student development was the influence of the student's peer group. Certain peer-group characteristics exerted more influence on student development than others. Specifically, the peer group's "values, attitudes, self-concept, and socioeconomic status" were far more influential than "the peer group's abilities, religious orientation, or racial composition" (Astin, 1993, p. 363).

Faculty had some impact on student development. Research-oriented faculty had a considerably different effect on undergraduates than student-oriented faculty. Heavily research-oriented faculty were significantly associated with student dissatisfaction with higher education and with lower student cognitive and affective development. An institution with a heavily student-oriented faculty had very positive effects on undergraduates' satisfaction and on their cognitive and affective development (Astin, 1993).

General education had little, if any, impact on student development in most institutions. Astin (1993) explained this result as the outcome of general education programs that lacked focus.

Evidence from a variety of sources indicates that the significant changes for college undergraduates most probably occur as aggregate outcomes. That is, these changes are not due to any one experience but, rather, are due to a series of connected experiences over a period of time. Some of the experiences occur in class, but others occur outside the classroom and involve such activities as interacting with faculty, living on campus as well as living off campus, associating with peers, studying in an academic major, and participating in the intellectual, cultural, and social life of the campus (Terenzini & Pascarella, 1994).

Summary of Involvement Effects

Some of Astin's (1993) findings about student involvement confirmed findings reported in his 1977 study. For example, living on campus during one's first year had positive effects on student retention (students returning to the college for their sophomore years). However, other findings from the 1977 study were not confirmed in 1993. In particular, increases in political liberalism did not occur as they had in the 1977 study. Unlike the 1960s and 1970s, today's colleges and universities are more equally made up of liberal and conservative students.

Financial aid did not seem to have the positive effects on students as it had in the 1960s and 1970s. In fact, Pascarella and Terenzini (1991) reported that the effects of financial aid were mixed, at best, and contradictory, at worst. The one type of aid that had positive effects on student development was aid awarded on merit rather than on need. Astin (1993) wondered if the difference lay in the student's understanding of the reason for receiving the aid.

Heavy involvement in studies had particularly noticeable effects on a student's academic development. This finding is so obvious that one would be alarmed if the result were different. Students develop academically when they spend "a considerable amount of time studying, attending classes, and using a personal computer, as well as engaging in academically related activities that require student involvement" (Astin, 1993, p. 382). The converse is true as well; students who ignore studies and avoid engaging in academic work do not grow academically. We all know students who major in self-indulgence, rather than in a program of studies. Note Astin's caution that "academic development does not seem to be facilitated by frequent use of multiple-choice exams"(1993, p. 382).

Frequent student interaction with faculty has very positive effects on student development (and, I suspect, on faculty development as well). Astin (1993) found that students who regularly interact with faculty increase their GPAs, and they are more likely to complete their degrees, graduate with honors, and pursue graduate or professional studies. Other positive effects of interacting with faculty include increased involvement in social activism, campus leadership, and cultural events (Astin, 1993).

Involvement with other students positively influences sensitivity to cultural diversity and produces greater satisfaction with student life in general. Of some surprise to Astin (1993) was the finding that involvement in a social fraternity or sorority did not influence student satisfaction. However, sorority or fraternity involvement did have positive effects on growth in leadership and exerted a significant influence on alcohol consumption (Astin, 1993).

Working while attending college has clear outcomes for student development. Full-time work interferes with completing the degree, getting good grades, participating in cultural events and other activities on campus, and obtaining in-depth knowledge of one's discipline. Students who worked full-time reported feeling overwhelmed with multiple demands (Astin, 1993). Like high school students who work part-time (Steinberg & Dornbusch, 1991), college students who work full-time not only see their school performances suffer but they also turn to smoking cigarettes regularly.

Working part-time off campus had effects on students that closely resembled the outcomes in students who worked full-time. However, Astin (1993) found a completely opposite set of outcomes in students who worked part-time on campus. Working part-time on campus was "positively associated with attaining a bachelor's degree and with virtually all areas of self-reported cognitive and affective growth" (Astin, 1993, p. 388). Astin explained the positive results of part-time on-campus work stem from the very type of involvement the work provided. "Compared to students who spend an equivalent amount of time working off campus, students who are employed on campus are, almost by definition, in more frequent contact with other students and possibly with faculty" (Astin, 1993, p. 388).

CHAPTER SUMMARY

One of the prominent social and individual issues encountered in the middle grades centers on the transitions that occur from the elementary to middle school and from the middle school to the high school. Early adolescents have specific developmental tasks to accomplish, and the middle school was formed to promte achievement of these developmental tasks. Whether the middle school does enable early adolescents to achieve these developmental tasks is debated. Evidence indicates that early-maturing adolescents find the middle school frustrating and stifling.

Empirical findings strongly suggest that early adolescents pay for the transition from a K–6 elementary school to a junior high school. Effects are worse when students make several transitions.

Naturalistic studies have gained data on what it means to early adolescents to be a middle school student and how they construct that meaning. They seek and use information to succeed in their new school settings, and they employ communication strategies to cope. Another critical factor to succeeding as a middle school student is understanding the transition to be a regular, expected event that provides evidence of maturing.

A national task force examined middle school education and made eight recommendations based on an understanding of the developmental tasks of early adolescents. The task force maintained middle school education could be transformed only if the climate in schools became one of trust and communication.

The current assessment of American high school education is that we miseducate students. Sources of concern include declining standardized test scores and poor ratings when compated to German and Japanese students, especially in comprehension of mathematics and natural science. However, there is evidence of good high schools in the United States, as naturalistic studies have revealed.

The social caste system is alive and well in American high schools. Schools typically have a group of students who form an elite cadre, and names for this cadre vary. Coleman (1961) referred to these students as the "leading crowd" and everyone else as outsiders. In some Detroit high schools, there are two broad categories of students: the jocks and the burnouts. Social groupings in most high schools typically encompass more than two broad categories.

The consequences of high school underachievement can be long-lasting. An extensive, longitudinal study showed that chronic underachievers suffer negative outcomes in adult life and indicated that the reasons for such underachievement involve serious problems with making commitments and feeling motivated.

Current thinking about the effects of college on undergraduate student development suggests several things, including:

- a growing interest in culture over the undergraduate years;
- influence of peers on the values, attitudes, and self-concepts of undergraduates;
- faculty influence on cognitive and affective development of students (this influence is positive if the college has a student-oriented faculty);
- little impact of general education unless the general education program is focused and expects the same of all students;
- increased time spent at work to earn money for tuition and other expenses; and
- greater receptivity to cultural diversity.

We turn next to another ecological niche for adolescents; namely, work.

CHAPTER
9

ADOLESCENTS, WORK, AND CAREER DEVELOPMENT

A Boy Who Has Worked Since Early Adolescence

Sid is a 16-year-old male who lives in a midwestern town with a population of about 38,000 people. He is going to be a junior at the local high school. Sid has three siblings; a younger brother named Bobby who is 9, an older brother named Thomas who is 19, and an older sister named Sally who is 20. His mother manages a cafe (called "Grounds" by its customers) that specializes in coffee. Sid used to work at the cafe. His father is a self-employed carpenter. Recently, he was away from home working on carpentry jobs during which time Sid and he drifted apart. When his father returned, the two had severe difficulties getting along. Sid moved out of his home and sublet a room from a friend at the cafe for nearly the whole summer.

As the summer progressed, Sid's uncle helped to get him and his dad talking again. Eventually, Sid began working for his father, and things between them started to get better. When I spoke to Sid, he was planning to move back home in the next two weeks.

Sid had worked at Grounds about 20 hours a week for the past two years until his mother was offered the job of managing the cafe; the store owners do not permit the manager to supervise relatives. Because the position of manager was a very good opportunity for his mother and for his family, Sid seemed to accept that he had to end his job at Grounds.

Our conversation took place in the cafe over lunch, a day before the start of school. Sid was on his way for a job interview at a shoe repair shop. Things looked promising; this would be his second interview with the owner.

"When I worked at Grounds, I used to work four hours after school—from 3:30 to about 7:30 P.M. Then I'd get home around 8:00, do my homework, and spend some time with my family. I'd do homework until 10:00 or 10:30. We all ate together. My family would wait for me to come home before we'd have supper.

"I worked 20 hours a week. To begin with, I made $4.25 an hour, then $4.50.

"Work didn't fit in to what I wanted to do. I had much less time to spend with friends, to do things I enjoy. I wanted to go out for clubs that meet after school, but I couldn't because of work. I really cut back on spending time with my friends. There were breaks now and then when I'd be able to get together with them. But I've had much less time to spend with friends, to do things I enjoy.

"I worked to save money and to get money to spend. I was able to save until this summer when I was living away from my family and had to pay rent. Rent was a lot higher than I had expected. I had to pay $50 a month. I was subleasing from an older friend at work. It was a big mistake to have moved out and rented a place. All my savings are gone now.

"But it was also a mistake because I think it's very important to have a relationship with your father. The apartment was a place to hide, and I didn't have any discipline. I could go out when I wanted and do what I wanted. Not that I always want discipline, but I see the need for it.

"I'm still not living at home. I'm with my grandparents now. I plan to move back into the house in a few weeks, now that my dad and I are talking again. An uncle helped my dad and me start talking once more.

"I work with my dad now. He pays me $4.00 an hour, and I'm learning a lot. He's been teaching me about electricity recently. And it's more important that Dad and I build a relationship again than that he pay me lots of money.

"Working affected my schooling. My grades definitely went down. I'd come home tired and couldn't put full effort into my studies.

"I've got a new job lined up at a shoe repair shop, and it will begin in a few weeks. I'll only work until 6:00 P.M., so I'll get home earlier and have more time to put into my studies. I'm not sure just what I'll be doing. Probably things like dyeing shoes and selling shoes. I bought my first pair of shoes with my own money from the guy who owns the place.

"I work because I have to. I want money so I no longer get hand-me-downs. I saved up and got new pants and shoes. Most of my friends come from families with more money than mine. If they want to go to a movie, their dads give them $10.00. If I want to go, I have to spend money I've made.

"Work has taught me the value of money and of bargains. Most people my age don't understand that a dollar is not just paper. Four dollars for me is an hour's worth of good work.

"If I didn't work, at home there's always things to do. I'd have time to do those things. I'd have more free time to be with friends. None of my friends work.

"I don't have many regrets about working. I've learned so much. I don't get as much time with my family and friends. I can't just drop everything and play football with my friends like I would like to at times. But I've learned so much from working. Like at Grounds, I learned how to deal with angry customers and not take their anger personally. For instance, a customer got upset that we were out of a certain type of pastry, and I just had to remember that 'the customer is always right' and remember 'none of this was my fault.'

"This year I want to do more things with my friends. And still be a kid while I do have a chance."

I told Sid about some of the research that says teenagers who begin to work long hours start smoking and even using drugs to relieve their stress (Greenberger & Steinberg, 1986). When asked his reaction to the findings, Sid replied, "I don't see people at the high school smoking or using drugs because of stress, but because it is popular. I read in the newspaper that drug use is going down, but I don't believe it.

Alcohol use is going up among teens I would never have thought would drink. Even among teens who are members of SADD (Students Against Drunk Driving).

"To relieve my stress, I ride my mountain bike. I bought it myself. We've never had a TV at home, so I read a lot—science fiction, Stephen King, Tolkien, Central American mythology, Susan Cooper. Books with neat artwork inspire me to read them. I guess you'd say I do judge a book by its cover.

"I've been taking ceramics every year in high school and like to work with clay. When I get stressed during school, I go into my teacher's ceramics studio and make something out of clay. It helps relieve my tension and release my aggression."

Sid expresses clearly his attitudes toward work, money, and responsibility. Do his views suggest a maturity regarding these issues? What are your conclusions about the effects working has had on Sid's schoolwork, his relations with peers, and with his family? Many of the ideas present in this case study will be addressed in this chapter on the impact of work on adolescents.

In this chapter, we also review other topics pertinent to adolescents and work. For instance, this chapter includes a discussion of identity formation and adolescents' understandings of work, a review of adolescents' desires to succeed in the working world, gender differences regarding career development, and a look at adolescents who do not go on to college but, rather, enter the work force. In addition, we look at training programs for youths considered at risk of being unemployed, at the Armed Forces as an employer of adolescents, and at the impact of college on career development and career prospects. We begin with a look at identity formation and gender differences in career formation.

IDENTITY FORMATION AND GENDER DIFFERENCES IN CAREER DEVELOPMENT

This section focuses on (a) the progress of adolescents toward achieving an occupational identity and (b) the relationship between gender and achieving occupational identity. **Occupational identity** is the extent of a person's interest in and commitment to working—and, frequently, interest in and commitment to a particular type of work.

Recall the identity-formation model developed by Marcia (1964, 1966, 1967, 1980). He postulates four categories of identity status: diffusion, foreclosure, moratorium, and achievement (see Chapter 4). In brief, identity diffuse individuals are people who are drifting and have made no personal decisions about such fundamental choices as career, religion, or politics. Identity foreclosed individuals have adopted the values of others (for instance, one's parents) without any struggle or crisis. Identity moratoriums are people who are in crisis over which values to choose. Identity achieved individuals have emerged from the crisis of moratorium with their own sets of commitments to work, religion, and politics.

One of the main aspects distinguishing the various identity statuses is the extent of occupational exploration and the extent of personal commitment to occupational choice. Let's look at a detailed discussion of one study of gender differences in the styles of forming an occupational identity in late adolescence.

Gender and the Formation of Occupational Identity

Harold Grotevant and William Thorbecke (1982) studied 83 white adolescents (41 males and 42 females). Fifty-four had just completed their junior year of high school (30 males and 24 females). Twenty-nine had just graduated from high school (11 males and 18 females). Nearly all the adolescents came from upper-middle-class families.

Grotevant and Thorbecke's (1982) research was based on certain assumptions. One is that males and females develop identity using different processes. Evidence does confirm that the processes of exploration and commitment that mark the paths to identity formation occur differently for males and females (Josselson, 1987; Marcia, 1980; Orlofsky, Marcia, & Lesser, 1973). Matina Horner (1972), for instance, has demonstrated that highly capable adolescent females desire to succeed but fear the price that success will exact on them personally and socially.

From early childhood, males and females are socialized differently about identity. Males are raised to focus on doing things, and the consistent press on males is to identify an occupational goal and pursue it. According to Sally Archer (1985), adolescent males do not consider family roles and responsibilities when thinking about career dilemmas. Males assume that selecting a career is their paramount responsibility (Archer, 1985). Such singular focus is not present for females.

For females, the pressing issues related to identity formation—especially in these times of cultural changes regarding gender roles—involve three things.

- Females seek to establish and maintain interpersonal relationships.

- Females focus on resolving conflicts between commitments to a family and to a career. In Archer's (1985) research, 90% of the females anticipated conflicts over family and career. Also, nearly all these late adolescents were concerned how career/family dilemmas could be resolved satisfactorily.

- Masculine, feminine, and androgynous individuals make career decisions differently. Masculine individuals, for instance, prefer analytic or logical decision making and value instrumentality. Feminine individuals prefer intuitive or emotional decision making and value expressiveness. Androgynous individuals use both types of decision making and value both instrumentality and expressiveness (Archer, 1985; Grotevant & Thorbecke, 1982).

Masculine and feminine characteristics are seen as two aspects of personality or, in Bem's (1978) terms, dimensions of personality. Androgynous individuals incorporate characteristics considered masculine as well as characteristics considered feminine. **Instrumentality** is an overall characteristic associated with masculinity, and signs of instrumentality include dominance, independence, assertiveness, competitiveness, and orientation toward achievement. **Expressiveness** is an overall characteristic associated with femininity, and signs of expressiveness include submissiveness, kindness, empathy, nurturance, and cooperation. An androgynous individual might, for example, be an excellent team leader, listen carefully to a friend's problems, strive hard to win a game of basketball, and cook a great spaghetti dinner. Do you imagine this androgynous person is a male or a female? An androgynous person could be male or female.

Four Predictions About Gender and Occupational Identity

Grotevant and Thorbecke (1982) made four predictions about gender differences in styles of occupational identity formation in late adolescence.

- Males and females who possess the instrumental and analytic qualities of masculinity will actively engage in exploring occupational choices.

- Males and females who use the feminine qualities of expression of feelings and reliance on intuition will explore occupational choices less actively than masculine types.

- Androgynous individuals will achieve more progress in forming an occupational identity than either the masculine or feminine types. By using both instrumental and expressive qualities, androgynous individuals explore career options thoroughly.

- Motivation to succeed will be positively related to identity achievement. Grotevant and Thorbecke (1982) framed identity achievement in terms of Marcia's identity status model and in terms of vocational goals, interests, and talents.

Grotevant and Thorbecke (1982) gathered data using several instruments, including Marcia's interview schedule. They considered six dimensions reflect the extent to which one has achieved identity. The first three dimensions—occupation, religion, and politics—are straight from Marcia's model. The other three dimensions—friendship, sex roles, and dating—were added by the authors.

Another instrument was a 23-item true-false inventory about vocational identity. Scores are computed in terms of the clarity and stability of a person's goals, interests, and talents. A sample item is, "I have a clear idea of what my talents are." High scores on this instrument are indicative of having achieved **vocational identity**.

Grotevant and Thorbecke (1982) also used the Extended Personal Attributes Questionnaire (PAQ) (Spence, Helmreich, & Holahan, 1979), a 40-item self-report instrument, to assess personal understandings of masculinity and femininity. The PAQ measures the presence of instrumental and expressive qualities. Androgynous individuals score high on both types of qualities.

Grotevant and Thorbecke (1982) also measured **achievement motivation** on four dimensions: (*a*) preference for difficult and challenging tasks (**mastery**), (*b*) desire to win when competing with others (**competitiveness**), (*c*) desire to exert oneself (**work**), and (*d*) lack of concern whether others disapprove (**personal unconcern**).

In addition, the researchers used an instrument that assesses socially desirable responses (answers the respondents think will make them look good in the eyes of others). If people give many socially desirable responses, answers to other inventories are suspect.

Results of the Grotevant and Thorbecke Study

Eighty-seven individuals entered Grotevant and Thorbecke's (1982) study, and seventy (80.1%) provided usable data. Seventeen subjects were eliminated because coders could not reliably judge their Identity Status Interview responses and/or because the subjects had skipped parts of the PAQ. The 70 subjects remaining in the study were equally divided between males ($n = 35$) and females ($n = 35$). Forty-five of the subjects had just completed their junior year of high school, and 25 had just graduated from high school.

Findings related to gender and age.   Significant gender differences emerged regarding exploration of options and commitment to choices. Males explored options more than females ($p < .05$), and females demonstrated more commitment to choices ($p < .05$). Furthermore, more high school graduates were classified as identity achieved and more juniors as identity diffuse ($p < .05$).

Findings related to the researchers' predictions.   You may recall that Grotevant and Thorbecke (1982) made four predictions about gender differences and occupational identity formation in adolescence. Their first prediction was that males and females who possess the instrumental and analytic qualities of masculinity would actively engage in exploring occupational choices. This prediction received partial support, but males' responses strongly correlated with the social desirability instrument. Once the effects of social desirability were removed, the statistically significant correlation between masculinity and vocational identity disappeared (Grotevant & Thorbecke, 1982).

The second prediction was that males and females who use the feminine qualities of expression of feelings and reliance on intuition would search occupation choices less actively than masculine types. This prediction was demonstrated to be true, except that males who used the feminine quality of expressiveness actively engaged in occupational exploration.

The third prediction was that androgynous adolescents would achieve more progress in forming an occupational identity than either the masculine or feminine types. This prediction also turned out to be true. Identity achievers were much more likely to have an androgynous orientation than more strictly masculine or feminine orientations ($p < .001$).

Grotevant and Thorbecke's (1982) fourth prediction was that motivation to succeed would be related positively to identity achievement. There were some significant findings, but not always in the direction predicted, particularly in terms of gender differences. Recall that achievement motivation has four dimensions: mastery, competitiveness, work, and personal unconcern. Recall also that identity formation in this study referred to vocational identity, exploration of occupational choices, and commitment to occupational choice. I have presented in Table 9-1 the findings in terms of male and female responses to the various dimensions.

As Table 9-1 illustrates, preference for difficult, challenging tasks differentiated males from females for both vocational identity and commitment to occupational choice. Females had significantly greater preference than males for a vocational identity involving hard work. Females expressed strong negative responses about

TABLE 9-1   **Gender Differences, Occupational Identity, and Achievement Motivation**

OCCUPATIONAL IDENTITY FORMATION	MASTERY	
	Males	Females
Vocational Identity	< .001	ns
Exploration	ns	ns
Commitment	< .01	ns
	WORK	
Vocational Identity	ns	< .01
Exploration	ns	ns
Commitment	ns	ns
	COMPETITIVENESS	
Vocational Identity	ns[*]	< .05
Exploration	ns	ns
Commitment	ns	ns
	PERSONAL UNCONCERN	
Vocational Identity	< .05	ns
Exploration	ns	ns
Commitment	ns	ns

[*]Socially desirable responses correlated significantly for males.
ns = not significant

SOURCE: From "Sex Differences in Styles of Occupational Identity Formation in Late Adolescence," by H. D. Grotevant and W. L. Thorbecke. In *Developmental Psychology*, 1982, *18*, 396–405. Reprinted by permission of the author.

competitiveness and vocational identity. Finally, males showed significantly less concern than females about the negative reactions of others.

How did Grotevant and Thorbecke (1982) explain their findings? They focused on four topics: styles of achieving occupational identity, specificity of the results, the ongoing evolution of identity formation, and implications for vocational counselors.

Styles of achieving occupational identity. In terms of achieving an occupational identity, both males and females were very much alike on three dimensions measured: identity status, motivation to achieve, and vocational identity (Grotevant & Thorbecke, 1982). Males, however, had used clearly different styles than females to achieve an occupational identity. For males, commitment to a career was part of an acceptance of instrumental values, challenging tasks, and lack of concern over negative evaluations by others. For females, occupational identity was related to preferences to work hard but to avoid competition.

Specificity of the results. While the results look promising in identifying patterns related to formation of an occupational identity, it would be conjecture to assume these findings extend to other dimensions of identity formation (Grotevant

& Thorbecke, 1982). Achieving vocational identity is one task in a multidimensional life; the types of exploration and commitment needed in other domains may differ significantly. In short, what Grotevant and Thorbecke (1982) found about occupational exploration and commitment may not apply to religion, politics, gender roles, friendship, or dating.

The ongoing evolution of identity formation.   What could explain the high percentage of adolescents in identity achievement in Grotevant and Thorbecke's (1982) study? Their explanation is that identity formation is a continuous process of exploration and commitment, an evolving spiral of cycles in which breadth and depth of knowledge change as a person assimilates experience. In terms of occupational identity, the adolescents had explored career options and had made tentative commitments to career choices. Their exploration and commitment in other domains of identity may have been less substantial. Experience and education may also influence the youths to modify their choices or to understand and accept these choices more fully as they gain more knowledge about the careers.

Grotevant and Thorbecke (1982) considered their study was conducted during a time of relative balance and harmony in the adolescents' lives. None of the subjects had yet been challenged by the realities of living away from home that they would encounter when they began working full-time or went away to college. Once the separation from home and family began, these adolescents would likely renew their explorations—and, perhaps, even experience the uncertainties of commitment associated with the moratorium phase of identity formation (Grotevant & Thorbecke, 1982).

Implications for vocational counselors.   The results of the Grotevant and Thorbecke (1982) study are in line with other research indicating adolescent males and females do not deal with vocational identity in the same way. The results support the need to tailor vocational counseling programs to individual differences, and to identify for adolescents possible problems they will experience when they enter fields dominated by the other sex.

ADOLESCENTS IN THE WORKPLACE

Considerable attention has been given to the difficulties youths have experienced in the 1980s and early 1990s finding work. Unemployment problems affect adolescents from all ethnic groups, but rise dramatically for black and other nonwhite teenagers. For example, during 1984, unemployment in the United States averaged 7.5%, but for teenagers, overall unemployment averaged 18.9% and for black teenagers, 42.7%. These trends in youth unemployment have not suddenly appeared but, according to U.S. government statistics, represent a steady trend extending over many decades (Betsey, Hollister, & Papageorgiou, 1985).

One possible **confounding factor** (something that throws interpretations into disarray) is confusing school attendance trends with trends in unemployment. For instance, between the 1960s and middle 1980s, the unemployment rate for nonwhite youths increased, but so did their school enrollment rates. Statistics gathered over these same three decades indicate youths attending school were less likely than other

Several researchers have investigated changes over time in the career aspirations and achievement of females (Astin, 1984; Astin & Myint, 1971; Farmer, 1976; Gustafson & Magnusson, 1991; Harmon, 1989). Let's look at a longitudinal study that investigated career aspiration of two cohorts of females.

Lenore Harmon (1989), a faculty member at the University of Illinois at Urbana-Champaign, has been studying changes over time in the career aspirations of females since 1968. She collected data from 300 college freshmen (average age 18) in 1968 and did a follow-up investigation on a subsample of these women in 1974 and once again in 1981 with the individuals who completed her 1974 questionnaire. Her return rates were 74% in 1974 and 79% in 1981. In 1983, Harmon collected data from a new sample of college freshmen females ($n = 250$), whose average age was 18.

Harmon's questionnaire included items on life plans, educational aspirations, career aspirations, and occupational alternatives considered. A comparison of demographic data in the 1968 and 1983 freshmen indicated the groups did not differ in terms of age, socioeconomic status, family size, and parents' educational levels.

Significant questions emerge in Harmon's longitudinal study. How did the 1968 sample change over time? Do the females in the 1983 sample resemble the 1968 freshmen or those females 6 or 13 years later?

The 1968 sample clearly changed over time (Harmon, 1989). Whereas in 1968, less than 30% expected to work all their adult lives, by 1981, 67% said they expected to work most of their lives. In comparison, an even higher percentage (73%) of the 1983 freshmen females expected to work all their lives. One could conclude that a significant cohort difference occurred between 1968 and 1983 regarding late adolescent females' life plans regarding work.

1968 and 1983 freshmen had nearly identical educational aspirations, with the majority (59.9% and 60.4%, respectively) aspiring to graduate from college and nearly 40% aspiring to complete postbaccalaureate degrees. Whereas 30% of the 1968 freshmen women intended to earn a master's degree, by 1981, only 10% had achieved their aspirations; in 1968, 3% intended to earn a doctorate but less than 1% had done so by 1981. Harmon wondered if the 1983 freshmen would achieve their educational expectations, which were very similar to the aspirations of their 1968 counterparts.

The 1983 freshmen resembled the 1968 sample when they were 30-year-old women (in 1981) in terms of aspiring to careers in business more than careers in social service fields. However, the 1983 freshmen were unlike the 1968 sample at any age in terms of occupational alternatives they considered; the 1983 group considered careers in science, math, and medicine much more often than females in the other group.

Harmon (1989) considered the changes she detected between the 1983 females and the women in her 1968 sample could be attributed to historical factors. Growing up in the 1970s had taught her 1983 sample the need for female employment and the desirability of careers not open to females just 13 years earlier. The 1983 freshmen also were much more likely than the 1968 freshmen to have grown up in dual-career families (61% of the mothers of the 1983 sample worked versus 45% of the mothers of the 1968 sample). Harmon also suggested many more of the 1983 sample may have come from single-parent homes in which the mother was the breadwinner.

On the whole, historical changes (inflation and technological advances and societal phenomena, such as feminism) in the 13 years of Harmon's studies caused the 18-year-old females of 1983 to aspire for nontraditional careers and to consider work would involve much of their adult time. It was clear that career openings available to the 1983 cohort were much less available or anticipated for late adolescent females in 1968.

FIGURE 9-1
Employment Rates for Black and White Male 16- to 24-Year-Olds

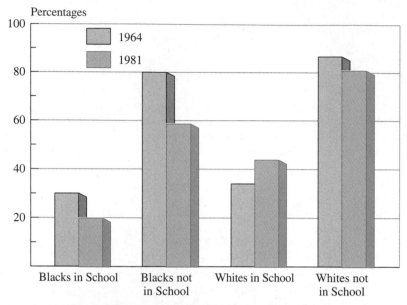

SOURCE: Adapted from *Youth Employment and Training Programs: the YEDPA Years* edited by
C. L. Betsey, R. G. Hollester, and M. R. Papageorgiou, 1985, Washington, DC: National Academy Press.

youths to be employed (Betsey et al., 1985). The employment rates for these in-school and out-of-school youths differed, however, according to gender and ethnic/racial group membership.

The employment rates of white male adolescents and young adults enrolled in school increased nearly 10% between 1964 to 1981 (from 34% to 43.4%), and declined by 5.6% (from 86.7% to 81%) for their counterparts not in school. Over the same time period, the employment rates of black male adolescents and young adults declined sharply, whether they were in or out of school; the rate of employment declined 10% for in-school black males between 1964 and 1981 (from 30% to 20.1%), and dropped nearly 23% between 1964 and 1981 (from 80.5% to 5.8%) for out-of-school black males. Thus, white males in school saw a 10% *increase* in employment from 1964 to 1981, whereas black males enrolled in school saw a 10% *decrease*. An average of 84% of white males not in school found work over these same years, whereas by 1981, employment for out-of-school blacks had declined nearly 23% (from 80.5% to 57.8%). By 1981, black males were much less likely than white males to find employment, whether they stayed in school or dropped out (Betsey et al., 1985). This comparison of white and black male employment rates for 16- to 24-year-olds is depicted in Figure 9-1.

Employment trends for black and white 16- to 24-year-old females noticeably differed between 1964 and 1981. White females increased their employment by roughly 20%—whether they were enrolled in school (23.3% to 43%) or were out of school (47.3% to 68.3%). Black females in school slightly increased their employment from 15.4% to 17.2% over the period 1964 to 1981. Black females who dropped out of school saw a corresponding 5% drop in employment over these years

Unemployment problems affect youth of all ethnic groups but rise dramatically for youths who are not white.

(from 48% to 43%). Thus, white females experienced increasing rates of employment while black females experienced a marginal increase if they were in school and a decreasing rate of employment once they left school. These data are portrayed in Figure 9-2.

An analysis of causes of unemployment among youth provides sobering information for adolescents, particularly for blacks. According to Charles Betsey and his associates (1985), the total unemployment rate in 1978 for all white 16- and 17-year-olds was 13.8%; for all blacks of the same age, the unemployment rate was 44%. For

FIGURE 9-2
Employment Rates for Black and White Female 16- to 24-Year-Olds

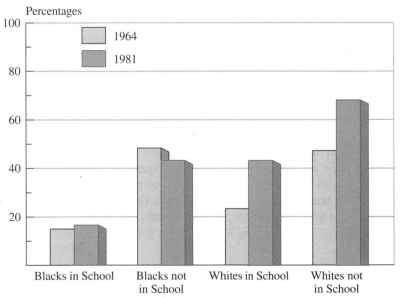

SOURCE: Adapted from *Youth Employment and Training Programs: The YEDPA Years* edited by C. L. Betsey, R. G. Hollester, and M. R. Papeorgiou, 1985, Washington, DC: National Academy Press.

18- and 19-year-olds, 9% of whites were unemployed and 38% of blacks. For nearly all of these youths, the primary cause of unemployment was not that they had quit their jobs but that they had lost their jobs. This probability was much higher for blacks than for whites, but did affect all ethnic/racial groups. These figures disconfirm a widely held view that high rates of youth unemployment occur because youths quit work. These youths encounter unemployment problems because they typically find work in fields with higher probabilities of being laid off or of being fired (Betsey et al., 1985).

Many adolescents want a job so they can earn their own money. Some, of course, have to work to help their families get by. Given their desire for work and the federal concern of problems with youth unemployment, it may surprise you to learn that some researchers consider working during the high school years endangers adolescent development (Greenberger, 1988; Greenberger & Steinberg, 1986; Greenberger, Steinberg, & Vaux, 1981; Steinberg, Greenberger, Garduque, Ruggiero, & Vaux, 1982; Steinberg, Greenberger, Vaux, & Ruggiero, 1981). We look at this research now.

Negative Consequences for Adolescents in the Workplace

Ellen Greenberger (1988) questions the merit of allowing high school students to work extended hours in the labor market. Her concerns summarize longitudinal research that she, Laurence Steinberg, and other colleagues conducted during the 1980s (Greenberger, 1988; Greenberger & Steinberg, 1986; Greenberger, et al., 1981; Steinberg, Greenberger, Garduque, Ruggiero, & Vaux, 1982; Steinberg et al., 1981). They concluded that individuals who argue in favor of involving high school students in the working world do not grasp the negative consequences such work has on middle adolescents (Steinberg et al., 1982). What data support this conclusion, and how did the researchers go about conducting their inquiries?

Greenberger and Steinberg (1986) studied several hundred adolescents in the tenth and eleventh grades at four high schools in the greater Los Angeles metropolitan area. From this large sample, they selected students who were holding their first part-time jobs ($n = 211$) and used a comparison group of 319 adolescents who had never worked. Most participants were white (82%), some were Hispanic (10%), and the rest were black or Asian (8%). From this research, several papers and one book were published (Greenberger, 1988; Greenberger & Steinberg, 1981, 1983, 1986; Greenberger et al., 1982; Greenberger et al., 1981; Greenberger, Steinberg, Vaux, & McAuliffe, 1980; Ruggiero, Greenberger, & Steinberg, 1982; Steinberg, 1982; Steinberg, Greenberger, Garduque, Ruggiero, & Vaux, 1982; Steinberg, Greenberger, & Jacobi, 1981; Steinberg, Greenberger, Garduque & McAuliffe, 1982). These studies are synthesized in two published works: Greenberger (1988) and Greenberger and Steinberg (1986).

A question pursued by the researchers was whether working while going to high school promotes the development of autonomy and social integration (Greenberger, 1988). By **autonomy**, the researchers meant such attributes as "self-reliance, constructive work habits, knowledge of business and money concepts, and experience in financial decision-making" (Greenberger, 1988, p. 25). By **social integration**, they meant a person's life has structure and significance, the person experiences decreased feelings of alienation and isolation, and—broadly conceived—a person feels "a sense of participation in the larger society, ties to generations other than (one's) own, and commitment to the norms of adult society" (Greenberger, 1988, p. 29).

Greenberger and Steinberg's (1986) overall findings indicated adolescent development suffers when high school students spend long hours at work. The researchers concluded such work requires spending long hours in roles and tasks that are boring, restrictive, and unrelated to developing autonomy and social integration. The work also interferes with academic work, family relations, and peer interactions.

Specifically, in their cross-sectional survey, the researchers found that working has the following effects on high school students.

- Working adolescents attain greater levels of self-reliance and dependability.

- Working adolescents do not, however, achieve greater concern for others nor increased social cooperation skills. This finding contradicts expectations that working alongside people of different cultural and ethnic backgrounds would increase tolerance for diversity.

- Working diminishes involvement in family, peer, and school activities. In fact, working adolescents miss more school, spend less time on homework, and earn lower grades than their nonemployed peers.

- Working adolescents develop cynical attitudes toward work. In particular, they express more tolerance for unethical behavior (for instance, stealing from their employers) than nonworking peers.

- Working adolescents use drugs, alcohol, and cigarettes more than nonworking teenagers (Greenberger & Steinberg, 1986).

Greenberger and Steinberg (1986) were troubled by these findings. They wondered if an explanation for their results could be that working did not produce these effects, but, rather, that their research subjects were cynical when they started their jobs. Perhaps work available to teenagers attracts high school students who are uninvolved with family, peers, and school. Perhaps youths in high school get jobs because they need money to buy drugs, alcohol, and cigarettes.

Only a longitudinal study would permit testing whether changes over time occur as a function of working while also attending high school. As a follow-up to their cross-sectional studies (Greenberger & Steinberg, 1981; Greenberger et al., 1980), Steinberg and his associates (Steinberg, Greenberger, Garduque, Ruggiero, & Vaux, 1982) completed a longitudinal study of 176 adolescents. This study provided the opportunity to check the unexpected findings of their cross-sectional research and also provided the means to see if changes over time differentiate working from nonworking high school students.

The 176 adolescents in the longitudinal study were in grades ten and eleven. Seventy-five (42.6%) had not worked prior to the study, were not working when it began, but were employed one year later; 101 (57.4%) did not work during any portion of the study nor prior to the start of the study. Nearly all the subjects were white (82%), some were Hispanic (9.7%), and the rest were black or Asian (8.3%). These ethnic/racial figures mirror those in Greenberger and Steinberg's (1986) cross-sectional study. Twenty-three percent were from professional families (lawyers, doctors, bankers), 33% were from white-collar families (accountants, sales personnel), and 44% were from blue-collar families (factory workers, construction workers).

The study lasted a year. On several occasions during that year, the adolescents filled out instruments that measured four areas of development: personal and social responsibility; involvement with family, school, and peers; and cynicism toward work, preoccupation over material things, and acceptance of illegal and unethical behavior in the workplace.

Steinberg and his colleagues (Steinberg, Greenberger, Garduque, Ruggiero, & Vaux, 1982) found a set of nine specific findings that clearly supported the earlier results of the cross-sectional study. Working contributed to developing personal, but not social, responsibility, diminished involvement with family, peers, and school, and elicited negative behaviors not seen in youths who did not work. Let's look at the nine findings more specifically.

- Personal responsibility increased as hours working increased. However, there were gender differences in self-reliance, which increased for girls who worked but decreased for boys.

- Neither social tolerance nor social involvement was affected by working with people from varied economic and ethnic backgrounds.

- Working adolescents spent significantly less time on schoolwork and expressed less enjoyment of school. However, working did not affect the students' school attendance or the students' grades.

- Working created emotional distances between girls and their families. The more hours girls worked, the greater was the decline in the closeness they felt with their families. Working positively influenced emotional closeness between boys and their families. When adolescents did not work long hours during high school, family emotional bonds actually increased.

- While work did not significantly affect the amount of time working adolescents spent with peers, as hours on the job increased, emotional closeness with peers significantly declined.

- As youths spent more hours working, they developed greater acceptance of unethical and illegal business practices. This trend was noticed particularly among adolescents from white-collar families, in contrast to youths from blue-collar and professional families.

- Boys' materialism increased the more they worked, but not girls'. The younger adolescents became more materialistic the more they worked, but not the older adolescents.

- Cynicism toward work was associated with the adolescent's social class. Adolescents from blue-collar and white-collar families developed more cynicism, whereas the youths from professional families did not.

- Cigarette smoking increased as work hours increased, particularly among white-collar and blue-collar youths and among older adolescents. Marijuana use increased, particularly as the older students spent more time on the job (Steinberg, Greenberger, Garduque, Ruggiero, & Vaux, 1982).

Two overarching themes bear discussion in these results: gender differences and costs to adolescents. We start by discussing gender differences.

Gender Differences in Adolescent Work Experiences

At least four kinds of evidence support the conclusion that the effects of working influence the development of autonomy differently for males and females (Steinberg, Greenberger, Garduque, Ruggiero, & Vaux, 1982).

- Girls, but not boys, showed gains in self-reliance.
- Girls, but not boys, showed increased interest in jobs that permit decision making.
- Girls' educational expectations increased, but the boys' did not.
- Working diminished family closeness among girls but actually increased family closeness among working boys.

Steinberg and his colleagues (Steinberg, Greenberger, Garduque, Ruggiero, & Vaux, 1982) interpreted this last finding as the impact of the girls' gaining greater distance from family supervision, thereby gaining autonomy from their family's insularity.

Why would there be gender differences in the effects of working on the development of autonomy? Steinberg and his associates (Steinberg, Greenberger, Garduque, Ruggiero, & Vaux, 1982) offered two possibilities. First, they suggested that perhaps the girls obtained jobs that foster independence, whereas the boys worked in jobs that inhibit autonomy. The authors rejected this hypothesis as implausible since no research indicated girls get jobs offering more autonomy than the jobs boys get (Steinberg, Greenberger, Garduque, Ruggiero, & Vaux, 1982). Teenagers' jobs, on the whole, are repetitious and dull. Take, for example, the experiences afforded in a fast-food restaurant. "Little is at stake when (the adolescent) recites some variant of 'What can I get you?'" (Greenberger & Steinberg, 1986, p. 114).

A second alternative suggested for gender differences in the development of autonomy is that getting a job in adolescence departs from the expectations girls hold for themselves. In contrast, for boys, taking a job is less an act of independence and more an act of conforming to others' expectations. While Steinberg and his associates (Steinberg, Greenberger, Garduque, Ruggiero, & Vaux, 1982) do not express the following view, it struck me that the effect of working in banal jobs may be an affront to boys' expectations about their self-efficacy.

Costs to Adolescents

Another theme worth discussing is the academic and social prices adolescents pay for early employment, especially when they work 20 or more hours a week. Evidence clearly demonstrates work hours reduce the adolescents' involvement in school, diminish their emotional bonds with friends, and, particularly in the case of girls, reduce emotional ties with their families.

Steinberg and his colleagues (Steinberg, Greenberger, Garduque, Ruggiero, & Vaux, 1982) acknowledged that the effect on adolescent development of these diminished involvements was as yet uncertain. One view asserts that these dimin-

Work, Adolescents, and Cross-Cultural Data: The Netsilik Eskimos

Cross-cultural research in 186 preindustrial societies has noted that people in nearly every society consider adolescence a time for both males and females to learn productive skills. These skills are considered essential in the adolescents' cultures for gaining social status as an adult and for attracting a spouse (Schlegel & Barry, 1991).

Most ethnographic studies have ignored providing full descriptions of adolescents at work. When ethnographers do comment on adolescent work, they typically limit their descriptions to noting boys work with their fathers and girls work with their mothers.

An example of parent tutelage of adolescents in a preindustrial society can be found in Asen Balikci's (1970) study of the Netsilik Eskimos. Balikci noted that fathers treat their children the same until they reach age 4 or 5, at which time, some distinctions emerge in father-son and father-daughter relationships.

After the age of four or five, the father-son relationship grew more intense. The boy watched his father at work, patiently and silently, observing each gesture. The father continued to make various toys, often miniature models of weapons and other articles of the material culture like sleds.

With these the boy actively imitated the adult hunter's postures. A father might even set up sea gull snares for his small son in order for him to play with the bird. Learning proceeded exclusively through observation and imitation; no formal teaching whatsoever took place.

By the time he was ten or eleven, the boy had become his father's helper. On the migration track, he no longer sat on the sledge, but tried to push and pull with the others. He accompanied his father on hunting and fishing trips, performing various light but useful tasks. He rarely asked questions. Instead his father would briefly instruct him before or after a task, when necessary. This always took place in context and in reference to the particular situation at hand. During adolescence the authority of the father remained very strong, and the boy undertook no hunting trips on his own or without his father's approval. His attitude was one of complete submissiveness. It was only very gradually that the son acquired autonomy of action.

Relations between father and daughter lacked this intimacy and, of course, engaged in none of the collaborative aspects of the father-son tie.

ished involvements represent, in actuality, moving away from the milieu of childhood and denote the transition toward adulthood. The researchers cautioned that the transition for these working adolescents may occur before the youths should relinquish what the milieu of childhood has to offer. "We raise seriously the question of whether 15- and 16-year-olds who commit 20 to 25 hours weekly to a part-time job may be missing out on important socialization and learning experiences that occur in other settings" (Steinberg, Greenberger, Garduque, Ruggiero, & Vaux, 1982, p. 394).

Another cost for working adolescents is the increased use of cigarettes and marijuana when work pressures place stress on the adolescents. The researchers discovered that as work hours increase, particularly when they exceed 15 to 20 hours a week, so too does the adolescent's likelihood of starting to use marijuana (Steinberg, Greenberger, Garduque, Ruggiero, & Vaux, 1982).

These findings are controversial and not immune to criticism. Some college students who have read the studies by Greenberger and her associates (Greenberger,

. . . . At all times girls past eight or nine years of age tried to be helpful to their fathers in small matters such as handing over an object to the father when asked to do so, etc. The mother-daughter relationship was much more significant . . . . Already at the age of seven or eight a girl began to interrupt her play in order to participate in her mother's activities. First she collaborated with the mother, accompanying her while cutting fresh ice, getting water, or gathering moss. Gradually she began to perform many of the women's tasks by herself whenever asked to do so by her mother. Soon her functions as household helper became very important. Often young girls were seen carrying infant siblings on their backs. Sewing and skin work were learned somewhat later. After a girl reached the age of eleven or twelve, just as father and son began to collaborate closely, so mother and daughter worked on similar tasks.

. . . . As (male siblings) grew, they increasingly collaborated and worked together, either with their father or by themselves. A patterned division of tasks existed during such cooperation, the older brother assuming initiative and decision-making, and the younger respectfully obeying.

Eskimo male adolescents learn by observing and imitating their fathers.

Relations between younger sisters were much more intimate and playful. They talked much more freely to each other, giggling and joking, and were very expressive of their affection. This closeness of sisters was expressed both at play and at work (From *The Netsilik Eskimo*, by A. Balikci, pp. 105–107. Copyright © 1970 by Waveland Press. Reprinted by permission).

1988; Greenberger & Steinberg, 1986) question the validity of generalizing findings about adolescents in Orange County, California to adolescents elsewhere. Rather than feeling dismay that working adolescents spend, rather than save, the money they earn, one college student felt perplexed that the researchers would even consider such behavior to be a matter for concern. "At least they aren't stealing the things they want," was the way this student put it. What this student did not acknowledge was that income from part-time jobs during high school can give adolescents a false sense of affluence, especially when everyday needs, such as shelter, clothing, and food, are being paid for by parents. Finally, college students who worked during high school did not recognize themselves in the research reported by Greenberger and her associates (Greenberger, 1988; Greenberger & Steinberg, 1986). While the effects of working may have been detrimental to the California teenagers, midwestern college students said they found work gave them a sense of freedom and was enjoyable.

EMPLOYMENT TRAINING FOR YOUTHS AT RISK

Not all youths are able to find work, as we saw in an earlier section. For some youths, their chances of being unemployed are greater because their educations and/or social skills are poor. In this section, we examine programs to make such youths employable.

Preparing youths for fulfilling, productive adult work is one of the paramount tasks of society. We know that developing an identity fundamentally involves selecting an occupation. At times, occupational choice is not stable; people change jobs and even lines of work two or more times in their adult lives.

The dangers to society—not only to individuals or to families—when people cannot find work are frightening. Civil unrest in metropolitan areas of the United States provides stark examples of what happens when many young people have no hope for a job, let alone a productive future.

The Job Corps
In 1964, the United States government established the Job Corps as one of President Lyndon Johnson's "Great Society" programs. This program is still in existence in many locations throughout the United States.

The Job Corps provides training in a residential setting for out-of-school youths. Job Corps training and services include basic education, vocational training, health care, and job placement. Training takes up to 30 weeks, and nearly 50% of the participants drop out prior to completing their training (Betsey et al., 1985).

Job Corps participants range in age from 14 to 21, come from impoverished families, and are considered to be at a severe disadvantage educationally—reading levels seldom reach even sixth grade proficiency. Most Job Corps participants are male (70%), nearly all participants are high school dropouts (90%), and the great majority are from ethnic/racial minority groups (75%). Thirty percent of the participants are female, and, of this group, most are without children; however, 9% of Job Corps residents are single mothers with young children.

Renewal of Job Corps funding went through precarious times in the late 1960s and in the 1970s as legislators questioned the success of the program. For instance, one study indicated that 18 months after Job Corps training, the earnings of participants did not differ from earnings of youths who dropped out within the first three months of training (Woltman & Walton, 1968). The early evaluation findings suggested the Job Corps had a short-term, noticeable impact that quickly withered.

Other evaluation studies done more recently and using more sophisticated designs and more extensive data-gathering procedures indicate Job Corps programs work (Mallar, Kerachsky, Thornton, & Long, 1982; Wholey, 1986). The study by Mallar and his colleagues (1982), commonly referred to as the *Mathematica evaluation*, was a longitudinal study with a large sample and a comparison control group.

Mallar and his associates (1982) studied 3,800 youths for up to four and one-half years after Job Corps training. The sample included 2,800 Job Corps participants and 1,000 nonparticipants who were, in all other respects, similar to the Job Corps students. Although attrition rates generally plague longitudinal studies, the Mathematica evaluation retained 70% of its sample over the four and one-half year period.

The evaluators took measures on multiple factors, including employment, education, physical health, criminal behavior, and weekly earnings. Findings in all areas significantly favored Job Corps participants, except for in the first six months following training when Job Corps participants had more difficulty finding work or finding good-paying jobs (Betsey et al., 1985). Specifically, for three and one-half years after training, Job Corps participants

- worked about 13% more per year than nonparticipants,
- earned 28% more per year than nonparticipants,
- received less welfare or unemployment compensation than nonparticipants,
- had a significantly greater likelihood of earning a high school diploma or of completing the General Equivalency Diploma (GED),
- reported significantly less health problems than nonparticipants, and
- had significantly fewer arrests for serious crimes (Betsey et al., 1985).

Another study identified factors that predicted success in Job Corps training for 85 adolescents (mean age of 18.8) enrolled in a Job Corps center in the southwestern United States (Gallegos & Kahn, 1986). The majority of the participants (53%) were female; 34% were Hispanic, 30% white, 16% Asian, 10% Native American, 7% black, and 3% not identified. The focus of the study was to assess background factors that would predict success or failure for enrollees.

The researchers designated successful Job Corps participants as individuals who had graduated or who were still in the program nine months following enrollment. Eighty-five individuals were placed in this group. The researchers designated unsuccessful Job Corps participants as individuals who dropped out of the program. This group numbered 40.

The researchers gathered information on ten categories: (*a*) school and employment, (*b*) self-concept, (*c*) peer relations, (*d*) relations with family members, (*e*) socioeconomic indicators, (*f*) social adjustment indicators, (*g*) age, (*h*) ethnic group membership, and (*i*) geographical place of residence. Several categories distinguished successful from unsuccessful participants.

- Participants whose homes were in the Southwest region where the training center was located fared worse than participants who came from other parts of the country. The Job Corps center appeared to have been too close to familiar distractions (home, friends, locales) for individuals who dropped out of the program.
- Participants enrolled in school or employed just prior to entering the program tended to succeed in Job Corps. Other participants were much more likely to drop out of the training.
- Ethnicity associated very significantly ($p < .004$) with success. Successful participants were Asian (100% of the Asians who enrolled succeeded), white (71%), black (67%), Hispanic (58%), and Native American (54%).

■ Successful participants made more reliable estimates of the length of time needed to complete Job Corps training. They realized training would take longer than did the individuals who dropped out (Gallegos & Kahn, 1985).

The researchers analyzed all these factors associated with success and noted they formed "a pattern of characteristics that repeatedly have been associated with success or nonsuccess in helping youth find meaningful employment and roles in society" (Gallegos & Kahn, 1986, p. 176). Rather than endorsing a simplistic recommendation to enroll only youths whose histories indicate successful past adjustment, the authors said the challenge for the Job Corps center was to find methods of reaching the high percentage of Job Corps enrollees who do not stay with the program (Gallegos & Kahn, 1986).

New Youth Initiatives in Apprenticeship

In 1977, the U.S. Department of Labor funded projects with schools and employers to provide registered apprenticeship training in nonconstruction jobs. Minority and impoverished adolescents were the intended beneficiaries of one program, the New Youth Initiatives in Apprenticeship (NYIA). Incentives to employers were subsidies to cover one-half of the apprentice wages and program screening and training of applicants. The ultimate goal of the NYIA program was to place apprentices in positions of employment after graduation from high school. Thus, the program offered high school students part-time paid employment in a skilled trade and placement in a job following graduation.

Eighty-two percent of the NYIA participants were white and 93% were male. The average GPA of the participants was B-. Nearly all participants (96%) graduated from high school.

Betsey and his associates. (1985) concluded the program was not effective in reaching minority youths and did not lead to any significant differences in wages. Because the follow-up data were gathered less than two years following high school graduation, the researchers suggested program effects might not be noticed yet. Nonetheless, they considered the program results to have been disappointing (Betsey et al., 1985).

Labor Market Programs for Out-of-School Adolescents

Several programs designed to increase economic independence and employment opportunities for at-risk youths have focused on overcoming various deficiencies, such as poor work habits, lack of basic skills, such as reading and writing, and ignorance about job opportunities fitting their interests. Let's look at data from one of these programs, Alternative Youth Employment Strategies (AYES).

The AYES program used three alternative approaches at sites in New York City, Miami, and Albuquerque to reach unemployed, delinquent 16- to 21-year-old dropouts. The three alternative approaches were:

■ full-time work, with counseling and job placement services;

■ full-time classroom instruction in basic education, vocational and prevocational education, with counseling and job placement services; and

■ part-time work and part-time training, counseling, and job placement services.

Program participants were mostly minority male adolescents. While demographics varied across the sites, black and Hispanic youths accounted for up to 75% of the students. In all, over 1,000 adolescents took part in the training. The assessment of program effects included a control group of nonparticipants.

Data on program outcomes were collected three times: immediately after the program, three months after the program, and eight months after the program. The basic findings were that program participants were more likely than nonparticipants to be fully employed eight months after the program. Outcomes did not depend on which alternative training approach was used (Betsey et al., 1985).

Betsey and his associates (1985) commented on the lack of differences in program outcomes for the three alternative approaches. They note that several studies had reported similar results for alternative treatment approaches and that this result (lack of different outcomes for alternative approaches) has been found in other studies of job training programs. Betsey and his colleagues (1985) suggest three explanations for such a strong and persistent finding.

- "The types of instruction have equal effects."

- "Students select the type of program best suited to their needs."

- "Sample sizes are too small to detect small differences in outcomes controlling for size, treatment, and other variables" (Betsey et al., 1985, p. 123).

These explanations suggest that people are unsure what produces the consistent finding that the programs work despite using different methods. Betsey and his associates (1985) imply in their third explanation that differences are present but cannot be detected due to research and measurement constraints.

The School-to-Work Transition Program

Some programs aim at helping youths make the transitions from school to work. The William T. Grant Foundation, which commissions and funds research regarding school-age youths at risk, sponsored a national commission to study youth and America's future. This study is known as the youth in transition project. Several working papers of this commission focus on adolescents and work. The commission concluded, "American society today lacks a clear, accepted conceptual model of youth transition from school to work—how youth are and should be related to the experiences of work and learning" (Charner & Fraser, no date, p. 2). Noting that such a model existed until the late 1940s, the commission described the features of such a model.

- Compulsory formal education extended through high school.

- Upon completing high school, adolescents—especially males—joined the labor force full-time.

- Schooling provided basic education rather than vocational preparation.

- On-the-job training sufficed for most positions because skill requirements were low.

- Mobility and communication were limited.

- Populations concentrated where jobs existed.

These features promoted swift and direct transitions from school to work (Charner & Fraser, no date).

Dramatic changes in technology, mobility, communications media, and specialized, technical jobs have altered the assumptions regarding requirements to work. Schooling has become both a means to impart basic education and an opportunity to prepare adolescents for independent living. However, the highly technical working world today is impossible to enter without preparatory training, and the traditional high school curriculum does not offer such preparation. A proposed solution is to provide work experience while youths are enrolled in high school.

Adults in the 1940s, 1950s, and 1960s asserted that working while still a high school student was a positive experience. (This conclusion, of course, runs counter to the findings of Greenberger and Steinberg (1986) reported earlier in this chapter.) Experts maintained that having adolescents work with adults in real jobs solved the problem that high schools had become places keeping adolescents removed from vital involvement with adults and the working world requiring adult habits and skills (National Panel on High School and Adolescent Education, 1976).

For eight years, researchers studied adolescents in the Youth in Transition project. The study began in 1966 with a national sample of 2,213 tenth grade boys attending public high school. Over the eight-year duration of the project, 1,628 individuals remained in the study (71.5% of the original sample). Except for a disproportionate loss of school dropouts from the study, the sample remaining after eight years significantly resembled the original participants in the study (Bachman & O'Malley, 1984).

The Youth in Transition project investigated the impacts of school and work on adolescent males. The initial impetus for the study was to identify the causes and effects of not completing high school. The researchers chose an all-male sample because they asserted dropping out of school has widely disparate consequences for males and females and because they did not have the capabilities for conducting separate sets of analyses (Bachman & O'Malley, 1984). Twenty years after beginning the study, the researchers believed their findings apply also to females, but regretted their inability to support their assertion with research data.

The objectives of the study were fivefold:

- to assess the extent to which factors present in tenth grade predict educational and occupational achievements (some of these factors were family background, emotional state, self-concept, values, academic skills, and intelligence);
- to evaluate the influence of educational achievement on occupational achievement;
- to investigate the consequences of dropping out of high school, specifically, by comparing occupational achievements of high school graduates with achievements of dropouts;
- to discover if different high schools have noticeably different impacts on student occupational achievement; and

■ to measure the impact of experiences after high school (for example, military service, marriage, parenthood, education, and work) on individual conduct, beliefs, and viewpoints (Bachman & O'Malley, 1984);

Findings From the Youth in Transition Project

Let's look at findings regarding predictors of educational and occupational achievement, level of education and occupational consequences, and consequences of dropping out of school.

Several factors present in tenth grade are highly predictive of educational achievement. These factors are family background, intelligence, ninth grade GPA, plans for college, negative school attitudes, school curriculum, delinquent behavior, and failing grades. The researchers in the Youth in Transition project concluded that family background and ability provide indirect impacts on educational attainment by contributing to individual expectations about academic failure and success (Bachman & O'Malley, 1984).

Over the course of the study, neither earnings nor rates of employment were significantly related to the participants' amount of education. However, this finding hardly surprised the researchers since their research participants were just beginning their careers. Given time, they felt certain wages would correlate positively with level of education (Bachman & O'Malley, 1984).

Educational attainment in this project extended over a continuum ranging from high school dropout to graduate work at a university. When studying the consequences of dropping out of high school, the researchers struggled to find a reasonable comparison group. They reasoned that high school graduates who did not go to college formed the most reasonable comparison group. Basing comparisons on dropouts and high school graduates led to few significant differences; the groups were alike in the types of jobs held, job status, hourly wages, and job satisfaction. The one difference was that dropouts ran twice the chance of being unemployed, regardless of ability or family background (Bachman & O'Malley, 1984).

The Youth in Transition study looked solely at the effects on males during the transition from school to work. We turn next to research about adolescent females and work.

Adolescent Female Participation in Employment and Training Programs

The federal government's employment and training programs began in the middle 1960s, and they focused primarily on helping males overcome barriers to employment. Program developers considered males' employment needs more important than females', and considered unemployed males to be at greater risk of criminal behavior than unemployed females. Thus, between 1964 and 1979, females made up less than half of the participants in employment and training programs.

As social, political, and economic constraints changed in this century, young women's economic needs became a recognized issue in this country. Impoverishment has disproportionately affected females. Research shows that unemployment during young adulthood has a damaging effect on the long-term earnings and work histories of females, particularly black females (Simms, 1985). Adolescent females have increased their participation in employment and training programs since 1979. By the first quarter of 1979, females were a majority of all participants. The females seemed better qualified than the males, perhaps because the programs required females to have more education and prior work experience (Simms, 1985).

A longitudinal study conducted by the Urban Institute followed 12,000 adolescents (ages 14 to 21) over a two-year period (Simms & Leitch, 1983). The study compared employment and training program participants with nonparticipants. Nearly equal numbers of males and females participated, and far fewer males had completed high school. In fact, the school dropout rates for white males were double the rate for white females enrolled in the programs.

The researchers consistently found that females in these employment and training programs had greater qualifications than males. One hypothesis is that the females hold less traditional attitudes toward work than their same-age male peers. In particular, they expect they will have to work outside the home, and, thus, they have been preparing for that reality. While female participants endorsed the view that "a woman's place is in the home," they said they expected to be working outside the home at age 35. If economic realities were to improve and eliminate the need to work, female participants in government-sponsored employment and training programs would select to drop out of the work force (Simms & Leitch, 1983).

The typical female participant was from a minority ethnic group (black or Hispanic primarily) or a low-income white family. They were much more likely than the male participants to be a parent; this finding, of course, does not take into account that males may have fathered a child and escaped parental responsibilities. The female mothers were likely to be single-parent heads of households.

What have been the outcomes for females who participate in these government sponsored programs? One consistent finding is that female participants increase their earnings. For instance, over a two-year period, white females in on-the-job training increased their earnings by 23%, and during the same period, black females increased their earnings by nearly 39%. The data do not show that the females received higher hourly wages but, rather, indicate the wage gains resulted from working more hours for over 90% of the females. In contrast, a higher percentage of the gains for male participants was due to higher hourly wages (Simms, 1985).

Female participants also experienced other gains, such as completion of GED programs, graduation from high school, and enrollment in college. Upon completing these employment and training programs, female participants had reduced dependency on welfare and engaged in significantly less criminal behavior than nonparticipants. Nonetheless, women with children seemed hindered from taking advantage of opportunities following graduation from one of these programs, probably because they found it difficult to afford day-care for their children (Simms, 1985).

We have looked at various programs to help adolescents gain and keep employment. One major employer of adolescents coming out of high school is the United States military. Advertisements encouraging enlistment tout the career opportunities available as a soldier and the doors that open in civilian life for the veteran. What do we know about youths who join the armed forces? We turn to this question in the next section.

YOUTHS WHO ENLIST IN THE ARMED FORCES

The military is a significant employer of young males and females in the United States. Since the United States instituted the all-volunteer military, there has been a need to screen applicants. A good screening device would reduce **military attrition** (leaving the military) and increase selection of qualified candidates. Newell Eaton, Mary Weltin, and Hilda Wing (1982) assessed the validity of the Military Applicant Profile (MAP) as a screening instrument used with male applicants who did not graduate from high school.

The 4,278 research subjects were divided into four age-groups: 1,006 17-year-olds, 1,102 18-year-olds, 1,275 19- and 20-year-olds, and 895 individuals 21 years old and over. Sixty-six percent of the research subjects were white, 26% were black, 5% were Hispanic, and the remaining 3% were of some other ethnic/racial group.

The one significant predictor of attrition turned out to be the applicant's education level. Soldiers who had not graduated from high school were significantly more likely ($p < .001$) to leave the military (Eaton et al., 1982).

A longitudinal study of 2,408 males investigated which psychosocial factors predict military enlistment (Johnson & Kaplan, 1991). The majority of participants (62%) were white, 25% were black, 9% were Hispanic, and 3% were from another ethnic/racial group. Some of the factors investigated were ethnic/racial identity, socioeconomic class, life stressors, criminal history, and peer relationships. Robert Johnson and Howard Kaplan (1991) followed their subjects from 1972 (when the individuals were seventh-graders) into the 1980s. Of the 2,408 people in the study, 491 (20.4%) enlisted in the military. All the enlistees were in their late adolescence (none was over 20 years of age). A higher proportion of black and Hispanic adolescents entered the military than stayed in civilian life, whereas the reverse was true for whites (Johnson & Kaplan, 1991).

Of the 491 individuals who enlisted in the military, a disproportionately high percentage were from working-class families, particularly among ethnic minorities. Factors that induced enlistment were peer rejection, submission to punitive authority,

Several factors influence an adolescent to enlist in the military: job experience, educational opportunities, the county's unemployment rate, and pay incentives.

life crises (for instance, attempted suicide and family moves), arrest records, and desire for peer-group associations (Johnson & Kaplan, 1991).

David Balkin and Sid Groeneman (1985) tested whether pay incentives attract adolescents to enlist. They studied 5,993 males between 16 and 21 years of age. None of the research participants were in the military at the time of the study and none had ever been in the military. Findings indicated youths are much more likely to enlist when pay incentives are present. Similar results were found with Australian youths, who indicated financial incentives form the major reason they enlist in their country's version of the National Guard (Bollen & Cotton, 1991). However, emphasis on the role of financial incentives was questioned by Petersen's (1989) research, which dismissed the strength of any single factor, such as economic considerations, to account for adolescent enlistment in the military. Petersen (1989) proposed that several factors influence a youth's decision to join the military, including the desire to gain job experience, educational opportunities, the current rate of unemployment in the country, and pay incentives.

One factor that does not seem associated with enlistment is coming from a military family. Gary Bowen (1986) conducted a study of 931 men in the Air Force. The sample was randomly selected, with 40% ($n = 372$) coming from the officer ranks and 60% ($n = 541$) from enlisted personnel. After two interviews conducted two years apart, the researchers concluded enlisted men whose fathers have made a career of the military are quite unlikely to consider staying in the military (Bowen, 1986).

Bowen's (1986) findings about the unlikelihood of sons of career military men joining the armed forces contradict earlier findings (Faris, 1981). The significance of Bowen's findings lies first in the fact that military planners cannot count on recruiting to career positions adolescents who have been raised in a military life. Second, the findings suggest that male adolescents raised in a military family do not see occupational identity commitments in terms of the values their fathers modeled for them.

Many researchers have documented the consequences for youths who join the armed forces. Some researchers extol the developmental opportunities afforded by military service and other researchers excoriate the developmental consequences induced by military service. Perhaps the conclusions disclose the values of the persons doing the research.

A critic of the effects of military service on youths is Chaim Shatan (1977), who severely disparaged the developmental consequences that Marine Corps training had on recruits. He referred to the outcome as "bogus manhood and bogus honor" and believed the authoritarian mystique of the Marine Corps subverts and deforms character development in young men. According to Shatan, the appeal of the Marine Corps for late adolescent males emerges from the youths' confusion in forging an identity in civilian life and their attraction to the Marine Corps' emphasis on endurance, fitness, and authority.

There are some positive consequences traced to military service. For instance, youths who drop out of high school and enlist in the armed forces are more likely to complete their high school educations than youths who do not enlist (Kolstad &

Owings, 1986). Studies of Israeli youths—who, unlike American adolescents, are required to serve in their country's military—indicate that they look to military service as a means to give definite shape to their vocational identities (Orr, Liran, & Meyer, 1986). Australian youths, who indicate that pay incentives are their major inducement to enlist, also indicate they join the military for enjoyment of that life itself (Bollen & Cotton, 1991).

A good portion of late adolescents enter college as a means to increase their chances for entering a career that will be personally and financially fulfilling. The next section of this chapter focuses on effects of college on career choice and career development.

CAREER CHOICE AND DEVELOPMENT DURING COLLEGE

Studies of the effects of college on career choice and development are marred by their cross-sectional nature. While researchers may conclude that college produces career maturation for undergraduates, failure to use rigorous longitudinal methods weakens their case that college attendance influences career development (Pascarella & Terenzini, 1991). Such changes may not be the effects of extended college attendance but, rather, may occur as students grow older or result because students with less mature career plans leave college.

Despite those needed qualifications concerning what we know about the effects of college on career choice and development, there is a body of scholarship that consistently demonstrates upper-division students engage in significantly more critical thinking about careers than first- or second-year students. This thinking involves formulating career plans, obtaining accurate knowledge about a career, and making clear career choices (Pascarella & Terenzini, 1991). Feeling the pressure of impending graduation seems to spur many students to develop their career development skills.

Helen Astin (1977), a career development specialist, maintains that a large number of undergraduates use college to implement, rather than to select, a career. The single most useful predictor of a student's career choice at the end of college remains the initial choice made when the student enters college (Braxton, Brier, Herzog, & Pascarella, 1988; Ethington, Smart, & Pascarella, 1987; Tusin & Pascarella, 1985). This evidence implies little change occurs about career choice during a student's years in college.

These rosy views of college students' choices of careers may not match the experience of some readers of this text. Many students change majors multiple times during college, and up to two-thirds of all undergraduates alter their career plans many times (Pascarella & Terenzini, 1991). Several reasons are suggested for these changes.

One reason offered by Astin (1977) is that students learn some fields (for instance, medicine and engineering) are extremely competitive and opt for other choices. Learning that some careers offer meager employment possibilities or few financial rewards can also lead students to alter their plans. One student, attracted to work in zoos, told me she still thought such a job would be fun but had changed her mind because the salary prospects were so low.

Most students would recognize their own experience of career choice and development during college as one of searching. Pascarella and Terenzini (1991) note that adolescents engage in considerable rethinking and sharpening of their career plans while in college.

Graduation from college definitely has significant positive effects on gaining a job with occupational status. The means for measuring occupational status is fairly complicated, is overwhelmingly associated with educational level, and is significantly influenced by the income obtained from the job. Three highly prestigious jobs, for instance, are medical doctor, investment banker, and judge.

Pascarella and Terenzini (1991) note that educational level has the single most important impact on occupational status across one's life span, and they conclude that graduating from college opens up employment opportunities with more occupational status than are available to individuals without a college education. Analysis of data from several national studies on the determinants of career and economic success confirm Pascarella and Terenzini's assertion. In short, a consistent body of scholarship indicates graduation from college leads to occupations with nearly double the status of jobs available to high school graduates (Jencks et. al., 1979).

Several factors favor college graduates over high school graduates. Obviously one of these factors is the increasingly sophisticated demands of jobs that require education beyond the high school curriculum. Other factors include access to stable positions and access to promotions in managerial and professional careers. Furthermore, even when unemployed, college graduates have advantages for reentering the work force. These advantages include "increased accuracy of occupational information and efficiency in job search, increased regional mobility to take advantage of employment opportunities, and an enhanced network of personal contacts, some of which date back to college days" (Pascarella & Terenzini, 1991, p. 488).

Chapter Summary

Finding meaningful work has long been considered a primary task of development. Several issues of development pertinent to adolescence come into play when studying adolescents, work, and career choice.

One issue is identity formation. Of particular importance is the exploration of options, as represented in Marcia's (1964, 1966, 1967, 1980) moratorium status, and by commitment to choices, as represented by Marcia's achievement status.

Another issue in the area of adolescents, work, and career choice is the development of more abstract cognitive competencies, called "formal operations" by Piaget (1983). Examples of formal operations include understanding probabilities, appreciating long-term consequences, having a future time perspective, and considering possibilities in terms of an "as if" approach. An instance of the as if approach is, "What would the world be like if men, rather than women, were expected to be nurturant to children?" Another instance is, "What would my life be like if I became a high school math teacher?"

A third issue in adolescents, work, and career choice is the role of the desire to achieve. Sometimes this desire is termed achievement motivation or the motivation to succeed. Gender differences come into play here because fear of success has been linked to gender and identity formation.

A fourth issue in adolescents, work, and career choice involves gender differences. As an example, there is evidence that most adolescent girls do not really explore career possibilities but, rather, go through the motions (what is called "pseudo exploration") and put career decisions on hold until issues of marriage and family are settled in their lives (Archer, 1985).

A fifth issue is the experience of adolescents—particularly middle adolescents—who work during their high school years. Some very influential research (Greenberger & Steinberg, 1986; Steinberg, Greenberger, Garduque et al., 1982) asserts that adolescents who attend high school and also work several hours pay a price socially and psychologically.

A sixth issue in adolescents, work, and career choice is the influence career development plays in the process of forming a secure adult identity. This process involves not only high school programs that promote career exploration but also college experiences that lead to reaching closure on tasks related to career maturity (Pascarella & Terenzini, 1991).

A seventh issue involves what one prominent study called "the forgotten half" (William T. Grant Foundation, 1988). By this phrase, the researchers meant the great numbers of youths who enter the work force and do not go to college. As a group, these late adolescents are much less known than college students, who form a more accessible research population.

An eighth issue involves another less explored group of late adolescents. These are the youths who enter the Armed Forces. While pay incentives offer some attraction for enlistment, other factors, such as job experience, educational opportunities, and the prospect for employment, also matter.

Ninth, there is the issue of youths who are at risk of not forming an occupational identity. These are youths who are often impoverished, have done poorly in school, and have poorly developed problem-solving skills. Training programs have been devised to assist such youths. One program to assist career development in these individuals is the Job Corps.

Finally, there is the role of college in the formation of a career identity. Many students change career choices more than once during their undergraduate years. Late adolescents engage in considerable rethinking and sharpening of their career plans while in college. Graduation from college definitely has significant positive effects on gaining a job with occupational status.

We have completed this review of adolescents, work, and career development. In the next chapter, we look at the influence of electronic media, especially television, on adolescents.

ADOLESCENTS AND ELECTRONIC MEDIA, PARTICULARLY TELEVISION

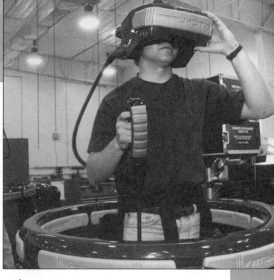

"Television Is Like a Companion, Especially When I'm Alone"

Rose is a high school sophomore. She is a good student and gets mostly grades of A or B. Rose is in several honors classes in her high school and recently took a college course arranged through her high school's advanced placement program. She got a high B from the college instructor.

Rose watches TV a lot, on average, about six hours a day. Such viewing habits place her among the "heavy viewers." For one week, Rose kept track of all the TV programs she watched. She said it had been a typical week when we talked about what was on her list and why she watched the programs she chose.

"I love TV, but TV is not my first choice. I prefer going out with my boyfriend. I suppose people who don't have TV find other things to do, like read a book or go outside. I do read. I just finished *A Separate Peace* (Knowles, 1966), and I want to read *The Color Purple* (Walker, 1982), but it's always checked out of the library. I've asked my dad to see if he can find me a copy. I read *Newsweek* too each week.

"When you watch TV, there's lots of other things you can do at the same time, like do your hair or paint your nails or do your homework or talk on the phone. But when you read a book, you can't do anything else.

"TV is like a companion, especially when I'm alone. It gives me something to do when I'm alone and feeling lonely."

Rose then reviewed her list of all the shows she had watched throughout the week. You may notice, as she did, a clear pattern to the shows she selected. You may note, as well, that she never once mentioned watching MTV. When I pointed that out to her, Rose commented, "I watch MTV real briefly sometimes. I don't watch MTV much though. It's kind of boring to just watch videos all the time.

"On Saturday, I only watched a few shows. I sleep in on Saturdays. I watched 'Gossip' because I like to find out about stars and what they are doing. Then I watched 'Cops' and 'Code 3' because of all the action. Then, my boyfriend got off work and dropped over, and we went out to play pool." Rose's total television viewing on Saturday amounted to 2.5 hours.

"On Sunday, I watched 'Gossip' again, for the same reasons I gave before. Then I watched part of a movie called *9 to 5* for an hour. Turned to watch comedy shows for the rest of the evening. I did a lot of other things while the TV was on: did my hair, talked on the phone." Rose watched TV for 6.25 hours on Sunday.

"On Monday, I got up around 6 A.M. and turned on 'Cartoon Express'. It gives me something to do while I'm getting ready for school. It's like my parents, who listen to National Public Radio while they are getting ready for work. When I got back from school in the afternoon, I watched 'Geraldo' and 'Oprah'. They're cool shows and have neat people on. I watched comedy shows the rest of the evening 'cause they're funny. While they're on, I'm doing other things too, like talking on the phone, doing my hair." Rose watched TV for 7.5 hours on Monday.

"On Tuesday, same thing in the morning—'Cartoon Express' while I put on my makeup and fix my hair. I went out with my boyfriend after school so I didn't watch 'Geraldo' or 'Oprah'. Turned on 'Jeopardy' at 5:00 P.M., then watched a bunch of comedy shows until 9:00. At 9:00, I watched 'We're Expecting' because it was true to life and showed what it is like to be pregnant and have a baby—both the good things and the nasty stuff. You should see the program. It is really something." Rose watched TV for 4.5 hours on Tuesday.

"On Wednesday, same thing in the morning as I've said before. After I get home from school, I basically watch the same things until 7:00 P.M. I watched 'Unsolved Mysteries' because it is about real life situations and people, and it's neat to see what people's lives are like. I watched 'Tales from the Crypt' at 9:00 P.M. because it's gross and disgusting." Rose spent 6 hours watching TV on Wednesday.

"On Thursday, I watched all the same programs as before until 7:00 P.M. Then, I watched 'Top Cops' and 'Street Stories' because they're real-life dramas. I watched 'Picket Fences' at 9:00 P.M. because it was about a man who had a case of Hodgkins disease. It was all about him dying and efforts to save him by injecting fetal tissue into his brain." On Thursday, Rose watched TV for 7.5 hours.

"On Friday, I watched all the regular shows I've mentioned before. Then, I watched a show about criminals the police are trying to arrest, and I watched a show about ghosts. I believe in ghosts. After that, I watched a horror film because it's disgusting and gross." Rose watched TV for 8 hours on Friday.

During this one week, according to Rose's account, she watched TV for 42.25 hours in all. She admits she doesn't give full attention to all the shows that she turns on. She occupies herself doing other things, such as homework or talking on the phone, while the TV is going. There seems to be evidence that Rose selects TV because there is nothing else available to her. Unlike Marshall McLuhan (1964; McLuhan & Fiore, 1967), who maintained TV is an all-involving medium, Rose sometimes gives it her full attention and at other times uses it for background presence. She says books take more undivided attention; she reads one or more books a week.

There seems some strong evidence for what is called the *default hypothesis* in Rose's viewing habits; she watches TV when there is nothing else to do. When something more attractive comes along, she chooses it over TV. What she especially prefers over TV is to be with her boyfriend.

This chapter looks at electronic media and adolescents. One form of electronic media is radio. American adolescents listen to the radio primarily to hear music. I devote considerable space in this chapter to discussing television and adolescents. We look at hypotheses offered for why people watch TV, the amount of television adolescents view regularly, and the role of television in socializing viewers. Television provides viewers opportunities to vicariously learn about emotions and exposes viewers to considerable violence and portrayals of human sexuality. Researchers debate the impact of television on cognitive performance. Information-processing theorists have examined the cognitive skills required to view television programs.

We begin with an analysis of the phenomenon of television and its impact on human culture. We turn to the views of Marshall McLuhan.

ELECTRONIC MEDIA AND AMERICAN CULTURE

The ideas of the Canadian scholar Marshall McLuhan became suddenly popular in the United States in the 1960s. While fairly complex, McLuhan's thesis was that the contemporary human environment is *fundamentally technological* (McLuhan, 1951, 1962, 1964, 1989; McLuhan & Fiore, 1967). McLuhan maintained that technological advances are extensions of the human species, and that few people are aware of how pervasively technology influences human life. In McLuhan's words, "all media are extensions of some human faculty," and he gave these examples: "The book is an extension of the eye . . . clothing an extension of the skin . . . [and] electric circuitry an extension of the central nervous system" (McLuhan & Fiore, 1967, pp. 26–40). Regarded by some scholars as narrow minded and dogmatic (O'Neill, 1991), but lauded by others as our champion in outgrowing the printed word (West, 1969), McLuhan's ideas are probably best considered "preliminary efforts to explore a radical cultural change in communication" (Bissell, 1989, p. 5).

For McLuhan, the most revolutionary technological influence is the marriage of electronic media, primarily television, with communication satellites. We now live, said McLuhan (1989), in a *global village* that has become *global theater*. His assertion proved true during the Persian Gulf War when CNN, NBC, ABC, and CBS carried live news broadcasts within the midst of battle zones, and videotaped replays taken from fighter jets showing television viewers actual strikes on Iraqi targets. In McLuhan's words, "with the satellite as a proscenium arch around the planet, the planet itself is now a stage on which everybody can do his thing" (1989, p. 4).

According to McLuhan, because of the electronic media revolution, Americans of today perceive the world and ourselves differently than did Americans of the 1940s or 1950s. However, McLuhan asserted few people realize the revolutionary change on our human sensory faculties television and other electronic media have produced.

At the age of 10, my daughter said she could not imagine a quality life without radio, television, and video cassettes. Please note: we are talking about transistor radios that turn on immediately, cable television that provides at least 20 channels to view, and video cassettes that bring into the home a variety of visual entertainment unavailable even in the 1970s. "What did people do with their time before these inventions were commonplace?" seems to have been my daughter's puzzlement.

American adolescents go to movies at least once a month, and few would dream of going alone.

Much of this chapter is about television and adolescents. Some attention is paid to radio. Because I believe the most pervasive influence on Americans is television, I have given more attention to that electronic medium than to any other.

I had intended to include information about motion pictures and adolescents. From early through middle adolescence, teenagers report they increasingly go to movies, and "over 50% of young people aged 12 through 17 report at least monthly attendance" (Fine, Mortimer, & Roberts, 1990, p. 247). Unfortunately, there has been almost no research on adolescent interest in motion pictures.

Some researchers describe adolescent motion picture viewing as a social activity (Schramm, Lyle, & Parker, 1961). Few adolescents I know would dream of going to a movie alone. This adolescent behavior is considered evidence of the **social activity hypothesis**, which maintains that adolescents engage in some behaviors only when with members of their peer groups. The social activity hypothesis has been extended to explain adolescents' renting and watching video cassettes in groups. A high proportion of these are R- or X-rated films. "One suspects that the combination of pressure and bravado inherent in the adolescent peer group helps to explain why much adolescent viewing involves" these types of films (Fine et al., 1990, p. 248).

Radio programs are an important source of entertainment and information for adolescents. We look next at adolescents and radio.

ADOLESCENTS AND RADIO

What is the primary reason adolescents turn on the radio? The answer is probably obvious: to listen to music. While television has a few programs devoted to adolescents' musical tastes and one complete television network (MTV), many radio stations play music to attract adolescent audiences. Most adolescents like rock, rap, and other forms of contemporary popular music (Lull, 1992), and few turn to talk shows or classical music stations. This assertion, of course, must be qualified. Considerable individual differences mark not only adolescent use of the radio, but of all electronic media (Fine et al., 1990). However, on the whole, teenagers primarily listen to the radio to hear music.

Some adults have voiced concerns over the explicit sexual content in contemporary popular music, as well as concerns over the advocacy of violence and anarchy in some songs. Publication of lyrics to several rap groups' songs has enabled adults to read first-hand the explicit messages of sex, violence, and degradation of women in much of this music (Stanley, 1992). However, efforts to provide a ratings system for contemporary music—a ratings system similar to the one applied to motion pictures—has met with resistance and allegations of censorship (Gore, 1987).

Radio use increases as children enter adolescence. In fact, researchers found an association between parental absence from the home and adolescents' increased use of radio. While television viewing decreased during this time, radio listening increased (Brown, Childers, Bauman, & Koch, 1990).

Adolescents prefer to do homework with the radio or TV on. When given a choice to study with or without a radio or TV playing, most students from grades five through nine chose to turn the radio or TV on (Patton, Routh, & Stinard, 1986). However, this preference for at least music in the background is not unique to adolescents. I frequently hear music coming from radios in several of my colleagues' offices at Kansas State University, and while writing this section of Chapter 10, I put on some compact discs to listen to music. I have frequently listened to "Jazz in the Night" from radio station KANU in Lawrence, Kansas, while completing this book.

Radio as a Public Information Medium Because adolescents turn so frequently to radio, efforts have been made to promote health care in radio spots. Radio spots that encouraged seat belt use were much more successful than television spots, at least as measured by adolescents' self-reports of increased seat belt usage (Gantz, Fitzmaurice, & Yoo, 1990).

Efforts to reach adolescents about the dangers of smoking through public service announcements (PSAs) on radio have faced obstacles from the radio industry. Problems stem from the reluctance of radio station operators to run these PSAs unless celebrities convey the taped message (Hammond, Freimuth, & Morrisen, 1990). Perhaps this reluctance stems from a fear of offending listeners who smoke. Radio stations may figure PSAs not delivered by celebrities are not worth the risk of losing listeners and, thereby, revenues from advertising. There was a backlash in beef growing states against radio stations that played songs of K. D. Lang, a recording star who openly protests against eating meat products. One could conclude that the solution to this obstacle for airing radio spots about smoking is self-evident—get celebrities to present the messages. Why not contact some radio stations in your area to find out what they say about running PSAs against smoking?

ADOLESCENTS AND TELEVISION

In this section, we turn to research concentrating on the role and impact of television in the lives of adolescents. The amount of research attention given television has been high, and most of the conclusions have been critical. There is a constant theme, sometimes explicit and at other times tacit, that television has not lived up to its promise. An early assessment was that television is a vast wasteland (Minow, 1961 as cited in Murray, 1993); this assessment has not been softened in recent scholarship (Huston, Donnerstein, Fairchild, Feshbach, Katz, Murray, Rubinstein, Wilcox, & Zuckerman, 1992). The critics want television to do more, particularly in the area of educating viewers. A counterview, however, was expressed by a contributor to the *New Yorker* who commented, "When you consider television's awesome power to educate, aren't you thankful it doesn't?" (Reilly, 1965, as cited in McLuhan & Fiore, 1967, p. 128).

McLuhan, who extolled the impact of television, countered that disappointment with television stemmed from mistaking television as a lesser form of print, rather than recognizing it for a complete breakthrough in communication technology. He said television demands different sensory responses than other communication technology (McLuhan & Fiore, 1967).

In fact, McLuhan (1964; McLuhan & Fiore, 1967) argued television extends the human sensory system so that all of the senses are simultaneously involved. (I am not sure how he thought TV involves smell, taste, or touch.) He considered television demands active participation, whereas other media—print and radio, in particular—require passive participation (McLuhan, 1964). In his words, "Television demands participation and involvement in-depth of the whole being. It will not work as background. It engages you" (McLuhan & Fiore, 1967, p. 125).

I have no doubt that television can completely capture a person's attention. I saw my daughter as a toddler totally enthralled with "Sesame Street"; she would literally begin jumping up and down in excitement when the opening credits for the program appeared on the screen. And yet, I have also seen her thoroughly involved in books she is reading or music she is listening to or music she is playing on the viola. While some television programs have great interest for me, I doubt anything will ever replace the sense of wonder and awe I felt when first hearing Beethoven's *Ninth Symphony*. At times, books completely capture my imagination, and I become fascinated with the ideas the authors present. I recall being utterly enthralled as an undergraduate with Plato's metaphor of the cave and not caring whether the ideas in *The Republic* (1960) were true or false but just feeling carried along by the power of the words themselves. My point is that I acknowledge television has a considerable influence on the human mind, but I believe McLuhan gets carried away in his views, and I wonder how a person could test his ideas.

One influential notion about television is the **default hypothesis**. In this notion, television viewing is explained as an activity people engage in when they cannot do other things. In other words, people watch television for lack of anything else to do. They watch TV because they are not involved in any interfering activities and because a TV set is available. Opportunity to watch television and lack of opportunity to do something else describe the activities of various groups in the United States. Some of these groups are children, the elderly, homemakers, impoverished groups, and people in institutions (Huston et al., 1992).

A counter to the default hypothesis is the **displacement hypothesis**, which maintains television viewing replaces more worthwhile activities. Examples given of more worthwhile activities displaced by television are reading books, exercising, and concentrating on homework (Fine et al., 1990). We return to the displacement hypothesis when covering television and cognitive performance.

The default hypothesis, which assumes that people watch TV because they have nothing better to do, may explain the noted drop in television viewing during the middle adolescent years. During these years, youths have access to cars, are allowed to spend more time away from home, and place greater importance on doing things with their friends (Huston et al., 1992). Thus, having other things they can do, adolescents need not select TV by default. One adolescent boy I know said he could not understand how his parents could spend so much time watching TV when there were other, more interesting things to do; he played sports with his friends several hours a day.

Various researchers report that television viewing increases steadily until age 6 then levels off somewhat to slightly less than 3 hours a day as the child enters school (Huston et al., 1992; Liebert & Sprafkin, 1988). By the age of 12, viewing reaches an average of around 4 hours a day. Then, as Aletha Huston and her colleagues claim, television viewing "declines in adolescence" (1992, p. 12). From age 14 to age 16, adolescents watch TV, on average, around 3.75 hours a day. Frankly, I find this claim of a decline puzzling because the decrease amounts to about 15 minutes a day. Certainly adolescent viewing time never drops below the 3 hours preadolescents spend watching TV. Is a 15 minute decline of any practical significance in a 24-hour day?

How Adolescents Spend Their Time

Reed Larson has devised some ingenious procedures to obtain information on how adolescents spend their time. He gives adolescents electronic beepers, signals them at random times, and has them indicate what they are doing at those moments (Larson, 1989, Larson & Richards, 1991a). In one study, 392 early adolescents studied over several months indicated they frequently were bored, regardless of their activity. Over 25% of the respondents were watching TV when they were beeped. What is also interesting is that the only activity the adolescents reported more often than watching television was being in class (Larson & Richards, 1991a).

In an earlier study using the same methods, 483 adolescents indicated television viewing was a common activity that rivaled socializing with friends (Larson, 1989). But, in another study with 401 early adolescents, many of the youths shifted from watching TV to listening to music (Larson et al., 1989). Many TV programs—for instance, cartoon shows—that had appealed to the adolescents when they were younger no longer did, and other than rock music programs and soap operas, these adolescents did not become interested in other types of TV programs (Larson et al., 1989).

Larson and his colleagues (1989) concluded that both television viewing and listening to music are adolescent social activities, but television viewing involves the family and listening to music involves friends. "Adolescents who do watch more TV are those who spend more time with the family overall" (Larson et al., 1989, p. 583).

The shift to spending time with peers, to listening to music, and moving away from families provides a social marker for the beginning of early adolescence. "In

Adolescents Use of VCRs in Rural Saudi Arabia

Video cassette recorders (VCRs) are a common household item in American homes. Since the late 1970s, VCRs have also been common items in middle- and upper-class Saudi Arabian homes.

The use of VCRs in Saudi Arabia brings to light two competing facts of life. One, Saudi society is deeply conservative, and exposure to values from other cultures is regarded with great concern and suspicion. Second, much of Saudi Arabia is isolated and offers few sources of entertainment. Movie theaters and live stage performances are forbidden. The two television channels are run by the government and have poor quality broadcast signals. Rural adolescents from middle- and upper-middle-class families in particular are left with many idle hours.

Gender socialization is clearly understood and enforced in Saudi Arabia. While adolescent males may drive cars and move about freely, females are typically restricted to their homes unless shopping or attending school. In rural areas in particular, Saudi females seen unsupervised outside their homes are considered unchaste and bring a disgrace on themselves and their families.

Saudi Arabian society enforces the traditional female responsibilities of child care and household chores, but, in many cases, middle-class families have hired servants for these duties. The resulting circumstance is that Saudi adolescent females face strong pressures to adopt their culture's values and also have many hours with nothing to do.

It may surprise you that a very conservative country with deeply held religious values would permit VCRs at all. Well, VCRs are allowed in Saudi Arabia, and Saudi rental businesses make available video cassettes from all over the world. Adolescents indicate a preference for cassette films from India, Egypt, and the United States. One study disclosed that in Saudi Arabian cities, the highest users of VCRs are young, single females (Abuzinada, 1988).

What do we know about VCR use among rural Saudi Arabian adolescents? Are there gender differences in what adolescents prefer to watch? Do Saudi adolescents defy parents over videos they watch? Do Saudi adolescents think VCRs threaten their Saudi culture?

Abdellatif Al-Oofy and Drew McDaniel (1992) investigated the impact of VCR viewing on rural

this sense and in conjunction with other indicators, adolescence can be thought to begin when a young person begins to seriously invest him or herself in the popular youth music of the day" (Larson et al., 1989, p. 597).

Television Viewing and the Disappearance of Childhood Innocence
Relaxation of television censorship in the 1980s led to television images and program content that would have been prohibited earlier. The sexual content of television soap operas became increasingly more daring, and prime-time programs tested earlier limits with portrayals of sexual relationships and increasingly explicit violence.

Cable television has daily brought into homes motion pictures far more explicit and daring than network shows. Uncensored, R-rated films have become a common entertainment staple for children and early adolescents. During the month of March,

Saudi adolescents. They drew a random sample of 66 male and 34 female high school students in Saudi villages. The males were between 16 and 19 years old, and the females were between 15 and 18 years old.

The females were much more frequent VCR viewers than the male adolescents. The adolescent boys watched VCRs less than three hours a day, but the girls watched, on average, four hours daily, and many girls watched more than four hours a day. These daily viewing habits indicate Saudi adolescent females are heavy VCR viewers.

Saudi adolescent males and females also differed in the types of VCR programs preferred. Saudi boys preferred sports videos, whereas none of the girls liked sports videos. Saudi adolescent girls preferred romance films.

Nearly 60% of the females said they preferred videos from Egypt, and 24% preferred videos from India. Half of the males said they preferred videos from the United States, and one-third preferred videos from Egypt. Very few (9%) of the Saudi females preferred videos from the United States. These gender differences are intriguing because they indicate males prefer video programs from a Western culture, whereas females prefer videos from Middle Eastern and Indian cultures.

Al-Oofy and McDaniel (1992) found the Saudi girls are much less likely ($p < .001$) than the Saudi boys to indicate they watch videos against their parents' wishes. Over 71% of the males said they watched videos their parents had forbidden, whereas over 85% of the females said they followed their parents' restrictions on video viewing. These viewing habits of rural Saudi adolescents need to be compared to the viewing habits of their urban peers; 33% of urban adolescent males and 18% of females watched videos forbidden by their parents (such as thrillers and pornographic films). The only difference between rural and urban Saudi adolescents was the much higher percentage of rural adolescent males who defied their parents' restrictions on video use.

Finally, the rural adolescent females considered VCRs to be more of a threat to Saudi culture than did the males ($p < .011$). Half of the females and 20% of the males considered videos are a very strong danger to Saudi culture. The greatest concerns were over X-rated and R-rated films. (Al-Oofy & McDaniel, 1992).

1993, homes with cable television were able to watch such R-rated films as *Blood Games*, *Carnal Crimes*, *Cyborg*, *Exposure*, *The Hand that Rocks the Cradle*, and *Tough Guys Don't Dance*. According to a cable TV magazine, these films contain nudity, explicit language, violence (some graphic violence), strong sexual content, adult themes, and adult sexual themes *(The Cable Guide*, 1993). The images contained in such programs have a powerful impact on a child's imagination and serve to remove a child's innocence. However, exposure to these images certainly does not provide emotional maturity. College students tell me that because of television and video cassette films, their younger siblings are aware of topics they were ignorant of until late adolescence. What do the developmental consequences of these explicit images of violence, sex, and the degradation of women portend for this younger generation as it grows older?

My concern over this exposure of children and early adolescents to explicit violence and sex on television stems not only from an intuitive belief about the negative short-term effects such images induce. I am also persuaded by research on a related area—effects of long-term exposure to pornography—that suggest the R-rated films available on cable TV harm children's and adolescents' understandings of sexual relations and of women. Dolf Zillmann (1989) noted that exposure to pornography desensitizes male and female viewers' to victims of rape and increases beliefs that females are sexually insatiable. Long-term effects of exposure to this type of video material induces both males and females to consider "women as willing recipients of any male sexual urge . . . or as oversexed, highly promiscuous individuals" (Huston et al., 1992, p. 50).

Television and Socialization

Television programs affect adolescent understandings of gender roles, emotions, violent behavior, and sexuality. In this section, we look at each topic in turn.

Gender Roles and Television

One hypothesis claims that television programming contains sexist messages, and the more a person watches TV, the more the person will cultivate sexist views (Gerber, Gross, Morgan, & Signorielli, 1986). This idea is called the **cultivation hypothesis**. The cultivation hypothesis helps to explain research that indicates the most negative attitudes toward females are held by "girls who watched the most television" (Huston et al., 1992, p. 29).

Content analysis of television shows since the 1950s indicates that women have been portrayed as incompetent, dependent, valued for their looks, passive, helpless, and overly concerned with their appearances (Huston et al., 1992). More recently, female television characters have become more autonomous and work in nontraditional careers, such as law; many are shown living affluent lives.

Female characters on television may be shown to lead lives quite unlike the lives of most real women (Huston et al., 1992). Television mothers, for instance, seem unbothered by sex discrimination, child care, household chores, or finances. When we watched the "Cosby Show" at the height of its popularity, my wife and I wondered who cleaned that constantly immaculate house since both parents had full-time, demanding professional careers and the program never suggested the Huxtables had a maid. Not even the bathroom was ever dirty. The only messy place was the adolescent son's bedroom. With three or four teenagers, does that seem likely?

At least two groups of researchers have conducted longitudinal studies on the effects of television viewing on early adolescents' perceptions about gender roles (Morgan, 1982; Wroblewski & Huston, 1987). These studies have applied the cultivation hypothesis.

Michael Morgan (1982) studied 349 sixth through tenth grade students over a two-year period. The focus of the study was to determine the relationship between watching television and forming attitudes toward women who work. Most of the youths in the study (98%) were white, and slightly more than half (55%) were female.

The students were given a five-item true-false scale on sex-role stereotypes, with most items focusing on women in the workplace. A sample item is, "Women have just as much chance to get big and important jobs, but they just aren't interested" (Morgan, 1982, p. 949). Morgan (1982) considered responses *sexist* if they denied women are discriminated against, said women are less interested in success than men, and said women are happier being homemakers. The inventory was administered in both the fall and the spring. In addition to answering the sex-role scale, the students were asked to estimate how many hours a day they watch TV.

More sexism was noted in students who watched the most television. Among the girls, longer exposure to television was associated with the development of increasingly sexist views. For boys, television viewing did not correlate with changing views toward women and work, but initial sexism scores for boys were related to increased TV watching over the course of the study (Morgan, 1982).

In 1987, Morgan extended his research by conducting a longitudinal investigation of the sex-role attitudes, sex-role behaviors, and television viewing habits of 287 early adolescents. Fifty-three percent of the sample were male. All the adolescents were students in the eighth grade of a rural Minnesota school system, and most came from lower-middle-class families.

Morgan (1987) gathered data twice—once in the fall and once in the spring. He asked the adolescents how many hours they watched television after dinner and before bedtime. He also administered seven items about household chores, and for each item "asked if each was something only boys should do, only girls, or either boys or girls" (Morgan, 1987, p. 273). He asked which of the household chores they performed. The seven chores were washing the dishes, taking out the garbage, mowing the lawn, cleaning the house, making the bed, helping with house repairs, and cooking.

Morgan's (1987) results showed that the adolescents who watched the most television tended to endorse traditional male and female divisions of household chores. Television viewing did not relate to actual gender typing of chores performed, but over time, extensive TV viewing did lead to greater congruence between traditional sex-role attitudes and sex-role behaviors. Remarking on these two studies, Huston and her colleagues (1992) concluded the findings suggest adolescents who watch television programs a great deal also develop stereotyped beliefs and attitudes about sex.

Roberta Wroblewski and Huston (1987) studied sixty-five 10- to 13-year-olds to see whether their viewpoints about gender and occupations had been influenced by increased TV portrayals during the 1980s of women in occupations traditionally considered men's work. Thirty-five of the research subjects were male, 30 were female, and all subjects came from a small town in Kansas. The researchers obtained information about the early adolescents' knowledge of (a) traditionally masculine and feminine occupations, (b) television portrayals of occupations, and (c) real-life occupations infrequently seen on television shows. Examples of these three sets of occupations are provided in Table 10-1 on the following page.

The early adolescents indicated much more knowledge about televised occupations and occupations they see in real life than about occupations that the researchers

TABLE 10-1　**Occupations Categorized by Gender Typing and Predicted Source of Knowledge for an Early Adolescent**

	PREDICTED INFORMATION SOURCE		
GENDER TYPE	Real life	TV	Neither
Male	Mail carrier	Lawyer	Podiatrist
	Dentist	Private detective	Insurance sales
Female	School nurse	Model	Data entry clerk
	Cafeteria server	Secretary	Contralto

SOURCE: Adapted from "Televised Occupational Stereotypes and Their Effects on Early Adolescents: Are They Changing?" by R. Wroblewski and A. C. Huston, 1987, *Journal of Early Adolescence, 7,* p. 288.

had predicted would be unknown to the youths. The research participants considered the televised occupations more gender-typed than jobs in real life. They were more critical of male involvement in televised occupations that are traditionally feminine than they were about male involvement in such jobs in real life. They considered masculine jobs more prestigious than feminine jobs. The girls in the study "preferred masculine television occupations to feminine real life occupations" (Wroblewski & Huston, 1987, p. 295). Boys were quite critical of male participation in feminine occupations. The researchers concluded that television portrayals influence girls to reconsider socialized gender schemas toward masculine occupations they are familiar with, regardless of the source of their information.

Emotions and Television

Researchers have looked at three topics regarding television and emotions: (*a*) the influence of watching TV on emotions, (*b*) the influence of one's emotional state on TV programs a person selects to watch, and (*c*) the effects of TV on viewer beliefs and ideas about emotions (Huston et al., 1992). Let's look at each topic in turn.

The influence of watching TV on emotions.　Emotional responses to television include fear, anger, happiness, sadness, surprise, suspense, and boredom. According to evidence cited by Huston and her colleagues (1992), some affective responses to television can endure for weeks.

Television can arouse or dampen emotions. For instance, as children become older they become more physically aroused by romantic scenes on TV. Horror films and suspense films also increase arousal. However, some TV programming can dampen emotions; as a general example, consider the finding that adults who felt annoyed when they began watching programs unrelated to their feelings of irritation became more relaxed and less annoyed (Huston et al., 1992).

Emotional responses to television programs are closely associated with changes in cognitive development. What scares younger children (for instance, cartoon characters changing into monsters), does not scare older children because they realize the events are implausible. Older children become frightened by television portrayals of events that seem plausible to them, such as nuclear destruction.

Furthermore, empathic responses to a televised character's emotional state are clearly associated with the ability to take someone else's point of view (Huston et al., 1992). As you may recall, empathy means understanding another person's feelings and/or experiences. Empathic responses to a televised character's emotional state denote understanding what the character is feeling.

The influence of one's emotional state on TV programs a person selects to watch.   Zillmann (1982; Bryant & Zillmann, 1984; Zillmann, Herzel, & Medoff, 1980) has investigated whether people's emotional arousal influences their choices of programs to watch. He tests this by using laboratory conditions, such as different types of music, to induce negative, positive, or neutral affect and then permits his research subjects to choose to watch televised comedies, game shows, dramas, or nothing at all (Zillmann, 1982).

People who are bored turn to programs offering excitement, and people under stress look for programs offering relaxation (Zillmann, 1982). Individuals under extreme distress seem to not watch any television (Huston et al., 1992). What is not known about viewer choice of TV programs is the influence of unconscious motivations. A long body of scholarship has clearly linked emotions and the human unconscious; see Freud's work, in particular, such as his *New Introductory Lectures in Psychoanalysis* (Freud, 1933/1964).

The effects of TV on viewer beliefs and ideas about emotions.   Television shows provide extensive opportunities to learn about human emotions. These pro-

Adolescents experiencing new emotions of romance and sexual attraction may use television video cassettes to explore their feelings.

grams depict a wide variety of emotions, including anger, greed, grief, lust, surprise, happiness, sadness, and excitement. Viewers may learn to identify expressions of certain emotions, develop beliefs about the frequency with which certain emotions occur, and realize that certain emotions are related to specific situations. Huston and her colleagues stated television viewers may learn to "accept social expectations regarding emotional expressions and behavior and come to believe in certain models of emotional responsiveness, experience, expression, and behavior" (1992, p. 43).

Systematic research on the affective content of television programs—and of the portrayal of the consequences of emotions—is uncommon. Huston and her colleagues (1992) recommended that systematic studies be carried out to learn what emotions are portrayed, the circumstances in which TV characters experience these emotions, what happens once the emotions are expressed, and the social rules identified as governing expression of emotions. I suspect such research would show TV portrayals of emotions are one-dimensional and without enduring consequences. You seldom see portrayed the long-lasting effects of a life crisis or of grief over the death of a character in the show.

We do know, however, that television portrayals of emotions have considerable influence on adolescent development. We know from Bandura's (1973) research that observing televised behavior can have a profound impact on learning new behaviors. Adolescents experiencing new emotions of romance and sexual attraction can use television and video cassettes to explore these feeling, and can even use these filmed programs to vicariously act out their feelings. Adolescent interest in rock music videos and in soap operas exposes adolescents to vulgar portrayals of sexuality, to debasing sex-role stereotypes, and to fantasized versions of interpersonal relationships. The frequent use on TV programs of violence as a solution to problems may well condition adolescent viewers to violently resolve human conflicts in the real world. Killing and death occur frequently on television programs; seldom do you see a main character feeling remorse or grief over someone's death, and even less frequently do deaths have long-term impacts on characters in programs that air weekly. Do adolescent viewers learn from TV programs how to respond with nurturance and love to someone else, how to negotiate conflict nonviolently, or how to express the feelings of distress that grief brings?

Violence and Television

While I have devoted a whole chapter to violence and American adolescents, and in that chapter discuss television violence, I want to focus here on two topics not covered in Chapter 13. These topics are the content of televised violence and the callousness induced by viewing TV violence.

The content of television violence includes property destruction, personal assaults, war-related injuries and deaths, and mass killings. Some of the violence is real—as in the news shows about natural disasters or the Persian Gulf War—and some is staged—as in made-for-TV movies. Of alarm is that children's programming contains five to six times the number of violent acts as prime-time shows aimed at adults. By the time most American children leave elementary school, they will have seen on TV no less than 8,000 individuals murdered and more than

100,000 acts of violence (Huston et al., 1992). Before they become teenagers, American youths who are heavy TV viewers (those who watch more than four hours a day) will see on TV at least 200,000 acts of violence (Huston et al., 1992).

Because viewing televised violence and aggression is strongly associated with the development of attitudes that favor physical conflict to resolve problems, one can see the concerns over a generation of youths who have not only been raised on "Sesame Street" and "Mister Roger's Neighborhood" but have also witnessed a legion of violent characters on television solve their problems by violent means. Extensive evidence indicates that people exposed to television programs depicting violence in sexual contexts become insensitive to women and develop tolerance for rape and other sexual forms of violence (Huston et al., 1992).

Sexuality and Television

According to a Harris poll, the great majority of American adults are concerned about the influence of television on children's values and behavior (Harris and Associates, 1987). Sixty-seven percent said they thought television fosters adolescent sexual involvement, and most considered television a source of education about sexuality for adolescents. However, most adults thought television portrays sexuality unrealistically.

One longitudinal study investigated children's exposure to television programs with sexual content and sexual activity five years later (Peterson, Moore, & Furstenberg, 1984). Results indicated no significant relationship between viewing TV programs with sexual content around age 11 and sexual activity around age 16. Huston and her colleagues (1992) suggested that exposure to televised images of sexuality have muted effects, at most, and concluded there was no evidence to support the assertion that TV viewing during late middle childhood and early adolescence leads to sexual activity as an adolescent. However, they admit "there are no experimental studies . . . in which children or adolescents have been exposed to the explicit sexual depictions that often occur on pay-cable channels" (Huston et al., 1992, p. 48). Given the need for informed consent from parents for any research involving minors, it is doubtful such experimental research will ever be conducted in the United States.

We have been reviewing information about effects of television on emotions, attitudes toward violence, and attitudes toward sexuality. Another topic worthy of discussion is the impact of television on cognitive performance.

Television and Cognitive Performance   The subject of television and cognitive performance can be looked at from two perspectives: (*a*) the impact of watching television on intellectual development and (*b*) how viewers process television information. Let's look at each perspective in turn.

The Impact of Television on Intellectual Development

David Shaffer cites several studies negating claims that TV "deadens young minds or transforms children into social isolates" (1989, p. 603). It is true that children in

During the 1970s, an unusual opportunity presented itself to John Murray and Susan Kippax, two faculty members at Marquarie University in Sydney, Australia. They learned that a small Australian community, which previously had had no TV reception, was about to gain access to television. The researchers had the opportunity to analyze the impact of TV on individuals in the community if they could find similar communities which differed only in the extent of exposure to TV. They found three towns within fifty miles of each other. All had a population of around 2,500, and were quite similar in socioeconomic level and ethnic composition.

At the beginning of the study, the first town had had TV reception for five years, the second town was just getting TV reception, and the third town was not scheduled to gain access to TV signals for at least another year. The researchers referred to these communities as the High-TV town, the Low-TV town, and the No-TV town, respectively.

During the ensuing year, Murray and Kippax (1977, 1978) interviewed mothers, fathers, and children between the ages of 8 and 12. A total of 282 families participated in the interviews. A breakdown of who was interviewed in each town is provided in the accompanying table. A total of 404 adults and 128 children participated in the study.

The interviews occurred in the people's homes. The parents completed information about demographics and discussed their views about the uses of TV, their programming preferences, and their evaluation of TV and other media. The adults also kept a record of a full week of television viewing. The chil-

Town	Mothers	Fathers	Girls	Boys
High-TV	76	52	20	13
Low-TV	95	50	30	27
No-TV	79	52	13	25
Total	250	154	63	65

dren presented their ideas about the uses of TV, their evaluation of TV and other media, the reasons they watched TV, and how they spent their time.

Adults' Responses   In both the High-TV and Low-TV towns, mothers watched TV more than did the fathers ($p < .005$), and parents in the Low-TV town watched TV more frequently than parents in the High-TV town ($p < .001$). Parents in the Low-TV town preferred dramas, documentaries, and sports programs. The adults in the High-TV town preferred quiz shows.

Adult evaluations of the quality of television differed according to whether the respondent lived in the High-TV, Low-TV, or No-TV town. Parents in the No-TV community were much more likely than parents in the other towns to say television is interesting ($p < .01$) and exciting ($p < .001$). Murray and Kippax (1977) noted that parents in the High-TV town had the least positive attitudes toward television.

On the whole, the adults thought TV is capable of producing good effects. Adults in each community were convinced that TV increases knowledge of the news. In the No-TV town, parents said TV would increase family interaction and keep people off the streets, but the people with longer exposure to TV began reevaluating the consequences of TV. Once the novelty of TV wore off, people watched less than they

communities without television spend their time enjoying other entertainment, such as reading comics and listening to the radio, and, when television is introduced, "children simply substitute TV viewing for these other roughly equivalent forms of entertainment" (Shaffer, 1989, p. 603).

did in the beginning. Adults in the High-TV town considered radio more important than television.

During the week in which the adults kept a record of TV viewing, individuals with no access to TV spent more time than adults in the High-TV and Low-TV towns listening to the radio, reading, listening to music, visiting friends, and going to movies. Interest in hobbies and taking care of animals was highest in the High-TV town, and next highest in the Low-TV town.

Adults in the No-TV town considered television mostly offers entertainment, whereas their counterparts in the High-TV and Low-TV towns said television provides both entertainment and information.

Children's Responses Children in the High-TV town and in the Low-TV town watched television the same amount. Around 60% of children in each town watched three or more hours a day, 30% watched one to two hours daily, and only 10% watched less than one hour a day. The impact of TV viewing on children's use of other media was revealed by comparing the number of hours children in all three towns spent with media other than TV. Children in the No-TV town listened to the radio, listened to records, and read comic books much more than children in the other towns ($p < .001$). However, children in the High-TV town listened to the radio and to records more than the children in the Low-TV town. The researchers concluded that as the novelty of TV wears off, children return to other forms of entertainment.

The children thought television provides both information and entertainment. Children from the No-TV town most considered television is a form of entertainment. Children in the Low-TV town, whose teachers used the public television programs in their classrooms, were more likely to see television as a form of information.

Children in all three towns reacted to television positively. Around three-fourths thought TV is very enjoyable, and nearly the same proportion thought TV is very interesting. Around 63% considered TV very exciting. Murray and Kippax (1978) pointed out that the more exposure children had to TV, the less interest they expressed in it. For instance, two-thirds of the children in the High-TV town said they watch TV when they are bored, whereas only 39% of the children in the Low-TV town gave this response. As a confirmation of the default hypothesis, the children with more exposure to TV found viewing television loses its novelty and becomes an activity to turn to when nothing else is available.

How did the children in these towns spend their leisure time? Children in the towns with TV spent considerably more time playing with friends than children in the No-TV town. We've already mentioned that children without TV listened to the radio, listened to records, and read comic books more than the other children; they also went to see movies more than children in the two towns with television reception.

Murray and Kippax (1977, 1978) concluded that the impact of TV on children's social behavior produces a short-term decline until viewing television loses its novelty effect. Over time, children who have access to TV return to interacting with their friends, reading books, engaging in hobbies, and sitting around doing nothing.

There is evidence to support the assertion that television helps cognitive development—and there is evidence to support the counter-claim that it obstructs cognitive development. The researchers who maintain television helps cognitive development note that positive effects depend on what programs are watched

(Huston et al., 1992; Shaffer, 1989). Those who assert that television viewing obstructs cognitive development point out that children who watch TV have poorer reading skills and spend less time reading (Corteen & Williams, 1986). However, the preponderance of evidence supports counter-intuitive results—namely, watching television has long-term, significantly positive impacts on time spent reading (Morgan & Gross, 1982). Huston and her associates (1992) maintain that children can watch television and become good readers, depending on how much they practice reading and depending on their attitudes toward reading.

The evidence leads me to conclude that adolescent reading is not endangered by heavy viewing of television, but that reading comprehension may very well be imperilled. Michael Morgan and Larry Gross reported their surprise that "heavy viewers in early adolescence read more in later adolescence" (1982, p. 85). They tempered this positive finding with the concern that heavy viewers of television process "print content more superficially," and noted that "although adolescent heavy viewers may spend more hours reading, they certainly seem to be comprehending less" (Morgan & Gross, 1982, p. 85).

Effects of television on academic achievement are extremely difficult to measure. Various studies produce as a whole what researchers gently call "mixed results." Some studies show a positive correlation between TV viewing and academic achievement, some show a negative correlation, and others show no correlation. Significant influences in all these studies appear to be the viewer's IQ, gender, and age. Morgan and Gross (1982) noted that younger children and children with lower IQs actually seem to do better in school if they watch television; however, these researchers also pointed out that academic performance declines in older students and in students with higher IQs if they watch much television.

Huston and her colleagues (1992) concluded that the research on television viewing and academic performance pointed to no single effect. More than watching television is involved when youths do poorly or do well in school. One must also take into account the individual's desire to achieve, level of intelligence, and family system. The primary finding would appear to be that there is no single pattern to the effects of television viewing on academic performance.

How Viewers Process Televised Information

McLuhan (1964; McLuhan & Fiore, 1967) asserted that television technology had revolutionized the human central nervous system. He maintained that TV involves the whole human being. While McLuhan's notion that the medium is the message attracted many thinkers, finding how to test his assertions has been a very difficult challenge. The current opinion is that there is little, if any, evidence to support the thesis that television viewing produces enduring changes in cognitive processing.

McLuhan's assertion that television viewing is an active rather than passive activity has been shown in research. However, his belief that TV viewing is an all-involving activity has been challenged. Evidence shows that television viewing is a selective process of allocating attention to specific aspects of programs. Selective attention seems to be highly correlated with the viewer's noticing what

W. Andrew Collins (1982) termed *perceptually salient features*. What count as perceptually salient features clearly alter as individuals age. My 2-year-old daughter's joy at seeing Big Bird gave way to rapt attention as she grew older to cartoon characters, such as the Smurfs and Jem; now, as a 16-year-old, she pays attention to Oprah Winfrey.

Efforts to explain cognitive processing of television information make clear use of information-processing concepts and implicit use of Piagetian concepts. Collins (1982) has noted that how viewers process television information depends on skill in (*a*) paying attention to main program events, (*b*) organizing these events in orderly fashion, and (*c*) making inferences about causal relationships implied in the program.

Adults and adolescents have wider experiences and greater familiarity with living than children, and thus can draw on such "walk around" knowledge to understand television programs. Because much of what children watch on TV is intended for older audiences, they see programs that are basically incomprehensible to them. Prior to age 9 or 10, children lack the necessary cognitive skills and life experiences to comprehend TV programs intended for adults (Huston et al., 1992).

One vital cognitive-processing skill in comprehending television is **temporal integration** (Collins, 1979, 1982).This skill enables a viewer to infer associations linking different parts of a program. Skill in temporal integration increases with age. Whereas adolescents would understand the connection between scenes of a murder, an arrest, and a courtroom trial, children probably would not. Temporal integration is particularly needed when the connection of events is implied, rather than explicitly shown, and the viewer must infer characters' intentions. Huston and her colleagues give an excellent example: "When the camera cuts from a scene in which two people are dining in a romantic setting to a bedroom with the morning light shining in, children do not infer the intervening events well" (1992, p. 93).

CHAPTER SUMMARY

One of the most pervasive and significant influences in 20th century technology has been the advance of electronic media, particularly television. American adolescents are not the only group to feel the effects of TV, and there is some evidence that adolescent TV viewing actually dips a bit from the average hours preadolescents spend watching television daily.

Whether the impact of television has been as fundamental as the Canadian scholar Marshall McLuhan claimed is open to debate. He asserted that television has led to an extension of the human central nervous system and has produced a revolution in human cognitive processing. He also maintained critics who faulted TV for failing to live up to higher cultural standards mistakenly believed TV is no different than the print medium. While many thinkers have been attracted to McLuhan's analysis, researchers have found testing his ideas to be an elusive task.

Radio is one electronic medium that greatly interests adolescents. The primary reason adolescents listen to the radio is to hear music they enjoy. An examination of some of this music has led to a call for a ratings system similar to the one that the motion picture industry imposed on itself—plus accusations that such a ratings system amounts to censorship.

Two ideas offered to explain television viewing are the *default hypothesis* and the *displacement hypothesis*. The former idea states people watch TV for lack of anything else to do. The latter maintains TV viewing replaces more worthwhile activities, such as reading books.

Children's TV viewing increases to about three hours a day by the time they enter school. By the age of 12, TV viewing reaches an average of four hours daily and then slightly declines during early and middle adolescence.

Early adolescents spend increased time listening to the radio and learning the popular music of the day. There is some belief that a marker of the beginning of adolescence is a youth's serious investment in listening to music with peers.

Television socializes children and adolescents in at least four areas: gender roles, emotions, violent behavior, and sexuality. The more TV youths watch, the more likely they are to espouse traditional sex-role attitudes. This finding is particularly true for girls.

Television viewing can either dampen or arouse emotions. Emotional responses depend partly on cognitive ability to understand what is being portrayed. Younger children, for instance, become fearful when cartoon characters change into monsters, whereas older children realize these situations are implausible.

A person's affective state can influence the type of TV program he or she prefers to watch. Bored individuals turn to programs offering stimulation, and individuals under stress look for programs offering relaxation.

Many human emotions are portrayed on TV. Systematic research on the affective content of television programs and of the consequences of specific emotions, however, is sparse.

How TV programs portray emotions can provide social learning for viewers. Viewers learn to identify how emotions are expressed, develop beliefs about how frequently certain emotions are expressed, and identify the link between emotions and personal situations.

Both fictional and documentary TV programs portray considerable amounts of violence. Before leaving elementary school, the average American child will have witnessed at least 8,000 televised murders and over 100,000 other acts of violence. The more people are exposed to violence, the more disposed they are to accept violence as a normal coping response.

Most American adults believe TV fosters adolescent sexual activity and portrays human sexuality unrealistically. However, longitudinal studies do not confirm that watching TV influences adolescent sexual activity.

Debate rages over the impact of TV on cognitive performance. Overall, research results are mixed on this topic. Assertions that TV viewing leads to reduced time reading have not been confirmed, but there does seem evidence that heavy TV viewing negatively affects reading comprehension.

Viewing television does require cognitive-processing skills that allow the viewer to pay attention to salient program features. The viewer must be able to organize the multiple TV images into an order, and must make inferences about causal relationships implied in discrete images.

One vital cognitive-processing skill for watching TV is *temporal integration*. This skill enables a viewer to infer relations about program images that occur over the span of a program. This skill increases with age and experience.

CHAPTER 11

COPING WITH LIFE CRISES DURING ADOLESCENCE

CASE STUDY

An Adolescent with Diabetes

Laura is 23 years old. She grew up on a farm in northern Kansas and graduated from college two years ago. She worked in a hospital for one year and is now a residential hall supervisor for young, single mothers who are part of an employment training program. Laura has been diabetic since her preteen years.

"I was 9 when I developed diabetes. I had been ill—losing a lot of weight, very irritable—and wetting the bed. My mom got very concerned and took me to our family physician. She did some blood tests. This was during the school year, and I was competing in a track meet when they told me I had diabetes.

"I had just won the 100-yard dash, and a school nurse came out and pulled me off the field and said, 'You're really sick.' Then I saw my mom, and we all went to the doctor's office. Then my dad came in from farming in the field. The doctor told us I had diabetes, and she knew of a famous specialist she recommended I see. He was about a five-hour drive away. The doctor said we needed to leave right away, so they packed me up and told me to drink nothing but tea and water and to lie down on the trip.

"When we started the trip, my blood sugar was 618. Normal is below 180. Everyone was very nervous, and people were afraid I'd go into a diabetic coma on the trip. People at the diabetes clinic were surprised I hadn't gone into a coma by the time we arrived.

"During the trip, I kept asking, 'Mom, will I have to have shots?' I hated shots. Mom kept reassuring me I wouldn't have to have any. And then, of course, that's what they gave me. I think Mom feels a little guilty about that still. Now I give myself shots all the time, and they don't bother me.

"They started giving me insulin right away and kept me in the hospital for two weeks. Mom could stay with me the whole time.

"What I remember feeling, basically, was fear. And the fear grew the longer I was there, especially because of all the diabetics I saw who had complications. There were amputees, people on dialysis machines, people with severe nerve damage—all as a result of their diabetes—and all of them were older than me. They were adolescents or in their 20s.

"My physician kept saying I could lead a normal life as long as I managed my diabetes. I thought I was going to die. I was sure I was going to die. After about two weeks, they gave me enough confidence that I knew I could manage my illness.

"At first I took two shots a day—the first at 7 A.M. and the second at 6 P.M. I'd take insulin at 7 A.M., lie on the couch until 7:30, eat breakfast, and then go to school. Mom packed me snacks so that at 10:00, I could have a bit to eat (bread and peanut butter or apples and peanuts).

"It became important to me that other kids not know I ate these snacks. I always tried to hide it from the other kids because they thought I was getting special treatment. A lot said that to me.

"I did well until four years later when puberty set in. Definitely. Things were OK until 13, when puberty set in.

"I started rebelling against my disease as a young adolescent. I started eating candy. It made me really sick. The 'now satisfaction' of being an adolescent was all important to me. I felt invincible. I was so angry because I couldn't escape diabetes. I think in a way I was trying to kill myself. There were times I wouldn't take my shots. I would overeat.

"Controlling diabetes is very difficult. You must be in complete control of every bit of food you eat because of how food affects your blood sugar level. Your blood sugar is like your fuel system, like the gas that runs a car. I have to be sure that the food I'm eating will neither raise nor lower my blood sugar. I must do this every time I eat.

"If your blood sugar level is too high, the glucose level builds up and damages the capillaries of the blood supply. It literally eats away your body, so to speak. These are layman terms, not what a physician would say.

"If your blood sugar is too low, it is not as damaging, but it can kill you if it stays too low. But, usually, the liver will kick in to bring the glucose level back up when your blood sugar level gets too low.

"A normal blood sugar count is between 80 and 160. Or at least that is a safe range. Most of us start having reactions about 60 or below. I've had mine get as low as 32. When it gets low, I become very lethargic, start shaking a lot, feel hot and irritable—incredibly irritable—and feel very hungry. I become willing to eat anything.

"It was very difficult having diabetes during adolescence—dealing with hormones and emotions. Insulin is a hormone. I don't know what insulin does other than stabilize glucose levels, but I'm sure it does other things. It just seems logical that, as a hormone, insulin would have some other effects.

"As a teenager, I was running away from diabetes. I wanted to be part of the normal group. I didn't have enough self-confidence at that time to say, 'I'm a diabetic, and I can't have fries, hamburgers, a shake, and candy bars.'

"My parents were not going to allow me to go with anyone unless I told the person I was a diabetic. So, I lied to my parents. I'd wear my ID bracelet out the front door and then take it off. I did everything in my power to hide that I was a diabetic.

"I hated not having control. You feel like you lose control when you are diabetic. It becomes even worse when you are an adolescent.

"I was convinced everyone was thinking I had this special disease and, because of that, I was trying to convince everyone I was normal and could do anything. So I tried out for everything: cheerleading, volleyball, basketball, 4-H. I made all the varsity teams and was head cheerleader for the boys' sports.

"I never went into a coma during high school, despite all I did, and that amazes everyone. Me, too, when I look back on it. When I got to college, stress really hit more.

"Diabetes reacts to changes in stress. When I am stressed, my blood sugar level rises, which affects me physically, makes me feel ill. And that affects my mood, and I become real angry and bitter and negative.

"Now, I recognize these changes and try to find what is stressing me. I decide if I can change it, and if I can, I do. If I can't, I cry and let myself feel. I'll let myself feel the stress instead of packing it inside and denying it.

"The most important thing I've learned is to live day by day. Sometimes hour by hour. With diabetes, there are so many factors that come into play that I've had to let go of trying to be the perfect diabetic. That just created more stress for me. Diabetes is a stressor that never goes away. I've learned I'm not 'Diabetic Laura', but, rather, I'm Laura first and my diabetes is second. I have accepted I have diabetes, and now I control it. It no longer controls me.

"I have to plan ahead all the time. As I sit here, I have in my purse crackers, life savers, insulin, an extra syringe. You never know.

"A lot of people live moment to moment, and others don't know when they will have lunch. When I finish my midmorning snack, I think ahead to when I will have lunch and where I will be when I take my insulin. I now take four shots a day.

"I have to plan out my day. Most other people are moment to moment. That gets difficult in other areas of my life. I want all other areas to be planned. Like my career, my education. I let go by getting more control. I don't think I overdo this planning. I don't externalize it; I keep it a secret. I'm always prepared so that other people don't need to change their schedules.

"But, this is different than when I was 9 or an adolescent and not wanting others to know I am diabetic. I now tell people I am diabetic because their knowledge helps keep me on my regimen. Other people, I found out, care and will support me by not suggesting things I can't do. For instance, they won't offer me M&Ms or offer me a drink of their soda. Rather than suggest going to McDonald's for a Big Mac, they suggest having salads. Makes me feel they really care."

Laura's life is clearly affected by how she perceives her diabetes. She has developed numerous mechanisms and procedures for maintaining control over her life. In this effort, she has obtained the help of people in whom she confides. During her early and middle adolescent years, she notes she rebelled because diabetes had control of her. Laura recognizes the reality of her situation. She has a chronic disease that can kill her if conditions are just right. The presence of other stressful circumstances also contributes to changes in her diabetic condition. Later in this chapter, we look at the relationship between stressful life events and physical health. There ia a box devoted to life stress and the onset of diabetes.

We go now from this story of Laura and how her life has changed because she must cope with diabetes to the more general concept of what it means to cope with a life crisis. We begin with a discussion of why some experiences are considered crises.

The changes and transitions that mark adolescence provide the impetus for learning coping strategies. In earlier chapters, we discussed several of the significant life domains in which adolescents experience change: for instance, puberty, thinking capacities, social and moral perspectives, family interactions, and peer relations. Each of these developments, as we have seen, can create stress and demand effective coping skills.

In this chapter, the focus is on how adolescents cope with specific types of uncommon life crises. The types of crises to be reviewed do not represent normal markers of growth for adolescent development, nor do they represent transitions adolescents are expected to face in our society. Rather, they represent unexpected crises in adolescents' lives. The types of life events we investigate are (a) life as a runaway, (b) the divorce of one's parents, and (c) the deaths of parents, siblings, and friends. We also look at the relationship between stressful life events and physical health.

A MODEL TO UNDERSTAND COPING WITH LIFE CRISES

Crises involve major life transitions or very distressing situations. These experiences are crises for two reasons: (a) they threaten an individual's social and psychological balance, and (b) the person's typical coping responses prove inadequate to handle the situation. The paradox of life crises is that, while they pose a serious threat, they impel the development of new coping skills and may lead to greater growth and maturity (Baldwin, 1978; Bloom, 1977; Caplan, 1964; Parad, 1965). Offer and his associates (Offer, 1969; Offer and Offer, 1975) have noted that adolescents commonly adapt to family tragedies, such as a parent's death, by developing new cognitive skills and personal resources. However, crises do not come with a guarantee that the affected individual will respond adaptively. For these reasons, crises are considered "dangerous opportunities."

Rudolf Moos (1986; Moos & Schaefer, 1986) has developed an approach to understanding how individuals cope with life crises. He proposes that understanding the outcome of coping with a crisis involves the following aspects: background and personal factors, event-related factors, environmental factors, appraisal of the event, adaptive tasks, coping skills, and crisis outcome. The interplay of these aspects is presented in Figure 11.1.

A concern I have with the Moos model is that it seems to be pointing only in one direction; namely, toward the box in Figure 11.1 entitled "Outcome of event or transition." In the model, cognitive appraisal, adaptive tasks, and coping skills are the mediating factors whereby an individual can move from the background and personal factors, event-related factors, and environmental factors to some form of crisis resolution. However, the impact of resolving a specific crisis on adaptation to new situations remains overlooked. Outcomes of crises bode either good or ill for an individual and point to the future. I suggest adding a box denoting the individual's future with an arrow from the outcome box. This modification is portrayed in Figure 11.1.

Background and personal factors include gender, race, religious beliefs, temperament, and self-concept. **Event-related factors** are situation specific and would include, for instance, data on the extent to which the crisis was anticipated and the

FIGURE 11-1   A Model to Understand Coping with Life Crises

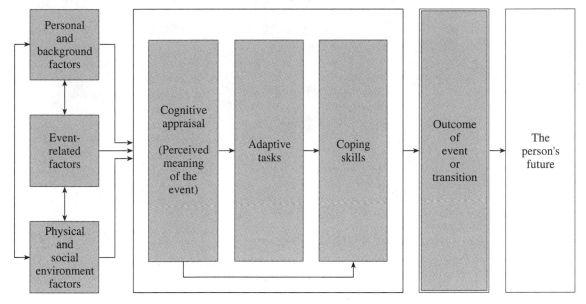

Time of event   Resources brought to or acquired during crisis

SOURCE: Adapted from "Life Transitions and Crises: A Conceptual Overview," by R. H. Moos and J. A. Schaefer. In R. H. Moos (Ed.), *Coping with Life Crises: An Integrated Approach*, pp. 1–28. Copyright © 1986 by Plenum Publishing. Reprinted by permission.

extent to which the individual is responsible for the crisis. **Environmental factors** include the quality and accessibility of family relationships, the availability of counseling, and the support of friends. These elements are present at the time of the event. **Cognitive appraisal** of a crisis is influenced by one's background and personal factors, event-related factors, and environmental factors. Cognitive appraisal triggers adaptive tasks and coping skills. The outcomes of a crisis are determined by the interaction of all these factors, the tasks of adaptation, and the various coping skills.

According to Moos (Moos & Schaefer, 1986), human beings employ five major **adaptive tasks** to cope with life crises. In the following presentation of the five major adaptive tasks, I use bereavement over a friend's death as an example to illustrate each task.

1. **Establish the meaning of the event and comprehend its personal significance.** The individual employs this task throughout crisis resolution. For instance, an adolescent faced with the death of friend must initially accept such a loss intellectually and, at later points, integrate the loss into a view of the world.

2. **Confront reality and respond to the situational requirements of the event.** This task is dictated by the event itself. For instance, an adolescent whose friend has died will make plans to attend the funeral and think about what to say to the friend's bereaved parents.

Coping includes such factors as race, religious beliefs, support of friends, and the extent to which the crisis was anticipated.

3. **Sustain interpersonal relations.** One of the fundamental lessons we have learned is that social support greatly assists individuals in mastering crises (Aneshensel & Frerichs, 1982; Balk, 1981, 1983a; Barrera, 1981; Barrett, 1978; Hirsch, 1980; Klass, 1988; Osterweis, Solomon, & Green, 1984; Silverman, 1975; Vachon, Sheldon, Lancee, Lyall, Rogers, & Freeman, 1980). An adolescent whose friend has died needs to sustain relationships with other friends and with family members in order to deal with the stress and confusion presented by such an event. There is little doubt that sharing one's feelings and thoughts and hearing other perspectives prove beneficial to someone coping with a significant loss.

4. **Maintain emotional balance.** Significant losses produce painful, unsettling feelings. The distress over the death of a friend can produce unexpected and intense emotional reactions. It is not uncommon for deaths of friends to leave adolescents overwhelmed with anger, confusion, fear, and perhaps even despair. A vital aspect of this adaptive task is to maintain some element of hope.

5. **Preserve a satisfactory self-concept and maintain a sense of self-efficacy.** Significant losses can shake an individual's self-confidence and threaten the person's self-image. Evidence suggests, however, that positive crisis resolution is intertwined with positive self-image (Balk, 1990b; Labouvie-Vief, Hakim-Larson, & Hobart, 1987; Petersen, 1988; Petersen & Hamburg, 1986). Thus, it is essential for individuals faced with crises to maintain a sense of personal control over events and belief in their abilities to influence outcomes. The death of a friend can shake an adolescent's sense of competency. At times, the grief adolescents feel is so intense and so long-lasting that they fear they will never regain any hope or balance in their lives. In fact, individuals who grieve acutely may begin to fear they are going crazy because of the intensity of their feelings.

In addition to these five adaptive tasks, Moos (Moos & Schaefer, 1986) identifies three domains of coping skills: appraisal-focused coping, problem-focused coping, and emotion-focused coping. **Appraisal-focused coping** involves the skills of logical analysis, mental preparation, cognitive redefinition, and cognitive avoidance or denial. **Problem-focused coping** involves the skills of seeking information and support, taking action, and identifying alternatives. **Emotion-focused coping** involves the skills of emotional control, emotional release, and emotional acceptance.

The linchpin of this model of coping is individual appraisal of the life crisis. We turn next to studies of some important influences on adolescent appraisal of life events.

Perceived Impact of Life Events During Adolescence: Influences of Gender, Ethnicity, and Exposure

The coping model followed in this chapter emphasizes the importance of cognitive appraisal of an event (Moos & Schaefer, 1986). Three researchers at UCLA tested whether adolescents' appraisals of life events are mediated by gender, ethnicity, or previous exposure to the events.

Michael Newcomb, George Huba, and Peter Bentler (1986) studied 1,018 high school students in Los Angeles. A plurality of the adolescents (42%) were in tenth grade, while approximately 37% were in the eleventh grade and 21% in the twelfth grade. Nearly two-thirds (65.7%) were female. The majority of participants (60%) were white, 18% were black, 15% were Hispanic, and 7% were Asian.

The adolescents completed a questionnaire about 39 life events. For each event, the adolescents indicated on a five-point scale ranging from very unhappy to very happy how they would feel if the event occurred to them. They also indicated whether they had experienced the event in the past 12 months and whether they had experienced the event more than 12 months ago.

Thirty-six of the 39 items grouped into clusters: family and parents, accidents and illness, sexuality, autonomy, relocation, deviancy, and distress. A sample item from each cluster is provided in Table 11-1.

Three of the 39 items did not group into any cluster. These items were "got religion," "met a teacher I liked," and "sibling moved out." At least on the face of

TABLE 11-1   Clusters of Life Events

Life Event Cluster	Item
Family and Parents	Parents argued or fought
Accidents and Illness	Death in the family
Sexuality	Fell in love
Autonomy	Got own stereo or TV
Relocation	Changed schools
Deviance	Trouble with the law
Distress	Ran away from home

SOURCE: Adapted from "Desirability of Various Life Change Events Among Adolescents: Effects of Exposure, Sex, Age, and Ethnicity" by M. D. Newcomb, G. J. Huba, and P. M. Bentler, 1986, *Journal of Research in Personality, 20,* pp. 212–213.

Age Differences in Coping with Distress

Examination of age differences in coping with stressful events across the life span have been obstructed by two alternative possibilities. One, age differences may represent real changes over time in how people cope with stressful life events. Second, age differences may occur because the types of stressful life events change over the life span.

A significant body of scholarship argues that coping skills deteriorate as people grow older and, in particular, asserts that elderly peoples' coping skills become more rigid and less responsive to the demands of situations (Chanowitz & Langer, 1981; Guttman, 1964, 1974; Langer & Benevento, 1978; Okun, 1976; Pfeiffer, 1977; Schultz, Hoyer, & Kay, 1980). In contrast, just as impressive a body of scholarship argues that coping skills show resiliency, novelty, adaptability, and flexibility as people age and learn from experience (Carpi & Elder, 1986; Cornelius & Caspi, 1987; Denney, 1982; Eysenck, 1983; Vaillant, 1977).

Karen Rook, David Dooley, and Ralph Catalano (1991) examined how individuals of different ages coped with the same type of life stressors in order to

remove the contradictions regarding changes in coping over the life span. They studied how people 18 years and older cope with financial stress. They chose financial stress because it is a problem people of all ages face. They also reasoned coping with financial problems provides indicators of how people handle other life stressors, such as interpersonal conflict.

Rook, Dooley, and Catalano's (1991) sample consisted of 8,376 individuals in the Los Angeles metropolitan area interviewed by phone. The subjects were selected randomly. The great majority of the interviews (93%) were conducted in English, and the remaining 7% in Spanish. The interviews were conducted over a period of four years. A total of 604 individuals randomly chosen from the total sample were recontacted three months after their first interviews.

The researchers restricted their analysis to the 388 people reinterviewed who were employed or were actively seeking work. This sample was 46% male and 54% female. Two-thirds of the sample were white. The age breakdown for the sample was 18 to

things, the last item looks to be a good fit for the family and parents cluster of life events.

After reviewing all the responses, Newcomb, Huba, and Bentler (1986) identified ten life events that would make the adolescents most happy. Eight of these items were from two clusters (sexuality and autonomy), and two items were from the group of items not part of a cluster. These ten items were:

- *fell in love* and *started dating* from the sexuality cluster,

- *started driving*, *got own stereo or TV*, *making own money*, *vacationed without parents*, *decided about college*, and *joined a club or group* from the autonomy cluster, and

- *met a teacher I liked* plus *got religion*, two of the three items not part of a life events cluster.

408

34 ($n = 195$), 35 to 59 ($n = 158$), and 60 and older ($n = 35$). They chose these age ranges to remain consistent with earlier studies.

Rook, Dooley, and Catalano (1991) gathered data on two categories of coping behaviors: problem-focused coping and emotion-focused coping. Younger respondents (18- to 34-year-olds) were significantly more likely than the other age-groups to have employed both problem-focused coping (such as cutting back on expenses and seeking a better paying job) and emotion-focused coping (such as expecting a better standard of living would come). The middle-aged workers (35- to 59-year-olds) significantly differed with the older workers on one problem-focused strategy: efforts to improve their job situations.

Middle-aged workers were more likely than the younger workers to become depressed when using some problem-focused coping skills, especially cutting back on expenses. Younger workers who tried to increase their funds by borrowing money or refinancing a loan reported more depression than other age-groups.

Overall, Rook, Dooley, and Catalano (1991) made three major conclusions.

- Younger people use coping strategies much more distinctive than strategies tried by middle-aged and older workers. For example, they reduce their expenses and try to get better jobs.

- Coping strategies that benefit middle-aged workers, such as borrowing money or simply waiting out the difficulty, leave younger workers feeling depressed, whereas other coping strategies that benefit younger workers, such as cutting back on spending money, leave middle-aged workers depressed.

- Older workers seem more immune to common financial stressors that hit the younger and middle-aged workers. However, the relatively small sample size of the older workers made the researchers hesitate to draw many conclusion about this age-group (Rook et al., 1991).

Gender differences were pronounced. Females had more extreme perceptions of events than males. That is to say, when the adolescents considered events undesirable, females considered them more undesirable than did males. Conversely, when events were perceived to be desirable, "the significant differences were all in the direction of the females perceiving the events as more desirable than the males" (Newcomb et al., 1986, p. 214). Females perceived the autonomy events as much more desirable than the males, while on all other clusters, "females' perceptions were significantly more undesirable than the males'" (Newcomb et al., 1986, p. 214).

Although the males and females perceived the impact of events differently, they identified the same events as the ones with greatest impact. That is, there was a significant correlation ($p < .001$) between the rank order of events given by the males and females. What this means is that, while they differed in their perceptions of how desirable or how undesirable events are, the males and the females reached a high degree of consensus about the rank order of the events themselves.

Whites, Asians, and Hispanics did not differ in their perceptions of any of the life event clusters. However, ethnic/racial differences were pronounced between the black adolescents and the other groups of students. Specifically, Hispanics and blacks differed in their perceptions of distress, deviance, and relocation life events. Black adolescents viewed distress and deviance events more negatively than did Hispanics, and viewed relocation more positively than did Hispanics. Asians and blacks differed in their perceptions of family and parent events, relocation events, and distress events. Black adolescents considered family and parent and relocation events more positively than did the Asians, whereas they viewed distress events more negatively than Asians. Blacks and whites differed in their perceptions of four clusters of life events: autonomy, relocation, deviance, and distress. Blacks considered autonomy and relocation events produce more happiness than whites, and perceived distress and deviance events produce more unhappiness than did whites (Newcomb et al., 1986).

Newcomb, Huba, and Bentler (1986) speculated that the blacks' differences with the other ethnic/racial groups' perceptions emerged from the life experiences these groups have in American society. Specifically, they assert that "moving is more associated with upward social mobility for Blacks and the more negative reactions to Deviance and Distress events may be because greater penalties are handed out by society for such 'transgressions' committed by Blacks" (Newcomb et al., 1986 p. 224).

When they considered exposure to events, Newcomb, Huba, and Bentler (1986) discovered that adolescents who had experienced an event viewed it more positively than adolescents who had not experienced the event. This influence of exposure was true in nearly every case. The experienced adolescents even gave desirable ratings to a few events that the inexperienced rated undesirable. These life events came from more than one cluster and, specifically, involved the remarriage of a parent, a parent's changing jobs, the loss of virginity, gaining new friends, going to therapy, and stealing something valuable.

How does the Moos model help us understand adolescent coping with life crises? The model will prove helpful only if it can accommodate the experiences of adolescents as they grapple with significant, traumatic events. The power of the model is tested by assessing whether it remains true to adolescents' experiences when a significant loss is being examined.

We can get an idea of an event-related factor when talking to an adolescent who feels responsible for a friend's death because she believes that she should have driven him home when he had been drinking. When we learn an adolescent's family has a history of self-disclosure and emotional closeness, we have some evidence of environmental factors. We can also see if the types of adaptation and coping employed to deal with specific kinds of losses match the adaptive tasks and coping skills identified by Moos (Moos & Schaefer, 1986).

In the rest of this chapter, we examine specific types of life crises experienced by adolescents. As you read these sections, see if the Moos model helps you understand how adolescents cope with these crises. We begin with significant losses in an adolescent's life.

SIGNIFICANT LOSSES IN AN ADOLESCENT'S LIFE

Loss and separation are part of development, indeed, part of human existence (Havighurst, 1952; LaGrand, 1986). Patricia Weenolsen (1988) maintains that adolescents necessarily experience losses as their physical and cognitive developments lead to changes in self-concept, loss of childhood innocence and dependency, and the emergence of increased autonomy and responsibility.

Much of socialization in this country is directed toward enabling an individual to develop a sense of separateness and autonomy (Bloom-Feshbach, Bloom-Feshbach, & Associates, 1987; Erikson, 1963, 1968; Kaplan, 1987). Gilligan (1982), of course, as we have seen in earlier chapters, has argued strongly that emphasis on autonomy and separation dismisses the value of and considerable investment in intimacy and cooperation manifested in female development.

Social patterns in our country reinforce the expectations of autonomy and separateness presented in Erikson's model of psychosocial development. Several expected separations, with their implied gains in autonomy, mark development from childhood through late adolescence. For example, we expect initial separation from home around age 5 or 6, when a child goes to kindergarten, separation from the security of self-contained classrooms around age 12 or 13, when an early adolescent enters a middle-school or a junior high school, and separation from one's family of origin around age 18 or 19, when a youth goes to college, enlists in the armed forces, marries, and/or joins the workforce.

These types of separations are associated with expected losses. They are part of **normal developmental transitions**, and a child or adolescent who adjusts poorly to them is a cause for some concern (Blackham & Silberman, 1975; Chess & Thomas, 1984; Rutter, 1975). Intervention methods can be employed to assist children and adolescents to cope well with these expected transitions (Danish & D'Augelli, 1980; Danish, Smyer, & Nowak, 1980).

A common view in the field of adolescent development is that normal developmental transitions, coupled with management of **unexpected losses** (events such as the death of a friend or theft of a valued possession), prepare individuals to handle other losses in their lives. In other words, one would expect that developmental transitions and unexpected losses prepare adolescents to cope with separations that produce irrevocable losses, which are not part of the expected developmental process, and which critically tax already mastered coping skills.

In the crises we study in this chapter, adolescents suffer irrevocable losses and are introduced to the excruciating pain of grief. These losses basically say to the individuals, "Whether you are ready to cope with this life crisis is not up for negotiation. You have no choice." The life crises we study are (*a*) life as a runaway, (*b*) parental divorce, and (*c*) death and bereavement.

COPING WITH LIFE AS A RUNAWAY

Times have changed our perspectives about the incidence and prevalence of adolescent runaways. In 1974, Derek Miller argued running away from home is extremely rare except among American youths. It is important to dispel this notion that ado-

Youths who gravitate to the streets have been robbed of their childhoods and exist without any vision of an open future.

lescents in other cultures do not respond to life pressures by running away. In the 1980s, articles appeared about runaways in Canada, England, Hungary, India, and the Soviet Union (Chockalingham, 1983; Grynaeusz & Pressing, 1986; Hartman, Burgess, & McCormack, 1987; Howe, Burgess, & McCormack, 1987; Kufeldt & Nimmo, 1987; McMullen, 1986; Oustimenko, 1984; Singh, 1984). Our focus here is on adolescent runaways in the United States.

Running away can take various forms, ranging from being absent over night without parental permission to striking out on one's own with the realization people at home would not be glad if you returned (Kimmel & Weiner, 1985). Official police reports of runaways (that is, police reports of arrests of youths whose crime is "running away") suggest somewhat less than 160,000 adolescents run away each year (Kimmel & Weiner, 1985). Many experts estimate that the true number of runaways each year in this country ranges between 500,000 and 1,000,000 (Adams & Gullotta, 1983; Kimmel & Weiner, 1985; Schiamberg, 1988). F. Ivan Nye and Craig Edelbrock (1980) have estimated that before they reach 18, one in eight adolescents (12.5%) will have run away as a response to distress in their lives.

My interest in this section is youths who gravitate to the streets, mobilized by rage, the products of disintegrating, impoverished communities (Lefkowitz, 1987; Leighton, 1959). These youths have grown up with chronic fear of being abandoned; they have been robbed of their childhoods and exist without any visions of an open future (Lefkowitz, 1987). They have lost hope. They present cases of **learned helplessness**, youths whose socialization has taught them that their efforts will have no effect on producing outcomes they desire (Balk, 1983d; Dweck, 1978; Dweck & Elliot, 1983; Seligman, 1975). Their running away from home is a desperate act to rewrite their life stories (Lefkowitz, 1987).

Running away is seen by some writers as a healthy response to dreadful life circumstances. Gerald Adams and Thomas Gullotta (1983), for instance, acknow-

Running Away in Preindustrial Cultures, Particularly the Hopi

Studies in preindustrial societies indicate females are more likely than males to run away from home to escape difficulties, usually to escape consequences of antisocial behavior. Another common reason adolescents run away is to escape from the burdens of adult responsibilities. Sometimes, the adolescent runs away to escape shame over doing poorly in adult roles and responsibilities.

Alice Schlegel, a professor of anthropology at the University of Arizona, indicated Hopi boys commonly hide overnight from parents (Schlegel & Barry, 1991). Schlegel also noted that by adolescence, Hopi males are given such an extreme freedom of movement that running away is no longer a possible behavior. Hopi adolescent males can stay away from home when they wish, and, thus, they can escape family conflicts and tensions easily without resorting to the dramatic gesture of running away.

Hopi adolescent females are not given the freedom of movement allowed adolescent males. Staying away from home overnight is seen as run-ning away when the females don't have their parent's permission. The trigger for Hopi adolescent females to run away is typically conflict with their mothers over restrictions on their freedom. Hopi females run to a place of refuge, however, and not to the urban streets mainstream American runaways turn to. The Hopi adolescent female typically runs to a female relative, who helps the runaway calm down and encourages her to return home once everyone's anger is dissipated.

Unlike the adolescent runaway from the majority American culture, whose running has been preceded by a history of chronic ill feelings and distrust between the adolescent and parents, running away in preindustrial cultures is a short-term response to an immediate situation. Seldom do runaways in preindustrial societies fail to return home after a short time. Unlike the modern day American adolescent who runs away into danger and anonymity, the preindustrial adolescent runs away to a friendly refuge and returns once adult anger at home diminishes (Schlegel & Barry, 1991).

ledge that running away can present a healthy coping response to intolerable home circumstances and can signify considerable insight about a troubled family. We take up these views later in the section about personal maladjustment of runaways.

I want to dispel any romantic illusions about the situations these runaway youths have experienced or their prospects once they are on their own on the street. What they are often leaving are continual messages that they do not matter; they get this from their families, their schools, and their surroundings. What they are often going to is chaos and anarchy.

Without the nurturance and support of stable families and communities, these youths never develop hope, senses of mastery and self-efficacy, and senses of achievement and competency. These youths come from families and, perhaps, communities that are best described as *socially disorganized* and *disintegrating* (Leighton, 1959). Family conflict and parental mistreatment have marked their development (Garbarino, Wilson, & Garbarino, 1986). Their personal coping styles are characterized by maladjustment (Adams & Gullotta, 1983). Let us look at each of these primary factors that contribute to runaway behavior in these youths.

Socially Disorganized, Disintegrating Communities

Several years ago, Alexander Leighton directed a remarkable study about the emergence of psychiatric disorders in certain sociocultural environments (Hughes, Tremblay, Rapoport, & Leighton, 1960; Leighton, 1959; Leighton, Harding, Macklin, Macmillan, & Leighton, 1963). The investigators studied communities in Nova Scotia, Canada marked by various **indicators of social disintegration** (extreme poverty, high frequency of broken homes, widespread ill health, high frequency of juvenile delinquency, and high frequency of hostility). Leighton and his associates persuasively demonstrated a significant contrast between stable and unstable communities in the development of psychiatric disorders in the population. Social disintegration was shown to be a major influence in the development of mental illness.

A significant contribution from the Leighton project (sometimes referred to as *the Stirling County study*) is the hypothesis that certain essential strivings mark human personality. Leighton (1959) postulated that disintegrating, unstable communities frustrate individuals from achieving these strivings. The **essential human strivings** are (*a*) physical security, (*b*) sexual satisfaction, (*c*) the expression of hostility, (*d*) the expression of love, (*e*) the securing of love, (*f*) the securing of recognition, (*g*) the expression of creativity, (*h*) orientation in terms of one's place in society and the places of others, (*i*) the securing and maintaining of membership in a definite human group, and (*j*) a sense of belonging to a moral order (Leighton, 1959).

The relative importance of the strivings (Leighton also refers to them as *human sentiments*) varies at different points in one's life. Take, as an example, the essential human sentiment to secure recognition. The worth and the importance of types of recognition will differ markedly for a 6-year-old girl whose teacher puts a happy face on her spelling paper and the same person at age 17 who earns a National Merit Scholarship.

When the sociocultural environments of runaway youths are considered, it is apparent that attaining most, if not all, of these essential strivings is frustrated. Hostility is expressed freely, but not in any constructive manner. Random murder and assault are common, as are physical and sexual abuse at home and gang fights in the streets; life is often at the mercy of uncaring strangers. Some of the youths belong to gangs, and in this way have secured membership in a definite human group. For most, the moral order is dominated by a cynicism and hopelessness and a notion that human existence is "nasty, brutish and short" (Hobbes, 1651/1960, p. 82). School has become a place of torment and futility, rather than an environment giving recognition for achievement and encouraging expressions of creativity. Runaways have learned from experience that their survival is of little consequence to other people.

Family Conflict

At least 80% of runaways leave home due to family conflict between the parents and the adolescents, as well as between the parents themselves (Adams & Gullotta, 1983; Schiamberg, 1988). Parenting styles, discussed in Chapter 6, are relevant here; many runaways were raised by authoritarian or laissez-faire parents and dysfunctional family communication is common in runaways' lives (Adams & Gullotta, 1983; Loeb, Burke, & Boglarsky, 1986).

Ineffective communication between parents and adolescents is a significant factor prompting adolescents to run away from home (Adams & Gullotta, 1983; Caton, 1986; Kimmel & Weiner, 1985; Garbarino et al., 1986; Schiamberg, 1988). Estrangement marks the family relationships. The adolescents see their parents as unwilling to listen and understand, and the parents consider their adolescents as untrustworthy, disobedient, and disrespectful. Conflict-resolution skills are poorly developed in these families (Farber, Kinast, McCoard, & Falkner, 1984), and disagreements over such topics as clothes and curfew hours escalate into major battles (Schiamberg, 1988). The fear of abandonment mentioned by Lefkowitz (1987) reveals itself in family uncertainty over roles, hesitancy with self-disclosure, concern over becoming vulnerable, and fear of rejection (Adams & Gullotta, 1983). Fear of rejection paralyzes relations between parents and their adolescents, engenders family conflict, and eventually induces the adolescent to run away (Gullotta, 1979; Spillane-Greco, 1984a, 1984b). The Circumplex Model discussed in Chapter 6 would identify these families as "chaotically disengaged."

Parental Mistreatment

Chronic mistreatment from parents is a common part of most runaways' histories. Douglas Kimmel and Irving Weiner (1985) report that the majority of runaway youths living in New York City emergency shelters mention being physically abused by their parents. Runaways report sexual abuse as another reason for running away from home (Gullotta, 1979; James, Burgess, & McCormack, 1987; Leigh, 1986; Schiamberg, 1988). National survey statistics confirm that parental mistreatment is a chief contributing cause leading adolescents to run (Garbarino et al., 1986).

Echoing the conclusion mentioned earlier that running away from these circumstances represents a sign of health, Mimi Silbert and Ayala Pines (1981, cited in Garbarino, Wilson, & Garbarino, 1986) posit that running away offers a way out of an impossible situation. Coping successfully with what faces runaways once they are on the street is not assured, however, regardless of how healthy and adaptive their acts of running away may have been (Weisberg, 1985).

Personal Maladjustment

Psychological comparisons of runaways to youths who do not run away disclose several types of dysfunctional or even pathological behaviors typical of runaways. Suicidal threats, vandalism, and truancy are associated more with runaways than with other youths (Schiamberg, 1988). In comparison to other youths, runaways exhibit greater defensiveness, more anxiety, and less impulse control (Leigh, 1986). Runaways also exhibit a host of problems, such as alcohol abuse, less favorable self-concepts, depression, poorly developed interpersonal skills, few friends, and feelings of inferiority (Garbarino et al., 1986). Adams and Gullotta (1983) cite several psychological studies that portray runaway youths as severely maladjusted, hostile, dependent, impulsive, and suffering from serious personality disorders, such as schizophrenia.

Caution should be used in drawing conclusions about the personal maladjustment of runaways. Many of the psychological studies focus on youths diagnosed as disturbed or adjudicated as delinquent before they ran away. Sampling problems arise because the studies exclude from the sample psychologically adjusted youths who are runaways.

A large body of sociological scholarship contradicts the conclusion that runaways are personally maladjusted. The sociological literature depicts running away as an adaptive response to life pressures and a form of excitement. While balancing the psychological interpretations with these sociological views, Adams and Gullotta (1983) note that sampling problems characterize the sociological literature because it overlooks runaways in treatment or correctional institutions (runaways with adjustment problems). Citing national survey and in-depth interview data reported in 1976, Adams and Gullotta conclude that a typical runaway has poor peer relationships, low academic goals, poor self-concept, and difficulties relating with parents and teachers. However, Adams and Gullotta do not conclude from these findings that runaways are seriously disturbed but, rather, that their living skills are deficient.

Running Away as a Coping Strategy

As a response to an intolerable situation, running away may be adaptive. As a step toward reconstructing a life, running away fits with some of the adaptive tasks and coping skills mentioned by Moos and Schaefer, (1986)—for instance, understanding the personal significance of the event, logically appraising the situation, and dealing with the reality of the situation.

But what resources do runaways have to deal with the environments they run to? What are the prospects that these youths will engage other adaptive tasks or sets of coping skills needed to master the crisis? There should be no illusions that being on their own on the street has done anything other than introduce a new series of crises into runaways' lives. The future for a runaway youth is bleak.

One consequence of running away is increased likelihood of committing criminal acts (Adams and Gullotta, 1983; Schiamberg, 1988). To survive on the street, runaways may sell drugs, become prostitutes, or steal, all behaviors the youths did not engage in before running away.

Youths who live on the street want work. The prospects of employment, however, are dismal for these youths, particularly if they are not white. As Lefkowitz notes,

> Out of work, out of school, often out of their homes, an estimated 1.4 million young men and women, most in their late teens and early twenties, drift. When they do manage to latch onto a job, it's often temporary, rarely pays more than the minimum wage, and infrequently offers a full week's work. The argument is often advanced that if minority youngsters can be persuaded to return to school and earn their diplomas, they will have a much better shot at getting a job with some promise. The kids know better. All they have to do is look at their friends who did stick it out, who did graduate. The unemployment rate of 1983 black high school graduates was 37.5 percent, as against a 23.5 percent unemployment rate for white high school dropouts. With such bleak prospects, it is not a stunning surprise to find that one-third of young inner-city black males in a national survey say they have a better chance of supporting themselves through crime than in the legitimate job market [emphasis in the original] (From *Tough Change*: *Growing*

The clearest empirical evidence of coping responses among these youths is provided by Lefkowitz (1987), who mentions that some turn to social support and some
specifically ask others for help. However, experiences have taught most of these runaway youths to expect nothing of benefit from adults. These youths must rely on some
outside intervention in the form of programs that overcome the barriers of race and
social class. In short, they must trust someone else to help them. Surprisingly, many of
these youths are still hoping to find someone they can trust (Lefkowitz, 1987).

COPING WITH FAMILY DISRUPTION AND DISCORD

We now turn our attention from running away from dysfunctional homes to a look
at the crises adolescents face in disruptive homes. The divorce rate in the United
States tells us the prevalence of family disruption and discord in this century. Almost
every college class has a significant minority of students whose parents have
divorced.

Demographic information suggests that divorce rates have been increasing since
the late 1950s, so that by the 1980s, one divorce occurred for every 2.04 marriages
(Adams & Gullotta, 1989; Hacker, 1983). Anthony Jurich and Wesley C. Jones
(1986) suggest that census data indicate a slowing down of divorce, but these
authors agree that the number of divorces in the United States remains high, as do
the number of families and the number of children affected by divorce.

One-third to one-half of adolescents in this country are affected by parental
divorce (Jurich & Jones, 1986). A large proportion of children growing up in the
1990s (69.2%) are doing so in single-parent families or in stepfamilies (Bureau of
the Census, 1991b). It is estimated that for all white children born in 1980, 38% will
live in single-parent households before they are 16 years old, and for all black children, 75% will be members of such families by age 16 (Adams & Gullotta, 1989).

A common outcome of parental divorce is that children live in a single-parent
home without a father. E. Mavis Hetherington and her associates (1972; Hetherington, Cox & Cox, 1982; Hetherington & Deur, 1971) have reported noticeable differences in the social behavior of girls and boys who grew up in a home without a
father. For instance, boys exhibit some difficulties with gender-role identification
prior to adolescence, but by their adolescent years, most boys have learned socially
accepted gender roles. A different pattern of influence is seen in girls, however.
Problematic effects on girls begin to emerge during adolescence and early adulthood. Most girls from father-absent homes begin dating and engage in sexual intercourse earlier than other girls. In addition, girls in father-absent homes exhibit
tension and insecurity when interacting with males, express low self-esteem, perceive scant control over influencing their lives, and as young adults, are less happy
in their marriages than their father-present counterparts.

David Reinhard (1977, cited in Adams & Gullotta, 1989) reports that few adolescents, even though unhappy that the divorce occurred, express negative feelings

about their parents' decisions. Robert Weiss, in fact, quotes as typical these words of a 17-year-old male, who said, "In the long run—I feel sort of like I shouldn't say it—but a lot of kids are better off if their parents do get divorced" (1986, p. 73).

Coping Tasks When Parents Divorce

Judith Wallerstein (1986) presents six tasks that children of divorce must accomplish. She followed 131 children from 60 divorced families. She studied the children at the time of the divorce, 18 months later, 5 years after the divorce, and again 10 years after the divorce. The tasks are Wallerstein's synthesis of how the children coped.

The first task is to *acknowledge the reality of the marital rupture*, a task akin to establishing the meaning and understanding the personal significance of the situation and confronting reality and responding to the requirements of the external situation in the Moos model (Moos & Schaefer, 1986). This task was accomplished by Wallerstein's subjects within the first year of the divorce.

The second task is to *disengage from parental conflict and return to customary activities*. Problem-focused and emotion-focused coping skills, such as studying hard at school and spending time with friends, enable adolescents to accomplish Wallerstein's second task. Most of the children in Wallerstein's study accomplished this task within the first 12 to 18 months following the divorce.

The third task is to *resolve the loss*; this task is usually the hardest task to accomplish. A considerable source of help in accomplishing this task is social support from friends and regular visits between the child and the noncustodial parent. Such actions serve to sustain interpersonal relationships. Wallerstein (1986) noted it takes many years for the child to absorb the loss and come to terms with the changes the divorce imposes on self-esteem, family roles, and self-efficacy.

The fourth task is to *resolve anger and self-blame*. Wallerstein (1986) notes that children are unlikely to accept the idea of a "no-fault divorce," are likely to attribute blame to one or both parents, and are very likely to harbor feelings of anger and self-blame for several years. The new perspectives that come with changes in adolescent social reasoning provide the means to resolve the anger and blame directed toward parents and self regarding the divorce. Jurich and Jones (1986) note that adolescents often respond with protest, particularly angry protest, to parental separation and divorce, and arguments over custody and confusion about loyalty can leave adolescents moody and irritable, seeming to themselves to be unable to control their emotions. Two coping strategies that apply here are **cognitive redefinition** (gaining a different perspective on the crisis) and **emotional release** (expressing one's feelings) (Moos & Schaefer, 1986).

Task five is to *accept the permanence of the divorce*. Unlike death, the divorce can be undone, and children typically invoke a fantasy that their parents will remarry (Wallerstein, 1986). Adolescents seem more capable than children of relinquishing the "restoration fantasy" that their parents will reunite. The first two adaptive tasks presented by Moos and Schaefer (1986)—establish the meaning of the event and comprehend its personal significance, and confront reality and respond to the situational requirements of the event—apply to accepting the permanence of the divorce.

The sixth task is to *achieve realistic hope regarding relationships*. An integral part of this task for a youth is achieving a realistic vision of his or her ability to love and be loved. Such a task becomes complex for an adolescent faced with the normal developmental tasks of forming an identity and entering into intimate friendships. Moos's adaptive task of preserving a satisfactory self-concept and maintaining a sense of self-efficacy applies to Wallerstein's sixth task (Moos & Schaefer, 1986).

Wallerstein (1986) notes that only long-term follow-up studies will reveal how well children of divorce accomplish the sixth task. Her preliminary results were not promising regarding long-term effects on personal development (Wallerstein, Corbin, & Lewis, 1988). Interpersonal troubles characterized the lives of young adults who were raised as children of divorce. Many of her subjects appeared to be drifting, were suspicious of interpersonal commitments, and demonstrated serious long-term developmental consequences as a result of their parents' divorce.

Increased Sense of Responsibility and Maturity

Weiss (1986) investigated the experiences of adolescents growing up in single-parent households. He noted that the single mothers delegate to their adolescents new responsibilities, particularly the care of younger children. These adolescents became aware of financial pressures and their parents' feelings of insecurity because both parents tended to confide in them after the divorce. The adolescents viewed with pride their abilities to handle adult worries and concerns, and saw themselves as much more mature than peers from two-parent homes. On the other hand, there was a wistfulness to their perceptions of their maturity; they regret that, in comparison to their friends, they had been given less time to remain dependent on their parents. Weiss concludes that parental divorce produces unexpected demands for autonomy and responsibility that teenagers can fulfill; coping with parental divorce "may lead to growth . . . . which leads to self-esteem, independence, and a genuine sense of competence" (Weiss, 1986, p. 73).

Economic Impacts of Parental Divorce

A considerable effect of divorce is the downward economic mobility imposed on single-parent households, particularly those headed by females (Bureau of the Census, 1991a; Jurich & Jones, 1986; Parish, 1987; Schiamberg, 1988). Jurich and Jones (1986) posit that early, middle, and late adolescents respond quite differently to the effects of less money. Early adolescents respond most negatively of the three age-groups because they are influenced most by peer pressures to value status achieved through what money can buy; wearing the "right" clothing, for example. Middle adolescents cope better than early adolescents because they typically have developed social networks more intimate than available to early adolescents and are therefore able to find alternative outlets to money (Jurich & Jones, 1986). Late adolescents fare best with the economic strains imposed on single-parent households; many in this age-group assume earning power for the family by entering the workforce, sometimes at the cost of delaying or foregoing plans for high school graduation or entrance to college.

Social support provides the key factor in adjusting to parental divorce. On this point, researchers seem in clear agreement (Haviland & Scarborough, 1981; Hetherington et al., 1976; Jurich & Jones, 1986; Lutz, 1983; Visher & Visher, 1979; Wallerstein, 1986;

Wallerstein & Kelly, 1974). The link between this research finding and Moos's third adaptive task of sustaining interpersonal relationships may be obvious.

In short, divorce proves traumatic for both children and adolescents. Of great concern are the interpersonal difficulties late adolescents of divorced parents exhibit. There is some gain in increased maturity because they have to grow up faster than their peers. Economic hardships almost always attend mothers and their children following a divorce.

Family disruption by divorce is becoming a more common adolescent crisis. It is likely that coping with divorce is more common in the lives of adolescents than coping with the death of a parent, sibling, or friend. We turn next to adolescent experiences with death and bereavement.

COPING WITH DEATH AND BEREAVEMENT

Coping with death and bereavement challenges more adolescents than many people apparently realize. The distress and destabilizing effects of grief present not only severe challenges to coping but also serious obstacles to managing the psychosocial transitions that mark adolescence. Indeed, a monograph on bereavement published by the National Institute of Medicine characterized bereavement as a serious risk to health and identified adolescents as a particularly vulnerable population (Osterweis et al., 1984).

A body of scholarship pertaining to adolescent grief experiences began to emerge in 1981. Articles have appeared in disparate sources and have focused on such topics as reactions to a parent's death, a sibling's death, and an adolescent's impending death due to a terminal illness. Little research attention has been given to adolescent reactions to a friend's death. On the whole, interest in adolescent bereavement has not caught the attention of the mainstream of adolescence researchers. In the early 1990s, a special issue of *Journal of Adolescent Research* was devoted to death and adolescent bereavement.

The nonnormative aspect of death and bereavement during adolescence may explain the apparent lack of interest in this topic. Difficulties dealing with death may offer another explanation. It is certainly clear that interest in identity formation and in the sexual behavior of teenagers is far more prominent in the adolescent research literature than interest in teenage bereavement; however, given the growing concern over adolescent vulnerability to sexually transmitted diseases and to the increased likelihood of teenagers' contracting AIDS, the prelude to more research on bereavement among adolescents and young adults may be in our midst.

Death and grief are more common experiences for adolescents than adults have acknowledged. The sharp rise in adolescent deaths due to automobile accidents accounts partially for the increased incidence of adolescent familiarity with grief. The increasing incidence of adolescent suicides provides another bit of evidence that adolescents are more familiar with grief than adults have acknowledged. Over 30% of a representative sample of Kansas State University undergraduates reported the death of a close friend or family member within the preceding 12 months (Balk, 1990a); these findings were met, at first, with astonishment by some campus administrators, but have been replicated in subsequent investigations (Balk, 1991a) and corroborated by other campus sources (for example, the Dean of Student Life, the University Counseling Services, and the Religious Activities Coordinator). Louis LaGrand's (1981, 1986) survey of college undergraduates in the state of New York also indicated that experience with death is not as rare among late adolescents as we might like to believe.

Bereavement produces intense and enduring emotional stress which outsiders seldom appreciate (Balk, 1981; Osterweis et al., 1984; Silver & Wortman, 1980). Bereavement impacts many areas of an individual's life, for instance, self-concept and identity formation, interpersonal relations, schoolwork, family involvement, and overall psychological well-being. Bereavement presents adolescents with an extremely serious life crisis at a time when their development is marked by significant physical, cognitive, moral, interpersonal, and psychosocial transitions. Bereavement can impair successful completion of developmental tasks and present obstacles to what otherwise would have been normal transitions to young adulthood. For instance, the psychiatrist Robert Pynoos, an international authority on trauma in childhood, remarked on the impact of bereavement on a very bright high school senior, whose grades plummeted in the aftermath of a sibling's death, whose admission to a prestigious university was thereby denied, and whose career aspirations were forestalled (personal communication, December 12, 1988). As Dr. Pynoos noted, this case exemplifies the types of consequences for adolescents who experience bereavement at critical points in their development.

Adolescent bereavement researchers commonly present findings about personality, self-concept, ability to converse about the death, crying, effects on family and friends, various emotional responses, use of social support, and/or effects on school work. Scant attention has been paid to religion as a means of coping with bereavement during adolescence. In addition, the impact of a friend's death has yet to be investigated thoroughly, few measures have been developed to gather data on the effects of bereavement, and very little longitudinal research has been conducted.

Coping With a Parent's Death

One of the developmental tasks of adolescence is forging an identity separate from one's parents, and fulfilling this task involves gaining autonomy and independence (Erikson, 1968). Researchers have developed a keen interest in the quality of separation occurring in late adolescence, the association between separation and parenting styles, and the relation between identity status and separation (Bell, Avery, Jenkins, Feld, & Schoenrock, 1985; Campbell, Adams, & Dobson, 1984; Marcia, 1980; Moore, 1984, 1987; Sullivan & Sullivan, 1980; Waterman, 1982).

While bereavement researchers seem unanimous that parental grief over a child's death is unparalleled in intensity and duration (Cook & Oltjenbruns, 1989; DeSpelder & Strickland, 1987; Klass, 1988; Raphael, 1983), the death of a parent creates excruciating anguish for an adolescent. The anguish is complicated by tensions over the developmental crisis of dependency versus autonomy that marks adolescent-parent relations (Crook & Eliot, 1980; McNeil, 1989; Raphael, 1983). Parental death is considered the most significant loss an adolescent can experience (Raphael, 1983).

Patricia Murphy's (1986-1987) research with college students who had experienced the death of a parent indicated adolescents who report fewer grief responses to their parents' deaths also report greater feelings of loneliness and lower self-esteem. Murphy inferred that issues of unresolved grief were interfering in the lives of these late adolescents. Counseling and clinical psychologists as well as pastoral counselors on the Kansas State University campus have mentioned that unresolved bereavement often emerges as a primary reason students seek professional help from university counseling staff (Fallon, personal communication, May 22, 1988; Newton, personal communication, February 20, 1989; Wilander, personal communication, May 24, 1988). Rachel Aubrey (1977) and Debra Floerchinger (1991) drew attention to the same phenomenon in their separate reviews of students seeking help at university counseling centers.

Ross Gray (1987a, 1987b) studied 50 adolescents between the ages of 12 and 19 who had experienced a parent's death. The majority of his research participants were female (68%), the deaths had occurred, on the average, 28.6 months prior to the study, and the average age of the participants when the parents died was 14.9. All the deaths had occurred during the participants' adolescence.

Gray used several data-gathering approaches: the Beck Depression Inventory (BDI), an instrument to measure depression (Beck, 1967); the Imaginary Audience Scale, an instrument to measure sensitivity to the perceptions of others (Elkind & Bowen, 1979); a measure of informal support; the Differential Diagnostic Technique (DDT), an instrument to measure personality development in terms of three categories: aggression/ independence, passivity/dependence, and a personality balanced between these first two categories (Weininger, 1986); and an in-depth interview.

The scores of Gray's (1987a, 1987b) participants on the BDI were higher than depression scores reported for nonbereaved American high school students; these results are suggestive of the overall effect of parental death on feelings of depression in adolescents. Gray (1987b) acknowledged that, lacking a control group of nonbereaved adolescents, conclusions about his sample must be made with caution.

Perceptions of social support significantly differentiated depression scores of the bereaved adolescents. Participants who reported low social support had much higher BDI scores than adolescents whose social support was perceived to be high. Furthermore, depression scores were significantly lower for the adolescents who indicated they held religious or spiritual beliefs. Adolescents whose personalities were characterized as balanced had lower scores on the Imaginary Audience Scale in contrast to adolescents characterized as aggressive/ independent.

Gray (1987b) uncovered significant findings regarding school performance and the age of the bereaved adolescents. Average grades dropped much more for adolescents 15 years old and under who had lost a parent. Gray (1987b) noted that changes in cognition during early adolescence may be obstructed when the youth is coping with a traumatic loss. Other researchers have noted that cognitive functions sometimes regress temporarily during bereavement (Furman, 1974; Raphael, 1983). Of concern for adolescent development is whether interference with cognitive development during early adolescence can be overcome later. Should recovery of the lost ground not occur, the implications for overall development become obvious, not only in the area of academic pursuits but also in emotional development, moral reasoning, social perspective taking, and even career opportunities.

The amount of time elapsed since the parent's death did not differentiate responses given by the adolescents. Balk (1981, 1983a) reported the same findings in his study of adolescent responses to sibling death. However, Hogan (1988) noted in her study of adolescent sibling bereavement that changes could be identified when two time periods were selected for making comparisons: the first 18 months after the death and more than 18 months after the death. Like Balk's and Gray's studies, Hogan's study was **retrospective** (subjects were asked to remember past events), not longitudinal, and thus their findings about effects of time on adolescent bereavement reactions may apply to changes in memory as much as to verifiable changes in mourning.

As discussed in the section on coping with parents' divorce, adolescent females in fatherless homes exhibit awkwardness toward males and engage in promiscuous behavior with males (Hetherington, 1972; Hetherington et al., 1982; Hetherington & Deur, 1971). Elyce Wakerman (1984) appeals to Hetherington's findings to explain the reactions of adolescent females whose fathers have died; she notes that these girls fall in love later than girls living with biological fathers or stepfathers. They also tend to idealize their deceased fathers. For instance, Wakerman found that girls whose fathers had died were much more likely than girls from divorced parents to describe their fathers as warm, loving, special, and tender. They were also much less likely to see their deceased fathers as indifferent, weak, and irresponsible. Divorced fathers took much criticism and measured up very poorly to the image of the deceased fathers (Wakerman, 1984).

Roberta Goodman (1986) studied 30 adolescents following the death of a parent. She interviewed the adolescent and the surviving parent separately and in private. No adolescent in Goodman's study was in psychiatric treatment; Goodman wanted to focus on the grief reactions of normal adolescents, an approach followed by other researchers of adolescent grief (Balk, 1981; Gray, 1987a, 1987b; Hogan, 1987) and recommended by earlier investigators of childhood mourning (Cain, Fast, & Erickson, 1964). Focusing solely on individuals in clinical treatment presents sampling biases unless the researcher intends to generalize findings to other individuals in clinical treatment.

Goodman's (1986) subjects reported physical complaints, changes in school attendance and academic performance, and alterations in sleeping and eating habits. The adolescents and their surviving parents held similar expectations about normal signs of mourning, and these expectations matched what the adolescents reported about their actual grief reactions. Support from the surviving parent proved to be valuable in resolving grief, as did talking with peers and with other individuals whose parents had died. These positive findings about social support from peers were not replicated in Gray's (1987a, 1987b, 1988) research. On the whole, Goodman's findings are more unqualifiedly optimistic regarding the bereavement process and outcomes than are the findings reported by other researchers.

Coping With a Sibling's Death

In the United States, sibling death presents an adolescent with an unexpected life crisis. Although mortality rates rise during the teenage years, adolescents in this country are not expected to cope with the death of a sibling. As stated above, recent studies conducted at Kansas State University and with college students in the state of New York have indicated that experience with death is far more common among college undergraduates than many adults realize (Balk, 1990, 1991a; LaGrand, 1981, 1986); still, the death of a sibling is much less common than the deaths of parents, grandparents, or friends.

The atypical aspect of sibling death during adolescence may account for the phenomenon that, when a family is grieving the death of a child, adolescent siblings become forgotten mourners. This is not to say adolescents are more forgotten than younger children during a family's time of grief; it is seemingly the case, however, that society accords the extraordinary pain of parental grief more credence and compassion than the pain of sibling grief. Perhaps some people believe mourning is beyond the realm of possibility when the individual is not yet an adult.

Adolescents bereaved over a sibling's death resemble their nonbereaved counterparts on measures of self-concept (Balk, 1981, 1983a; Hogan, 1987; Hogan & Balk, 1989; Morawetz, 1982). In their longitudinal study of adolescent reactions to sibling death, Mary Guerriero and Stephen Fleming (1985) found that in the first year of their study, bereaved adolescents' self-concepts were healthier than the self-concepts of nonbereaved adolescents. Although these differences did not hold over time, the self-concept scores of the bereaved youths never dipped lower than the scores of the nonbereaved adolescents.

Emotional responses of adolescents grieving siblings' deaths become intense and apparently diminish over time, but a lingering sense of grief manifests itself in confusion, depression, anger, and guilt (Balk, 1981, 1983a). One bereaved adolescent said, "My emotions were confused. Sometimes I'd cry a lot and then at other times, I'd just sit around and not feel anything. I wasn't happy but I wasn't sad. I still feel confused because I don't know answers—and about my emotions, like one minute I'll be happy and I'm kind of like my mom, someone will say something about Phil and she won't be in a good mood any longer, and she'll go downhill" (Balk, 1981, p. 285).

Guerriero and Fleming (1985) reported that depression was high initially for bereaved adolescents but did not remain high over time. By the third year of bereavement, their subjects' depression scores on a standardized instrument resembled the depression scores of nonbereaved adolescents. [Balk (1981, 1983a) found depression in bereaved adolescents persists.] The differences between Guerriero and Fleming's findings and those of Balk are possibly due to their different data-gathering methods; Balk used retrospective self-reports, which asked participants to remember earlier experiences, and Guerriero and Fleming used a standardized instrument administered several times in a follow-up study.

Guerriero and Fleming (1985) speculated that the responses of their adolescent subjects may have been influenced by their uniformly stable home conditions. Family communication and emotional closeness (called **family coherency**) significantly differentiate bereavement responses of adolescents following a sibling's death

(Balk, 1981, 1983a). In families marked by emotional closeness and personal communication between family members, bereaved teenagers are left feeling shocked, numb, lonely, and afraid after their siblings die; over time, the adolescents share their feelings with other family members and report an enduring sense of depression, but no longer report feeling afraid, lonely, or numb. Confusion and guilt about the deaths are practically nonexistent for these teenagers. In families marked by emotional distance and sparse personal communication, bereaved adolescents report they initially feel guilty and angry, but are unlikely to feel shocked, numb, afraid, or lonely. Over time, these adolescents report feeling confused about their siblings' deaths and report a sense of relief that the ordeal of grief is over (Balk, 1983a).

Mothers' views of their bereaved teenagers' self-concepts and grief reactions significantly differ with the views of the teenagers and with the views held by fathers regarding the teenagers. The fathers' views of their teenagers' self-concepts and grief reactions fundamentally agree with what teenagers report about themselves (Hogan & Balk, 1989). These findings are controversial; other researchers have reported a greater congruence between the reports of mothers and their adolescents and less congruence between the reports of fathers and their adolescents (Demo, Small, & Savin-Williams, 1987). In addition, mothers are expected to understand their children better than fathers because children are more likely to engage in self-disclosure with their mothers than with their fathers.

Religion took on increasing importance for many of the bereaved adolescents whom Balk (1981, 1991c) studied, but this turn to religion occurred only after considerable questioning of and anger toward God. For instance, one adolescent said, "At times religion didn't help me at all. It does at times now. You know, the way they explain about heaven and that. It sounds like a nice place for him" (Balk, 1981, p. 298).

LaGrand (1986) concluded that some bereaved college students build acceptance of their losses on a foundation of religious belief. In his study of adolescents bereaved over the death of a parent, Gray (1987a, 1987b) reported that teenagers with religious beliefs scored significantly lower on the Beck Depression Inventory than teenagers without religious beliefs. Religion and religious beliefs also play a noticeable part in resolution of sibling grief (Balk, 1981, 1991c).

The evidence seems clear that religious beliefs interact with the process of adolescent mourning. It would be imprudent to infer that adolescent bereavement resolution favors the religious believer. As of now, the evidence indicates that specific bereavement reactions differentiate religious from nonreligious teenagers. For example, after the death, the religious teenagers report more confusion, whereas the other teenagers report more depression and fear. Current evidence also indicates religious belief does not necessarily make coping with a sibling's death any easier (Balk, 1991c). An excellent effort at synthesizing the role of religion in human coping has been initiated by Kenneth Pargament and his associates (Ensing & Meerdink, 1988; Pargament, 1988a, 1988b; Reilly & Falgout, 1988; VanderMeulen & Warren, 1988). A review of religion in the lives of bereaved adolescents is available in a chapter by Balk and Hogan (in press).

Gender differences distinguish adolescents' bereavement reactions. As time elapses, females are more likely than males to report feeling confused about their siblings' deaths. Females older than the sibling who died are less likely to feel shocked in the first few weeks following the death than are other adolescents. Males older than the sibling who died are more inclined than other adolescents to feel afraid in the first few weeks following the death (Balk, 1981, 1983a).

Grades and study habits are noticeably affected following a sibling's death, with a decrease in both reported by a significant proportion of bereaved adolescents (Balk, 1981, 1983a, 1983b, 1983c; Hogan, 1987). Bereaved adolescents report trouble concentrating on schoolwork. As one adolescent said, "I didn't put as much importance on my studying. I wouldn't say like it really affected me like I didn't want to study or anything, but I think I probably was not as motivated. I studied less. I just had so much on my mind. I was busy thinking about myself and thinking about everything I was going through. I didn't feel like I had to study. I guess I thought I kind of had an excuse" (Balk, 1981, p. 294).

Over time, grades and study habits return to normal for most teenagers, but not for all. The return of grades and study habits to normalcy seems most attributable to the teenager's acceptance that personal goals and achievements are expected despite the deaths of their siblings; it is not as clear why academic interests and skills remain below previous standards for a minority of teenagers (Balk, 1981, 1983a, 1983b, 1983c).

In Guerriero and Fleming's (1985) study, physical health deteriorated over time for bereaved adolescents and remained different than the physical health of non-bereaved adolescent controls over a four-year period. Bereaved adolescents consistently reported more symptoms; furthermore, bereaved adolescent females had poorer indices of physical health following sibling death and had greater death anxiety than males (Guerriero & Fleming, 1985).

Coping With a Friend's Death

Intimacy with peers, manifest as emotional investment in and caring for the lives of a few other youths, marks the development of many adolescents. These changes in peer relations influence and are influenced by changes in social and moral reasoning, and they provide many of the environmental conditions for adolescents to overcome the egocentrism of the adolescent years. In Chapter 7, we discussed peer relations in detail.

Given the significance of friends in the lives of adolescents, it is surprising that so little research has been conducted on the reactions of adolescents to the death of a friend. The paucity of research is doubly perplexing considering the incidence of violent deaths from accidents, suicide, and murder that accompany adolescent risk taking. Many adolescents will know a peer who dies, will be deeply affected by the death, and, yet, will be less likely to be seen as bereaved because bereavement for family members is more readily recognized (Raphael, 1983). LaGrand (1985) refers to adolescents bereaved over a friend's death as *forgotten grievers*. In the same vein, Fred Sklar and Shirley Hartley (1987, 1990) describe bereaved friends as a *hidden population*.

At least three identifiable subgroups make up this hidden population of bereaved friends: (*a*) the elderly, (*b*) adult dyads analogous to marital partnerships, and (*c*) adolescents and young adults. Sklar and Hartley (1987) obtained data from open-ended interviews with college students and from essays written by members of a mutual support group. The authors concluded that bereavement over a friend's death closely parallels the mourning process experienced over the death of a family member.

In Balk's (1990a, 1991a) survey work with college undergraduates, he found many of the youths knew a close friend who had died during the college student's middle adolescent years. Over 30% of the sample reported that a close friend had died within the preceding 12 months, and over 45% reported the death of a close friend within the past two years. Ellen Zinner (1985) and LaGrand (1981, 1986) have documented the need for colleges and universities to respond directly to student deaths and student bereavement.

One response to bereavement on the college campus is the **Death Response Team** (**DRT**) initiated at the University of Minnesota (Rickgarn, 1987). The objective of the DRT is to provide trained volunteers capable of delivering educational and therapeutic services to student groups after the death of a student. Among services provided are group facilitation, follow-up consultation, and referrals for individuals who need counseling. The DRT is composed of staff members of the counseling center and the mental health clinic on campus. Ralph Rickgarn (1987) notes that some institutions with limited professional resources would need to provide training for DRT team members about grief reactions and grief interventions; team members in these institutions would be faculty, local clergy, students, and community residents.

In summary, a mounting body of scholarship paying attention to death and adolescent bereavement has emerged. Researchers have studied several topics, primarily, emotional responses with peers, relationships with family members, self-concept, schoolwork, and physical health. Implicit in all this scholarly attention is the finding that adolescents are more acquainted with grief over a death than commonly acknowledged.

STRESSFUL LIFE EVENTS AND PHYSICAL HEALTH: VULNERABILITY TO INJURY AND DISEASE

We shift now to the links between stressful life events and vulnerability to injury and disease. First, I want to explore the phenomenon of stress. Then, we will discuss life events that act as stressors in adolescence.

The Concept of Stress   The term **stress** has two unusual aspects: how old it is and how imprecisely it is used. The *Oxford English Dictionary* (OED) traces the word *stress* back to 14th-century English. By the 14th century, the word had already acquired several different meanings:

- a stimulus—what we now call a *stressor*—that is, something that provokes a stress response,

- a force requiring change of one's adaptive capabilities—what we now call *strain*,

- a mental state—what we now call the *experience of being distressed*, and

- a physical reaction or response—what we now refer to as the *general adaptation syndrome* (Seyle, 1982).

Michael Rutter (1983) gives an excellent overview of this material.

Today, there are literally thousands of research studies that focus on stress. But, as Mason said in a review of research on stress, "the single most remarkable historical fact concerning the term *stress* is its persistent, widespread usage in biology and medicine in spite of almost chaotic disagreement over its definition" (1975, p. 6).

Rutter (1983) asks why, given the ambiguity surrounding the concept of stress, is there such an immense outpouring of scientific interest in it. Two reasons seem plausible. First, the concept draws our attention to phenomena that are important and interesting. Second, despite the ambiguity of the concept, no agreement has been reached on what term will provide an unequivocal replacement for the word *stress*.

Some life events produce distressed reactions. Already in this chapter, we have looked at some primary examples of such life events—parental divorce and running away from home, for instance. I want to review a specific model of viewing stress—namely, Hans Seyle's (1982) general adaptation syndrome—and then discuss the role of life events as instrumental in producing a stress response in adolescents.

Seyle's General Adaptation Syndrome

Seyle was a noted researcher who investigated the effects of stress on animals. From his observations of animal responses to continued exposure to noxious stimuli, Seyle (1982) devised his concept of a **general adaptation syndrome** (**GAS**). Let's look at what Seyle said occurs when a living organism experiences stress.

First, there is an **alarm stage**. The animal detects the presence of stress and attempts to eliminate it. If these attempts fail, then the second stage occurs.

Second, there is a **resistance stage**. The body makes all-out efforts to fight the stress. A good example is the body's immune system attempting to fight off a massive infection. If resistance efforts fail, then the organism succumbs to the third stage.

Third, there is the **exhaustion stage**. The body's coping efforts to resist have failed, the stress persists, and strain on the organism increases to the point of exhaustion.

Stress, Distress, and Eustress

Often what we mean by the term *stress* is the reaction to a painful or noxious stimuli. Examples are getting a speeding ticket, getting into a fight with a close friend, or realizing you have lost all of your keys. We call such a reaction **distress**.

Seyle (1982) has brought to our attention the fact that some stimuli demand a response, but, rather than being noxious or unpleasant, these stimuli are energizing and pleasant and experienced as very positive. He calls such stimuli **eustress**. Examples are hearing a profoundly moving piece of music; Beethoven's *Ninth Symphony* has this affect on some people. Other examples are spending time with a close friend you have not seen for a long time, or reconciling with a loved one after a nasty fight.

We know that all individuals do not respond to the same types of events with the same stress reactions. Some people find distressing what others perceive as neutral or eustressing. Speaking before a group of people terrifies some individuals, is just a matter-of-fact experience for other people, and is a thrilling experience for others. I recall the reaction of one member of our university's basketball team when given the chance to shoot free throws when his team was behind by one point and there was no time left on the clock. He delighted in these situations and, while I doubt he would have used the term *eustress* to describe his reaction, clearly such situations energized him. For other players, such a situation presents only dread, and one imagined that they wanted to be as far away from the free-throw line as possible in these circumstances. Actually, it is hard to imagine someone as competitive as a college basketball player feeling neutral over such an experience.

For some time, stress research with humans overlooked the critical role of perception of events in determining what a situation means to an individual. For instance, Thomas Holmes and Richard Rahe (1967) developed a list of 43 life events considered to produce different amounts of stress for an individual. The top 3 life events on the list are death of a spouse, divorce, and marital separation, followed by such events as being sentenced to jail, experiencing personal injury or illness, and getting married. Each event was given a set value of the life change units the situation would demand; for instance, death of a spouse was given the highest value of 100, and getting married was assigned 50. The extent of adjustment expected in someone's life is calculated by adding up the value of the life change units in the person's recent schedule of events.

One concern with this approach is that it ignores personal interpretation of the event. It is as though the item "shooting free throws with no time left on the clock" was considered to require the same number of life change units no matter who was shooting the free throws. James Johnson (1986) has attempted to overcome this problem.

Johnson (1986) produced a 46-item life events checklist to assess the amount of stress in children's and adolescents' lives. Examples of items on the list are moving to a new home, experiencing the divorce of one's parents, making the honor roll, and getting your own car. Johnson provided a needed refinement to earlier approaches that ignore the personal appraisal of an event. In Johnson's approach, the adolescent is asked to indicate for each event that has occurred over the past 12 months (*a*) whether it was a good or bad event and (*b*) what impact it had on the adolescent (no effect, some effect, moderate effect, or great effect).

Most approaches in stress research with youths have not used the refinements introduced by Johnson (1986). Much more common is a form of the Holmes and Rahe (1967) approach. The most influential approach is that of R. Dean Coddington (1972a, 1972b), who produced a life events scale for identifying the role of stressful life events in the onset of childhood diseases.

The logic of Coddington's scale is that various life events require a differing degree of adjustment. He started with the assumption that, on an adjustment scale of 1 to 1,000, the birth of a sibling would be a 500. He quantified the amount of adjustment each event required in terms of a youth's age. He asked over 200 experts in child and adolescent development to rate all other events on the list in terms of their relationships to the birth of a sibling. The value finally given for each life event on the list was calculated by computing the average score of all his key informants and dividing the scores by 10 (Coddington, 1972b). The higher the score, the greater adjustment demanded by the event.

Coddington (1972a) formed bases for age-graded criterion scores by obtaining data from 3,256 children and adolescents. Table 11-2 presents values for several of the items on the Coddington list. As you review the table, note that in almost all cases, more is required of junior high school students (early adolescents) than of any other age-group in childhood or adolescence.

Research grounded in Coddington's approach has led to definitive conclusions about several relationships. First, a positive relationship exists between life stress and the frequency of accidents in children's lives. Research has also shown a positive relationship between the cumulative effects of life changes and the presence of a range of physical problems, such as rheumatoid arthritis, abdominal pains, and respiratory illnesses. Increases in life stress are positively related to increases in health problems of youths with chronic illnesses, and the presence of life changes is positively related to a variety of general indicators of illness, such as visits to a physician and number of school days missed due to illness.

Overall, the research suggests a positive relationship between cumulative life changes and a youth's physical health status. Such findings are consistent with research conducted on adults (Cohen, 1979; Lazarus, 1978). However, because the research is **correlational**—it identifies associations or relationships that exist between phenomena—we are not certain about the exact nature of the relationship between life changes and the health status of youths. It is often tempting to interpret correlational research as disclosing causes and effects when what it actually discloses is that variables are related, but not necessarily in a cause and effect manner.

TABLE 11-2   Adjustment Demanded of Four Age-Groups When Specific Life Events Occur

	AGE-GROUP			
LIFE EVENT	PRESCHOOL	ELEMENTARY SCHOOL	JR. HIGH	SR. HIGH
Death of sibling	59	68	71	68
Divorce of parents	78	84	84	77
Death of parent	89	91	94	87
Being hospitalized	59	62	59	58
Death of close friend	38	53	65	63
Using drugs	—	61	70	76
Failing school	—	57	62	56
Parent remarries	62	65	63	63
Birth of sibling	50	50	50	50
Change school	33	46	52	56

SOURCE: From "The Significance of Life Events as Contributing Factors in the Diseases of Children" by J. S. Heisel, S. Ream, R. Raitz, M. Rappaport, and R. D. Coddington. In *The Journal of Pediatrics*, 1973, *83*, 119–123.

Research has identified a positive relationship between serious athletic injuries and adolescents' experiences of life stress.

However, these qualifications aside, let us look at three topics related to life changes and adolescent physical health: life events and the frequency of accidents, life events and various health conditions, and life stress and the onset of diabetes.

Life Events and the Frequency of Accidents

Accidents are the major cause of death among children and adolescents. For this reason alone, but probably for others as well, some researchers became interested in identifying factors that contribute to accidental injuries in youths. Let's look at one of these studies.

Eligio Padilla, Damaris Rohsenow, and Abraham Bergman (1976) studied 103 seventh grade boys. They asked the boys to fill out a version of Coddington's (1972a, 1972b) life events checklist in terms of the past 12 months. Then, the researchers selected the boys who scored in the upper 27% ($n = 28$) and those boys who scored in the lower 27% ($n = 28$) and followed these boys over the next 5 months.

Interviewers met with the 56 boys over the next 5 months to obtain information about the occurrence and severity of accidents. The interviewers did not know any of the boys' stress scores. They gathered information on the weekly total of accidents in each of six categories:

- accidents resulting in no injury (for instance, falling off a bike, bumping into the piano),
- accidents resulting in injury, but not requiring first aid,
- accidents resulting in injury and requiring first aid,
- accidents resulting in injury and requiring a medical doctor's or nurse's attention,
- accidents resulting in injury and requiring hospitalization, and
- accidents resulting in death.

Life Stress and the Onset of Diabetes

everal fascinating studies have looked at the relationship between life events and the onset of juvenile diabetes. As early as 1971, one study reported that adolescents with diabetes were significantly more likely than youths with other types of illnesses (for instance, asthma or cystic fibrosis) to have experienced serious family disturbances, particularly parental divorce or death (Stein & Charles, 1971). The significant relationship between parental loss and the onset of diabetes in the lives of early adolescents was again reported in 1980 (Leaverton, White, McCormick, Smith, & Sheikholislam, 1980). In this study, diabetic youths were matched with a set of healthy adolescents on age, gender, race, and socioeconomic status. The authors concluded that loss of a parent was a possible significant factor in the emergence of juvenile diabetes (Leaverton et al., 1980).

Other studies also report a significant relationship between stressful life events and problems in controlling diabetes (Bradley, 1979; Chase & Jackson, 1981; Grant, Kyle, Teichman, & Mandels, 1974; Johnson & McCutcheon, 1980). In a study by H. Peter Chase and Ginny Jackson, retrospective accounts of life events over the preceding three

months indicated middle adolescents who had experienced stress showed several biomedical problems indicative of difficulties controlling diabetes.

Chase and Jackson (1981) suggested that diabetic adolescents with an internal locus of control experience more difficulty regulating their diabetes when environmental events become distressing; the researchers conjectured that when diabetic adolescents realize disturbing life events are beyond their control, expectations that they should be in control of these events create medical problems. Johnson (1986) provides some confirmation of this conjecture. He cites an unpublished manuscript in which he and his colleagues report negative life events were associated with problems in diabetes control; positive life events seemed to be unrelated to diabetes control, however (Brand, Johnson, & Johnson, 1986).

The onset of diabetes also affects family interactions and coping strategies, as indicated in the case study opening this chapter and corroborated by research conducted by Stuart Hauser and his colleagues (Hauser, DiPlacido, Jacobson, Paul, Bliss, Milley, Lavori, Vieyra, Wolsdorf, Herskowitz, Willett, Cole, & Wertlieb, 1993; Hauser, Jacobson,

After five months, boys with higher stress scores reported significantly more accidents than boys with lower stress scores. These results are presented in Table 11-3. Note that every category except fatalities had occurrences, and the boys with high stress scores had more than twice as many reported accidents as the boys with low stress scores.

One possible explanation for the accidents could be that some boys engage in much more risk-taking behavior than other boys. The researchers got a measure of the boys' risk-taking behaviors by observing them in four situations: once playing basketball, once wrestling, and twice playing soccer. With judges obtaining at least 80% inter-rater reliability regarding how risky a boy's behavior was, the researchers placed 25% ($n = 14$) in a low-risk category, 45% ($n = 25$) in a medium-risk category, and 30% ($n = 17$) in a high-risk category. Statistical tests indicated that life stress scores were much stronger predictors of accidents than was risk-taking behavior.

Lavori, Wolsdorf, Herskowitz, Milley, Bliss, Wertlieb, & Stein, 1990; Hauser, Jacobson, Milley, Wertlieb, Wolsdorf, Herskowitz, Lavori, & Bliss, 1992). In particular, Hauser and his colleagues have demonstrated families with diabetic youths (children and adolescents) use appraisal-focused, problem-focused, and emotion-focused coping strategies differently than the families of youths with acute illnesses.

Hauser and his associates (1993) found mothers of diabetic youths were more likely ($p < .001$) than mothers of acutely ill youths to appraise their families as consensual units, not merely a collection of relatives. Fathers of diabetic youths were more likely ($p < .0001$) than fathers of acutely ill youngsters to judge that their families had mastered the impact of the illness. Diabetic adolescents were more likely ($p < .006$) than acutely ill youths to describe their families as interacting groups, rather than as collections of separate but related individuals (Hauser et al., 1993).

Mothers of diabetic youths were more likely ($p < .0001$) than mothers of acutely ill youths to mention using such problem-focused strategies as seeking support, looking for alternate rewards, and using new approaches to resolve problems. Fathers of diabetic youths mirrored their wives' discussions of problem-focused strategies, and significantly differed ($p < .03$) from fathers of acutely ill youths in these matters. Diabetic adolescents were much more likely ($p < .0008$) than their acutely ill peers to mention problem-focused coping strategies in their families, such as seeking alternate rewards, looking for support from others, and relying on self; this self-reliance expressed itself in the diabetic adolescents' perceptions that their families were less likely to get information about their present problems (Hauser et al., 1993).

Mothers of diabetic youths were more likely ($p < .002$) than mothers of acutely ill youngsters to express their emotions outside their families. Fathers of diabetic youths mirrored their wives' discussions of this emotion-focused strategy and were more likely ($p < .003$) than the fathers of acutely ill youths to express their emotions within their families. Diabetic adolescents indicated more than acutely ill youths ($p < .0009$) that they expressed their feelings to people outside their families, and they were less likely to downplay personal awareness of their emotions and the emotions of the rest of their family members (Hauser et al., 1993).

TABLE 11-3   Frequency of Accidents for Seventh Grade Boys with High and Low Life Event Stress Scores

Type of Accident	Boys with Low Scores	Boys with High Scores
No injury	112	382
No first aid needed	186	363
First aid needed	94	174
Medical professional needed	3	24
Hospitalization needed	0	4
Fatality	0	0
Total	395	946

SOURCE: Adapted from "Predicting Accident Frequency in Children" by E. R. Padilla, D. J. Rohsenow, and A. B. Bergman, 1976, *Pediatrics, 58*, p. 225.

Two other studies with older adolescents found a positive relationship between serious athletic injuries and experiences of life stress. One study was conducted with high school students (Coddington & Troxell, 1980), and the other with college students (Bramwell, Wagner, Masuda, & Holmes, 1975). The types of events experienced prior to the injuries were family deaths and parental illnesses, separations, and divorces. Johnson (1986) noted that such findings suggest that injuries to children and adolescents may result because family stress leads people to ignore or misinterpret information indicating danger.

Life Events and Various Health Conditions

In 1962, Roger Meyer and Robert Haggerty published a pioneering article on family stress and childhood illness. The researchers followed 100 children over the course of one year. Every two weeks, throat cultures were taken from each child to determine if streptococcal infection was present. In addition, family members kept a diary of upsetting events encountered during the two-week period. They also recorded any illnesses in the family during that two-week period.

Meyer and Haggerty (1962) found that an increased level of upsetting events preceded streptococcal infection in the children. While some streptococcal infections occurred with no record of stressful events, Meyer and Haggerty reported that the probability of children's developing an infection significantly increased when stressful events were present in the family. Rather than saying the upsetting events cause the infections, Meyer and Haggerty suggested upsetting events contribute to the development of the infections by making the youths more vulnerable.

A variety of other illnesses (rheumatoid arthritis, appendicitis, and hemophilic bleeding) have been found to be exacerbated when life stress increases (Heisel, Ream, Raitz, Rapaport, & Coddington, 1973). In all three types of illness, youths were found to have experienced significantly higher life stress during the preceding 12 months than a sample of healthy children.

Some youths suffer recurrent pain; researchers have found in several studies that within 6 to 12 months prior to the onset of the pain, the youths had experienced aversive events. For instance, nearly one-third of 100 adolescents being treated for recurrent chest pains reported significantly stressful events, such as moving or changing schools, in the past 6 months (Pantell & Goodman, 1983). The researchers used the Coddington (1972a) scale to gather life event data.

In another study, early adolescents suffering recurrent abdominal pain reported significantly higher life stress scores on the Coddington scale than a control group of healthy children (Hodges, Kline, Barbero, & Flanery, 1984). The researchers included a comparison group of 67 early adolescents being treated in a psychiatric outpatient clinic. These individuals also had scores significantly higher than members of the healthy control group. The life stress scores of the youths with abdominal pain and the youths in psychiatric treatment exceeded the life stress scores of the healthy research participants by two standard deviations.

In summary, a large body of research indicates that negative, distressing life events are associated with a variety of physical health problems in adolescence. While we must bear in mind that the studies are correlational and do not disclose the exact nature of how life events and physical health are related, we may assuredly say that stressful life events contribute to various forms of adolescent vulnerability to injury and disease.

CHAPTER SUMMARY

In this chapter, we have reviewed coping with critical life events during adolescence. These events include running away to live on the streets, divorce of parents, bereavement over a death, and vulnerability to injury and disease. These life events present considerable challenges to adolescents' coping skills.

A theme in this chapter is that coping successfully with a crisis can lead to greater growth and maturity. Without suggesting that the dangerous opportunities presented by crises lead to fairy tale endings of happiness, there are indications that some adolescents do achieve developmental gains from the ordeals presented by their losses. For instance, while persisting troubles are evident in the lives of children of divorce 10 years after their parents' separations, some data indicate that coping leads to greater perceptions of self-control, responsibility, competence, and autonomy (Weiss, 1986). In the initial year of grief, bereaved adolescents actually demonstrate healthier self-concepts than nonbereaved peers (Guerriero & Fleming, 1986). Perhaps because of the demands on adaptation presented by bereavement, the self-concepts of bereaved adolescents demonstrate resiliency in all studies measuring self-concept (Balk, 1981, 1983a, 1990; Hogan, 1987; Martinson, Davies, & McClowry, 1987). Outside observers, such as teachers, friends, coaches, and employers, consistently have acknowledged in personal conversations that coping with bereavement produces empathy and maturity in adolescents greater than seen in their nonbereaved peers. Even desperate runaways, who have little to hope for, remain open to finding someone they can believe in (Lefkowitz, 1987). Overall, evidence from several quarters warrants concurring with Offer (1969) that adolescents often adapt to life tragedies, use them as means of growth and adjustment, and proceed a bit more quickly than their nonaffected peers into adulthood.

The Moos model for understanding coping with life crises was presented as a means to comprehend how adolescents cope when faced with losses. This model identifies five adaptive tasks and three sets of coping skills. Here, I review the adaptive tasks in terms of the different cases we have studied.

Establish the meaning of the event and comprehend its personal significance. Adolescents who run away to live on the streets are said to be making a desperate attempt at reconstructing their lives. The act of running away often indicates that the adolescent's home life is intolerable; to cope with a distressing home environment, runaways choose to become homeless. Adolescents whose parents divorce are forced to accept the rupture in their families and the impact that the divorce will have on them; at some point, the issue of reduced family finances becomes personally meaningful for an adolescent of divorced parents. Adolescents bereaved over a death must come to terms with the permanent loss of a loved one (a parent, sibling, friend, or themselves, if terminally ill). Bereaved adolescents must come to terms with their own mortality, with the apparent randomness at loose in the universe, and with the implications that random happenings have for believing the world is ultimately trustworthy.

Confront reality and respond to the situational requirements of the event. Runaways act out of a decision that their home lives are intolerable; leaving represents for them a healthy response. On the streets, they confront new situational stressors and often turn to criminal activity as a means of survival. Runaways may find emergency shelters in which to live. Adolescents of divorce must acknowledge the fact of their parents' marital dissolution and accept the permanence of the situation; they seem less vulnerable to the reunion fantasies that children envision. Bereaved adolescents are forced to respond to immediate demands (for instance, making plans for a funeral, attending the funeral, and talking with others about the death) and to cope with the effects of grief on ordinary activities (for instance, effects on concentration and on school work).

Sustain interpersonal relations. Runaways go to people on the street and, in some cases, become members of youth gangs. They look for someone they can trust, but typically have few friends and may have developed few interpersonal skills. Adolescents of divorce use conversations with friends and parents as means to resolve the losses in their lives; as time passes following a divorce, female adolescents seem more at risk of developing inappropriate relations with males. A crucial achievement for adolescents of divorce is to maintain and/or recover realistic expectations about interpersonal relationships. Bereaved adolescents turn to family members and friends as sources of information and support.

In all of these types of recovery from loss, interpersonal relations are noticeably strained. In some cases, the relationships worsen, thereby removing some important adaptive potentials from the adolescent's repertoire. An underlying thread to all of the losses we have covered is that each one involves a fundamental rupture in interpersonal relationships.

Maintain emotional balance. Runaways are considered by many sources to be impulsive, depressed, defensive, and anxious; at best, such a portrait accents the considerable challenge that life on the streets poses to maintaining emotional balance. Adolescents of divorced parents need to remove themselves from parental conflicts, to resolve feelings of anger, and to recover from self-blame and feelings of guilt. Bereaved adolescents are faced with a host of emotions that accompany grief, and must deal with feelings of guilt, confusion, depression, anger, fear, and loneliness, to name a few. These feelings endure longer than commonly expected, and their intensity is seldom appreciated by outsiders.

Preserve a satisfactory self-concept and maintain a sense of self-efficacy. Runaways are often described as suffering from impoverished self-concepts reinforced by experiences of failure in school and by assessments of their limited opportunities in the working world. The sense of helplessness and futility experienced by these youths is most resistant to change. Adolescents of divorce work on this adaptive task in their long-term efforts to resolve the impact of the divorce on their options, prospects, and expectations. Bereaved adolescents resolve grief differently as a function of self-concept; a sign of bereavement resolution is the adolescent's desire to plan for the future. The return of hope, marked by investing in goals, presents clear evidence that bereaved adolescents believe in their abilities to attain desired outcomes.

We have completed the chapter on coping with life crises. The next chapter focuses on juvenile delinquency. We begin with a case study of one adolescent who had difficulty coping with his dysfunctional home life.

CHAPTER
12

DELINQUENCY

CASE STUDY

"Every Time I Do Something Wrong, I Pray"

Randy is a late adolescent. He is husky, about 5' 9" tall, and weighs about 165 pounds. His teeth are jammed together and overlap in spots. When he smiles, he looks friendly. Because he is in a methadone maintenance program, his dull, sleepy appearance could be due to his medication. His long, stringy hair appears not to have been washed for several days. When we spoke, he was wearing a dirty, white t-shirt. His faded blue jeans were worn away at the knees, and his boots extended halfway up his calves.

Randy's body is scarred in several places. One scar above his right eye extends approximately six inches across his forehead. He also has scars on his chin, below his jaw, and on his back. His right forearm is severely scarred from a serious motorcycle accident.

As an early and middle adolescent, Randy was involved in a lot of delinquent activities, some status offenses (behaviors prohibited only for youths), and many criminal offenses. He got into a lot fights, drank a lot of alcohol, and used heroin. After hearing his story, you wonder how he is still alive.

Randy and I talked in an outpatient mental health clinic where he was a client. I have not edited his language, which gets crude at times.

"When I went to grade school, I was skinny and small. My teeth were all messed up. I couldn't eat for a long time. I was sickly. I started working out with weights. People used to pick on me, and I'd let them get away with it. When I got to high school, I was built up where boys couldn't bully me anymore. I'd get in a fight and pull their eyeballs out and grab their privates, do many things.

"At the time I'm fighting, it seems I'm getting a kick out of it, but afterwards, I'm sorry. Then it's too late. I've been in a lot of gang fights. I've been shot, stabbed in the back. It may sound like I'm bragging, but I'm not.

"One day in high school I was in a secluded part of the school and there were six or seven black kids there. I had to go through them to get where I was going. I was polite. I said, 'Excuse me.' I got about five feet from them and one of them shot a paper clip at the back of my head. Even being outnumbered like that, I asked, 'Which one of you motherfuckers did that?' I started for them. It just so happened I looked over in the parking lot and there were a bunch of buddies of mine. I yelled that I needed help. The black dudes had split by the time my buddies arrived. I was about 16 years old then.

"It was about the time I started taking drugs. I started out smoking weed, shooting reds. I started getting my first taste of heroin. I also was sniffing glue—anything to get loaded on.

"I had an old station wagon, and my friends and I would drive around. One night, we started for the drive-in. We were all loaded on reds, and when I pulled in, I heard a shrill whistle. I got out of the car and there was a bunch of cowboys. They were all seven or eight years older than me and my buddies. There were about six or seven of them.

"There was this one big dude about 25 years old. He had a beard, and he was big. We got out of the car, and this friend of mine said, 'We have a problem with this cowboy. He's hassling us.'

"I got two pop bottles from the car and started toward the cowboy. He said, 'I can whip any three of you motherfuckers.' I said, 'I bet you can't.' I threw a pop bottle, and it hit him right square in the face. It shattered.

"I got into a fight with this other one, and we were on the ground. He was on the bottom. I was pulling at his face. The other guys took off running down the road.

"Then the one I hit with the pop bottle got up and asked which one of us hit him with the bottle. I said, 'I did, motherfucker.' He outweighed me. He said, 'Will you fight me man to man?' Well, I ran toward him and knocked the shit out of him. He tried to pick me up, so I grabbed his balls and twisted until he fell over. He ended up on the bottom. I stuck my finger in his eye and started ripping his face. My friend said, 'Move your hand, move your hand!' I said, 'I already got him.' My friend wanted to kick him. He did and busted the guy's nose. The guy got up and was bleeding real bad. I wanted to get another pop bottle and go for him again, but we took off.

"When I was in the car, I felt my back hurting. When I got out, I noticed I was bleeding. I had been stabbed in the back during the fight. I was afraid of going to the hospital, afraid of getting caught. I went to a doctor. I lied and told him I slipped and fell on some glass. Ever since then, I've always carried a knife. Things like that have always been happening to me.

"My folks were pretty poor. I remember living in an adobe hut at one time. My dad and I never got along. My parents are both alcoholics. Growing up with them wasn't good. My dad's an alcoholic, and he made my mom one.

"Let me tell you about my parents, about how they disciplined me and my sister. Well, they used to beat the hell out of her. It was sickening. My folks would come home drunk, come into my room, and slap the hell out of me. I'd let them do it. Once I beat the hell out of my old man. I left home after that. I would just go back to wash my clothes and eat and then I would take off.

"Here's something else about my folks. I guess they believe in God. They think they're religious, but they aren't most of the time.

"Every time I do something wrong, I pray. All the things I've done, all the people I've hurt. My life has been violent. I'm depressed most of the time."

Randy's story is one of violence, poverty, an interrupted education, and harsh but inconsistent parents. He has found opportunities blocked and has learned from observation of peers and parents to be aggressive. He acts impulsively. He admits to engaging in many delinquent acts, mostly criminal in nature—for instance, physical assault and possession of drugs. He runs around with a group of males who are violent. All of these parts of his story point to a history of repeated antisocial acts. His involvement in a methadone maintenance program gives some promise that he intends to turn his life around. However, Randy has serious obstacles to overcome if he is to prevent his delinquent behavior from becoming adult antisocial behavior.

Randy thus introduces this chapter's look at delinquency. In this chapter, we review types of delinquent offenses, gender differences in delinquent activity, college students and antisocial behavior, and the prevalence of delinquent behavior among the majority of adolescents. We will read about causes of delinquency and whether delinquent behavior predicts an adult life of crime. Finally, we will review programs to treat delinquents and programs to prevent delinquency. We begin with a review of what juvenile delinquency is.

JUVENILE DELINQUENCY, STATUS OFFENSES, AND CRIMINAL OFFENSES

What is **juvenile delinquency**? It is behavior of children and adolescents prohibited by legal statutes. Age limits are placed on delinquent behavior, but the exact upper and lower limits vary from state to state. Most states use 18 as the upper age limit, but some use 16 or 17. The lower age limit also varies, but experts recommend 10 as a meaningful cutoff point (Trojanowicz & Morash, 1992).

What types of actions constitute delinquent behavior? State laws forbid youths from engaging in two types of offenses: status offenses and criminal offenses. **Status offenses** are behaviors that are prohibited only for youths. In other words, if adults engage in these behaviors, they do not break the law, but youths can be arrested if they do these things. Examples of status offenses are truancy from school, running away from home, breaking curfew, and incorrigibility (that is, being unmanageable or out of parental control).

Criminal offenses are actions that are illegal for adults and juveniles. Examples of criminal offenses include murder, rape, burglary, vandalism, shoplifting, and possession of drugs. One system of classifying criminal offenses distinguishes crimes against people (for example, assault or robbery) from crimes against property (for example, vandalism). Another classification system differentiates between violent crimes (for instance, assault) and theft (for instance, shoplifting).

Although criminal offenses are illegal for both adults and juveniles, it is uncommon for a youth who commits a criminal offense to be tried as an adult. Later in this chapter, we will look at the implications of judicial views toward adolescents who commit criminal offenses.

The typology of offenses (status versus criminal) has some practical as well as theoretical value. Data suggest that adolescents who commit criminal offenses are more likely than status offenders to commit criminal acts as adults. We return to this issue when discussing proposed causes of delinquency. Let us turn next to a discussion of the number of adolescents in custody.

Adolescents in Custody

In 1991, the U.S. Department of Justice published a report on adolescents in custody (Krisberg, DeComo, Herrera, Steketee, & Roberts, 1991). In this report, criminal offenses were labeled *delinquent offenses*, while status offenses retained the same name.

The federal government keeps track of the number of juveniles held in custody for criminal and status offenses. This record is called a **one day census**. Over a ten-year period from 1979 to 1989, the number of status offenders in the one day census remained fairly stable—9,085 for the one-day count in 1979, 9,019 in 1985, and 9,090 in 1989. The number held in custody for criminal offenses, however, increased dramatically—45,126 in 1979, 57,743 in 1985, and 66,132 in 1989. These numbers amount to nearly a 47% increase over the ten years (Krisberg et al., 1991).

These ten-year data clearly indicate that while the number of status offenders placed in custody hardly changed, there was a noticeable increase in detected criminal actions by adolescents. However, when Federal Bureau of Investigation (FBI) data are investigated, the trends seem less clear. For the period 1979–1989, the greatest number of criminal acts committed by individuals under the age of 18 occurred in 1979, with nearly a 17% decrease in criminal offenses by the year 1989. However, by 1989, violent juvenile crimes, such as murder, rape, and assault, were slightly higher than 1979 figures (Federal Bureau of Investigation [FBI], 1990).

Juvenile arrests for criminal offenses peaked at nearly 740,000 in 1979, and declined by 22.3% to 575,000 in 1984. Between 1985 and 1988, the number of arrests for criminal offenses stayed fairly constant—around 600,000 (Krisberg et al.,

Between 1979 and 1989, the number of adolescents held in custody for status offenses remained fairly stable, while the number held for criminal offenses increased dramatically.

1991). In fact, between 1978 and 1988, juvenile arrests for criminal acts declined by nearly 19%—from 738,094 in 1978 to 598,690 in 1988. Thus, the ten-year trend was for mid-decade decline in the number of arrests and then a slight increase that remained level for the rest of the decade.

Gender Differences in Delinquent Activity

Gender differences in juvenile delinquency leap off the page. Males are involved in far more criminal behaviors that come to the attention of the legal authorities. This gender difference in delinquency has remained constant since investigators began looking at delinquent activity (Trojanowicz & Morash, 1992).

Criminal offenses by juveniles declined for both males and females between 1978 and 1988. However, males were arrested nearly four times more frequently than females over those ten years. In each category of arrest, the gender differences are striking—males were arrested 7 times more often for violent crimes, 3.7 times more often for property crimes, and 6.8 times more often for drug crimes (Krisberg et al., 1991).

FBI data of arrest rates between 1965 and 1989 support the conclusion that males engage in criminal activities far more frequently than females. Never once over those 24 years did the rate of juvenile arrests drop below a ratio of four males for every female. In 1965, for instance, the arrest rate per 1,000 males was 7 times greater than the arrest rates for females. In 1978, the arrest rate was 4.3 times greater for males than for females. While male arrests still significantly outstripped arrests of females, another issue that emerged in the 1978 data was that female arrests had increased over 200% (compared to less than a 60% increase in male arrests). By 1988, the arrest rate for males was 4 times greater than the arrest rate for females, but was 20% less than the 1978 arrest rate. The arrest rate for females in 1988 was 13% less than the 1978 rate (FBI, 1990).

College Students and Antisocial Behavior

Few college students are young enough to commit status offenses. Thus, on one hand, it is misleading to consider college student behavior in this chapter. But, on the other hand, consider the evidence that antisocial behavior has a history that dates back to childhood (Bandura, 1964/1980; Robins, 1966; Snyder & Patterson, 1987). This evidence suggests that antisocial behaviors in college are extensions of delinquent behaviors from younger years.

The major stimulus for college students' antisocial behaviors is alcohol consumption. Researchers in Great Britain studied the drinking patterns of 270 college students (125 males; 145 females) (West, Drummond, & Eames, 1990). They noted that over one-fourth of the students admitted to vandalizing property and/or assaulting other people after drinking. Males were much more inclined than females to acknowledge drinking led them to commit antisocial acts.

Richard Dodder and Stella Hughes (1987), two researchers in the United States, demonstrated that collegiate drinking is strongly implicated in willingness to commit antisocial acts. Other researchers have also linked problem drinking and collegiate antisocial behavior (Sher & Alterman, 1988). Thus, alcohol consumption, a behavior that is a status offense, is strongly implicated as a significant factor in college students engaging in antisocial behavior.

Adolescent Antisocial Behavior Considered Cross-Culturally

Cultural anthropologists Alice Schlegel and Herbert Barry (1991) emphasize that behaviors considered antisocial in one cultural setting may be accepted as normal in a different culture. Resorting to a fist fight, for instance, in American society may be acceptable within limits, but in other cultures would be evidence of severe disorder. In short, the criterion that must be applied when examining antisocial behavior is the standard for acceptable behavior in the culture being investigated.

Youths in several preindustrial cultures behave in antisocial ways. The behaviors considered antisocial include abusive speech, vandalism, stealing, drunkenness, fighting, sexual misconduct, and misuse of drugs. In most preindustrial societies, boys, rather than girls, are documented as the greater perpetrators of antisocial behavior. However, belief that girls do not act antisocially may be due to lack of attention by researchers, not due to inactivity by girls (Schlegel & Barry, 1991).

What researchers have documented about adolescents' antisocial behavior in preindustrial societies is shown in Table 12-1. The information indicates in how many cultures the behavior has been observed and which gender engaged in the behavior.

TABLE 12-1 ■ Adolescents' Antisocial Behavior in Preindustrial Societies

ANTISOCIAL BEHAVIOR	ADOLESCENT MALES	ADOLESCENT FEMALES
Theft	9	1
Physical Violence	7	1
Verbal Abuse	4	0
Sexual Activity	3	3
Drug Use	2	0
Property Destruction	1	0
Other	6	2

SOURCE: Adapted from *Adolescence: An Anthropological Inquiry* (Chapter 8) by A. Schlegel & H. Barry, 1991, New York: The Free Press.

As the table indicates, the most common types of antisocial behavior in preindustrial societies are theft and physical assault. These two forms of deviant behavior are also very problematic in industrial societies. In fact, two general categories of criminal offenses in industrial societies are violent crimes and theft.

Adolescent antisocial behaviors typically occur in societies in which youths spend time primarily with their age-mates. In most preindustrial societies, adult relatives are expected to be the principal companions of adolescents. In those societies, antisocial behavior from adolescents is quite uncommon, because the adolescents spend time learning productive skills in the company of adults. Deviant behavior seems a clear outcome of spending time outside of adult supervision.

Some preindustrial societies tolerate antisocial behavior. A chief example is provided by societies whose economies require adolescent males work with their peers without adult supervision. This circumstance can result in such antisocial behavior as theft. Among the African Masai, for instance, adolescent males herd cattle. At times, the boys band together to steal cattle to increase the size of their own herds.

Masai adolescent males at times steal cattle to increase their own herds.

THE PREVALENCE OF SELF-REPORTED DELINQUENT BEHAVIOR

The notion of status and criminal offenses emphasizes the legal view of delinquent behavior. This view highlights arrests and convictions of adolescents for committing delinquent acts. Another view of juvenile delinquency emphasizes engaging in behaviors that adolescents know are violations of the law, and make them liable to adjudication if the behaviors come to the attention of a law-enforcement agency.

This second view of delinquent behavior recognizes that some willful and knowledgeable violations of the law do not necessarily become known to authorities. This view overcomes the problem of counting as delinquent behaviors only those actions that authorities punish. What this second view emphasizes is undetected delinquent behavior, and research suggests adolescents engage in an incredible number of both status and criminal offenses that the authorities never prosecute.

Two older studies used self-report procedures to determine the incidence and prevalence of undetected delinquent acts (Gold, 1970; Vaz, 1965). In his study of 1,639 middle-class boys between the ages of 13 and 19, Edmund Vaz learned that older boys (15- to 19-year-olds) engage in considerably more delinquent behaviors than younger boys (13- and 14-year-olds). For instance, 52% of the older boys admitted vandalizing property compared to 45% of the younger boys; 26% of the older boys stayed out all night without their parents' permission compared to 19.5% of the younger boys; and 25% purchased alcoholic beverages compared to 3% of the younger boys.

Martin Gold's (1970) research included 358 high school males between the ages of 13 and 16; 13.6% were 13 years old, 29.8% were 14 years old, 26.8% were 15 years old, and 29.8% were 16 years old.

As in Vaz's (1965) research and in the earlier work of Sheldon Glueck and Eleanor Glueck (1950), Gold's (1970) middle adolescent males (the 15- and 16-year-old subjects) admitted to engaging in more delinquent behaviors than did the early adolescents. For instance, 55% of the 15- and 16-year-olds admitted shoplifting, 50% admitted stealing money, 64% admitted drinking, 35% admitted vandalizing property, and 30% admitted engaging in gang fights. In comparison, 51% of 13- and 14-year-olds admitted they shoplifted, 43% stole money, 47% drank, 27% vandalized property, and 21% engaged in gang fights. Less than 10% of the 13- and 14-year-olds said they had been involved in armed robbery, assaulting their parents, or running away from home; at least 10% of the 15- and 16-year-olds admitted to all of those acts. These comparisons are presented in Table 12-2 on page 446.

Hershel Thornburg (1975) made a startling conclusion borne out by data from Vaz (1965) and Gold (1970). He concluded that the great majority of juveniles engage in delinquent behaviors—both status and criminal offenses—for which they are not arrested. He estimated that as many as 90% of adolescents at some time or other commit acts that would land them in custody if traced to them by the police. Informal surveys of college students in classes I teach confirm Thornburg's assertion. Nearly all the students admit to having done things that were against the law; the most frequent violations were underage drinking.

TABLE 12-2   Self-Reported Delinquent Behaviors of Early and Middle Adolescents

DELINQUENT ACTS	EARLY ADOLESCENTS (n = 112)	MIDDLE ADOLESCENTS (n = 146)
Shoplifting	51%	55%
Stealing Money	43%	50%
Drinking	47%	64%
Vandalizing	27%	35%
Gang Fighting	21%	30%
Armed Robbery	8%	10%
Assaulting Parents	7%	10%
Running Away	7%	10%

SOURCE: Adapted from *Delinquent Behavior in an American City* (p. 69) by M. Gold, 1970, Belmont, CA: Brooks/Cole.

One would rightly conclude from these self-report data that delinquent behaviors are more prevalent than adults might typically expect. Adults do not usually consider most adolescents antisocial. However, adults are concerned about youths whose behavior threatens society, and efforts have been made to uncover the causes of these threatening types of delinquent activity. We turn next to theories developed to explain delinquency.

CAUSES OF JUVENILE DELINQUENCY

A few well-established theories about what causes juvenile delinquency have been developed. We will look at four attempts to explain delinquency: the classical view, social learning theory, blocked opportunity theory, and Gisela Konopka's research with delinquent females.

The Classical View   One proposed explanation for criminal behavior is called the **classical view**. First proposed in the 18th century, this view asserts all human beings exercise free will to achieve goals of pleasure and use reason to select means to attain their goals. Criminals differ from law-abiding people only in the means they choose to attain goals of pleasure. Criminals freely choose to commit crimes to achieve goals, while law-abiding people choose other means.

A derivative of the classical view of criminal behavior is that only swift and harsh punishment for criminal acts influences a criminal to choose to obey the laws. This view is quite active today with police. Police deal with juvenile delinquents pragmatically and according to the law. The police officer does not have time, or usually the inclination, to focus on background or psychological aspects that explain a youth's deviant behavior. The police are law-enforcement officers, not psychologists or social workers, and the classical view fits the police officers' view of juvenile delinquency (Trojanowicz & Morash, 1992).

Social Learning Theory

Alternatives to the classical view of delinquent behavior are psychological and sociological explanations. One influential psychological explanation is Bandura's social learning theory (Bandura, 1973; Bandura & Walters, 1963). We explored this theory in Chapter 1.

Social learning theory explains delinquency as a result of copying behaviors of role models who are held in high esteem and who provide rewards. The key role models in a youth's life are parents and peers. Parents of delinquent youths provide inconsistent discipline, show little if any regard for how their children act, and frequently behave in antisocial ways themselves. Research provides strong support for the influence of social learning in the development and persistence of delinquent behavior (Trojanowicz and Morash, 1992).

One longitudinal study of delinquent youths singled out parents' poor behavior management and inconsistent discipline as major factors in the lives of the juveniles (Craig & Glueck, 1963; Glueck & Glueck, 1950). One consequence of this poor parental control is that the children developed little if any impulse control. The Gluecks (1950) concluded that a childhood history of deviancy is the prelude to an adult life of crime.

Blocked Opportunity Theory

A very influential sociological explanation of juvenile delinquency is **blocked opportunity theory** (Cloward & Ohlin, 1960; McCandless, 1970). This theory considers delinquent acts to be violations of conventional societal norms that are expected activities in a deviant subculture. To achieve any dominance in a delinquent milieu, individuals must engage in activities proscribed by mainstream society. Because a delinquent subculture pressures members to engage in delinquent behaviors, changing an individual's deviant behavior depends on changing the norms of his or her peer group (Cloward & Ohlin, 1960).

Blocked opportunity theory suggests membership in a delinquent subculture is the pathway to a criminal career. By a *delinquent subculture*, Richard Cloward and Lloyd Ohlin (1960) mean gangs. We look at gangs in greater detail in Chapter 13.

Adolescent offenders who do not belong to a delinquent subculture are less likely to continue breaking the law. As Cloward and Ohlin phrased it, the delinquent acts of solitary offenders are "transitory phenomena, more susceptible to social control" (1960, p. 12). Members of a delinquent subculture, however, are seen to be part of "criminal apprenticeship programs" (Trojanowicz & Morash, 1992, p. 64).

Blocked opportunity theory maintains that delinquency occurs because youths face barriers to achieve approved economic and social goals. Conforming to social norms merely produces frustration. The theory maintains delinquent subcultures are lower-class phenomena because individuals in an underclass face severe obstacles to achieving sanctioned economic and social goals. In short, the youths begin breaking the law to obtain goals that society holds forth but blocks the youths from achieving legally.

Research with adolescent males from various economic strata has given guarded support for the theory of blocked opportunities. Studies of gangs and of middle-class youths in Chicago, for instance, indicate a marked discrepancy in the youths' beliefs about the availability of legitimate opportunities (Short, 1990). Some of these views

Margaret Shaw and David Riley (1989), two British researchers, interviewed a representative sample of 751 adolescents age 14 to 15 years old in England and Wales. Their study focused on self-reported delinquent offenses, parental supervision, and association with friends. The interviews took place in the adolescents' homes. In addition to the adolescents, the researchers interviewed parents; in 98% of the cases, they interviewed the mother. Eight percent of the adolescents lived with both biological parents, 8% with a biological parent and a stepparent, 10% with a single mother, and 2% with a single father. All socioeconomic levels were equally represented in the sample.

The interviewers showed the adolescents a set of 21 cards, each naming a separate offense. The offenses ranged from less serious acts, such as breaking windows in an empty house and traveling on a bus without paying the fare, to more serious acts, such as arson, burglary, and taking money from others by force. The adolescents sorted the cards into two piles (acts committed and acts not committed), and they indicated how often they had committed an act in the past 12 months. The researchers defined *delinquency* as the commission of one or more acts

during the past 12 months. They also asked the adolescents about the delinquent behavior of their friends.

Parental supervision was considered to be the extent of the parent's knowledge of the adolescent's whereabouts when away from home, who the adolescent was with, and what the adolescent was doing. The researchers divided parents into two categories: high supervision and low supervision. The high supervision parents said they almost always knew where their adolescents were, what they were doing, and with whom.

Extent of Delinquency   Nearly one-half (49%) of the males and nearly two-fifths (39%) of the females reported committing at least one delinquent act in the previous 12 months. Shaw and Riley (1989) pointed out that these figures were much higher than official reports of delinquency (based on police arrests). Only 12 of the males (3.2%) and 4 of the females (1%) had police records. The researchers also pointed out it was uncommon for youths to be given more than a warning.

Much of the delinquency the adolescents admitted to involved minor offenses. However, 19% of the sample admitted committing five or more offenses

were linked to ethnic/racial identity as well as social class. "White boys and middle-class boys tended to perceive legitimate opportunities as available to a greater extent than did black and lower-class boys, and gang boys of both races were the least optimistic in this regard" (Short, 1990, p. 145). Other writers assert that research support for the blocked opportunity theory is weak, at best (Trojanowicz & Morash, 1992). It is clear that 1960s social reforms built on the blocked opportunity theory, such as the Model Cities Program and the War on Poverty of the Lyndon Johnson presidency, were a dismal failure (Marris & Rein, 1973; Moynihan, 1969).

Blocked opportunity theory points very directly at means for overcoming delinquency. For example, educational programs are often proposed to overcome blocked opportunities. We look at some of these efforts later in this chapter.

during the previous 12 months. The researches said this group involved more serious offenders.

Nearly equal proportions of males and females were in the serious offenders group (21% and 17%, respectively). It was just as likely for a girl or a boy to report vandalizing property or stealing. The British researchers found this lack of gender difference worthy of note. You may recall that American female adolescents placed in residential care at The Villages during the 1980s had become much more aggressive and difficult to handle than females placed there in the 1970s (see Chapter 9).

Parental Supervision and Friends' Involvement in Delinquency Delinquency was linked to the extent of parental supervision, and gender differences emerged when parental supervision and delinquency were analyzed. For adolescents with low parental supervision, nearly the same percentage of males and females (56% and 55%, respectively) reported delinquent acts. However, for adolescents with high supervision, boys were much more likely than girls (41% and 29%) to be delinquent. The researchers noted that parents were more likely to closely supervise their adolescent daughters than their sons.

Adolescent males who said their friends committed delinquent acts were eight times more likely than other adolescent males to commit delinquent offenses. Furthermore, males who went out with friends three or more times weekly were twice as likely to engage in delinquent acts. In many cases, these peers had committed nine or more delinquent acts during the past year.

Adolescent females who said their friends were delinquents were 15 times more likely than other adolescent females to commit delinquent acts. Girls who said their friends would not care if they stole things were twice as likely as other adolescent females to be delinquent.

A particularly relevant influence on female delinquency was the combination of low parental supervision and association with delinquent friends. This same association did not emerge for delinquent boys; rather, association with delinquent peers seemed to outweigh any influence from parents. However, the delinquent males could hardly be considered to have been raised by involved parents, regardless of the level of parental supervision. The delinquent males were not only away from home with friends more often than other boys but were expected to return home later (Shaw & Riley, 1989).

Gisela Konopka's Research with Delinquent Females To this point in my discussion of juvenile delinquency, the emphasis has been almost exclusively on males. Cloward and Ohlin (1960) give no voice to juvenile delinquency in the lives of females. Konopka (1966) was an author who saw that female delinquency was being overlooked.

Konopka said her question after reading a decade of studies on delinquency was, "What about the *girl* in trouble? What do we know about her? How can we help her?" (From *The Adolescent Girl in Conflict,* by G. Konopka, p. 3, 11, 41, 55–57, 103. Copyright © 1966 by Prentice-Hall, Inc. Reprinted by permission). She noted that authors of significant studies on delinquency acknowledged in personal communication with her that more needed to be known about female delinquents, but that the much smaller number of female delinquents had led them to focus exclusively on males.

Konopka said all experts on delinquency acknowledge that female adolescents have more influence on delinquent behavior than commonly believed. As examples, she pointed out that gang fights occur because of rivalry over girls, girls seem to temper boys' criminal behavior, and girls are particularly important because of their influence as mothers of the coming generation of children.

Konopka (1966) conducted extensive, intimate interviews and observations with 100 girls in police custody in Minnesota and with 76 pregnant girls in homes for unwed mothers. She gained clinical case information by living in the same facilities as the girls. Her reports are filled with rich, qualitative understanding of the stories of these girls' lives.

Konopka's (1966) method was to listen, be available, and observe. She followed the institutional rules that governed the girls' lives. "I went with the girls through such odd rigid ceremonies of their institutional life as waiting silently in line for the door to the dining room to open" (Konopka, 1966, p. 11). By being present, Konopka set the stage to interview the girls and conduct group meetings with them.

Konopka (1966) identified some major themes present in these girls' lives. First, the girls were acutely lonely. Second, they wished for a return of the dependency permitted them as children. Third, they felt helpless.

Puberty had caught the girls off guard and led to sexual experimentation and feelings of personal disgust. Their searches for identity had been overwhelmed because they felt uncared for, unprotected, friendless, and besieged by anonymity. Konopka (1966) believed the personal key to understanding delinquent girls is to appreciate and understand their feelings of helplessness amid insensitive, depersonalizing adults.

For the girls in Konopka's (1966) study, their experiences with adults were marked by bitterness, disappointment, brutality, and hypocrisy. Women in their lives provided ineffectual and indecisive role models. Men were particularly nasty and harsh. Adults refused to listen, to try even to understand them, and basically ignored the girls. Konopka provided this quote from a 14-year-old who said, "What I especially don't like about adults and especially teachers is that they don't let you finish what you have to say. When you start to explain something, they say, 'Oh no! Oh no . . . !'" (Konopka, 1966, p. 55). A quote from another girl expresses her skepticism of adults (her age was not given), "I don't understand adults. The adults say they never got into trouble, that they never had any problems. How is that possible? I don't believe them. They lie . . . . Why do they act so perfect? I think they just try to push us into the ground and make us feel like nothing" (Konopka, 1966, p. 57).

Konopka (1966) concluded there are deeply embedded social factors that produce female delinquents. Changing cultural mores, in particular the shift in society to nontraditional gender roles, emphasized to these girls—all from lower-class homes—that they would not succeed in life. Their home lives had been dreadful, and the idea of a traditional marriage had promised escape from their intolerable family situations. But, now, society was encouraging women to work and get ahead. The only work opportunities the girls saw as available to them involved drudgery and poverty—and did not promise a means to get ahead and certainly not a means to be taken care of by someone else.

You will hear in Konopka's (1966) analysis an appeal to the blocked opportunity theory. Konopka wrote, "The delinquent girl suffers, like many boys, from lack of opportunity, from lack of success. But her drive toward success is never separated from her need for people, for interpersonal involvement" (Konopka, 1966, p. 41).

All of the girls in Konopka's (1966) study had acted out sexually. Their offense commonly was that they had been sexually active. You will not find adolescent males charged with such an offense.

Konopka (1966) made a compelling argument that a double standard punishes girls, but not boys, for engaging in sex. She doubted that girls engage in more sex than boys, and argued that research evidence indicates boys are more sexually active than girls. Society has harsher responses to adolescent female sexuality because of the consequences sexual acting out can have for girls, but does not bring those consequences to bear in the life of a boy who impregnates a girl. Konopka also said social mores assert that for females—but not for males—sexual intercourse and pregnancy involve the whole personality. By this, Konopka meant sexuality is more than an isolated act for girls; it involves their whole beings and senses of identity.

The question certainly deserves raising, as Konopka (1966) has done, why sexual activity is judged delinquent in females but tolerated in adolescent males. I think it is critical for you to analyze the implications involved in finding girls at fault for engaging in sex with boys, but in overlooking boys' complicity for engaging in that same behavior. Do you think a double standard exists? Do you think adolescent sexual activity is delinquent behavior at all? If it is, should it apply only to girls? Under current statutes, a very high proportion of high school students are engaged in this delinquent behavior.

Overwhelmed with despair about overcoming loneliness, the delinquent girls in Konopka's (1966) study tried one of two approaches to cope. They either lost themselves in the anonymity of a crowd or in the fantasy of a love relationship that seemed all too close to the story of Cinderella. Losing their identities in a crowd allayed some of the yearning for belonging and acceptance, but only temporarily and never substantively. Being rescued by "Prince Charming" provided intensely fantasized relief in virtually every female Konopka studied. The girls deeply resented anyone who questioned the reality of their fantasy relationships with Prince Charming.

What is particularly sad about these common means used to cope with loneliness is the deep hurt these efforts eventually produce. While joining a crowd or losing oneself to a fantasy do offer temporary relief, such coping measures "increase the estrangement, make the wound deeper, [and] increase the hurt" (Konopka, 1966, p. 103). Desperate efforts to gain friendship, identity, and intimacy lead to further abandonment, self-doubt, and disappointment.

The self-doubt that builds when the delinquent girls receive continual feedback that they do not matter to other people—and cannot matter to themselves—produces an increasingly low self-esteem. Suicidal thoughts and actions become common because the girls think of themselves as fundamentally bad and worthless.

A Summary of Konopka's Findings

What dominates the picture Konopka (1966) painted of delinquent girls is a cycle of loneliness, desperate attempts to gain acceptance, feelings of helplessness and estrangement, and self-hate. The self-hate turns inward, most dramatically in suicide, and outward in acts of verbal and physical aggression against others. Researchers have confirmed three of Konopka's findings: effects of puberty, childhood traumas, and changing social mores about the role of women on female delinquent behavior.

Roberta Paikoff, Jeanne Brooks-Gunn, and Michelle Warnen (1991) tested the effects of hormonal status on depression and aggression in 72 white girls between 10 and 14 years of age over a two-year period. Hormone changes were predictive of delinquent behavior observed one year later. However, when certain statistical procedures were introduced to data analysis, the most powerful predictor of delinquency was emotional expression, rather than hormonal levels or physical maturation.

L. B. Bowers (1990) analyzed literature and concluded that evidence has established a relationship exists between physical and sexual abuse in childhood and subsequent female delinquency. The girls most vulnerable to later delinquent behavior had no supportive adults to whom they could reveal the abuse and from whom they could seek help to overcome being victimized. As Konopka (1966) had noted, delinquent girls find adults to be anonymous, unreliable, and arbitrary.

Ronald Berger (1989) analyzed literature to see whether changing social mores, especially the effects of changing gender roles, influence female delinquent behavior. Konopka (1966) had found the girls she interviewed to be deeply distressed that

One issue of growing concern for some observers is the increased involvement of female delinquents in crimes against people.

the traditional roles ascribed to females had changed. Berger (1989) concluded evidence from other sources supported the notion that changing social mores create distress and role strain for girls who turn to delinquency—primarily in the form of sexually acting out.

One issue of growing concern for some observers is that female delinquents have increased their involvement in crimes against people. A 20-year longitudinal study of youths placed in residential care at The Villages of Kansas showed that females admitted during the 1980s committed far more violent crimes than girls admitted in the 1970s, and showed that violent offenses during the 1980s were less gender-related (Balk, Murray, Nelson, & Johnson, 1993). For example, during the 1970s, the more common delinquent behaviors for boys were physical aggression, property damage, and theft, and for girls, sexual activity. In the 1980s, the more common delinquent behaviors for boys were physical aggression, property damage, and theft, and for girls, sexual activity, physical aggression, suicidal gestures, and theft.

We thus finish our discussion of some major explanations for the causes of delinquency. Another concern about delinquent behavior is whether it foreshadows a life of adult crime. Cloward and Ohlin (1960) maintained that membership in a delinquent subculture serves as a training ground for entree to an adult criminal career. They also said solitary offenders are much less likely to turn to crime as adults. What does research say about delinquency as a precursor to adult criminal behavior?

DELINQUENCY: PRECURSOR TO ADULT CRIMINAL BEHAVIOR?

Longitudinal studies indicate that a moderately strong relationship exists between adolescent antisocial behavior and adult criminal activity. The relationship becomes stronger as the seriousness of adolescent antisocial behavior increases. A record of extremely delinquent behavior is singularly predictive of criminal activity as an adult. Thus, the more seriously delinquent the adolescent, the more likely that individual will behave criminally as an adult.

Let's look at two longitudinal studies that investigated the links between juvenile delinquency and adult criminal behavior. The first is the Youth in Transition study, and the second is Lee Robins's study of adults who were deviant children.

The Youth in Transition Study The Youth in Transition study (Bachman, 1972; Bachman, Green, & Wirtanen, 1971; Johnston, O'Malley, & Eveland, 1978; O'Malley, Bachman, & Johnston, 1977) was conducted over a period of eight years. The purpose of the study was to identify the causes and consequences of dropping out of school. Topics investigated included educational achievement, occupational achievement, job satisfaction, self-esteem, motives, emotions, values, job attitudes, and self-reported delinquent behavior.

All subjects in the study were male. The study began with 2,213 tenth grade boys from all U.S. states but Hawaii and Alaska. The researchers collected data several times over the eight years. When the study ended, the research participants were 23 years old, and all but 219 of them had remained in the study. However, only 73% of the 2,213 individuals ($n = 1,608$) completed all the data instruments, causing the researchers to restrict analyses to those individuals. The researchers paid attention to

Robert J. Sampson and John H. Laub (1990), faculty members respectively at the University of Illinois at Urbana-Champaign and Northeastern University, used the longitudinal data set gathered by the Gluecks (1950, 1968) to test two hypotheses about adult criminal behavior. They tested, first, whether antisocial behavior in childhood is predictive of adult criminal behavior. Second, they tested whether adult attachment to social institutions such as the family and work, is associated with a lessening of adult criminal behavior.

The Gluecks' (1950, 1968) sample included 500 boys with persistent histories of delinquency and 500 boys with no histories of delinquency. The Gluecks interviewed their research participants on three occasions: at age 14, at age 25, and at age 32. They retained 88% of the sample for the 18-year duration of the project, a truly remarkable achievement in a longitudinal study.

Sampson and Laub (1990) took these longitudinal data and reanalyzed them to determine if childhood history and/or adulthood experiences have a bearing on the deviant and criminal behavior of adults. Their first focus was on juvenile delinquency as a predictor of adult criminality.

HYPOTHESIS 1:
Childhood Antisocial Behavior Predicts Adult Criminal Behavior

Childhood delinquency was highly predictive of adult criminal behavior and deviancy. As examples, consider that 64% of the delinquent sample inducted into the military were arrested for infractions while in the armed forces, whereas only 20% of the nondelinquent sample committed infractions while they were soldiers. Most were in the military because of the large buildup of American forces during World War II.

Other indicators of adult deviancy and criminality followed the same pattern as arrests for military infractions. In comparison to the nondelinquents, the delinquents engaged in excessive drinking, had significantly more arrests, and were much more likely to gamble and use prostitutes. In fact, the delinquents were five times more likely than their nondelinquent peers to be arrested by age 25 and seven times more likely to be arrested by age 32.

We know that many youths report they have committed acts that deviate from norms expected of youths and commit other acts that are officially considered delinquent behaviors (for instance, drinking alcohol or stealing a car). Sampson and Laub (1990) found that generally minor delinquent acts (such as smoking cigarettes, skipping school, and breaking

the relationship between delinquent behavior during adolescence and behavioral development during adulthood. Specifically, the researchers wanted to see how powerfully delinquent behaviors predict drug use, educational attainment, and criminal activity as young adults.

The researchers categorized delinquent behaviors into three types: (*a*) theft and vandalism, (*b*) physical assault, and (*c*) antisocial behavior in school, such as disrupting classes, getting into fights, and skipping school. Note that drug use, which is a criminal offense, was not categorized as a type of delinquent act.

Did adolescent delinquency predict drug use? Lloyd Johnston, Patrick O'Malley, and Leslie Eveland (1978) found that it did. It was clear, for instance, that 18- and curfew) were of negligible assistance in predicting adult criminal behavior. Juvenile offenses that were crimes, rather than status offenses, were predictors of adult criminal behavior. Sampson and Laub concurred with the Gluecks that childhood delinquency is a prologue to adult criminality.

HYPOTHESIS 2:
Adult Attachment to Social Institutions Lessens Crime in Adulthood

Sampson and Laub (1990) tested how job stability, commitment to educational goals, and attachment to one's spouse influence adult behavior. They discovered adult criminality was associated with uneven employment and poor work habits—that is, with job instability. They also determined that a history of continued employment and good work habits are associated with moving away from a life of crime.

Subjects committed to educational and occupational advancement were much less likely to be adult criminals, whereas individuals with few if any educational or occupational aspirations were highly likely to be criminals as adults. Commitment to occupational advancement is related to Marcia's (1966, 1980) idea of occupational identity, and, thus, a potential link between Marcia's four identity statuses, juvenile delinquency, and adult criminal behavior emerges as an area worth researching.

Which identity status would you expect to be associated with juvenile delinquency and adult crime: identity diffusion, foreclosure, moratorium, or achievement?

Adults with strong attachments to their spouses and their families were much less likely to be adult criminals than were adults with weak spousal attachments and lack of commitment to their families. In short, measures of attachment to family, work, and the community at large were highly predictive of adult criminal activity when these attachments were weak or nonexistent.

The significance of Sampson and Laub's (1990) findings is threefold. First, a history of serious juvenile delinquency prepares youths for a life of crime as adults. Deviancy persists over the life span when youths engage consistently in serious antisocial acts. Second, crime lessens when adults are attached to traditional social institutions; this second finding indicates that adult involvement in or rejection of criminal activity is influenced strongly by social conditions. For instance, in a society marked by high unemployment, opportunities to gain a stable job history and stable work habits greatly decrease, and influences to turn to crime increase. Third, these findings emphasize that both childhood development and adult development play important roles in movements to or movements from criminal behavior.

19-year-old drug users had engaged in serious other forms of delinquency before they began using drugs.

The reverse was not the case, however. Drug use did not precede other forms of delinquency. That is, adolescents did not begin using drugs and then become seriously delinquent. All the evidence suggests delinquent behaviors precede drug use and foreshadow it.

Did adolescent delinquency predict the level of educational attainment? Again, findings were clear. The researchers found a strong negative relationship between delinquency and educational attainment. That is, the more the adolescent was engaged in delinquent behavior, the less he achieved academically (O'Malley et al., 1977).

This finding of a strong negative relationship between delinquency and educational attainment may come as no surprise. Consider the findings presented in Chapter 7 that dissatisfaction with school, dissatisfaction with schoolwork, low motivation to achieve in school, and dislike of classmates among sixth-graders predicted delinquency among ninth-graders (Cowen, Pederson, Babijian, Izzo, & Trost, 1973; Parker & Asher, 1987; Roff, Sells, & Golden, 1972). In fact, the greatest predictor of poor school achievement for the adolescents in the Youth in Transition study was antisocial behavior in school (Bachman & O'Malley, 1984).

Did adolescent delinquency predict adult criminal behavior? The researchers found strong, positive relationships between criminal activity and three types of delinquent behaviors: theft, vandalism, and interpersonal assaults (Johnston et al., 1978).

One should not take these conclusions too seriously. While the association between types of delinquent behavior and adult criminal acts was statistically significant, the practical import was negligible. Adolescent theft and vandalism accounted for less than 5% of all the influences associated with adult criminality; interpersonal assaults accounted for less than 3%. Thus, the researchers could *not* account for over 92% of the influences on adult criminal activity. The researchers found some relationship between delinquency and adult criminality, but this relationship was small (Gold & Petronio, 1980).

Lee Robin's Follow-Up Study of Deviant Children

Lee Robins (1966) conducted a fine follow-up study of individuals identified during their childhoods as **sociopathic personalities**. A sociopathic personality was the term applied to individuals who would now be called **antisocial** or **psychopathic personalities**. Characteristics of these individuals include inadequate moral development, lack of feelings of guilt, impulsive behavior, low tolerance for frustration, exploitation of other people's weaknesses, rejection of authority, callous disregard for other people's rights and well-being, and blaming personal failure on others (Carson, Butcher, & Coleman, 1988).

Robins (1966) traced the development of 473 individuals (350 males and 123 females) originally seen in a child guidance clinic in St. Louis, Missouri in the 1930s. Each had been diagnosed as a sociopathic personality. Robins matched these individuals with a control group of 100 people in terms of age, gender, socioeconomic status, IQ, race, and neighborhood. The controls had not been diagnosed during their childhoods as sociopathic personalities.

Robins's (1966) data underscored the greater vulnerability of males to engage in antisocial behavior as adolescents and adults. Sociopathic adult behaviors were exhibited almost exclusively by males from the child guidance sample. Ninety-four of the 473 children (19.9%) developed antisocial personalities as adults, and 85% of them ($n = 80$) were males. On a positive note, 379 children (80.1%) did not develop antisocial personalities as adults.

Boys referred to the clinic for theft developed antisocial personalities significantly more often than boys referred for all other reasons put together. Insubordination to authority emerged as another important sign of incipient sociopathic adult personality. Although a rare reason for the referral, theft had the same predictive value for the development of sociopathic personalities in girls as it did for boys. For girls, sexual behavior was the sole referral reason that predicted an adult sociopathic personality at a statistically significant rate. At the same time, however, boys referred for sexual problems had a good chance for healthy adult development. Robins (1966) noted that sexual mores had changed considerably since the 1930s, and she questioned whether female sexual activity under current standards would hold the same predictive value for girls' becoming antisocial as adults.

The core of Robins's findings is that a record of extremely delinquent behavior is singularly predictive of adult antisocial activities. In addition to theft, which held the greatest predictive value, 13 other adolescent behaviors were associated significantly ($p < .001$) with adult antisocial behaviors. These other behaviors were

- inability to hold a job,
- incorrigibility,
- staying out at night beyond curfew,
- associating with children of bad reputation,
- impulsive, reckless behavior,
- truancy,
- running away from home,
- lying without apparent motive,
- lack of guilt over antisocial acts,
- sexual perversion,
- sexual intercourse, and
- verbal aggression.

Seven of these behaviors were significantly present among early adolescents who became adult sociopaths. These seven were lying without apparent motive, lack of guilt, recklessness, sexual perversion, incorrigibility, staying out late at night, and bad companions.

The effects of adolescent antisocial symptoms on adult behaviors is made strikingly clear when adult outcomes for other children are considered. Among psychiatrically disturbed children who did not have a history of antisocial symptoms, approximately 25% were functioning well as adults. However, six or more antisocial behaviors were highly predictive of problems in adulthood (Robins, 1966).

Socioeconomic level during childhood did not correlate significantly with development of an antisocial personality. The significant negative home factor that influenced children was the father's antisocial behavior, not his socioeconomic status. Effects of modeling thereby come into play, and give further credence to the social learning explanation for delinquency (Bandura, 1973, 1986; Bandura & Walters, 1963).

Identifying youths who are antisocial is one thing, and such identification is important. But can anything be done to intervene with these youths? We look next at some intervention programs.

INTERVENTION PROGRAMS: TREATING DELINQUENTS AND PREVENTING DELINQUENCY

When discussing delinquency treatment and prevention programs, a good starting point is the question "On which theory about the causes of delinquency is this program based?" In this section, I present data about four interventions, each stemming from a different theory about the causes of delinquency. The first is an approach based on social learning theory.

Gerald Patterson's Notion of Family Mismanagement

Gerald Patterson is a psychologist who uses social learning theory as a framework to help parents regain control of delinquent children. Patterson begins from the behaviorist credo that behaviors resistant to change have a history of reinforcement. In the case of delinquent youths, he says their antisocial behavior stretches back in nearly every case to their childhoods (Snyder & Patterson, 1987).

At his organization, the Oregon Social Learning Center, Patterson and his colleagues have worked for nearly 20 years to train parents to manage antisocial, aggressive youths who have committed multiple criminal offenses. Outside observers have singled out Patterson's approach for its careful and extensive development, clear description, and rigorous assessment methods (Gordon & Arbuthnot, 1987).

Four specific parenting skills Patterson teaches are monitoring children's actions, disciplining behavior, using rational problem-solving skills, and providing social reinforcement. Each skill is something found among parents who raise normal children (Patterson & Stouthamer-Loeber, 1984). Both clinical experience with families with delinquent children and reviews of literature on antisocial children persistently have indicated parents seldom keep track of their delinquent children's whereabouts. These parents provide inconsistent discipline, fail to support prosocial behavior, and engage in disruptive communication when attending to problems. Delinquents themselves consider inadequate nurturance and discipline from parents to be the primary explanation for their behavior (Goldstein, 1990).

It is crucial to grasp the fact that parents and children interact mutually. Youths influence their parents, rather than simply being influenced by their parents. Poor parenting skills produce defiant children who make their parents' lives more troublesome (Snyder & Patterson, 1987).

Patterson and Magda Stouthamer-Loeber (1984) studied early adolescent and middle adolescent boys in 206 families. Nearly all of the boys (99.4%) were white. The boys ranged in age from 10 to 17. Nineteen of the youths (9.2%) had juvenile court records, and 21 (10.3%) admitted they engaged in a high rate of delinquent behavior.

Measures taken on the four family management skills indicated parents of the delinquent youths had problems enforcing discipline, using rational problem solving, and providing social reinforcement. They had more success monitoring the behavior of the younger boys than of the older delinquent children. As the youths' activities became increasingly less monitored, their delinquent activities increased significantly ($p < .0001$).

Patterson and Stouthamer-Loeber (1984) concluded that disrupted parental monitoring played a central role in the boys' delinquent behavior. The more serious repeat offenders, in fact, were from the families in which monitoring was least active.

The authors speculated that disrupted parental monitoring fosters delinquency in two ways. On the one hand, it increases boys' chances to engage in socially prohibited behaviors. On the other hand, it fosters continuous and successive delinquent acts. Thus, disrupted parental monitoring contributes not only to trying out delinquent behaviors but also to repeating these actions (Patterson & Stouthamer-Laeber, 1984).

A key component in Patterson's efforts to teach parents better family management skills is treatment that lasts beyond the center's training sessions. Donald Gordon and Jack Arbuthnot (1987) concluded that little if any evidence supports the efficacy of short-term training (5 to 10 hours) to teach parents better skills of managing delinquent children. Typically, Patterson's training sessions run for 17 or more hours, with nearly the same number of follow-up hours after training.

As an example of Patterson's extended involvement with parents, consider his work with parents and early adolescents who had committed multiple criminal offenses (Marlowe, Reid, Patterson, & Weinrott, 1986). Parents were randomly assigned to the family management skills training program or to other sources of treatment in the community. Patterson's skill training focused on setting rules, monitoring behavior, disciplining behavior, and solving problems. The training lasted over 20 hours, and each family received 15 hours of follow-up during the year.

While their parents were in the training program, the adolescents committed significantly fewer offenses than the youths whose parents had been referred to other sources of help. Furthermore, the youths in Patterson's experimental program were placed in custody for far fewer days than their counterparts. Patterson and his colleagues noted that a decrease in delinquent acts accompanied an increase in enjoyable family interaction (Marlowe et al., 1986).

Interventions Based on Blocked Opportunity Theory

In the 1960s, interventions based on the theory that delinquency results from obstacles to achieving the material and social standards of the middle-class (Cloward & Ohlin, 1960) were extensively funded. The interventions derived from such a view of delinquency were social action programs intended to provide equal opportunity in education, housing, job training, and employment. Programs developed to provide these opportunities are called the Community Action Programs (CAP).

The CAP began in the middle 1960s as part of President Lyndon Johnson's War on Poverty. A major resource for the CAP was the earlier work of President John F. Kennedy's Committee on Juvenile Delinquency. The most influential consultants to this committee were the authors of the blocked opportunity theory, Richard Cloward and Lloyd Ohlin.

The CAP was funded for over $30 million and began programs in several American cities. Evaluations of these programs, as well as other programs of the War on Poverty, assert they were dismal failures. The failures were traced to bureaucratic incompetence, various corrupt political practices at local sites, and questionable assumptions about the causes of juvenile delinquency (Marris & Rein, 1973; Moynihan, 1969).

Interventions Based on Changing Behaviors Through Counseling

Some programs allege that juvenile delinquents can be changed by means of counseling or psychotherapy. The point of these programs is to assist individuals learn delay of gratification or to help parents learn better discipline and management skills. There is little evidence, however, that psychotherapy programs have been successful in reducing or preventing delinquency. In fact, "there are disturbing reports that psychological interventions may be more destructive than constructive for young people" (Adams & Gullotta, 1989, p. 412).

In a study of a psychological intervention conducted with 506 male juvenile delinquents in the 1930s, the researchers randomly placed half of the youths ($n = 253$) and their families in a treatment group that received counseling for over five years (Powers & Witmer, 1951). In addition to counseling, the treatment group received several types of services ranging from tutoring to summer camp scholarships. The 253 youths placed in the control group situation received no services and participated in the study only by providing information about themselves. Joan McCord (1978; McCord & McCord, 1959) provided two follow-up analyses of the results of the intervention.

According to McCord (1978), short-term results showed no differences in delinquent activity between the treatment and the control group subjects. Members of each group committed nearly the same number of crimes during their adolescence, and when they became young adults engaged in criminal behavior with almost the same frequency. However, 30 years later, data suggested that the treatment program had done more harm than good. Thirty years later, individuals who had been in the counseling program as adolescents

- had committed significantly more crimes than their control group counterparts,
- showed more signs of alcoholism and of serious mental illness,
- held lower status jobs,
- expressed less satisfaction with their jobs, and
- had a higher incidence of death.

Various explanations have been offered for why the treatment group members ended up experiencing more problems than the members of the control group. One

There is little evidence that psychotherapy programs have had success in reducing or preventing delinquency.

explanation is that the intervention led the adolescents to have high expectations not fulfilled in later life (McCord, 1978). This explanation sounds like a version of the blocked opportunity theory.

Another explanation is that the program led the adolescents in the treatment group to believe they needed special help. The intervention, in other words, was blamed for fostering dependency. Rather than empowering the adolescents to gain autonomy and self-direction, the program led the boys to label themselves as helpless (McCord, 1978).

Interventions Based on Education and Skills Development

One education intervention did succeed with a group of early adolescent juvenile delinquents (Bowman, 1959). In this intervention, 60 eighth grade boys were identified by junior high school staff as having below-average scholastic ability and as doing poorly in school. Over 40% had police records. The researchers randomly assigned 40 of the boys to alternative classrooms with 20 students each; 20 were selected at random to remain in the school's traditional classrooms.

Teachers in the alternative classrooms provided individual attention to the boys, used small groups, and developed projects out of expressed student interests. The teachers based grading in the alternative classrooms on the progress each student demonstrated. Discipline was considered to be firm, consistent, and based on negotiating issues.

Results showed clear evidence, over the short-term at least, that the alternative classrooms produced beneficial results.

- At the end of the first semester, all the experimental group members were given the choice of returning to their regular classrooms. Ninety-five percent (38 out of 40) chose to remain in the alternative settings.
- Attendance at school improved for the students in the alternative classrooms, but the number of days absent from school increased for the control group subjects.
- School officials and the police indicated delinquent behaviors decreased 33% for members of the alternative classrooms and increased 300% for members of the control group.
- Follow-up regarding work history indicated employers considered boys in the alternative classrooms to be much better workers than the other boys. They also held their jobs longer than members of the control group.
- One feature that did not differentiate boys in the alternative classrooms from their control group counterparts was performance on standardized tests of achievement.
- Compared to boys in the control group, boys in the alternative classrooms said they liked school more.

One explanation for the results of the educational intervention is that it empowered the boys to be autonomous and self-directed. The alternative classrooms enabled the boys to experience school success—even if their standardized achievement test scores did not change—by offering them power to make decisions about classroom activities.

Criteria for success were measured in terms of progress. Such an approach avoided comparisons with criteria that made the boys look inadequate. The alternative classrooms led the boys to see themselves as able to succeed, and interrupted a history of schooling that had led the boys to consider themselves failures and to disrupt traditional classrooms.

What is not mentioned in the report of the intervention is how the boys handled returning to traditional classrooms once their eighth grade experience ended. There is no mention whether similar alternatives were implemented for later grades or if alternative classrooms were put into effect for other disruptive students.

Nagging concern also remains over the dramatic differences in delinquent behaviors between the boys in the alternative classrooms and the control group boys kept in traditional classrooms. The control group boys surely knew about the alternative classroom milieu. What if the control group boys were reacting strongly in rebellion against the fact that they had been excluded from the special arrangement? Were they frustrated at seeing more opportunities blocked?

Intervention programs are aimed at changing problematic behavior. Another approach aims at preventing problem behaviors from developing. We look next at models developed to prevent juvenile delinquency.

Prevention Models   Raymond Lorion, Patrick Tolan, and Robert Wahler (1987) argue that the public health model of prevention offers the most fruitful approach for designing efforts to prevent delinquency. This model categorizes prevention into three types: (*a*) efforts that prevent the onset of delinquent behavior, (*b*) efforts that work to stop early delinquent behaviors from continuing and getting worse, and (*c*) efforts that work to prevent serious offenders from continuing in a life of crime. Traditionally, these three approaches are called, respectively, **primary prevention**, **secondary prevention**, and **tertiary prevention**. Lorion and his colleagues contend that our current level of understanding and skill make secondary prevention of juvenile delinquency the approach most likely to succeed and provide outcomes society will value.

Community psychologists who have engaged in secondary prevention efforts are less sanguine about the prospects for success in diverting delinquents from antisocial behavior. For instance, community psychologists at the University of Illinois indicated their efforts were subverted by politicians and judicial experts who redirected community funds from programs designed to keep youths from developing court records and being officially labeled as delinquents (Rappaport, 1977). Other researchers looking at nearly 60 studies of community efforts to work with delinquents reported the programs were largely ineffective (Gottschalk, Davidson, Gensheimer, & Mayer, 1987). Such results are sobering, to say the least, particularly with the rise in the incidence and prevalence of violent crimes committed by adolescents (Eron & Gentry, 1993; FBI, 1992).

CHAPTER SUMMARY

This chapter looked at behaviors labeled delinquent. Delinquent behaviors involve actions of children and adolescents prohibited by legal statutes. There are two kinds of delinquent behaviors: status offenses and criminal offenses. A status offense involves behavior prohibited only for youths, such as truancy. A criminal offense is illegal regardless of the perpetrator's age. An example is shoplifting. One classification system categorizes criminal offenses as crimes against people and crimes against property. Another system categorizes criminal offenses as violent crimes and theft.

The number of adolescents held in custody for status offenses between the years 1979 and 1989 remained stable. However, the number held for criminal offenses increased nearly 47% in that same time frame.

Males are involved much more than females in delinquent activities. When compared to females, males are arrested much more often for violent crimes, drug crimes, and property crimes. FBI data gathered between 1965 and 1989 show the rate of juvenile arrests has been greater for males during every year, and never once did the ratio drop below four males for every female arrested.

While most college students are beyond the age limit for being considered delinquent, this chapter provided a brief look at antisocial behavior of college students. Imposing evidence indicates antisocial behaviors have histories that date back to childhood. Alcohol is the main influence associated with collegiate antisocial behavior.

Self-reported delinquent behaviors indicate adolescents engage in an incredible number of status and criminal offenses not prosecuted by authorities, primarily because the perpetrators do not become known to the authorities. The greatest rise in delinquent behaviors occurs around 15 to 16 years of age.

The main explanations for delinquency are (a) a willful violation of laws to obtain goals of pleasure, (b) observation of antisocial role models held in esteem, and (c) frustration over blocked opportunities. One researcher has linked female delinquency to acute loneliness, despair, changing social norms about gender roles, intolerable family situations, and a retreat into fantasy. Another researcher, using social learning theory, focuses on modifying poor parental skills to overcome children's antisocial behaviors.

Longitudinal studies indicate a moderately strong relationship exists between adolescent delinquency and adult criminal behavior. The relationship becomes stronger as the severity of the delinquent acts increases. There is also a greater likelihood that adolescents who commit crimes with other delinquents will continue to commit crimes as adults. Another strong influence on developing a pattern of adult antisocial behavior is being raised by an antisocial father.

Treatment programs have had poor results in reducing or preventing juvenile delinquency. Massive federal efforts in the 1960s and 1970s had, at best, negligible success. Counseling programs in the 1930s proved harmful to the adult development of the juveniles. Education programs seem to have some basis for claiming success, at least in the short run. Social learning theory, in particular, has had demonstrated success in reducing juvenile offenses.

We have now completed our review of juvenile delinquency. In the next chapter we review adolescent violence, a topic strongly related to delinquency. We begin with a case study about an adolescent who was raped by someone she thought was a friend.

VIOLENCE AND AMERICAN ADOLESCENTS

"No One Would Believe Me"

The freshman orientation seminar was about to begin. Students were spread about the classroom. They wore the usual college uniform of jeans, expensive running shoes, and t-shirts. Some wore shorts. One of the students was Helen, an 18-year-old freshman.

Helen's first semester in college was going OK academically. Well, better than OK—quite well. She was majoring in prelaw and liked her courses.

Helen had done well all through school, even after the incident in her sophomore year of high school. In college, grades definitely were not a problem, but her loneliness and her isolation from others were becoming more difficult to bear. The informal arrangement of who sat where in the orientation seminar accentuated her lack of connection to anyone else. She was in the front row, and the desks to her left and her right were vacant.

This freshman orientation seminar was interesting. Many different speakers provided information on a variety of topics, such as study skills, campus resources, career decision making, and university policies and procedures. Today, someone from the university's Women's Resource Center was going to speak. The speaker's name was Judy.

Judy began talking calmly but—Helen particularly noticed this—quite forcefully about personal control and self-esteem and each woman's right to decide who uses her body. She talked about women being entitled to feel angry and to express their anger when violated sexually or physically.

"Oh my God," thought Helen, "she's going to talk about rape." Suddenly Helen's memory took her back to her hometown, three years ago, to an incident in her house that she'd kept locked inside her because "no one would believe me."

At the time, Helen was 15. She had curly brown hair, amazingly blue eyes, and stood about 5' 3" tall. She lived in a small farming town, with about 5,000 people. She was a sophomore in high school and had a part-time job working at a store. She liked the people she worked with. All of them were her friends.

One afternoon after work, Henry, an 18-year-old high school senior, who also worked at the store, gave Helen a ride home. When he dropped her off at her house, he asked if he could get something to drink. "Sure," said Helen. Henry was a friend, her pal; she trusted him.

Helen's parents were both at work, so there was no one else in the house other than Henry and herself. She got both of them something to drink, and they went into the living room to sit down and talk. That's when it started.

Henry began to touch her. She was uncomfortable, and embarrassed. She wanted him to stop. She asked him to stop. She said, "No, Henry, don't." But he didn't stop. Henry was much stronger than Helen, and he was raping her.

Helen felt stunned. She couldn't believe this was happening to her—and in her own home. She was shocked that someone she thought was her friend was doing this to her. She also was scared, just plain terrified. She feared no one would come to make Henry quit, and she feared her parents would come home and think she was to blame.

When Henry finished raping her, he got up, got dressed, said, "Thanks, slut," and went back to his car. Helen just lay there on the floor a while, feeling almost numb. She wondered what to do now.

She didn't tell her parents what happened—ever. Partly, she kept quiet because she wanted to protect them from such horrible news; partly, she didn't tell them because she feared they would not believe her.

Socially, Henry really did a job on Helen after he raped her. He returned immediately to work and boasted that he and Helen had had sex. He said she had asked him into her house. She was "easy," said Henry. If Helen had thought about talking to someone at work about being raped, Henry had preempted that possibility.

After a while, it was clear to Helen that people at work felt differently about her. Henry had not only raped her body, he had taken away her reputation. Henry had been very confident he could do to her what he wanted and that she would keep her mouth shut. Henry was right on the latter point.

Helen closed herself off after the rape. It was as if she began operating on autopilot. She stopped being friendly, worked hard to become invisible, and kept to herself. She basically spent the rest of her high school years as if sleepwalking.

Her grades did not suffer. Keeping good grades is probably what saved Helen's self-esteem. It proved she had control over something, maybe not over people who could turn on her, but over her mind.

Helen was different than many females who deny that a rape ever took place. Helen always knew Henry had raped her, but she felt she had no possibility of getting anyone to believe her. It took some time for her to process all her thoughts and feelings about the event. She did all this processing on her own.

Helen spent about two years hurting and being frightened all the time. The fact that she could concentrate on schoolwork did not surprise her—schoolwork was her refuge—but it does make some people wonder how she could have focused on studies when so frightened and hurt. At times, she thought about killing herself when the pain became really bad, but she managed not to destroy herself.

Around the age of 17, Helen began to look at the rape differently. Possibly, the attention paid to rape in the popular media helped her realize she had permission to feel angry about what had happened. Whatever the reasons, Helen was less afraid and much more aware that what Henry had done to her was wrong.

During her senior year, Helen still kept to herself. She continued making good grades. She decided to go to law school when she finished college. It seemed to her that the rape had something to do with her decision to go to law school.

And now, here she was in her freshman orientation seminar, listening about the right to be angry over rape and about women's rights to be believed when they are raped. The tears started to gently stream down her face. After three years, she had found someone who would believe her story. She could let someone else know the secret she had feared no one else would believe. She wept for relief.

This chapter is about adolescent violence. We look at adolescent victims as well as adolescent assailants. Topics covered in this chapter include the prevalence of violence in America and theories about the causes of violence. Some factors, such as family violence and media violence, prompt adolescents to act violently. The availability of guns in this country greatly adds to the number of violent acts adolescents perpetrate. Physical assaults, murders, and sexual assaults are three types of violence adolescents perpetrate. Gang activity has produced an alarming increase in physical assaults, murders, and sexual assaults. Dating violence and date rape are two forms of violence that affect a growing percentage of females, and males who engage in such violence view this quite differently than their victims. The chapter closes with a look at three populations of American youths vulnerable to being assaulted: gay and lesbian adolescents, Asian-American adolescents, and Hispanic adolescents.

VIOLENCE IN AMERICA

Stories in American newspapers highlight the growing tendency of American youths to engage in **interpersonal violence**, violence between people. For instance, after an argument with his half-brother, a 17-year-old teenager systematically shot to death his half-brother, mother, and stepfather over a four hour period. A friend looked on while the first two killings took place, and he did not notify the police until several hours later (Saladino, 1993).

Stories abound of youth murders motivated by vengeance and greed. Adolescents are murdered for their running shoes or athletic jackets; females are sexually assaulted; youth gangs indiscriminately kill and maim people in drive-by shootings.

While I am not claiming that the majority of American youths resorts to violence as a solution to problems, it is sobering to realize that violence (automobile accidents, homicides, and suicides) accounts for most deaths of adolescents in this country (Fisher & Shaffer, 1990). Black youths, particularly males, are especially vulnerable to being murdered (Federal Bureau of Investigation [FBI], 1992).

In June of 1990, *The Atlantic Monthly*, a magazine published in Boston, printed an article on violent crime and its impact on the lives of American urban youths (Zinsmeister, 1990). The information was very chilling. For instance,

- over a four-month period, 102 adolescents and children in Detroit were shot, nearly all by other youngsters;
- of 168 teenagers at an inner-city health clinic in Baltimore, nearly three-fourths knew someone who had been shot and one-fourth had witnessed a murder; and
- all of the 168 teenagers in the Baltimore inner-city clinic had been assaulted, and slightly less than 10% had been raped (Zinsmeister, 1990).

Murder is the leading cause of death for children in American inner cities. Around 50% of the murderers are other youths. These statistics are particularly grim for blacks. Data indicate over 1,000 black children were murdered in 1988, a 50% increase over the number of black children murdered in 1985 (Zinsmeister, 1990). Information also indicates that the murder rate in the adolescent and young adult black populations has actually lowered the expected life span for black Americans by almost four months (McCord & Freeman, 1990; National Center for Health Statistics, 1993). No other ethnic/racial group has experienced such a development.

Prevalence of Violence in America

The homicide rates for 15- to 24-year-old males in several countries will provide a good starting point for illustrating the problem of violence in America. As indicated in Table 13-1, the homicide rate for 15- to 24-year-old males in the United States exceeds the European rates by seven to ten times, on average. The American rate exceeds the Canadian rate by four times, the Australian by three, and the Japanese by over forty-three times (Fingerhut & Kleinman, 1990).

Federal Bureau of Investigation (1992) data have indicated that around 70 individuals are murdered each day in this country. While not confined to any age-group,

TABLE 13-1   Homicide Rates of 15- to 24-Year-Old Males in Selected Countries, With a Comparison to Rates in the United States*

Country	Data Year	Rate per 100,000	Difference With U. S.
United States	1987	21.9	—
Japan	1987	0.5	43.8 times less
Denmark	1986	1.0	21.9 times less
West Germany	1987	1.0	21.9 times less
England & Wales	1987	1.2	18.3 times less
Switzerland	1987	1.4	15.6 times less
France	1986	1.4	15.6 times less
Sweden	1987	2.3	9.5 times less
Australia	1987	2.5	8.8 times less
Canada	1986	2.9	7.5 times less
Finland	1986	3.0	7.3 times less
Norway	1986	3.3	6.6 times less
Israel	1985	3.7	5.9 times less
New Zealand	1985	4.4	5.0 times less
Scotland	1987	5.0	4.4 times less

*Based on statistics the World Health Organization gathered between 1985 and 1987.

SOURCE: Adapted from "International and Interstate Comparisons of Homicide among Young Males" by L. A. Fingerhut and J. C. Kleinman, 1990, *Journal of the American Medical Association, 263.*

murder does especially affect youths—particularly minority group males. When deaths due to suicide, war, lawful use of force by the police, or state executions are excluded, the contrast in the murder rates of white and black youths is stark. As of 1988, national data showed that the homicide rate for black male adolescents was nearly nine times greater than the homicide rate for white male adolescents, and four times greater for black female adolescents than for white female adolescents (National Center for Health Statistics, 1990a; Hammond & Yung, 1993). Analyses indicate that between 1988 and 1990, the homicide rate for middle and late adolescent males (15- to 19-year-olds, in particular) had risen 55% (Centers for Disease Control, 1990a). In the United States, it is now estimated that murder will be the cause of death for

- 1 out of every 27 black male adolescents,
- 1 out of every 117 black female adolescents,
- 1 out of every 205 white male adolescents, and
- 1 out of every 496 white female adolescents (Slaby, 1994).

The data indicate that the most likely murderer of a black adolescent is another black adolescent. What could be the cause of this remarkable and disturbing set of statistics? We are no longer so ignorant that we accept facile racial inferiority theories, think that certain racial groups are inherently more savage, or find ways to blame victims for what is perpetrated against them (Ryan, 1971). But, what in American society leads to this preying of blacks on blacks? One analysis places the fundamental blame on a destruction of intact families, and says this devastation has had an eroding effect on the socialization of a whole cohort of youths who are without hope and certainly without attachments to an intact family system (Whitehead, 1993).

Do you think the roots of black violence on other blacks stem partially or in whole from the long-term effects of a governmental system which has kept a significant proportion of blacks trapped in structural poverty, made them permanent mem-

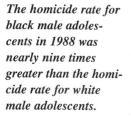

The homicide rate for black male adolescents in 1988 was nearly nine times greater than the homicide rate for white male adolescents.

Theories About Violence

The psychoanalysts would have us believe that humans are engaged fundamentally in a losing battle to control aggressive impulses. The starkest portrayal of this view of human nature is given by Freud (1930/1957) in his monograph *Civilization and Its Discontents*. Karl Menninger (1966), the famous American psychiatrist, believed humans are pitted in conflict against each other and against themselves. These conflict views of human nature form the bases of other writers' descriptions of human beings as a uniquely aggressive, violent species (Ardrey, 1966; Lorenz, 1966). One author from the conflict-ridden days of the 1960s depicted humans as naked apes who evolved from killer gorillas (Morris, 1967).

In a persuasive essay in *The American Psychologist*, Richard Lore and Lori Schultz (1993) argue that Americans make two questionable assumptions about human aggression. The first assumption is that humans are innately aggressive. The second assumption is that societal efforts to control aggression will lead to severe restraints on human freedom.

Lore and Schultz (1993) disagree with these assumptions. They note that several animal species can act as aggressively as humans, but develop means of inhibiting violence. Chimpanzees, lions, lemurs, rats, rhesus, monkeys, and hyenas are examples. They also note that several countries have developed cultures and instituted social policies, such as gun control, that greatly reduce violent incidents.

American violence is sometimes attributed to a "frontier" mentality, blamed on the hordes of desperate, impoverished immigrants who settled this land. Comparisons with Canada and Australia, both of which were frontiers settled by immigrants, indicate American violence cannot be so readily explained by the appeal to the frontier metaphor. Furthermore, Australia was a continent taken over by very rough individuals—convicts in the main—and, thus, the American attempt to explain violence as the legacy of our ancestors holds little weight. More to the point, neither Canada nor Australia has homicide rates even close to the rate in the United States.

bers of an underclass, and led to the destruction of familial and other social systems (Hamburg, 1992; Murray, 1984)? **Structural poverty** refers to impoverishment based in the very demographics of society and resistant to change, even if there is economic growth. An **underclass** comprises people who are trapped in structural poverty. Is there greater likelihood for black adolescents to be murdered than adolescents in other ethnic/racial groups because there is more witnessing of violence and, thereby, more learning of violent solutions in black communities? Are such suggestions themselves infected with stereotypes and racism?

According to data on victims of violent crimes, nearly 1.5 million people over the age of 12 are injured annually in this country due to physical attacks (Bureau of Justice Statistics, 1990). Abuse and neglect produce 1.6 million injured children annually (National Center on Child Abuse and Neglect, 1988). One out of every 130 people under the age of 20 is given medical care for injuries caused by violence (Slaby, 1994).

Several groups are especially vulnerable to violent assault. We have already seen the grim statistics about the murder of black youths. Females are more vulnerable than males to injuries from sexual assault (Sorenson & Bowie, 1994). Gay and lesbian youths are targets of physical assault, sometimes perpetrated by members of their own families (Dark, 1994). Asian-American youths often become victims of hate crimes and of family violence (Chen, 1994). Hispanic youths between the ages of 12 and 24 are victims of violent crime more often than any other group of Hispanics (Soriano, 1994).

Over the past several years, children and adolescents placed in residential facilities by state agencies have been more aggressive and dangerous than youths placed in these facilities during the 1960s and 1970s. These assertions were confirmed in a 20-year follow-up of youths placed in the care of The Villages of Kansas. Youths admitted during the 1980s were more difficult to control than youths admitted during the 1970s. Males were more aggressive than females in each decade, but females admitted in the 1980s were more violent than males admitted in the 1970s. During the 1980s, male aggression at The Villages exceeded male aggression in the 1970s (Balk, Murray, Nelson, & Johnson, 1993).

CIRCUMSTANCES FOSTERING VIOLENCE

Except in unusually stressful circumstances or times of actual psychosis, humans seldom are randomly, unpredictably violent. Even the senseless acts of drive-by shootings seem to have a perverted logic, once you understand the social milieu of gangs, which promote these attacks.

In this section, we investigate social circumstances that foster human interpersonal violence. These include violence in the family, violence in the media, the availability of guns, the use of alcohol and other substances, and economic constraints.

Violence in the Family

For many youths, their families provide an introduction to interpersonal violence. What the youths witness in their families, as well as experience as victims of assault, provide lessons in how to be violent. Of course, by living in a violent home, youths may become victims of family violence; they run risks of injury or death.

The incidence and prevalence of family violence in this country are quite high. Several factors are associated with the alarmingly high rates of American family violence, including (*a*) frequency of interaction between family members, (*b*) proximity to each other, (*c*) intensity of involvement, (*d*) dependence of some family members on others, and (*e*) greater cultural acceptance of domestic violence than of violence outside the home (Slaby, 1994). Look carefully at these five factors. Are not the first four factors what one expects of families? What else besides America's acceptance of domestic violence could explain American family violence?

Parental arguments that result in violence frighten children. These conflicts can scar children emotionally, but they also serve as powerful lessons in how to resolve interpersonal difficulties. No doubt, esteemed models acting aggressively influence children to act aggressively (Bandura, 1973; Bandura & Walters, 1963). In short, parents are one of the first sources from whom many youths learn about interpersonal aggression.

Sibling violence against one another is far more widespread than many people have apparently been willing to acknowledge (see Chapter 5). Older, more powerful siblings find easy targets for aggression in their vulnerable, younger brothers and sisters. Being the victims of sibling aggression leads some youths to turn aggressive against others.

Physical aggression against children is the most direct source of family violence children experience. The forms of parental aggression against children are multiple; the most dire are physical and sexual abuse. Punitive disciplinary tactics (such as slaps or spanking) are common ways that parents assault children. Some writers view threats of violence as actual acts of violence against children (Slaby, 1994). In addition to directly assaulting family members, parents endorse aggression by encouraging violence outside the home and by permitting other family members to attack each other.

Violence in the Media   Media coverage of state executions has a fleeting influence in lowering capital crimes (crimes for which the penalty is death). Whereas the homicide rate drops during the week of an execution covered by the media, and in the following week as well, the supposed deterrent effect of capital punishment lasts no longer. By the second week after the execution, the homicide rate returns to its former level (Phillips, 1984, as cited in Lore & Schultz, 1993). The conclusion is that media coverage has only a short-term effect in deterring murderous violence.

Conversely, a very strong link has been established between watching violence on television and acting aggressively. The effects on children are both immediate and long-term. Longitudinal studies have documented the clear influence of viewing television violence on boys' violent behavior as adolescents and adults (Comstock, 1986; Huesmann, Eron, Lefkowitz, & Walder, 1984). As George Comstock put the matter, "A large majority of studies record a positive association between exposure to television and film violence and aggressive and antisocial behavior, and although there are decided differences in the size of the majority, there is no type of design, no variety of measure, and no category of persons for which there is not a majority of positive findings" (1986, p. 180).

Brandon Centerwall (1992) dramatically chronicled the effects of violent television programs on the increase in white murder rates in this country. He tracked homicide rates and television ownership in the United States for a 30-year period (1945–1975). Fifteen years following the rise in television ownership (during the 1960s), homicide rates of whites began to rise. Centerwall's argument is that children raised on television begin to show the impact of viewing violent programs when they reach their adolescent years. He has equally grim statistics showing the same pattern in Canadian homicide rates and television ownership.

Centerwall (1992) acknowledged that we should not discount the significance of other influences on murder rates, such as poverty, stress, and alcohol. However, he emphasized the very strong association between the introduction of television in the 1950s and a doubling of the murder rate in the middle to late 1960s. Centerwall attributed extensive exposure to television during childhood as the cause of the majority of murders committed in this country.

Viewing violence on television and in films has effects on viewers' attitudes and values as well as overt behavioral consequences. People become indifferent toward victims of violence, increase their distrust of others, and more readily accept violence as proper behavior (Cline, Croft, & Currier, 1973; Murray, 1980; Murray, Rubenstein, & Comstock, 1972). Social scientists no longer ask whether viewing television violence leads to real-world violence, but accept the evidence as conclusive and look now to ways to reduce the negative effects on children who view television violence (Murray, 1993).

Availability of Guns

Over half of all violent crimes juveniles perpetrate involve guns (Lewandowski & Forsstrom-Cohen, 1986). Easy access to firearms is considered the main reason for most murders in this country. Three-fifths of all murders in the United States (60%) are caused by guns, and guns account for 71% of the murders of all middle and late adolescents. As a comparison, less than 24% of homicides in other industrialized countries are caused by firearms (Fingerhut & Kleinman, 1990). Of course, guns are also used to cause injury. In fact, the proportion of nonfatal injuries from gunshot wounds exceeds the proportion of deaths due to firearms eightfold (Rice et al., 1989).

How adolescents get guns varies. In some cases, the gun belongs to the youth's parents. In other cases, the youth steals the gun or buys it. Regardless of how juveniles get firearms, the multiplicity of guns in this country and the efforts of some groups to protect unhindered access to guns has made it fairly easy for adolescents to obtain loaded weapons. As of 1990, Americans owned an estimated 140 million rifles, 60 million handguns, and about 3 million semiautomatic assault weapons (firearms that discharge many bullets per second) (Ewing, 1990).

Adolescents are taking firearms to school with increasing frequency. Four sets of statistics bear out this alarming finding.

- Between 1985 and 1989, the number of firearms confiscated from California elementary and junior high school students increased 43%.

- Between 1985 and 1989, the number of guns confiscated in California high schools increased 50%.

- Between 1987 and 1988, incidents involving guns in Florida high schools increased 42%.

- National survey data of high school students let us infer that on any given day, 135,000 boys take guns to school, and another 270,000 bring a gun to school at least once during their secondary education (Ewing, 1990).

Use of Alcohol and Other Substances

Charles Ewing (1990) reports that the use of alcohol and other drugs plays a significant part in juvenile killings. Youths intoxicated or on drugs often start out to commit a robbery and end up killing their victims. There is also another connection between killings and drugs—many youths kill others in the effort to get money to buy drugs. Over 60% of physical assaults are perpetrated by adolescents who used drugs or drank alcohol before the attacks (Lewandowski & Forsstrom-Cohen, 1986).

One explanation for the role of alcohol in youth homicides is the power of alcohol to lower inhibitions. Alcohol reduces a human's power to reason, to plan, and to restrain behavior, and allows a person to act on violent impulses (Lewandowski & Forsstrom-Cohen, 1986).

Less is known about the disinhibiting power of other substances, such as marijuana. However, several instances of murderous rampages have been blamed on PCP, sometimes called "angel dust" (Slaby, 1994), and the corresponding rise in juvenile drug abuse and in juvenile homicides cannot escape notice (Ewing, 1990).

Economic Constraints

The homicide rates are greatest in countries with the greatest gaps between the wealthy and the impoverished (Hawkins, 1990, cited by Slaby, 1994). The rates of violent crime are also highest in impoverished urban areas (Hamparian, Schuster, Dinitz, & Conrad, 1978). Charles Silberman (1978) argued that homicide rates increase because people denied opportunities become frustrated and turn violent. You may note Silberman's (1978) explanation seems derived from the blocked opportunity notions of Cloward and Ohlin (1960).

The American disparity between the wealthy and the poor is easily noticeable, especially to the impoverished. Television promotes possession and consumption of material goods. We are shown daily what life is like for the rich and famous. The blocked opportunity theory would argue that awareness of these disparities and of this economic discrimination produces violence. As Silberman summarizes this opinion, "The close association of violent crime with urban lower class life is a direct result of the opportunities that are *not* available" (1978, pp. 117–118).

David Hamburg (1992) insists the most profound obstacles challenging efforts to reduce and prevent youth violence come from the experiences of being part of an underclass. These experiences involve severe poverty, broken families, blocked

The most profound obstacles challenging efforts to reduce and prevent youth violence come from the experience of being part of an underclass.

Adolescent Violence in Preindustrial Cultures

I n Chapter 12, I reported cross-cultural data on adolescent antisocial behavior in preindustrial societies. In this section, the focus is on one of the more severe forms of antisocial behavior— namely, violence. The two forms of antisocial behavior most frequently noted in preindustrial cultures are theft and violence. You may recall that criminal offenses in industrialized societies are sometimes catalogued as crimes against people and crimes against property.

Rarely does adolescent violence in preindustrial societies turn fatal. For example, in one Ethiopian culture, adolescent violence never goes beyond shoving and wrestling provoked by verbal mockery gone too far. However, among some Indian tribes of northern Mexico, when adolescents are allowed to drink alcohol at celebrations, they have been noticed to become drunk and insult their elders, sometimes going so far as to threaten them with knives.

Male adolescent violence correlates positively with certain cultural characteristics, including

- high peer competition ($p < .002$),
- adult antisocial behavior ($p < .015$),
- adult sexual promiscuity ($p < .021$), and
- adult deviance in general ($p < .006$) (Schlegel & Barry, 1991).

However, adolescent violence correlates negatively with other cultural characteristics, such as

- high peer cooperation ($p < .01$),
- conformity to cultural values ($p < .03$),
- adolescent trust of adults ($p < .011$), and
- attachment with mother in infancy ($p < .001$) (Schlegel & Barry, 1991).

In short, in cultures that promote peer competition, discourage peer cooperation, and indulge in adult promiscuity and deviance, adolescent males are likely to commit violence.

opportunities, and "isolation from reliably nurturant human contacts" (Hamburg, 1992, p. 191).

TYPES OF ADOLESCENT VIOLENCE

In this section, we look at three types of violence that adolescents perpetrate. These forms of violence are physical assaults, murders, and sexual assaults.

Physical Assaults The percentage of adolescent crimes involving violence is nearly four times greater than the percentage of violent adult crimes (37% to 10%). Another difference between adult and adolescent physical assaults is that most adolescent assailants attack individuals they do not know or attack people with whom they are casually acquainted. However, adult assailants typically attack family members and other individuals they know (Lewandowski & Forsstrom-Cohen, 1986). The difference is attributed to gang violence, which is often directed at strangers or rival gang members known only by sight (Lewandowski & Forsstrom-Cohen, 1986).

The most common adolescent violent offense is physical assault. Such assaults extend from fist fights to brutal beatings. In their study of violent adolescents in California, Jarad Tinklenberg and Frank Ochberg (1981) concluded there are five broad categories of physical assaults perpetrated by youths: (*a*) instrumental, (*b*) emotional, (*c*) felonious, (*d*) bizarre, and (*e*) dyssocial. See Table 13-2 for an explanation of each.

Who are the victims of adolescent physical assaults? The great majority are other adolescents. Some sobering statistics from the 1980s are that 6 out of every 100 early adolescents were victims of assault, and 8 out of every 100 middle adolescents were victims (Hamburg, 1992). As Hamburg notes, "These rates are about twice as high as the rate for people aged twenty and over" (1992, p. 191).

The rates may actually be much worse than what is given above. Rodney Hammond and Betty Yung (1993) report that, at best, one-third of all assaults against adolescents are reported to authorities. Even the assaults that are reported are considered to underestimate the prevalence and severity of adolescent victimization by other youths. Why? The instruments used to record the information are subject to such problems as "memory failure, lying, miscoding, misinterpretation, and reluctance to self-identify as a victim" (Hammond & Yung, 1993, p. 143). In short, violence against adolescents is probably much more prevalent than official data indicate.

TABLE 13-2   Five Types of Adolescent Physical Assault

INSTRUMENTAL
This type of violent crime is planned, calculated, impersonal, and motivated by intent to harm or eliminate the victim. An example is the stalking and rape of a stranger.

EMOTIONAL
This type of violent crime occurs impulsively and usually between individuals who know each other. The perpetrators may be angry or afraid. An example is a boyfriend's assault on his girlfriend when she tells him she wants to break up.

FELONIOUS
This type of violent crime involves assaults that occur in the commission of another crime and without premeditated intent to harm the victim. An example is shooting a store owner who resists a robbery.

BIZARRE
This type of violent crime involves psychotic acts. Often, these crimes involve sadism and excessive brutality. An example is kidnapping, torturing, and dismembering a victim.

DYSSOCIAL
These criminal acts are normative behavior in some violent subcultures. An example is carrying out violent reprisals against a member of a rival gang or using drive-by shootings of strangers as the initiation rite into the gang.

SOURCE: Adapted from "Patterns of Adolescent Violence: A California Sample" by J. R. Tinklenberg and F. M. Ochberg, *Biobehavioral Aspects of Aggression* (pp. 136–137) edited by D. Hamburg and M. Trudeau, 1981, New York: Liss.

Murders   In their study of dangerously violent adolescent offenders, Donna Hamparian and her colleagues (Hamparian, Schuster, Dinitz, & Conrad, 1978) reported a very small percentage (less than 2%) of youth offenses in the early and middle 1970s involved murder. Since those days, the rate of adolescent homicide has increased. By 1988, juvenile homicide arrests accounted for more than 10% of all arrests for murder in this country (Ewing, 1990). Ewing (1990) says social indicators are very grim regarding predictions of the rate of juvenile homicides, which he estimates will increase by at least 7% during the 1990s. Such an increase would mean that by the end of the 20th century, nearly one-fifth of all arrests for murder in this country will involve adolescents. For a country that had over 4,200 murders in 1987 alone, the implication is that by the end of the 1990s, adolescents will murder at least 1,000 people each year, or nearly three individuals a day.

The factors that influence adolescent violence in general play a substantial role in adolescent murder. The major factors are child abuse, poverty, access to firearms, and drugs. To take but one factor into account, reports of child abuse have increased dramatically since 1976; between 1976 and 1987, the number of reports of child abuse increased 127%. Ewing (1990) notes that such data very probably only scratch the surface, as many cases of childhood abuse never come to light.

Of relevance for this section on adolescent homicide is the substantial correlation between child abuse and subsequent adolescent homicide. The legacy of the epidemic of child abuse will be a corresponding increase in the numbers of adolescent homicides and abused children (Ewing, 1990).

The great majority of adolescents who kill are between 15 and 17 years of age (that is, middle adolescents). Very few juveniles arrested for manslaughter or murder are younger than 15. Ninety-three percent of juvenile killers are male; their victims are usually not family members but, rather, strangers or acquaintances. Girls who kill seldom murder strangers, but, more typically, family members or acquaintances (Ewing, 1990).

Far more black adolescents are arrested for murder than adolescents in any other ethnic/racial group. In the late 1980s, over 57% of all adolescents arrested for murder were black. Hispanic youths accounted for nearly 25% of juvenile homicide arrests. These figures indicate a disparity between arrests for murder and black and Hispanic representation in the total population. Ewing (1990) acknowledges that, even with the greater likelihood that police will arrest black and Hispanic youths rather than white, many more adolescent murders are committed by black and Hispanic youths than by members of any other ethnic/racial group.

Again, we are faced with the question of why. Why are many more adolescent murders committed by black and Hispanic youths than by members of any other ethnic/racial group? Are we seeing the outgrowth of obstructions to opportunity and the effects of being part of a permanent economic underclass (Lemann, 1991)? If so, why has the response turned violent in this generation when the response was definitely much less violent in the 1960s? Has the disparity between the "haves" and the "have nots" become more noticeable or actually that much greater (Edsall, 1988)? Is the answer to be found in the ready availability of firearms? The answer is probably a mixture of several sociocultural factors, including among them, blocked opportunities, the experience of being part of an underclass, and the disparity between the haves and the have nots.

Sexual Assaults   Juvenile sexual offenses are underreported. Part of the reasoning leading to this assertion is that victims frequently keep silent about being attacked. Gail Ryan (1991a) noted juveniles arrested for sexual assault for the first time had, on average, assaulted six other individuals prior to the arrest.

About 15% of the arrests of dangerously violent adolescents in the study by Hamparian and her colleagues (1978) were for sexual assault; out of a total of 985 arrests for violence, 140 were for sexual assault. If Ryan's (1991a) estimate of one arrest for every seven individuals assaulted is correct, the juveniles had actually assaulted nearly 1,000 people.

Self-reports indicate nearly 60% of male children who are sexually abused are victimized by adolescents. These figures lead Ryan (1991a) to estimate that, in 1986 alone, 70,000 boys were victims of adolescent sexual assault. Furthermore, self-reports indicate around 25% of females sexually abused as children were attacked by adolescents. Using 1986 data, Ryan (1991a) extrapolates that adolescents victimized 110,000 girls in that year alone. She estimated further that up to 7% of all females under the age of 18 are victims of adolescent sex offenders.

Over half of adolescent sexual assaults (55%) are against someone the adolescent knows—for instance, a neighbor's child. About 40% of sexual assault victims are related to the adolescent. Strangers account for, at most, 5% of victims selected by juvenile sexual offenders. Nearly all offenders are at least ten years older than their victims, who, on average, are about 6 when assaulted (Ryan, 1991b).

Most adolescent sexual offenders (93%) are male. The majority are white, live with both parents, and, possibly, were victims of sexual abuse themselves. About one-third have been arrested for some nonsexual offense, such as shoplifting. Although many live with both parents, the trauma of parental loss—divorce or death of a parent—is common (Ryan, 1991a).

Ryan (1991a) calculates that, at most, 2 out of every 1,000 adolescent males engage in sexual assault. She figures that this small proportion of the male adolescent population accounts for over 20% of the rapes committed in this country. She acknowledges that critics consider her "2 in every 1,000" estimate much too conservative. What is not clear is whether the critics think these adolescents commit more than 20% of the rapes in this country.

This concludes our discussion of types of adolescent violence. Next, we turn to a particular form of adolescent violence; namely, gang violence.

GANGS

Los Angeles is a city of gangs. There are Chinese gangs and Central American gangs, Vietnamese and Cambodian gangs, Phillipino [sic], Korean, and Samoan gangs. There are white gangs. The oldest street gang in L.A., dating back to the thirties, is Mexican-American . . . . But the white hot glare of public interest focused sharply on gangs only a little more than two and a half years ago. And then it centered on the ghetto gangs, the Bloods and the Crips (Bing, 1991, p. xiv).

The concern over the violence of the Bloods and the Crips is illustrated clearly by an account in Ewing's (1991) book *Kids Who Kill*. The Crips and the Bloods wear gang colors—Crips blue and Bloods red. Ewing (1991) tells how two teenage Bloods murdered a 16-year-old Crips gang member on an L.A. mass transit bus. They killed him, they said, because he was wearing a Los Angeles Dodgers baseball cap, which just happens to be blue.

Other gang incidents highlight why youth gangs have become a national concern. Gangs engage in drive-by shootings of randomly selected strangers. Gang members injure and kill each other in shootouts, and they also kill innocent bystanders caught in the crossfire. Gang activity and gang organization are spreading across the country from large metropolitan areas, such as Los Angeles and Washington, D.C., to small towns. One of the ironies is that correctional facilities and prisons become fertile grounds for recruiting gang members (Knox, 1991).

In this section, we will look at theories about gangs, statistics about gang members, and information about gang violence. We begin with a discussion of theories about gangs.

Theories About Gangs   Three main theories to explain youth gangs are *strain theory*, *cultural deviance theory*, and *dysfunctional families*. We studied a derivative of strain theory in the discussion in Chapter 12 of Cloward and Ohlin's (1960) blocked opportunity theory. (Note that the subtitle of the Cloward and Ohlin (1960) book, *Delinquency and Opportunity*, mentions gangs.)

The fundamental idea of **strain theory** is that youths in an impoverished underclass strive to solve the problem of their economic oppression. Finding no doors opening on the world of economic advancement, the youths experience strain over the obstacles preventing attainment of their economic aspirations. This strain leads to frustration, discontent, and anger; however, rather than becoming helpless, the youths develop their own economic opportunity program—the gang (Goldstein & Soriano, 1994; Knox, 1991).

Cultural deviancy theory explains youth gangs as the creation of adolescents who follow behavioral norms that vary considerably from the norms of mainstream society. Norms in the youth gang subculture include endorsement of gratuitous violence, instant gratification, rebellion against social restraints such as laws, and group autonomy (Cohen, 1966).

In his study of a Puerto Rican youth gang in Chicago, Felix Padilla (1992) said the gang members did not perceive their behaviors as deviant. While they recognized that their business (selling drugs) was illegal and violated traditional social norms, the gang members thought the gang offered them "the only course of action still available to them and with which they [could] challenge existing constraints in and domination by mainstream society" (Padilla, 1992, p. 4).

Padilla's portrait seems a clear confirmation of the blocked opportunity explanation of gangs. Perhaps the issue of deviancy depends on who does the labeling, not just on the consequences of the gang behaviors for people doing the labeling.

Dysfunctional families as the cause of gangs (Bloch & Niederhoffer, 1958) is the theory Armando Morales (1992) uses to explain Hispanic gangs in Los Angeles. Morales maintains that adolescents turn to gang membership to achieve the nurturance, support, and protection denied them in their biological families. Invariably, their families are beset by drug addiction, alcoholism, chronic illness, impoverished housing, physical and emotional abuse, and parental discord. Morales says the gang provides members "affection, understanding, recognition, loyalty, and emotional and physical protection" (1992, p. 137).

Delinquents attribute their antisocial behavior most often to dysfunctional family environments (Goldstein, 1990). The delinquents speak of the gang as a family. In George Knox's (1991) massive synthesis of research about gangs, he concluded that gangs serve as surrogate families for their members.

Statistics About Gang Membership   Accurate data about gangs are elusive. Researchers have grave difficulties collecting valid and reliable firsthand information. In addition, gang members may be suspicious of researchers and thus unwilling to discuss their gangs.

In the 1980s, efforts were made to uncover information about gang membership in urban areas considered to have the most gang activity. Results indicated most gang members are male, are between 12 and 21 years of age, and come from poorer sections of the city. Most gangs comprise ethnic and racial minority youths, and it is very uncommon for members of different ethnic groups to be members of the same gang (Miller, 1974).

In the early 1980s, a survey of police in this country showed gangs are not confined to metropolitan areas. Some of these gangs are in smaller towns and were linked to gangs in big cities. Whereas Arnold Goldstein and Fernando Soriano (1994) consider this belief in gang franchising to be mostly a myth, police are convinced otherwise. The case of Topeka, Kansas provides data for consideration.

Police in Topeka indicate gang leaders in Chicago, Detroit, and Kansas City make occasional efforts to establish a foothold in Topeka (Taschler, 1993c). *NBC Nightly News* on October 5, 1993, featured a story about the growing gang violence in Topeka, and people have noted there are more homicides in Topeka than in San Diego, a city 20 times larger than Topeka. A national newspaper ran a story on school violence and featured, among other cities, Topeka (Guttman, 1993). This reference to Topeka gang problems ought to, if nothing else, highlight how serious gangs have become. Hardly a booming metropolitan area, even the capitol city of Kansas is having gang-related problems.

By the late 1980s, it was clear that gangs were found in every state, with particular concentrations in California, Illinois, and Florida. The number of youths in these gangs was estimated to be less than 120,000 (Spergel, Ross, Curry, & Chance, 1989).

The estimate that gang members total less than 120,000 seems surprisingly low given the growing concern over the spread of youth gangs. Knox's (1991) evidence of the membership in gangs within correctional facilities and prisons indicates gang membership exceeds the number found on the street. Knox's data suggests gangs are endemic to offender populations and are present in every state of the United States. There seems little evidence that these gang members leave their gangs once released from prison.

In the words of one midwestern police officer who is a specialist on youth gangs, "Gangs are like cancer. If you leave them alone, they'll spread" (Taschler, 1993a,

p. 1A). As an example, police in Wichita, Kansas estimated gang membership doubled in their town in 1991 and noted that gang violence had increased 50% by the following year. As of 1992, an estimated 1,200 gang members lived in Wichita, and police predicted that, if these gangs became entrenched, gang activity would spread to smaller Kansas towns (Taschler, 1993a).

Today's gangs are still predominantly male; females commit, at most, 5% of gang-related crimes. Today, youths enter gangs earlier and stay longer than gang members did previously, except for females, who still enter later than males and leave earlier. Whereas the age range of gang members used to extend from 12 to 20, it now extends from 9 to 30.

The reason for including younger gang members is linked directly to dealing in drugs. Juveniles are used as messengers, lookouts, and **mules**—that is, individuals who carry drugs from one point to another. Children are recruited because the juvenile justice system is predisposed to treat younger perpetrators less harshly than older adolescents and young adults (Goldstein & Soriano, 1994). To illustrate this point, consider the following story: police in Garden City, Kansas (a town of about 24,000 people) met 15-year-old-gang members from Detroit at the bus depot, confiscated the drugs the youths were sent to deliver, and placed the youngsters on the next bus back to Detroit.

Older gang members stay in the gang for two reasons. The first is the money available from dealing drugs. The second is there are few opportunities for them in the regular workforce. Ironically, as Padilla graphically illustrates, even in gangs, worker exploitation is in force; only the gang's main leaders benefit from the work of everyone else in the gang, and the other members occupy a "permanent position as minimum wage earners" (1992, p. 6).

Leaving the gang can occur via many avenues. Some gang members marry and leave the gang, some find legitimate employment, others become too old, and some are killed (Goldstein & Soriano, 1994). Many are sentenced to prison, but, in these cases, they join gangs on the inside (Knox, 1991). One ex-gang member from the 1970s, who is now a police officer in Wichita, Kansas, said he left his gang when given the choice of prison or the military; he chose the military (Taschler, 1993b).

Gang Violence   Gang violence has increased substantially since the 1970s. Relatively few gang homicides were reported in the 1950s and 1960s, but by 1980, the city of Los Angeles alone reported 351 deaths due to gang violence (Goldstein & Soriano, 1994). By the year 1989, nearly 40% of all the murders in Los Angeles were gang-related (Ewing, 1990).

Police who work with gangs have come to understand their utter disregard for life and the lack of remorse gang members feel for their victims. "Their appetite for vengeance and destruction defies understanding" (Taschler, 1993d, p. 1A). Two examples from Wichita, Kansas illustrate the point.

- In 1992, gang members went to the home of a rival gang member, knocked on the front door, and shot in the face the person who opened the door. The victim was the mother of the rival gang member. In retaliation, the woman's son took members of his gang and did the same thing to the mother of one of the rival gang's members.

- In 1993, gang members were at the grave site for the burial of one of their own killed in gang-related violence. "A rival gang moved into the cemetery, walked right past police, and attacked the rival gang members attending the funeral" (From "An Ounce Prevention," by J. Taschler. In *The Topeka Capital-Journal*, Jan. 31, 1993, *119*, 1A–2A; "Ex-gang Member Joins Other Side," by J. Taschler. In *The Topeka Capital-Journal*, Feb. 2, 1994, *119*, 1A–2A; "Mind-set of Gangs: No Remorse," by J. Taschler. In *The Topeka Capital-Journal*, Feb. 2, 1994, *119*, 1A–2A. Reprinted by permission).

Startling statistics on gang killings are now common in nearly every major American city. These cities report increases in gang membership and a corresponding increase in gang violence and murder. For instance, Chicago police reported gang killings increased nearly 30% between 1987 and 1988 (from 47 to 60) (Ewing, 1990). The ex-gang member now on the Wichita police force said the major difference between gangs today and when he was a member is "they're more violent . . . . macho to these guys is you kill someone" (Taschler, 1993b, p. 2A).

Several things prompt gang violence. The chief spur is the desire to remove competition in the drug trade. Other sources of gang violence are conflict over territory ("turf"), perceived insults, prejudice, and jealousy over girls (Goldstein & Soriano, 1994).

Access to guns makes the turn to violence so deadly. Whereas before, gangs had chains, bricks, bats, knives, and zip guns, today, they have automatic weapons. Knox (1991) suggests that one means to understand the organizational features of gangs is to identify whether the weapons they use are low-threat (for instance, clubs, rocks, and knives) or high-threat (military ordnance and automatic weapons); the higher threat the weapons present, the greater the formal organization of the gang.

One form of gang violence, exemplified by what New York police call **wolf packs**, is especially disquieting. Wolf packs are "informal bands of youthful marauders who come together solely to attack, rob, rape, and sometimes kill" (Ewing, 1990, p. 103). The most infamous act of a wolf pack involved the multiple rapes and attempted murder of a female jogger in New York City's Central Park. The perpetrators said they thought it was fun. Wolf pack incidents occur, on average, three times a day in New York (Ewing, 1990).

Gang violence is organized and involves a group of individuals. Another form of violence, despite its prevalence, typically occurs on an individual level. I am referring to dating violence and date rape. We look at these topics next.

DATING VIOLENCE AND DATE RAPE

Some heterosexual relationships have an underside of coercion and victimization. One form of this violence is physical abuse. Another form is coerced sexual intercourse; that is, **rape**. In this section, we look at dating violence and date rape as they affect high school and college students.

High School Students

Dating violence affects about 10% of high school students (Roscoe & Callahan, 1985) but increases to 22% for college students (Sorenson & Bowie, 1994). Reports of dating violence exclude rape or other sexual assault and concentrate on physical injuries, verbal assaults, and threats of violence. Jealousy and anger are the primary motives for dating violence, and most incidents occur once the partners have been dating each other steadily (Burke, Stets, & Pirog-Good, 1989; Makepeace, 1986; Roscoe & Callahan, 1985).

Emotional trauma is three times greater for females than for males following dating violence. The victims generally seek help from friends, if they seek help at all. Many females even consider the violence a sign of their partner's love. In most cases, the female reasons her boyfriend became violent because she denied him sex. Males say they become violent with a date to exert power over her or to intimidate her (Sorenson & Bowie, 1994).

In 1992, a nationwide survey of high-achieving high school students—all were juniors or seniors, all had at least a B average, and 97% planned to attend college—produced some disturbing findings about what these adolescents thought a female means when she says "No." Nearly half of the students said that when a female was being affectionate and passionate, she was willing to continue sexual activity, even if she told her partner she wanted to quit. Males and females did not differ on this point ("Teens Believe," 1992).

Thirty-one percent of the respondents knew someone who had been the victim of date rape. In the previous year's national survey, 24% had said they knew a date rape victim. Drinking alcohol had been involved in practically all the date rapes: both parties had been drinking in 45% of the rapes, the assailant in 42%, and the victim in 13%. The survey results also indicated proportionately more Hispanic students (25%) had been date raped than high school girls from any other ethnic/racial group.

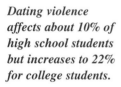

Dating violence affects about 10% of high school students but increases to 22% for college students.

Among females in the other ethnic/racial groups, 21% of the blacks had been raped, 13% of the whites, and 9% of the Asian-Americans ("Teens Believe," 1992).

In a study of adolescent sexuality conducted by Robert Coles and Geoffrey Stokes (1985) 14% of the girls reported they had been raped. The assailant was a boyfriend or an acquaintance in almost half the cases. When discussing adolescent rape, Herant Katchadurian (1990) noted that by the time they reach adolescence, males accept the use of force with females and have established reasons to justify its use.

As many as 25% of middle to late adolescent females are considered to be victims of date rape. Females between the ages of 16 and 19 are considered especially vulnerable (Sorenson & Bowie, 1994). Both Suzanne Ageton (1983) and Mary Koss (1988) indicate that over half of all sexual assaults of adolescents occur on dates, either in the victim's or assailant's home or car.

How do adolescent female rape victims respond? One alarming finding is that most victims do not think the assault fits the definition of rape and, therefore, they refrain from reporting the attack to the police. Psychological reactions involve feelings of fear, anxiety, self-blame, loss of self-esteem, and depression. A majority of rape victims develop some type of **sexual dysfunction** (problems that interfere with sexual relations), such as aversion to sex or **vaginismus** (painful contractions of the sphincter muscle of the vagina). Some women report **flashbacks** (vivid recall of the event) (Ageton, 1983; Burgess & Holmstrem, 1979/1986; Burnam, Stein, Golding, Siegel, Sorenson, Forsythe, & Teller, 1988; Koss, 1988). Susan Sorenson and Patricia Bowie (1994) indicate there is concern that adolescent rape victims may develop **delayed stress reactions** (intense responses occurring some time after the event) long after the rape, but acknowledge there are no data about the incidence or prevalence of such problems.

College Students

As early as 1957, researchers reported that up to one-quarter of all college females surveyed reported their dates had attempted to force them to engage in sexual intercourse (Kanin, 1957; Kilpatrick & Kanin, 1957). Fifteen percent of college males in a 1984 study admitted they had forced dates to have intercourse despite their dates' protests (Rapaport & Burkhart, 1984). Other studies report date rape prevalence rates on college campuses range from 5% to 25% (Kilpatrick, Veronen, & Best, 1984; Koss, 1985; Russell, 1984).

U.S. Department of Justice crime statistics for 1988 indicate the number of reported rapes on university and college campuses totaled 266 (FBI, 1989). The report for 1991 showed a 46% increase ($n = 388$) in reported rapes (FBI, 1992). Data from a nationwide survey of college students indicated only 58% of rape victims report the crime (Koss, 1988). If this figure is applied to the FBI data, we can estimate that at least 377 rapes were committed on university and college campuses in 1988; in 1991, the estimated figure of actual rapes would be 550.

The Ms. Magazine Study

Because prevalence rates of date rape on college campuses varied so widely from one study to the next, *Ms. Magazine* commissioned a nationwide survey of sexual assault on university and college campuses (Koss, Gidycz, & Wisniewski, 1987).

Both males and females were surveyed, and—despite some sampling difficulties regarding ethnic representation—the study clarified the prevalence of date rape in college settings.

The investigators surveyed 6,159 students: 3,187 (51.7%) were female, and 2,972 (48.3%) were male. Only 91 students (1.5%) declined to participate. Koss (1988) cautions that her sample was not fully representative of college students across the country for two reasons. One, minority students were not as well represented as whites; and two, over 67% of the colleges and universities contacted refused the researchers permission to survey their students.

Most students in the sample (86%) were white, the average age of the sample was 21, and a plurality of the sample (39.5%) was Catholic. A breakdown of the sample's demographic characteristics is provided in Table 13-3.

Students answered a self-report inventory. The instrument asked questions about such experiences as having sexual intercourse against one's will because the other person used physical force and engaging in forms of intercourse (for example, oral sex) against one's will because the other person used physical force. Validation procedures using interviews with randomly selected males and females indicated very high correlations between what people reported on the inventory and what they reported in interviews several months afterwards (Koss, 1988).

TABLE 13-3 ■ Characteristics of the *Ms. Magazine* Sample

	FEMALES		MALES		TOTAL	
MARITAL STATUS	NUMBER	PERCENTAGE	NUMBER	PERCENTAGE	NUMBER	PERCENTAGE
Single	2,709	85	2,675	90	5,384	87.4
Married	351	11	267	9	618	10.0
Divorced	127	4	30	1	157	2.6
ETHNIC/RACIAL IDENTITY						
White	2,740	86	2,556	86	5,296	86.0
Black	223	7	178	6	40	16.5
Hispanic	96	3	89	3	185	3.0
Asian	96	3	119	4	215	3.5
Native American	32	1	30	1	62	1.0
RELIGIOUS PREFERENCE						
Catholic	1,243	39	1,189	40	2,432	39.5
Protestant	1,211	38	1,010	34	2,221	36.1
Jewish	127	4	149	5	276	4.5
Other or None	606	19	624	21	1,230	19.9
TOTAL	3,187	52	2,972	48	6,159	100.0

SOURCE: Adapted from "Hidden Rape: Sexual Aggression and Victimization in a National Sample in Higher Education" by M. P. Koss, *Rape and Sexual Assault, Volume II* (pp. 6–7) edited by A. W. Burgess, 1988, New York: Garland Publishing Company.

One-eighth of the females (12.1%) reported males had attempted to rape them, and 15.4% reported they had been raped. While nearly three-fourths of the males (74.8%) indicated they had not attempted to force females to have sex, a significant minority (25.2%) had engaged in some form of sexual assault: 3.3% had tried to rape a date, and 4.4% had raped one or more dates.

Women in private colleges (14%) and in major universities (17%) reported a considerably higher rate of rape than females in religiously affiliated schools (7%). Rape and ethnic/racial identity of victims correlated significantly ($p < .002$), as did rape and ethnic/racial identity of assailants ($p < .001$). Table 13-4 provides data about the ethnic/racial identity of victims and perpetrators of rape on college campuses.

In sheer numbers, white females were by far the ethnic/racial group most victimized, but in terms of prevalence rates, Native American females were victimized far more. You may recall the caution Koss (1988) gave about making inferences to groups other than whites; namely, that minority students were not as well represented as whites.

The average age for the women when they were raped was 18.5. Nearly all the women knew their assailants, and nearly 60% were on dates when the rapes occurred. The dominant feelings for the women during the rape were anger, fear, and depression.

Over two-thirds of the women did not inform the police of the rapes, and for the one-third who did contact the authorities, they did not consider the police to be at all supportive. What surprised the researchers was that 42% of the victims reported having had sex again with their assailants. Whether these incidents were also coerced was not determined. In time, nearly all of the women (87%) reported they broke off their relationships with the men who raped them. Two-fifths said they believed it was likely they would be sexually assaulted again (Koss, 1988).

The males who raped were 18.5 years old, on average, when the rapes occurred. Most frequently, they forced women to have sex in a house off campus or in an automobile. Almost always, they knew the female, and over 60% raped their dates.

TABLE 13-4 **Ethnic/Racial Identity of Victims and Perpetrators of Rape on College Campuses***

	VICTIMS		PERPETRATORS	
ETHNIC/RACIAL IDENTITY	Number	Percentage	Number	Percentage
White	438	16	102	4
Black	22	10	18	10
Hispanic	11	12	6	7
Asian	7	7	2	2
Native American	13	40	0	0

*Percentages based on total number of students per ethnic/racial group.

SOURCE: Adapted from "Hidden Rape: Sexual Aggression and Victimization in a National Sample in Higher Education" by M. P. Koss, *Rape and Sexual Assault, Volume II* (p. 12) edited by A. W. Burgess, 1988, New York: Garland Publishing Company.

The large majority of male rapists (74%) were drinking or using **psychoactive drugs** (for instance, marijuana, amphetamines, hallucinogens, and cocaine) when they attacked their victims. The rapes usually followed heavy petting. They said the women had not at all been clear about not wanting to have intercourse, but they did acknowledge using physical force. The most commonly reported emotion for males during a rape was pride. Nearly half of the males (47%) expected they would engage in forced sex again (Koss, 1988).

We have finished the section on date violence and date rape. Next we turn to a discussion of certain groups who seem particularly vulnerable to aggression.

ADOLESCENT GROUPS VULNERABLE TO VIOLENCE

In this section, we look at three populations of American youths vulnerable to violence: gay and lesbian adolescents, Asian-Americans, and Hispanics. We have already noted in an earlier section the particular risk for black adolescents—especially for males—of violent deaths.

Gay and Lesbian Adolescents

Fear of the AIDS epidemic and a deep-seated **homophobia** (irrational fear of homosexuality) in American society have led to increased violent attacks against gay and lesbian youths. Lawrence Dark (1994) reports that several organizations, such as the National Gay and Lesbian Task Force, indicate a rise in hate crimes against homosexuals in the United States. One environment where violence against gays and lesbians has increased is the college campus (Dark, 1994). While not providing any data to support his assertion that information about **gay bashings** (violent assaults against homosexuals) is suppressed, Dark (1994) intimates that conservative politicians have denounced any efforts to investigate violence against homosexual youths.

Data suggest there has been a rise in hate crimes against homosexuals in the United States.

One source of information about violence directed against homosexual adolescents indicates the incidence of gay bashing has increased (Hunter, 1990). In her report, Joyce Hunter (1990) presented self-report data from gay and lesbian adolescents who had been assaulted in New York City. Slightly less than half the adolescents considered they had been targeted specifically because of their homosexuality. Over 60% of gay-targeted assaults were from family members.

Asian-American Adolescents

In the last section we saw the term *hate crime* being used to describe attacks against homosexuals. Asian-American youths are vulnerable to hate crimes motivated by racial prejudice.

The most dramatic demonstration of hate crimes against Asian-Americans came during the 1992 Los Angeles riots. According to Shium Chen (1994), over 3,000 businesses owned by Asian-Americans were destroyed or severely damaged, dozens of Asian-Americans were physically assaulted, some were shot, and two were killed.

Following the L.A. riots, a national conference on violence looked at hate crimes perpetrated against Asian-Americans. Without exception, all Asian-American youths were said to have experienced some form of threat or to have been assaulted. Chen (1994) noted that Asians are fourth in a rank order of victims of hate crimes, preceded by blacks, Jews, and homosexual men.

Reports from the United States Commission on Civil Rights confirm this stark picture. In 1986, the Commission said hate crimes against Asian-Americans were present throughout the country, and reconfirmed in 1992 that violent assaults against Asian-Americans had become widespread (U. S. Commission on Civil Rights, 1986, 1992).

Hispanic Adolescents

Specific data about assaults against homosexuals and Asian-American youths are harder to come by than data about violence perpetrated against Hispanic adolescents. For instance, during the decade of the 1970s, the homicide rate for Hispanic males in Los Angeles increased by almost 300% (from a rate of 9 per 100,000 to nearly 33 per 100,000). Most of the deaths were gang-related (Soriano, 1994).

National data indicated that between 1979 and 1986, the rate at which Hispanics were victimized by violent crime exceeded the rate for whites and nearly equalled the rate for black victimization. These rates were 40 out of every 1,000 blacks, 37 out of every 1,000 Hispanics, and 29 of every 1,000 whites (Soriano, 1994).

On the whole, the data indicate that Hispanic youths are more at risk than non-Hispanics of being victims of robbery as well as victims of aggravated assault. Hispanic males are more likely than non-Hispanic males to be victims of violent crime (49.5 per 1,000 versus 36.3 per 1,000, respectively). Hispanic females are more likely than non-Hispanic females to be victims of violent crime (25 per 1,000 versus 21.9 per 1,000, respectively) (Soriano, 1994).

Hispanic youths are more inclined to report assaults when they know their assailants. If a stranger assaults them, less than 43% of Hispanic adolescents inform the police. However, if an acquaintance perpetrates the assault, nearly 70% of Hispanic victims report the crime (Soriano, 1994). Of course, these data mean that between 30% and 57% of assaults against Hispanic youths go unreported. Non-

Hispanics, however, seem even more hesitant than Hispanics to report assaults perpetrated by individuals they know (47% to 68.5%) (Soriano, 1994).

EFFECTS OF VIOLENCE

The effects of violence are twofold. First, adolescents who witness violence in their families are more likely to become part of the cycle of violence as adults. Second, violence produces long-lasting emotional trauma.

The Cycle of Violence

Children who witness family violence, particularly chronic sexual and/or physical abuse, are at risk of perpetrating violence themselves when they become older, especially if they are male, or of becoming a victim of violent assault at an older age, especially if they are female (Jaffe, Sudermann, & Reitzel, 1992). The association between witnessing family violence as a child and becoming a perpetrator or victim of violence during adolescence is what is meant by the **cycle of violence**.

The many changes associated with adolescence amplify the emotional and interpersonal problems that accrue during a childhood marked by family violence. Adolescent attacks on others and violence against self (that is, suicide) are the most obvious symptoms associated with a history of family violence (Grusznski, Brink, & Edelson, 1988; Jaffe et al., 1992). Other effects associated with observing family violence are:

- a fourfold increase in the likelihood for adolescent males to assault their dates,
- a greater probability for adolescent males convicted of violent offenses to repeat these crimes, and
- a one-third greater chance for adolescent females to be victims of date rape and other forms of assault (Jaffe et al., 1992).

Emotional Trauma Caused by Violence

Individuals who experience traumatic life events, such as aggravated assaults, can experience emotional reactions whose intensity and duration are far greater than suspected by unaffected outsiders (Silver & Wortman, 1980). The enduring emotional trauma of violence has been likened to the psychologically disabling conditions seen in many soldiers years after they were involved in combat (Foa & Rothbaum, 1992).

Some of the symptoms of the enduring emotional trauma of violence are depression, difficulties getting to sleep or staying asleep, nightmares, anxiety and fear, severe self-doubt, and constant rumination about the violent incident (Foa & Rothbaum, 1992). Because adolescents are the most likely victims of violence perpetrated by adolescents, we have the very worrisome prospect that a significant proportion of our contemporary adolescent population will enter adulthood still trying to cope with emotional trauma. These emotional effects will change not only these adolescents but also others in their lives.

Efforts to overcome the disabling psychological conditions produced by violence seek to help the individuals cope with the extreme anxiety they feel. Some of these efforts involve teaching means to increase tolerance for stress (Foa & Rothbaum,

TABLE 13-5 ▪ Adaptive Response to Violent Assault and the Model for Understanding Responses to Life Crises Developed by Moos (1986)

ADAPTIVE RESPONSES TO VIOLENT ASSAULT	COPING RESPONSES IN MOOS MODEL
Increase stress tolerance	Maintain emotional balance
Develop new coping skills	Three domains of coping: emotion-focused, problem-focused, and appraisal-focused
Learn deep relaxation	Maintain emotional balance
Behave assertively	Preserve self-concept and maintain self-efficacy
Find new stability with marriage or dating partner	Sustain interpersonal relationships

SOURCE: Adapted from "Adaptive Strategies and Recovery from Rape" by A. W. Burgess and L. L. Holmstrom, 1979, *American Journal of Psychiatry*, *136*; "Post-Traumatic Stress Disorder: Clinical Features and Treatment" by E. B. Foa and B. O. Rothbaum, *Aggression and Violence Through the Life Span* edited by R. DeV. Peters, R. J. McMahon, and V. L. Quinsey, 1992, Newbury Park CA: Sage; "Psychological Sequelae to Rape: Assessment and Treatment Strategies" by D. G. Kilpatrick, L. J. Veronen, and P. A. Resick, *Behavioral Medicine: Assessment and Treatment Strategies* edited by D. M. Doleys, R. L. Meredith, and A. R. Cimenero, 1982, New York: Plenum; "Life Transitions and Crises: A Conceptual Overview" by R. H. Moos and J. A. Schaefer, *Coping with Life Crises: An Integrated Approach* edited by R. H. Moos, 1986, New York: Plenum; and "A Comparative Outcome Study of Behavioral Group Therapy for Sexual Assault Victims" by P. A. Resick, C. G. Jordan, S. A. Girelli, C. K. Hutter, and S. Marhoefer-Dvorak, 1988, *Behavior Therapy*, *19*.

1992), to develop new coping skills (Moos, 1986), to learn deep relaxation procedures (Kilpatrick, Veronen, & Resick, 1982), to gain new stability in interpersonal relations (Burgess & Holstrom, 1979), and to behave assertively (Resick, Jordan, Girelli, Hutter, & Marhoefer-Dvorak, 1988).

You may see in these approaches some of the thinking used to describe coping with life crises in Chapter 11. Among these coping processes for victims of violence, you can see an emphasis on establishing the personal significance of the event, confronting the reality of the situation, sustaining interpersonal relationships, maintaining emotional balance, preserving a satisfactory self-concept, and maintaining a sense of self-efficacy (Moos & Schaefer, 1986). These similarities are shown in Table 13-5.

CHAPTER SUMMARY

This chapter provides some disturbing information about adolescent experiences in the United States. We have seen that violence perpetrated by adolescents is often directed against other adolescents. As the evidence indicates, adolescents are both perpetrators and victims of violence.

One view of human violence is that we are a uniquely aggressive species, and efforts to inhibit our aggressive tendencies would prove both fruitless and damaging to social freedoms. Recently, this view has come under critical scrutiny, and proposals have been made for preventing and reducing the incidence and prevalence of violence in American society.

Rates of violence in the United States are staggering. About 7 in every 100 adolescents are victims of violent crimes. These rates vary considerably from one ethnic/racial group to another. Black adolescents, by far, have a much higher risk of being murdered than adolescents in any other ethnic/racial group.

Various circumstances foster violence. In this chapter, we looked at five: violence in the family, violence in the media, availability of guns, use of alcohol and other substances, and economic constraints.

Adolescents engage in three major types of violence: physical assaults, murders, and sexual assaults. The percentage of adolescent crimes involving violence is nearly four times greater than the percentage of violent adult crimes. Evidence suggests most adolescent victims of violence do not report what happened to them.

The rise of gang violence has led to increased attention on gangs themselves. We examined theories about gangs, statistics about gang membership, and gang violence.

The prevalence of violence on dates, including sexual assault and rape, has become an issue of grave concern. Ten percent of all high school students are involved in dating violence, and this figure more than doubles for college students. The best estimates are that up to 14% of high school females and 15.4% of college females have been date raped.

Evidence suggests only one-third of all rapes are reported to the authorities. Females report they felt angry, afraid, and depressed during the rape, whereas males report feeling proud. Often the female believes the assault did not fit the definition of rape, and seldom do males acknowledge the woman did not consent to have sex.

Some groups of adolescents are particularly vulnerable to violence. In addition to blacks and females, gay and lesbian adolescents, Asian-Americans, and Hispanics are at risk of being victims of violence.

The effects of violence are twofold. First, individuals who witness family violence have a much greater likelihood of becoming part of the cycle of violence. Second, violence produces long-lasting emotional trauma.

We have completed this study of violence and American adolescents. Next, we turn to a chapter on adolescents and human sexuality. We begin with a case study of a late adolescent male discussing his experience with and feelings about sexuality.

CHAPTER 14

ADOLESCENCE AND HUMAN SEXUALITY

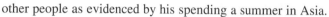

"I Would Like to Have Sex, But Feel It Is Not the Best Thing for Me Now"

Frank is a white 23-year-old male college senior majoring in human development. He has extended his education by pursuing a second major in Christian education. He seeks opportunities to expand his awareness of other cultures and other people as evidenced by his spending a summer in Asia.

My conversation with Frank took place in my office. Frank organized his presentation chronologically.

"When I was about 4 or 5, I was playing doctor with some other kids. When I got home, I didn't realize my parents had found out. They were furious and spanked me. I never knew why I was being punished. They just said, 'You shouldn't do that.'

"Playing doctor showed me there were physical differences between girls and boys. Being punished did not get me to stop, but to be more careful next time. I didn't see any reason to stop.

"It was probably in elementary school when I first became aware I was sexual. I used to think differences between males and females were just physical. We didn't talk in junior high school sex classes about emotional or cognitive differences between boys and girls. I didn't know much then about gender differences.

"In fifth grade—I was 10—as I was starting to develop physically, my parents would make comments, such as, 'You're getting hair under your arms.' It embarrassed me, made me shy away from asking girls out.

"I was not close to my parents, and to avoid them and to avoid questions about why I wasn't dating, I worked, so I always had an excuse not to be home or not to be dating. I had a paper route, and then, when I was older, worked in fast-food places. I was shy, and the work gave me an excuse to avoid my parents and questions about dating.

"During junior high school, we lived in a really small town. I didn't get along with the other kids very well. There wasn't anything to do except go to school and go home. Nearest place to go on a date was about 20 miles away. I didn't have the means. I played a lot of video games.

"My interest in sex remained pretty low until junior high school. Through human sexuality class, I became really interested in it. The easiest way to find out for me was through pornography—soft core pornography like *Playboy*—in bookstores. My parents wouldn't buy it, and I certainly couldn't. This was in seventh grade when I was 12 or 13.

"By looking at the magazines, I found out what sex was. There would be letters from people telling what they did. I learned about what went on when people had sex. At the time, I considered it a reliable source, but now, I don't think of it that way. These books and magazines skewed my idea of women and how women relate to people and what they want from men.

"In my junior year of high school, my family moved to a larger town—about 8,000 people—where I really felt at home. I began to learn about gender differences as opposed to sex differences. Learned from really good friends who were girls about relationship problems they were having with their boyfriends. For instance, how hurt they felt when their boyfriends cheated on them. Learned that sex was more than an S-R phenomenon like I had thought from what *Playboy* presented.

"I was not sexually active at this time. I was someone the girls felt they could talk with. All my life, I've had an easier time sitting down talking with females than with males. Where that comes from, I don't know. It made my male friends pretty jealous.

"Kids at school in this large town were quite active sexually. A lot of people talked about sex, and they were not lying about having sex. But, I still think a lot of the guys just made up stories.

"My guess is that 80% of the kids back in the small town we had moved from were sexually active in high school. There was nothing else to do but go have sex. There were some pregnancies, but not so much STDs.

"In the next town, I'd guess about 50% to 60% of the kids were active. The high school had about 500 students. Maybe not continuously active. Maybe it is better to say 50% were experienced.

"We moved again in my senior year and went to a much larger town. My high school had about 3,300 students, and I'd say 70% were active. I was not sexually active, but no one knew that. Because I hung out with so many girls, the guys thought I was sexually active.

"Some of the girls openly told me they were having sex. Not with more than one partner. I think, at most, 10% of the girls were not monogamous. But, their boyfriends were active with more than one person.

"Even though I wasn't sexually active, I would have liked to have been. I was too shy to go about doing it. But if researchers had asked me, I'd have lied and said I was active just as a boost to my ego. I'd have probably said I was having sex once or twice a week.

"I don't think the kids who are sexually active are lying. I think it would be more correct to say they are sexually experienced rather than actively having sex. I think at least 70% to 80% of high school students are sexually experienced. My guess is that 20% to 25% are actively having sex—at least once a month.

"I knew that older girls did initiate younger boys on occasion. I saw that happen a few times. A guy would go out with a girl one or two years older than he, and then they would have sex. I'm not sure it was the girl's intention. I know the guys went out with the girls because they had heard the girls were sexually experienced. The two would stay together maybe two or three months. They'd have sex a couple of times. Then they'd break up.

"On this college campus, I don't think students as a whole are promiscuous. I think the underclassmen—freshmen, sophomores—are more sexually active with multiple partners than are the upperclassmen. I think by the time they become juniors and seniors, they get more serious emotionally.

"In my freshman year of college, I dated a little, but not to any great degree by any stretch of the imagination. No serious relationship with anyone. We didn't go very far sexually—only kissing, making out, petting.

"Sophomore year, my roommate introduced me to a girl named Maureen, and we started going out. It was really kind of bad. I didn't think it was bad at the time. I was really uncomfortable with the relationship, but I kept that pretty much hidden from her and from myself. I'd get really jealous when she was not with me. A lot of my other friendships suffered since I didn't spend time with them.

"Maureen and I went out for nine or ten months. We'd go out and do things together, but end up someplace making out. It was pretty much just a physical relationship. We never had sex, but came close a few times. Usually, someone would come home and interrupt us. It was really frustrating at the time. Looking back, I'm glad it worked out that way.

"We didn't communicate a lot while we went together. We communicated better after we broke up. We hung out for a couple months.

"By the start of my junior year, I'd broken up with Maureen. I now realized the importance of getting to know people before starting to date them. Now saw it was important to know someone well before I dated them. By the end of my relationship with Maureen, I knew there had to be more to relationships than just making out. All I had been doing was living out a physically based relationship, and I'd learned there wasn't much there at all.

"I started hanging out with another girl. I'll call her 'Kris'. We started to date after a couple of months. I was attracted to her. She was pretty, friendly, nice. She wasn't very funny, I remember. After a month or so, our relationship started to get physical, and we sat down and talked about what our goals in the relationship were—what we were going to do, what not do.

"I said I didn't want to French-kiss or go beyond that because that is what I had done with Maureen. I didn't want to get into another physical relationship. She agreed. And that decision really freed us up.

"Kris and I went together for about nine months. After about two months going out, we got pretty serious about each other. One afternoon, we were looking at picture albums from her family, her high school, stuff like that, and she suddenly just became catatonic. She just curled up and was completely withdrawn for at least two hours. I was really shocked. Kris never really talked about it afterwards.

"The more I pieced together, I found out she had a lot of problems stemming from childhood sexual abuse. She seemed to get worse the longer we were together. I became more and more stressed being around her. I finally said to her, 'I can't deal with this. We need to be friends.'

"She thought I meant just step back and eventually we would get back together. A month or so later, I said clearly we were not going out again. It wasn't until several months later that I could tell her the real reasons I'd broken up with her.

"I wanted nothing to do with dating after my experiences with Kris and Maureen. I could only think of pain and stress. During this time, I learned more how to express my feelings and communicate on a friendship level. I learned the importance of knowing someone well before making a commitment to date. Dating means committing oneself to a romantic, intimate relationship with someone. Going out on dates is not the same as dating.

"During my senior year, I've met a lot of female friends and just have spent time getting to know them. I am not and have not been dating anyone. Before I begin dating someone now, I will know everything there is to know about that person.

"Having sex is a very intimate thing. It means a commitment to someone else. I have not had sex. Came close several times. In earlier adolescence, I had opportunities but was too shy to take advantage of it. Now I think having sex is too powerful a thing and it could destroy you by just messing around in casual relationships.

"Sexual activity goes far beyond physical activity. Encompasses our whole being. It is also a mental and an emotional activity. Don't have to be having sex physically, but you can be involved in fantasy. And I think that adversely affects how I relate to someone. I would like to have sex, but feel it is not the best thing for me now."

Frank's comments about adolescent sexuality tie in with several themes in this chapter, as well as with such topics as reactions to early adolescent physical development and gender differences versus sex differences. Notice Frank's comments about the prevalence of teenage sexual activity, his concept, "sexually experienced," and his growing understanding of the role of communication in relationships. Note also his comments on what he would have told researchers if asked in high school if he was sexually active. When you compare Frank's story with the evidence we have about adolescents and human sexuality, he will probably strike you as an atypical adolescent.

This chapter looks at several aspects involved in adolescent sexuality. We look at survey data about adolescent sexual activity and at what adolescents understand about human sexuality. The increasing incidence of sexually transmitted diseases highlights the risks for adolescents who engage in casual, unprotected sex. Most adolescents are heterosexual in orientation, but there are homosexual adolescents. We look at pregnancy and parenthood during adolescence, at programs that work with pregnant adolescents and with female adolescent mothers, and at efforts to teach human sexuality in the elementary and secondary grades.

THE SEXUALLY CHARGED CLIMATE IN THE UNITED STATES

Does anyone doubt that the United States is a sex-charged social climate? Advertisements promoting instant gratification and continuous consumption use sexual themes to sell their products. More and more films, television programs, and books have explicitly sexual contents—at times, only related peripherally to the main story. Children in homes with cable television have access to R-rated films that supposedly they cannot pay admission to see in a movie theater. Popular music is increasingly graphic in portraying sexual activity.

One example from professional football illustrates the sex-charged climate Americans live in. After being outside the United States since the early 1970s, a woman who had been born and raised in the U.S. returned for a vacation during the Christmas holidays. A football game featuring the Dallas Cowboys was on TV. The woman watched part of the game and said what astonished her were the cheerleaders. She could hardly believe the outfits they wore or the amount of time the TV cameras turned to show them. As she said, "I guess I shouldn't be surprised, but I never thought professional football teams would start using sex to sell their games."

Sex seems literally to be on sale everywhere in this country. The "900" and "800" phone numbers that involve sex talk are blatant examples. Magazines found in nearly every convenience store promote sexual fantasies. Video rental stores frequently have adult movie sections that only adults are supposed to enter. Many rock stars flaunt their sexuality and their disdain for traditional mores regarding behavior. With these images, American society throws sexual experiences, fantasies, and misinformation into the lives of children and adolescents.

As we look at the sexually charged climate in the U.S., three questions emerge: (a) how do adolescents behave sexually? (b) what do adolescents really know about sexuality? and (c) what questions do adolescents have about sexuality? In this chapter, I address each of these questions in turn.

SEXUAL BEHAVIOR DURING ADOLESCENCE

The Prevalence of Sexual Intercourse

A review of adolescent sexual behavior between 1930 and 1990 concluded adolescents had become increasingly involved in more casual, less committed sexual activity. The data indicated a steady rise in adolescent sexual intercourse and noted that age of sexual initiation had steadily declined (Dyk, Christopherson, & Miller, 1991).

Both national survey data and survey data gathered in rural Kansas confirm this conclusion; American teenagers engage in explicit sexual activity—particularly intercourse—far more than many adults want to acknowledge (Barnes, Wright, Ninas-Scheffel, Wyrick, & White, 1990; Coles & Stokes, 1985; Wright & Barnes, 1986). For instance, in a national survey of a randomly selected sample of 1,067 adolescents (52% urban, 26% suburban, and 22% rural) conducted in the mid-1980s, half of the boys reported they had been no more than 13 years old when they first engaged in sexual intercourse. Only 1% of the boys said they felt sorry, and 60% said they were glad. For girls, less than 20% reported intercourse as early as age 13, but for all girls who had intercourse, 11% said they were sorry about the first time, 61% felt ambivalent, and only 23% said they were glad. In nearly all cases, the young boys and girls had sex for the first time with an older adolescent of the opposite sex (Stokes, 1985). Kansas data indicated that 17- and 18-year-old high school girls were introducing early adolescent boys to sexual intercourse (Wright & Barnes, 1986).

The Kansas data and the national survey data indicate that most adolescents engage in sex. Less than 5% of all boys in the national survey were still virgins by age 16, and less than 12% of girls by age 17. The pressure to engage in sex, while commonly attributed to peers, was more self-imposed by rural Kansas teenagers, and ongoing sexual relations seemed in many cases to involve teenagers' confusing sexual feelings for affection and signs of caring (Wright & Barnes, 1986). Curiosity was a prime motive for Kansas boys to have sex the first time, whereas girls reported they had sex the first time because they were in love with their sex partners (Wright & Barnes, 1986). In the national survey, adolescents expressed similar motives (Stokes, 1985).

Despite common worries that they may not be good sex partners, the great majority of adolescents (81% of boys and 70% of girls) continue to have sex because they enjoy intercourse very much (Stokes, 1985). Not uncommonly, the adolescents have multiple partners.

The casual attitude and open pleasure that the more recent cohorts of adolescents express toward sex may shock adults. The extensive interviews given by adolescents in the national survey drive home the extent of teenage freedom to engage in sexual activity. Both boys and girls talked at length about masturbation, sexual techniques, birth control, abortion, and pornographic media—films, books, and magazines (Stokes, 1985).

Alcohol was less involved in first intercourse for rural Kansas adolescents than for adolescents across the country. Continued sexual activity, however, involved alcohol consumption for both samples of teenagers. Geoffrey Stokes quoted as typical of the national sample an 18-year-old female, who said, "I've found that I've messed around with people only because I've been drunk and they've been drunk" (1985, p. 117). David Wright and Howard Barnes (1986) discovered that drinking alcohol was associated with frequent sexual intercourse among rural Kansas adolescents.

Is There an Epidemic of Adolescent Sexual Activity?

Data from the late 1970s, now nearly 15 years old, indicated that over half of sexually active adolescent males (55%) had up to five sex partners, and one-quarter had more than ten. Thirty-eight percent of sexually active adolescent females had up to five sex partners, and 6% had more than ten. Thus, approximately 80% of all sexually active boys had multiple sex partners, as did 44% of sexually active girls (Hass, 1979). There is no reason to suggest that adolescents of today engage in sex less frequently than their adolescent counterparts from the 1970s. If anything, the more recent data suggest that today's adolescents are more permissive, more active, and more careless.

Some writers argue strongly against the assertion that adolescents frequently engage in sexual intercourse (Olsen, Jensen, & Greaves, 1991). They claim that inflated figures of adolescent sexual activity occur because other researchers only calculate the proportion of adolescents who have had intercourse for the first time. The basis for this argument seems ill-founded. Concerns over adolescent sexual practices stem from data about the frequency of adolescent sexual intercourse, the number of adolescent pregnancies, and adolescent vulnerability to sexually transmitted diseases. The concerns do not seem based on the number of adolescents who have had sex once.

According to Joseph Olsen, Larry Jensen, and Paul Greaves, the valid measure of sexual activity is whether a "person has had sexual intercourse more often than once during the past three months" (1991, p. 442). Their calculations from national survey data of the late 1970s indicated between 58% and 66% of 15- to 19-year-old females had sex more than once a month. The percentages of males between 17 and 21 who were sexually active was 60%. Olsen, Jensen, and Greaves considered these figures signified adolescent sexual activity was "substantially less . . . than has been previously reported" and certainly not the symptom of an epidemic (1991, p. 419).

Most, if not all, other studies conclude that adolescent sexual activity in the United States is at epidemic proportions. Let's review several of these studies.

David Rowe and Joseph Rodgers (1991) conducted a national survey of both Danish and American adolescents between 14 and 21 years of age. The researchers applied a **public-health concept** that new cases of a disease occur when susceptible people become infected by carriers of the disease. In the case of their study, the "disease" was sexual intercourse, "susceptible people" were virgins, and "disease carriers" were nonvirgins. The sexual activity of Danish youths and of American white adolescents did fit the model. However, the model did not fit the activity of Hispanic and black American adolescents. Of considerable import to the argument that most American adolescents are substantially engaging in sexual intercourse, Rowe and Rodgers reported that the ratio of nonvirgins to virgins was so extreme that the notion of carriers and susceptible people could not be tested. Most American youths were carriers—in other words, nonvirgins.

National survey data reported by Stokes (1985) indicated most adolescents frequently engage in sex after the first time, and Sandra Hofferth (1990) reported in a separate national study that intercourse three times or more a month was the norm for at least 65% of the 15- to 19-year-old females surveyed. Less than 19% of the females in Hofferth's study said they did not engage in sex at least three times a month.

Other writers reporting on adolescent sexual practices since 1930 have said sexual intercourse increased in the 1980s and have reported that, by age 17, nearly 60% of all adolescents in the 1980s were sexually experienced (Dyk et al., 1991). According to national survey data, the adolescents who were more likely to be sexually active had parents who were not college graduates, had below-average school grades, or were black (Dyk et al., 1991).

Research with 230 early and middle adolescents in Oregon indicated widespread high-risk behaviors that the researchers said could only, in fairness, be termed "promiscuous" (Biglan, Metzler, Wirt, Ary, & Associates, 1990). Some research has linked **adolescent promiscuity** to several unusual circumstances and/or to psychological problems. For instance, associations have been found between adolescent promiscuity and histories of physical and sexual abuse (Cavaiola & Schiff, 1988), emotional vulnerability (Bleiberg, 1988), antisocial behavior (Biglan et al., 1990; Konopka, 1966), and psychiatric disturbances (Green, 1986). However, the widespread engagement in premarital sexual intercourse by early, middle, and late ado-

Masturbation During Childhood, Adolescence, and Adulthood

Sigmund Freud based the core of his theory of personality development on human sexuality and the conflict that ensues as desires for immediate gratification meet societal restraints. While his views about childhood sexuality were met with shocked opposition, today we understand that there are elements of erotic pleasure in infancy and childhood. John Dacey (1982) maintains that by the age of 4 or 5, most children have enjoyed playing with their sex organs.

Masturbation is an area of adolescent sexual behavior that researchers have not investigated well (Dreyer, 1982). Despite the inadequacies of studies on adolescent masturbation—for instance, inadequate samples, inadequate data collection techniques, and inadequate data analysis—a consistent message of increasing tolerance for and acceptance of masturbation has emerged.

Nearly 50 years ago, Alfred Kinsey and his associates (1948) reported that nearly all male adolescents masturbate. Kinsey and his associates (1953) also reported about one-third of grade school females and around three-fifths of high school and college females masturbate.

More recent national survey data indicated that, of adolescents who admitted they masturbate, 90% began before age 15 (Stokes, 1985). Studies during the early 1970s reported that 50% of males and 30% of females first masturbated before age 15 (Dreyer, 1982). By age 18, masturbation is estimated to involve between 60% and 85% of boys, depending on the study one reads, whereas for girls, the figures

are less clear. John Gagnon and William Simon (1969) claimed two-thirds of females by the age of 16 masturbate until achieving orgasm. Philip Dreyer (1982) said that 60% of girls between the ages of 16 and 19 reported they masturbate at least some of the time. Studies on campuses indicated half of the female students masturbate at least once a week (Dreyer, 1982).

Shame about masturbating and reticence to discuss their masturbatory behavior marked the reactions of over two-thirds of the adolescents in Stokes's (1985) national study. While Adams and Gullotta (1989) offered firm resolve that giving up qualms about masturbation and accepting it as natural and pleasant is all that adolescents need to know, adolescents do not seem to have accepted those notions. In fact, other than an intellectual agreement that masturbation is an acceptable part of growing up, boys consider the subject matter something to keep hidden. "A 15-year-old California boy who said he masturbated, but 'not often at all,' was asked if there were 'some guys among your friends who are known for doing it quite a bit.' His answer: 'They wouldn't be my friends if they were known for doing it'" (Stokes, 1985, p. 65). Girls in the national study expressed the same sort of reticence about the topic.

Nearly 70% of all boys and girls who acknowledged masturbating said they enjoy it, but few, if any, found it an easy topic to discuss. Girls, in particular, said they find masturbating satisfying because they could reach orgasms doing it, but they

lescents suggests it is too simple to attribute casual involvement in sex to some form of psychological problem.

Abstinence (refraining from sexual intercourse) is definitely not the norm for the majority of American adolescents. In contrast to the claim Olsen, Jensen, and Greaves (1991) made, I have not found that people are as bothered by the numbers of adolescents who engage in sex for the first time as by the numbers who engage in frequent, careless sex.

considered the subject, as one 15-year-old girl said, "so personal . . . [and] none of your business" (Stokes, 1985, p. 67).

Do sexually active adolescents masturbate more than their less sexually active peers? Dreyer asserted that boys in ongoing sexual relationships stop masturbating, whereas girls in ongoing sexual relationships increase their masturbatory activity because masturbating releases "sexual tensions built up as a result of sexual activities which do not result in orgasm" (1982, p. 564). National survey data, however, indicated both males and females reported they masturbate less when they have an ongoing sexual relationship (Excerpts from *Sex and the American Teenager,* by Robert Coles and Geoffrey Stokes, Copyright © 1985 by Rolling Stone Press. Reprinted by permission of HarperCollins Publishers, Inc.).

We may be in the midst of a **cohort change** regarding the acceptability of masturbation. While many individuals have engaged in masturbation, until recently, the practice was considered embarrassing and wrong. Today, there is a radical shift in some quarters which seems to promote masturbation. Popular artists, such as Madonna, openly sing about masturbating; some television shows such as "Seinfeld," develop material around the topic; and some films, such as *Lethal Weapon*, suggest the main character masturbates. A music video entitled "She Bop" made obvious allusions to female **voyeurism** (obtaining pleasure by looking at sexual objects or pictures) and sexual pleasure achieved through masturbating. The video ended with the performers entering heaven, providing the clear message that masturbation is not a sin (Lewis, 1990).

A cohort of males born in the depression era and interviewed in their 40s reluctantly admitted they occasionally masturbated. These men acknowledged their immediate sense of pleasure was followed by feelings of guilt (Vaillant, 1977). Adult males one generation younger than this cohort admitted they masturbated between 75 to 100 times a year, or about once every four days (Athanasiou, 1976).

Similar findings among adult females suggested that cohort changes about masturbation began in the 1970s. Shere Hite (1976) reported upwards of 82% of her sample of females, many of whom were college graduates, reported masturbating regularly. Dreyer (1982), as mentioned earlier, said 60% of middle to late adolescent females masturbate at least now and then, and claimed 50% of undergraduate females masturbate at least once a week. Newcomb (1984) indicated young adult women around age 25 said they masturbate about once every four days and that sexually active women masturbate even more often.

What do you think about the assertion that masturbation has become more acceptable? Do you think there has been an increase in the prevalence of masturbation? Is it possible that there has not been an increase in the prevalence of masturbation but, rather, an increase in the willingness of individuals to admit engaging in the practice? Would an increase in willingness to admit masturbating count as evidence that masturbation is now considered normal?

WHAT DO ADOLESCENTS REALLY KNOW ABOUT HUMAN SEXUALITY?

Sources of Information

Adolescents learn about human sexuality from a variety of sources, not all of them reliable. School, parents, friends, and the media are the main sources of information about such topics as reproduction, birth control, masturbation, homosexuality, and sexual techniques. According to one national study, over 40% of adolescents who engage in sexual intercourse say their sexual partners are their primary sources of

Over 40% of adolescents who engage in sexual intercourse say their sexual partners are their primary sources of information about sexual techniques.

information about sexual techniques (Stokes, 1985). Sexually active college students surveyed at Iowa State University indicated they obtain more information about sexuality from peers and from reading than from any other sources (Andre, Dietsch, & Cheng, 1991).

Reliability of Information   How accurate is adolescent understanding of human sexuality? Despite the rise in mandatory sexual education in the schools, surveys in Kansas and across the country indicate adolescents seldom have fundamental knowledge about reproduction. Stokes considered adolescents' "lack of fundamental sexual knowledge . . . when combined with the level of sexual activity, can only be called alarming" (1985, p. 33). What is also alarming is the adolescents' mistaken confidence in their knowledge about human sexuality.

To illustrate this point, consider adolescent responses to a question on Stokes's (1985) national survey—"When can a woman get pregnant?" There were five possible responses and the survey asked respondents to select the one which was best. The choices were:

- when she has sexual intercourse the first time,
- when she has sexual intercourse before she is 16 years old,
- when she has sexual intercourse several times during the month,
- when she does *not* have intercourse, but the boy climaxes near the opening to her vagina, and
- all of the above.

Fifty-five percent chose the correct answer, "all of the above." The rest of the adolescents thought one of the other answers was the best choice. For instance, 18%

chose "when she has sexual intercourse the first time" and 23% chose "when she has intercourse several times during the month" (Stokes, 1985).

In Wright and Barnes's (1986) Kansas study, the adolescents were asked a more specific question about the risk of pregnancy. The question was worded, "During a woman's menstrual cycle, when is her risk of getting pregnant the greatest?" Seven choices were provided, and very few respondents chose the correct response, "Two weeks before her period is due." More than 93% of early adolescent females and 81% of middle adolescent females chose the wrong responses. Wright and Barnes wrote, "It is especially noteworthy that more males than females . . . could answer this question correctly" (1986, p. 26). Let me point out, however, that 85% of early adolescent males and 71% of middle adolescent males did not know the correct answer.

What seems clear from these survey data is that a high percentage of adolescents know many sexual terms, a high percentage of adolescents know many ways to engage in sex, but an alarmingly high percentage of adolescents misunderstand some important basics about human reproduction. Adolescents may fear pregnancy—although frequently, alcohol overcomes that fear—but they do not know when a female is most likely to become pregnant. Do they have any questions about human sexuality?

WHAT QUESTIONS DO ADOLESCENTS HAVE ABOUT SEXUALITY?

National survey data indicate adolescents find sex education in schools to be boring and, frequently, provided too late (Coles & Stokes, 1985). Stokes asserted that "in an effort to avoid controversy, schools embrace boredom" (1985, p. 38).

Few adolescents reported that their parents are approachable about sexual information. In the national survey, "only about a third (36%) say they would ask their parents for any desired sexual information, while almost half (47%) would turn to friends, sex partners, or siblings" (Stokes, 1985, p. 36). Data from the Kansas study suggest it may be a good thing many adolescents do not turn to their parents for sexual information; a significant proportion of parents barely made passing marks on a test about basic sexual knowledge (Wright & Barnes, 1986).

But, what do adolescents desire to know? Adolescents from middle school through high school consistently want to know more about birth control, sexually transmitted diseases, sexual feelings, and how to say "no." Parents, interestingly enough, also want more information on these subjects in order to pass the knowledge on to their children (Wright & Barnes, 1986).

The Kansas adolescents expressed more interest in friendship, social support, and expressions of affection than in engaging in sexual activity (Wright & Barnes, 1986). The Kansas researchers speculated that adolescents have difficulty distinguishing affection and caring from sexual feelings, and they engage in intercourse because they think that is how to express affection and caring. Dreyer reported that the adolescent increase in sexual activity reflects, primarily, a desire to gain identity and fulfillment, and is not merely the result of "uncontrolled impulse gratification or wanton promiscuity" (1982, p. 569).

The national survey provided less reason to think adolescents engage in sex because they confuse sexual feelings and affection, or are attempting to achieve greater personal identity and fulfillment. A casual attitude toward sex and toward sex partners, particularly among males, was noticeable. Most girls expressed more interest in ongoing relationships. At the same time, however, breaking up with boyfriends was common for girls and it was unusual for females to wait very long before entering new sexual relationships (Stokes, 1985).

Until now, the focus of this chapter has been adolescent heterosexual activity and interests. We turn next to a discussion of adolescents and homosexuality.

HOMOSEXUALITY AND ADOLESCENTS

Estimates of the percentages of the total population who are homosexual vary from a low of 2% to a high of 12% (Gonsiorek & Weinrich, 1991). These results, particularly the lowest figures, must be taken with considerable caution. People who disclose they are homosexual often face consequences if the information is traced back to them. The most consistent figure in this country for the number of adult male homosexuals is 6% of the population, but such data "represent an absolute minimum and . . . represent homosexual individuals who are relatively open and who live within tolerant or cosmopolitan communities" (Gonsiorek & Weinrich, 1991, p. 4). According to data gathered by Dreyer (1982), few American males and even fewer females report having had any homosexual contact during adolescence. At most, 2% to 3% report engaging in a continuing homosexual relationship.

In the industrial and postindustrial Western societies, homosexuals face intolerance and negative consequences should their homosexual preferences become known. Until recently, gay men and lesbians were court martialed from the United States armed forces because of their sexual orientations. At least one sailor was murdered because he was gay. Efforts to change this policy were met with opposition, and as of 1994, soldiers could not be required to divulge their sexual orientation but could still be court martialed for openly practicing homosexuality. Other examples of homophobia can be given.

Gay bashing is not uncommon. Harassment during adolescence is a common theme homosexuals mention (Herek, 1991; Sears, 1991). Insight into some adolescents' perceptions of their homosexual longings and preferences are found in the autobiographical portraits provided by gay and lesbian individuals (Garrord, Smulyan, Powers, & Kilkenny, 1992; Sears, 1991). Many of these portraits recount both harassment and anxiety—harassment from others who found the homosexuality offensive and anxiety should others discover the adolescent's homosexual orientation.

What do we know about adolescent homosexuality in the United States? There have been few studies of adolescent homosexuality. However, Dreyer (1982) asserted that American adolescents express widespread acceptance of homosexuality. National survey data challenge Dreyer's assertion (Stokes, 1985), as do discussions I have had with adolescents—gay, lesbian, and straight. Stokes (1985) said 75% of American adolescent females and 84% of adolescent males express disgust about

Adolescent Homosexuality in Preindustrial Cultures

Anthropological investigations of societies outside the industrialized West have turned up extensive permissiveness toward adolescent homosexuality (Schlegel & Barry, 1991). For instance, these preindustrial societies use very controlled rituals in which younger boys perform oral sex on older boys. Schlegel and Barry (1991) consider these rituals a form of dominance and power of older males over younger.

A few preindustrial societies permit one sex to engage in homosexual relations but forbid the other sex to do the same. However, usually when a society permits homosexual behavior, it does so for all adolescents. In these societies, adolescents engage in homosexual relations eagerly and with enjoyment, but rarely do they continue homosexual relations as adults. In the majority of these pre-industrial societies, adolescent homosexuality appears to be a form of social control that protects individuals from heterosexual relations before they are ready (Schlegel & Barry, 1991).

There are, of course, some individuals who continue to engage in homosexual relations as adults. These societies seem to tolerate such behavior, but not approve it. Schlegal and Barry (1991) found no society that permitted ritualized adolescent homosexuality banned adult homosexual practices.

For some reason I was unable to discern, the anthropological discussion of adult homosexuality in preindustrial societies barely touches on lesbianism. There is a suggestion, however, that these societies do not practice a double standard of tolerating adult male homosexuals but outlawing adult lesbians.

homosexual acts. Girls do, however, appear to be more tolerant of homosexuals than boys; several boys' reactions about male homosexuality were nothing less than hatred, and boys feared being identified as gay much more than did girls (Stokes, 1985).

Efforts to account for homosexuality in adolescence employ four main approaches. The first is the psychoanalytic view, which maintains that homosexuality is an aberration caused by never having resolved the oedipal complex of early childhood. According to Freud (1914/1957), as a child, the homosexual never formed a satisfying identification with his or her same-sex parent and, therefore, never developed mature adult heterosexual relations. Research evidence confirming the psycho-analytic interpretation of homosexuality is weak, at best (Dreyer, 1982).

A **biological explanation** has been offered to explain homosexuality as the result of genetic coding. "The presumption is that there is a gene determining sexual preference or orientation" (Kirsch & Weinrich, 1991, p. 24). Some theorists consider such an approach a very promising avenue to gain understanding (Gonsiorek & Weinrich, 1991), but others consider environmental factors, particularly social psychological factors, to be more influential determinants of sexual preference (Money & Ehrhardt, 1972).

Social learning theory explains homosexuality as conditioned behavior that results from a history of satisfying sexual experiences with someone of one's own gender (Dreyer, 1982). Although lauded for its neutral stance toward homosexuality, social learning theory is considered to have no supporting research evidence (Dreyer, 1982).

A fourth approach to explaining homosexuality is ecological (Chilman, 1982). This approach emerged from observations of girls' interactions at all-female summer camps. Chilman (1982) argued that girls became lonely and homesick and turned to other campers as well as counselors for affection and support. The extent to which the campers then became homosexual depended on whether the adult leaders were openly homosexual.

Chilman's (1982) observations hardly explain the homosexual preferences of the adult female counselors. We must question what accounts for the leaders' overt homosexuality.

One could hardly use the summer camp experiences as a version of what anthropologists have reported about approval of adolescent homosexuality in preindustrial societies. Most of the girls in the camp did not participate enthusiastically in the homosexual activities. It was "the sexual orientation of camp leaders," rather than a large societal endorsement, affecting the development of a homosexual lifestyle in the camp (Chilman, 1982, p. 62).

Chilman's (1982) account seems less an explanation of homosexual orientation and more a description of transitory experiences of lonely girls taken advantage of by adults. Even Chilman noted that most of the girls became considerably anxious, rather than pleased, with the camp's homosexual turn, and she pointed out that the great majority of the girls discontinued their homosexual behavior once they returned to their homes.

ADOLESCENTS AND SEXUALLY TRANSMITTED DISEASES

As we have seen, many adolescents frequently engage in sexual intercourse. It is not uncommon for sexually active adolescents to have many sex partners. It is less common for adolescents to practice safe sex by using condoms. "Of sexually active adolescents, only 47% of females and 25% of males, respectively, report using condoms" (DiClemente, 1990b, p. 9).

There are various reasons why adolescents do not, as a rule, use condoms. One reason is that adolescents often have sex impulsively and while intoxicated, and therefore they are not prepared to use condoms. Some adolescents, wanting to keep up the appearances of not being sexually active, do not purchase condoms because buying them would ruin their images. To purchase condoms is an admission that the teenager is actively planning to engage in sex—a painful admission for some adolescents.

The pattern of adolescent sexual activity, including not using condoms, makes adolescents vulnerable to sexually transmitted diseases. Research indicates that of all sexually active people in the U.S., 10- to 19-year-olds "have the highest rates of gonorrhea, syphilis, and chlamydia in the population" (Henggeler, Melton, & Rodrigue, 1992, p. 58). Those three diseases form part of what are called sexually transmitted diseases.

Sexually Transmitted Diseases

There is a group of infectious diseases that people contract primarily through sexual contact with someone who is infected. At one time, these diseases were called venereal diseases, but the preferred term today is sexually transmitted diseases (STDs).

There has been a rise in new cases of STDs, and adolescents are one of the age-groups most affected. The rise in new cases of STDs is positively associated with a similar rise in the frequency of casual sex (Kilby, 1986).

In this section, we look at five of the most common and troubling STDs. These are chlamydial infections, gonorrhea, syphilis, herpes, and AIDS.

Chlamydial Infections

Chlamydial infections have become the most prevalent of sexually transmitted diseases in North America (Kilby, 1986). Caused by a parasite, chlamydia is difficult to diagnose. It can lead to infertility in women and to blindness. An infected woman can transmit chlamydia to her infant when the baby passes through the birth canal.

According to Donald Kilby (1986), casual sex with multiple partners primarily accounts for the high number of infected females in the United States. Approximately 5% of American female college students have been diagnosed with chlamydia (Kilby, 1986). The method of treating chlamydia is to use such medication as "tetracycline, erythromycin or their derivatives" (Kilby, 1986, p. 141).

Gonorrhea

Gonorrhea is caused by bacteria and must be "transmitted from one sexual partner to another through direct contact of one infected mucous membrane with another" (Kilby, 1986, p. 159). The number of reported cases increased dramatically between the 1950s and 1980s. However, for every reported case, it is estimated another 1.5 cases go unreported. Since 1980, the number of reported cases of gonorrhea in the general population has dropped considerably—from over 1 million in 1980 to less than 691,000 in 1990 (National Center for Health Statistics, 1992). Yet, between 1985 and 1989, early adolescent females experienced an alarming increase in the incidence of gonorrhea; from 1970 to 1984 the rate of gonorrhea among early adolescent females averaged 64.8 per 100,000 individuals, but averaged 97.1 between 1985 and 1989. The rate of infection among middle adolescents remained steady during that same time period, and the rate among late adolescents actually declined (Centers for Disease Control, 1985, 1990b).

Between 50% and 60% of infected females show no symptoms of gonorrhea, whereas nearly all infected males have a thick, creamy, greenish yellow discharge from the penis. Many males and females infected with gonorrhea find urinating to be quite painful. If gonorrhea spreads through the bloodstream, it can cause heart problems, liver difficulties, and brain tissue damage (Kilby, 1986). Gonorrhea is generally treated with antibiotics. Penicillin used to be an effective means of treating gonorrhea, but this STD developed resistance to penicillin in the 1970s (Kilby, 1986).

Syphilis

Syphilis is caused by a bacterial microorganism and has been known since biblical times. Syphilis is contracted through sexual intercourse in most cases, but an infected woman can transmit the disease to her fetus through the placenta. Both the penis and the vulva may develop sores.

Unlike other STDs discussed so far, syphilis develops in four phases, going from an incubation phase of about three weeks to a final phase, which may occur within five years of being infected. If this STD progresses through its four phases, the results can affect almost any major organ and are fatal (Kilby, 1986).

During the decade of the 1980s, we saw an increase in the number of reported syphilis cases in the United States—from about 69,000 in 1980 to 134,000 in 1990. Whereas the rate of reported syphilis cases among early and middle adolescents remained constant between 1970 and 1989, the rate of cases among late adolescents increased, particularly between 1985 and 1989 (Centers for Disease Control, 1985, 1990b). The method of treating syphilis is penicillin or comparable medicine for individuals with penicillin allergies (Kilby, 1986).

Herpes

Herpes, called both **herpes simplex** and **genital herpes**, is caused by a virus and is incurable. The symptoms are sore, reappearing lesions and blisters. Genital herpes is painful, and, because it has recurring attacks, produces serious psychological harm in many infected individuals.

By the middle 1980s, genital herpes was ranked fifth among the most prevalent STDs (Kilby, 1986). The mode of transmission is usually sexual, but "you can also catch herpes simplex by touching an active lesion or fluid-filled blister, and then soon after, touching a part of your body or somebody else's" (Kilby, 1986, pp. 124–125). Herpes infections can be passed to a fetus during labor; while rare, such infections kill between 40% and 60% of all newborns who contracted the disease during birth. By using caesarean section, infected women can avoid transmitting the disease to their infants.

AIDS

In the 1980s, **acquired immunodeficiency syndrome (AIDS)** became the newest and most feared of all the STDs. As late as 1983, the total number of known cases of AIDS in the United States was 800, but by 1989, there were 33,000 reported cases of infected adolescents and adults. Black and Hispanic adolescents seem to be nearly four times more at risk for developing AIDS than other adolescents (National Center for Health Statistics, 1991).

AIDS is caused by a virus that affects the human immune system and prevents the body from fighting infections. This virus is called **human immunodeficiency virus (HIV)**. The incubation period of this virus widely varies, and it is believed that some individuals may carry the virus for up to ten years before they show signs of being infected. There is no cure for AIDS, and life expectancy after HIV develops into AIDS is three years.

A person can contract HIV through sexual contact with an infected individual, through contaminated intravenous drug needles, or through contaminated blood. There have been some unusual cases in Florida of dental patients who were infected by their dentist, and cases of hospital personnel infected when they jabbed themselves with needles that had been used with infected patients in medical procedures.

AIDS is caused by a virus that affects the human immune system. As yet, there is no cure, and life expectancy after contracting this STD is three years.

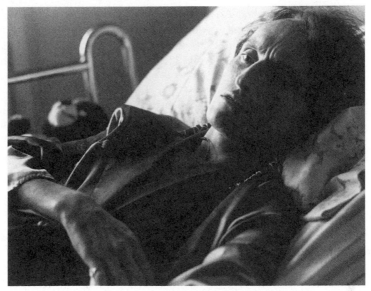

While most infected individuals in the United States during the 1980s were homosexual males and/or intravenous drug users, the majority of known AIDS cases around the world were heterosexuals. Today, the incidence of heterosexual AIDS cases in the U.S. is growing, and the heterosexual population no longer takes shelter in the idea that this STD affects only the gay population.

As mentioned above, the virus that causes AIDS has an incubation period of undetermined length. The first sign that the AIDS infection is taking over is the appearance of **opportunistic diseases**. These are diseases that the human body usually fights successfully, but cannot when infected by AIDS (Kilby, 1986).

There is growing concern that the incubation period of HIV in adolescents lasts longer than it does in adults. An adolescent could become infected but not show any symptoms for up to ten years. Evidence indicates from 40% to 50% of AIDS cases identified since 1981 in 20- to 24-year-olds resulted from infection during adolescence (Henggeler et al., 1992). The chances that these infected youths have transmitted HIV to unsuspecting sexual partners is quite high—as are the prospects that their sex partners have, in turn, infected others, and so on. These likelihoods have clinical workers and researchers very concerned that an AIDS epidemic is lying dormant, waiting to show itself when the vulnerable adolescent population grows a bit older. Ralph DiClemente (1990a, 1990b, 1992) has discussed strategies to reduce the risk of adolescent vulnerability to HIV infection. These include using social learning theory to develop personal controls, using the mass media to educate adolescents about HIV infection, and increasing adolescents' interpersonal skills.

Adolescent Understanding of STDs

Knowing that sexually active adolescents remain ignorant about basic human reproduction provides little comfort. Such ignorance has not led them to abstain from sexual intercourse, which in turn makes them vulnerable to STDs. Do sexually active adolescents understand about these diseases?

The National Adolescent Student Health Survey (NASHS) (1989), a carefully designed national investigation of a representative sample of adolescents, demonstrated that a significant number of adolescents are ignorant or misinformed about STDs. The survey sampled 11,419 eighth and tenth grade students; all 50 states were represented. The researchers concluded that many teenagers

- do not know how to avoid STDs,
- cannot identify common symptoms of STDs,
- do not know how to care for STD infection, and
- are misinformed about adolescent access to public health care for STDs (NASHS, 1989).

Prevention of STDs

The NASHS determined that over 30% of all adolescents do not know that most people get STDs through sexual contact. Over two-thirds (67.3%) thought washing after sex is an effective means to avoid STD infection. Over half (55%) believed taking birth control pills will prevent STD infection. About 25% did not know using condoms prevents STD infection (NASHS, 1989).

Common Early Signs of STD Infection

One-third of the respondents did not know a common early symptom is a sore on the sex organ. Nearly 45% did not know that a discharge of pus from the sex organ is a common early sign of STD infection. Forty-one percent did not know painful urination is a common early sign (NASHS, 1989).

STD Treatment

Nearly half of all the respondents believed that eating special foods is an effective remedy for STD infection. Forty-three percent did not know it is harmful to wait and see if STD symptoms disappear. Over two-thirds (68.2%) did not know the harm that is caused when someone infected stops taking medicine once the STD symptoms disappear (NASHS, 1989).

Adolescent Access to Public Health Care

Over three-fourths of the respondents (76%) believed incorrectly that the Public Health Department must inform the parents when an underage adolescent (less than 18 years old) is infected with an STD. Almost 80% believed public-health clinics need a parent's permission to treat patients under 18 years of age. Almost 40% indicated they did not know where to seek medical help for STD infection. Girls, more than boys, said it would be difficult to pay for medical treatment and to obtain transportation to a clinic (NASHS, 1989)

Thus concludes this section on sexually transmitted diseases, which are but one serious consequence of sexual intercourse. Another consequence is pregnancy.

It may surprise you to learn that adolescent pregnancy rates were much higher in the 1950s and 1960s than they are today.

ADOLESCENT PREGNANCY

Since the Carter presidency in the late 1970s, adolescent pregnancy has been regarded as a grave problem needing federal attention. During the 1970s, adolescent pregnancies among 15- to 19-year-olds increased by almost 38% (from 839,000 in 1970 to 1,151,000 in 1980) (Voydanoff & Donnelly, 1990). Today, it would be difficult "to pick up any newspaper or popular magazine without being reminded of the one million teenagers who become pregnant each year" (Vinovskis, 1988, p. 23). Adolescent pregnancy rates have remained at 11.0 per 100,000 individuals since the middle 1980s.

While few would cavalierly dismiss concerns over the many adolescent pregnancies each year, it may surprise you to learn that adolescent pregnancy rates were much higher in the 1950s and 1960s than they were in the 1970s· or than they are today. One reason for higher rates would be earlier marriages. Another reason would be that abortions were illegal in the 1950s and 1960s. Yet, recognizing that adolescent pregnancy has been an issue in this country for several decades should indicate prevention efforts have been notably unsuccessful.

Pregnancy rates are higher for older adolescents than for younger, and higher for black adolescents than for white. As an example, in 1985, the pregnancy rate for 18-

and 19-year olds (16.6 per 100,000) was more than twice the rate for 15- through 17-year-olds (7.1 per 100,000). Black adolescents between the ages of 15 and 19 had a pregnancy rate of 18.6, compared to 9.3 for white adolescents of the same age (Vinovskis, 1988).

Factors Associated With Adolescent Pregnancy

Becoming pregnant during adolescence is clearly associated with several factors. Four important factors are contraceptive use, socioeconomic status, individual aspirations, and assessment of consequences.

Contraceptive Use

Consistent use of contraceptives by sexually active adolescents is the exception, rather than the rule. Dreyer (1982) reported that 50% of college students and 80% of high school students do not regularly use any form of birth control. Adolescents' resistance to contraceptive use most frequently stems from (a) a perception that contraceptives interfere with enjoying sex, (b) a belief that planning for sex is wrong, (c) anxiety and embarrassment over buying contraceptives, and (d) fear that their parents will discover they are sexually active (Coles & Stokes, 1985).

Patricia Voydanoff and Brenda Donnelly (1990) reported that, in a sample of 937 sexually active adolescent females, 253 never used contraceptives, 365 sometimes used them, and 319 always used contraceptives. Of those who never used contraceptives, two-thirds ($n = 169$) got pregnant, compared to only 4.1% ($n = 13$) of those adolescents who always used contraceptives. About one-third ($n = 122$) of the adolescents who sometimes used contraceptives got pregnant. These data are presented in Figure 14-1.

Socioeconomic Status

Dyk, Christopherson, and Miller (1991) indicated lower socioeconomic status (SES) is strongly associated with adolescent sexual activity. Research studies report higher rates of pregnancy in adolescents from lower-SES families than from middle- and upper-SES families (Voydanoff & Donnelly, 1991). Other researchers confirmed that low SES is a demographic descriptor for a significant number of sexually active adolescents who become pregnant (Barnett, Papini, & Gbur, 1991). Dreyer (1982), who analyzed several studies that linked lower SES and adolescent pregnancy, cautioned readers to resist concluding that a lower SES background causes higher rates of adolescent pregnancy. Dreyer also indicated there is no substantive evidence that lower-SES adolescent females became pregnant to achieve identity.

Individual Aspirations

Pregnancy is more likely in adolescents with low educational and occupational aspirations than in those with high aspirations. Even when other factors, such as contraceptive use and family SES background, are taken into account, pregnant adolescents are more likely to have lower career aspirations than their nonpregnant peers (Voydanoff & Dreyer, 1990).

As in all correlation studies, there is no certainty about casual direction in these studies linking lower aspirations with higher rates of adolescent pregnancy.

FIGURE 14-1   Sexually Active Adolescents: Pregnancy and Contraceptive Use

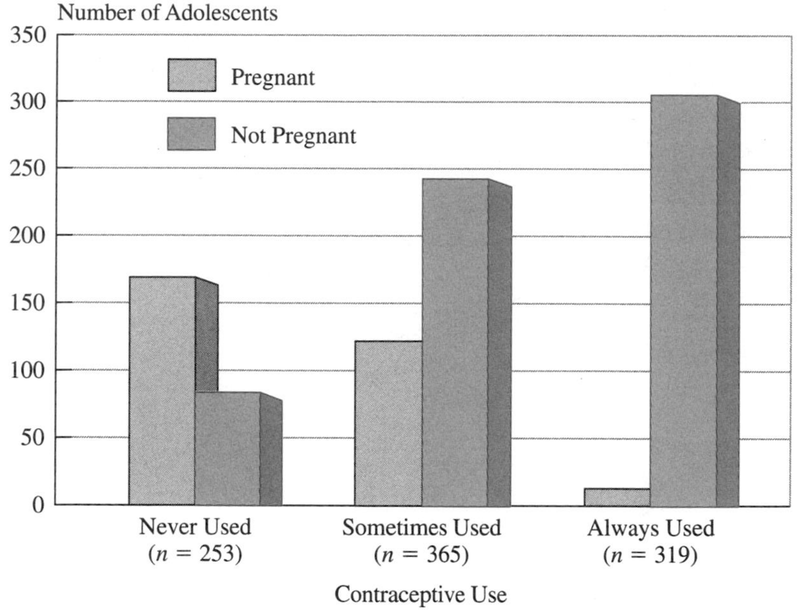

SOURCE: From *Adolescent Sexuality and Pregnancy* (p. 44) by P. Voydanoff and B. W. Donnelly, 1991, Newbury Park, CA: Sage.

Becoming pregnant may lead some adolescents to lower their educational and career aspirations, whereas others who become pregnant may consider even finishing high school irrelevant to achieving independence as an adult (Voydanoff & Donnelly, 1990).

For adolescents with long-term educational and occupational goals, pregnancy presents a severe obstacle to attaining their aspirations. They are more likely to avoid such a severe obstacle, whereas adolescents who do not have such "aspirations are not as likely to see an early pregnancy as such a threat" (Voydanoff & Donnelly, 1990, p. 58).

Assessment of the Consequences of Pregnancy

Sexually active teenagers, on the whole, despite risky sexual behavior that increases their chances of pregnancy, consider becoming pregnant a disaster. However, some adolescents do not judge pregnancy to be disastrous, and they are much more likely to become pregnant. Voydanoff and Donnelly (1990) reported that high school students in North Carolina whose families strongly disapproved of adolescent pregnancy were less likely to become pregnant than their peers whose families did not share these views.

Adolescents in some preindustrial cultures view pregnancy quite differently than American adolescents. Many preindustrial cultures accept premarital adolescent pregnancy as long as marriage soon follows. In some cultures where daughters are expected to marry the person chosen by their parents, females have used premarital pregnancy to force their parents to accept an otherwise unwanted suitor. However, the concern in many preindustrial cultures about premarital adolescent pregnancy is over property rights; the parents become concerned that paternal claims on the daughter's child will lead to unwanted alliances and exchanges of property the parents would otherwise be able to fight (Schlegel & Barry, 1991).

Responses to Pregnancy

What are the responses of the over 1 million adolescents in the United States who learn each year that they are pregnant? Their personal choices are reduced to two options: to give birth or to abort. The moral reasoning that adolescents employ about such decisions was covered in Chapter 5.

Abortion

Stokes's (1985) national survey data showed that adolescents consider abortion a very serious issue. These national findings indicated that adolescent judgments about abortion are, at best, marginally influenced by age, SES, or place of geographic residence (urban, rural, or suburban). Voydanoff & Donnelly (1991) found that age was associated with aborting a fetus or bringing it to term; pregnant middle adolescents were more likely to give birth, whereas early and late adolescents were more likely to choose abortion.

Adolescent views about abortion are influenced by religion, race, and sexual experience. Catholic adolescents are much less likely than other adolescents to approve of abortion, and Catholic adolescents who choose abortion are much more inclined than others to feel guilty. Blacks are more likely than whites to condone abortion, and virgins are less likely than sexually experienced adolescents to sanction abortion (Stokes, 1985). Dreyer (1982) as well as Voydanoff and Donnelly (1991) reported that abortion rates for black adolescents are higher than the rates for white adolescents.

Adolescents find the abortion choice troubling, even when they support the right of a female to choose how to handle her pregnancy. Some adolescents express concern over using abortion "as an easy escape from consequences they ought to face, or foresee and try to avoid" (Stokes, 1985, p. 130). Boys, perhaps not surprisingly, are more likely than girls to consider abortion to be an effort to escape from consequences. Girls, on the other hand, seem more inclined to weigh the abortion decision within the context of an adolescent's life (for instance, if the pregnant girl is poor) and to express concern over possible abuse of the right to choose. One abuse of concern to adolescents is the decision to use abortion as the primary means of birth control.

Males seem to avoid facing the consequences of pregnancy in real life. In fact, very few males participate in family planning clinics aimed at high-risk adolescents. Because males who do participate most likely differ from males who do not participate, evaluating the impact of adolescent pregnancy and parenthood programs directed at males is difficult.

Adoption or Parenthood

Some pregnant adolescents choose to carry their fetuses to full term and then place the children with adoption agencies. We look now at some studies on adolescents' decisions to place their infants for adoption.

One issue that distinguishes adolescent mothers who choose adoption over keeping the baby is the perception that they are not capable of providing good homes for their infants (Resnick, Blum, Bose, Smith, & Toogood, 1990). In a study of 118 unmarried adolescent mothers—half had chosen adoption and the other half had chosen to raise their children—the adolescent mothers who elected to keep their children said adoption was too emotionally upsetting to consider. The young women who elected adoption had higher educational and career aspirations than the other adolescent mothers, and also were from higher-SES families living in the suburbs (Resnick et al., 1990). Other studies have shown a greater likelihood for white adolescent females to select adoption over parenthood (Warren & Johnson, 1989) and a much greater likelihood of Hispanic adolescent females to select parenthood over adoption (Berger, Kyman, Perez, Menendez, Bistritz, & Goon, 1991).

Kathleen Herr (1989) determined that pregnant adolescents who select adoption are children of mothers who favor adoption. Her study included 125 female adolescents, all of whom were in a comprehensive adolescent pregnancy program. These females had few pregnant peers who had decided to raise their babies. Several demographic and interpersonal variables were *not* significantly associated with the decision to place a baby for adoption; these nonsignificant variables included age of the adolescent mother, her school grades, and her extent of involvement in the pregnancy program.

One concern of professionals who work with pregnant teenagers is the impulsive decision making adolescents exhibit in the choice to be a parent, rather than place their infants with an adoption agency (Weinman, Robinson, Simmons, Schreiber, & Stafford, 1989). Evaluation of the decisions of 474 pregnant adolescents to raise their infants or place them for adoption indicated that a significant proportion who initially planned on adoption switched at the last minute to parenthood. The great majority of the adolescents in the study were between 14 and 17 years of age, but an increasing number of the pregnant adolescents were between 10 and 13 years old (Weinman et al., 1989). Seventy percent were black or Hispanic, 75% were impoverished, and all but 12% were unmarried.

Of considerable concern for the researchers was the alarming incidence of psychosocial problems and health risks among the adolescents who switched from adoption to parenting. For instance, the adolescents often had histories of substance abuse, their pregnancies were not desired, their babies were born premature, and their labors were complicated (Weinman et al., 1989). Adolescents who choose to raise their infants may face economic difficulties. Although Dreyer (1982) considered the evidence about negative economic consequences for adolescent mothers unconvincing, most other researchers are less optimistic. Widespread, pervasively negative effects occur in the areas of education, employment, income, and dependency on welfare (Voydanoff & Donnelly, 1991). For instance, adolescent parents attain lower levels of education and lower paying jobs with less occupational prestige than other adolescents attain as they age. Females who give birth during adolescence, in particular, are more likely than other females to have annual incomes below $25,000 (Voydanoff & Donnelly, 1991).

Adolescents Giving Birth

When an adolescent chooses to give birth, whether she plans to raise the child or place it for adoption, both mother and child face sobering consequences. First, let's consider consequences for the child.

Fetal and infant death rates are higher among pregnant adolescents than for any other age-group in the United States (Dreyer, 1982; Voydanoff & Donnelly, 1991). Fetal mortality is higher among black adolescents than white adolescents (National Center for Health Statistics, 1990b; Voydanoff & Donnelly, 1991). Six percent of the babies born to mothers under 15 years of age die in their first year of life, many from sudden infant death syndrome (SIDS) (Dreyer, 1982; Voydanoff & Donnelly, 1991).

Babies born to early and middle adolescents have a higher incidence of physical and mental problems than other babies. For instance, by age 5, children of young mothers are shorter than other 5-year-olds and are more likely to have hearing problems (Vandenberg, 1978, as cited in Chilman, 1982). Furthermore, children born to young mothers are more likely than other babies to be mentally retarded and to have learning disabilities (Dreyer, 1982). Children of young mothers get poor health care, and are seen much more frequently in emergency medical care facilities than other babies (Vandenberg, 1978, as cited in Chilman, 1982). Voydanoff and Donnelly (1991) reported that, due to the many cases of premature births, children of adolescent mothers are more vulnerable than other infants to neurological problems, such as epilepsy and cerebral palsy.

For the adolescent, giving birth also has some sobering consequences. Labor is often prolonged and may involve such complications as toxemia (blood poisoning due to kidney problems or difficulties with other human organs) and anemia (an excess of white blood cells) (Voydanoff & Donnelly, 1991). Other consequences include higher maternal death rates, extreme gains in weight, and greater likelihood of giving birth prematurely (Vandenberg, 1979, as cited in Chilman, 1982; Voydanoff & Donnelly, 1991).

Because we know of the risks associated with adolescent pregnancy, it would seem reasonable to expect programs would have been developed to address these risks. We turn next to these programs.

Teen Pregnancy and Parenting Programs

With adolescent pregnancy rates unchanged since the 1980s, one could argue two seemingly contradictory theses. On one hand, you could argue that prevention efforts have stemmed the tide of increase in adolescent pregnancy. On the other hand, you could argue that prevention efforts have made no appreciable impact on

A Program for Pregnant Adolescents and Adolescent Mothers

Project Redirection was established in the 1980s as a pilot program at four separate sites in the United States (Boston, New York, Phoenix, and Riverside, California). Janet Quint (1991) evaluated the impact of the program on its 805 participants and on a comparison group; the number of adolescents in the comparison group was not identified, but Quint said they were chosen carefully.

All participants in Project Redirection and in the comparison group were adolescent females—either pregnant or mothers. None had graduated from high school, and all were eligible for aid for dependent children (AFDC). Nearly 90% of the Project Redirection participants were black (43.5%) or Hispanic (44.7%), all were under 17 years of age when they entered the program, and over 70% received AFDC. Nearly all (93.6%) had never been married. About 75% said their mothers had been adolescent parents.

The program connected the adolescents with both educational and medical services, provided workshops on parenting and employment skills, and offered both individual and group counseling. Project Redirection also paired each teenager with an adult female role model whose job was to be the adolescent's teacher and friend. A high percentage of community women (78%) left the program, and the adolescents frequently found it hard to trust and care for the women who replaced the individuals who had left.

After five years, evaluation findings indicated that Project Redirection participants had higher employment rates, worked more hours a week, and earned higher incomes (Quint, 1991). Project Redirection participants had better parenting skills, and their children were better behaved than children in the comparison group. While adolescents in both the project and in the comparison group were considered reasonably good parents, observations suggested Project Redirection participants created homes better suited for children. Significant gains were not seen, however, in high school graduation rates for members of either group (Quint, 1991).

decreasing pregnancy during adolescence. I believe that *on a national basis*, the continuous rate of adolescent pregnancy from one year to the next makes it difficult to argue that pregnancy prevention has been effective. A decrease in rates would seem to be a reasonable criterion to measure effectiveness.

In some local situations, one can argue that prevention efforts have made an appreciable impact based on a decrease in pregnancy rates. One apparently successful program developed in New York used small group techniques. The small groups included both males and females, and the group agenda was primarily educational. The education portion emphasized five major areas:

- problems that adolescent parents face,
- adolescents' rights to make personal choices,
- contraception,
- values, and
- decision making.

The program also stressed abstinence from premarital intercourse (Moyse-Steinberg, 1990). Research asserted that three-year evaluative data support the power of the program to promote responsible sexual behavior. Dominique Moyse-Steinberg (1990) based her evaluation on longitudinal results indicating significant attitudinal, behavioral, and informational changes about reproduction, sexual activity, and birth control.

Over a ten-year period, one program provided health care and education to adolescent mothers and medical care to their babies. This program took place in a mother-baby clinic. Jill Rabin, Vicki Seltzer, and Simcha Pollack (1991) looked at the ten-year data on 498 mothers who had participated in the program, and compared the outcomes with data on 91 mothers who used family planning services following delivery. The mother-baby clinic participants had much better school attendance than their counterparts, higher rates of high school graduation, better employment histories, and more regular use of contraceptives. The continued existence of the mother-baby clinic over a decade was tied clearly to acceptance from and use by the community's teenagers.

Another prevention and parenting program is the Hull House Adolescent Family Like Project (Marsh & Wirick, 1991). Hull House is a famous community program in Chicago.

The Hull House program was located in two public-housing projects, and over a four-year span, 335 adolescents took part in program services. All were either pregnant or mothers, all were living in poverty, all were considered to be blocked from opportunities, and all but two participants were black.

The Hull House program provided practical counseling and offered education about child development, parenthood, health, and human sexuality. Participants' understanding of all four educational areas markedly increased. On a practical level, their use of contraceptives also increased, but the program had no effect whatsoever on the incidence of repeat pregnancies. Evaluators considered the frequent use of the counseling and the health services demonstrated adolescents valued these program components more than any other aspect of the Hull House approach (Marsh & Wirick, 1991).

EDUCATION ABOUT HUMAN SEXUALITY IN THE SCHOOLS

Adolescents obtain information about human sexuality from five major sources: school, parents, peers, the media, and sex partners. In this section, we look at human sexuality education in the schools and discuss some community concerns associated with these education programs.

National survey data indicated clear support from adults and adolescents for sex education in American schools (Katchadourian, 1990). However, individual communities or interest groups within communities may strongly oppose any teaching of human sexuality that offends personal, religious, or community values, particularly when the curriculum is seen as being forced upon some people against their will.

A Test Case:
The Kansas Plan

A test case for implementing a human sexuality curriculum in the schools was offered in the late 1980s by the state of Kansas. The Kansas legislature mandated that human sexuality curricula be incorporated into all accredited elementary and secondary schools. Legislators expected information about human sexuality would be integrated with other curriculum topics. Considerable attention was given to promoting successful implementation of the mandate, and evaluators conducted a study of program implementation efforts (Balk, 1989; Balk & Camp, 1988; Camp, 1990).

The evaluation study identified several divisive issues about the implementation of human sexuality curricula in Kansas schools. We take up two of the issues here: resistance to the mandate and the "opt out" provision.

Resistance to the Mandate

While there was evident support for including human sexuality in the curriculum, resistance to the mandate was noticeable from many sources. Teacher resistance stemmed from discomfort over presenting detailed, explicit information about human sexuality; teachers also resisted the additional hours required for in-service training. Some teachers could see no way to fit these new curriculum demands into an already jammed school day (Balk, 1989). Evaluators concluded that in many school districts, teachers are "either uninformed about what part they will play in the implementation process or they have not been trained adequately enough to effectively educate students about human sexuality" (Camp, 1990, p. 61).

School administrators seemed ambivalent about the mandate and, while they expressed support for the concept, several showed no signs of actually making efforts to implement human sexuality topics across the curriculum. There were some clear possibilities that integrating human sexuality into a curriculum presented unique obstacles. Administrators who lacked specific training related to human sexuality education were not likely to put in place successful implementation strategies (Camp, 1990).

Community resistance was evident in both vocal opposition to the legislative mandate and in reluctance to participate in planning efforts. Local planning groups that obtained community involvement listened to doubts about and support for the mandate and devised acceptable strategies to present human sexuality information in their schools. The accepted view among many in Kansas was that community resistance would be the most difficult obstacle to overcome; but analysis of interview responses indicated the teachers, rather than community residents, had the lowest level of support for implementing the mandate (Camp, 1990).

The "Opt Out" Provision

The Kansas mandate emphasized the importance of integrating human sexuality education into the whole curriculum rather than making human sexuality a separate topic. At the same time, the regulation allowed parents to refuse to let their children participate—to "opt out" of the education. The opt out provision enables parents to require their children be removed from the classroom whenever the curriculum topic is sexuality.

This provision in the regulation, which emerged as a compromise to handle volatile groups opposed to human sexuality education in the schools, was criticized by educators and by other citizen groups concerned over the dangers of ill-informed and sexually active youths. A question raised by several sources was how could elementary and secondary school students be required to complete credits in some areas, such as history or math, but be permitted to opt out of a state mandated educational requirement in human sexuality. Observers said many schools had one or more students not taking part in the human sexuality curriculum (Balk, 1989).

Other Approaches to Sex Education

Other school systems have developed sex education programs for adolescents. For instance, in North Carolina, school counselors and teachers implemented a nine-week curriculum to teach human sexuality in the seventh grade. This approach had four components: (*a*) informed parental consent, (*b*) small groups of same-sex participants, (*c*) human sexuality topics, and (*d*) direct involvement of the school counselor in all aspects of the program. The pregnancy rate among early adolescents dropped during the year in which the program was tried (Dycus & Costner, 1990).

Nearly 1,200 Oregon high school students surveyed about use of health education (53% female; 47% male) indicated that sex education was one of three services they would be most inclined to use; the other two services were counseling and nutrition/body weight education. Over half (51%) indicated they engage in sexual intercourse, but only a quarter indicated they would request information about contraception or about AIDS (Hawkins, Spigner, & Murphy, 1990).

One group of researchers in Utah report favorably about three experimental programs to enhance early and middle adolescent acceptance of abstinence (Olsen, Weed, Ritz, & Jensen, 1991). Analysis of results indicated that female participants felt more positive than males about abstinence, and posttest outcomes demonstrated that the emphasis on abstinence in these programs elicited favorable attitudes among the participants.

A sex education course in Mexico City with nearly 400 female adolescents showed that attendance alone had no effect on changing the girls' continued sexual activity or their use of contraceptives. However, when the program discussed relationships with sex partners, where to obtain contraceptives, and information about sexuality, the girls altered their sexual activity, particularly by increasing the use of contraceptives (Pick-deweiss, Diaz-Loving, Andrade-Palos, & David, 1990).

CHAPTER SUMMARY

Sexual themes and temptations permeate American society. TV, movies, books, 517magazines, popular music, and even professional football frequently place sex before the American public. Such dominant cultural themes continually encourage early, middle, and late adolescents to act on their sexual drives and feelings.

National and regional survey data indicate the great majority of American adolescents are sexually active. Half of all boys in one national survey had engaged in sexual intercourse by age 13, usually with an older adolescent girl who had initiated the contact. Most adolescents continue to have sex because they enjoy intercourse very much. Multiple sex partners are not uncommon over the adolescent years. Some researchers argue that claims about an epidemic of adolescent sexual activity are unwarranted. Do you think national data indicating 60% to 70% of adolescents engage in sexual intercourse at least three times a month—and without protection against pregnancy or sexually transmitted diseases (STDs)—warrant concern?

Adolescents learn about human sexuality from a variety of sources—primarily, school, parents, friends, and the media. Sex partners are the primary sources of information about sexual techniques for around 40% of adolescents. College students gain information primarily from conversations with peers and from reading material. However, despite their open discussion of sex and their widespread engagement in sexual intercourse, adolescents remain basically misinformed about basic topics, such as reproduction and STDs.

Adolescents say they want to know more about contraception, STDs, sexual feelings, and how to say "no." Parents express desire to know the same information, particularly so they can intelligently discuss sex with their children. Most adolescents consider school efforts to teach human sexuality to be boring and too late. Resistance to teaching human sexuality in the schools comes from a multitude of sources: teachers, administrators, community groups, and parents. However, most American adults and adolescents think human sexuality ought to be taught in elementary and secondary schools.

Sound data about the extent of homosexuality among American adolescents are difficult to uncover. Less than 3% of American teenagers report participating in continuing homosexual activity. Because homosexuals run severe risks of reprisals should their sexual preferences become known, many investigators think the proportion of the population that is homosexual exceeds the 6% who consistently admit their orientations.

Some non-Western preindustrial societies approve of homosexual practices during adolescence. Few of their adolescents continue to practice homosexuality as adults, but are tolerated if they do so. The American society, however, on the whole is openly intolerant of homosexuality. Despite some researchers' claims that American adolescents accept and tolerate homosexuality, most data indicate they consider homosexuality repugnant. Most American adolescent males, in particular, express an irrational hatred of homosexuals and a fear of being considered gay.

Because adolescents engage so frequently in unprotected sex with different partners, they run high risks of contracting and transmitting STDs. Five of the most common STDs are chlamydia, gonorrhea, syphilis, herpes, and AIDS. National data indicate a significant proportion of adolescents is ignorant or misinformed about prevention of STDs, symptoms of STDs, treatment for STDs, and confidential access to public health care.

Since the late 1970s, federal attention has focused on adolescent pregnancy as a matter of grave national importance. Over one million unmarried teenagers become pregnant every year. Pregnancy rates are higher for older adolescents and black adolescents than for younger adolescents and white adolescents.

Despite their casual, even careless approach to sexual intercourse, most adolescents consider pregnancy to be a disaster. Once pregnant, an adolescent faces two choices: to give birth or to abort. Abortion is a troubling issue for the majority of adolescents. Few choose abortion without serious deliberation. Females are more inclined to weigh the abortion decision within the overall context of the pregnant adolescent's life. Males are more likely than females to express concern against using abortion as a way to avoid consequences that should be faced. However, males seem to avoid facing these consequences in real life. In fact, very few males participate in family planning clinics aimed at high-risk adolescents. Because males who do participate most likely differ from males who do not participate, evaluating the impact of adolescent pregnancy and parenthood programs directed at males is difficult.

Adolescents who decide against abortion are faced with two options: to raise the child or place the infant for adoption. Females who select adoption frequently come from higher income families and have higher educational and occupational aspirations than those who choose to raise their children.

Many adolescents who choose to become an active parent say the adoption decision is too upsetting to consider. However, professionals who work with pregnant teenagers express concern over the impulsivity that frequently marks the choice to raise the child. Also, many young mothers face both psychological and health risks stemming from histories of substance abuse or of psychiatric hospitalizations. While some researchers debate whether parenthood negatively affects adolescents economically, most data indicate widespread negative consequences in income, employment, education, and welfare dependency.

Adolescent pregnancies result in higher fetal and infant death rates than pregnancies in any other age-group. Adolescent mothers are more likely to give birth prematurely, and, thus, their babies have a higher incidence of mental and physical problems than babies carried to full term.

Adolescents who decide to give birth experience some sobering consequences. Their labor is often prolonged and complicated. Maternal death rates are higher for adolescents than for any other age-group.

On the national level, pregnancy prevention programs have been singularly unsuccessful in reducing the rate of adolescent pregnancies. However, some local programs claim evaluation findings indicate their services positively impact the pregnancy rate.

Several programs provide quality health care to pregnant adolescents and to young mothers and their babies. Some of these programs report their participants have better high school graduation rates, better employment histories, more regular use of contraceptives, and improved parenting skills.

Most Americans support the introduction of human sexuality as a curriculum matter for elementary and secondary schools. One statewide effort to teach human sexuality on a kindergarten through twelfth grade basis was mandated in the state of

Kansas. Implementing the mandate uncovered various types of resistance from a multiplicity of groups. School programs that succeed in teaching human sexuality involve many community stakeholders in planning the curriculum.

This concludes our discussion on adolescence and human sexuality. We turn next to the final chapter, a discussion of psychological disorders during adolescence. We begin with a case study of a schizophrenic adolescent.

PSYCHOLOGICAL DISTURBANCES DURING ADOLESCENCE

CASE STUDY

"I Stopped Talking to Everyone When I Was 13"

Walter is a white male in his early 20s. Walter told me about himself when I met him at the mental health clinic he visits regularly. He prefers to talk about his view of the world, and his eyes become intense and his face rigidly set when he is deterred from presenting his worldview. When he discusses his philosophy of life, his voice becomes high-pitched, his demeanor animated, and his gestures more pronounced and frequent.

He asks seemingly disarming questions while passing someone he knows in the hall of the mental health clinic. For example, he asked me, "Can I see you for a minute?" I said, "Sure, Walter." His next statement was, "Who do you think is the world's greatest statesman?" His look changed from casual to quite intense. At times, Walter seems disappointed with all the "mortals" he must tolerate. See if you think he has unusual thought patterns.

"I'm aware now that I've lived all my life as an intellectual robot. A spirit. Not a *Homo sapiens*, not human, but more like a robot. You see, basically, my life has been a struggle to suppress and to know what I consider is crime.

"I consider myself a police officer—a special police officer. Not a city policeman or an FBI agent. I consider myself a police officer. I consider the universe itself is dominated by organized crime. It's very simple. To lie is to commit a crime. Everything is hypocrisy. Acting, play acting, theatrics, melodrama, drama, propaganda, falsehood, everything. International diplomacy is based on hypocrisy. It's very simple. I found all this out two or three years ago when I was 19 years old. I began to gradually evolve into this self-awareness.

"I never knew my father. I don't know where he is. I don't know who he is. I've been told things about my father, intelligence reports as you might call it. I've been told that he's been down to Guatemala, that he is an employee in an air base in Alaska, and that he's been near the Mexican border. My mother told me this. The truth of it I don't know. My mother lives here in this town.

"The first time I got out of the state hospital, I lived at home with my mother and grandmother. I didn't have a job. Virtually, I've never been employed in my life. Well, actually once. When I was 14, I worked as a caretaker and a gardener for someone while they were on vacation. When I was in the state hospital, I worked, but I didn't demand payment, although I could have. Except for that, I haven't worked.

"I have a variety of activities. I spend a lot of time studying in libraries. I have a number of library cards. I spend an awful lot of time checking out books and researching, studying, examining, investigating. I travel to the library by car. I have a driver's license, but most of the time, I'm emotionally not stable enough to drive. That is, my mind is too busy thinking and daydreaming to drive. I passed the driver's test though.

"I don't get together with people very much. I haven't had a social life since I stopped speaking to everyone when I was 13. I stopped speaking to everyone at school, and the neighbors had already boycotted me since I was in second grade. I had a row with my parents, and the relatives boycotted me because of the row with my parents. The neighbors had had this big hassle with my grandmother, and they ostracized me. I wasn't allowed to play with their children. I stopped talking to everybody.

"I feel it was simply they were nothing but boys. To play the hypocrite with them and to try to appease them with foolishness, I was better off not speaking to them and taking anything they dish out. Speaking to them and being stomped on. It was that simple. I wasn't gonna be stomped on. I took guff, but it was nothing compared to what they planned to dish out if I were to give them the diplomatic leverage of just speaking to them or giving them any form of recognition.

"I went into isolation for three years. I went underground. From the time I was 13 until I was 16, I didn't speak. Then, between 16 and 19, I was in almost complete isolation. I was completely underground. Completely! I didn't even go shopping. I stayed in the house all day. I spent my time researching what's been happening on this planet.

"It's shocking to think that the world capitulates to the I. Q. Farben Industry. When I was 17, I began to understand that. I began to figure it out and to have a theory. Between 17 and 19 years of age, I was seriously researching. I came aboveground when I was committed. I've been aboveground ever since. But, I could go underground anytime I wanted to. If I would become in danger, any form of physical danger, I would go underground.

"When I was 10 years old, I made a study of communism. All that propaganda they do in the comics. Now, you take that same propaganda and you throw it at the Fascists and you can't. The Nazis, the Fascists, and the Warlords of China and the military war order of Japan, the Axis powers, you can't. It's very simple. Fascism is simply an alliance of capitalists, clerics, and military.

"I'm not a communist, not a Fascist. I'm not anything. I am a police officer, to police. Right now I'm trying to understand myself.

"I discovered a secret international organization called 'The Madrid Regime'. It started in 1928 in Madrid, Spain. Supposedly, it was a Roman Catholic organization, but non-Catholics were allowed to join it. I suspect that it was responsible for the rise of Hitler, Mussolini, and the hell that Hitler brought on this world.

"It's very simple why I was committed to the hospital. I broke windows at home. I was hostile, uncooperative. My mother said there was no other course of action. Had I been amiable and all of that, perhaps she would have let me stay home.

"I was hospitalized. When I was hospitalized . . . . well, it was simply ranting and raving about conditions in the home that I felt were unjust. I would rather not discuss it. But, I will put it in a nutshell. The home is not the Garden of Eden. It's that simple. Not that I'm any kind of pimp or Fascist or anything, just that from your earliest memory until your present memory, you've been nothing but a regimented soldier in a barracks. It might be a little bit repressive. I think I made it clear, and I said it very passively and subtly.

"Now, getting back to the situation. It's so simple. The Madrid Regime has the mind of a puppet. It has the financial dynasty and international industrial power under their control. Power, not financial power, not economic power, not the military power, and not power through asking, and not power through diplomacy. But power through organization.

"Basically, my life's history has been with myself. I've been unaware of my self-esteem. I've been very blind. I've been conceited, but I haven't known I was conceited. I was completely ignorant of self-love. I didn't have official knowledge of self-respect. I was unaware of the 'I'. The 'I am'. Walter Lott is simply an individual. A human being. A *Homo sapiens*, unaware of dignified self-esteem and respectful of self-love. In other words, he doesn't know completely. He's unaware of the 'I'. That's my problem.

"If free choice is enforced, it would be free choice as to what kind of clothes you should wear. There would be free choice not to wear anything. The police would protect everyone. Now, they got these sex psychopath laws, these antisex laws. The dress code, the sex censorship law. If they were abolished and there was free choice, life would be a lot better.

"But there is one thing. You do have pornography. You see, it's like this; in the name of suppressing pornography, they suppress the truth about free choice. Pornography is not the truth about sex. It's not the truth about free choice. It's just a bunch of slimy filth. So the big bullies control both sides of the propaganda, both sides of the action, to suppress the truth. Not just about sex, but about life. About the right of free choice. Not to persecute, not to bully, not to torment, but the truth. Have power over self, not power over others.

"It's very simple. This lie that men are masculine and women are feminine is just a big hoax. Everyone knows it. If anyone who stands up and says that they are going to maintain this hypocrisy—actually, if I had my way, they would be put up against a wall and shot.

"It's free choice. I'm not saying that a woman can't say she wants to be feminine. Or the man can't say he wants to be masculine. I'm saying that they have no right to cram that down the throats of everyone else. If they want to be that way, let them. You can't force others to be that way. It should be free choice."

Walter has been diagnosed as schizophrenic. His problems developed gradually during his childhood and adolescence. His schizophrenia did not come about as the result of a specific life trauma, but, rather, emerged over the course of years. His problems are considered much less likely to disappear, therefore, than if they resulted from some specific life event.

An early sign that Walter had psychiatric problems was his considerable diffi-culty getting along with other people. He says he stopped talking to anyone when he was 13, says he felt ostracized by neighbors, and mentions they would not allow him to play with their children. He thinks of people as bullies and tormentors.

He says with all seriousness, "It's very simple," and then gives a complex expla-nation of what is going on in the world. He has some insight into his own difficul-ties and the interpersonal problems that evolved as he developed.

He talks about having gone underground, studying about the world and politics intensely, and not coming out until he was committed. Rather than committed to a belief or a point of view, Walter is referring to being committed to the state hospital.

This chapter is about psychological disturbances during adolescence. We discuss distinctions between normality and abnormality, the prevalence of psychological disturbances during adolescence, and the difference between internalized and exter-nalized disturbances. Two types of internalized disturbances that affect adolescents are depression and schizophrenia. Two types of externalized disturbances that affect adolescents are suicide and substance abuse.

SEVERE DISORDERS AND NORMAL PROBLEMS

The psychoanalysts consider the adolescent years to be a time of severe tumult and disorder. They maintain that stresses brought on by sexual drives, societal prohibi-tions, and a resurgence of the oedipal conflict of early childhood create serious psy-chological troubles for adolescents. Earlier in the book, we studied these views when looking at the storm and stress theory of adolescence.

Offer (1969; Offer & Offer, 1975; Offer, Ostrov, Howard, & Atkinson, 1988) has persuasively challenged the notion that adolescence is a time marked by severe dis-orders. Cross-national, multiethnic, dual-gender, and longitudinal studies using Offer's self-image inventory (the OSIQ) provide no support for Anna Freud's (1958/1969; 1969/1971) assertion that the one thing normal about adolescence is abnormality. I suspect that the psychoanalysts based their pessimistic views about adolescents not on a representative sample of youths, but on the 20% of youths whom Offer (1969) has noted experience adolescence as troubling and tumultuous. Psychoanalysts are much more likely to work with disturbed adolescents than with youths adapting well to life.

Unlike the 20% of adolescents who were emotionally upset, the great majority of youths in Offer's studies were relatively calm and coped well with developmental tasks. In his eight-year longitudinal study of male adolescents, Offer (1969) was impressed with their abilities to deal effectively with severe life crises, such as the death of a parent, financial problems in the home, or serious injury to a sibling.

A 12-year longitudinal study of 634 adolescents indicated that adolescent devi-ancy seldom results in serious consequences for psychological development and typ-ically stems from challenges to conform. The adolescents who engaged in problematic behavior desired personal autonomy, were uninterested in traditional religious and academic goals, felt critical of society, and tolerated rule breakers. The adolescents who were least likely to engage in problematic behavior were not concerned over personal autonomy, valued academic achievement and religious involvement, accepted society uncritically, and were intolerant of rule breakers (Jessor & Jessor, 1984).

These findings did not differ, for the most part, for males and females, nor were there age differences or changes over time for early, middle, and late adolescents. The findings highlighted that a significant proportion of adolescents engage in behaviors that deviate from conventional norms, but these adolescents' challenges to established authority neither fill their lives with tumult nor indicate their psyches are severely disordered.

In short, the great majority of adolescents cope well with stress and do not develop severe disorders, and the very essence of adolescence is normality rather than abnormality. These conclusions raise the question, "What does it mean to be abnormal?"

What Does It Mean to Be Abnormal?

When college professors talk about normal and abnormal behavior, students commonly inquire what it means to be abnormal. This inquiry is not a glib challenge. Much damage can be done by labeling someone *abnormal* when, in reality, the individual merely differs from the group in power. A chief example is the policy in the former Soviet Union of placing political dissidents in psychiatric institutions. Insensitivity to cultures different from one's own is another example. For instance, inappropriate labeling occurs when white psychiatrists label Hispanics *excessively dependent* because of deep bonds to their families of origin and to their extended families.

Ideas of abnormality presuppose an understanding of normality. Walter Hirsch said, "We do not know what normal is, and what an exact definition of normality consists of. Our conceptions of normality differ considerably, depending on our orientation, be it cultural, social, psychological, or medical"(1962, as cited in Offer & Sabshin, 1967, p. 97). What criteria are offered to distinguish normality from abnormality?

Criteria for Judging Abnormality

Five criteria offered as standards of abnormality are:

- deviations from statistical norms,
- deviations from social norms,
- personal distress,
- personal immaturity, and
- maladjustment.

As a statistical concept, *normality* is considered to be the major portion of the continuum of human behavior along the normally distributed bell-shaped curve. Extreme scores at either end of the curve are considered **deviations from statistical norms** and are judged to be abnormal. Normal behavior comprises from 68% to 90% of human behavior, depending on what one uses as cutoff scores (1 or 2 standard deviations from the mean). This statistical criterion applies well to some psychological traits, such as aggressiveness, because extreme aggressiveness or extreme passivity suggest maladaptation. However, the statistical criterion applies quite poorly to other psychological traits, such as intelligence. Under the statistical criterion, both genius and mental retardation would be labeled *abnormal* (Coleman & Broen, 1972).

Behavior that does not conform to the majority is considered a **deviation from social norms**. Using this criterion, abnormality is the judgment of the majority against nonconformers. One example provided already is the treatment of political dissidents in the former Soviet Union. This criterion assumes that it is in the best interest of society and of the individual to act in conformity with the prevailing values and activities of the majority. This standard is vulnerable to temporal and cultural relativism. For instance, while we consider slavery to be fundamentally wrong, 150 years ago, the white citizens of the United States were deeply divided over the status of Negroes and over the institution of slavery. The social norm criterion causes us to wonder whether that which we accept in the 1990s as normal will be considered reprehensible and abnormal by future generations. Perhaps you have some suggestions to make.

Feelings of personal distress—anxiety, depression, guilt—may indicate abnormality, particularly when the feelings are chronic. However, one expects a person to feel distressed in some circumstances. Consider the sorrow experienced over the loss of a friend or the anger felt at being cheated out of something you deserved and wanted. In fact, in these circumstances, lack of personal distress would be considered abnormal. Four yardsticks applied to judging whether feelings of personal distress are abnormal are (*a*) the intensity of the feelings, (*b*) the frequency of their

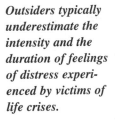

Outsiders typically underestimate the intensity and the duration of feelings of distress experienced by victims of life crises.

occurrence, (*c*) the duration of the feelings, and (*d*) the situation that produced the feelings. Yet, as Roxanne Silver and Camille Wortman (1980) have pointed out, victims of serious life crises (rape, bereavement, life threatening injury) find outsiders typically underestimate the intensity and duration of their feelings of distress.

A fourth criterion for judging abnormality is to consider whether behavior indicates **personal immaturity**; that is, whether the behavior is inappropriate for one's age. Temper tantrums and extreme dependency on others are considered abnormal in adolescents and, thus, as signs of personal immaturity. However, while examples of some behaviors are fairly easy to label *immature* and, therefore, *abnormal*, this criterion begs the question of what behaviors signify maturity and normality.

The fifth criterion—**maladjustment**—identifies abnormality as coping ineffectively with demands. In this regard, maladjustment impedes optimal growth and functioning. One example of maladjustment is alcoholism. The major criticism of this criterion is that it is essentially negative and fails to consider that adjusting to demands does not necessarily imply a person is fulfilling his or her potential. The strength of the criterion is its utility in clinical assessment (Coleman & Broen, 1972).

Given the conceptual difficulty of establishing standard criteria for abnormality, are we simply to shrug off the issue as an academic debate. Does the issue lack any practical significance?

I think the need to identify criteria for judging abnormality is obvious—mental health professionals work with some adolescents who are severely troubled. More than 7 million American youths suffer from mental disorders that can affect them throughout their lives (National Advisory Mental Health Council, 1990). We would hardly consider adolescents who are clinically depressed, suicidal, schizophrenic, or addicted to drugs or alcohol to be merely eccentric deviants from social norms. They have maladapted to life. Thus, I have found it useful to adopt James Coleman and William Broen's (1972) criterion that abnormality is maladjustment that hinders and obstructs optimal growth and development.

PREVALENCE OF PSYCHOLOGICAL DISTURBANCES DURING ADOLESCENCE

Psychological and social problems affect many adolescents around the world. A group of international scholars contributed information about the prevalence of these problems in their own countries (Hurrelman, 1994). The countries represented included advanced industrialized nations (Canada, Finland, Germany, Japan, Norway, Spain, Sweden, the Netherlands, the United Kingdom, and the United States), industrialized nations (Czechoslovakia, Hungary, Poland, and Russia), and developing as well as partially industrialized nations (Argentina, Brazil, China, India, Korea, Mexico, the People's Republic of China, and Singapore).

Cross-national differences and similarities emerged in the reports from these various countries. Scholars from all but one nation mentioned delinquency was a problem, and substance abuse was mentioned in all but two accounts. Scholars from about one-third of the nations said adolescent violence was on the rise. Extremist political behavior (riotous resistance to lawful authority) was mentioned for adolescents in four nations. Very few scholars mentioned adolescent pregnancy, running away, or unemployment as adolescent problems. Anxiety over school achievement plagued adolescents in five countries. Eating disorders were considered problems in four advanced industrialized nations.

Other than violence, which was reported as a problem among United States adolescents, the psychological and social problems of Canadian and United States adolescents mirrored each other. The psychological and social problems of United States adolescents included delinquency, depression, eating disorders, substance abuse, suicide, and violence. Table 15-1 provides an overview of psychological and social problems considered troublesome for adolescents in 22 countries.

The international prevalence of delinquency and substance abuse is worthy of note. Often, the first issue scholars addressed was the prevalence of these disorders in their countries. There was a pattern to some problems, such as eating disorders (prevalent in advanced industrialized nations) and extremist political behavior (prevalent in industrialized or partially industrialized nations).

What would enable adolescents in Finland and Sweden to have so few psychological and social problems when compared to adolescents in other advanced industrialized nations? What would lead scholars not to mention running away, pregnancies, and unemployment as serious problems for a significant proportion of adolescents in the United States? Does it seem reasonable that the only psychological and social problem for adolescents in China is delinquency? What do you suppose leads researchers in any country to highlight some problems but not to mention others?

According to Ann Masten (1991), there are five patterns of psychological disturbances during adolescence. These patterns are delinquency, suicidal behavior, depression, eating disorders, and schizophrenia. As previously mentioned, more than 7 million American youths suffer from mental disorders that can affect them their whole lives.

Categorizing psychological disturbances as either internalized or externalized is a popular approach (Achenbach, 1966; Colten, Gore, & Aseltine, 1991). **Internalized disturbances** are disorders whose primary symptoms are cognitive, emotional, or psychosomatic. Examples include schizophrenia, depression, anxiety, and suicidal thoughts. **Externalized disturbances** are disorders whose primary symptoms are overt actions against oneself or others. Examples are substance abuse, sexual acting out, and suicidal acts.

In this chapter, we look at four types of severe disorders that some adolescents experience. Two of these disorders are internalized disturbances—depression and schizophrenia—and two are externalized—suicide and substance abuse. Five other types of problems experienced by troubled youths—running away, violence, eating disorders, promiscuity, and juvenile delinquency—have been treated in earlier chapters. We look at the internalized disturbances first, starting with depression.

DEPRESSION

While there was, at one time, belief that depression was strictly an adult disorder, it is now clear that depression is a serious problem for a significant minority of the adolescent population in many countries of the world. In the mid-1980s, in fact,

TABLE 15-1 ■ Psychological and Social Problems of Adolescents in Twenty-Two Countries

	ANXIETY	DELINQUENCY	DEPRESSION	EATING DISORDERS	EXTREMIST POLITICS	PREGNANCY	RUNNING AWAY	SUBSTANCE ABUSE	SUICIDE	UNEMPLOYMENT	VIOLENCE
ARGENTINA		X						X		X	X
BRAZIL		X			X		X	X			
CANADA		X	X	X		X		X	X		
CHILE		X						X	X		
CHINA		X									
CZECHOSLOVAKIA		X			X			X			
FINLAND			X					X	X		
GERMANY	X	X	X	X				X			X
HUNGARY		X	X		X			X	X		
INDIA		X			X			X			
JAPAN	X	X		X					X		X
KOREA		X						X			X
MEXICO		X				X	X	X			
NETHERLANDS		X	X				X	X	X		
NORWAY		X	X					X	X	X	
POLAND	X	X	X					X	X		
RUSSIA	X	X						X			
SINGAPORE	X	X	X					X	X		
SPAIN		X	X			X		X	X		X
SWEDEN		X	X						X		
UNITED KINGDOM	X	X	X					X			X
UNITED STATES	X	X	X	X				X	X		X

SOURCE: Adapted from *International Handbook of Adolescence* edited by K. Hurrelmann, 1994, Westport, CT: Greenwood Press.

depression had become the most rapidly expanding area in the field of adolescent psychiatry (Hodgman, 1983).

A clear picture of the prevalence of depression in adolescence is difficult to obtain. One reason is that different studies use different criteria to identify depression, and another is that researchers often demonstrate insensitivity to developmental differences that separate children and adolescents. For instance, 12 studies of the prevalence of depression grouped early childhood, middle childhood, and adolescent subjects together without discriminating between these age-groups (Finch, Casat, & Carey, 1990). Why is this distinction important to uphold? For one reason, the emotional, cognitive, and physical development of children and adolescents differ remarkably. To consider depressed 3- to 5-year-olds, 6- to 9-year-olds, and 14- to 17-year-olds experience fundamentally the same developmental phenomena is a bit of gross ignorance.

Studies of **nonclinical populations** of adolescents (individuals not being seen by mental health professionals) report rates of depression ranging from 18% to 28%. As might be expected, studies of **clinical populations** (individuals being seen by mental health professionals) report much greater percentages of depressed youths (Ehrenberg, Cox, & Koopman, 1990; Kaplan, Hong, & Weinhold, 1984; Klee & Garfinkel, 1982; Reynolds, 1984).

An instrument commonly used to identify depression is the Beck Depression Inventory (BDI) (Beck, 1978). This 21-item inventory includes questions on such topics as weight loss, sleep disturbances, feelings of failure, crying, and suicidal thoughts. The instrument has very good psychometric properties of reliability and validity, and has been used successfully with clinical and nonclinical adolescent samples (Izard & Schwartz, 1896; Strober, Green, & Carlson, 1981; Teri, 1981). Responses to each BDI item range from 0 to 3; overall responses to the 21-item inventory can thus range from 0 to 63. Scores for adolescents are grouped in the following manner:

- 0 to 10—no depression
- 11 to 16—mild depression
- 17 to 20—borderline depression
- 21 to 29—moderate depression
- 30 to 40—severe depression
- 41 to 63—extreme depression (Burns, 1980)

Growing evidence suggests that some severe depressions occur in adolescents with family histories of depression (Beardslee, Keller, & Klerman, 1985). Genetic influences on depression are suggested by studies of the family histories of victims of affective disorders (Petti & Larson, 1987).

William Reynolds (1984) studied over 2,800 high school students by giving them the BDI, and found 18% met criteria for moderate to severe depression. In another study, BDI scores for 385 junior and senior high school students indicated 22% were mildly to severely depressed (Kaplan et al., 1984). BDI scores of Canadian high school students indicated 31.4% were mildly to severely depressed (Ehrenberg et al, 1990).

Depression rates rise considerably when clinical populations are studied. Steven Klee and Barry Garfinkel (1982) noted that two-thirds of 30 consecutive adolescent admissions to a psychiatric hospital were for depression. Reynolds (1984) reported depression is the primary problem for 40% of all adolescents referred to mental health professionals.

Symptoms of Adolescent Depression

What are the symptoms of adolescent depression? Not uncommonly, depressed adolescents suffer from harsh consciences and painful feelings of guilt (Petti & Larson, 1987). Depressed adolescents manifest such core symptoms as loss of self-esteem, negative self-thoughts, and despondency (White, 1989).

Are depressed adolescents like depressed adults? John Conger (1991) maintains that it is mostly in severe and extreme cases of depression that adults and adolescents present similar symptoms. Several researchers have concluded that much adolescent depression goes undetected because it is more difficult to diagnose than its adult forms (Carlson & Strober, 1983; Ehrenberg et al., 1990; Hodgman, 1983; Izard & Schwartz, 1986). Offer and his colleagues (1988) have referred to the disturbing cross-cultural evidence that the problems of many depressed youths remain hidden from adults and from mental health professionals.

Irving Weiner (1980) argued that until age 17, adolescents seldom manifest symptoms associated with adult depression. He gave two reasons. One is that early adolescents are more inclined to do things than to reflect on their lives. Thus, depressed early adolescents may continue to be active, unlike depressed adults, who are often marked by inactivity. Another reason is that the developmental tasks of early and middle adolescence present such serious challenges to self-esteem that depressed adolescents disguise their feelings in order to protect themselves. Feeling incompetent causes great distress to an adolescent already beset by self-consciousness and by doubt over self-worth.

The ongoing stress from expected developmental tasks, such as forging an identity, developing intimate friendships, and deciding on a vocation, present further complications for depressed adolescents. Adolescents become depressed when faced with feelings of incompetence and of being unlovable. Dependency on adults may also lead to depression as the adolescent both fights against and demands such dependence (Petti & Larson, 1987).

Early Adolescent Depression

Early adolescents disguise their feelings of depression (Weiner, 1980), and they are likely to be aggressive (Petti & Larson, 1987). When distressed over loss or disappointment, early adolescents behave restlessly, have difficulties concentrating, and cling to and/or flee from others. Let's look at each manifestation.

Restlessness is one way early adolescents defend themselves against depression; they keep busy to overcome feeling depressed (Weiner, 1980). A down side of this restlessness is that it leads easily to boredom, a problem that fans the depressive flames for early adolescents.

Flights to people seem to be efforts to gain acceptance, while escapes from people are efforts to avoid rejection. Constant efforts to be with others keep the early adolescent stimulated and active. Restlessness is associated with the flights to people. A constant effort to win friends enables the depressed adolescent to avoid depressive moods, thoughts, and feelings.

Difficulties concentrating are frequently accompanied by fatigue and by irrational concerns over physical health. Not uncommonly, adults attribute these physical symptoms to the developmental changes of early adolescence, rather than to depression (Weiner, 1980).

Depressed early adolescents may engage in problem behaviors as signals for help. While once considered core symptoms of depression, problem behaviors are now considered secondary symptoms in a depressed adolescent (White, 1989). Problem behaviors may take such forms as temper tantrums or delinquent acts. One sign that the adolescent is actually appealing for help is that the adolescent behaves so overtly that being caught is virtually assured (Weiner, 1980). Other signs are that the problem behaviors can be traced to a specific upsetting experience and that the behaviors are very unlike the youth's usual way of acting. Thus, problematic behaviors of depressed early adolescents differ markedly from the deviant behavior of typical juvenile delinquents.

Middle Adolescent Depression

Rates of depression increase in the middle adolescent years. Evidence of this increased prevalence came from a review of public health data regarding mental health care (Weiner, 1980). This review found that greater proportions of older adolescents than younger adolescents were diagnosed and treated for depression: on average, 3.3% of early adolescents were considered depressed, 6.1% of middle adolescents, and 10% of late adolescents. Invariably, in each age-group, more females than males were depressed, especially in the middle and late adolescent years.

Gender differences in depression primarily emerge during the middle adolescent years. Evidence suggests that female rates of adolescent depression are three times greater than the rates for males (White, 1980). In their study of Canadian youths, Marion Ehrenberg, David Cox, and Raymond Koopman (1990) found no gender differences for early adolescents, but significantly more middle adolescent girls than boys were depressed. Other studies make clear that adolescent girls are more vulnerable than boys to depression (Kandel & Davies, 1982; Shaffer, 1986; Weisman, Lea, Holzer, Myers, & Tischler, 1984). Conger (1991) suggests that gender intensification accounts for this difference, and he submits that increased flexibility in sex roles could produce a decline in female depression.

Late Adolescent Depression

The cognitive skills of reflection and self-analysis lead depressed late adolescents to manifest mood and thought disorders more clearly. Late adolescents can reflect more than early adolescents on issues of identity, the future, and the world in which they live. Developmental tasks, such as establishing a separate identity or choosing what to do with one's life, become fertile fields in which a portion of late adolescents become moderately to extremely depressed (White, 1989).

Anxiety and alienation are two aspects of depression found in both middle and late adolescence (Kashani & Orvaschel, 1988; Weiner, 1980; White, 1989). Signs of anxiety in adolescents include excessive concerns about past behavior, difficulties relaxing, extreme need for reassurance from others, and conspicuous self-consciousness (Strauss & Lahey, 1987). Alienation in adolescents manifests itself in withdrawal from planning for the future, lack of connection to the values of one's society, and cynicism that nothing really matters (Conger, 1991). Alienated late adolescents are primarily concerned about escaping feelings of loneliness, insignificance, or incompetency (Weiner, 1980).

Given the severity of adolescent depression, you may have asked what can be done to help depressed adolescents. Next, we discuss treatment for adolescent depression.

Treatment for Adolescent Depression

Longitudinal studies have indicated that severe feelings of depression are long-lasting and recurrent (Reynolds, 1984; Welner, Welner, & Fishman, 1979). Chronically severely depressed adolescents present formidable challenges to professionals who treat depression. Some evidence indicates psychiatric drugs—particularly lithium carbonate and tricyclic antidepressants—provide effective treatment for chronically severely depressed adolescents (Petti & Larson, 1987). The side effects of these drugs must be carefully monitored because improper dosages can prove fatal.

On a more positive note, the majority of depressed adolescents can be helped. For instance, adolescents whose depression stems from a life event (such as breaking up with a boyfriend or a girlfriend) are very receptive to treatment. In fact, recovery from these types of **situational depressions** frequently occurs without professional help (White, 1989).

Adolescents with histories of habitual failure and feelings of being helpless to influence outcomes are quite resistant to treatment. Recurrent experiences of failure, in fact, make an adolescent vulnerable to suicide should an important relationship disappear. While antidepressant drugs may lift the spirits of such an adolescent, he or she needs intensive psychotherapy with a therapist who appreciates the struggles the youth has faced and is facing. At times, only hospitalization can protect such an adolescent from harming him- or herself or someone else.

SCHIZOPHRENIA

Schizophrenia (an internalized disturbance) is a **psychopathological disorder**. Psychopathological disorders involve severe and pervasive distortions in perceiving, behaving, thinking, and feeling. Researchers have ruled out the possibility that schizophrenia is directly transmitted genetically. However, a disposition to develop the disorder is transmitted genetically. This type of disposition has been termed a **diathesis**. Contemporary authors have replaced the term *diathesis* with the term **vulnerability**. In essence, the terms mean the same thing (Cancro, 1988).

Vulnerability to Schizophrenia During Adolescence

Schizophrenia is the most frequently occurring psychopathological disorder in adolescence (Conger, 1991; Weiner, 1980). Schizophrenia typically leads to very serious, long-lasting problems for the majority of adolescents who develop the disorder. More than half of all adolescents who develop schizophrenia make no recovery and require continual care.

There is considerable debate about the prevalence of schizophrenia. Current evidence indicates that 1% of the American population experiences schizophrenia at some time in their lives. Joseph White (1989) reported that 100,000 new cases are diagnosed each year.

The individuals most at risk for developing schizophrenia are middle adolescents, late adolescents, and young adults. Individuals in the age-group of 17 to 25 seem most vulnerable (White, 1989). While some adults in their 40s and even in their 50s develop schizophrenia, such occurrences are rare (Weiner, 1980; White, 1989). Males are more susceptible than females to developing schizophrenia during adolescence, whereas females seem more susceptible as adults (Conger, 1991). Researchers have yet to determine whether these different points of vulnerability for males and females are due (*a*) to more tolerance in adolescent females whose schizophrenia has remained under control, (*b*) to biological or cultural stressors that affect males and females differently, or (*c*) to a combination of the first two factors (Babigian, 1985).

Symptoms of Schizophrenia

Detecting schizophrenia in adolescents is difficult. Adolescent schizophrenia has symptoms that resemble other disorders. Some schizophrenic adolescents appear to be primarily depressed, whereas others appear to be primarily antisocial. However, depression and antisocial behavior are secondary symptoms of adolescent schizophrenia, and once these secondary symptoms abate, the persistence of the primary symptoms leave no doubt what the real problem is. The primary symptoms of schizophrenia are disordered thinking, poor emotional control, peculiar speech patterns, quite limited interpersonal contact, and feelings of persecution (Conger, 1991; White, 1989). Difficulty diagnosing adolescent schizophrenia stems from the probability that normal adolescents will, at some time, exhibit disordered thinking, poor emotional control, peculiar speech patterns, and feeling they are under everyone's scrutiny. Perhaps it was the difficulty of distinguishing schizophrenic adolescents from normal adolescents that led Anna Freud (1969/1971) to declare that adolescents are abnormal.

Causes of Schizophrenia

What causes schizophrenia? For a time, it was very popular to identify dysfunctional family communication as the cause of schizophrenia. In other words, researchers believed a person developed schizophrenia because the family gave conflicting messages and produced emotional turmoil (Bateson, Jackson, Haley, & Weakland, 1956; Fromm-Reichmann, 1948).

The mounting evidence favors a biochemical and/or genetic origin for schizophrenia. The biochemical model says that increased levels of **dopamine** impair brain functioning and produce schizophrenic reactions. Dopamine is a chemical in the brain. As evidence for the dopamine hypothesis, researchers note that when people take certain drugs that increase dopamine levels, primary symptoms intensify in schizophrenic individuals and emerge (at lower levels) in healthy individuals (Goldenberg, 1990; White, 1989).

Genetic theories are founded on the significant occurrence of schizophrenia in identical twins, but the much less likely occurrence in fraternal twins (Conger, 1991;

Vulnerability to Psychological Disorders from Childhood to Adulthood

In the early 1970s, a group of researchers began a 17-year longitudinal study of three groups of individuals, all of whom ranged from 7 to 12 years of age when the study began (Erlenmeyer-Kimling, Cornblatt, Bassett, Moldin, Hildoff-Adomo, & Roberts, 1990). The three groups were (a) 43 children whose parents suffered depression, (b) 63 children whose parents had schizophrenia, and (c) 100 children whose parents were normally adjusted. Of these 206 children, the researchers had completed follow-up interviews with 156 individuals by the late 1980s—44 from schizophrenic parents, 33 from depressed parents, and 79 from normally adjusted parents.

The issue at hand was to determine how well children whose parents' psychological adjustments greatly varied would fare during adolescence and adulthood. None of the children had been in treatment for any psychiatric difficulties when they entered the study.

By early adulthood 23%, of the individuals were considered psychologically maladjusted. The greatest risk for poor adjustment was run by children of schizophrenic parents; nearly half of these individuals (45.4%) followed up in adulthood were disturbed. A much smaller percentage of children from depressed parents (24.2%) and of children from normally adjusted parents (10.1%) were considered to be psychologically maladjusted in adulthood.

Of considerable significance is the ability of the researchers to track the trajectory of disorders that emerged between early adolescence and early adulthood. The researchers gained data on the global adjustment of these individuals at four points in time: when they were, on average, 14, 17, 21, and 24 years old.

When the subjects of this project entered the study, available data indicated they were all well-adjusted. However, over the next five to six years, changes began to appear in some children who, by their young adulthood, manifested clear psychiatric problems. Other children continued to give every indication of being well-adjusted.

As the study progressed, differences between dysfunctional and adjusted adolescents became more pronounced. The individuals who began showing impairments in late middle childhood and early adolescence began exhibiting signs of chronic adjustment difficulties.

The individuals whose descent into psychopathology became most severe were those who experienced a psychotic episode requiring hospitalization for six months or more. By the time these individuals reached young adulthood (around age 24), they were significantly less well-adjusted than any of the subjects who had never had a psychotic episode ($p < .001$).

The histories of individuals who became dysfunctional over time differed from the histories of well-adjusted individuals. The researchers pointed out that it was not easy to predict the life course any person would take toward psychopathology; some individuals had very poor adjustment beginning in their early adolescent years; others, at one time, were functioning quite well but then their adjustment scores plummeted; and others went back and forth between functional and dysfunctional behavior.

What did not seem debatable, however, was the greater vulnerability to developing psychological disorders faced by children of schizophrenic parents. Yet, for those dysfunctional individuals from depressed parents, their adjustment in late adolescence and early adulthood was deemed the poorest of all.

White, 1989). Confirming evidence also comes from studies of adopted children. When their biological relatives had a history of this disorder, the presence of schizophrenia was nearly six times greater than it was among individuals not biologically related (Conger, 1991). Extensive follow-up studies with 311 Danish youths who were considered at either high or low risk for developing schizophrenia emphasized schizophrenia resulted from an interaction between stressful environmental circumstances (extremely inadequate parenting and being raised in an impersonal institution, for instance) and genetic predisposition (Conner, Mednick, & Parnas, 1990).

The presence of schizophrenia in close biological relatives does not predict a person will necessarily develop this disorder. In fact, evidence indicates it is unlikely that another relative will develop the disease. For one thing, except in the case of identical twins, relatives' genes are not the same. Even in the case of identical twins, when one develops schizophrenia, the likelihood of the other twin becoming schizophrenic is less than half—about 40% (White, 1989).

Some correlational studies have identified vulnerabilities to developing schizophrenia. Prior to developing the disorder, preschizophrenic adolescents typically come from highly stressful family environments, lack any contact with peers, and behave antisocially toward their families (Conger, 1991; Weiner, 1980). Preschizophrenic males become much more defiant of authority and much more aggressive than other adolescent boys; preschizophrenic females become more passive and more emotionally immature than other adolescent girls.

Treatment of Adolescent Schizophrenia

Treatment of adolescent schizophrenia involves a combination of approaches: psychiatric hospitalization, antischizophrenic drugs, psychotherapy, and family involvement. The goals of treatment are (*a*) to reduce the acutely disruptive symptoms, (*b*) to improve psychological functioning, and (*c*) to re-engage contact with reality. Once this first set of goals is achieved, the goal of treatment is to promote continuing recovery following discharge from the hospital (White, 1989). Because of remarkable advances in drug therapy, many individuals who will never be cured of their schizophrenic conditions can live independent, productive lives that are relatively symptom free.

Recovery From Adolescent Schizophrenia

As stated in the beginning of this section on schizophrenia, recovery from the disorder favors less than half of all adolescents who are affected. A rule of thumb is that the earlier the age of onset, the less likely the prospects for recovery. Pooling data from several follow-up studies of schizophrenic adolescents, Weiner (1980) reported full recovery for only 23%. Of the remaining affected adolescents, 25% showed some improvement, but experienced occasional psychotic episodes, and 52% made little or no progress whatsoever.

In addition to age of onset, other factors influence adolescent recovery from schizophrenia. A chief factor is whether the disorder seems to have been a gradual or sudden development. Recovery favors youths whose schizophrenia is the result of situational issues, such as stressful life events or crises over developmental tasks, but the outcome is poor for youths whose symptoms develop gradually over time (White, 1989).

Other factors have been linked to recovery. Among these are the person's level of adjustment prior to the onset of the disorder, the extent to which the person's thought processes deteriorate while schizophrenic, the attitude of the adolescent's family, and the frequency of relapses (Conger, 1991; White, 1989).

We have completed our discussion of two internalized disturbances that affect adolescents. Next, we turn to two examples of externalized disturbances—suicide and substance abuse. First, we discuss suicide.

SUICIDE

Official figures indicate that approximately 30,000 people in the United States commit suicide each year. The highest rate occurs among white males 65 years of age and older. While commonly considered an adolescent phenomenon, suicide is far more prevalent among the elderly (Conger, 1991; National Center for Health Care Statistics, 1985; Petti & Larson, 1987; U.S. Bureau of the Census, 1989).

The common perception that suicide is an adolescent phenomenon probably stems from the marked increase in the rate of adolescent suicide. Among 15- to 24-year-olds, the suicide rate has increased 300% since 1950 (White, 1989). Current annual figures indicate approximately 6,000 adolescents intentionally kill themselves each year. Such a death rate, which averages out to around 16 adolescent suicides daily, has made suicide the third leading cause of death among adolescents (Cook & Oltjenbruns, 1989; Curran, 1987; Petti & Larson, 1987; White, 1989). The two leading causes of adolescent death are accidents and homicide. Thus, violence claims the majority of adolescents who die.

It may be obvious to you that the prevalence of suicidal thoughts would be much higher than the prevalence of actual and attempted suicides. One study of 1,601 early and middle adolescents (ages 13 through 16) provides an estimate of the prevalence of suicidal thoughts in this age-group. Approximately 19% of the adolescents said they had thought about suicide; suicidal thoughts were more prevalent among the girls (23%) than among the boys (14%). There were also gender differences in the frequency of suicidal thoughts; 5% of the boys and 10% of the girls reported they frequently thought about suicide. When compared to their peers who said they had not thought about killing themselves, the adolescents with suicidal thoughts were involved in more delinquent behaviors, used drugs more often, had more problems with their health, and sought medical attention more often (Choquet & Menke, 1990).

Official figures about suicide are criticized for seriously underreporting the actual number of cases. Several experts are convinced that up to two-thirds of suicides get listed as accidents, primarily to prevent further troubles for bereaved survivors (Cook & Oltjenbruns, 1989; Petti & Larson, 1987; White, 1989). Thus, some experts estimate that up to 100,000 deaths in the United States each year are self-inflicted.

For every **completed suicide** (sometimes called a "successful suicide"), experts estimate there are 50 attempts. **Attempted suicides** that do not result in death are sometimes called **parasuicides**.

Adolescent parasuicides seldom involve much planning but, rather, seem to be impulsive acts. Females are much more likely than males to attempt suicide.

However, males are more likely than females to use highly lethal means for killing themselves, such as guns and hanging. Girls are more likely to use passive means, such as sleeping pills.

Failure to kill oneself in a suicide attempt frequently leads adults and the adolescent's peers to ostracize the individual. The parasuicide is viewed as a matter of gross manipulation, rather than an act of desperation and a cry for help (Curran, 1987). Such reactions typically intensify the distressing situation the adolescent wants to escape and thus increase the likelihood the adolescent will try again.

Characteristics of Suicidal Adolescents   Several major factors are associated with adolescent suicide. For instance, males who are above average in intelligence and who have entered puberty earlier than their peers are more likely to attempt suicide (Shaffer & Fisher, 1981). Other important characteristics associated with suicidal adolescents include

- feelings of depression,
- low self-esteem and poor self-image,
- excessively high parental expectations,
- use of drugs and alcohol,
- breakdowns in communication with parents or friends,
- a history of other suicide attempts, and
- a major confrontation with someone the adolescent considers important (Curran, 1987; Petti & Larson, 1987).

Investigators of completed suicides conduct inquiries called **psychological autopsies**. Their inquiries have revealed a small set of motives influence youths to kill themselves. Some youths are influenced by several of these motives. These motives include a desire to

- get help,
- escape from a difficult situation,
- punish individuals who have hurt the adolescent,
- join someone who has died, and
- assert independence in a world in which the youth feels no control (Curran, 1987).

David Curran (1987) has noted that adults and nonsuicidal adolescents view the motives for suicide quite differently than suicidal youths. More frequently than not, suicidal youths perceive suicide as an effort to escape an intolerable situation or to get help; adults and nonsuicidal peers typically consider suicidal acts stem from self-pity, hostility toward others, and clumsy efforts to manipulate other people (Curran, 1987).

These different perceptions about motives for suicide help explain myths that have emerged about suicide. Let's look at three of these myths.

Myths About Suicide

The first myth about suicide is that people who talk about suicide do not actually carry out the threat. In reality, about 75% of individuals who commit suicide communicate their intentions in hints or in clear statements. Such communication frequently is ignored or dismissed as a means to get attention (Rickgarn, 1983).

The second myth is that suicidal individuals are fully intent on dying. In reality, most individuals who attempt suicide are ambivalent about living or dying. A growing belief is that suicide attempts are signals for help from distressed individuals (Rickgarn, 1983). As discussed above, the most common response of adults to a suicide attempt is to view the attempt as a gesture to get attention, particularly when the adolescent selected a means very unlikely to prove lethal.

A third myth about suicide is that improvement in a suicidal person signals the risk has passed. In reality, severely depressed individuals are likely at greatest risk when their moods seem unexpectedly to be on the upswing. Improvement can indicate the adolescent's distress has passed because the youth now has a plan to end his or her troubles (Rickgarn, 1983).

Rules for Dealing With Suicidal Adolescents

Are there any rules to consider when someone talks about committing suicide? Here are seven rules.

First, take the threat seriously. Consider the communication a cry for help that could result in death if ignored.

Second, ask the person about his or her plans. If you are not sure, but think there is a chance, directly ask if the individual is considering ending his or her life. Being direct does not put the idea into the person's head or give the person permission. As Ralph Rickgarn noted, "the person is often relieved and able to begin an exploration of alternatives"(1983).

Third, find out how the person intends to carry out the act. Assessing the proposed method will indicate how likely the act will prove lethal. Jumping off the tenth floor of a dorm or shooting oneself in the head clearly has greater chances of proving lethal than "a nebulous idea with little feasibility of success" (Rickgarn, 1983).

Fourth, look for clues about the person's mood. Does the individual feel helpless, guilty, or exhausted, for example? Does the person want to die or feel ambivalent about dying? "The greater the desire to die, the higher the risk" is Rickgarn's (1983) warning.

Fifth, determine if the person has attempted suicide before. Individuals with histories of suicide present a clear risk of carrying out another attempt (Curran, 1987).

Sixth, indicate your concern, but do not promise total confidentiality. To help the person may require discussing the situation with someone else. Part of this help may require referring the youth to trained professionals and accompanying the adolescent to ensure the appointment is kept (Rickgarn, 1987).

Seventh, get the person to enter into a contract with you promising *not* to attempt suicide and promising to discuss alternatives with you should suicide remain an option. Rickgarn says, "It sounds strange, but it works" (1983).

Treatment of Suicidal Adolescents

Treatment of adolescents who attempt suicide occurs in two phases. As a first phase, acute, 24-hour care must be provided to reduce the danger the adolescent presents to him- or herself and to begin efforts at marshalling resources for coping once the youth is released from the hospital.

The second phase of care involves ongoing counseling with a skilled, knowledgeable therapist once the youth leaves the hospital. Many complicated issues color the goals and outcomes of therapy with suicidal adolescents. For instance, suicidal adolescents are quite sensitive to signs of rejection, and therapists may trigger unexpected reactions merely by being distracted during a session (Curran, 1987). In addition, success in therapy may present considerable risks to the adolescent; because the therapy is working, the relationship with the therapist will be ending. Separation from the therapist can create anxieties that trigger suicidal thoughts and, perhaps, suicidal actions (Curran, 1987).

Including the family in a suicidal adolescent's therapy may be important in some cases, but rigid insistence on family involvement in therapy sessions can work against the adolescent's being in treatment, especially at the beginning. "While it is accepted that the family is often the major component in the development of the problem of suicidality in their adolescent son or daughter, it must be recognized that they may not always be able to become part of the solution" (Curran, 1987, p. 157).

We have completed the section on adolescent suicide. We next take up a set of behaviors that frequently are present in suicidal individuals—substance abuse.

SUBSTANCE ABUSE

The mortality rate of individuals in the 15- to 24-year-old age-group has startled many observers. As stated earlier, the chief causes of death are some form of violence: accidents, homicide, and suicide. The mortality rate exceeds that of any other age-group in the United States. These mortality figures run in sharp contrast to the overall good physical health of most adolescents and young adults. However, look at the significant contributing factors to the high mortality rate: drug-related behaviors, such as alcohol consumption and use of illicit substances (for example, crack).

I have been given advice to take a bold stand and acknowledge recreational use of drugs is not harmful and actually correlates with popularity. I consider such advice intemperate given the sharply adverse consequences that follow for individuals and for society when drugs become a source of entertainment.

Besides the lethal consequences of substance abuse, other adverse outcomes also are worth mention. For the nation as a whole, the economic costs of substance abuse are more than four times the costs of cancer and nearly three times the costs of cardiovascular diseases, the leading causes of death in adults (Okwumabua, 1990). In addition to national economic costs and the chances of dying, substance abuse makes adolescents vulnerable to a legion of other problems, such as contracting contagious diseases, becoming addicted, dropping out of school, and becoming pregnant (Newcomb & Bentler, 1989). Researchers have known since at least the 1970s that substance abuse correlates positively with adolescents' antisocial behaviors and emotional problems, and represents a serious risk factor predicting psychopathology (Cohen, Brook, Cohen, Velez, & Garcia, 1990).

Campaigns promoting drug abstinence—for example, the "Just Say No" campaign—face many powerful obstacles. Saying no to drugs is one message in the national media, but many more messages in the same media extol the use of drugs. Pharmaceutical companies compete with one another for customers who will buy the painkiller most prescribed by doctors, and breweries put forth blatant messages that drinking beer is an essential part of having a good time. Many television shows and movies show characters using illicit drugs are having a good time. The American society "clearly says yes to a wide range of licit and illicit drugs" (Okwumabua, 1990, p. 396). Hank Resnik (1990) provided a similar evaluation in a document about drug use published by the U.S. government.

Types of Substances

Substance use and abuse obviously involve specific substances that people consume. The types of substances I am referring to are called **psychoactive drugs**. A psychoactive drug alters one's mood, as well as how one thinks, feels, and behaves. The psychoactive drugs adolescents most commonly use are alcohol, marijuana, stimulants, depressants, cocaine, crack, hallucinogens, and heroin. Here, I discuss the effects of alcohol in some detail, and also discuss briefly the effects of the other psychoactive drugs adolescents most commonly use.

Alcohol

Alcohol is a psychoactive drug with beneficial effects when used moderately. For instance, alcohol produces relaxation, appetite stimulation, and mild euphoria. When used to excess, alcohol has toxic effects, such as hangovers for immediate consequences and liver damage for chronic, excessive consumption (Lewy & Josephson, 1989).

How does alcohol work on the body? Once the body ingests alcohol, the stomach or the small intestine directly absorbs nearly all the alcohol a person has drunk. Alcohol, thus, quickly enters the bloodstream and circulates to every part of the body containing water. Although quickly absorbed into the body, alcohol remains in the body for a relatively long time. The liver can process about one ounce of alcohol per hour; three ounces of alcohol will still be circulating in decreasing amounts up to three hours later (Lewy & Josephson, 1989).

Attempting to sober up by drinking coffee or taking a cold shower simply has no impact on eliminating alcohol from the body. In fact, pouring black coffee into someone who is intoxicated has the effect of stimulating the person and often fooling onlookers into thinking this individual is able to operate an automobile (Lewy & Josephson, 1989).

Alcohol reaches the brain within minutes. Its first effects are to act as a stimulant, but, quickly, alcohol depresses human judgment and inhibition. Sexual inhibitions, for instance, are depressed by alcohol consumption, and a few college students have told me they engaged in sexual acts they would never have consented to if sober.

Alcohol impairs motor performance, depth perception, reaction time, and night vision. As you may have guessed, a person impaired in these physical abilities presents a considerable risk to self and to others when driving an automobile (Lewy & Josephson, 1989).

After drinking too much alcohol, a person will experience a hangover. His or her body will begin to experience the symptoms of withdrawal from alcohol intoxication. Because hangovers are unpleasant, people try homemade remedies to treat them. Two common approaches are to drink a small amount of alcohol (called "the hair of the dog") or to take a depressant drug, such as Valium. These remedies actually keep alcohol in a person's body. Another approach is to take stimulant drugs, such as amphetamines. These drugs camouflage alcohol withdrawal symptoms. Robert Lewy and Eric Josephson (1989) say the best cure for a hangover comes from sleep, liquids, aspirin, and time.

The long-term effects of alcohol abuse are profound. Alcohol abuse leads to a damaged heart, damaged central nervous system, damaged liver, and damaged gastrointestinal system. For instance, alcohol intoxication increases risk for high blood pressure, destroys brain cells, interferes with the production of normal clotting agents, and obstructs digestion (Lewy & Josephson, 1989).

Other Psychoactive Drugs

I will discuss briefly in this section the effects of the other psychoactive drugs adolescents commonly use. We will begin with marijuana.

Marijuana is a plant that, when ingested, can produce feelings of contentment. Its effects on the body are fairly rapid, and the typical duration for the effects of a single marijuana cigarette is around four hours. Some marijuana users report such intoxicating effects as hallucinations, panic, apathy, paranoia, and delusions. While there is debate over marijuana's ability to produce physical addiction, psychological dependence in heavy users has been noted. Claims that smoking marijuana leads to lung cancer are confounded by the fact that marijuana smokers frequently smoke tobacco. Heavy marijuana use is associated with use of other drugs, such as barbiturates, amphetamines, or cocaine. Withdrawal from marijuana produces such symptoms as inability to sleep, nausea, irritability, and sweating (Arif & Westermeyer, 1988; Josephson, 1985; Morofka, 1989).

Stimulants are drugs that produce arousal and feelings of being alert; **amphetamines** are a major type of stimulant. Amphetamines begin to affect the body within 30 minutes and last for prolonged (if indeterminate) periods. They increase wakefulness and improve motor skills, particularly on simple, repetitive tasks. Amphetamine users become talkative and confident of their abilities; they feel energetic because amphetamines induce the release of adrenalin. Intoxication symptoms include hypertension, lack of sleep, mood swings, confusion, convulsions, and, possibly, death. Withdrawal symptoms include exhaustion, apathy, depression, and sleep disturbances (Arif & Westermeyer, 1988; Josephson, 1985; Morofka, 1989).

Depressants are psychoactive drugs that slow down the central nervous system; **barbiturates** and **tranquilizers** are major types of depressants. They have an anesthetic effect on the body, and begin to act in 20 minutes or less. The duration of their effects varies widely depending on the type of depressant taken. Some barbiturates can last up to 40 hours. People who drink alcohol and use barbiturates at the same time run a considerable risk of killing themselves by inducing severe restrictions on circulatory and respiratory functions. Intoxication symptoms include irritability, mood swings, confusion, constricted pupils, and memory impairments. Withdrawal can involve visual hallucinations, nausea, anxiety, nightmares, and coma (Arif & Westermeyer, 1988; Josephson, 1985; Morofka, 1989).

Cocaine is a psychoactive drug that is highly addictive and produces feelings of euphoria and well-being. **Crack** is a derivative of cocaine made by mixing baking soda with cocaine; crack produces instant feelings of euphoria that last about 30 minutes and then leave the individual depressed. The physical effects of cocaine include increased heart rate, blood pressure, body temperature, and breathing. A common response to remove the depression that follows the ebb of cocaine's euphoric effects is to take more cocaine. Intoxication effects include mood swings, dilated pupils, chills and sweating, insomnia, confusion, convulsions, and, possibly, death. Withdrawal symptoms include exhaustion, depression, sleep disorders, and hyperactivity (Arif & Westermeyer, 1988; Josephson, 1985; Morofka, 1989).

Hallucinogens are also called **psychedelic drugs**; they induce the central nervous system to emit elaborate fantasies, and they alter perceptions of self and of time. Examples of these drugs are mescaline, PCP, and LSD. The effects of these drugs are psychological, rather than physical, and are unpredictable. While these drugs do not produce physical or psychological dependence, there are cases of induced psychosis, which required the victim to be hospitalized for psychiatric care. Intoxication effects are hypertension, dilated pupils, extreme mood swings, amnesia, violence, convulsions, and the possibility of death. There are no reported withdrawal effects from hallucinogens, although PCP induces flashbacks accompanied by erratic violence, hyperactivity and nervousness, and **catalepsy** (a form of being in a "conscious coma") (Arif & Westermeyer, 1988; Josephson, 1985; Morofka, 1989).

Heroin is an addictive drug that produces a sense of peace and calmness for about four hours before it wears off. Heroin is a member of the **opiate** family of drugs. Opiates are obtained by processing the opium poppy. Besides heroin, other opiates include morphine, darvon, demerol, and codeine. These opiates are powerful painkillers. All of the opiates possess addictive powers, and regular heroin users can rapidly become addicted. Intoxication effects of heroin include reduced breathing, decreased heart rate, drowsiness, and reduced consciousness. Chronic heroin users develop a need for greater dosages because the body builds a tolerance for dosages that initially produced euphoria. Withdrawal symptoms are very painful, and include muscle cramps, vomiting, diarrhea, dehydration, irritability, loss of appetite, severe panic attacks, and hypertension (Arif & Westermeyer, 1988; Josephson, 1985; Morofka, 1989; White, 1989).

Use versus Abuse   The concept of substance abuse is unclear. When does use of a substance turn into abuse? Does one drink of alcohol or one trial of a marijuana cigarette constitute abuse? Few people would think so, but for some, there is no fine line to be drawn between use and abuse. For others, the difference between recreational use and excessive use (abuse) of psychoactive drugs needs to be acknowledged.

Various professions give different definitions to substance abuse. Using drugs without a prescription is a medical notion of abuse, whereas not following a pharmacist's written directions is another profession's definition. Some civil libertarians have argued that the problem of abuse derives from efforts to constrict choice; this argument maintains "by restricting the availability of a given substance, we increase its market value, [and] create an underground culture of users not amenable to help and suppliers not subject to taxation" (Horan & Straus, 1987, p. 314). Civil liberties arguments against restrictions on individuals are usually countered by pointing to evidence about the varied costs society endures because individuals abuse drugs: costs in health care, lost productivity, crime, and lost lives.

Frequency, amount, and types of adverse consequences are three criteria proposed as means to distinguish use from abuse. John Horan and Lawrence Straus (1987) consider abuse a matter of damage to body tissue and ongoing psychological problems. Michael Newcomb and Peter Bentler (1989) suggest regular use of mind- or mood-altering substances indicates abuse, regardless of the frequency, amount, or adverse consequences. Jebose Okwumabua (1990) notes that abuse is indicated when a person's consumption of a drug interferes with the person's daily life or adversely affects development: for instance, producing criminal behavior, fostering economic dependence, and endangering oneself, other people, or property. Under these various definitions, an adolescent who causes an accident while drinking under the influence is an example of substance abuse, even if the occurrence was a one-time matter. My personal preference is to define abuse as frequent indulgence, rather than isolated incidents.

We know that people agree that substance abuse occurs, even though different notions of abuse exist. What is known about the prevalence and trends of adolescent substance abuse?

Prevalence of Adolescent Substance Abuse

In a longitudinal study of life stress and coping in the lives of 1,033 adolescents, Mary Ellen Colten, Susan Gore, and Robert Aseltine (1991) gathered information on alcohol consumption and drug use. The students were high school sophomores, juniors, and seniors; 44.2% were boys, 57.8% were girls, and the students ranged in age from 15 to 18. Over three-fourths of the adolescents ($n = 795$) lived with both parents, 21% ($n = 217$) lived with one parent, and the remaining 2% ($n = 21$) lived without either parent.

A goal of the study was to identify the prevalence of drinking and drug use problems, and to see if prevalence of problem behavior is related to gender and/or parental presence in the home.

A high school student was considered to have a drinking problem if that individual (a) had consumed five or more drinks at one time in the past 30 days, (b) drank alcohol at least once a week, or (c) had problems with parents, employers, school officials, or the police due to drinking. A high school student was considered a drug user if that individual had used any of the illicit psychoactive drugs during the preceding year (Colten et al., 1991).

When compared to girls of all ages, significantly more older boys had drinking problems. These problems were also age-related. Eleventh and twelfth grade boys were two to three times as likely as eleventh and twelfth grade girls to have drinking problems. However, in tenth grade, the girls were more likely than the boys to have drinking problems. One explanation for the drinking problems in tenth grade girls was that they tended to drink with older boys (Colten et al., 1991).

No gender differences appeared for high school drug use. Nearly 31% of the girls used drugs, as did 29% of the boys. Boys used hallucinogens and steroids more than girls, but there were no gender differences in the use of any other drugs (Colten et al., 1991).

Adolescents in two-parent households were much less likely to have drinking problems or to use drugs than adolescents with one or both parents absent from the home. The difference was most noticeable in drug use by females from homes without one or both parents ($p < .001$). Boys from nonintact homes did use drugs more than boys from two-parent households, but while statistically significant, the differences were less dramatic ($p < .05$) than what was found in female drug use (Colten et al., 1991).

Colten and her colleagues (1991) identified both drinking problems and drug use within a sample of high school students. Do we have any notion of when adolescents begin consuming illicit substances?

Age When Substance Use Begins

Findings from national surveys on drug use have suggested today's middle and late adolescents start using illicit substances at earlier ages than their counterparts from previous generations. For example, nearly half of high school seniors in 1984 reported having tried illicit drugs by tenth grade; a bit more than one-third of 1975 seniors reported similar experiences in tenth grade (Okwumabua, 1990).

A 1984 survey found alcohol is the predominant drug used and abused by adolescents; 92% of the sample used alcohol, 37% engaged in one or more episodes of heavy drinking, and 5% used alcohol daily (Johnston, O'Malley, & Bachman, 1985). While a minority of adolescents used other illicit drugs—amphetamines (23%),

Nothing rivals alcohol as the adolescent's drug of choice.

sedatives and tranquilizers (16%), hallucinogens (14%), and cocaine (13%)—nothing rivalled alcohol as the adolescent's drug of choice. Other studies corroborate these national survey findings (Horan & Straus, 1987; Johnston et al., 1988; Okwumabua, 1990). Let's look at the extensive 1987 and 1991 national surveys commissioned by the National Institute on Drug Abuse (Johnston et al., 1988, 1992).

The 1987 and 1991 surveys sampled high school seniors in approximately 135 public and private high schools throughout the United States, and administered questionnaires with a representative sample of late adolescents and young adults up to age 29. Eleven states were not included, among them, Nevada, Wyoming, Kansas, Vermont, North Dakota, and South Dakota. Because only graduating seniors were included in the sample, the exclusion of high school dropouts represents a sampling bias regarding the total late adolescent and young adult population in this country. These sampling procedures have been used since 1976 (Johnston et al., 1988, 1992).

Illicit Drug Use by Age-Group

1987 graduating seniors, college students, and young adults showed a sharp decline in the use of cocaine compared to use by earlier samples. This was the first time all three groups decreased cocaine use. This decline continued to be seen in all groups surveyed in 1991 (Johnston et al., 1992). The investigators attributed the decline to the growing national awareness of the dangers of cocaine use.

Use of some other illicit drugs also declined among all age-groups. Seniors, college students, and young adults reported less use of marijuana and amphetamines than reported by earlier samples. However, over-the-counter stimulants doubled in use between 1982 and 1991; about 23% of graduating seniors were using the drugs to stay awake (Johnston, et al., 1992) as compared to about 13% in 1982.

Other illicit drug use stayed fairly stable. When compared to use reported by earlier samples, heroin use remained the same for the 1987 seniors (0.6%), college students (0.2%), and young adults (0.2%) but dropped in 1991 slightly for seniors. Tranquilizer use continued to decline for high school seniors (3.6%), college students (2.4%), and young adults (3.5%). The three illicit drugs considered to have the greatest use and, therefore, the most impact on 1987 seniors, college students, and young adults were marijuana, cocaine, and amphetamines. However, noticeable declines in the use of all three substances by all three age-groups were found in 1991. In Table 15-2, you can see the annual prevalence rates for three drugs by age-group as determined in each survey. Marijuana continues to be an illegal substance used by about one-fourth of all people in these three age-groups.

Males in each of the age-groups were much more likely than females to use illicit drugs, especially at higher levels of consumption (Johnston et al., 1988, 1992). Males, for instance, used marijuana daily at two to three times the rate of females. However, there was one glitch to these data indicating higher male usage of illicit drugs. Female high school seniors in 1987 used amphetamines and tranquilizers—both uppers and downers—more than male high school seniors and used them at the same rate as males in 1991. No gender differences emerged in amphetamine and tranquilizer use among college students and young adults for 1987 or 1991.

On the whole, college students' use of several illicit drugs matches use by other individuals of the same age who are not in college. In 1987, noncollege late adoles-

TABLE 15-2   1987 and 1991 Prevalence Rates for Marijuana, Cocaine, and Amphetamines

| | AGE-GROUPS | | | | | |
| | SENIORS | | COLLEGE STUDENTS | | YOUNG ADULTS | |
ILLICIT DRUGS	1987	1991	1987	1991	1987	1991
Marijuana	36%	24%	37%	27%	35%	24%
Cocaine	10%	3.5%	14%	4%	16%	6%
Amphetamines	12%	8%	7%	4%	9%	4%

SOURCE: Adapted from *Illicit Drug Use, Smoking, and Drinking by America's High School Students, College Students, and Young Adults: 1975–1987* by L. D. Johnston, P. M. O' Malley, and J. G. Bachman, 1988, Rockville, MD: National Institute on Drug Abuse and *Smoking, Drinking, and Illicit Drug Use among American Secondary School Students, College Students, and Young Adults, 1975–1991* by L. D. Johnston, P. M. O'Malley, and J. G. Bachman, 1992, Rockville, MD: National Institute on Drug Abuse.

cents used several drugs much more than college students. In particular, 1987 college student intake of the following substances was less than the rate of their same-age, noncollege peers: cocaine, crack, amphetamines, barbiturates, and tranquilizers (Johnston et al., 1988). The 1991 college seniors also had lower rates of usage than their noncollege, young adult peers for these drugs (Johnston et al., 1992).

Alcohol Use by Age-Group

In the 1987 and 1991 surveys, nearly all the high school seniors reported they drink alcohol, and occasions of heavy drinking are pervasive. "Heavy drinking" was considered having five or more drinks in a row during the last two weeks. For 1987 seniors, 38% reported heavy drinking, and for 1991 seniors, 30% reported heavy drinking. Since 1984, about one-third of high school seniors have reported heavy drinking. A much higher percentage of 1987 males (46%) than females (29%) reported occasions of heavy drinking; the figures for 1991 were 38% for males and 21% for females.

A high percentage of the college students (43%) reported occasions of heavy drinking in 1987 and 1991. College students reported slightly less daily use of alcohol than their same-age, noncollege peers (6% versus 6.6% in 1987 and 4.1% versus 4.5% in 1991). However, occasions of heavy drinking were much more prevalent among 1987 and 1991 college students (43% for college seniors in both surveys compared to around 33% for their same-age, noncollege peers). On a daily basis, college males reported they drink more than females (8.8% to 3.9% in 1987 and 6.1% to 2.5% in 1991).

Gender differences in drinking become pronounced during college. Since these national surveys began in 1975, the percentage of college males who drink heavily has gradually increased. As mentioned above, 43% of college students reported drinking heavily on occasion, but more than half of all college males said they drank heavily compared to around one-third of college females. National surveys have not shown a comparable increase in occasions of heavy drinking by noncollege males. In fact, same-age noncollege peers have had a steady decline in heavy drinking since 1980.

Conclusions About Adolescent Substance Abuse

From the 1987 and 1991 surveys, we can draw the following conclusions:

- 57% of 1987 high school seniors and 37% of 1991 high school seniors tried marijuana,

- 36% of 1987 and 1991 high school seniors tried some illicit substance other than marijuana,

- daily use of marijuana dropped sharply between 1982 and 1991 among female high school seniors (from 18% to 6%) and dropped a bit less for males (from 23% to 12%),

- by their mid-20s, 80% of young adults in 1987 tried marijuana, and 60% tried some other illicit substance (the researchers did not report such information for 1991),

- 17% of 1987 high school seniors and 8% of 1991 high school seniors tried cocaine; 6% in 1987 and 3% in 1991 tried crack,

- by age 27, 40% of young adults in 1987 tried cocaine,

- 3% of 1987 and 1991 high school seniors smoked marijuana daily, and 15% of 1987 seniors versus 9% of 1991 seniors reported smoking marijuana daily at some time,

- nearly 5% of 1987 high school seniors and 4% of 1991 high school seniors drank alcohol daily; 38% of 1987 seniors and 32% of 1991 seniors had five or more drinks in a row during the past two weeks, and

- 54% of college males in 1987 and 43% in 1991 had five or more drinks in a row during the past two weeks (Johnston et al., 1988, 1992).

We know types of substances used, as well as age and gender differences involved in adolescent substance consumption. We know that some adolescents consume illicit substances excessively. What do we know about factors that foreshadow adolescent use or abuse of drugs? We look first at longitudinal data identifying personality and parenting factors associated with adolescent responses to the availability of marijuana. Then, we look at factors involved in adolescent abuse of drugs.

Personality and Parental Factors Foreshadowing Adolescent Marijuana Use

Some writers have given considerable emphasis to the role peers play in adolescent drug use (Kaplan, Martin, & Robbins, 1982). The popular phrase "Just say no" is considered advice to help youths withstand peer pressure to use drugs. A prominent drug use prevention program called DARE (Baker, 1982) emphasizes teaching elementary school children coping skills to overcome peer pressures, with the clear inference that learning a wide variety of ways to say "no" will enable a child to refrain from drug use. There is, however, some evidence that emphasizing skills to negate peer pressure ignores more significant factors that foreshadow an adolescent's decision to use drugs.

Jack Block, a psychologist at the University of California at Berkeley, and his colleagues have produced impressive longitudinal data about personality and parenting factors that foreshadow early and late adolescent drug use (Block, Block, & Keyes, 1988; Shedler & Block, 1990). Their longitudinal work followed over 100 individuals from age 3 to age 18. They collected data when the children were 3, 4, 5, 7, 11, 14, and 18 years of age. About 67% of the youths were white, 25% were black, and 12% were Asian. The study retained 78% of its 130 research participants ($n = 101$) over its duration.

Block and his associates were interested in the longitudinal effects of personality and parenting on adolescent development, particularly on drug use. They gathered data on **ego-resiliency** and **ego-control**. Some of the behaviors attributed to ego-resiliency were acting resourcefully, taking initiative, being energetic, self-reliant and confident, and adjusting well to stress. Some of the behaviors attributed to ego-control were delaying gratification, planning ahead, coping with minor frustrations, and having stable moods, rather than rapid mood shifts. Data were obtained from clinical psychologists' interviews with the children and from teachers' ratings.

The researchers also gathered data on how the mothers and fathers interacted with their children. The parents completed an inventory about their child-rearing behaviors. The researchers visited the homes of all the children, gathering impressions of the home environments and observing interactions between each child and his or her parents.

Early Adolescent Marijuana Use

At age 14, the youths answered questions about their use of drugs, as well as about many other topics, such as peer relations, schoolwork, family relations, and personal ambitions. The adolescents indicated which, if any, drugs on a list they had used. The list identified such drugs as wine, beer, liquor, tobacco, marijuana, amphetamines, tranquilizers, barbiturates, hashish, and heroin. The youths indicated how often they used the drugs (from never to once a week or more frequently).

Two groups of early adolescents emerged: **drug users** and **drug nonusers**. Personality and parenting factors that dated from as early as age 3 distinguished drug users from nonusers, primarily around use of marijuana. Nearly half of the youths (49%) had never used marijuana, whereas of the 51% who were considered drug users, 13% used it once or twice and 10% used marijuana more than once a week.

Early adolescent females who used marijuana were characterized by lack of ego-resiliency and absence of ego-control. They had difficulties delaying gratification, were rebellious, nonconforming, and hostile toward others, held low personal aspirations, and wanted to be independent. During their preschool and elementary school years, these girls had been described as greedy, inconsiderate, prone to blame others when things went wrong, likely to cry when stressed, and disliked by many of their peers.

For early adolescent males who used marijuana, ego-resiliency and drug use were not related, but drug use was highly related to absence of ego-control. These males lacked fear, disliked intellectual matters, enjoyed sensuous experiences, were rebellious and unconforming to authority, relied on subjective interpretations, acted impulsively, desired to be independent, believed in their physical attractiveness, were self-indulgent, and were interested in the opposite sex. During their preschool and elementary school years, these boys had been considered inconsiderate, defiant, domineering, uncooperative, easily frustrated, hostile, risk-takers, and lacking resources to recover from setbacks.

Mothers of early adolescent female drug users had expressed disappointment in their daughters during the preschool and elementary school years. The mothers often seemed angry with their daughters and thought their daughters had forced them to miss out on much of life. They had difficulty disciplining their daughters, and gave them considerable latitude, even at an early age, to question their mothers' decisions. Fathers of early adolescent female drug users gave no encouragement to the girls to succeed, had, at best, lax and inconsistent rules, and favored their daughters becoming independent at a young age.

No parenting factors foreshadowed early adolescent drug use by boys. Block and his colleagues (1988) wondered if these findings indicated girls are more responsive to family dynamics than are boys, and wondered if parental behaviors more easily influence daughters than sons during the early and middle childhood years.

Late Adolescent Marijuana Use

During the middle adolescent years, a shift occurred regarding drug use in Block's longitudinal study (Shedler & Block, 1990). Analyses indicated that by age 18, there were three groups of adolescents vis-à-vis marijuana use: abstainers, experimenters, and frequent users. **Abstainers** (28.7% of the sample) had never used marijuana or any other drug, **experimenters** (35.6%) had tried marijuana anywhere from once or twice to up to once a month, and **frequent users** (19.8%) used marijuana once a week or more often. None of the experimenters had used more than one other drug (besides marijuana), whereas the frequent users had tried one or more other drugs. Approximately 16% of the youths could not be grouped with any of the others; these adolescents were users of other drugs, but not of marijuana.

Significant psychological differences distinguished between abstainers, experimenters, and frequent users. Significant personality characteristics dating from early childhood and middle childhood foreshadowed each group's decisions about using marijuana. We look at each group in turn.

Abstainers.   These adolescents had good high school academic records (3.0 GPA). They were tense, emotionally confined, socially inept, and isolated from others. They valued delaying gratification and reaching objectivity in their decisions. They judged behavior moralistically. Their peers did not particularly like them. As far back as age 7, these youths had been sad and gloomy, lacking in curiosity and energy, and unresponsive to other people. Their mothers were cold, distant, and insensitive to their needs. These mothers had neither praised their children during their early years nor encouraged them in their tasks; paradoxically, these mothers had pressured their children to perform correctly and had criticized them severely when their performances did not meet the mothers' standards. Their fathers were authoritarians, who squelched expressions of spontaneity and demanded strict adherence to rules. The fathers disliked spending time with their children and seemingly made sure their children disliked being with them. These fathers "played a telling role in their [children's] character development" (Shedler & Block, 1990, p. 627).

Frequent marijuana users.   These adolescents had low C averages in their high-school work (2.3 GPA). By age 18, other people found them undependable, devious, impulsive, selfish, lacking in interpersonal warmth, and openly hostile. It may not surprise you to learn other people did not like them. These frequent marijuana users were prone to blame others for their difficulties, were distrustful, and were concerned solely for what they could gain from interpersonal relations. Jonathan Shedler and Block (1990) described these adolescents as troubled, alienated, and expressly antisocial. All of these characteristics fit Offer's (1969) descriptions of the 20% to 25% of American youths whose lives are filled with turmoil, storm, and stress.

As far back as the age of 7, these youths had noticeable problems getting along with peers. They had been deceitful even then, lacked self-confidence, thought of themselves as unsatisfactory, and did not identify with adults they thought were admirable. Other children took advantage of them. By the age of 11, they were easily distracted, avoided stressful situations, gave up easily when challenged, and disliked change.

. Like the mothers of the abstainers, the mothers of frequent marijuana users were emotionally cold, unresponsive to their children, and negligent regarding their children's safety. These mothers offered their children infrequent praise or encouragement and, conversely, pressured them to perform well. They seemed unaware of how to encourage success in any way other than by threatening, belittling, and pressuring. The fathers had little, if any, impact on the development of these youths into adolescent marijuana users.

Experimenters.   These adolescents had high school academic records no different than the records of the abstainers (3.0 GPA). They had close personal relationships, were generous and sympathetic with others, and were liked by their peers. They had poise in social situations, and were sought out by peers for advice. They had proven themselves trustworthy and productive. They could delay gratification. In short, unlike abstainers or frequent marijuana users, late adolescent experimenters had strong senses of well-being and senses of personal worth. One would say they were marked by ego-resiliency and by ego-control, whereas the abstainers were marked by overcontrol and lack of resiliency and the frequent users by undercontrol and lack of resiliency.

As early as the age of 7, the experimenters were already warm and responsive in interpersonal relations, were pleased with their achievements, acted energetically, handled stress well, were dependable, and were self-confident. By the age of 11, they were cooperative, were liked by adults, enjoyed learning, confronted stressful situations rather than running from them, trusted others, were talkative, and made social contacts easily.

The mothers of experimenters accepted their children's ideas, interacted spontaneously with them, valued their children's creativity, were relaxed when around them, and encouraged them. They protected their children and were patient with them. These children enjoyed being with their mothers. Their fathers were responsive to the children's needs, offered reasons for rules rather than being autocratic, and permitted their children to participate in making decisions.

Implications of These Longitudinal Findings About Adolescent Marijuana Use

What can we conclude from these findings? The implications group into two general categories: assertions about overall psychological development and assertions about drug prevention efforts. We take up each set of assertions in turn.

Assertions about psychological health.   Shedler and Block (1990) asserted that both the frequent users and the abstainers showed signs of psychological maladjustment. The fact that frequent users were maladjusted came as no surprise to the researchers, but signs of maladjustment in the abstainers led Shedler and Block to conclude that it is critical to rethink what it means for adolescents in contemporary American society to use marijuana.

They noted that abstaining from marijuana use during adolescence was—statistically speaking—deviant behavior for the late adolescent American. This concept of determining normalcy and deviancy by statistical comparisons fits what we discussed about normality at the beginning of this chapter. However, I am loathe to argue in favor of behavior on the grounds that "everyone else is doing it." Perhaps you think otherwise on this matter, and certainly there is some logic to the notion that the widespread prevalence of a behavior makes it normal for the society. However, at that rate, what would we say about the prevalence of housing discrimination against certain groups in some cities? Are we left with deciding that what is normal is a matter of contemporary societal expectations? Given the survey data gathered over the past several years, it is difficult to argue against the view that— because more adolescents try marijuana than do not— abstaining deviates from the statistical norm. But even this argument does have limits, as Shedler and Block (1990) note, when they restrict the sense of normality to the 36% of the adolescents who moderate their use of marijuana.

A more complicated analysis comes in what Shedler and Block (1990) say about the need to understand marijuana use within the overall context of adolescent development. They maintain that experimentation with marijuana is a sign of the developmental task of struggling to choose one's own values; in short, they consider the experimenters to be in the midst of a healthy developmental crisis known as the moratorium stage of identity formation (Josselson, 1987; Marcia, 1980). After reflecting on Block and Shedler's data, I have inferred that abstainers do not have the ego strength to try situations prohibited by authority, and frequent users are stuck in the rootlessness of identity diffusion.

It is crucial, absolutely crucial in fact, not to misrepresent Shedler and Block's (1990) conclusions. They do not contend that experimenting with marijuana made some adolescents psychologically healthy, that frequent use made some adolescents maladjusted, and that refraining from marijuana made other adolescents maladjusted. Rather, their longitudinal data support the conclusion that many factors involving personality formation and parenting behaviors contribute to making experimenters psychologically healthy and to making frequent users and abstainers maladjusted. In other words, the relative adjustment of the experimenters preceded their experimenting with marijuana, just as the relative maladjustment of the frequent users and the abstainers preceded their responses to the chance of using marijuana.

Shedler and Block's (1990) findings do not extend to an argument to legalize drugs. Their findings do suggest that infrequent to occasional use of marijuana does not prove detrimental and, in fact, such use seems a foregone conclusion for a significant proportion of youths growing up in this era of American society.

It would be intemperate, to say the least, to maintain that these findings support the notion that recreational use of drugs makes a person popular or improves psychological development—as though experimenters were popular or adjusted because they had used marijuana. In fact, concern over being misrepresented led Shedler and Block to write that their study did *not* support or "remotely encourage" any opinion "that drug use might somehow improve an adolescent's psychological health" (1990, p. 628).

Assertions about drug prevention efforts.   These findings do lead to doubts about the efforts made to prevent drug use by inoculating youths against peer pressures. Shedler and Block's (1990) data suggest personality development and parenting styles may have as much influence, if not more, on adolescent drug use as peers. Their findings point toward interventions that employ family life education, foster parenting skills, and promote character development during childhood.

Now that we have finished our discussion on Shedler and Block's (1990) longitudinal data, we have one last question to consider. Why do adolescents abuse substances?

Why Do Adolescents Abuse Substances?

The reasons for substance abuse are complex. Many factors lead substance users to be substance abusers. One format for looking at the motivations to abuse substances is to consider both individual factors and environmental factors.

Individual Factors

Several individual factors have been identified in adolescent substance abuse. Poor social skills, poor self-image, and antisocial behavior have been identified as antecedents to adolescent substance abuse. While drug use is common among delinquents, researchers assert that delinquency precedes drug use (Donovan, Jessor, & Jessor, 1983; Johnston, O'Malley, & Eveland, 1978). Other individual factors considered important include poor school performance, lack of religious commitment, and even shyness in the first grade (Okwumabua, 1990). Horan and Straus (1987) suggest that all these conclusions about individual factors may be based on questionable data since the researchers relied on retrospective accounts offered by individuals after they had been using drugs for some time.

Environmental Factors

The major environmental factors that are considered influential in producing adolescent substance abuse are conflictual interpersonal relations with peers, family members, or other individuals. Both peers and parents are considered to provide

The Incidence and Prevalence of Drug Abuse Among Native Americans and Alaskan Natives

Research data collected over a 10-year period documented that alcohol was, without doubt, the most abused drug among Native American youths. The other drugs abused by Native Americans were, respectively, "marijuana, tobacco, inhalants, stimulants, and cocaine" (Trimble, 1992, p. 251). The 10-year study also indicated:

- 75% of Native American early adolescents have tried marijuana,
- 30% of Native American youths have used inhalants (such as sniffing glue), and
- 5% have tried heroin (Trimble, 1992).

The data indicated Native Americans are exposed to many illegal substances much earlier than other youths in this country.

An 11-year study of drug use by Alaskan youths produced results quite similar to the pattern found among Native Americans in the continental United States. Native Alaskan youths had a prevalence rate for drug use higher than any other ethnic group in Alaska. What concerned researchers was that adolescent drug use in Alaska was on the upswing, while national findings reported a decline everywhere else.

The overriding concern of substance abuse researchers and therapists is the disproportionately high number of Native American youths at risk for being lifetime drug or alcohol abusers. Youths in boarding schools for Native Americans seem particularly vulnerable to becoming heavy drug users. About one-fifth of all Native American youths were enrolled in these schools in the late 1980s. Joseph Trimble (1992) reports 53% of Native American adolescents in one school were considered already to be alcoholics, and notes in another boarding school, 25% of the youths got drunk every weekend.

strong modeling forces in an adolescent's decision to turn to drugs (Horan & Straus, 1987; Okwumabua, 1990). Shedler and Block (1990) noted that frequent marijuana users had mothers who were cold, unresponsive, and belittling. In particular, dysfunctional family systems and ineffective parental discipline are cited as significant environmental influences on adolescent drug use (Jessor & Jessor, 1978; Kandel, 1982). We have already mentioned in the beginning of this section the concerns felt over societal tolerance for and extolling of drug use.

CHAPTER SUMMARY

While some writers have described the adolescent years as tumultuous by nature, research evidence indicates only a minority of adolescents experience such emotional turmoil that it would be correct to label them psychologically disturbed. In this chapter, we looked at some of the severe emotional difficulties that adolescents in turmoil experience.

Severely disturbed adolescents are considered to be abnormal. The intense psychological disorders that plague these adolescents set them apart from their unaffected age-mates. Disturbed adolescents have adapted poorly to life and are hindered from achieving optimal development. Criteria for determining their abnormality usually point to excessive reactions to internal or external situations. Other criteria point to deviations from statistical and social norms.

Experts frequently differentiate internalized from externalized psychological problems. The former are disorders whose primary symptoms are cognitive, emotional, or psychosomatic; an example is depression. Externalized disturbances are disorders whose primary symptoms are overt actions against oneself or others, such as suicide.

In this chapter, we reviewed four types of severe disorders manifested in adolescents in turmoil. Two are internalized disorders—depression and schizophrenia, and two are externalized—suicide and substance abuse.

It has proven difficult to obtain a clear picture of the prevalence of adolescent depression. One difficulty stems from failure to establish criteria to identify depression. Between 18% and 28% of the adolescent population not in clinical treatment is considered to suffer from depression; these individuals would be what Daniel Offer (Offer et al., 1988) has called "quietly disturbed adolescents." Depression is the primary problem for 40% of all adolescents referred to mental health professionals.

Schizophrenia is the most frequently occurring psychopathological disorder in adolescence, and it typically produces serious, chronic difficulties for individuals who develop the disorder during adolescence. The actual number of schizophrenics is debated. Individuals most at risk are 17- to 25-year-olds. Symptoms include disordered thinking, poor emotional control, peculiar speech patterns, and extreme sensitivity about scrutiny from other people. Causes of schizophrenia seem more and more likely to be biochemical and/or genetic. Treatment includes psychiatric hospitalization, medication, psychotherapy, and involvement of the family.

Suicide has increased in the 15- to 24-year-old age range by 300% since 1950. Official figures indicate about 6,000 adolescents take their own lives each year, and suicide is the third leading cause of adolescent death. However, several experts on suicide believe two-thirds of all suicides are listed as accidents in efforts to spare bereaved survivors. Factors associated with suicide include feelings of depression, low self-esteem, excessively high parental expectations, communication breakdown, and substance use. Among other motivations, suicidal youths express a desire to get help, to escape from difficulties, and to punish others. We looked at some myths about suicide and some rules to follow when with a person at risk for suicide.

Alcohol and other substance abuse contribute to adolescent death, antisocial behaviors, and development of psychopathological disorders. In addition to alcohol, adolescent substance abuse involves other psychoactive drugs, such as marijuana, stimulants, depressants, cocaine, crack, hallucinogens, and heroin. Distinctions are made between substance use and abuse. Three criteria proposed as means to distinguish use from abuse are frequency of consumption, amount consumed, and adverse consequences following consumption. Alcohol abuse significantly affects more older male adolescents than females, and no other substance rivals alcohol as the adolescents' drug of choice. There are no gender differences found in high school students' drug use overall.

The majority of high school seniors, college students, and young adults do not use illicit substances. Both personality factors and parenting styles foreshadow adolescents' responses to the availability of marijuana. For adolescents who do use illicit drugs, the three most frequently consumed are marijuana, cocaine, and amphetamines. Late adolescents who do not go to college use several drugs, such as cocaine, crack, amphetamines, barbiturates, and tranquilizers more than college students. Environmental factors and individual factors have been identified in adolescent substance abuse.

This concludes Chapter 15. We move on to the last portion of this book, an epilogue, which contains my thoughts about adolescents and the future.

EPILOGUE:

Facing the Future

What are we to make of prospects for adolescents? Are we to conclude that these are terrible times beset by promiscuity, violence, and moral relativism? Or are these times of momentous opportunity symbolized by technological and artistic ingenuity and by advances in social justice? Do we face the future with feelings of ambiguity and dread because, to borrow Charles Dickens's line, we live in the best and the worst of times?

I remain optimistic for the human race and for the world that adolescents will inherit as adults. Part of this optimism comes from my temperament I suppose; I expect things can turn out all right, even though I realize tragedy marks all of our lives sooner or later. Part of my optimism stems from my reading of history. How often have people bemoaned the future and considered their society's youths were hopeless? The majority of youths from generation to generation accept the challenges and responsibilities that adults transfer from generation to generation.

I think we face enormous challenges in stemming the epidemic of violence that seemingly has overtaken American society. What is promising is to see adults in my generation say enough to this insanity of unlimited gun use and to hear adolescents in my daughter's generation express outrage over acquiescence that nothing can be done to stem assaults and murders of their peers.

We see a revolution occurring in American willingness to provide opportunities, regardless of a person's race, religion, or gender. The pockets of hate that protest these gains in civil rights are gladly only that—pockets of intolerance, which most people find abhorrent. I expect the world of work and of politics to be more gender-fair and racially balanced as my daughter's generation assumes adult responsibilities and begins to raise their own children.

I suspect we will continue to have a portion of adolescents who find growing up to be a difficult and emotionally troubling journey. By the time this generation of adolescents is writing the college textbooks—if indeed advances in electronic media do not do away with textbooks as we know them—I expect there will be widespread acceptance that the majority of adolescents develop with relative calm, marred most likely by conflict with their parents.

Of course, we cannot readily forecast the future. So much change has occurred since I was a young adult that I fully expect marvels will continue. I expect my daughter to partake in this future, along with the rest of her generation.

What will be the key events that all people will remember as world changing? The binding question for individuals of my generation is "Where were you when Kennedy was shot?" For my mother and my father's generation, that question was "Where were you when Pearl Harbor was bombed?" as well as the question about Kennedy. For my daughter and her generation, that question is "Where were you when the shuttle blew up?" It is sobering for adults in my generation to realize that none of the current generation of adolescents was alive when Kennedy was shot. Will there be another landmark event, such as the Kennedy assassination or the bombing of Pearl Harbor, that captures the imagination of a generation? Almost surely.

I do not expect some troubles to disappear unless tremendous breakthroughs occur. Schizophrenia will continue to haunt a small portion of the population. I expect child abuse to continue even if we institute family life education and parenting workshops on a national scale. I expect adolescents from this current generation to take the lead in efforts to cure schizophrenia and to work against child abuse. Unfortunately, some adolescents from this generation will develop schizophrenia, and others who have been abused will repeat this cycle of violence in their own homes.

I hope scientists in my generation find a cure for AIDS before my daughter becomes a young adult. The prospects for this world should a cure be not be found are indeed scary. It is sobering to realize that many adolescents have contracted HIV and won't learn their condition for several years, after infecting many individuals.

These are serious thoughts about the need for changes and the need for committed individuals willing to accept the challenges presented to adults. When I think of my daughter and of her friends, and of the college students I have met during my time at Kansas State University, I understand the reason my optimism wins out over any temptations to give up.

With the close of this epilogue, this book on adolescent development from early through late adolescence comes to an end. It was a pleasure to write, and because I am interested in the book's communication value, I hope readers will welcome my invitation to send me their ideas about the book. Adolescent development is a dynamic process and the primary readers of this book know adolescence firsthand.

References

Abraham, K. G. (1986). Ego-identity status among Anglo-American and Mexican-American adolescents. *Journal of Adolescence, 9,* 151–166.

Abramowitz, R. H., Petersen, A. C., & Schulenberg, J. E. (1984). Changes in self-image during early adolescence. In D. Offer, E. Ostrov, & K. I. Howard (Eds.), *Patterns of adolescent self-image* (pp. 19–28). San Francisco, CA: Jossey-Bass.

Abuzinada, Z. A. (1988). *The diffusion and uses of video cassette recorders among adult members of an extended community in the Kingdom of Saudi Arabia.* Unpublished doctoral dissertation, The Ohio State University, Columbus, OH.

Achenbach, T. M. (1966). The classification of children's psychiatric symptoms: A factor-analytic study. *Psychological Monographs* (Whole No. 615).

Adams, G. M., & deVries, H. A. (1973). Physiological effects of an exercise training regimen upon women aged 52 to 79. *Journal of Gerontology, 28,* 50–55.

Adams, G. R. (1976). Personal identity formation: A synthesis of cognitive and ego psychology. *Adolescence, 12,* 151–164.

Adams, G. R. (1978). Racial membership and physical attractiveness effects on preschool teachers' expectations. *Child Study Journal, 8,* 29–41.

Adams, G. R., Abraham, K. G., & Markstrom, C. A. (1987). The relations among identity development, self-consciousness, and self-focusing during middle and late adolescence. *Developmental Psychology, 23,* 292–297.

Adams, G. R., Bennion, L., & Huh, K. (1989). *Objective measure of ego identity status: A reference manual.* (Available from Gerald Adams, Dept. of Family Studies, Univeristy of Guelph, Guelph, Ontario, Canada.)

Adams, G. R. & Crane, P. (1980). An assessment of parents' and teachers' expectations of preschool children's social preference for attractive or unattractive children and adults. *Child Development, 51,* 224–231.

Adams, G. R. & Fitch, S. A. (1982). Ego stage and identity status development: A cross-sequential analysis. *Journal of Personality and Social Psychology, 43,* 574–583.

Adams, G. R. & Gullotta, T. (1983). *Adolescent life experiences.* Pacific Grove, CA: Brooks/Cole.

Adams, G. R. & Gullotta, T. (1989). *Adolescent life experiences.* (2nd ed.) Pacific Grove, CA: Brooks/Cole.

Adams, G. R. & Jones, R. M. (1983). Female adolescents' identity development: Age comparisons and perceived child-rearing experience. *Developmental Psychology, 19,* 249–256.

Adams, G. R. Openshaw, D. K., Bennion, L., Mills, T., & Noble, S. (1988). Loneliness in late adolescence: A social skills training study. *Journal of Adolescent Research, 3,* 81–96.

Adams, G. R. & Shea, J. (1979). The relationship between status, locus of control, and ego development. *Journal of Youth and Adolescence, 8,* 81–89.

Adams, G. R., Shea, J., & Fitch, S. A. (1979). Toward the development of an objective assessment of ego-identity status. *Journal of Youth and Adolescence, 8,* 223–237.

Adelson, J. (1971). The political imagination. In J. Kagan & R. Coles (Eds.), *Twelve to sixteen: Early adolescence* (pp. 106–143). New York: Norton. (Originally published in *Daedalus,* 1971, *100,* 1013–1050).

Adelson, J. (1986). *Inventing adolescence: The political psychology of everyday schooling.* New Brunswick, NJ: Transaction Books.

Adelson, J., Green, B., & O'Neil, R. (1969). Growth of the idea of law in adolescence. *Developmental Psychology, 1,* 327–332.

Adelson, J. & O'Neil, R. (1966). Growth of political ideas in adolescence: The sense of community. *Journal of Personality and Social Psychology, 4,* 295–306.

Ageton, S. (1983). *Sexual assault among adolescents.* Lexington, MA: Lexington Books.

Ahrons, C. & Rodgers, R. (1987). *Divorced families: A multidisciplinary view.* New York: Norton.

Alasker, F. D. (1989). Perceived social competence, global self-esteem, social interactions and peer dependence in early adolescence. In B. H. Schneider, G. Attili, J. Nadel, & R. P. Weissberg (Eds.), *Social competence in developmental perspective (pp. 390–392).* Boston: Kluwer Academic.

Allgozzine, O. (1977). Perceived attractiveness and classroom interaction. *Journal of Experimental Education, 46,* 63–66.

Allport, G. W. (1951). *The use of personal documents in psychologial science.* New York: Social Science Research Council.

Allport, G. W. (1961). *Pattern and growth in personality.* New York: Holt, Rinehart & Winston.

Allport, G. W. (1965). *Letters from Jenny.* New York: Harcourt Brace Jovanovich.

Allport, G. W., Bruner, J. S., & Jandorf, E. M. (1941). Personality under social catastrophe: An analysis of 90 German refugee life histories. *Character & Personality, 10,* 1–22.

Al-Oofy, A. & McDaniel, D. O. (1992). Home VCR viewing among adolescents in rural Saudi Arabia. *Journal of Broadcasting & Electronic Media, 36,* 217–223.

American College of Physicians Health and Public Policy Committee. (1986). Eating disorders: Anorexia nervosa and bulimia. *Annals of Internal Medicine, 105,* 790–794.

American Psychiatric Association. (1987). *Diagnostic and statistical manual of mental disorders* (3rd ed., rev.). Washington, DC: Author.

Anastasi, A. (1988). *Psychological testing* (6th ed.). New York: Macmillan.

Anderson, B. W. (1975). *Understanding the Old Testament* (3rd ed.). Englewood Cliffs, NJ: Prentice-Hall.

Anderson, R. C. (1984). Role of the reader's schema in comprehension, learning, and memory. In R. C. Anderson, J. Osborn, & R. J. Tierney (Eds.), *Learning to read in American schools: Basal readers and content texts* (pp. 243–257). Hillsdale, NJ: Erlbaum.

Andre, P. (1987). *Drug addiction: Learn about it before your kids do.* Deerfield Beach, FL: Health Communications.

Andre, T., Dietsch, C., & Cheng, Y. (1991). Sources of sex education as a function of sex, coital activity, and type of information. *Contemporary Educational Psychology, 16,* 215–240.

Aneshensel, C. S. & Frerichs, R. R. (1982). Stress, social support, and depression: A longitudinal causal model. *Journal of Community Psychology, 10,* 363–376.

Aneshensel, C. S. & Gore, S. (1991). Development, stress, and role restructuring: Social transitions of adolescence. In J. Eckenrode (Ed).), *The social context of coping* (pp. 55–77). New York: Plenum.

Applebee, A. N., Langer, J. A., & Mullis, I. V. S. (1986). *Writing: Trends across the decade, 1974–1984.* Princeton, NJ: Educational Testing Service.

Archer, S. (1982). The lower age boundaries of identity development. *Child Development, 53,* 1551–1556.

Archer, S. (1985). Career and/or family: The identity process for adolescent girls. *Youth and Society, 16,* 289–314.

Ardrey, R. (1966). *The territorial imperative.* New York: Atheneum.

Arif, A. & Westermeyer, J. (1988). *Manual of drug and alcohol abuse: Guidelines for teaching in medical and health institutions.* New York: Plenum.

Aronfreed, J. (1968). *Conduct and conscience: The socialization of internalized control over behavior.* New York: Academic Press.

Asher, S. R. & Coie, J. D. (Eds.). (1990). *Peer rejection in childhood.* New York: Cambridge University Press.

Asher, S. R. & Dodge, K. A. (1986). Identifying children who are rejected by their peers. *Developmental Psychology, 22,* 444–449.

Asher, S. R. & Gottman, J. M. (Eds.). (1981). *The development of children's friendships.* New York: Cambridge University Press.

Asher, S. R. & Hymel, S. (1981). Children's social competence in peer relations: Sociometric and behavioral assessment. In J. D. Wine & M. D. Smye (Eds.), *Social competence* (pp. 125–157). New York: Guilford.

Asher, S. R., Markell, R. A., & Hymel, S. (1981). Identifying children at risk in peer relations: A critique of the rate of interaction approach to assessment. *Child Development, 52,* 1239–1245.

Asher, S. R. & Renshaw, P. D. (1981). Children without friends: Social knowledge and social skill training. In S. R. Asher & J. M Gottman (Eds.), *The development of children's friendships* (pp. 273–296). New York: Cambridge University Press.

Asher, S. R. & Wheeler, V. A. (1986). Children's loneliness: A comparison of rejected and neglected peer status. *Journal of Consulting and Clinical Psychology, 53,* 500–505.

Astin, A. W. (1977). *Four critical years.* San Francisco, CA: Jossey-Bass.

Astin, A. W. (1984). Using longitudinal data to study college impact. In S. A. Mednick, M. Harway, & K. M. Finello (Eds.), *Handbook of longitudinal research. Volume Two. Teenage and adult cohorts* (pp. 62–70). New York: Praeger.

Astin, A. W. (1991). *Assessment for excellence: The philosophy and practice of assessment and evaluation in higher education.* New York: Macmillan.

Astin, A. W. (1993). *What matters in college: Four critical years revisited.* San Francisco, CA: Jossey-Bass.

Astin, H. S. (1984). The meaning of work in women's lives: A sociopsychological model of career choice. *The Counseling Psychologist, 12,* 117–126.

Astin, H. S. & Myint, T. (1971). Career development of young women during the post high school years. *Journal of Counseling Psychology Monograph, 18,* 369–393.

Atanasoff, S. E. (1989). *How to survive as a teen: When no one understands* (Rev ed.). Scottsdale, PA: Herald Press.

Athanasiou, R. (1976, February). Frequency of masturbation in adult men and women. *Medical Aspects of Human Sexuality,* 121–124.

Atkinson, R. C. & Shiffrin, R. M. (1968). Human memory: A proposed system and its control processes. In K. W. Spence & J. T. Spence (Eds.), *The psychology of learning and motivation: Advances in research and theory.* Volume 2 (pp. 89–195). New York: Academic Press.

Attie, I. & Brooks-Gunn, J. (1992). Developmental issues in the study of eating problems and disorders. In J. H. Crowther, D. L Tennenbaum, S. E. Hofboll, & M. A. P. Stephens (Eds.), *The* *etiology of bulimia nervosa: The individual and familial context* (pp. 35–58). Washington, DC: Hemisphere.

Aubrey, R. R. (1977). Adolescents and death. In E. R. Prichard, J. Collard, B. A. Drevitt, A. H. Kutscher, I. Seeland, & N. Lefkowitz (Eds.), *Social work with the dying patient and family* (pp. 131–145). New York: Columbia University Press.

Babigian, H. M. (1985). Schizophrenia: Epidemiology. In H. I. Kaplan & B. J. Sadock (Eds.), *Comprehensive textbook of psychiatry/IV*. (4th ed.). (pp. 643–650). Baltimore: Williams & Wilkins.

Bachman, J. G. (1972). *Young men in high school and beyond: A summary of findings from the Youth in Transition project.* Ann Arbor, MI: Institute of Social Research.

Bachman, J. G., Green, S., & Wirtanen, I. (1971). *Youth in transition. Vol. III: Dropping out — Problem or symptom?* Ann Arbor, MI: Institute of Social Research.

Bachman, J. G. & O'Malley, P. M. (1984). The Youth in Transition project. In S. A. Mednick, M. Harway, & K. M. Finello (Eds.), *Handbook of longitudinal research. Volume Two: Teenage and adult cohorts* (pp. 121–140). New York: Praeger.

Bailey, S. L. & Hubbard, R. L. (1991). Developmental changes in peer factors and the influence on marijuana initiation among secondary school students. *Journal of Youth and Adolescence, 20,* 339–360.

Baker, J. (1982). *Coping with drug abuse: A lifeline for parents.* Rockford, IL: DARE.

Baldwin, B. (1978). A paradigm for the classification of emotional crises: Implications for crisis intervention. *American Journal of Orthopsychiatry, 48,* 538–551.

Baldwin, J. M. (1906). *Thought and things: A study of the development and meaning of thought.* New York: Macmillan.

Balikci, A. (1970). *The Netsilik Eskimo.* Prospect Heights, IL: Waveland Press.

Balk, D. E. (1981). *Sibling death during adolescence: Self concept and bereavement reactions.* Unpublished doctoral dissertation, University of Illinois, Champaign-Urbana, IL.

Balk, D. E. (1983). Adolescents' grief reactions and self-concept perceptions following sibling death: A case study of 33 teenagers. *Journal of Youth and Adolescence, 12,* 137–161.

Balk, D. E. (1983b). Effects of sibling death on teenagers. *Journal of School Health, 53,* 14–18.

Balk, D. E. (1983c). How teenagers cope with sibling death: Some implications for school counselors. *The School Counselor, 31,* 150–158.

Balk, D. E. (1983d). Learned helplessness: A model to understand and overcome a child's extreme reaction to failure. *Journal of School Health, 53,* 365–370.

Balk, D. E. (1989). *Evaluating implementation of human sexuality curricula in Kansas schools.* A paper presented at the Annual Convention of the American Psychological Association, New Orleans, LA.

Balk, D. E. (1990a). *The many faces of bereavement on the college campus.* Paper presented at the Annual Convention of the American Psychological Association, Boston, MA. (ERIC Document Reproduction Service No. ED 326 794).

Balk, D. E. (1990b). The self-concepts of bereaved adolescents: Sibling death and its aftermath. *Journal of Adolescent Research, 5,* 112–132.

Balk, D. E. (Ed.). (1991a). Death and adolescent bereavement. [Special issue]. *Journal of Adolescent Research, 6*(1).

Balk, D. E. (1991b). Death and adolescent bereavement: Current research and future directions. *Journal of Adolescent Research, 6,* 7–27.

Balk, D. E. (1991c). Sibling death, adolescent bereavement, and religion. *Death Studies, 15,* 1–20.

Balk, D. E. & Camp, B. (1988). *Implementing the regulation for human sexuality curriculum in Kansas schools: Interviews with key informants.* Topeka, KS: Kansas Action for Children.

Balk, D. E. & Hogan, N. S. (in press). Religion and bereaved adolescents. In D. W. Adams & E. Deveau (Eds.), *Loss, threat to life, and bereavement: The child's perspective.* Amityville, NY: Baywood.

Balk, D. E., Murray, J. P., Nelson, S. F., & Johnson, J. (1992). *Twenty years of family life at The Villages: A report to the Executive Director.* Unpublished manuscript, Kansas State University, Department of Human Development and Family Studies, Manhattan, KS.

Balkin, D. B. & Groeneman, S. (1985). The effect of incentive compensation on recruitment: The case of the military. *Personnel Administrator, 28,* 563–598.

Bandura, A. (1965). Influence of models' reinforcement contingencies on the acquisition of imitative responses. *Journal of Personality and Social Psychology, 1,* 589–595.

Bandura, A. (1969). *Principles of behavior modification.* New York: Holt, Rinehart & Winston.

Bandura, A. (1973). *Aggression: a social learning analysis.* Englewood Cliffs, NJ: Prentice-Hall.

Bandura, A. (1977). *Social learning theory.* Englewood Cliffs, NJ: Prentice-Hall.

Bandura, A. (1980). The stormy decade: Fact or fiction? In R. E. Muuss (Ed.), *Adolescent behavior and society: A book of readings* (3rd ed.) (pp. 22–31). New York: Random House. (Reprinted from *Psychology in the Schools,* 1964, *1,* 224–231)

Bandura, A. (1986). *Social foundations of thought and action: A social cognitive theory.* Englewood Cliffs, NJ: Prentice-Hall.

Bandura, A. (1987). The self system in reciprocal determinism. *American Psychologist, 33,* 344–358.

Bandura, A. & Walters, R. H. (1959). *Adolescent aggression: A study of the influence of child-training practices and family inter-relationships.* New York: The Ronald Press.

Bandura, A., & Walters, R. H. (1963). *Social learning and personality development.* New York: Holt, Rinehart & Winston.

Bane, M. J. (1976). Marital disruption and the lives of children. *Journal of Social Issues, 32,* 103–117.

Bank, L., Patterson, G. R., & Reid, R. B. (1987). Delinquency prevention through training parents in family management. *Behavior Analyst, 10,* 75–82.

Barker, P. (1976). *Basic child psychiatry.* Baltimore: University Park Press.

Barnes, H. (**1991, Summer**). Adolescents: Risking their futures. *Action for Children*, pp. 1–2.

Barnes, H. L. & Olson. D. H. (**1985**). Parent-adolescent communication and the Circumplex Model. *Child Development, 56,* 438–447.

Barnes, H. L., Wright, D. W., Ninas-Scheffel, S. J., Wyrick, D. N., & White, C. P. (**1990**). *Relationship and sexual attitudes: An assessment of student-parent communication, knowledge, and behaviors.* Manhattan: Kansas State University, Department of Human Development and Family Studies.

Barnett, J. K., Papini, D. R., & Gbur, E. (**1991**). Familial correlates of sexually active pregnant and nonpregnant adolescents. *Adolescence, 26,* 457–472.

Barnett, M. A. (**1982**). Empathy and prosocial behavior in children. In T. M. Field, A. Huston, H. C. Quay, L. Troll, & G. E. Finley (Eds.), *Review of human development.* New York: Wiley.

Barnett, M. A. (**1987**). Empathy and related responses in children. In N. Eisenberg & J. Strayer (Eds.), *Empathy and its development.* New York: Cambridge University Press.

Barnett, M. A. & McCoy, S. J. (**1989**). The relation of distressful childhood experiences and empathy in college undergraduates. *Journal of Genetic Psychology, 150,* 417–426.

Barnett, M. A., McMinimy, V., Flouer, G., & Masbad, I. (**1987**). Adolescents' evaluations of peers' motives for helping. *Journal of Youth and Adolescence, 16,* 579–586.

Barnett, M. A., Thompson, M. A., & Pfeiffer, J. R. (**1985**). Perceived competence to help and the arousal of empathy. *Journal of Social Psychology, 125,* 679–680.

Barrera, M., Jr. (**1981**). Social support in the adjustment of pregnant adolescents: Assessment issues. In B. H. Gottlieb (Ed.), *Social networks and social support* (pp. 69–96). Beverly Hills, CA: Sage.

Barrett, C. J. (**1978**). Effectiveness of widows' groups in facilitating change. *Journal of Consulting and Clinical Psychology, 31,* 348.

Bateson, G., Jackson, D. D., Haley, J., & Weakland, J. (**1956**). Toward a theory of schizophrenia. *Behavioral Sciences, 1,* 256–264.

Baumrind, D. (**1967**). Child care practices anteceding three patterns of preschool behavior. *Genetic Psychology Monographs, 75,* 43–88.

Baumrind, D. (**1968**). Authoritarian vs. authoritative parental control. *Adolescence, 3,* 255–272.

Baumrind, D. (**1968, August**). *Naturalistic observation in the study of parent-child interaction.* Paper presented at the Annual Convention of the American Psychological Association, San Francisco.

Baumrind, D. (**1972**). An exploratory study of socialization effects on Black children: Some Black-White comparisons. *Child Development, 43,* 261–267.

Baumrind, D. (**1977, March**). *Socialization determinants of personal agency.* Paper presented at the biennial meeting of the Society for Research in Child Development, New Orleans.

Baumrind, D. (**1978**). Parental disciplinary patterns and social competence in children. *Youth and Society, 9,* 239–276.

Baumrind, D. (**1986**). Sex differences in moral reasoning: Response to Walker's (1984) conclusion that there are none. *Child Development, 57,* 511–521.

Baumrind, D. (**1991**). The influence of parenting style on adolescent competence and substance use. *Journal of Early Adolescence, 11,* 56–95.

Bayley, N. (**1955**). On the growth of intelligence. *American Psychologist, 10,* 805–818.

Bayley, N. (**1968**). Behavioral correlates of mental growth: Birth to thirty-six years. *American Psychologist, 23,* 1–17.

Beardslee, W. R., Keller, M. B., & Klerman, G. D. (**1985**). Children of parents with affective disorders. *International Journal of Family Psychiatry, 6,* 283–299.

Beavers, W. R. (**1977**). *Psychotherapy and growth: A family systems perspective.* New York: Brunner/Mazel.

Beavers, W. R. (**1982**). Healthy, midrange, and severely dysfunctional families. In F. Walsh (Ed.), *Normal family processes* (pp. 45–66). New York: The Guilford Press.

Beck, A. T. (**1967**). *Depression: Clinical, experimental, and theoretical aspects.* New York: Harper and Row.

Beck, A. T. (**1978**). *Beck Depression Inventory.* Revised. Philadelphia, PA: Center for Cognitive Therapy.

Beiser, H. R. (**1991**). Ages eleven to fourteen. In S. I. Greenspan & G. H. Pollock (Eds.), *The course of life. Vol. IV. Adolescence* (pp. 99–118). Madison, WI: International Universities Press.

Bell, H., Avery, A., Jenkins, D., Feld, J., & Schoenrock, C. (**1985**). Family relationships and social competence during late adolescence. *Journal of Youth and Adolescence, 14,* 109–119.

Bell, R. & Wildflower, L. (**1983**). *Talking with your teenager: A book for parents.* New York: Random House.

Bell, R. M. (**1985**). *Holy anorexia.* Chicago: University of Chicago Press.

Bem, S. L. (**1974**). The measurement of psychological androgyny. *Journal of Consulting and Clinical Psychology, 42,* 155–162.

Bem, S. L. (**1978**). Beyond androgyny: Some presumptuous prescriptions for a liberated sexual identity. In J. A. Sherman and F. L. Denmark (Eds.), *The psychology of women: Future directions in research.* New York: Psychological Dimensions.

Bem, S. L. (**1981**). Gender scheme theory: A cognitive account of sex-typing. *Psychological Review, 88,* 354–364.

Benenson, J. F. (**1990**). Gender differences in social networks. *Journal of Early Adolescence, 10,* 472–495.

Benenson, J. F. & Dweck, C. S. (**1986**). The development of trait explanations and self-evaluations in the academic and social domains. *Child Development, 57,* 1179–1187.

Bennion, L. D. & Adams, G. R. (**1986**). A revision of the Extended Version of the Objective Measure of Ego Identity Status: An identity instrument for use with late adolescents. *Journal of Adolescent Research, 1,* 183–198.

Bensinger, J. S. & Natenshon, A. H. (**1991**). Difficulties in recognizing adolescent health issues. In W. R. Hendee (Ed.), *The* *health of adolescents: Understanding and facilitating biological, behavioral, and social development* (pp. 381–410). San Francisco, CA: Jossey-Bass.

Berger, D. K., Kyman, W., Perez, G., Menendez, M., Bistritz, J. F., & Goon, J. M. (1991). Hispanic adolescent pregnancy testers: A comparative analysis of negative testers, childbearers, and aborters. *Adolescence, 26,* 951–962.

Berger, R. L. (1989). Female delinquency in the emancipation era: A review of the literature. *Sex Roles, 21,* 375–399.

Bergin, A. E. & Strupp, H. H. (1972). *Changing frontiers in the science of psychotherapy.* Chicago, IL: Aldine Atherton.

Berndt, T. J. (1989). Contributions of peer relationships to children's development. In T. J. Berndt & G. W. Ladd (Eds.), *Peer relationships in child development* (pp. 407–416). New York: Wiley.

Berry, J. W. (1980). Introduction to *Methodology.* In H. C. Triandis & J. W. Berry (Eds.), *Handbook of cross-cultural psychology. Volume 2. Methodology* (pp. 1–28). Boston: Allyn & Bacon.

Bethge, E. (1970). *Dietrich Bonhoeffer: Man of vision, man of courage.* (Translated by E. Mosbacher and others). New York: Harper & Row.

Betsey, C. L., Hollester, R. G., & Papageorgiou, M. R. (Eds.). (1985). *Youth employment and training programs: The YEDPA years.* Washington, DC: National Academy Press.

Beunen, G. P., Malina, R. M., Van't Hof, M. A., Simons, J., Ostyn, M., Renson, R., & Van Gernen, D. (1988). *Adolescent growth and motor performance: A longitudinal study of Belgian boys.* Champaign, IL: Human Kinetics Books.

Bichard, S. L., Aldon, L., Walker, L. J., & McMahon, R. J. (1988). Friendship understanding in socially accepted, rejected, and neglected children. *Merrill-Palmer Quarterly, 34,* 33–46.

Bick, I. J. (1990). Outatime: Recreationism and the adolescent experience in *Back to the Future. Psychoanalytic Review, 77,* 587–608.

Bick, I. J. (1992). Stella Dallas: Maternal melodrama and feminine sacrifice. *Psychoanalytic Review, 79,* 121–145.

Bigelow, B. J. (1977). Children's friendship expectations: A cognitive-developmental study. *Child Development, 48,* 246–253.

Biglan, A., Metzler, C. W., Wirt, R., Ary, D. V., & Associates. (1990). Social and behavioral factors associated with high-risk sexual behavior among adolescents. *Journal of Behavioral Medicine, 13,* 245–261.

Bing, L. (1991). *Do or die.* New York: HarperCollins.

Birren, J. E., Kinney, D. K., Schaie, K. W., & Woodruff, D. S. (1981). *Developmental psychology: A life-span approach.* Boston, MA: Houghton Miflin.

Bissell, C. T. (1989). Herbert Marshall McLuhan. In G. Sanders & F. Macdonald (Eds.), *Marshall McLuhan: The man and his message* (pp. 5–11). Golden, CO: Fulcrum.

Blackham, G. J (1967). *The deviant child in the classroom.* Belmont, CA: Wadsworth.

Blackham, G. J (1977). *Counseling: Theory, process, and practice.* Belmont, CA: Wadsworth.

Blackham, G. J & Silberman, A. (1975). *Modification of child and adolescent behavior.* (2nd ed.). Belmont, CA: Wadsworth.

Bleiberg, E. (1988). Adolescence, sense of self, and narcissistic vulnerability. *Bulletin of the Menninger Clinic, 52,* 211–228.

Blieszner, R. & Adams, R. G. (1992). *Adult friendship.* Newbury Park, CA: Sage.

Bloch, H. & Neiderhoffer, A. (1958). *The gang: A study in adolescent behavior.* New York: Philosophical Press.

Block, J., Block, J. H., & Keyes, S. (1988). Longitudinally foretelling drug usage in adolescence: Early childhood personality and environmental precursors. *Child Development, 59,* 336–355.

Bloom, B. L. (1977). *Community mental health: A general introduction.* Monterey, CA: Brooks/Cole.

Bloom, B. S., Madaus, G. F., & Hastings, J. T. (1981). *Evaluation to improve learning.* New York: McGraw-Hill.

Bloom-Feshbach, J., Bloom-Feshbach, S., & Associates. (1987). *The psychology of separation and loss: Perspectives on development, life transitions, and clinical practice.* San Francisco: Jossey-Bass.

Blos, P. (1941). *The adolescent personality: A study of individual behavior.* New York: D. Appleton-Century.

Blos, P. (1979a). Character formation in adolescence. In *The adolescent passage: Developmental issues* (pp. 171–191). New York: International Universities Press. (Reprinted from *The Psychoanalytic Study of the Child,* 1968, *22,* 162–186).

Blos, P. (1979b). The child analyst looks at the young adolescent. In *The adolescent passage: Developmental issues* (pp. 192–213). New York: International Universities Press. (Reprinted from *Daedalus,* 1971, *100,* 961–978)

Blos, P. (1979c). The genealogy of the ego ideal. In *The adolescent passage: Developmental issues* (pp. 319–369). New York: International Universities Press. (Reprinted from *The Psychoanalytic Study of the Child,* 1974, *29,* 43–88)

Blos, P. (1979d). The generation gap: Fact and fiction. In *The adolescent passage: Developmental issues* (pp. 11–22). New York: International Universities Press. (Reprinted from S. C. Feinstein, P. Giovacchini, & A. A. Miller (Eds.) (1971). *Adolescent psychiatry* (Volume 1, pp. 5–13). New York: Basic Books)

Blos, P. (1979e). The initial stage of male adolescence. In *The adolescent passage: Developmental issues* (pp. 117–140). New York: International Universities Press. (Reprinted from *The Psychoanalytic Study of the Child,* 1965, *20,* 145–164)

Blos, P. (1979f). Modifications in the classical psychoanalytic model of adolescence. In *The adolescent passage: Developmental issues* (pp. 473–497). New York: International Universities Press.

Blos, P. (1979g). Normative stages of adolescence. In *The adolescent passage: Developmental issues* (pp. 101–103). New York: International Universities Press.

Blos, P. (1979h). Preoedipal factors in the etiology of female delinquency. In *The adolescent passage: Developmental issues* (pp. 221–245). New York: International Universities Press. (Reprinted from *The Psychoanalytic Study of the Child*, 1957, *12*, 229–249)

Blos, P. (**1979i**). The second individuation process of adolescence. In *The adolescent passage: Developmental issues* (pp. 141–170). New York: International Universities Press. (Reprinted from *The Psychoanalytic Study of the Child*, 1967, *22*, 162–186)

Blos, P. (**1979j**). When and how does adolescence end? Structural criteria for adolescent closure. In *The adolescent passage: Developmental issues* (pp. 404–420). New York: International Universities Press. (Reprinted from S. C. Feinstein & P. Giovacchini (Eds.). (1976). *Adolescent psychiatry* (Volume 5, pp. 5–17). New York: Jason Aronson)

Boas, F. (**1950**). Foreword to *Coming of age in Samoa*. New York: Morrow. (Original work published 1928)

Boldero, J. & Moore, S. (**1990**). An evaluation of deJong-G:ervald's loneliness model with Australian adolescents. *Journal of Youth and Adolescence*, *19*, 133–147.

Bollen, I. D. & Cotton, A. J. (**1991**). *Ready Reserve concept survey of the Australian Defence Force*. Canberra, ACT, Australia: First Psychological Research Unit.

Bonhoeffer, D. (**1960**). *Prisoner for God: Letters and papers from prison* (R. H. Fuller, Trans.). New York: Macmillan.) Original work published 1953)

Boskind-Lodahl, M. (**1976**). Cinderella's stepsisters: A feminist perspective on anorexia and bulimia. *Signs, the Journal of Women in Culture and Society*, *2*, 324–356.

Boskind-White, M. (**1985**). Bulimarexia: A sociocultural perspective. In S. W. Emmett (Ed.), *Theory and treatment of anorexia and bulimia* (pp. 113–126). New York: Brunner/Mazel.

Boskind-White, M. & White, W. C. (**1986**). Bulimarexia: A historical-sociocultural perspective. In K. D. Brownell & J. P. Foreyt (Eds.), *Handbook of eating disorders* (pp. 353–366). New York: Basic Books.

Boskind-White, M. & White, W. C. (**1987**). *Bulimarexia: The binge/purge cycle* (2nd ed.). New York: Norton.

Bowen, G. L. (**1986**). Intergenerational occupational inheritance in the military: A reexamination. *Adolescence*, *21*, 623–629.

Bowers, L. B. (**1990**). Traumas precipitating female delinquency: Implications for assessment, practice, and policy. *Child and Adolescent Social Work Journal*, *7*, 389–402.

Bowman, P. H. (**1959**). Effects of a revised school program on potential delinquents. *The Annals of the American Academy of Political and Social Science*, *322*, 53–62.

Boyer, E. L. (**1983**). *High school: A report on secondary education*. New York: Harper & Row.

Boyer, E. L. (**1987**). *College: The undergraduate experience in America*. New York: Harper & Row.

Bradley, C. (**1979**). Life events and the control of diabetes mellitus. *Journal of Psychosomatic Research*, *23*, 159–162.

Brainerd, C. J. (**1978**). *Piaget's theory of intelligence*. Englewood Cliffs, NJ: Prentice-Hall.

Bramwell, S. T., Wagner, N. N., Masuda, M., & Holmes, T. H. (**1975**). Psychosocial factors in athletic injuries. *Journal of Human Stress*, *1*, 6–20.

Brand, A. H., Johnson, J. H., & Johnson, S. B, (**1986**). *The relationship between life stress and diabetic control in insulin-dependent diabetic children and adolescents*. Unpublished manuscript, University of Florida.

Bransford, J. D. & Johnson, M. V. (**1972**). Contextual prerequisites for understanding: Some investigations of comprehension and recall. *Journal of Verbal Learning and Verbal Behavior*, *11*, 717–721.

Bransford, J. D. & McCarrell, N. S. (**1975**). A sketch of a cognitive approach to comprehension: Some thoughts about understanding what it means to comprehend. In P. N. Johnson-Laird & P. C. Wason (Eds.), *Thinking: Readings in cognitive science* (pp. 377–399). Cambridge, England: Cambridge University Press.

Braxton, J., Brier, E., Herzog, L., & Pascarella, E. T. (**1988**). *Occupational attainment in the professions: The effects of college origins and college experiences on becoming a lawyer*. Paper presented at the meeting of Association for the Study of Higher Education, St. Louis.

Bronowski, J. (**1973**). *The ascent of man*. Boston, MA: Little, Brown.

Brooks-Gunn, J. (**1987**). Pubertal pressures: Their relevance for developmental research. In V. B. Van Hasselt & M. Hersen (Eds.), *Handbook of adolescent psychology* (pp. 111–130). New York: Pergamon Press.

Broude, G. J. (**1981**). The cultural management of sexuality. In R. H. Munroe, R. L. Munroe, & B. B. Whiting (Eds.), *Handbook of cross-cultural human development* (pp. 633–673). New York: Guilford.

Brown, B. B., Lohr, M. J., & McClenahan, E. L. (**1986**). Early adolescents' perceptions of peer pressure. *Journal of Early Adolescence*, *6*, 139–154.

Brown, B. B., Mounts, N., Lamborn, S. D., & Steinberg, L. (**1993**). Parenting practices and peer group affiliation in adolescence. *Child Development*, *64*, 467–482.

Brown, J. D., Childers, K. W., Bauman, K. E., & Koch, G. G. (**1990**). The influence of new media and family structure on young adolescents' television and radio use. *Communication Research*, *17*, 65–82.

Brownfield, D. & Thompson, K. (**1991**). Attachment to peers and delinquent behavior. *Canadian Journal of Criminology*, *33*, 45–60.

Bruch, H. (**1981**). Developmental considerations of anorexia nervosa and obesity. *Canadian Journal of Psychiatry*, *26*, 212–217.

Brusko, M. (**1987**). *Living with your teenager*. New York: Ivy Books.

Bryant, J. & Zillmann, D. (**1984**). Using television to alleviate boredom and stress: Selective exposure as a function of individual excitational states. *Journal of Broadcasting*, *28*, 1–20.

Bryson, M. F. & Reichlin, S. (1966). Neuroendocrine regulation of sexual function and growth. *Pediatric Clinics of North America, 13*, 423–436.

Buhrmester, D., Furman, W., Wittenberg, M. T., & Reis, H. T. (1988). Five domains of interpersonal competence in peer relations. *Journal of Personality and Social Psychology, 55*, 991–1008.

Bukowski, W. M., Newcomb, A. F., & Hoza, B. (1987). Friendship conceptions among early adolescents: A longitudinal study of stability and change. *Journal of Early Adolescence, 7*, 143–152.

Bulkeley, R. & Cramer, D. (1990). Social skills training with young adolescents. *Journal of Youth and Adolescence, 19*, 451–463.

Bureau of the Census. (1990). *Statistical abstract of the United States: 1990* (110th ed.). Washington, DC: U.S. Government Printing Office.

Bureau of the Census. (1991a). *Family disruption and economic hardship: The short-run picture for children.* Washington, DC: U.S. Government Printing Office.

Bureau of the Census (1991b). *Marital status and living arrangements: March 1990.* Washington, DC: U.S. Government Printing Office.

Bureau of Justice Statistics. (1990). *Criminal victimization in the United States, 1988. A national crime survey report.* Washington, DC: U.S. Department of Justice.

Burgess, A. W. & Holmstrom, L. L. (1986). Adaptive strategies and recovery from rape. In R. H. Moos (Ed.), *Coping with life crises: An integrated approach* (pp. 353–365). New York: Plenum. (Originally published in *American Journal of Psychiatry*, 1979, *136*, 1278–1282)

Burke, P. J., Stets, J. E., & Pirog-Good, M. A. (1989). Gender identity, self-esteem and physical and sexual abuse in dating relationships. In M. A. Pirog-Good & J. E. Stets (Eds.), *Violence in dating relationships: Emerging social issues* (pp. 72–93). New York: Praeger.

Burnam, M. A., Stein, J., Golding, J. M., Siegel, J., Sorenson, S., Forsythe, A. B., & Telles, C. A. (1988). Sexual assault and mental disorders in a community population. *Journal of Consulting and Clinical Psychology, 56*, 843–850.

Burns, D. D. (1980). *Feeling good: The new mood therapy.* New York: Morrow.

Burton, R. (1989). Family preservation at the expense of the child. *Justice for Children, 2*, 3–5.

Butterfield, H. (1957). *The origins of modern science: 1300–1800* (rev. ed.). New York: The Free Press.

Byrne, D. & Fisher, W. A. (Eds.). (1983). *Adolescents, sex, and contraception.* Hillsdale, NJ: Erlbaum.

The Cable Guide. (1993, March). Now showing. *13*, A2–A16.

Cain, A., Fast, I., & Erickson, M. (1964). Children's disturbed reactions to the death of a sibling. *American Journal of Orthopsychiatry, 34*, 741–752.

Callahan, C. M., Cornell, D. G., & Loyd, B. (1990). Perceived competence and parent-adolescent communication in high ability adolescent females. *Journal for the Education of the Gifted, 13*, 256–269.

Camp, B. (1990). *Implementing human sexuality education in Kansas schools: An examination of the process of educational change.* Unpublished master's thesis, Kansas State University, Manhattan, KS.

Campbell, E., Adams, G. A., & Dobson, W. R. (1984). Familial correlates of identity formation in late adolescence: A study of the predictive utility of connectedness and individuality in family relations. *Journal of Youth and Adolescence, 13*, 509–525.

Campbell, J. (1949). *The hero with a thousand faces.* Princeton, NJ: Princeton University Press.

Camus, A. (1948). *The plague.* (S. Gilbert, Trans.). New York: Knopf.

Camus, A. (1954). *The rebel.* (A. Bower, Trans.). New York: Knopf.

Camus, A. (1955). *The myth of Sisyphus and other essays.* (J. O'Brien, Trans.). New York: Vintage.

Cancro, R. (1985). History and overview of schizophrenia. In H. I. Kaplan & B. J. Sadock (Eds.), *Comprehensive textbook of psychiatry/IV.* (4th ed.) (pp. 631–643). Baltimore: Williams & Wilkins.

Caplan, G. (1964). *Principles of preventive psychiatry.* New York: Basic Books.

Carlson, G. & Strober, M. (1983). Affective disorders in adolescence. In D. P. Cantwell & G. Carlson (Eds.), *Affective disorders in childhood and adolescence: An update* (pp. 85–96). New York: Spectrum.

Carson, R. C., Butcher, J. N., & Coleman, J. C. (1988). *Abnormal psychology and modern life* (8th ed.). Glenview, IL: Scott, Foresman.

Case, R. (1985). *Intellectual development: Birth to adulthood.* Orlando, FL: Academic Press.

Caspi, A. & Elder, G. H. (1986). Life satisfaction in old age: Linking social psychology and history. *Psychology and Aging, 1*, 18–26.

Catania, A. C. (1993). Approaching Skinner. *Contemporary Psychology, 38*, 779–780.

Caton, C. L. (1986). The homeless experience in adolescent years. *New Directions for Mental Health Services*, No. 30, pp. 63–70. San Francisco: Jossey-Bass.

Cavaiola, A. A. & Schiff, M. (1988). Behavioral sequelae of physical and/or sexual abuse in adolescents. *Child Abuse and Neglect, 12*, 181–188.

Cebula, R. & Lopes, J. (1982). Determinants of student choice of undergraduate major field. *American Educational Research Journal, 19*, 303–312.

Centers for Disease Control. (1985). *Sexually transmitted disease statistics: 1984.* Atlanta, GA.

Centers for Disease Control. (1990a). Homicide among young Black males—United States, 1978–1987. *Morbidity and Mortality Weekly Report, 39*, 225–253.

Centers for Disease Control. (1990b). *Sexually transmitted disease surveillance: 1989.* Atlanta, GA.

Centerwall, B. S. (1992). Television and violence: The scale of the problem and where to go from here. *Journal of the American Medical Association, 267*(22), 3059–3063.

Chanowitz, B. & Langer, E. J. (1981). Premature cognitive commitment. *Journal of Personality and Social Psychology, 41*, 1051–1063.

Charner, I. & Fraser, B. S. (no date). *Youth and work: What we know, what we don't know, what we need to know.* New York: The William T. Grant Foundation.

Chase, H. P. & Jackson, G. G. (1981). Stress and sugar control in children with insulin-dependent diabetes mellitus. *Journal of Pediatrics, 98*, 1011–1013.

Chen, C. L. & Yang, D. C. (1986). The self-image of Chinese-American adolescents: A cross-cultural comparison. *International Journal of Social Psychiatry, 32*, 19–26.

Chen, S. A. (1992). *In pursuit of justice.* Washington, DC: Organization of Chinese Americans.

Chen, S. A. (1994). Vulnerable populations: Asian-Americans. In L. Eron & J. Gentry (Eds.), *Violence and youth: Psychology's response. Volume II. Papers of the American Psychological Association on Violence and Youth.* Washington, DC: APA.

Chess, S. & Thomas, A. (1984). *Origins and evolution of behavior disorders: From infancy to early adult life.* New York: Brunner/Mazel.

Chi, M. T. H. (1978). Knowledge structures and memory development. In R. S. Siegler (Ed.), *Children's thinking: What develops?* (pp. 73–96). Hillsdale, NJ: Erlbaum.

Chickering, A. (1974). The impact of various college environments on personality development. *Journal of the American College Health Association, 23*, 82–93.

Chilman, C. (1982). *Adolescent sexuality in a changing American society: Social and psychological perspectives* (2nd ed.). New York: Wiley.

Chockalingham, K. (1983). Recidivism among adult offenders. *Indian Journal of Social Work, 44*, 81–86.

Chomsky, N. (1968). *Language and mind.* San Diego, CA: Harcourt Brace Jovanovich.

Choquet, M. & Menke, H. (1990). Suicidal thoughts during early adolescence: Prevalence, associated troubles, and help-seeking behavior. *Acta Psychiatrica Scandinavica, 81*, 170–177.

Chumlea, W. C. (1982). Physical growth in adolescence. In B J. Wolman (Ed.), *Handbook of developmental psychology* (pp. 471–485). Englewood Cliffs, NJ: Prentice-Hall.

Church, R. L. & Sedlack, M. W. (1976). *Education in the United States.* New York: Free Press.

Clark, K. (1970). *Civilization: A personal view.* New York: Harper & Row.

Clifford, M. M. & Walster, E. (1973). The effects of physical attractiveness on teacher expectations. *Sociology of Education, 46*, 248–258.

Cline, V. B., Croft, R. G., & Currier, S. (1973). Desensitization of children to television violence. *Journal of Personality and Social Psychology, 27*, 1120–1134.

Cloward, R. A. & Ohlin, L. E. (1960). *Delinquency and opportunity: A theory of delinquent gangs.* Glencoe, IL: Free Press.

Coddington, R. D. (1972a). The significance of life events as etiological factors in the diseases of children: A study of a normal population. *Journal of Psychosomatic Research, 16*, 205–213.

Coddington, R. D. (1972b). The significance of life events as etiological factors in the diseases of children: A survey of professional workers. *Journal of Psychosomatic Research, 16*, 7–18.

Coddington, R. D. & Troxell, J. R. (1980). The effect of emotional factors on football injury rates: A pilot study. *Journal of Human Stress, 6*, 3–5.

Cohen, A. K. (1966). The delinquency subculture. In R. Giallombardo (Ed.), *Juvenile delinquency: A Book of readings.* New York: Wiley.

Cohen, F. (1979). Personality, stress, and the development of physical illness. In G. C. Stone, F. Cohen, N. E. Adler, & Associates (Eds.), *Health psychology: A handbook* (pp. 77–111). San Francisco: Jossey-Bass.

Cohen, P., Brook, J. S., Cohen, J., Velez, C. N., & Garcia, M. (1990). Common and uncommon pathways to adolescent psychopathology and problem behavior. In L. N. Robins & M. Rutter (Eds.), *Straight and devious pathways from childhood to adulthood* (pp. 242–258). Cambridge, England: Cambridge University Press. Coie, J. D. & Dodge, K. A. (1983). Continuities and changes in children's social status: A five-year longitudinal study. *Merrill-Palmer Quarterly, 29*, 261–281.

Coie, J. D., Dodge, K. A., & Kupersmidt, J. B. (1990). Peer group behavior and social status. In S. R. Asher & J. D. Coie (Eds.), *Peer rejection in childhood* (pp. 17–59). Cambridge: Cambridge University Press.

Coie, J. D., Lochman, J. E., Terry, R., & Hyman, C. (1992). Predicting early adolescent disorder from childhood aggression and peer rejection. *Journal of Consulting and Clinical Psychology, 60*, 783–792.

Colby, A. & Kohlberg, L. (1984). Invariant sequence and internal consistency in moral judgment stages. In W. M. Kurtines & J. L. Gewirtz (Eds.), *Morality, moral behavior, and moral development* (pp. 41–51). New York: Wiley.

Colby, A. & Kohlberg, L. (1987). *The measurement of moral judgment. Volume 1. Theoretical foundations and research validation.* Cambridge: Cambridge University Press.

Colby, A., Kohlberg, L., Gibbs, J., & Lieberman, M. (1983). A longitudinal study of moral judgment. *Monographs of the Society for Research in Child Development, 48*, 1–96.

Colby, A., Kohlberg, L., Speicer, B., Hewer, A., Candee, D., Gibbs, J., & Power, C. (1987). *The measurement of moral* *judgment. Volume 2. Standard issue scoring manual.* Cambridge: Cambridge University Press.

Coleman, J. C. (**1978**). Current contradictions in adolescent theory. *Journal of Youth and Adolescence, 7*, 1–11.

Coleman, J. S. (**1961**). *The adolescent society: The social life of the teenager and its impact on education.* New York: The Free Press.

Coleman, J. S. & Broen, W. E. (**1972**). *Abnormal psychology and modern life.* (4th ed.). Glenview, IL: Scott, Foresman.

Coles, R. & Stokes, G. (**1985**). *Sex and the American teenager.* New York: Harper Colophon.

Collins, W. A. (**1979**). Children's comprehension of television content. In E. Wartella (Ed.), *Children communicating: Media and development of thought, speech, and understanding* (pp. 21–52). Beverly Hills, CA: Sage.

Collins, W. A. (**1982**). Cognitive processing in television viewing. In D. Pearl, L. Bouthilet, & J. Lazar (Eds.), *Television and behavior: Ten years of scientific progress and implications for the eighties. Volume 2: Technical reviews* (pp. 9–23). Washington, DC: U.S. Government Printing Office.

Collins, W. A. (**1984**). *Development during middle childhood.* Washington, DC: National Academy Press.

Collins, W. A. (**1990**). Parent-child relationships in the transition to adolescence: Continuity and change in interaction, affects, and cognition. In R. Montemayor, G. Adams, & T. Gullotta (Eds.), *From childhood to adolescence: A transitional period?* (pp. 85–106). Beverly Hills, CA: Sage.

Colten, M. E., Gore, S., & Aseltine, R. H. (**1991**). The patterning of distress and disorder in a community sample of high school aged youth. In M. E. Colten & S. Gore (Eds.), *Adolescent stress: Causes and consequences* (pp. 157–180). New York: A. deGruyter.

Comstock, G. (**1986**). Television and film violence. In S. J. Apter & A. P. Goldstein (Eds.), *Youth and violence: Programs and prospects* (pp. 178–218). New York: Pergamon Press.

Conger, J. J. (**1991**). *Adolescence and youth: Psychological development in a changing world.* New York: HarperCollins.

Connell, W. F., Stroobant, R. E., Sinclair, K. E., Connell, R. W., & Rogers, K. W. (**1975**). *12 to 20: Studies of city youth.* Sydney: Hicks, Smith, & Sons.

Conner, T. D., Mednick, S. A., and Parnas, J. (**1990**). Two pathways to schizophrenia in children at risk. In L. N. Robins & M. Rutter (Eds.), *Straight and devious pathways from childhood to adulthood* (pp. 328–350). Cambridge, England: Cambridge University Press.

Conroy, P. (**1986**). *The prince of tides.* Boston: Houghton Miflin.

Cook, A. S. & Oltjenbruns, K. A. (**1989**). *Dying and grieving: Lifespan and family perspectives.* New York: Holt, Rinehart & Winston.

Cook, T. D. (**1985**). Postpositivist critical multiplism. In L. Shotland & M. M. Mark (Eds.), *Social science and social policy* (pp. 21–62). Beverly Hills, CA: Sage.

Coombs, R. H., Paulson, M. J., & Richardson, M. A. (**1991**). Peer vs parental influence in substance use among Hispanic and Anglo children and adolescents. *Journal of Youth and Adolescence, 20*, 73–88.

Cooper, C. R., & Cooper, R. G. (**1992**). Links between adolescents' relationships with their parents and peers: Models, evidence, and mechanisms. In R. D. Parke & G. W. Ladd (Eds.), *Family-peer relationships: Modes of linkage* (pp. 135–158). Hillsdale, NJ: Erlbaum.

Cooper, C. R., Grotevant, H. D., & Condon, S. M. (**1983**). Individuality and connectedness in the family as a context for adolescent identity formation and role-taking skill. In H. D. Grotevant & C. R. Cooper (Eds.), *Adolescent development in the family: New directions for child development* (pp. 43–60). San Francisco: Jossey-Bass.

Cornelius, S. & Caspi, A. (**1987**). Everyday problem-solving in adulthood and old age. *Psychology and Aging, 2*, 144–153.

Corteen, R. S. & Williams, T. M. (**1986**). Television and reading skills. In T. M. Williams (Ed.), *The impact of television: A natural experiment in three communities* (pp. 39–85). Orlando, FL: Academic Press.

Corter, C., Trehub, S., Boukydis, C., Ford, L., Celhoffer, L., & Minde, K. (**1978**). Nurses' judgments of the attractiveness of premature infants. *Infant Behavior and Development, 1*, 373–380.

Cowan, P. A. (**1991**). Individual and family life transitions: A proposal for a new definition. In P. A. Cowan & M. Hetherington (Eds.), *Family transitions* (pp. 3–30.). Hillsdale, NJ: Erlbaum.

Cowan, P. A. & Hetherington, M. (Eds.). (**1991**). *Family transitions.* Hillsdale, NJ: Erlbaum.

Cowen, E. L., Pederson, A., Babijian, H., Izzo, L. D., & Trost, M. A. (**1973**). Long-term follow-up of early detected vulnerable children. *Journal of Consulting and Clinical Psychology, 41*, 438–446.

Craig, M. & Glueck, S. J. (**1963**). Ten years experience with the Glueck social prediction scale. *Crime and Delinquency, 24*, 231–232.

Crisp, A. H., Palmer, R. L., & Kalucy, R. S. (**1976**). How common is anorexia nervosa? A prevalence study. *British Journal of Psychology, 218*, 549–554.

Crockett, L. J., Petersen, A. C., Graber, J. A., Schulenberg, J. E., & Ebata, A. (**1989**). School transitions and adjustment during early adolescence. *Journal of Early Adolescence, 9*, 181–210.

Crook, M. (**1988**). *Every parent's guide to understanding teenagers and suicide: Recognize the hidden signs.* Fortuna, CA: ISC.

Crook, T. & Eliot, J. (**1980**). Parental death during childhood and adult depression: A critical review of the literature. *Psychological Bulletin, 87*, 252–259.

Curran, D. K. (**1987**). *Adolescent suicidal behavior.* Washington, DC: Hemisphere.

Dacey, J. S. *Adult development.* Glenview, IL: Scott, Foresman.

Daniel, W. A. (1991). Meeting the health service needs of adolescents. In W. R. Hendee (Ed.), *The health of adolescents: Understanding and facilitating biological, behavioral, and social development* (pp. 499–511). San Francisco, CA: Jossey-Bass.

Daniels, D., Dunn, J., Furstenberg, F. F., & Plomin, R. (1985). Environmental differences within the family and adjustment differences within pairs of adolescent siblings. *Child Development, 56,* 764–774.

Danish, S. J. & D'Augelli, A. R. (1980). Promoting competence and enhancing development through life development intervention. In L. A. Bond & C. J. Rosen (Eds.), *Primary prevention of psychopathology* (Vol. 5., pp. 105–129). Hanover, NH: University Press of New England.

Danish, S. J., Smyer, M. A., & Nowak, C. A. (1980). Developmental interventions: Enhancing life-event processes. In P. B. Baltes & O. G. Brim (Eds.), *Life-span development and behavior* (Volume 3, pp. 340–346). New York: Academic Press.

Dark, L. (1994). Vulnerable populations: Gay and lesbian youth. In L. Eron & J. Gentry (Eds.), *Violence and youth: Psychology's response. Volume II. Papers of the American Psychological Association on Violence and Youth.* Washington, DC: APA.

Datan, N. & Ginsberg, L. (Eds.). (1975). *Life-span developmental psychology: Normative life transitions.* New York: Academic Press.

Delisle, J. R. (1990). The gifted adolescent at risk: Strategies and resources for suicide prevention among gifted youth. *Journal for the Education of the Gifted, 13,* 212–228.

Demo, D., Small, S., & Savin-Williams, R. (1987). Family relations in the self-esteem of adolescents and their parents. *Journal of Marriage and the Family, 49,* 705–715.

Denney, N. W. (1982). Aging and cognitive changes. In B. Wolman (Ed.), *Handbook of developmental psychology* (pp. 807–827). Englewood Cliffs, NJ: Prentice-Hall.

DeSpelder, L. A. & Strickland, A. L. (1992). *The last dance: Encountering death and dying.* (3rd ed.). Palo Alto, CA: Mayfield.

deVries, H. A. (1970). Physiological effects of an exercise training regimen upon men aged 52 to 88. *Journal of Gerontology, 25,* 325–336.

deVries, H. A. (1975). Physiology of exercise and aging. In D. S. Woodruff & J. E. Birren (Eds.), *Aging: Scientific perspectives and social issues* (pp. 257–276). New York: Van Nostrand.

Dewey, J. (1909). *Moral principles in education.* New York: Philosophical Library.

DiClemente, R. J. (1990a). Adolescents and AIDS: Current research, prevention strategies, and policy implications. In L. Temoshok & A. Baum (Eds.), *Psychosocial perspectives on AIDS: Etiology, prevention, and treatment* (pp. 51–64). Hillsdale, NJ: Erlbaum.

DiClemente, R. J. (1990b). The emergence of adolescents as a risk group for human immunodeficiency virus infection. *Journal of Adolescent Research, 5,* 7–17.

DiClemente, R. J. (Ed.). (1992). *Adolescents and AIDS: A generation in jeopardy.* Newbury Park, CA: Sage.

Dobson, J. C. (1984). *Preparing for adolescence.* NY: Bantam.

Dobson, J. C. (1986). *Dr. Dobson answers your questions about raising children.* Farmington Hills, MN: Tyndale.

Dobson, J. C. (1988). *Raising teenagers right.* Farmington Hills, MN: Tyndale.

Dobson, J. C. (1990). *Fighting for the hearts and minds of our children: America's second Civil War.* Irving, TX: Word Books.

Dodder, R. & Hughes, S. P. (1987). Collegiate drinking behavior: A test of neutralization theory. *Journal of Alcohol and Drug Education, 33,* 73–85.

Dodge, K. A., Pettit, G. S., McClaskey, C. L., & Brown, M. M. (1986). Social competence in children. *Monographs for the Society for Research in Child Development, 51*(2, Serial No. 181).

Donovan, J. E., Jessor, R., & Jessor, S. L. (1983). Problem drinking in adolescence and young adulthood: A follow-up study. *Journal of Studies on Alcohol, 44,* 109–137.

Dornbusch, S. M., Ritter, P. L., Leiderman, P. H., Roberts, D. F., & Fraleigh, M. J. (1987). The relation of parenting style to adolescent school performance. *Child Development, 58,* 1244–1257.

Douvan, E. & Adelson, J. (1966). *The adolescent experience.* New York: Wiley.

Dreyer, P. H. (1982). Sexuality during adolescence. In B. B. Wolman (Ed.), *Handbook of developmental psychology* (pp. 559–601). Englewood Cliffs, NJ: Prentice-Hall.

Dronkers, J. (1989). Working mothers and the educational achievements of their children. In K. Hurrelmann & U. Engel (Eds.), *The social world of adolescents: International perspectives* (pp. 185–198). Berlin: W. deGruyter.

DuRant, R. H. (1991). Overcoming barriers to health care access. In W. R. Hendee (Ed.), *The health of adolescents: Understanding and facilitating biological, behavioral, and social development* (pp. 431–452). San Francisco, CA: Jossey-Bass.

Dweck, C. (1975). The role of expectations and attributions in the alleviation of learned helplessness. *Journal of Personality and Social Psychology, 31,* 674–685.

Dweck, C. S. (1986). Motivational processes affecting learning. *American Psychologist, 41,* 1040–1048.

Dweck, C. S. & Elliott, E. S. (1983). Achievement motivation. In E. M. Hetherington (Ed.), P. H. Mussen (Series Ed.), *Handbook of child psychology, Vol. IV. Socialization, personality, and social development* (pp. 643–691). New York: Wiley.

Dycus, S. & Costner, G. M. (1990). Healthy early adolescent development (11–13 year olds): Implementing a human sexuality curriculum for seventh graders. *Elementary School Guidance and Counseling, 25,* 46–53.

Dyer, K. F. (1977). The trend of male-female performance differential in athletics, swimming, and cycling 1918–1976. *Journal of Biosocial Science, 9,* 325–338.

Dyk, P. H., Christopherson, C. R., & Miller, B. C. (1991). Adolescent sexuality. In S. J. Bahr (Ed.), *Family research: A sixty-*

year review, 1930–1990. Volume 1 (pp. 25–63). New York: Lexington Books.

Eaton, N. K., Weltin, M., & Wing, H. (**1982**). *Validity of the Military Applicant Profile (MAP) for predicting early attrition in different educational, age, and racial groups.* Alexandria, VA: Army Research Institute for the Behavioral and Social Sciences. (ERIC Document ED 242929.)

Eccles, J. P., Adler, T., & Kaczala, C. (**1982**). Socialization of achievement attitudes and beliefs: Parental influences. *Child Development, 53,* 310–321.

Eccles, J. S., Midgley, C., Wigfield, A., Buchanan, C. M., Reuman, D., Flanagan, C., & MacIver, D. (**1993**). Development during adolescence: The impact of stage-environment fit on young adolescents' experience in schools and families. *American Psychologist, 48,* 90–101.

Eckert, P. (**1990**). Adolescent social categories—Information and science learning. In M. Gardner, J. G. Greeno, F. Reif, A. H. Schoenfeld, A. Diseau, & E. Stage (Eds.), *Toward a scientific practice of science education* (pp. 203–217). Hillsdale, NJ: Erlbaum.

Edsall, T. B. (**1988**). The return of inequality. *The Atlantic Monthly, 261*(6), 86–94.

Egan, G. (**1990**). *The skilled helper: A systematic approach to effective helping.* (4th ed.). Pacific Grove, CA: Brooks/Cole.

Ehrenberg, M. F., Cox, D. N., & Koopman, R. F. (**1990**). The prevalence of depression in high school students. *Adolescence, XXV,* 905–912.

Eisenberg, A. R. & Garvey, C. (**1981**). Children's use of verbal strategies in resolving conflicts. *Discourse Processes, 4,* 149–170.

Elder, G. H. (**1991**). Family transitions, cycles, and social change. In P. A. Cowan & M. Hetherington (Eds.), *Family transitions* (pp. 3–30.). Hillsdale, NJ: Erlbaum.

Elizur, J. & Minuchin, S. (**1989**). *Institutionalizing madness: Families, therapy, and society.* New York: Basic Books.

Elkind, D. (**1967**). Egocentrism in adolescence. *Child Development, 38,* 1025–1034.

Elkind, D. (**1979**). *The child and society: Essays in applied child development.* New York: Oxford University Press.

Elkind, D. (**1981**). *The hurried child: Growing up too fast, too soon.* Reading, MA: Addison-Wesley.

Elkind, D. (**1984**). *All grown up and no place to go: Teenagers in crisis.* Reading, MA: Addison-Wesley.

Elkind, D. (**1987**). The child yesterday, today, and tomorrow. *Young Children,* May, 6–11.

Elkind, D. & Bowen, R. (**1979**). Imaginary audience behavior in children and adolescents. *Developmental Psychology, 15,* 38–44.

Ellis, N. B. (**1991**). An extension of the Steinberg accelerating hypothesis. *Journal of Early Adolescence, 11,* 221–235.

Emerick, B. B. & Easley, J. (**1978**). *A constructivist challenge to the validity of formal operations.* Paper presented at the annual meeting of the American Educational Research Association, Toronto.

Ennis, R. H. (**1975**). Children's ability to handle Piaget's propositional logic: A conceptual critique. *Review of Educational Research, 45,* 1–41.

Ennis, R. H. (**1976**). An alternative to Piaget's conceptualization of logical competence. *Child Development, 47,* 903–917.

Ennis, R. H. (**1978**). Conceptualization of children's logical competence: Piaget's propositional logic and an alternative proposal. In L. S. Siegel & C. J. Brainerd (Eds.), *Alternatives to Piaget: Critical essays on the theory* (pp. 201–260). New York: Academic Press.

Enright, R. D., Levy, V. M., Harris, D., & Lapsley, D. K. (**1987**). Do economic conditions influence how theorists view adolescence? *Journal of Youth and Adolescence, 16,* 541–559.

Ensing, D. S. and Meerdink, M. J. (**1988, August**). *The outcomes of religious coping.* In K. I. Pargament (Chair), *Investigations of religion and coping: Theoretical and empirical advances.* Symposium conducted at the meeting of the American Psychological Association, Atlanta, GA.

Entwisle, E. R. (**1990**). Schools and the adolescent. In S. S. Feldman & G. R. Elliott (Eds.), *At the threshold: The developing adolescent* (pp. 197–224). Cambridge, MA: Harvard University Press.

Epstein, N. B., Bishop, D. S., & Baldwin, L. M. (**1982**). McMaster Model of Family Functioning: A view of the normal family. In F. Walsh (Ed.), *Normal family processes* (pp. 115–141). New York: The Guilford Press.

Erikson, E. H. (**1958**). *Young man Luther.* New York: Norton.

Erikson, E. H. (**1961**). Youth: Fidelity and diversity. In E. H. Erikson (Ed.), *Youth: Change and challenge* (pp. 1–23). New York: Basic Books.

Erikson, E. H. (**1963**). *Childhood and society* (2nd ed.). New York: Norton.

Erikson, E. H. (**1968**). *Identity: Youth and crisis.* New York: Norton.

Erikson, E. H. (**1969**). *Gandhi's truth.* New York: Norton.

Erikson, E. H. (**1975**). *Life history and the historical moment.* New York: Norton.

Erikson, E. H. (**1982**). *The life cycle completed: A review.* New York: Norton.

Erikson, E. H., Erikson, J. M., & Kivnick, H. Q. (**1986**). *Vital involvement in old age: The experience of old age in our time.* New York: Norton.

Erlenmeyer-Kimling, L., Cornblatt, B. A., Bassett, A. S., Moldin, S. O., Hildoff-Adomo, U., & Roberts S. (**1990**). High-risk children in adolescence and young adulthood: Course of global adjustment. In L. N. Robins & M. Rutter (Eds.), *Straight and devious pathways from childhood to adulthood* (pp. 351–364). Cambridge, England: Cambridge University Press.

Eron, L. & Gentry, J. (**Eds.**). (**1994**). *Violence and youth: Psychology's response. Volume II. Papers of the American Psychological Association on Violence and Youth.* Washington, DC: APA.

Ethington, C., Smart, J., & Pascarella, E. T. (**1987**). Entry into the teaching profession: Test of a causal model. *Journal of Educational Research, 80,* 156–163.

Ewing, C. P. (1990). *Kids who kill*. Lexington, MA: Lexington Books.

Eysenck, H. J. (1983). Stress, disease, and personality: The "inoculation" effect. In C. J. Cooper (Ed.), *Stress Research* (pp. 121–146). New York: Wiley.

Farber, E. D., Kinast, C., McCoard, W. D., & Falkner, D. (1984). Violence in families of adolescent runaways. *Child Abuse and Neglect, 8,* 295–299.

Faris, J. H. (1981). The all-volunteer force: Recruitment from military families. *Armed Forces and Society, 7,* 545–559.

Farley, D. (1986, May). Eating disorders: When thinking becomes an obsession. *FDA Consumer,* 20–23.

Farmer, H. S. (1976). What inhibits achievement and career motivation in women? *The Counseling Psychologist, 6,* 12–14.

Federal Bureau of Investigation. (1989). *Uniform crime reports for the United States*. Washington, DC: U.S. Department of Justice.

Federal Bureau of Investigation. (1990). *Age-specific arrest rates and race-specific arrest rates for selected offenses, 1965–1989*. Washington, DC: Unified Crime Reporting Program.

Federal Bureau of Investigation. (1992). *Crime in the United States. 1991. Uniform crime reports*. Washington, DC: U.S. Department of Justice.

Feingold, A. (1988). Cognitive gender differences are disappearing. *American Psychologist, 43,* 95–103.

Feldhusen, J. F. & Hoover, S. M. (1986). A conception of giftedness: Intelligence, self concept, and motivation. *Roeper Review, 8,* 140–143.

Fenigstein, A., Scheier, M. F. & Buss, A. H. (1975). Public and private self-consciousness: Assessment and theory. *Journal of Consulting and Clinical Psychology, 43,* 522–527.

Fenzel, L. M. (1989). Role strains and the transition to middle school: Longitudinal trends and sex differences. *Journal of Early Adolescence, 9,* 211–226.

Feyerabend, P. (1975). *Against method: Outline of an anarchistic theory of knowledge*. London: Verso.

Finch, A. J., Casat, C. D., & Carey, M. P. (1990)., Depression in children and adolescents. In S. B. Morgan & T. M. Okwumabua (Eds.), *Child and adolescent disorders: Developmental and health psychology perspectives* (pp. 136–172). Hillsdale, NJ: Erlbaum.

Fine, G., Mortimer, J., & Roberts, D. (1990). Leisure, work, and the mass media. In S. S. Feldman & G. R. Elliott (Eds.), *At the threshold: The developing adolescent* (pp. 225–254). Cambridge, MA: Harvard University Press.

Fingerhut, L. A. & Kleinman, J. C. (1990). International and interstate comparisons of homicide among young males. *Journal of the American Medical Association, 263*(24), 3292–3295.

Finkelhor, D., Hotaling, G., & Sedlak, A. (1990). *Missing, abducted, runaway, and thrownaway children in America. First report: Numbers and characteristics. National incidence studies. Executive summary*. Washington, DC: U.S. Department of Justice.

Fischbein, S. (1977). Intra-pair similarity in physical growth of monozygotic and dizygotic twins during puberty. *Annals of Human Biology, 4,* 417–430.

Fischer, C. S. (1982). *To dwell among friends*. Chicago: University of Chicago Press.

Fischer, K. W. (1983). Illuminating the process of moral development. *Monographs of the Society for Research in Child Development, 48,* 97–107.

Fisher, P., & Shaffer, D. (1990). Facts about suicide: A review of national mortality statistics and records. In M. J. Rotheram-Borus, J. Bradley, & N. Obolensky (Eds.), *Planning to live: Evaluating and treating suicidal teens in community settings* (pp. 1–33). Tulsa, OK: University of Oklahoma Press.

Flavell, J. H. (1984). Discussion. In R. J. Sternberg (Ed.), *Mechanisms of cognitive development* (pp. 187–209). New York: W. H. Freeman.

Flavell, J. (1985). *Cognitive development*. (2nd ed.). Englewood Cliffs, NJ: Prentice-Hall.

Floerchinger, D. S. (1991). Bereavement in late adolescence: Interventions on college campuses. *Journal of Adolescent Research, 6,* 146–156.

Florito, J. & Dauffenbach, R. (1982). Market and nonmarket influences on curriculum choice by college students. *Industrial and Labor Relations Review, 36,* 88–101.

Foa, E. B. & Rothbaum, B. O. (1992). Post-traumatic stress disorder: Clinical features and treatment. In R. DeV. Peters, R. J. McMahon, & V. L. Quinsey (Eds.), *Aggression and violence through the life span* (pp. 155–170). Newbury Park, CA: Sage.

Food and Nutrition Board. (1989). *Recommended dietary allowances* (10th ed.). Washington, DC: National Academy Press.

Ford, M. R. & Lowery, C. R. (1986). Gender differences in moral reasoning: A comparison of the use of justice and care orientations. *Journal of Personality and Social Psychology, 50,* 777–783.

Fowler, J. W. (1981). *Stages of faith: The psychology of human development and the quest for meaning*. San Francisco: Harper & Row.

Fowler, J. W. (1991). Stages of faith consciousness. In F. K. Oser & G. Scarlett (Eds.), *Religious development in childhood and adolescence* (pp. 27–45). San Francisco: Jossey-Bass.

Frank, L. K. (1938). The fundamental needs of the child. *Mental Hygiene, 22,* 353–379.

Freeman, D. (1983). *Margaret Mead and Samoa: The making and unmaking of an anthropological myth*. Cambridge, MA: Harvard University Press.

Freeman, R. (1971). *The market for college trained manpower*. Cambridge, MA: Harvard University Press.

Freud, A. (1946). *The ego and the mechanisms of defense*. (C. Baines, Trans.). New York: International Universities Press.

Freud, A. (1969). Adolescence. In *The writings of Anna Freud* (Volume V, pp. 136–166). New York: International Universities Press. (Reprinted from *The Psychoanalytic Study of the Child*, 1958, *13*, 255–278)

Freud, A. (1971). Adolescence as a developmental disturbance. In *The writings of Anna Freud* (Volume VII, pp. 39–47). New York: International Universities Press. (Reprinted from S. Lebovici & G. Caplan (Eds.), *Adolescence: Psychosocial perspectives*, 1969, New York: Basic Books)

Freud, S. (1925). Analysis of a phobia in a five year old boy. In J. Strachey (Ed. and Trans.), *The standard edition of the complete psychological works of Sigmund Freud* (Vol. 3, pp. 149–289). London: Hogarth Press.

Freud, S. (1938a). The interpretation of dreams. In A. A. Brill (Ed. and Trans.), *The basic writings of Sigmund Freud* (pp. 181–549). New York: Random House.

Freud, S. (1938b). Three contributions to the theory of sex. In A. A. Brill (Ed. and Trans.), *The basic writings of Sigmund Freud* (pp. 553–629). New York: Random House.

Freud, S. (1938c). Psychopathology of everyday life. In A. A. Brill (Ed. and Trans.), *The basic writings of Sigmund Freud* (pp. 33–178). New York: Random House.

Freud, S. (1946). *Civilization and its discontents*. (J. Riviere, Trans.). (3rd ed.). London: Hogarth Press. (Original work published 1929)

Freud, S. (1957). On narcisissm: An introduction. In J. Strachey (Ed. and Trans.), *The standard edition of the complete psychological works of Sigmund Freud* (Volume 14, pp. 73–102). London: Hogarth Press. (Original work published 1914)

Freud, S. (1960). *A general introduction to psychoanalysis*. (J. Riviere, Trans.). New York: Washington Square Press. (Original work published 1935)

Freud, S. (1961). The ego and the id. In J. Strachey (Ed. and Trans.), *The standard edition of the complete psychological works of Sigmund Freud* (Volume 19, pp. 13–59). London: Hogarth Press. (Original work published 1923)

Freud, S. (1964). New introductory lectures on psycho analysis. In J. Strachey (Ed. and Trans.), *The standard edition of the complete psychological works of Sigmund Freud* (Vol. 22, pp. 5–182). London: Hogarth Press. (Original work published 1933)

Freud, S. (1966). *Introductory lectures on psychoanalysis*. (J. Strachey, Trans.). New York: Norton. (Original work published 1920)

Friedenberg, E. (1959). *The vanishing adolescent*. New York: Dell.

Frisch, R. E. (1974). A method of prediction of age of menarche from height and weight at ages 9 through 13 years. *Pediatrics*, *53*, 384–390.

Frisch, R. E. & Revelle, R. (1970). Height and weight at menarche and a hypothesis of critical body weight and adolescent girls. *Science*, *169*, 379–399.

Frisch, R. E. & Revelle, R. (1971). Height and weight at menarche and a hypothesis of menarche. *Archives of Diseases in Childhood*, *46*, 695–701.

Frisch, R. E., Revelle, R., & Cook, S. (1973). Components of weight at menarche and the initiation of the adolescent growth spurt in girls: Estimated total water, lean body weight and fat. *Human Biology*, *45*, 469–483.

Fromm-Reichmann, F. (1948). Notes on the development of schizophrenia by psychoanalytic psychotherapy. *Psychiatry*, *11*, 263–273.

Furman, E. (1974). *A child's parent dies*. New Haven, CT: Yale University Press.

Furman, W. & Bierman, K. L. (1983). Developmental changes in young children's conceptions of friendship. *Child Development*, *54*, 549–556.

Furman, W. & Buhrmester, D. (1985). Children's perceptions of the personal relationships in their social networks. *Developmental Psychology*, *21*, 1016–1024.

Furman, W. & Buhrmester, D. (1992). Age and sex differences in perceptions of networks of personal relationships. *Child Development*, *63*, 103–115.

Furman, W. & Gavin, L. A. (1989). Peers' influence on adjustment and development: A view from the intervention literature. In T. J. Berndt & G. W. Ladd (Eds.), *Peer relationships in child development* (pp. 319–340). New York: Wiley.

Furnham, A. & Kramers, M. (1989). Eating problems patients' conceptions of normality. *Journal of Genetic Psychology*, *150*, 147–153.

Fusco, P. (1992, July/August). Whose rescue? *Mother Jones*, *17*, 50–53.

Gagnon, J. & Simon, W. (1969). They're going to learn on the street anyway. *Psychology Today*, *3*, 46.

Gallagher, J. R. & Harris, H. I. (1958). *Emotional problems of adolescents*. New York: Oxford University Press.

Gallegos, G. E. & Kahn, M. W. (1986). Factors predicting success of underprivileged youths in Job Corps training. *The Vocational Guidance Quarterly*, *34*, 171–177.

Gantz, W., Fitzmaurice, M., & Yoo, E. (1990). Seat belt campaigns and buckling up: Do the media make a difference? *Health Communication*, *2*, 1–12.

Garbarino, J. & Guttmann, E. (1986). Characteristics of high-risk families: Parental and adolescent perspectives. In J. Garbarino, C. J. Schellenbach, & J. M. Sebes, (Eds.), *Troubled youth, troubled families: Understanding families at-risk for adolescent maltreatment* (pp. 121–148). New York: Aldine.

Garbarino, J., Wilson, J., & Garbarino, A. C. (1986). The adolescent runaway. In J. Garbarino, C. J. Schellenbach, & J. M. Sebes (Eds.), *Troubled youth, troubled families: Understanding families at-risk for adolescent maltreatment* (pp. 41–54). New York: Aldine.

Gardner, H. (1983). *Frames of mind: The theory of multiple intelligences*. New York: Basic Books.

Gardner, H. (1985). *The mind's new science: A history of the cognitive revolution*. New York: Basic Books.

Gardner, H. (1993). *Multiple intelligences: The theory in practice*. New York: Basic Books.

Garfinkel, P. E. (1981). Some recent observations on the pathogenesis of anorexia nervosa. *Canadian Journal of Psychiatry, 26,* 218–223.

Garrord, A., Smulyan, L., Powers, S. I., & Kilkenny, R. (1992). *Adolescent portraits: Identity, relationships, and challenges.* Boston: Allyn & Bacon.

Gavin, L. A. & Furman, W. (1989). Age differences in adolescents' perceptions of their peer groups. *Developmental Psychology, 25,* 827–834.

Geber, G. & Okinow, N. A. (1991). Chronic illness and disability. In W. R. Hendee (Ed.), *The health of adolescents: Understanding and facilitating biological, behavioral, and social development* (pp. 282–301). San Francisco, CA: Jossey-Bass.

George, P. S., Stevenson, C., Thomasen, J., & Beane, J. (1992). *The middle school — and beyond.* Alexandria, VA: Association for Supervision and Curriculum Development.

Gerber, G., Gross, L., Morgan, M., & Signorielli, N. (1986). Living with television: The dynamics of the cultivation process. In J. Bryant & D. Zillmann (Eds.), *Perspectives on media effects* (pp. 17–40). Hillsdale, NJ: Erlbaum.

Gergen, M. M. (1988). Building a feminist methodology. *Contemporary Social Psychology, 13,* 47–53.

Germain, C. B. (1990). Life forces and the anatomy of practice. *Smith College Studies in Social Work, 60,* 138–152.

Gerrold, D. (1988). *When Harlie was one.* New York: Bantam.

Gesell, A., Halverson, H. M., Thompson, H., Ilg, F. L., Costner, B. M., Ames, L. B., & Amatruda, C. S. (1940). *The first five years of life: A guide to the study of the preschool child.* New York: Harper & Row.

Gesell, A. & Thompson, H. (1929). Learning and growth in identical twins: An experimental study by the method of co-twin control. *Genetic Psychology Monographs, 6,* 1–123.

Gibbs, J. C. & Widaman, K. F. (1982). *Social intelligence: Measuring the development of sociomoral reflection.* Englewood Cliffs, NJ: Prentice-Hall.

Gibbs, J. T. (1985). City girls: Psychosocial adjustment of urban Black adolescent females. *SAGE: A Scholarly Journal on Black Women, 2,* 28–36.

Gilligan, C. (1977). In a different voice: Women's conceptions of self and of morality. *Harvard Educational Review, 47,* 481–517.

Gilligan, C. (1982). *In a different voice: Psychological theory and women's development.* Cambridge, MA: Harvard University Press.

Gilligan, C. (1986). Reply by Carol Gilligan. *Signs: Journal of Women in Culture and Society, 11,* 324–333.

Gilligan, C., Kohlberg, L., Lerner, J., & Belenky, M. (1971). Moral reasoning about sexual dilemmas: The development of an interview and scoring system. In *Technical Report of the Commission on Obscenity and Pornography,* Vol. 1. Washington, DC: U.S. Government Printing Office.

Glaser, B. G. & Strauss, A. L. (1967). *The discovery of grounded theory: Strategies for qualitative research.* Chicago: Aldine.

Glass, G. V., McGraw, B., & Smith, M. L. (1981). *Meta-analysis in social research.* Beverly Hills, CA: Sage.

Glueck, S. & Glueck, E. (1950). *Unraveling juvenile delinquency.* Cambridge, MA: Harvard University Press.

Glueck, S. & Glueck, E. (1968). *Delinquents and nondelinquents in perspective.* Cambridge: Harvard University Press.

Gold, M. (1970). *Delinquent behavior in an American city.* Belmont, CA: Brooks/Cole.

Gold, M. & Petronio, R. J. (1980). Delinquent behavior in adolescence. In J. Adelson (Ed.), *Handbook of adolescent psychology* (pp. 495–535). New York: Wiley.

Goldenberg, M. M. (1990). *Pharmacology for the psychotherapist.* Muncie, IN: Accelerated Development, Inc.

Goldstein, A. P. (1990). *Delinquents on delinquency.* Champaign, IL: Research Press.

Goldstein, A. P. & Soriano, F. I. (1994). Delinquent gangs. In L. Eron & J. Gentry (Eds.), *Violence and youth: Psychology's response. Vol. II. Papers of the American Psychological Association on Violence and Youth.* Washington, DC: APA.

Gonsiorek, J. C. & Weinrich, J. D. (1991). The definition and scope of sexual orientation. In J. C. Gonsiorek & J. D. Weinrich (Eds.), *Homosexuality: Research implications for public policy* (pp. 1–12). Newbury Park, CA: Sage.

Goodman, P. (1960). *Growing up absurd.* New York: Random House.

Goodman, R. A. (1986). *Adolescent grief characteristics when a parent dies.* Unpublished doctoral dissertation, University of Colorado, Boulder, CO.

Goodnow, J. & Burns, A. (1985). *Home and school: A child's-eye view.* Sydney: Allen & Unwin.

Goodwin, M. P. & Roscoe, B. (1990). Sibling violence and agonistic interaction among middle adolescents. *Adolescence, 25,* 451–467.

Gordon, D. A. & Arbuthnot, J. (1987). Individual, group, and family interventions. In H. C. Quay (Ed.), *Handbook of juvenile delinquency* (pp. 290–324). New York: Wiley.

Gordon, S. (1981). *The teenage survival book: The complete revised, updated version of you.* New York: Random House.

Gordon, S. (1985). *When living hurts.* New York: UAHC.

Gore, T. (1987). *Raising PG kids in an X-rated society.* Nashville, TN: Abingdon.

Gottman, J. M. & Parker, J. G. (Eds.). (1986). *Conversations of friends: Speculations on affective development.* New York: Cambridge University Press.

Gottman, J. M. & Parkhurst, J. T. (1980). A developmental theory of friendship and acquaintanceship processes. In W. A. Collins (Ed.), *Minnesota symposia on child development: Vol. 13: Development of cognition, affect, and social relations* (pp. 197–253). Hinsdale, NJ: Erlbaum.

Gottschalk, R., Davidson, W. S., Gensheimer, L. K., & Mayer, J. P. (1987). Community-based interventions. In H. C. Quay (Ed.), *Handbook of juvenile delinquency* (pp. 266–289). New York: Wiley.

Gould, R. L. (1978). *Transformations: Growth and change in adult life.* New York: Simon & Schuster.

Grant, I., Kyle, G. C., Teichman, A., & Mandels, J. (1974). Recent life events and diabetes in adults. *Psychosomatic Medicine, 36,* 121–128.

Gray, R. E. (1987a). *Adolescents faced with the death of a parent: The role of social support and other factors.* Unpublished doctoral dissertation, University of Toronto, Toronto, Canada.

Gray, R. E. (1987b). Adolescent response to the death of a parent. *Journal of Youth and Adolescence, 16,* 511–525.

Gray, R. E. (1988). The role of school counselors with bereaved teenagers: With and without peer support groups. *The School Counselor, 35,* 188–193.

Green, J. K. (1986). Psychiatric illness: Effects on sexual functioning in teenagers. *Medical Aspects of Human Sexuality, 20,* 26–32.

Greenberger, E. (1988). Working in teenage America. In J. T. Mortimer & K. M. Borman (Eds.), *Work experience and psychological development through the life span* (pp. 21–50). Boulder, CO: Westview Press.

Greenberger, E. & Steinberg, L. D. (1986). *When teenagers work.* New York: Basic Books.

Greenberger, E., Steinberg, L. D., & Vaux, A. (1981). Adolescents who work: Health and behavioral consequences of job stress. *Developmental Psychology, 17,* 691–703.

Greenberger, E., Steinberg, L. D., Vaux, A., & McAuliffe, S. (1980). Effects of part-time employment on family and peer relations. *Journal of Youth and Adolescence, 9,* 189–202.

Grimshaw, J. (1986). *Philosophy and feminist thinking.* Minneapolis, MN: University of Minnesota Press.

Gronlund, N. E. (1959). *Sociometry in the classroom.* New York: Harper & Brothers.

Grotevant, H. D. (1987). Toward a process model of identity formation. *Journal of Adolescent Research, 2,* 203–222.

Grotevant, H. D. & Adams, G. R. (1984). Development of an objective measure to assess ego identity in adolescence: Validation and replication. *Journal of Youth and Adolescence, 13,* 419–438.

Grotevant, H. D. & Cooper, C. R. (1986). Individuation in family relationships: A perspective on individual differences in the development of identity and role-taking skill in adolescence. *Human Development, 29,* 82–100.

Grotevant, H. D. & Thorbecke, W. L. (1982). Sex differences in styles of occupational identity formation in late adolescence. *Developmental Psychology, 18,* 396–405.

Grumbach, M. M. (1978). The central nervous system and the onset of puberty. In F. Falkner & J. M. Tanner (Eds.), *Human growth* (Vol. 2). *Postnatal growth.* New York: Plenum.

Grusznski, R. J., Brilnk, J. C., & Edelson, J. L. (1988). Support and education groups for children of battered women. *Child Welfare, 67,* 431–444.

Grynaeusz, E. & Pressing, L. (1986). A psychological examination of adolescents having escaped from home and child rearing institute: I. Background factors. *Magyar Pszichologial Szemle, 43,* 28–44. (English abstract in PsycLIT Database)

Guba, E. G. & Lincoln, Y. V. (1989). *Fourth generation evaluation.* Newbury Park, CA: Sage.

Gubrium, J. F. & Holstein, J. A. (1990). *What is family?* Mountain View, CA: Mayfield.

Guerra, N. G. & Slaby, R. G. (1990). Cognitive mediators of aggression in adolescent offenders. 2. *Developmental Psychology, 26,* 269–277.

Guerriero, A. M. (1983). *Adolescent bereavement: Impact on physical health, self-concept, depression, and death anxiety.* Unpublished masters's thesis, York University, Toronto, Canada.

Guerriero, A. M. & Fleming, S. J. (1985, June). *Adolescent bereavement: A longitudinal study.* Paper presented at the Annual Meeting of the Canadian Psychological Association, Halifax, Nova Scotia.

Guerriero-Austrom, M. & Fleming, S. J. (1990). *Effects of sibling death on adolescents' physical and emotional well-being: A longitudinal study.* Paper presented at the Annual Convention of the American Psychological Association, Boston, MA.

Guilford, J. P. (1967). *The nature of human intelligence.* New York: McGraw-Hill.

Gullotta, T. P. (1979). Leaving home: Family relationships of the runaway child. *Social Casework, 60,* 111–114.

Gunkel, H. (1907). *The legends of Genesis* (W. H. Carruth, Trans.). Chicago, IL: Open Court.

Gustafson, S. B. & Magnusson, D. (1991). *Female life careers: A pattern approach.* HIllsdale, NJ: Erlbaum.

Guttman, D. L. (1964). An exploration of ego configurations in middle and later life. In B. L. Neugarten & associates (Eds.), *Personality in middle and later life* (pp. 114–148). New York: Atherton Press.

Guttman, D. L. (1974). The country of old men: Cross-cultural studies in the psychology of later life. In R. A. LeVine (Ed.), *Culture and personality* (pp. 95–127). Chicago: Aldine.

Guttman, M. (1993). Prime time for school violence. *USA Weekend,* October 22–24, 4.

Hacker, A. (1983). *U. S.: A statistical portrait of the American people.* New York: Penguin.

Hagestad, G. O. (1988). Demographic change and the life course: Some emerging trends in the family realm. *Family Relations, 37,* 405–410.

Haim, A. (1974). *Adolescent suicide.* New York: International Universities Press.

Hains, A. A. (1989). An anger-control intervention with aggressive delinquent youths. *Behavioral Residential Treatment, 4,* 213–230.

Hale, S. (1990). A global developmental trend in cognitive processing speed. *Child Development, 61,* 653–663.

Hall, G. S. (1904). *Adolescence: Its psychology and its relations to physiology, anthropology, sociology, sex, crime, religion, and education.* (Vol. 1). New York: D. Appleton.

Hall, G. S. (1909). Evolution and psychology. In (no editor indicated), *Fifty years of Darwinism: Modern aspects of evolution* (pp. 251–267). New York: Henry Holt.

Hall, G. S. (1920). Introduction to R. A. Mackie's *Education during adolescence: Based partly on G. Stanley Hall's psychology of adolescence* (pp. xi–xv). New York: E. P. Dutton.

Halmi, K. A. (1987). Anorexia nervosa and bulimia. In V. B. Van Hasselt & M. Hersen (Eds.), *Handbook of adolescent psychology* (pp. 265–287). New York: Pergamon Press.

Hamburg, D. A. (1992). *Today's children: Creating a future for a generation in crisis.* New York: Times Books.

Hamburg, D. A., Mortimer, A. M., & Nightingale, E. O. (1991). The role of social support in improving the health of adolescents. In W. R. Hendee (Ed.), *The health of adolescents: Understanding and facilitating biological, behavioral, and social development* (pp. 526–542). San Francisco, CA: Jossey-Bass.

Hamilton, L. H., Brooks-Gunn, J., & Warren, M. P. (1985). Socio-cultural influences on eating disorders in professional female ballet dancers. *International Journal of Eating Disorders, 4,* 465–477.

Hammarskjold, D. (1964). *Markings.* (L. Sjoberg & W. H. Auden, Trans.). New York: Knopf.

Hammond, S. L., Freimuth, V. S., & Morrison, W. (1990). Radio and teens: Convincing gatekeepers to air health messages. *Health Communication, 2,* 59–67.

Hammond, W. R. & Yung, B. (1993). Psychology's role in the public health response to assaultive violence among young African-American men. *American Psychologist, 48,* 142–154.

Hamparian, D. M., Schuster, R., Dinitz, S., & Conrad, J. P. (1978). *The violent few: A study of dangerous juvenile offenders.* Lexington, MA: Lexington Books.

Hanson, N. R. (1972). *Patterns of discovery: An inquiry into the conceptual foundations of science.* New York: Cambridge University Press.

Haq, M. N. (1984). Age at menarche and the related issue: A pilot study of urban school girls. *Journal of Youth and Adolescence, 13,* 559–567.

Harding, S. (Ed.). (1987). *Feminism and methodology: Social science issues.* Bloomington, IN: University of Indiana Press.

Hardwick, P. J., Pounds, A. B., & Brown, M. (1985). Preventative adolescent psychiatry? Practical problems in running social skills groups for the younger adolescent. *Journal of Adolescence, 8,* 357–367.

Harlow, H. F. & Mears, C. (1979). *The human model: Primate perspectives.* Washington, DC: V. H. Winston.

Harmon, L. W. (1989). Longitudinal changes in women's career aspirations: Developmental or historical? *Journal of Vocational Behavior, 35,* 46–63.

Harris and Associates. (1987, February). *Attitudes about television, sex, and contraceptive advertising.* New York: Harris and Associates.

Hartman, C. R., Burgess, A. W., & McCormack, A. (1987). Pathways and cycles of runaways: A model for understanding repetitive runaway behavior. *Hospital and Community Psychiatry, 38,* 292–299.

Hartup, W. W. (1983). Peer relations. In E. M. Hetherington (Ed.), *Handbook of child psychology. Volume IV. Socialization, personality, and social development* (4th ed.) (pp. 103–196). New York: Wiley.

Hartup, W. W. (1989). Behavioral manifestations of children's friendships. In T. J. Berndt & G. W. Ladd (Eds.), *Peer relationships in child development* (pp. 46–70). New York: Wiley.

Hass, A. (1979). *Teenage sexuality: A survey of teenage sexual behavior.* New York: Macmillan.

Hastings, J. T. (1966). Curriculum evaluation: The why of the outcomes. *Journal of Educational Measurement, 3,* 27–32.

Hatch, T. C. & Gardner, H. (1986). From testing intelligence to assessing competences: A pluralistic view of intellect. *Roeper Review, 8,* 147–150.

Haubenstricker, J. & Seefeldt, V. (1986). Acquisition of motor skills during childhood. In V. Seefeldt (Ed.), *Physical activity and well-being* (pp. 41–102). Reston, VA: American Alliance for Health, Physical Education, Recreation, and Dance.

Hauser, S. T., Borman, E. H., Jacobson, A. M., Powers, S. I., & Noam, G. G. (1991). Understanding family contexts of adolescent coping: A study of parental ego development and adolescent coping strategies. *Journal of Early Adolescence, 11,* 96–124.

Hauser, S. T., DiPlacido, J., Jacobson, A. M., Paul, E., Bliss, R., Milley, J., Lavori, P., Vieyra, M. A., Wolsdorf, J. I., Herskowitz, R. D., Willett, J. B., Cole, C., Wertlieb, D. (1993). The family and the onset of its youngster's insulin-dependent diabetes: Ways of coping. In R. E. Cole & D. Reiss (Eds.), *How do families cope with chronic illness?* (pp. 25–55). Hillsdale, NJ: Erlbaum.

Hauser, S. T. & Greene, W. M. (1991). Passages from late adolescence to early adulthood. In S. I. Greenspan & G. H. Pollock (Eds.), *The course of life. Volume IV. Adolescence* (pp. 377–405). Madison, CT: International Universitites Press.

Hauser, S. T., Jacobson, A. M., Lavori, P., Wolsdorf, J. I., Herskowitz, R. D., Milley, J. E., Bliss, R., Wertlieb, D., & Stein, J. (1990). Adherence among children and adolescents with insulin-dependent diabetes over a four year longitudinal follow-up: II. Immediate and long-term linkages with the family milieu. *Journal of Pediatric Psychology, 15,* 527–542.

Hauser, S. T., Jacobson, A. M., Milley, J. E., Wertlieb, D., Wolsdorf, J., Herskowitz, R. D., Lavori, P., & Bliss, R. L. (1992). Ego development paths and adjustment to diabetes: Longitudinal studies of preadolescents and adolescents with insulin-dependent diabetes mellitus. In E. J. Susman, L. V. Feagans, & W. J. Ray (Eds.), Emotion, cognition, health, and development in children and adolescents (pp. 133–152). Hillsdale, NJ: Erlbaum.

Havighurst, R. (1952). *Developmental tasks and education.* New York: Longmans, Green.

Havighurst, R. J., Neugarten, B. L., & Tobin, S. S. (1968). Disengagement and patterns of aging. In B. L. Neugarten (Ed.), *Middle age and aging* (pp. 161–172). Chicago: University of Chicago Press.

Haviland, J. M. & Scarborough, H. S. (1981). *Adolescent development in contemporary society.* New York: Van Nostrand.

Hawkins, W. E., Spigner, C., & Murphy, M. (1990). Perceived use of health education services in a school-based clinic. *Perceptual and Motor Skills, 70*, 1075–1078.

Hayes, M. L. & Sloat, R. S. (1990). Suicide and the gifted adolescent. *Journal for the Education of the Gifted, 13*, 229–244.

Hazel, J. S., Schumaker, J. B., Sherman, J. A., & Sheldon-Wildgen, J. (1981). *ASSET: A social skills program for adolescents*. Champaign, IL. Research Press.

Heald, F. P. (1976). New reference points for defining adolescent nutrient requirements. In J. I. McKigney & H. N. Munro (Eds.), *Nutrient requirements in adolescence* (pp. 295–313). Cambridge, MA: The MIT Press.

Heisel, J. S., Ream, S., Raitz, R., Rappaport, M., & Codding-ton, R. D. (1973). The significance of life events as contributing factors in the diseases of children. *The Journal of Pediatrics, 83*, 119–123.

Hendee, W. R. (Ed.). (1991). *The health of adolescents: Understanding and facilitating biological, behavioral, and social development*. San Francisco, CA: Jossey-Bass.

Hendricks, M. (1982). Oral policy briefings. In N. L. Smith (Ed.), *Communication strategies in evaluation* (pp. 249–258). Beverly Hills, CA: Sage.

Henggeler, S. W., Melton, G. B., & Rogdigue, J. R. (1992). *Pediatric and adolescent AIDS. Research findings from the social sciences*. Newbury Park, CA: Sage.

Herek, G. M. (1991). Stigma, prejudice, and violence against lesbians and gay men. In J. C. Gonsiorek & J. D. Weinrich (Eds.), *Homosexuality: Research implications for public policy* (pp. 60–80). Newbury Park, CA: Sage.

Herkowitz, J. (1978). Sex-role expectations and motor behaviors of the young child. In M. V. Ridenour (Ed.), *Motor development: Issues and application* (pp. 83–98). Princeton, NJ: Princeton Book Company.

Herr, K. M. (1989). Adoption versus parenting decisions among pregnant adolescents. *Adolescence, 24*, 795–799.

Hetherington, E. M. (1972). Effects of father absence on personality development in adolescent daughters. *Developmental Psychology, 7*, 97–111.

Hetherington, E. M., Cox, M., & Cox, R. (1982). Effects of divorce on parents and children. In M. Lamb (Ed.), *Nontraditional families: Parenting and child development* (pp. 235–289). Hillsdale, NJ: Erlbaum.

Hetherington, E. M. & Deur, J. (1971). The effects of father absence on child development. *Young Children, 26*, 233–248.

Hill, J. P. & Holmbeck, G. N. (1986). Attachment and autonomy during adolescence. In G. T. Whitehurst, (Ed.), *Annals of child development* (Vol. 3, pp. 145–189). Greenwich, CT: JAI.

Hill, J. P. & Lynch, M. E. (1983). The intensification of gender-related role expectations during early adolescence. In J. Brooks-Gunn & A. C. Petersen (Eds.), *Girls at puberty: Biological and psychological perspectives* (pp. 201–228). New York: Plenum.

Hillerman, T. (1970). *The blessing way*. New York: Harper & Row.

Hillerman, T. (1978). *Listening woman*. New York: Harper & Row.

Hillerman, T. (1984). *The dark wind*. New York: Harper & Row.

Hinde, R. A., Titmus, G., Easton, D., & Tamplin, A. (1985). Incidence of "friendship" and behavior with strong associates versus non-associates in preschoolers. *Child Development, 56*, 234–245.

Hinton, S. E. (1967). *The outsiders*. New York: Vintage Press.

Hirsch, B. J. (1980). Natural support systems and coping with major life change. *American Journal of Community Psychology, 8*, 153–166.

Hite, S. (1976). *The Hite report: A nationwide study of female sexuality*. New York: Macmillan.

Hobbes, T. (1935). *Leviathan*. London: Cambridge University Press. (Originally published 1651)

Hodges, K., Kleine, J. J., Barbero, G., & Flanery, R. (1984). Life events occurring in families of children with recurrent abdominal pain. *Journal of Psychosomatic Research, 28*, 185–188.

Hodgman, C. H. (1983). Current issues in adolescent psychiatry. *Hospital and Community Psychiatry, 34*, 514–521.

Hofferth, S. L. (1990). Trends in adolescent sexual activity, contraception, and pregnancy in the United States. In J. Bancroft & J. M. Reinisch (Eds.), *Adolescence and puberty* (pp. 217–233). New York: Oxford University Press.

Hoffman, L. W. (1979). Maternal employment: 1979. *American Psychologist, 34*, 859–865.

Hoffman, L. W. (1989). Effects of maternal employment on the two-parent family. *American Psychologist, 44*, 283–292.

Hoffman, M. L. (1981). Perspectives on the differences between understanding people and understanding things: The role of affect. In J. H. Flavell & L. Ross (Eds.), *Social cognitive development* (pp. 67–81). Cambridge, England: Cambridge University Press.

Hoffman, M. L. (1982). Development of prosocial motivation: Empathy and guilt. In N. Eisenberg (Ed.), *The development of prosocial behavior*. New York: Academic Press.

Hogan, N. S. (1987). *An investigation of the adolescent bereavement process and adaptation*. Unpublished doctoral dissertation, Loyola University, Chicago.

Hogan, N. S. (1988). The effects of time on the adolescent sibling bereavement process. *Pediatric Nursing, 14*, 333–335.

Hogan, N. S. (1988). [*Sibling bereavement reactions and self-concept of 144 adolescents*]. Unpublished raw data.

Hogan, N. S. & Balk, D. E. (1990). Adolescents' reactions to sibling death: Perceptions of mothers, fathers, and teenagers. *Nursing Research, 39*, 103–106.

Hogan, N. S. & Greenfield, D. B. (1991). Adolescent sibling bereavement symptomatology in a large community sample. *Journal of Adolescent Research, 6*, 97–112.

Hogan, R. (1985). Review of the Offer Self-Image Questionnaire for Adolescents. In J. V. Mitchell, Jr. (Ed.), *The ninth mental measurements yearbook, Vol. II* (pp. 1079–1080). Lincoln, NE: The Buros Institute of Mental Measurements.

Holmes, T. H. & Rahe, R. H. (1967). The social readjustment rating scale. *Journal of Psychosomatic Research, 11*, 213–218.

Holton, G. (**1978**). *The scientific imagination: Case studies.* New York: Cambridge University Press.

Horan, J. J. & Straus, L. K. (**1987**). Substance abuse in adolescence. In V. B. Von Hasselt & M. Hersen (Eds.), *Handbook of adolescent psychology* (pp. 313–331). New York: Pergamon Press.

Horner, M. (**1972**). Toward an understanding of achievement-related conflicts in women. *Journal of Social Issues, 28,* 157–175.

Hortascu, N. (**1990**). Information search in relation to attributional foci: A developmental study. *Genetic, Social, and General Psychology Monographs, 116,* 337–353.

Howard, M. R. (**1975**). *Ego identity status in women, fear of success and performance in a competitive situation.* Unpublished doctoral dissesrtation, State University of New York at Buffalo.

Howe, J. W., Burgess, A. W., & McCormack, A. (**1987**). Adolescent runaways and their drawings. *Arts in Psychotherapy, 14,* 35–40.

Huberty, D. J. & Huberty, C. E. (**1986**). Sabotaging siblings: An overlooked aspect of family therapy with drug dependent adolescents. [Special issue]. *Journal of Psychoactive Drugs, 18,* 31–41.

Huesmann, L. R., Eron. L. D., Lefkowitz, M. M., & Walder, L. O. (**1984**). The stability of aggression over time and generations. *Developmental Psychology, 20,* 1120–1134.

Hull, J. D. (**1991, September 9**). Whose side are you on? *Time, 138,* 19.

Hughes, C. C., Tremblay, M. A., Rapoport, R. N., & Leighton, A. H. (**1960**). *People of Cove and Woodlot: Communities from the viewpoint of social psychiatry.* New York: Basic Books.

Hunter, J. (**1990**). Violence against lesbian and gay male youths. *Journal of Interpersonal Violence, 5,* 295–300.

Hurlock, E. B. (**1955**). *Adolescent development.* New York: McGraw-Hill.

Hurrelmann, K. (**1989**). The social world of adolescents: A sociological perspective. In K. Hurrelmann & U. Engel (Eds.), *The social world of adolescents: International perspectives* (pp. 3–26). Berlin: W. deGruyter.

Hurrelmann, K. (Ed.). (**1994**). *International handbook of adolescence.* Westport, CT: Greenwood Press.

Huston, A. C. (**1983**). Sex-typing. In E. M. Hetherington (Ed.), P. H. Mussen (Series Ed.), *Handbook of child psychology, Vol. IV. Socialization, personality, and social development* (pp. 387–468). New York: Wiley.

Huston, A. C. & Alvarez, M. M. (**1990**). The socialization context of gender role development in early adolescence. In R. Montemayor, G. R. Adams, & T. P. Gullotta (Eds.), *From childhood to adolescence: A transitional period?* (pp. 41–62). Newbury Park, CA: Sage.

Huston, A. C., Donnerstein, E., Fairchild, II., Feshbach, N. D., Katz, P. A., Murray, J. P., Rubinstein, E. A., Wilcox, B. L., & Zuckerman, D. (**1992**). *Big world, small screen: The role of television in American society.* Lincoln, NE: University of Nebraska Press.

Hyde, J. S. & Linn, M. C. (Eds.). (**1986**). *The psychology of gender differences: Advances through meta-analysis.* Baltimore: Johns Hopkins University Press.

Hymel, S. Wagner, E., & Butler, L. J. (**1990**). Reputational bias: View from the peer group. In S. R. Asher & J. D. Coie (Eds.), *Peer rejection in childhood* (pp. 156–186). New York: Cambridge University Press.

Imobekhai, S. Y. (**1986**). Attainment of puberty and secondary sexual characteristics in some rural and urban Nigerian adolescents. *Nigerian Journal of Guidance and Counseling, 2,* 48–55.

Inderbitzen-Pisaruk, H. & Foster, S. L. (**1990**). Adolescent friendships and peer acceptance: Implications for social skills training. *Clinical Psychology Review, 10,* 425–439.

Izard, C. E. & Schwartz, G. M. (**1986**). Patterns of emotion in depression. In M. Rutter, C. E. Izard, & P. B. Read (Eds.), *Depression in young people: Developmental and clinical perspectives* (pp. 33–70). New York: Guilford.

Jacklin, C. N. (**1989**). Female and male: Issues of gender. *American Pscyhologist, 44,* 127–133.

Jackson, J. & Cochran, S. D. (**1991**). Loneliness and psychological distress. *Journal of Psychology, 125,* 257–262.

Jacob, T. & Tennenbaum, D. L. (**1988**). *Family assessment: Rationale, methods, and future directions.* New York: Plenum.

Jaffe, P. G., Sudermann, M., & Reitzel, D. (**1992**). Working with children and adolescents to end the cycle of violence: A social learning approach to intervention and prevention programs. In R. DeV. Peters, R. J. McMahon, & V. L. Quinsey (Eds.), *Aggression and violence through the life span* (pp. 83–99). Newbury Park, CA: Sage.

James, M. D., Burgess, A. W., & McCormack, A. (**1987**). Histories of sexual abuse in adolescent male runaways. *Adolescence, 22,* 405–417.

James, W. (**1967**). Habit. In J. J. McDermott (Ed.), *The writings of William James: A comprehensive edition* (pp. 9–21). New York: The Modern Library. (Reprinted from *Psychology. Briefer Course.* Original work published 1892)

James, W. (**1985**). *The varieties of religious experience: A study in human nature.* Cambridge, MA: Harvard University Press. (Original work published 1901)

Jaquette, D. S. (**1980**). A case study of social-cognitive development in a naturalistic setting. In R. L. Selman (Au.), *The growth of interpersonal understanding: Developmental and clinical analyses* (pp. 215–241). New York: Academic Press.

Jencks, C. (**1985**). How much do high school students learn? *Sociology of Education, 58,* 128–135.

Jencks, C. Bartlett, S., Corcoran, M., Crouse, J., Eaglesfield, D., Jackson, G., McClelland, K., Mueser, P., Olneck, M., Schwartz, J., Ward, S., & Williams, J. (**1979**). *Who gets ahead? The determinants of economic success in America.* New York: Basic Books.

Jencks, C., Smith, M., Acland, H., Bane, M. J., Cohen, D., Gintis, H., Heyns, B., Michelson, S. (**1972**). *Inequality: A reassessment of the effect of family and schooling in America.* New York: Basic Books.

Jessor, R. & Jessor, S. L. (**1978**). *Problem behavior and psychological development: A longitudinal study of growth.* New York: Academic Press.

Jessor, R. & Jessor, S. L. (1984). Adolescence to young adulthood: A twelve-year prospective study of problem behavior and psycho-social development. In S. A. Mednick, M. Harway, & K. M. Finello (Eds.), *Handbook of longitudinal research. Vol. Two: Teenage and adult cohorts* (pp. 34–61). New York: Praeger.

Johnson, D. & Johnson, R. T. (1985). The internal dynamics of cooperative learning groups. In R. Slavin, S. Sharan, S. Kagan, R. Hertz-Lazarowitz, C. Webb, & R. Schmuck (Eds.), *Learning to cooperate, cooperating to learn* (pp. 103–124). New York: Plenum.

Johnson, J. H. (1986). *Life events as stressors in childhood and adolescence.* Beverly Hills, CA: Sage.

Johnson, J. H. & McCutcheon, S. M. (1980). Assessing life stress in older children and adolescents: Preliminary findings with the Life Events Checklist. In I. G. Sarason & C. D. Spielberger (Eds.), *Stress and anxiety.* Washington, DC: Hemisphere.

Johnson, R. J. & Kaplan, H. B. (1991). Psychosocial predictors of enlistment in the all-voluntary armed forces: A life-event history analysis. *Youth and Society, 22,* 291–317.

Johnston, L. D., O'Malley, P. M., & Bachman, J. G. (1985). *Use of licit and illicit drugs by America's high school students, 1975–1984.* (DHHS Publication No. ADM 82–1221). Washington, DC: U.S. Government Printing Office.

Johnston, L. D., O'Malley, P. M., & Bachman, J. G. (1988). *Illicit drug use, smoking, and drinking by America's high school students, college students, and young adults: 1975–1987.* Rockville, MD: National Institute on Drug Abuse.

Johnston, L. D., O'Malley, P. M., & Bachman, J. G. (1992). *Smoking, drinking, and illicit drug use among American secondary school students, college students, and young adults, 1975–1991.* Rockville, MD: National Institute on Drug Abuse.

Johnston, L. D., O'Malley, P. M., & Eveland, L. K. (1978). Drugs and delinquency: A search for causal connections. In D. G. Kandel (Ed.), *Longitudinal research on drug use: Empirical findings and methodological issues* (pp. 137–156). Washington, DC: Hemisphere.

Jones, E. (1953). *The life and work of Sigmund Freud. Vol. I. 1856–1900. The formative years and the great discoveries.* New York: Basic Books.

Jones, E. (1955). *The life and work of Sigmund Freud. Vol. II. 1901–1919. Years of maturity.* New York: Basic Books.

Jones, E. (1957). *The life and work of Sigmund Freud. Vol. III. 1919–1939. The last phase.* New York: Basic Books.

Jones, M. C. (1967). A report on three growth studies at the University of California. *Gerontologist, 7,* 49–54.

Josephson, E. (1985). Smoking, alcohol, and substance abuse. In D. T. Tapley, R. J. Weiss, T. Q. Morris, G. J. Subak-Sharpe, & D. M. Goetz (Eds.), *The Columbia University of Physicians and Surgeons complete home medical guide* (pp. 340–359). Mt. Vernon, NY: Crown.

Josselson, R. (1972). *Identity formation in college women.* Unpublished doctoral dissertation, University of Michigan, Ann Arbor, MI.

Josselson, R. (1973). Psychodynamics of identity formation in college women. *Journal of Youth and Adolescence, 2,* 3–52.

Josselson, R. (1987). *Finding herself: Pathways to identity development in women.* San Francisco, CA: Jossey-Bass.

Jupp, J. J. & Griffiths, M. D. (1990). Self-concept changes in shy, socially isolated adolescents following social skills training emphasizing role plays. *Australian Psychologist, 25,* 165–177.

Jurich, A. P. & Jones, W. C. (1986). Divorce and the experience of adolescents. In G. K. Leigh & G. W. Peterson (Eds.), *Adolescents in families* (pp. 308–336). Cincinnati, OH: South-Western.

Justice, B. & Duncan, D. F. (1976). Running away: An epidemic problem of adolescence. *Adolescence, 11,* 365–371.

Kandel, D. (1982). Epidemiological and psychosocial perspectives on adolescent drug use. *Journal of the American Academy of Child Psychiatry, 21,* 328–347.

Kandel, D. B. & Davies, M. (1982). Epidemiology of depressive mood in adolescents. *Archives of General Psychiatry, 39,* 1205–1216.

Kanfer, F. H. (1979). Personal control, social control, and altruism: Can society survive the age of individualism? *American Psychologist, 34,* 231–239.

Kanin, E. J. (1957). Male aggression in dating-courtship relations. *American Journal of Sociology, 63,* 197–204.

Kaplan, E. H. (1987). Development of the sense of separateness and autonomy during middle childhood and adolescence. In Bloom-Feshbach, J., Bloom-Feshbach, S., & Associates (Eds.), *The psychology of separation and loss: Perspectives on development, life transitions, and clinical practice* (pp. 136–164). San Francisco: Jossey-Bass.

Kaplan, H. B., Johnson, R. J., & Bailey, C. A. (1987). Deviant peers and deviant behaviors: Further elaboration of a model. *Social Psychology Quarterly, 50,* 277–284.

Kaplan, H. B., Martin, S. S., & Robbins, C. (1982). Application of a general theory of deviant behavior: Self-derogation and adolescent drug use. *Journal of Health and Social Behavior, 23,* 274–294.

Kaplan, S. L., Hong, G. K., & Weinhold, C. (1984). Epidemiology of depressive symptomatology in adolescents. *Journal of the American Academy of Child Psychiatry, 23,* 91–98.

Kashani, J. H. & Orvaschel, H. (1988). Anxiety disorders in mid-adolescence: A community sample. *American Journal of Psychiatry, 145,* 960–964.

Katchadourian, H. (1990). Sexuality. in S. S. Feldman & G. R. Elliott (Eds.), *At the threshold: The developing adolescent* (pp. 330–351). Cambridge, MA: Harvard University Press.

Kaufmann, W. (1980). *Discovering the mind. Vol. 3. Freud versus Adler and Jung.* New York: McGraw-Hill.

Keating, D. P. & Bobbitt, B. L. (1978). Individual and developmental differences in cognitive-processing components of mental ability. *Child Development, 49,* 155–167.

Kiell, N. (1964). *The universal experience of adolescence.* New York: International Universities Press.

Kilby, D. (1986). *Manual of safe sex.* Toronto: B. C. Decker.

Kilpatrick, C. & Kanin, E. J. (1957). Male sexual aggression on a university campus. *American Sociological Review, 22,* 52–58.

Kilpatrick, D. G., Veronen, L. J., & Best, C. L. (1984). Factors predicting psychological distress among rape victims. In C. R. Figley (Ed.), *Trauma and its wake: The study and treatment of post-traumatic stress disorders* (pp. 113–141). New York: Brunner/Mazel.

Kilpatrick, D. G., Veronen, L. J., & Resick, P. A. (1982). Psychological sequelae to rape: Assessment and treatment strategies. In D. M. Doleys, R. L. Meredith, & A. R. Ciminero (Eds.), *Behavioral medicine: Assessment and treatment strategies* (pp. 473–497). New York: Plenum.

Kimmel, D. C. & Weiner, I. B. (1985). *Adolescence: A developmental transition*. Hillsdale, NJ: Erlbaum.

King, P. M. (1986). Formal reasoning in adults: Review and critique. In R. A. Mines & K. S. Kitchener (Eds.), *Adult cognitive development: Methods and models* (pp. 1–21). New York: Praeger.

Kinsey, A. C., Pomeroy, W. B., & Martin, C. E. (1948). *Sexual behavior in the human male*. Philadelphia: Saunders.

Kinsey, A. C., Pomeroy, W. B., Martin, C. E., & Gebhard, P. H. (1953). *Sexual behavior in the human female*. Philadelphia: Saunders.

Kirsch, J. A. W. & Weinrich, J. D. (1991). Homosexuality, nature, and biology: Is homosexuality natural? Does it matter? In J. C. Gonsiorek & J. D. Weinrich (Eds.), *Homosexuality: Research implications for public policy* (pp. 13–31). Newbury Park, CA: Sage.

Kitchener, K. S., King, P. M., Wood, P. K., & Davison, M. K. (1989). Sequentiality and consistency in the development of Reflective Judgment: A six-year longitudinal study. *Journal of Applied Developmental Psychology, 10,* 73–95.

Klass, D. (1988). *Parental grief: Solace and resolution*. New York: Springer.

Klee, S. H. & Garfinkel, B. D. (1984). Identification of depression in children and adolescents: The role of the dexamethasone suppression test. *Journal of Child Psychiatry, 23,* 410–415.

Knowles, J. (1966). *A separate peace: A novel*. New York: Macmillan.

Knox, G. W. (1991). *An introduction to gangs*. Berrien Springs, MI: Vande Vere.

Kobak, R. R. & Sceery, A. (1988). Attachment in late adolescence: Working models, affect regulation, and representation of self and others. *Child Development, 59,* 135–146.

Koch, J. (1972). Student choice of undergraduate major field of study and private internal rates of return. *Industrial and Labor Relations Review, 26,* 680–685.

Koenig, L., Howard, K. I., Offer, D., & Cremerius, M. (1984). Psychopathology and adolescent self-image. In D. Offer, E. Ostrov, & K. I. Howard (Eds.), *Patterns of adolescent self-image* (pp. 57–71). San Francisco, CA: Jossey-Bass.

Kohlberg, L. (1969). Stage and sequence: The cognitive-developmental approach to socialization. In D. Goslin (Ed.), *Handbook of socialization theory and research* (pp. 347–480). Chicago: Rand McNally.

Kohlberg, L. (1971). *Structure issue scoring manual*. Unpublished manuscript. Cambridge, MA: Center for Moral Development and Education, Harvard University.

Kohlberg, L. (1976). Moral stages and moralization: The cognitive-developmental approach. In T. Lickona (Ed.), *Moral development and behavior: Theory, research, and social issues* (pp. 31–53). New York: Holt, Rinehart & Winston.

Kohlberg, L. (1980). *The meaning and measurement of moral development*. Worcester, MA: Clark University Press.

Kohlberg, L. (1981). *The philosophy of moral development: Moral stages and the idea of justice*. San Francisco: Harper & Row.

Kohlberg, L. & Gilligan, C. (1971). The adolescent as philosopher: The discovery of the self in a post-conventional world. *Daedalus, 100,* 1051–1086.

Kolstad, A. J. & Owings, J. A. (1986). *High school dropouts who change their minds about school*. Washington, DC: Office of Educational Research and Improvement. (ERIC Document ED 275800.)

Konopka, G. (1966). *The adolescent girl in conflict*. Englewood Cliffs, NJ: Prentice-Hall.

Koss, M. P. (1985). The hidden rape victim: Personality, attitudinal, and situational characteristics. *Psychology of Women Quarterly, 9,* 193–212.

Koss, M. P. (1988). Hidden rape: Sexual aggression and victimization in a national sample in higher education. In A. W. Burgess (Ed.), *Rape and sexual assault, Vol. II* (pp. 3–25). New York: Garland Publishing Company.

Koss, M. P., Gidycz, C. J., & Wisniewski, N. (1987). The scope of rape: Incidence and prevalence of sexual aggression and victimization in a national sample of students in higher education. *Journal of Consulting and Clinical Psychology, 55,* 162–170.

Kreipe, R. E. & Strauss, J. (1989). Adolescent medical disorders, behavior, and development. In G. R. Adams, R. Montemayor, & T. P. Gullotta (Eds.,), *Biology of adolescent behavior and development* (pp. 98–140). Newbury Park, CA: Sage.

Krisberg, B., DeComo, R., Herrera, N. C., Steketee, M., & Roberts, S. (1991). *Juveniles taken into custody: Fiscal year 1990 report*. San Francisco, CA: National Council on Crime and Delinquency.

Kufeldt, K. & Nimmo, M. (1987). Kids on the street have something to say: Survey of runaways and homeless youth. *Journal of Child Care, 3,* 53–61.

Kuhn, D. (1988). Cognitive development. In M. H. Bornstein & M. E. Lamb (Eds.), *Developmental psychology: An advanced textbook* (pp. 205–260). Hillsdale, NJ: Erlbaum.

Kuhn, T. S. (1962). *The structure of scientific revolutions*. Chicago: University of Chicago Press.

Kuhn, T. S. (1970). *The structure of scientific revolutions* (2nd ed.). Chicago: University of Chicago Press.

Labouvie-Vief, G., Hakim-Larson, J., & Hobart, C. J. (1987). Age, ego level, and the life-span development of coping and defense processes. *Psychology and Aging, 2,* 286–293.

Lacey, P. A. (**1990, April 18**). Let's not perpetuate our mistakes of the past as we prepare a new professorial generation. *The Chronicle of Higher Education*, pp. B1, B3.

Ladd, G. W., Profilet, S. M., & Hart, C. H. (**1992**). Parents' management of children's peer relations: Facilitating and supervising children's activities in the peer culture. In R. D. Parke & G. W. Ladd (Eds.), *Family-peer relationships: Modes of linkage* (pp. 215–253). Hillsdale, NJ: Erlbaum.

LaGrand, L. E. (**1981**). Loss reactions of college students: A descriptive analysis. *Death Studies, 5,* 235–247. (previously *Death Education*)

LaGrand, L. E. (**1985**). College student loss and response. In E. S. Zinner (Ed.), *Coping with death on campus* (pp. 15–28). San Francisco: Jossey-Bass.

LaGrand, L. E. (**1986**). *Coping with separation and loss as a young adult: Theoretical and practical realities.* Springfield, IL: Charles C. Thomas.

Lancaster, J. B. (**1984**). Evolutionary perspective on sex differences in the higher primates. In A. S. Rossi (Ed.), *Gender and the life course* (pp. 3–27). New York: A. deGruyter.

Langer, E. J. & Benevento, A. (**1978**). Self-induced dependence. *Journal of Personality and Social Psychology, 36,* 886–893.

Larson, G. (**1980**). *The Far Side Gallery 2.* Kansas City, MO: Andrews, McMeel & Parker.

Larson, K. (**1989**). Task-related and interpersonal problem-solving training for increasing school success in high-risk young adolescents. *RASE: Remedial and Special Education, 10,* 32–42.

Larson, R. W. (**1989**). Beeping children and adolescents: A method for studying time use and daily experience. *Journal of Youth and Adolescence, 18,* 511–530.

Larson, R. W. (**1990**). The solitary side of life: An examination of the time people spend alone from childhood to old age. *Developmental Review, 10,* 155–183.

Larson, R. W., Kubey, R., & Colletti, J. (**1989**). Changing channels: Early adolescent media choices and shifting investments in family and friends. *Journal of Youth and Adolescence, 18,* 583–599.

Larson, R. W. & Richards, M. H. (**1991a**). Boredom in the middle school years: Blaming schools versus blaming students. *American Journal of Education, 99,* 418–443.

Larson, R. W. & Richards, M. H. (**1991b**). Daily companionship in late childhood and early adolescence: Changing developmental contexts. *Child Development, 62,* 284–300.

Lattal, K. A. (**Ed.**) (**1992**). Reflections on B. F. Skinner and psychology. *American Psychologist, 47,* 1265–1533. [Special issue].

Lazarus, R. S. (**1978**). A strategy for research on psychological and social factors in hypertension. *Journal of Human Stress, 4,* 35–40.

Leaverton, D. R., White, C. A., McCormick, C. R., Smith, P., & Sheikholislam, B. (**1980**). Parental loss antecedent to childhood diabetes mellitus. *Journal of the American Academy of Child Psychiatry, 19,* 678–689.

Lefkowitz, B. (**1987**). *Tough change: Growing up on your own in America.* New York: Free Press.

Leigh, G. K. (**1986**). Adolescent involvement in family systems. In G. K. Leigh & G. W. Peterson (Eds), *Adolescents in families* (pp. 38–72). Cincinnati, OH: South-Western.

Leighton, A. H. (**1959**). *My name is Legion: Foundations for a theory of man in relation to culture.* New York: Basic Books.

Leighton, D. C., Harding, J. S., Macklin, D. B., Macmillan, A. M., & Leighton, A. H. (**1963**). *The character of danger: Psychiatric symptoms in selected communities.* New York: Basic Books.

Lemann, N. (**1991**). The other underclass. *The Atlantic Monthly, 268*(6), 96–110.

Lemov, P. (**1991, May**). The return of the orphanage. *Governing,* 31–35.

Lerman, H. (**1986**). *A mote in Freud's eye: From psychoanalysis to the psychology of women.* New York: Springer.

Levine, M. P. & Smolak, L. (**1992**). Toward a model of the developmental psychopathology of eating disorders: The example of early adolescence. In J. H. Crowther, D. L. Tennenbaum, S. E. Hofboll, & M. A. P. Stephens (Eds.), *The etiology of bulimia nervosa: The individual and familial context* (pp. 59–80). Washington, DC: Hemisphere.

Levinson, D. J., Darrow, C. N., Klein, E. B., Levinson, M. H., & McKee, B. (**1978**). *The seasons of a man's life.* New York: Knopf.

Lewandowski, L. J. & Forsstrom-Cohen, B. (**1986**). Neurological bases of youth violence. In S. J. Apter & A. P. Goldstein (Eds.), *Youth violence: Programs and prospects* (pp. 58–74). New York: Pergamon Press.

Lewin, K. (**1951**). Field theory and experiment in social psychology. In D. Cartwright (Ed.), *Field theory in social science: Selected theoretical papers by Kurt Lewin* (pp. 130–154). New York: Harper and Brothers. (Reprinted from *American Journal of Sociology*, 1939, *44,* 868–897)

Lewis, J. M. (**1978**). The adolescent in the healthy family. In S. C. Feinstein & P. L. Giovacchini (Eds.), *Adolescent psychiatry: Developmental and clinical studies.* Vol. 6 (pp. 156–170). Chicago: University of Chicago Press.

Lewis, L. A. (**1990**). *Gender politics and MTV: Voicing the difference.* Philadelphia: Temple University Press.

Lewy, R. & Josephson, E. (**1989**). Smoking, alcohol, and substance abuse. In D. T. Tapley, T. Q. Morris, L. W. Rowland, R. J. Weiss, G. J. Subak-Sharpe, & D. M. Goetz (Eds.), *The Columbia University of Physicians and Surgeons complete home medical guide* (rev. ed.). (pp. 356–379). Mt. Vernon, NY: Crown.

Liberty, C. & Ornstein, P. A. (**1973**). Age differences in organization and recall: The effects of training in categorization. *Journal of Experimental Child Psychology, 15,* 169–186.

Liebert, R. M. & Sprafkin, J. (**1988**). *The early window: Effects of television on children and youth* (3rd ed.). New York: Pergamon Press.

Lightfoot, S. L. (**1983**). *The good high school: Portraits of character and culture.* New York: Basic Books.

Lincoln, Y. V. & Guba, E. G. (1985). *Naturalistic inquiry*. Beverly Hills, CA: Sage.

Lo, C. (1991). Psychosocial correlates of problem drinking behavior and multiple drug-using behavior among collegians. *College Student Journal, 25*, 141–148.

Loeb, R. C, Burke, T. A., & Boglarsky, C. A. (1986). A large-scale comparison of perspectives on parenting between teenage runaways and nonrunaways. *Adolescence, 21*, 921–930.

Logan, D. D. (1980). The menarche experience in 23 foreign countries. *Adolescence, 15*, 247–256.

Longino, H. & Doell, R. (1983). Body, bias, and behavior: A comparative analysis of reasoning in two areas of biological science. *Signs, 9*, 206–227.

Lore, R. K. & Schultz, L. A. (1993). Control of human aggression: A comparative perspective. *American Psychologist, 48*, 16–25.

Lorenz, K. (1966). *On aggression*. New York: Harcourt, Brace & World.

Lorion, R. P., Tolan, P. H., & Wahler, R. G. (1987). Prevention. In H. C. Quay (Ed.), *Handbook of juvenile delinquency* (pp. 266–289). New York: Wiley.

Lounsbury, J. H. (1992). Perspectives on the middle school movement. In J. R. Irvin (Ed.), *Transforming middle level education: Perspectives and possibilities* (pp. 3–15). Boston: Allyn & Bacon.

Lowenthal, M. F., Thurnher, M., & Chiriboga, D. (1975). *Four stages of life: A comparative study of women and men facing transitions*. San Francisco: Jossey-Bass.

Lull, J. (Ed.). (1992). *Popular music and communication* (2nd ed.). Newbury Park, CA: Sage.

Lutes, C. J. (1981). Early marriage and identity foreclosure. *Adolescence, 16*, 809–815.

Lutz, P. (1983). The stepfamily: An adolescent perspective. *Family Relations, 22*, 367–375.

Lyons, N. P. (1982). *Conceptions of self and morality and modes of choice*. Unpublished doctoral dissertation, Harvard University, Cambridge, MA.

Lyons, N. P. (1983). Two perspectives: On self, relationships, and morality. *Harvard Educational Review, 53*, 125–145.

Maas, H. S. & Kuypers, J. A. (1975). *From thirty to seventy*. San Francisco: Jossey-Bass.

MacDonald, B. & Walker, R. (1975). Case study and the social philosophy of educational research. *Cambridge Journal of Education, 1*, 5.

MacFarlane, J. W. (1938). Studies in child guidance. Vol. 1. Methodology of data collection and organization. *Monographs of the Society for Research in Child Development, 3*(6).

Macht, J. (1990). *Poor eaters: Helping children who refuse to eat*. New York: Plenum.

Magnusson, D., Stratton, H., & Allen, V. L. (1985). Relation between expected peer sanctions for norm breaking and menarcheal age for girls with and without older friends. *Journal of Youth and Adolescence, 14*, 267–283.

Makepeace, J. M. (1986). Gender differences in courtship violence victimization. *Family Relations, 32*, 101–109.

Malina, R. M. (1978). Adolescent growth and maturation: Selected aspects of current research. *Yearbook of Physical Anthropology, 21*, 63–94.

Malina, R. M. (1990). Physical growth and performance during the transitional years (9–16). In R. Montemayor, G. R. Adams, & T. P. Gullotta (Eds.), *From childhood to adolescence: A transitional period?* (pp. 41–62). Newbury Park, CA: Sage.

Mallar, C., Keracksky, S., Thornton, C., & Long, D. (1982). *Evaluation of the economic impact of the Job Corps program: Third follow-up report*. Princeton, NJ: Mathematica Policy Research.

Marcia, J. E. (1964). *Determination and construct validity of ego identity status*. Unpublished doctoral dissertation, The Ohio State University, Columbus, OH.

Marcia, J. E. (1966). Development and validation of ego-identity status. *Journal of Personality and Social Psychology, 3*, 551–558.

Marcia, J. E. (1967). Ego identity status: Relationship to change in self-esteem, "general maladjustment," and authoritarianism. *Journal of Personality, 35*, 118–135.

Marcia, J. E. (1980). Identity in adolescence. In J. Adelson (Ed.), *Handbook of adolescent psychology* (pp. 159–187). New York: Wiley.

Marcia, J. E. & Friedman, M. L. (1970). Ego identity status in college women. *Journal of Personality, 38*, 249–263.

Marlowe, H., Reid, J. B., Patterson, G. R., & Weinrott, M. (1986). *Treating adolescent multiple offenders: A comparison and follow-up of parent training for families of chronic delinquents*. Unpublished manuscript. Eugene, OR.

Marris, P. & Rein, M. (1973). *Dilemmas of social reform: Poverty and community action in the United States*. Chicago: Aldine.

Marsh, J. C. & Wirick, M. A. (1991). Evaluation of Hull House teen pregnancy and parenting programs. *Evaluation and Program Planning, 14*, 49–61.

Marshall, C. & Rossman, G. B. (1989). *Designing qualitative research*. Newbury Park, CA: Sage.

Marshall, W. A. & Tanner, J. W. (1969). Variations in the pattern of pubertal changes in girls. *Archives of Disease in Childhood, 44*, 291–303.

Martin, R. P. (1985). Review of the Offer Self-Image Questionnaire for Adolescents. In J. V. Mitchell, Jr. (Ed.), *The ninth mental measurements yearbook. Vol. II* (p. 1080). Lincoln, NE: The Buros Institute of Mental Measurements.

Martinson, I. M., Davies, E. B., & McClowry, S. G. (1987). The long-term effects of sibling death on self-concept. *Journal of Pediatric Nursing, 2*, 227–235.

Mason, J. W. (1975). A historical view of the stress field. Part I. *Journal of Human Stress, 1*, 6–12.

Masson, J. M. (1984). *The assault on truth: Freud's suppression of the seduction theory*. New York: Farrar, Straus & Giroux.

Masten, A. S. (**1991**). Developmental psychopathology and the adolescent. In R. M. Lerner, A. C. Petersen, & J. Brooks-Gunn (Eds.), *Encyclopedia of adolescence* (pp. 221–227). New York, NY: Garland Publishing.

May, R. (**1969**). *Love and will*. New York: Norton.

McCall, R. B., Evahn, C., & Kratzer, L. (**1992**). *High school underachievers: What do they achieve as adults?* Newbury Park, CA: Sage.

McCandless, B. R. (**1970**). *Adolescents: Behavior and development*. Hinsdale, IL: Dryden.

McClelland, D. C., Atkinson, J. W., Clark, R. A., & Lowell, E. L. (**1953**). *The achievement motive*. New York: Appleton.

McCord, C. & Freeman, H. P. (**1990**). Excess mortality in Harlem. *New England Journal of Medicine*, 322(3), 173–177.

McCord, J. (**1978**). A thirty-year follow-up of treatment effects. *American Psychologist*, 33, 284–289.

McCord, J. & McCord, W. (**1959**). A follow-up report on the Cambridge-Somerville youth study. *Annals of the American Academy of Political and Social Science*, 322, 89–96.

McDavid, J. W. & Harari, H. (**1966**). Stereotyping of names and popularity in grade school children. *Child Development*, 37, 453–459. McGoldrick, M. & Carter, E. A. (1982). The family life cycle. In F. Walsh (Ed.), *Normal family processes* (pp. 167–195). New York: The Guilford Press.

McGoldrick, M. & Gerson, R. (**1985**). *Genograms in family assessment*. New York: Norton.

McHale, S. M. & Gamble, W. C. (**1987**). Sibling relationships and adjustment of children with disabled brothers and sisters. *Journal of Children in Contemporary Society*, 19, 131–158.

McLuhan, H. M. (**1951**). *The mechanical bride: Folklore of industrial man*. New York: Vanguard.

McLuhan, H. M. (**1962**). *The Gutenberg galaxy: The making of typographical man*. Toronto: University of Toronto Press.

McLuhan, H. M. (**1964**). *Understanding media: The extensions of man*. New York: McGraw-Hill.

McLuhan, H. M. (**1989**). A McLuhan mosaic. In G. Sanderson & F. Macdonald (Eds.), *Marshall McLuhan: The man and his message* (pp. 1–4). Golden, CO: Fulcrum.

McLuhan, H. M. & Fiore, Q. (**1967**). *The medium is the message*. New York: Bantam.

McMullen, R. J. (**1986**). Youth prostitution: A balance of power? *International Journal of Offender Therapy and Comparative Criminology*, 30, 237–244.

McNeil, J. N. (**1989**). Adolescence and death. In R. Kastenbaum & B. Kastenbaum (Eds.), *The encyclopedia of death*. Phoenix, AZ: Oryx Press.

Mead, G. H. (**1934**). *Mind, self and society from the standpoint of a social behaviorist*. C. W. Morris (Ed.). Chicago: University of Chicago Press.

Mead, M. (**1950**). *Coming of age in Samoa*. New York: Morrow. (Original work published 1928)

Mead, M. (**1952**). Adolescence in primitive and modern society. In T. M. Newcomb & E. L. Hartley (Eds.), *Readings in social psychology* (rev. ed.) (pp. 531–539). New York: Henry Holt. (Reprinted in abridged form from V. F. Calverton & S. D. Schmalhausen (Eds.), *The new generation*, 1930. New York: Macauley)

Meilman, P. W. (**1979**). Cross-sectional age changes in ego identity status during adolescence. *Developmental Psychology*, 15, 230–231.

Menninger, K. (**1966**). *Man against himself*. New York: Harcourt Brace Jovanovich.

Menninger, K. (**1973**). *Sparks: Reflections from the records of a pioneer psychiatrist*. New York: Thomas Y. Crowell.

Meyer, R. J. & Haggerty, R. J. (**1962**). Streptococcal infections in families. *Pediatrics*, 29, 539–549.

Mikesell, J. W. & Garbarino, J. (**1986**). Adolescents in stepfamilies. In J. Garbarino, C. J. Schellenbach, & J. M. Sebes, (Eds.), *Troubled youth, troubled families: Understanding families at-risk for adolescent maltreatment* (pp. 235–251). New York: Aldine.

Miller, D. (**1974**). *Adolescence: Psychology, psychopathology, and psychotherapy*. New York: Jason Aronson.

Miller, W. B. (**1974**). American youth gangs: Past and present. In A. Blumberg (Ed.), *Current perspectives on criminal behavior*. New York: Knopf.

Minow, N. N. (**1961, May**). *The "vast wasteland."* Address to the National Association of Broadcasters, Washington, DC.

Moe, R. (**1993**). *The last full measure: Life and death of the 1st Minnesota volunteers*. New York: Henry Holt.

Mohr, G. S. & Despres, M. A. (**1958**). *The stormy decade: Adolescence*. New York: Random House.

Money, J. & Ehrhardt, A. (**1972**). *Men and women, boys and girls*. Baltimore: Johns Hopkins University Press.

Montemayor, R. & Eisen, M. (**1977**). The development of self-conceptions from childhood to adolescence. *Developmental Psychology*, 13, 314–319.

Montemayor, R. & Hanson, E. (**1985**). A naturalistic view of conflict between adolescents and their parents and siblings. [Special issue]. *Journal of Early Adolescence*, 5, 23–30.

Moore, D. (**1984**). Parent-adolescent separation: Intrafamilial perceptions and difficulty separating from parents. *Personality and Social Psychology Bulletin*, 10, 611–619.

Moore, D. (**1987**). Parent-adolescent separation: The construction of adulthood by late adolescents. *Developmental Psychology*, 23, 298–307.

Moos, R. H. (**1986**). *Coping with life crises: An integrated approach*. New York: Plenum.

Moos, R. H. & Schaefer, J. A. (**1986**). Life transitions and crises: A conceptual overview. In R. H. Moos (Ed.), *Coping with life crises: An integrated approach* (pp. 1–28). New York: Plenum.

Morales, A. T. (**1992**). Therapy with Latino gang members. In L. A. Vargas & J. D. Koss-Chioino (Eds.), *Working with culture: Psychotherapeutic interventions with ethnic minority children and adolescents* (pp. 129–154). San Francisco: Jossey-Bass.

Morash, M. A. (**1980**). Working class membership and the adolescent identity crisis. *Adolescence*, 15, 313–320.

Morawetz, A. (1982). The impact on adolescents of the death in war of an older sibling: A group experience. *Series in Clinical and Community psychiatry: Stress and Anxiety, 8*, 267–274.

Morgan, M. (1982). Television and adolescents' sex-role stereotypes: A longitudinal study. *Journal of Personality and Social Psychology, 43*, 947–955.

Morgan, M. (1987). Television, sex-role attitudes, and sex-role behavior. *Journal of Early Adolescence, 7*, 269–282.

Morgan, M. & Gross, L. (1982). Television and educational achievement and aspiration. In D. Pearl, L. Bouthilet, & J. Lazar (Eds.), *Television and behavior: Ten years of scientific progress and implications for the eighties. Vol, 2: Technical reviews* (pp. 78–90). Washington, DC: U.S. Government Printing Office.

Moriarty, A. E. & Toussieng, P. V. (1976). *Adolescent coping*. New York: Grune and Stratton.

Morofka, V. (1989). Mental health. In J. M. Thompson, G. K. Mcfarland, J. E. Hirsch, S. M. Tucker, & A. C. Bowers (Eds.), *Mosby's manual of clinical nursing* (2nd ed.). (pp. 1506–1556). St. Louis: C. V. Mosby.

Morris, D. (1967). *The naked ape: A zoologist's study of the human animal*. New York: McGraw-Hill.

Moynihan, D. P. (1969). *Maximum feasible misunderstanding*. New York: Free Press.

Moyse-Steinberg, D. (1990). A model for adolescent pregnancy prevention through the use of small groups. *Social Work with Groups, 13*, 57–68.

Munroe, R. H., Munroe, R. L., & Whiting, B. B. (1981). Preface. In R. H. Munore, R. L. Munroe, & B. B. Whiting (Eds.), *Handbook of cross-cultural development* (pp. ix–xiv). New York: Garland.

Murdock. G. (1967). *Social structure*. New York: Free Press.

Murphy, P. A. (1986–1987). Parental death in childhood and loneliness in young adults. *Omega, 17*, 219–228.

Murray, C. (1984). *Losing ground: American social policy, 1950–1980*. New York: Basic Books.

Murray, J. P. (1980). *Television and youth: 25 years of research and controversy*. Boys Town, NE: Boys Town Center for the Study of Youth and Development.

Murray, J. P. (1993). The developing child in a multimedia society. In G. L. Berry & J. K Asamen (Eds.), *Children and television: Images in a changing sociocultural world* (pp. 9–22). Newbury Park, CA: Sage.

Murray, J. P. & Kippax, S. (1977). Television diffusion and social behaviour in three communities: A field experiment. *Australian Journal of Psychology, 29*, 31–43.

Murray, J. P. & Kippax, S. (1978). Children's social behavior in three towns with differing television experience. *Journal of Communication, 28*, 19–29.

Murray, J. P., Rubenstein, E. A., & Comstock, G. A. (Eds.). (1972). *Television and social behavior. Vol. 2. Television and social learning*. Washington, DC: U.S. Government Printing Office.

Muuss, R. E. (1988). *Theories of adolescence* (5th ed.). New York: Random House.

Mwamwenda, T. S. & Mwamwenda, B. B. (1989). Formal operational thought among African and Canadian college students. *Psychological Reports, 64*, 43–46.

Nagy, P. & Griffiths, A. K. (1982). Limitations of recent relating Piaget's theory to adolescent thought. *Review of Educational Research, 52*, 513–556.

The National Adolescent Student Health Survey: A report on the health of America's youth. (1989). Oakland, CA: Third Party.

National Advisory Mental Health Council. (1990). *National plan for research on child and adolescent mental disorders*. Rockville, MD: National Institute of Mental Health.

National Center for Health Care Statistics. (1985). *Vital statistics of the United States*. Washington, DC: U.S. Government Printing Office.

National Center for Health Statistics. (1990a). *Prevention profile: Health, United States, 1989*. Hyattsville, MD: U.S. Department of Health and Human Services (DHHS Publication No. PHS 90–1232).

National Center for Health Statistics. (1990b). *Vital statistics of the United States: 1988. Vol. II— Mortality, Part B*. Hyattsville, MD: U.S. Government Printing Office.

National Center for Health Statistics. (1991). *Health, United States, 1990*. Hyattsville, MD: Public Health Service.

National Center for Health Statistics. (1992). *Health, United States, 1991*. Hyattsville, MD: Public Health Service.

National Center on Child Abuse and Neglect. (1988). *Study of national incidence and prevalence of child abuse and neglect: 1988*. Washington, DC: U.S. Department of Health and Human Services.

National Commission on Excellence in Education. (1983). *A nation at risk: The imperative for educational reform*. Washington, DC: U.S. Government Printing Office.

National Panel on High School and Adolescent Education. (1976). *The education of adolescents: The final report and recommendations of the National Panel on High School and Adolescent Education*. Washington, DC: U.S. Government Printing Office.

Neimark, E. D. (1983). Adolescent thought: Transition to formal operations. In B. B. Wolman, G. Stricker, S. J. Ellman, P. Keith-Spiegel, & D. S. Palermo (Eds.), *Handbook of developmental psychology* (pp. 486–502). Englewood Cliffs, NJ: Prentice-Hall.

Nelson, C. (1990, September). Harvard's hollow core. *The Atlantic Monthly, 266*, 70–80.

Nettlebeck, T. & Wilson, C. (1985). A cross-sequential analysis of developmental differences in speed of visual information processing. *Journal of Experimental Child Psychology, 40*, 1–22.

Newcomb, A. & Bukowski, W. (1983). Social impact and social preference as determinants of children's peer group status. *Developmental Psychology, 19*, 856–867.

Newcomb, M. D. (1984). Sexual behavior, responsiveness, and attitudes among women: A test of two theories. *Journal of Sexual Marital Therapy, 10*, 272–286.

Newcomb, M. D. & Bentler, P. M. (1989). Substance use and abuse among children and teenagers. *American Psychologist, 44,* 242–248.

Newcomb, M. D., Huba, G. J., & Bentler, P. M. (1986). Desirability of various life change events among adolescents: Effects of exposure, sex, age, and ethnicity. *Journal of Research in Personality, 20,* 207–217.

Nguyen, N. A. (1992). Living between two cultures: Treating first-generation Asian Americans. In L. A. Vargas & J. D. Koss-Chioino (Eds.), *Working with culture: Psychotherapeutic interventions with ethnic minority children and adolescents* (pp. 2042–222). San Francisco: Jossey-Bass.

Nisan, M. & Kohlberg, L. (1982). Universality and variation in moral judgment: A longitudinal and cross-sectional study in Turkey. *Child Development, 53,* 865–876.

Noblit, G. W. (1987). Ideological purity and variety in effective middle schools. In G. W. Noblit & W. T. Pink (Eds.), *Schooling in social context: Qualitative studies* (pp. 203–217). Norwood, NJ: Ablex.

Noller, P. & Callan, V. (1991). *The adolescent in the family.* London: Routledge & Kegan Paul.

Noshpitz, J. D. (1991). Disturbances in early adolescence. In S. I. Greenspan & G. H. Pollock (Eds.), *The course of life. Vol. IV. Adolescence* (pp. 119–180). Madison, WI: International Universities Press.

Nye, I. F. & Edelbrock, C. (1980). Some social characteristics of runaways. *Journal of Family Issues, 1,* 147–150.

Ockerman, J. D. (1979). *Self-esteem and social anchorage of adolescent white, black, and Mexican-American students.* Saratoga, CA: R & E.

Oden, S. & Asher, S. R. (1977). Coaching children in friendship making skills. *Child Development, 48,* 495–506.

Offer, D. (1969). *The psychological world of the teenager.* New York: Basic Books.

Offer, D. (1984). *The adolescent: A psychological self-portrait.* New York: Basic Books.

Offer, D. & Franzen, S. A. (1979). *Mood development in the normal adolescent.* Paper presented at the Conference on the Adolescent and Mood Disturbance, Toronto, Canada.

Offer, D. & Howard, K. I. (1972). An empirical analysis of the Offer Self-Image Questionnaire for Adolescents. *Archives of General Psychiatry, 27,* 529–537.

Offer, D. & Offer, J. B. (1975). *From teenage to young manhood: A psychological study.* New York: Basic Books.

Offer, D., Ostrov, E., & Howard, K. I. (1977a). *The Offer Self-Image Questionnaire for Adolescents: A manual.* Chicago: Michael Reese Hospital and Medical Center.

Offer, D., Ostrov, E., & Howard, K. I. (1977b). The self-image of adolescents: A study of four cultures. *Journal of Youth and Adolescence, 6,* 265–280.

Offer, D., Ostrov, E., & Howard, K. I. (1982). *The Offer Self-Image Questionnaire for Adolescents: A manual* (rev. ed.). Chicago: Michael Reese Hospital and Medical Center.

Offer, D., Ostrov, E., Howard, K. I., & Atkinson, R. (1988). *The teenage world: Adolescents' self-image in ten countries.* New York: Plenum.

Offer, D. & Sabshin, M. (1974). *Normality: Theoretical and clinical concepts of mental health* (rev. ed.). New York: Basic Books.

Offer, D., Sabshin, M., & Marcus, D. (1965). Clinical evaluation of normal adolescents. *American Journal of Psychiatry, 121,* 864–872.

Ogle, L. T., Alsalom, N., & Rogers, G. T. (1991). *The condition of education, 1991. Vol. 1. Elementary and secondary education.* Washington, DC: National Center for Education Statistics.

Okun, M. A. (1976). Adult age and cautiousness in decision: A review of the literature. *Human Development, 19,* 220–233.

Okwumabua, J. O. (1990). Child and adolescent substance abuse: Etiology and prevention. In S. B. Morgan & T. M. Okwumabua (Eds.), *Child and adolescent disorders: Developmental and health psychology perspectives* (pp. 395–427). Hillsdale, NJ: Erlbaum.

Oleckno, W. A. & Blacconiere, M. J. (1990). Wellness of college students and differences by gender, race, and class standing. *College Student Journal, 24,* 421–429.

Olsen, J. A., Jensen, L. C., & Greaves, P. M. (1991). Adolescent sexuality and public policy. *Adolescence, 26,* 419–430.

Olsen, J. A., Weed, S. E., Ritz, G. M., & Jensen, L. C. (1991). The effects of three abstinence sex education programs on student attitudes toward sexual activity. *Adolescence, 26,* 631–641.

Olson, D. H., McCubbin, H. I., Barnes, H. L., Larsen, A., Muxen, M. J., & Wilson, M. (1983). *Families: What makes them work?* Beverly Hills, CA: Sage.

Olson, D. H., Portner, D. S., & Bell, R. (1982). Family adaptability and cohesion evaluation scales. In D. H. Olson, H. I. McCubbin, H. L. Barnes, A. Larsen, M. J. Muxen, & M. Wilson, (Eds.), *Family inventories: Inventories used in a national survey of families across the family life cycle* (pp. 5–24). St. Paul, MN: Family Social Service, University of Minnesota.

Olson, D. H., Russell, C. S., & Sprenkle, D. H. (1983). Circumplex Model of marital and family systems: VI. Theoretical update. *Family Process, 22,* 69–83.

Olson, D. H., Sprenkle, D. H., & Russell, C. S. (1979). Circumplex Model of marital and family systems. I. Cohesion and adaptability dimensions, family types, and clinical applications, *Family Process, 18,* 3–28.

O'Malley, P. M., Bachman, J. G., & Johnston, J. (1977). *Youth in transition. Final report: Five years beyond high school: Causes and consequences of educational attainment.* Ann Arbor, MI: Institute for Social Research.

O'Neill, J. (1991). *Plato's cave: Desire, power, and the secular functions of the media.* Norwood, NJ: Ablex.

Orlofsky, J. L. (1978). Identity formation, achievement, and fear of success in college men and women. *Journal of Youth and Adolescence, 7,* 49–62.

Orlofsky, J. L., Marcia, J. E., & Lesser, I. M. (1973). Ego identity status and the intimacy versus isolation of young adulthood. *Journal of Personality and Social Psychology*, 27, 211–219.

Orr, E., Liran, E., & Meyer, J. (1986). Compulsory military service as a challenge and a threat: Attitudes of Israeli twelfth graders towards conscription. *Israeli Social Science Research*, 4, 5–20.

Osborn, J. (1971). *The paper chase*. New York: Warner Books.

Osterweis, M., Solomon, F., & Green, M. (1984). *Bereavement: Reactions, consequences, and care*. Washington, DC: The National Academy Press.

Ostrov, E. & Offer, D. (1978). Loneliness and the adolescent. In S. C. Feinstein & P. L. Giovacchini (Eds.), *Adolescent psychiatry: Developmental and clinical studies. Vol. VI* (pp. 34–50). Chicago, IL: University of Chicago Press.

Ostrov, E., Offer, D., & Hartlage, S. (1984). The quietly disturbed adolescent. In D. Offer, E. Ostrov, & K. I. Howard (Eds.), *Patterns of adolescent self-image* (pp. 73–81). San Francisco, CA: Jossey-Bass.

Ostrov, E., Offer, D., & Howard, K. I. (1986). Cross-cultural studies of sex differences in normal adolescents' self-image. *Hillside Journal of Clinical Psychiatry*, 8, 183–192.

Ostrov, E., Offer, D., & Howard, K. I. (1989). Gender differences in adolescent symptomatology: A normative study. *Journal of the American Academy of Child and Adolescent Psychiatry*, 28, 394–398.

Oustimenko, S. F. (1984). Interpersonal relations of difficult adolescents. *Voprosy Psikhologii*, 1, 27–33. (English abstract in PsycLit Database).

Padilla, E. R., Rohsenow, D. J., & Bergman, A. B. (1976). Predicting accident frequency in children. *Pediatrics*, 58, 223–226.

Padilla, F. M. (1992). *The gang as an American enterprise*. New Brunswick, NJ: Rutgers University Press.

Page, R. M. (1991). Loneliness as a risk factor in adolescent hopelessness. *Journal of Research in Personality*, 25, 189–195.

Paikoff, R. L. & Brooks-Gunn, J. (1990). Physiological processes: What role do they play during the transition to adolescence? In R. Montemayor, G. R. Adams, & T. P. Gullotta (Eds.), *From childhood to adolescence: A transitional period?* (pp. 63–81). Newbury Park, CA: Sage.

Paikoff, R. L., Brooks-Gunn, J., & Warren, M. P. (1991). Effects of girls' hormonal status on depressive and aggressive symptoms over the course of one year. *Journal of Youth and Adolescence*, 20, 191–215.

Palla, B. & Litt, I. F. (1988). Medical complications of eating disorders in adolescents. *Pediatrics*, 81, 159–162.

Pantell, R. H. & Goodman, B. W. (1983). Adolescent chest pain: A prospective study. *Pediatrics*, 71, 881–886.

Parad, H. J. (1965). *Crisis intervention: Selected readings*. New York: Family Service Association of America.

Pargament, K. I. (1988a, August). *Conceptualization and study of religion and coping*. In K. I. Pargament (Chair), *Investigations of religion and coping: Theoretical and empirical advances*. Symposium conducted at the meeting of the American Psychological Association, Atlanta, GA.

Pargament, K. I. (1988b, Summer). God help me: Towards a theoretical framework of coping for the psychology of religion. *Psychologists Interested in Religious Issues Newsletter*, 13(2), 1–6.

Parish, T. S. (1987). Family and environment. In V. B. Van Hasselt and M. Hersen (Eds.), *Handbook of adolescent psychology* (pp. 168–183). New York: Pergamon Press.

Parker, J. G. & Asher, S. R. (1987). Peer relations and later personal adjustment: Are low-accepted children at risk? *Psychological Bulletin*, 102, 357–389.

Parker, J. G. & Gottman, J. M. (1989). Social and emotional development in a relational context: Friendship interaction from early childhood to adolescence. In T. J. Berndt & G. W. Ladd (Eds.), *Peer relationships in child development* (pp. 95–131). New York: Wiley.

Parkhurst, J. T. & Asher, S. R. (1992). Peer rejection in middle school: Subgroup differences in behavior, loneliness, and interpersonal concerns. *Developmental Psychology*, 28, 231–241.

Parsons, T. (1959). Psycho-analysis and social structure. *Psychoanalytic Quarterly*, 19, 371–384.

Pascarella, E. T. (1989). The development of critical thinking: Does college make a difference? *Journal of College Student Development*, 30, 19–26.

Pascarella, E. T. & Terenzini, P. T. (1991). *How college affects students: Findings and insights from twenty years of research.* San Francisco, CA: Jossey-Bass.

Patterson, G. R., DeBaryshe, B. D., & Ramsey, E. (1989). Developmental perspective on antisocial behavior. *American Psychologist*, 44, 329–335.

Patterson, G. R. & Stouthamer-Loeber, M. (1984). The correlation of family management practices and delinquency. *Child Development*, 55, 1299–1307.

Patton, J. E., Routh, D. K., & Steinard, T. A. (1986). Where do children study? Behavioral observations. *Bulletin of the Psychonomic Society*, 24, 439–440.

Payne, S., Summers, D. A., & Stewart, T. R. (1973). Value differences across three generations. *Sociometry*, 36, 20–30.

Pearson, G. H. J. (1958). *Adolescence and the conflict of generations*. New York: Norton.

Pellegrini, D. S. (1985). Social cognition and competence in middle childhood. *Child Development*, 56, 253–264.

Perry, E. (1993, August 20). Abortion doctor shot. *The Kansas City Star*, 113(337), A1, A6.

Perry, W. G. (1970). *Forms of intellectual and ethical development during the college years*. New York: Holt, Rinehart & Winston.

Pertschuk, M., Collins, M., Kreisberg, J., & Fager, S. S. (1986). Psychiatric symptoms associated with eating disorders in a college population. *International Journal of Eating Disorders*, 5, 563–568.

Peskin, H. (1967). Pubertal onset and ego functioning. *Journal of Abnormal Psychology*, 72, 1–15.

Petersen, A. C. (1983). Menarche: Meaning of measure and measuring meaning. In S. Golub (Ed.), *Menarche* (pp. 63–76). New York: Heath.

Petersen, A. C. (1988). Adolescent development. In L. W. Porter & M. Rosenzweig (Eds.), *Annual Review of Psychology, 39*, 583–607.

Petersen, A. C. & Hamburg, B. A. (1986). Adolescence: A developmental approach to problems and psychopathology. *Behavior Therapy, 17*, 480–499.

Petersen, A. C. & Taylor, B. (1980). The biological approach to adolescence: Biological change and psychological adaptation. In J. Adelson (Ed.), *Handbook of adolescent psychology* (pp. 117–155). New York: Wiley.

Petersen, R. (1989). Rationality, ethnicity, and military enlistment. *Social Science Information, 28*, 563–598.

Peterson, J. L., Moore, K. A., & Furstenberg, F. F. (1984). *Television viewing and early initiation of sexual intercourse: Is there a link?* Paper presented at the annual meeting of the American Psychological Association, Toronto, Ontario, Canada.

Petti, T. A. & Larson, C. N. (1987). Depression and suicide. In V. B. Von Hasselt & M. Hersen (Eds.), *Handbook of adolescent psychology* (pp. 288–312). New York: Pergamon Press.

Pfeiffer, E. (1977). Psychopathology and social pathology. In J. E. Birren & K. Schaie (Eds.), *Handbook of psychology and aging*, (pp. 650–671). New York: Van Nostrand Reinhold.

Phinney, J. S. (1989). Stages of ethnic identity development in minority group adolescents. *Journal of Early Adolescence, 9*, 34–49.

Piaget, J. (1929). *The child's conception of the world.* London: Routledge & Kegan Paul.

Piaget, J. (1972). Intellectual evolution from adolescence to adulthood. *Human Development, 15*, 1–12.

Piaget, J. (1983). Piaget's theory. In P. H. Mussen (Ed.), *Handbook of child psychology. Vol. 1. History, theory, and methods.* New York: Wiley.

Pick-deweiss, S., Diaz-Loving, R., Andrade-Palos, P., & David, H. P. (1990). Effect of sex education on the sexual and contraceptive practices of female teenagers in Mexico City. *Journal of Psychology and Human Sexuality, 3*, 71–93.

Pitt, R. B. (1983). Development of a general problem-solving schema in adolescence and early adulthood. *Journal of Experimental Psychology General, 112*, 547–584.

Plato. (1960). *The Republic.* Translated by B. Jowett. In *The Republic and other works* (pp. 9–316). New York: Doubleday.

Pollak, S. & Gilligan, C. (1982). Images of violence in Thematic Apperception Test stories. *Journal of Personality and Social Psychology, 42*, 159–167.

Pope, H. G., Hudson, J. I., & Yurgelun-Todd, D. (1984). Anorexia nervosa and bulimia among 300 suburban women shoppers. *American Journal of Psychiatry, 141*, 292–293.

Poppen, P. J. (1974). *The development of sex differences in moral judgment for college males and females.* Unpublished doctoral dissertation, Cornell University, Ithaca, NY.

Potok, C. (1967). *The chosen.* New York: Simon & Schuster.

Powers, E. & Witmer, H. (1951). *An experiment in the prevention of delinquency: The Cambridge-Somerville youth study.* New York: Columbia University Press.

Quay, H. C. (Ed.). (1987). *Handbook of juvenile delinquency.* New York: Wiley.

Quint, J. (1991). Project Redirection: Making and measuring a difference. *Evaluation and Program Planning, 14*, 75–86.

Quintana, S. M. & Kerr, J. (1993). Relational needs in late adolescent separation-individuation. *Journal of Counseling and Development, 71*, 349–354.

Rabin, J. M., Seltzer, V., & Pollack, S. (1991). The long-term benefits of a comprehensive teenage pregnancy program. *Clinical Pediatrics, 30*, 305–309.

Rando, T. A. (1988). *Grieving: How to go on living when someone you love dies.* Lexington, MA: Lexington Books.

Ransom, J. W., Schlesinger, S., & Derdeyn, A. P. (1979). A stepfamily in formation. *American Journal of Orthopsychiatry, 49*, 36–43.

Rapaport, K. & Burkhart, B. R. (1984). Personality and attitudinal characteristics of sexually coercive college males. *Journal of Abnormal Psychology, 93*, 216–221.

Raphael, B. (1983). *The anatomy of bereavement.* New York: Basic Books.

Raphael, D. (1979). Sequencing in female adolescents' consideration of occupational, religious, and political alternatives. *Adolescence, 14*, 73–80.

Rappaport, J. (1977). *Community psychology: Values, research, and action.* New York: Holt, Rinehart & Winston.

Rees, J. M. & Trahms, C. M. (1989). Nutritional influences on physical growth and behavior in adolescence. In G. R. Adams, R. Montemayor, & T. P. Gullotta (Eds.,), *Biology of adolescent behavior and development* (pp. 195–222). Newbury Park, CA: Sage.

Reilly, B. A. and Falgout, K. (1988, August). *The ecology of religious coping.* In K. I. Pargament (Chair), *Investigations of religion and coping: Theoretical and empirical advances.* Symposium conducted at the meeting of the American Psychological Association, Atlanta, GA.

Reinhard, D. W. (1977). The reaction of adolescent boys and girls to the divorce of their parents. *Journal of Clinical Child Psychology, 6*, 21–23.

Renshaw, P. & Asher, S. (1983). Children's goals and strategies for social interaction. *Merrill-Palmer Quarterly, 29*, 353–374.

Resick, P. A., Jordan, C. G., Girelli, S. A., Hutter, C. K., & Marhoefer-Dvorak, S. (1988). A comparative outcome study of behavioral group therapy for sexual assault victims. *Behavior Therapy, 19*, 385–401.

Resnick, M. D., Blum, R. W., Bose, J., Smith, M., & Toogood, R. (1990). Characteristics of unmarried adolescent mothers: Determinants of child rearing versus adoption. *American Journal of Orthopsychiatry, 60*, 577–584.

Resnik, H. (Ed.). (1990). *Youth and drugs: Society's mixed messages.* Rockville, MD: Office of Substance Abuse Prevention (DHHS Publication No. ADM 90–1689).

Rest, J. (1968). *Developmental hierarchy in preference and comprehension of moral judgment.* Unpublished doctoral dissertation, University of Chicago, Chicago, IL.

Rest, J. (1986). *Moral development: Advances in research and theory.* New York: Praeger.

Rest, J., Power, C., & Brabeck, M. (1988). Lawrence Kohlberg (1927–1987). *American Psychologist, 43,* 399–400.

Rest, J., Turiel, E., & Kohlberg, L. (1969). Relations between level of moral judgment and preference and comprehension of the moral judgment of others. *Journal of Personality, 27,* 225–252.

Retter, L. K. (1991). *A conceptual model of religiosity, sex education, and sexual knowledge as predictors of the sexual intercourse attitudes and behaviors of adolescents.* Unpublished master's thesis, Kansas State University, Manhattan, KS.

Reynolds, E. L. (1951). The distribution of subcutaneous fat in childhood and adolescence. *Monographs of the Society for Research in Child Development, 15,* 1–189.

Reynolds, W. M. (1982). Development of reliable and valid short forms of the Marlowe-Crowne social desirability scale. *Journal of Clinical Psychology, 38,* 119–125.

Reynolds, W. M. (1984). Depression in children and adolescents: Phenomenology, evaluation, and treatment. *School Psychology Review, 13,* 171–182.

Rice, D. P., MacKenzie, E. J., & Associates. (1989). *Cost of injury in the United States: A report to Congress.* San Francisco, CA: Institute for Health and Aging.

Richardson, D. W. & Short, R. V. (1978). Time of onset of sperm production in boys. *Journal of Biosocial Science, 5,* 15–25.

Ricketts, M. (1989). Epistemological values of feminists in psychology. *Psychology of Women Quarterly, 13,* 401–415.

Rickgarn, R. L. V. (1983). *The issue is suicide.* Minneapolis, MN: University of Minnesota.

Rickgarn, R. L. (1987). The Death Response Team: Responding to the forgotten grievers. *Journal of Counseling and Development, 66,* 197–199.

Ritter, B. (1988). *Sometimes God has a kid's face: The story of America's exploited street kids.* New York: Covenant House.

Roberts, L. R., Sarigiani, P. A., & Petersen, A. C. (1990). Gender differences in the relationship between achievement and self-image during early adolescence. *Journal of Early Adolescence, 10,* 159–175.

Robins, L. N. (1966). *Deviant children grown up: A sociological and psychiatric study of sociopathic personality.* Baltimore: Williams & Wilkins.

Robinson, A. (1990). Does that describe me? Adolescents' acceptance of the gifted label. *Journal for the Education of the Gifted, 13,* 245–255.

Roche, A. F. (1976). Growth after puberty. In E. Fuchs (Ed.), *Youth in a changing world: Cross-cultural perspectives on adolescence* (pp. 17–53). The Hague, Netherlands: Mouton.

Rodgers, C. (1961). *On becoming a person.* Boston: Houghton Miflin. *American Psychologist, 34,* 231–239.

Rodin, G. M., Daneman, D., Johnson, L. E., Kenshole, A., & Garfinkel, P. (1985). Anorexia nervosa and bulimia in female adolescents with insulin dependent diabetes mellitus: A systematic study. *Journal of Psychiatric Research, 19,* 381–384.

Rodriguez, J. (1990). Childhood injuries in the United States. *American Journal of Diseases of Childhood, 144,* 627–646.

Roff, M., Sells, S. B., & Golden, M. M. (1972). *Social adjustment and personality development in children.* Minneapolis, MN: University of Minnesota Press.

Rolfes, S. R. & DeBruyne, L. K. (1990). *Life span nutrition: Conception through life.* St. Paul, MN: West.

Rook, K. Dooley, D., & Catalano, R. (1991). Age differences in workers' efforts to cope with economic distress. In J. Eckenrode (Ed.), *The social context of coping* (pp. 79–105). New York: Plenum.

Roscoe, B. & Callahan, J. E. (1985). Adolescents' self-report of violence in families and dating relations. *Adolescence, 20,* 545–553.

Roscoe, B., Goodwin, M. P., & Kennedy, D. (1987). Sibling violence and agonistic interactions experienced by early adolescents. *Journal of Family Violence, 2,* 121–137.

Rosenberg, M. (1965). *Society and the adolescent self image.* Princeton, NJ: Princeton University Press.

Rossi, P. H. (1989). *Down and out in America: The origins of homelessness.* Chicago: University of Chicago Press.

Rossi, P. H. & Freeman, H. E. (1989). *Evaluation: A systematic approach* (4th ed.). Newbury Park, CA: Sage.

Rotenberg, K. J. & Mann, L. (1986). The development of the norm of the reciprocity of self-disclosure and its function in children's attraction to peers. *Child Development, 57,* 1349–1357.

Rotenberg, K. J. and Sliz, D. (1988). Children's restrictive disclosure to friends. *Merrill-Palmer Quarterly, 34,* 203–215.

Rotter, J. B. (1966). Generalized expectancies for internal versus external control of reinforcement. *Psychological Monographs, 80* (1, Whole No. 609).

Rowe, D. C. & Rodgers, J. L. (1989). Behavioral genetics, adolescent deviance, and "d": Contributions and issues. In G. R. Adams, R. Montemayor, & T. P. Gullotta (Eds.), *Biology of adolescent behavior and development* (pp. 38–67). Newbury Park, CA: Sage.

Rowe, D. C. & Rodgers, J. L. (1991). An "epidemic" model of adolescent sexual intercourse: Applications to national survey data. *Journal of Biosocial Science, 23,* 211–219.

Rubin, K. H., Hymel, S., & Mills, R. S. (1989). Sociability and social withdrawal in childhood: Stability and outcomes. *Journal of Personality, 57,* 237–255.

Ruggiero, M., Greenberger, E., & Steinberg, L. (1982). Occupational deviance among first-time workers. *Youth and Society, 13,* 423–448.

Rule, A. (1980). *The stranger beside me.* New York: Norton.

Russell, C. S. (1979). Circumplex Model of marital and family systems. III. Empirical evaluation with families. *Family Process, 18,* 29–45.

Russell, D. H. (1984). *Sexual exploitation: Rape, child sexual abuse, and sexual harassment.* Beverly Hills, CA: Sage.

Russell, G. F. M. (1979). Bulimia nervosa: An ominous variant of anorexia nervosa. *Psychological Medicine, 9,* 429–448.

Russo, T. S. (1991). *Factors influencing parents to discuss general and specific sexuality with their adolescent children.* Unpublished doctoral dissertation, Kansas State University, Manhattan, KS.

Russo, T. S., Barnes, H. L., & Wright, D. W. (1991). *Parental factors influencing parent-child communication about sexuality: Role differences between mothers and fathers.* Manuscript submitted for publication.

Rutter, M. (1975). *Helping troubled children.* New York: Plenum.

Rutter, M. (1983). Stress, coping, and development: Some issues and some questions. In N. Garmezy & M. Rutter (Eds.), *Stress, coping, and development in children* (pp. 1–41). New York: McGraw-Hill.

Rutter, M. (1990). Psychosocial resilience and protective mechanisms. In J. Rolf, A. S. Masten, D. Cicchetti, K. H. Nuechterlein, & S. Weintraub (Eds.), *Risk and protective factors in the development of psychopathology* (pp. 181–214). Cambridge, England: Cambridge University Press.

Rutter, M. & Garmezy, N. (1983). In E. M. Hetherington (Ed.), P. H. Mussen (Series Ed.), *Handbook of child psychology, Vol. IV. Socialization, personality, and social development* (pp. 775–911). New York: Wiley.

Rutter, M., Graham, P., Chadwick, O. F., & Yule, W. (1976). Adolescent turmoil: Fact or fiction? *Journal of Child Psychology and Psychiatry and Allied Disciplines, 17,* 35–56.

Ryan, C. M. (1990). Age-related improvement in short-term memory efficiency during adolescence. *Developmental Neuropsychology, 6,* 193–205.

Ryan, G. (1991a). Incidence and prevalence of sexual offenses committed by juveniles. In G. D. Ryan & S. L. Lane (Eds.), *Juvenile sexual offending: Causes, consequences, and correction* (pp. 9–15). Lexington, MA: Lexington Books.

Ryan, G. (1991b). Juvenile sex offenders: Defining the population. In G. D. Ryan & S. L. Lane (Eds.), *Juvenile sexual offending: Causes, consequences, and correction* (pp. 3–8). Lexington, MA: Lexington Books.

Ryan, W. (1971). *Blaming the victim.* New York: Random House.

Ryle, G. (1949). *The concept of mind.* London: Hutchinson.

Saladino, T. (1993, February 12). Teen accused of slaying his family one by one. *The Topeka Capital-Journal, 119*(104), 7B.

Sampson, R. J. & Laub, J. H. (1990). Crime and deviance over the life course: The salience of adult social bonds. *American Sociological Review, 55,* 609–627.

Savin-Williams, R. C. & Weisfeld, G. E. (1989). An ethological perspective on adolescence. In G. R. Adams, R. Montemayor, & T. P. Gullotta (Eds.,), *Biology of adolescent behavior and development* (pp. 249–274). Newbury Park, CA: Sage.

Scalf-McIver, L. & Thompson, J. K. (1989). Family correlates of bulimic characteristics in college females. *Journal of Clinical Psychology, 45,* 467–472.

Schave, D. & Schave, B. (1989). *Early adolescence and the search for self.* Westport, CT: Greenwood.

Schenkel, S. (1975). Relationship among ego identity status, field-independence, and traditional femininity. *Journal of Youth and Adolescence, 4,* 73–82.

Schiamberg, L. B. (1988). *Child and adolescent development.* New York: Macmillan.

Schlegel, A. & Barry, H. (1991). *Adolescence: An anthropological inquiry.* New York: The Free Press.

Schleidinger, S. (1984). The adolescent peer group revisited: Turbulence or adaptation? *Small Group Behavior, 15,* 387–397.

Schlundt, D. G. & Johnson, W. G. (1990). *Eating disorders: Assessment and treatment.* Boston, MA: Allyn & Bacon.

Schneider, S. (1986, April). Abortion clinic bombing: The war on sex. *Mademoiselle, 92,* 172–173+.

Schramm, W., Lyle, J., & Parker, E. B. (1961). *Television in the lives of our children.* Stanford, CA: Stanford University Press.

Schreiber, F. R. (1973). *Sybil.* Chicago: Regnery.

Schultz, N. R., Kaye, D. B., & Hoyer, W. J. (1980). Intelligence and spontaneous flexibility in adulthood and old age. *Intelligence, 4,* 219–231.

Scott, D. (1988). *Anorexia and bulimia nervosa: Practical approaches.* London, England: Croom Helm.

Sears, J. T. (1991). *Growing up gay in the South: Race, gender, and journeys of the spirit.* New York: The Haworth Press.

Sebes, J. M. (1986). Defining high risk. In J. Garbarino, C. J. Schellenbach, & J. M. Sebes, (Eds.), *Troubled youth, troubled families: Understanding families at-risk for adolescent maltreatment* (pp. 83–120). New York: Aldine.

Seligman, M. E. P. (1975). *Helplessness: On depression, development, and death.* San Francisco: W. H. Freeman.

Selman, R. L. (1976). Social-cognitive understanding: A guide to educational and clinical practice. In T. Lickona (Ed.), *Moral development and behavior: Theory, research, and social issues* (pp. 299–316). New York: Holt, Rinehart & Winston.

Selman, R. L. (1979, October). Children's ideas about friendship: A new theory. *Psychology Today,* 70–80, 114.

Selman, R. L. (1980). *The growth of interpersonal understanding: Developmental and clinical analyses.* New York: Academic Press.

Selman, R. L. (1981). The child as a friendship philosopher. In S. R. Asher & J. M Gottman (Eds.), *The development of children's friendships* (pp. 242–272). New York: Cambridge University Press.

Selman, R. L. & Schultz, L. H. (1990). *Making a friend in youth: Developmental theory and pair therapy.* Chicago, IL: The University of Chicago Press.

Seyle, H. (1982). History and present status of the stress concept. In L. Goldberger & S. Breznitz (Eds.), *Handbook of stress: Theoretical and clinical aspects* (pp. 7–17). New York: The Free Press.

Shaffer, D. (1986). Developmental factors in child and adolescent suicide. In M. Rutter, C. E. Izard, & P. B. Reed (Eds.), *Depression in young people: Clinical and developmental perspectives* (pp. 383–398). New York: Guilford Press.

Shaffer, D. & Fisher, P. (1981). The epidemiology of suicide in children and adolescents. *Journal of the American Academy of Child Psychiatry, 20,* 545–565.

Shaffer, D. R. (1989). *Developmental psychology: Childhood and adolescence* (2nd ed.). Pacific Grove, CA: Brooks/Cole.

Shain, L. & Farber, B. A. (1989). Female identity development and self-reflection in late adolescence. *Adolescence, 24,* 381–392.

Shantz, C. U. & Hobart, C. J. (1989). Social conflict and development: Peers and siblings. In T. J. Berndt & G. W. Ladd (Eds.), *Peer relationships in child development* (pp. 95–131). New York: Wiley.

Shatan, C. F. (1977). Bogus manhood, bogus honor: Surrender and transfiguration in the United States Marine Corps. *Psychoanalytic Review, 64,* 585–610.

Shaw, M. & Riley, D. (1989). Working towards clearer definitions: A national self-report study of teenage boys and girls in England and Wales. In M. W. Klein (Ed.), *Cross-national research in self-reported crime and delinquency* (pp. 67–87). Dordecht, Netherlands: Kluwer Academic Publishers.

Shedler, J. & Block, J. (1990). Adolescent drug use and psychological health: A longitudinal inquiry. *American Psychologist, 45,* 612–650.

Sher, K. J. & Alterman, A. I. (1988). The HK/MBD questionnaire: Replication and validation of distinct factors in a nonclinical sample. *Alcoholism: Clinical and Experimental Research, 12,* 233–238.

Shock, N. W. (1977). System integration. In C. E. Finch & L. Hayflick (Eds.), *Handbook of the biology of aging* (pp. 639–665). New York: Van Nostrand Reinhold.

Short, J. F. (1990). *Delinquency and society.* Englewood Cliffs, NJ: Prentice-Hall.

Siegler, R. S. (1989). Mechanisms of cognitive development. In M. S. Rosenzweig & L. W. Porter (Eds.), *Annual Review of Psychology, 40,* 353–379.

Silberman, C. E. (1978). *Criminal violence, criminal justice.* New York: Vintage Books.

Silberman, C. S. (1971). *Crisis in the classroom: The remaking of American education.* New York: Vintage Books.

Silbert, M. & Pines, A. (1981). *Runaway prostitutes.* San Francisco: Delancey Street Foundation. (unpublished manuscript)

Silver, R. C. & Wortman, C. B. (1980). Coping with undesirable life events. In J. Gardner & M. E. P. Seligman (Eds.), *Human helplessness: Theory and applications* (pp. 279–340). New York: Academic Press.

Silverman, L. K. (1986a). An interview with Elizabeth Hagen: Giftedness, intelligence, and the new Stanford-Binet. *Roeper Review, 8,* 168–171.

Silverman, L. K. (1986b). The IQ controversy: Conceptions and misconceptions. *Roeper Review, 8,* 136–140.

Silverman, P. R. (1980). *Mutual help groups: Organization and development.* Beverly Hills, CA: Sage.

Simmons, R. G. & Blyth, D. A. (1987). *Moving into adolescence: The impact of pubertal change and social context.* New York: A. deGruyter.

Simms, M. (1985). The participation of young women in employment and training programs. In C. L. Betsey, R. G. Hollister, & M. R. Papageorgiou (Eds.), *Youth employment and training programs: The YEDPA years* (pp. 462–485). Washington, DC: National Academy Press.

Simms, M. C. & Leitch, M. L. (1983). *Determinants of youth participation in employment and training programs with a special focus on young women.* Washington, DC: The Urban Institute.

Sinclair, D. (1978). *Human growth during adolescence.* New York: Oxford University Press.

Singh, A. (1984). The girls who run away from home. *Child Psychiatry Quarterly, 17,* 1–18.

Siri, W. K. (1956). The gross composition of the body. In J. H. Lawrence & C. A. Tobias (Eds.), *Advances in biological and medical physics Vol. IV* (pp. 239–280). New York: Academic Press.

Skinner, B. F. (1957). *Verbal behavior.* New York: Appleton-Century-Crofts.

Skinner, B. F. (1990). Can psychology be a science of mind? *American Psychologist, 45,* 1206–1210.

Sklansky, M. A. (1991). The pubescent years: Eleven to fourteen. In S. I. Greenspan & G. H. Pollock (Eds.), *The course of life. Vol. IV. Adolescence* (pp. 63–97). Madison, WI: International Universities Press.

Sklar, F. & Hartley, S. F. (1987). *Bereavement patterns in a "hidden" population.* Paper presented at the annual conference of the American Sociological Association, New York.

Sklar, F. & Hartley, S. F. (1990). Close friends as survivors: Bereavement patterns in a "hidden" population. *Omega, 21,* 103–112.

Slaby, R. (1994). Reduction and prevention of violence. In L. Eron & J. Gentry (Eds.), *Violence and youth: Psychology's response. Vol. II. Papers of the American Psychological Association on Violence and Youth.* Washington, DC: APA.

Small, M. Y. (1990). *Cognitive development.* San Diego, CA: Harcourt Brace Jovanovich.

Smith, H. (1989). *Religions of man.* New York: HarperCollins.

Snarey, J. R. (1985). Cross-cultural universality of social-moral development: A critical review of Kohlbergian research. *Psychology Bulletin, 97,* 202–232.

Snarey, J. R., Reimer, J., & Kohlberg, L. (1985). Development of social-moral reasoning among kibbutz adolescents: A longitudinal cross-cultural study. *Developmental Psychology, 21,* 3–17.

Snow, C. P. (1963). *The two cultures: And a second look.* London: Cambridge University Press.

Snow, C. P. (1970). *Last things.* London: Macmillan.

Snyder, J. & Patterson, G. R. (1986). The effects of consequences on patterns of social interaction: A quasi-experimental approach to reinforcement in natural interactions. *Child Development, 57,* 1257–1268.

Snyder, J. & Patterson, G. R. (1987). Family interaction and delinquent behavior. In H. C. Quay (Ed.), *Handbook of juvenile delinquency* (pp. 216–243). New York: Wiley.

Snyder, S. (1991). Movies and juvenile delinquency: An overview. *Adolescence, 26,* 121–132.

Solderman, A. K., Greenberg, B. S., & Linsangan, R. (1988). Television and movie behaviors of pregnant and non-pregnant adolescents. *Journal of Adolescent Research, 3,* 153–170.

Sorenson, S. & Bowie, P. (1994). Vulnerable populations: Girls and young women. In L. Eron & J. Gentry (Eds.), *Violence and youth: Psychology's response. Vol. II. Papers of the American Psychological Association on Violence and Youth.* Washington, DC: APA.

Soriano, F. I. (1994). Vulnerable populations: Hispanics. In L. Eron & J. Gentry (Eds.), *Violence and youth: Psychology's response. Vol. II. Papers of the American Psychological Association on Violence and Youth.* Washington, DC: APA.

Spearman, C. (1904). "General intelligence" objectively determined and measured. *American Journal of Psychology, 15,* 210–293.

Spence, J. T. & Helmreich, R. L. (1978). *Masculinity and femininity: Their psychological dimensions, correlates, and antecedents.* Austin, TX: University of Texas Press.

Spence, J. T., Helmreich, R. L., & Holahan, C. R. (1979). Negative and positive components of psychological masculinity and femininity and their relationships to neurotic and acting out behaviors. *Journal of Personality and Social Psychology, 37,* 1673–1682.

Spergel, I. A., Ross, R. E., Curry, G. D., & Chance, R. (1989). *Youth gangs: Problem and response.* Washington, DC: Office of Juvenile Justice an Delinquency Prevention.

Spillane-Greco, E. (1984a). Characteristics of a helpful relationship: A study of empathic understanding and positive regard between runaways and their parents. *Adolescence, 19,* 63–75.

Spillane-Greco, E. (1984b). Feelings and perceptions of parents of runaways. *Child Welfare, 63,* 159–166.

Sprinthall, N. A. & Collins, W. A. (1988). *Adolescent psychology: A developmental view.* New York: Random House.

Stake, R. E. (1967). The countenance of educational evaluation. *Teachers College Record, 68,* 523–540.

Stake, R. E. (1978). The case study method in social inquiry. *Educational Researcher, 7,* 5–8.

Stake, R. E. (1986). *Quieting reform.* Urbana: University of Illinois Press.

Stake, R. E. (1987). An evolutionary view of programming staff development. In M. F. Wideen & I. Andrews (Eds.), *Staff development for school improvement: A focus on the teacher* (pp. 55–69). New York: The Falmer Press.

Stake, R. E., Raths, J., Denny, T., Stenzel, N., & Hoke, G. (1986). *Final report: Evaluation study of the Indiana Department of Education gifted and talented program.* Champaign, Il: Center for Instructional Research and Curriculum Evaluation.

Stake, R. E. & Trumbull, D. (1982). Naturalistic generalizations. *Review Journal of Philosophy and Social Sciences, 7,* 1–12.

Stamford, B. A. (1972). Physiological effects of training upon institutionalized geriatric men. *Journal of Gerontology, 27,* 451–455.

Stanley, L. A. (1992). *Rap: The lyrics.* New York: Penguin.

Staton, A. Q. & Oseroff-Varnell, D. (1990). Becoming a middle school student. In A. Q. Staton, *Communication and student socialization* (pp. 72–99). Norwood, NJ: Ablex.

Stcyznski, L. E. & Langlois, J. H. (1977). The effects of familiarity on behavioral stereotypes associated with physical attractiveness in young children. *Child Development, 48,* 1137–1141.

Stein, S. P. & Charles, E. (1971). Emotional factors in juvenile diabetes mellitus: A study of early life experiences of adolescent diabetics. *American Journal of Psychiatry, 128,* 56–60.

Steinberg, D. (1983). *The clinical psychiatry of adolescence.* New York: Wiley.

Steinberg, L. (1981). Transformations in family relations at puberty. *Developmental Psychology, 17,* 833–840.

Steinberg, L. (1986). Latchkey children and susceptibility to peer pressure: An ecological analysis. *Developmental Psychology, 22,* 435–439.

Steinberg, L. (1988). Reciprocal relation between parent-child distance and pubertal maturation. *Developmental Psychology, 24,* 1–7.

Steinberg, L. (1989). Pubertal maturation and parent-adolescent distance: An evolutionary perspective. In G. R. Adams, R. Montemayor, & T. P. Gullotta (Eds.), *Biology of adolescent behavior and development* (pp. 71–97). Newbury Park, CA: Sage.

Steinberg, L. & Dornbusch, S. M. (1991). Negative correlates of part-time employment during adolescence: Replication and elaboration. *Developmental Psychology, 27,* 304–313.

Steinberg, L. D., Greenberger, E., Garduque, L., & McAuliffe, S. (1982). High-school students in the labor force: some costs and benefits to schooling and learning. *Educational Evaluation and Policy Analysis, 4,* 363–372.

Steinberg, L. D., Greenberger, E., Garduque, L., Ruggiero, M., & Vaux, A. (1982). Effects of working on adolescent development. *Developmental Psychology, 18,* 385–395.

Steinberg, L. D., Greenberger, E., Jacobi, M., & Garduque, L. (1981). Early work experience: A partial antidote for adolescent egocentrism. *Journal of Youth and Adolescence, 10,* 141–157.

Steinberg, L., Greenberger, E., Vaux, A., & Ruggiero, M. (1981). Effects of early work experience on adolescent occupational socialization. *Youth and Society, 12,* 403–422.

Steinberg, L. D. & Silverberg, S. (1986). The vicissitudes of autonomy in early adolescence. *Child Development, 57,* 841–851.

Sternberg, R. J. (1979). The nature of mental abilities. *American Psychologist, 34,* 214–230.

Sternberg, R. J. (1984). Mechanisms of cognitive growth: A componential approach. In R. J. Sternberg (Ed.), *Mechanisms* of cognitive development (pp. 163–186). New York: W. H. Freeman.

Sternberg, R. J. (1986). Identifying the gifted through IQ: Why a little bit of knowledge is a dangerous thing. *Roeper Review, 8,* 143–147.

Sternberg, R. J. (1988). Intellectual development: Psychometric and information-processing approaches. In M. H. Bornstein & M. E. Lamb (Eds.), *Developmental psychology: An advanced textbook* (pp. 261–295). Hillsdale, NJ: Erlbaum.

Sternberg, R. J., Conway, B. E., Ketron, J. L., & Bernstein, M. (1981). People's conceptions of intelligence. *Journal of Personality and Social Psychology: Attitudes and Social Cognition, 41,* 37–55.

Sternberg, R. J. & Downing, C. (1982). The development of higher order reasoning in adolescence. *Child Development, 53,* 209–221.

Sternberg, R. J. & Powell, J. S. (1983). The development of intelligence. In J. H. Flavell & E. M. Markman (Eds.), P. H. Mussen (Series Editor), *Handbook of child psychology. Vol. III. Cognitive development* (pp. 341–419). New York: Wiley.

Sternberg, R. J. & Rifkin, B. (1979). The development of analogical reasoning processes. *Journal of Experimental Child Psychology, 27,* 195–232.

Stokes, G. (1985). The social profile. In R. Coles & G. Stokes, *Sex and the American teenager* (pp. 31–144). New York: Harper & Row.

Stone, L. J. & Church, J. (1973). *Childhood and adolescence* (3rd ed.). New York: Random House.

Storr, A. (1988). *Solitude: A return to the self.* New York: The Free Press.

Strauss, A. L. & Corbin, J. (1990). *Basics of qualitative research: Grounded theory procedures and techniques.* Newbury Park, CA: Sage.

Strauss, C. C. & Lahey, B. B. (1987). Anxiety. In V. B. Von Hasselt & M. Hersen (Eds.), *Handbook of adolescent psychology* (pp. 332–350). New York: Pergamon Press.

Streitmatter, J. L. (1989). Identity development and academic achievement in early adolescence. *Journal of Early Adolescence, 9,* 99–111.

Streitmatter, J. L. & Pate, G. S. (1989). Identity status development and cognitive prejudice in early adolescents. *Journal of Early Adolescence, 9,* 142–152.

Strober, M., Green, J., & Carlson, G. (1981). Utility of the Beck Depression Inventory with psychiatrically hospitalized adolescents. *Journal of Affective Disorders, 3,* 281–290.

Strong, B. & DeVault, C. (1989). *The marriage and family experience.* (4th ed.). St. Paul, MN: West.

Stuart, H. C. (1946). Normal growth and development during adolescence. *New England Journal of Medicine, 234,* 666–672, 693–700, 732–738.

Sullivan, H. S. (1953). *The interpersonal theory of psychiatry.* New York: Norton.

Sullivan, K. & Sullivan, A. (1980). Adolescent-parent separation. *Developmental Psychology, 16,* 93–99.

Super, D. E. (1957a). *The psychology of careers.* New York: Harper & Row.

Super, D. E. (1957b). *Vocational development: A framework for research.* New York: Columbia University.

Suppe, F. (1977). Afterword—1977. In F. Suppe (Ed.), *The structure of scientific theories* (pp. 617–730). Urbana, IL: University of Illinois Press.

Szmulker, G. I., Eisler, I., Gillies, C., & Hayward, M. E. (1985). The implications of anorexia nervosa in a ballet school. *Journal of Psychiatric Research, 19,* 177–181.

Tanner, J. M. (1962). *Growth at adolescence.* Oxford, England: Blackwell Scientific Publications.

Taschler, J. (1993a, January 31). An ounce of prevention. *The Topeka Capital-Journal, 119*(92), 1A–2A.

Taschler, J. (1993b, February 2). Ex-gang member joins other side. *The Topeka Capital-Journal, 119*(94), 1A–2A.

Taschler, J. (1993c, February 3). Gang members don't like being hassled, police learn. *The Topeka Capital-Journal, 119*(95), 1A-2A.

Taschler, J. (1993d, February 2). Mind-set of gangs: No remorse. *The Topeka Capital-Journal, 119*(94), 1A-2A.

Task Force on Education of Young Adolescents. (1989). *Turning points: Preparing American youth for the 21st century.* Washington, DC: Carnegie Council on Adolescent Development.

Teens believe "no" means "yes." (1992, November 25). *Manhattan Mercury, 84*(249), C3.

Terenzini, P. T. & Pascarella, E. T. (1994). Living with myths: Undergraduate education in America. *Change, 26*(1), 28–32.

Teri, L. (1981). The use of the BDI with adolescents. *Journal of Abnormal Child Psychology, 10,* 277–284.

Terman, L. M. & Oden, M. H. (1947). *The gifted child grows up: Twenty-five years follow-up of a superior group.* Stanford, CA: Stanford University Press.

Terman, L. M. & Oden, M. H. (1959). *The gifted group at midlife: Thirty-five years follow-up of the superior group, genetic studies of genius.* Stanford, CA: Stanford University Press.

Thissen, D., Bock, R., Wainer, H., & Roche, A. (1976). Individual growth in stature: A comparison of four growth studies in the USA. *Annals of Human Biology, 3,* 529–542.

Thornburg, H. D. (1975). *Development in adolescence.* Monterey, CA: Brooks/Cole.

Thornburg, H. D. (1980). Early adolescents: Their developmental characteristics. *The High School Journal, 63,* 215–221.

Thornton, J. L. (1991). Permanency planning for children in kinship foster homes. *Child Welfare, LXX,* 593–601.

Thurstone, L. L. (1938). *Primary mental abilities.* Chicago, IL: University of Chicago Press.

Tinklenberg, J. R. & Ochberg, F. M. (1981). Patterns of adolescent violence: A California sample. In D. Hamburg & M. Trudeau (Eds.), *Biobehavioral aspects of aggression* (pp. 121–140). New York: Liss.

Tisak, M. S., Tisak, J., & Rogers, M. J. (1989, March). *The influence of social rules on children's and adolescents' concepts of peer relations.* Paper presented at the Biennial Meeting of the Society for Research in Child Development, Kansas City, MO. (ERIC Documentation Reproduction No. ED 312075.)

Tobin-Richards, M.H., Boxer, A. M., & Petersen, A. C. (1983). The psychological significance of pubertal change: Sex differences in perceptions of self during early adolescence. In J. Brooks-Gunn & A. C. Petersen (Eds.), *Girls at puberty: Biological and psychological perspectives* (pp. 127–154). New York: Plenum.

Tomko, T. N. & Ennis, R. H. (1979). *Evaluation of informal logic competence: Rational Thinking Reports No. 3*. Urbana, IL: Bureau of Educational Research.

Toulmin, S. E. (1961). *Foresight and understanding*. London: Hutchinson.

Toulmin, S. E. & Goodfield, J. (1962). *The architecture of matter*. New York: Harper & Row.

Trimble, J. E. (1992). A cognitive-behavioral approach to drug abuse prevention and intervention with American Indian youth. In L. A. Vargas & J. D. Koss-Chioino (Eds.), *Working with culture: Psychotherapeutic interventions with ethnic minority children and adolescents* (pp. 246–275). San Francisco: Jossey-Bass.

Trojanowicz, R. C. & Morash, M. (1992). *Juvenile delinquency: Concepts and control* (5th ed.). Englewood Cliffs, NJ: Prentice-Hall.

Turley, J. M. & Derdeyn, A. P. (1990). Use of a horror film in psychotherapy. *Journal of the American Academy of Child and Adolescent Psychiatry, 29*, 942–945.

Turner, S. M. & Mo, L. (1984). Chinese adolescents' self-concept as measured by the Offer Self-Image Questionnaire for Adolescents. *Journal of Youth and Adolescence, 13*, 131–143.

Tusin, L. & Pascarella, E. T. (1985). The influence of college on women's choice of teaching as a career. *Research in Higher Education, 22*, 115–134.

Tyler, R. W. (1942). General statement on evaluation. *Journal of Educational Research, 35*, 492–501.

Unger, R. K. (1988). Psychological, feminist, and personal epistemology: Transcending contradiction. In M. Mccanney Gergen (Ed.), *Feminist thought and the structure of knowledge* (pp. 124–141). New York: New York University Press.

Unger, R. K. (Ed.). (1989). *Representations: Social constructions of gender*. Amityville, NY: Baywood.

Unger, R. K. (1990). Imperfect reflections of reality: Psychology constructs reality. In R. T. Hare-Mustin & J. Marecek (Eds.), *Making a difference: Psychology and the construction of gender* (pp. 102–149). New Haven, CT: Yale University Press.

Unger, R. K. & Crawford, M. E. (1992). *Women and gender: A feminist psychology*. Philadelphia, PA: Temple University Press.

Urberg, K. A., Cheng, C. & Shyu, S. (1991). Grade changes in peer influence on adolescent cigarette smoking: A comparison of two measures. *Addictive Behaviors, 16*, 21–28.

U.S. Bureau of the Census. (1989). *Statistical abstract of the United States, 1989*. Washington, DC: U.S. Government Printing Office.

U.S. Commission on Civil Rights. (1986). *Recent activities against citizens and residents of Asian descent*. Washington, DC: U.S. Government Printing Office.

U.S. Commission on Civil Rights. (1992). *Civil rights issues facing Asian Americans in the 1990s*. Washington, DC: U.S. Government Printing Office.

Vachon, M., Sheldon, A. R., Lancee, W. J., Lyall, W. A., Rogers, J., & Freeman, S. (1982). Correlations of enduring stress patterns following bereavement: Social network, life interaction, and personality. *Psychological Medicine, 12*, 783–788.

Vaillant, G. E. (1977). *Adaptation to life*. Boston: Little, Brown.

Van Scotter, R. D. (1991). *Public schooling in America: A reference handbook*. Santa Barbara, CA: ABC-CLIO.

VanderMeulen, K. & Warren, R. K. (1988, August). *The complexities of religion and coping*. In K. I. Pargament (Chair), *Investigations of religion and coping: Theoretical and empirical advances*. Symposium conducted at the meeting of the American Psychological Association, Atlanta, GA.

Vaz, E. W. (1965). Middle-class adolescents: Self-reported delinquency and youth culture activities. *Canadian Review of Sociology and Anthropology, 2*, 52–70.

Vernon, M. E. L. (1991). Life-style, risk taking, and out-of-control behavior. In W. R. Hendee (Ed.), *The health of adolescents: Understanding and facilitating biological, behavioral, and social development* (pp. 162–180). San Francisco, CA: Jossey-Bass.

Vernon, P. E. (1971). *The structure of human abilities*. London: Methuen.

Vinovskis, M. A. (1988). *An "epidemic" of adolescent pregnancy? Some historical and policy considerations*. New York: Oxford University Press.

Visher, E. & Visher, J. (1979). *Stepfamilies: A guide to working with stepparents and stepchildren*. New York: Brunner/Mazel.

Volosinov, V. N. (1976). *Freudianism: A Marxist critique*. (I. R. Titunik, Trans.; N. H. Bruss, Ed.). New York: Academic Press.

Von Rad, G. (1962). *Old Testament theology* (Vols. 1–2). (D. M. G. Stalker, Trans.). London: Oliver and Boyd.

Voydanoff, P. & Donnelly, B. W. (1991). *Adolescent sexuality and pregnancy*. Newbury Park, CA: Sage.

Wakerman, E. (1984). *Father loss: Daughters discuss the man that got away*. Garden City, NY: Doubleday.

Walker, A. (1982). *The color purple: A novel*. New York: Harcourt Brace Jovanovich.

Walker, L. J. (1984). Sex differences in the development of moral reasoning: A critical review. *Child Development, 55*, 677–691.

Walker, L. J. (1986). Sex differences in the development of moral reasoning: A rejoinder to Baumrind. *Child Development, 57*, 522–526.

Walker, L. J. (1989). A longitudinal study of moral reasoning. *Child Development, 60*, 157–166.

Wallerstein, J. S. (1986). Children of divorce: The psychological tasks of the child. In R. H. Moos (Ed.), *Coping with life crises: An integrated approach* (pp. 35–48). New York: Plenum. (Reprinted from *Journal of Social Issues*, 1979. *35*, 97–111)

Wallerstein, J. S., Corbin, S. B., & Lewis, J. M. (1988). Children of divorce: A 10-year study. In E. M. Hetherington & J. D. Arasteh (Eds.), *Impact of divorce, single parenting, and stepparenting on children* (pp. 197–214). Hillsdale, NJ: Erlbaum.

Wallerstein, J. S. & Kelly, J. B. (1974). The effects of parental divorce: The adolescent experience. In E. Anthony & A. Koupernik (Eds.), *The child in his family: Children as a psychiatric risk.* (Vol. 3, pp. 479–505). New York: Wiley.

Ward, M. & Lewko, J. H. (1987). Adolescents in families adopting older children: Implications for service. *Child Welfare, 66,* 539–547.

Ward, M. & Lewko, J. H. (1988). Problems experienced by adolescents already in families that adopt older children. *Adolescence, 23,* 221–228.

Warner, J. (1993, May/June). The assassination of Dr. Gunn: Scare tactics turn deadly. *Ms., 3,* 86–87.

Warren, K. C. & Johnson, R. W. (1989). Family environment, affect, ambivalence and decisions about unplanned adolescent pregnancy. *Adolescence, 24,* 505–522.

Warren, M. P. (1983). Physical and biological aspects of puberty. In J. Brooks-Gunn & A. C. Petersen (Eds.), *Girls at puberty: Biological and psychosocial perspectives* (pp. 3–28). New York: Plenum.

Watanabe, H. K. (1985). A survey of adolescent military family members' self-image. *Journal of Youth and Adolescence, 14,* 99–107.

Waterman, A. S. (1982). Identity development from adolescence to adulthood: An extension of theory and a review of research. *Developmental Psychology, 18,* 341–358.

Waterman, A. S. (1985). Identity in the context of adolescent psychology. In A. S. Waterman (Ed.), *Identity in adolescence: Processes and contents* (pp. 5–24). San Francisco, CA: Jossey-Bass.

Waterman, A. S., Geary, P. S., & Waterman, C. K. (1974). A longitudinal study of changes in ego identity status from the freshman to the senior year at college. *Developmental Psychology, 10,* 387–392.

Waterman, A. S. & Goldman, J. A. (1976). A longitudinal study of ego development at a liberal arts college. *Journal of Youth and Adolescence, 5,* 361–369.

Waterman, A. S. & Waterman, C. K. (1971). A longitudinal study of changes in ego identity status during the freshman year at college. *Developmental Psychology, 5,* 167–173.

Waters, B. (1987). The importance of sibling relationships in separated families. *Australian and New Zealand Journal of Family Therapy, 8,* 13–17.

Watson, J. D. (1968). *The double helix: A personal view of the discovery of the structure of DNA.* New York: Signet Books.

Watterson, B. (1990). *The authoritative Calvin and Hobbes.* Kansas City, MO: Andrews, McMeel & Parker.

Webber, M. (1991). *Street kids: The tragedy of Canada's runaways.* Toronto, Canada: University of Toronto Press.

Wechsler, D. (1974). *Wechsler Intelligence Scale for Children.* New York: Psychological Corporation.

Weenolsen, P. (1988). *Transcendence of loss over the life span.* New York: Hemisphere.

Weiner, I. B. (1980). Psychopathology in adolescence. In J. Adelson (Ed.), *Handbook of adolescent psychology* (pp. 288–312). New York: Pergamon Press.

Weininger, O. (1986). *The Differential Diagnostic Technique, a visual-motor projective test: Research and clinical work.* Springfield, IL: Charles C. Thomas.

Weinman, M. L., Robinson, M., Simmers, J. T., Schreiber, N. B., & Stafford, B. (1989). Pregnant teens: Differential pregnancy resolution and treatment implications. *Child Welfare, 68,* 45–55.

Weinmann, L. L. & Newcombe, N. (1990). Relational aspects of identity: Late adolescents' perceptions of their relationships with parents. *Journal of Experimental Child Psychology, 50,* 357–369.

Weinstein, R. J., Trickett, P. K., & Putnam, F. W. (1989, August). *Sexual and aggressive behavior in girls experiencing child abuse and precocious puberty.* Paper presented at the Annual Convention of the American Psychological Association, New Orleans, LA.

Weisberg, D. K. (1985). *Children of the night: A study of adolescent prostitution.* Lexington, MA: Lexington Books.

Weisman, M. M., Lea, P. J., Holzer, C. E., Myers, J. K., & Tischler, G. L. (1984). The epidemiology of depression: An update on sex differences in rates. *Journal of Affective Disorders, 7,* 179–188.

Weiss, L. & Lowenthal, M. F. (1975). Life-course perspectives on friendship. In M. F. Lowenthal, M. Thurnher, & D. Chiriboga (Eds.), *Four stages of life: A comparative study of women and men facing transition* (pp. 48–61). San Francisco: Jossey-Bass.

Weiss, R. S. (1986). Growing up a little faster: The experience of growing up in a single-parent household. In R. H. Moos (Ed.), *Coping with life crises: An integrated approach* (pp. 35–48). New York: Plenum. (Reprinted from *Journal of Social Issues, 1979. 35,* 97–111)

Welner, A., Welner, Z., & Fishman, R. (1979). Psychiatric adolescent inpatients—Eight- to ten-year follow-up. *Archives of General Psychiatry, 36,* 698–700.

Wentzel, K. R. & Erdley, C. A. (1993). Strategies for making friends: Relations to social behavior and peer acceptance. *Developmental Psychology, 29,* 819–826.

West, R. (1969). *McLuhan and the future of literature.* London: The English Association.

West, R., Drummond, C., & Eames, K. (1990). Alcohol consumption, problem drinking, and anti-social behavior in a sample of college students. *British Journal of Addiction, 85,* 479–486.

When foster care ends, home is often the street. (1991, January-February). *Youth Law News,* 10–11.

White, C. S. (1987). Developing information-processing skills through structured activities with a computerized file-management program. *Journal of Educational Computing Research, 3,* 355–375.

White, J. L. (1989). *The troubled adolescent*. New York: Pergamon Press.

White, R. W. (1976). *The enterprise of living: A view of personal growth*. (2nd ed.) New York: Holt, Rinehart & Winston.

Whitehead, B. D. (1993). Dan Quayle was right. *The Atlantic Monthly, 272*(4), 47–84.

Whitney, E. N. & Hamilton, E. M. N. (1987). *Understanding nutrition* (4th ed.). St. Paul, MN: West.

Wholey, J. S. (1986). The Job Corps: Congressional use of evaluation findings. In J. S. Wholey, M. A. Abramson, & C. Bellavita (Eds.), *Performance and credibility: Developing excellence in public and nonprofit organizations* (pp. 245–255). Lexington, MA: Lexington.

The William T. Grant Foundation Commission on Work, Family, and Citizenship. (1988). *The forgotten half: Noncollege youth in America*. New York: The William T. Grant Foundation.

Williams, R. L., Schaefer, C. A., Shisslak, C. M., Gronwaldt, V. H., & Comerci, G. D. (1986). Eating disorders and behaviors in adolescent women: Discrimination of normals and suspected bulimics using the eating attitudes tests and eating disorder inventory. *International Journal of Eating Disorders, 5*, 879–894.

Wills, T. A. & Vaughan, R. (1989). Social support and substance abuse in early adolescence. *Journal of Behavioral Medicine, 12*, 321–339.

Wilson, R. S. (1976). Concordance in physical growth for monozygotic and dizygotic twins. *Annals of Human Biology, 3*, 1–10.

Winter, J. S. D. (1978). Prepubertal and pubertal endocrinology. In F. Falkner & J. M. Tanner (Eds.), *Human growth. Vol. 2. Postnatal growth*. New York: Plenum.

Wolf, T. (1988). *I'll be home before midnight and I won't get pregnant*. New York: Random House.

Woltman, H. R. & Walton, W. W. (1968). *Evaluation of the War on Poverty: The feasibility of benefit-cost analysis for Manpower programs*. Unpublished report prepared for the U.S. General Accounting Office. Bethesda, MD: Resource Management Corporation.

Woodruff, D. S. & Birren, J. E. (1972). Age changes and cohort differences in personality. *Developmental Psychology, 6*, 252–259.

Woodruff, D. S. (1977). *Can you live to be 100?* New York: Chatham Square Press.

Woodward, J. C. & Kalyan-Masih, V. (1990). Loneliness, coping strategies, and cognitive styles of the gifted rural adolescent. *Adolescence, 25*, 977–988.

Wong, M. M. & Csikszentmihalyi, M. (1991). Affiliation motivation and daily experience: Some issues on gender differences. *Journal of Personality and Social Psychology, 60*, 154–164.

Wright, D. W. & Barnes, H. L. (1986). *Teenage sexual behavior and pregnancy: A needs assessment for a rural Kansas community*. Unpublished report, Kansas State University.

Wright, D. W. & Barnes, H. L. (1989). A strategic planning approach to reducing adolescent pregnancy. *Family Perspective, 23*, 151–163.

Wroblewski, R. & Huston, A. C. (1987). Televised occupational stereotypes and their effects on early adolescents: Are they changing? *Journal of Early Adolescence, 7*, 283–297.

Wylie, R. C. (1989). *Measures of self-concept*. Lincoln, NE: University of Nebraska Press.

Youniss, J. & Smollar, J. (1985). *Adolescent relations with mothers, fathers, and friends*. Chicago, IL: University of Chicago Press.

Yussen, S. R. (1977). Characteristics of moral dilemmas written by adolescents. *Developmental Psychology, 13*, 162–163.

Zajonc, R. B. (1986). The decline and rise of scholastic aptitude scores: A prediction derived from the confluence model. *American Psychologist, 41*, 862–867.

Zillmann, D. (1982). Television and arousal. In D. Pearl, L. Bouthilet, & J. Lazar (Eds.), *Television and behavior: Ten years of scientific progress and implications for the eighties. Vol. 2: Technical reviews* (pp. 53–67). Washington, DC: U.S. Government Printing Office.

Zillmann, D. (1989). Effects of prolonged consumption of pornography. In D. Zillmann & J. Bryant (Eds.), *Pornography: Research advances & policy considerations* (pp. 127–157). Hillsdale, NJ: Erlbaum.

Zillmann, D., Herzel, R. T., & Medoff, N. J. (1980). The effect of affective states on selective exposure to televised entertainment fare. *Journal of Applied Social Psychology, 10*, 332–339.

Zinsmeister, K. (1990). Growing up scared. *The Atlantic Monthly, 265*(6), 49–66.

Zinner, E. S. (1985). *Coping with death on campus*. San Francisco: Jossey-Bass.

Ziv, A. & Gadish, O. (1990). Humor and giftedness. *Journal for the Education of the Gifted, 13*, 332–345.

Name Index

Subject Index

PHOTO CREDITS

CHAPTER 1

3 Jean-Claude Lejeune/Stock Boston **6** (top left) Mary Kate Denny/ PhotoEdit; (top right) Jean-Claude Lejeune/Stock Boston; (bottom) David Young-Wolff/PhotoEdit **10** Bobbi Carrey/THE PICTURE CUBE **23** Frances M. Cox/Stock Boston **39** Robert A. Isaacs/Photo Researchers, Inc.

CHAPTER 2

43 (right) Tony Freeman/PhotoEdit; (bottom) Courtesy of David Balk **44** Courtesy of David Balk **53** (left) Jeff Greenberg/THE PICTURE CUBE; (right) Lawrence Cherney/FPG International; **58** Michael Newman/PhotoEdit **65** (left) Jerry Berndt/Stock Boston; (right) Felicia Martinez/PhotoEdit **78** PhotoEdit

CHAPTER 3

85 David Carmack/Stock Boston **91** (left) Bob Daemmrich/ Stock Boston; (middle) Bohdan Hrynewych/Stock Boston; (right) Tony Freeman/PhotoEdit **98** Peter Menzel/Stock Boston **107** (left) Ulrike Welsch/PhotoEdit; (right) Tony Freeman/Photo-Edit **116** (left) Barbara Ries/Photo Researchers Inc.; (right) Ulrike Welsch/Photo Researchers Inc. **122** Sarah Putnam/THE PICTURE CUBE

CHAPTER 4

127 Bill Gillette/Stock Boston **131** Billy E. Barnes/Stock Boston **141** Lionel Delevingne/Stock Boston **164** Jeff Greenberg/PhotoEdit **168** Peter Southwick/Stock Boston **173** Rhoda Sidney/PhotoEdit

CHAPTER 5

179 Michael Dwyer/Stock Boston **185** (left) Myrleen Ferguson/PhotoEdit; (right) Spencer Grant/Photo Researchers, Inc.; **191** (left) Catherine Ursillo/Photo Researchers, Inc.; (right) Jeff Greenberg/ PhotoEdit **205** (top left) S. Takatsuno/THE PICTURE CUBE; (top right) Barbara Ries/Photo Researchers, Inc.; (bottom left) S. Takatsuno/THE PICTURE CUBE; (bottom right) Rafael Marcia/Photo Researchers, Inc. **216** Robert Brenner/PhotoEdit **222** Michael Newman/PhotoEdit

CHAPTER 6

231 Mike Mazzaschi/Stock Boston **252** John Coletti/THE PICTURE CUBE **269** Dorothy Littel/Stock Boston

CHAPTER 7

275 Jeffry W. Myers/Stock Boston **288** Don Klumpp/The Image Bank **291** Jim Whitmer/Stock Boston **302** Tony Freeman/ PhotoEdit **305** Gale Zucker/Stock Boston;

CHAPTER 8

313 Bob Daemmrich/Stock Boston **328** Tony Freeman/PhotoEdit **340** Courtesy of Kansas State University Archives **343** (left) Courtesy of Kansas State University Archives; (right) Richard Pasley/Stock Boston

CHAPTER 9

349 Michael Newman/PhotoEdit **359** S. Takatsuno/THE PICTURE CUBE **365** Lawrence Migdale/Stock Boston **373** Norman Rowan/Stock Boston

CHAPTER 10

379 Courtesy of Cary Conover **382** David Young-Wolff/PhotoEdit **391** Tom McCarthy/PhotoEdit

CHAPTER 11

401 David Ulmer/Stock Boston **406** PhotoEdit **412** Dorothy Littel/Stock Boston **431** Ellis Herwig/THE PICTURE CUBE

CHAPTER 12

439 Billy E. Barnes/PhotoEdit **442** MacDonald/THE PICTURE CUBE **444** Hubertus Kanus/Photo Researchers, Inc. **452** Cleo Photography/PhotoEdit **460** Bob Daemmrich/Stock Boston

CHAPTER 13

465 Rhoda Sidney/PhotoEdit **469** Mark Reinstein/FPG International **474** Katina Thomas/Photo Researchers Inc. **483** Tom Prettyman/PhotoEdit **487** Dorothy Littel/Stock Boston

CHAPTER 14

493 Spencer Grant/Stock Boston **502** Ron Chapple/FPG International **509** Therese Frare/ THE PICTURE CUBE **511** (left) L. Willinger/ FPG International; (right) Arthur Tilley/ FPG International

CHAPTER 15

525 J. Gerald Smith/Photo Researchers Inc. **530** Michael Grecco/ Stock Boston **549** Cleo Photography/THE PICTURE CUBE